Nuclear War Survival Skills

Updated and Expanded 2022 Edition Regarding Ukraine Russia and the World

Cresson H. Kearny

with Foreword by Dr. Edward Teller

2022 Updated and Expanded Edition Pages
Authored by Steven E. Harris

Original Edition Published September, 1979,
by Oak Ridge National Laboratory,
a Facility of the
U.S. Department of Energy

1987 Update and 1999 Hormesis Update Published by the
Oregon Institute of Science and Medicine
Cave Junction, Oregon

2022 Update and Additions Edition Remastered and Published by
KnowledgePublications Corporation
ISBN: 978-1-60322-070-5

www.NuclearWarSurvivalSkills.com

First printing May 1987
Second printing November 1988
Third printing September 1990
Fourth printing April 1999
Fifth printing November 2001
Digitally Remastered for On Demand Publishing 2006 (KPC)
1987 Edition for World Wide Free Download 2011 (KPC)
On Demand Publishing Create Space 2012 (KPC)
On Demand Publishing World Wide Amazon KEP 2022 (KPC)
On Demand Publsihing World Wide Amazon KDP 2022 (KPC)

ISBN: 978-1-60322-070-5

Contents

NUCLEAR WAR SURVIVAL SKILLS

This book should be in every American home and place of business. It should be a part of all civilian and military defense preparations.

In this nuclear age, prior preparation and knowledge are the primary elements of survival during a nuclear war or a nuclear crisis especially one caused by terrorists or by an accidental missile launch. This book provides that essential knowledge.

(from the 2022 Update Author). The original intent of Nuclear War Survival Skillls (NWSS) was for it to be printed on water resistant paper that would not fall apart if it got soaked and the same goes for the cover. Printing out the PDF at home and having Amazon get you an On Demand INSTANTLY a printed copy of this book the same day or overnight for most of the industruialized world does NOT lend itself to this ability. The intent is to get the information into your hands whether on a phone, tablet, kindle or a printed book as close to INSTANT as possible.

The Oregon Institute of Science and Medicine, a 501.c3 org and the Robinson Family that founded it and their generations of children have been and always will be a long time friend of the late Cresson Kearny. They still have (and hopefully will continue to manufacture) copies of NWSS with these water resistant abilities. Its not water proof, just quite water repelling. If this is before a disaster I HIGHLY encourage you to get one of these copies. In 2022 they are about $20+. Go to www.RobinsonBooks.com and then click on OTHER and you will see NWSS. I encourage you to get Cresson's other book Jungle Snafus and Remedies at the same time. The military food and tools and methods in there will help your preparedness.

Oregon Institute of Science and Medicine
2251 Dick George Road
Cave Junction, OR 97523
www.OISM.org

OISM also has the "Fighting Chance" DVD sets and other information that may be of benefit to you for pre-disaster preparedness.

If you are reading this and there is a nuclear emergency in the world and nuclear devices are going off then listen to me carefully. You are in good hands with what you have in your hands right now. This is all you need for now. It is all in here. Cresson Kearny and many many dedicated people have spent their whole lives dedicate to brining you what you are reading now. The odds of you making it with the knowlegde in this book are very good.

Foreword

There are two diametrically opposite views on civil defense. Russian official policy holds that civil defense is feasible even in a nuclear war. American official policy, or at any rate the implementation of that policy, is based on the assumption that civil defense is useless.

The Russians, having learned a bitter lesson in the second world war, have bent every effort to defend their people under all circumstances. They are spending several billion dollars per year on this activity. They have effective plans to evacuate their cities before they let loose a nuclear strike. They have strong shelters for the people who must remain in the cities. They are building up protected food reserves to tide them over a critical period.

All this may mean that in a nuclear exchange, which we must try to avoid or to deter, the Russian deaths would probably not exceed ten million. Tragic as such a figure is, the Russian nation would survive. If they succeed in eliminating the United States they can commandeer food, machinery and manpower from the rest of the world. They could recover rapidly. They would have attained their goal: world domination.

In the American view the Russian plan is unfeasible. Those who argue on this side point out the great power of nuclear weapons. In this they are right. Their argument is particularly impressive in its psychological effect.

But this argument has never been backed up by a careful quantitative analysis which takes into account the planned dispersal and sheltering of the Russian population and the other measures which the Russians have taken and those to which they are committed.

That evacuation of our own citizens can be extremely useful if we see that the Russians are evacuating is simple common sense. With the use of American automobiles an evacuation could be faster and more effective than is possible in Russia. To carry it out we need not resort to the totalitarian methods of the iron curtain countries. It will suffice to warn our people and advise them where to go, how to protect themselves. The Federal Emergency Management Administration contains the beginnings on which such a policy might be built.

The present book does not, and indeed cannot, make the assumption that such minimal yet extremely useful government guidance will be available. Instead it outlines the skills that individuals or groups of individuals can learn and apply in order to improve their chances of survival.

This book is not a description of civil defense. It is a guide to "Stop-gap" civil defense which individuals could carry out for themselves, if need be, with no expenditures by our government. It fills the gap between the ineffective civil defense that we have today and the highly effective survival preparations that we could and should have a few years from now. However, if we go no further than what we can do on the basis of this book, then the United States cannot survive a major nuclear war.

Yet this book, besides being realistic and objectively correct, serves two extremely important purposes. One is: it will help to save lives. The second purpose is to show that with relatively inexpensive governmental guidance and supplies, an educated American public could, indeed, defend itself. We could survive a nuclear war and remain a nation.

This is an all-important goal. Its most practical aspect lies in the fact that the men in the Kremlin are cautious. If they cannot count on destroying us they probably will never launch their nuclear arsenal against us. Civil defense is at once the most peaceful and the most effective deterrent of nuclear war.

Some may argue that the Russians could evacuate again and again and thus, by forcing us into similar moves, exhaust us. I believe that in reality they would anger us sufficiently so that we would rearm in earnest. That is not what the Russians want to accomplish.

Others may say that the Russians could strike without previous evacuation. This could result in heavy losses on their part which, I hope, they will not risk.

Civil defense as here described will not eliminate the danger of nuclear war. It will considerably diminish its probability.

This book takes a long overdue step in educating the American people. It does not suggest that survival is easy. It does not prove that national survival is possible. But it can save lives and it will stimulate thought and action which will be crucial in our two main purposes: to preserve freedom and to avoid war.

Edward Teller

Keep in Touch and Keep UP to Date.

PO BOX

In 1979 and 1987 you just published a book and that was it. Maybe you had a PO Box where people could write you but this is the year 2022 so we will tell you how to keep in touch with us. The field of nuclear expertise is a small one and we will all come together in times of difficulty to feed you the best actionable knowledge (not information) that you can benefit from. In the civil defense field. We all either know each other or are separated by only one person. At the writing of this update, a nuclear device has not been detonated on the earth in anger since 1945. If the situation becomes direr before I do a 2023 update for this book, follow us at the methods below to get the latest information.

WEBSITE

www.NuclearWarSurvivalSkills.com Any updates or notices on changes will be put up on this website.

TWITTER

https://twitter.com/BookNwss or @BookNWSS on twitter.

TELEGRAM

https://t.me/nwssbook Is a Telegram Channel. It can have unlimited members and it allows us to communicate one way, from us to you without limitation and it might be something people younger than me are comfortable with. If we form an NWSS Telegram GROUP where we can all chat and people can ask questions and experts can answer them we will announce that GROUP via the website, Twitter and the above telegram channel.

CONFERENCE CALL.

After the rush of people that got the NWSS book in March of 2022 a good friend told me, "Hey, dummy. Why did you not have a weekly Q&A conference call or something!!". "Great Idea!!!" I stated. If the world situation escalates I will announce when and how we will have some form of a large group meeting, video, audio, text, etc....(at least once a week). You can ask questions and myself and experts more nuclear qualified than myself can answer them directly. We will record these calls and then make them available to everyone. If you are asking a question, a million other people are probably thinking the same thing. If you want to sign up to be on the list for a 'conference call' there is a signup link at www.NuclearWarSurvivalSkills.com Please use your best email that you get daily and this is where I say that I have about a million other things to do in life than to SPAM you. All Subject lines of emails from us will start with "NWSS: blah blah blah. etc..." They will all start with NWSS in the start of the Subject Line.

EMAIL

Email: nwssbook (at) protonmail (dot) com For Personal, Professional, Corporate, or Enterprise Assistance. We know 'everyone' in the field and can get you the help you need. MEDIA: PUT your Media ORG and TIME and DATE Needed in the Subject Line Please. I can't guarantee how often I'll be checking because of the flood of emails I'll get. If you want to help me help people. I'll do it. If you are a large corporate entity with resources that you want to volunteer to help us with what you see we are doing, contact me.

STEVEN HARRIS WEBSITE:

www.Harris1234.com has my other food, water, power, electricity, prepareness subjects on it and I will make this my site that will lead to anything else I have up there to help you.

CRESSON KEARNY COMBAT PROVEN TOOLS

This is a little promo here for Cresson's best practices. I inherited his original items used in the making of the book Jungle Snafus and Remedies. Some of these date back to WWII and Vietnam and the first Gulf War. He gave me specific instructions on how and what to do regarding companies putting these items back into production for the benefit of the NATO War Fighter and the public.

You really need to get a copy of Jungle Snafus and Remedies from the used market or buy a brand new copy from www.RobinsonBooks.com (click on OTHER). The details on everything below are in that book. Please get the book before contacting me.

THE JUNGLE HAMMOCK

Gary Clark did his version of the jungle hammock without knowing about Cresson. I found Gary and called him and Cresson was still alive then. The 3 of us talked and Cresson approved of what Gary had done and I sent Cresson's details and best practices to Gary. Gary has since retired and Dutchware Gear now sells the hammocks at junglehammock.com but I do not know if they are currently keeping up with what Cresson called Jungle Platoon Best Practices. If you want your hammock to be up to Cresson Kearny Warfighter's best practices contact me.

THE PANAMA SOLE.

The panama sole boot pattern or tread has been copied and copied to the point its not like the original that Cresson made and tested when he help found the Jungle Training Center in Panama before/during WW2. I have sent scans of this to 2 boot manufactures but I have no idea of they did anything with it. Does not look like it. Any boot manufactures that want 3D scans or plaster molds of the original pattern, I have Cressons original boots from when he made them in WW2.

THE JUNGLE BOAT.

This is a breath inflatable boat combat-proven and tested to hold 3 warfighters with full pack loads (WW2 / Vietnam Era Loads). It has been under fire, in combat, and the concept is still valid today. It took 87-year-old Cresson about 8 minutes to breathe inflate it, it rolls up, weight is about 7 pounds and it will cross rivers, lakes, and Cresson even took it 25 miles out into the Pacific Ocean off the coast of Panama and had a US Army or Navy boat meet him and pick him up. I have 2 different variants of the boat. Cresson wanted these back in production for use by the WarFighter. NOTE: All of these items do NOT have to go through 'Military Approval". Special Forces today have these things called Military Credit Cards and they buy what they need.

About the Author

When the U.S. Atomic Energy Commission authorized me in 1964 to initiate the Civil Defense Project at Oak Ridge National Laboratory, one of the first researchers I recruited was Cresson H. Kearny. Most of his life has been preparation, unplanned and planned, for writing this guide to help people unfamiliar with the effects of nuclear weapons improve their chances of surviving a nuclear attack. During the past 15 years he has done an unequaled amount of practical field work on basic survival problems, without always conforming to the changing civil defense doctrine.

After I returned to my professional duties at Princeton in 1966, the civil defense effort at Oak Ridge National Laboratory was first headed by James C. Bresee, and is now headed by Conrad V. Chester. Both have wholeheartedly supported Kearny's down-to-earth research, and Chester was not only a co-developer of several of the survival items described in this book, but also participated in the planning of the experiments testing them.

Kearny's concern with nuclear war dangers began while he was studying for his degree in civil engineering at Princeton — he graduated summa cum laude in 1937. His Princeton studies had already acquainted him with the magnitude of an explosion in which nuclear energy is liberated, then only a theoretical possibility. After winning a Rhodes Scholarship, Kearny earned two degrees in geology at Oxford. Still before the outbreak of World War II, he observed the effective preparations made in England to reduce the effects of aerial attacks. He had a deep aversion to dictatorships, whether from the right or left, and during the Munich crisis he acted as a courier for an underground group helping anti-Nazis escape from Czechoslovakia.

Following graduation from Oxford, Kearny did geological exploration work in the Andes of Peru and in the jungles of Venezuela. He has traveled also in Mexico, China, and the Philippines.

A year before Pearl Harbor, realizing that the United States would soon be at war and that our jungle troops should have at least as good personal equipment, food, and individual medical supplies as do exploration geologists, he quit his job with the Standard Oil Company of Venezuela, returned to the United States, and went on active duty as an infantry reserve lieutenant. Kearny was soon assigned to Panama as the Jungle Experiment Officer of the Panama Mobile Force. In that capacity he was able to improve or invent, and then thoroughly jungle-test, much of the specialized equipment and rations used by our jungle infantrymen in World War II. For this work he was promoted to major and awarded the Legion of Merit.

To take his chances in combat, in 1944 the author volunteered for duty with the Office of Strategic Services. As a demolition specialist helping to limit the Japanese invasion then driving into the wintry mountains of southern China, he saw mass starvation and death first hand. The experiences gained in this capacity also resulted in an increased understanding of both the physical and emotional problems of people whose country is under attack.

Worry about the increasing dangers of nuclear war and America's lack of civil defense caused the author in 1961 to consult Herman Kahn, a leading nuclear strategist. Kahn, who was at that time forming a nonprofit war-research organization, the Hudson Institute, offered him work as a research analyst. Two years of civil defense research in this "think tank" made the author much more knowledgeable of survival problems.

In 1964 he joined the Oak Ridge civil defense project and since then Oak Ridge has been Kearny's base of operations, except for two years during the height of the Vietnam war. For his Vietnam work on combat equipment, and also for his contributions to preparations for improving survivability in the event of a nuclear war, he received the Army's Decoration for Distinguished Civilian Service in 1972.

This book draws extensively on Kearny's understanding of the problems of civil defense acquired as a result of his own field testing of shelters and other survival needs, and also from an intensive study of the serious civil defense preparations undertaken by other countries, including Switzerland, Sweden, the USSR, and China. He initiated and edited the Oak Ridge National Laboratory translations of Soviet civil defense handbooks and of a Chinese manual, and gained additional knowledge from these new sources. Trips to England, Europe, and Israel also expanded his information on survival measures, which contributed to the *Nuclear War Survival Skills.* However, the book advocates principally those do-it-yourself instructions that field tests have proved to be practical.

Eugene P. Wigner

Eugene P. Wigner, Physicist, Nobel Laureate, and
the only surviving initiator of the Nuclear Age.
May, 1979

About the 2022 Update Author

About Steven Harris and these updates. The author of Nuclear War Survival Skills (NWSS through this book) is Cresson H. Kearny. I met Cresson in 1996 a the Doctors for Disaster Preparedness meeting. He started a friendship and a mentorship with me that lasted until he passed away in 2004.

I spent 1000's of hours with him between meetings and on the phone and we'd send preparedness items back and forth in the mail and I started to continue the work of his other book, Jungle Snafus and Remedies, with the US Military.

Another person that I had a similar relationship from DDP with was Edwin York. He was at Los Alamos in WWII and did development on the first atomic weapons and then his life continued in the field of nuclear weapon development and the protection from the effects of nuclear weapons.

Through those years and beyond, they gave me a very very firm understanding of the hows and whys of what was written in this book, what was not written, and why. Ed gave me a much greater understanding of the Effects of Nuclear Weapons, which is the title of the famous book which I am the only publisher to keep in print. I even made reproductions of the 'bomb computer' in the back of the book when I was selling the copies I produced. It's still for sale on Amazon by my company, but it no longer includes the bomb computer but there are 'online' versions of it. NOTE: The "Bomb Computer" in the book is a circular slide ruler, it's not an electronic computer.

I started my journey in preparedness in 1993 and it continues to this day. I taught a great deal on batteries and power to different elements of the US Military starting in 2003 and it has continued to this day. Now a great deal of what I teach and consult for just falls under the title of "Science and Technology" or S&T.

This includes items such as food and water which through my Test and Evaluation (T&E) with Cresson and others I have gained a broad yet specific expertise in. My food technology, methods, and tools are being used by civilians, government, military, USA, and others around the world. My main area of expertise is all forms of power, energy, batteries, power generation, transmission, storage, harvesting, and much more. Power is my passion, and all that goes with it. Food technology, preservation, storage, and other unusual methods and applications are just plain fun for me.

During the March of 2022 Ukraine invasion, there was a great deal of nuclear concern among many. Many people communicated with me about NWSS and asked me about updates to the book. My answer was the same. The book was timeless. No changes needed to be made to it.

People that I admire and respect illustrated the need for clarification for the year 2022. In fact, that *I* should be the person to make the clarification of more modern tools and methods and dispel some new modern myths. They convinced me.

For example, the fuel for the bucket stove is twisted newspaper and the insulation for expedient cold weather clothing is newspaper. Who has scrap newspaper today? Not many homes do. However, we do have plenty of amazon boxes. That can be a source of fuel for the bucket stove.

Using a single filament of a cotton string in a lamp made from a glass jar and cooking oil is still valid however we have things that did not exist when Cresson wrote the book. We now have lithium-ion batteries and LED-based lights. Many of my favorites lights, that I preached about and taught about to the people who admonished me to write this update, have modes that go down to 1 lumen for the minimum needed illumination. Too often the light is marketed by its brightest setting. "1000 lumens, see 2 miles!" Digital electronics control the light and some go down to as low as 1 lumen of light and the light will literally run for an entire week or more on one charge. Some even have a display that tells you the length of time the light will run at the selected brightness level. Much like the single piece of string in a cooking oil lamp giving minimum necessary illumination, the right LED light can do this as well.

The only dosimeters when this book was written was the yellow civil defense ones that worked on static charge (and those are good) but people are buying "Modern" dosimeters and "radiation meters" off Amazon, eBay, and other market places and they do not understand that those meters when exposed to a level of radiation beyond their measurement range error out at zero rather than error out high. So a $120 dosimeter that tells you the current reading of radiation may only go up to 1000 microrads, which is 1 millirad. That is NOT an amount of radiation to be concerned with regarding your health and nuclear fallout. We wish it was that low. However, when the Geiger-Mueller tube inside that small device gets more than 1001 microrads it does not say ERROR HIGH it gives you a reading of ZERO. So there is more radiation than it can measure but it is telling you there is no radiation. So I was strongly urged to make people aware of these concerns and other options available to them in the year 2022 and beyond.

Also when this book was written its focus was on mutually assured destruction and 10,000 nuclear devices from the Soviets coming over the north pole and hitting the USA. Those devices were also around 1 megaton in size and there were 10, 20, even 50 megatons (mt) bombs. Today, my sources tell me that even 250 kiloton (kt) (0.250 megatons) is a rarity and the most common large nuclear weapon we have in inventory is 100 kiloton (0.100 megatons). This is because the delivery systems are so much more accurate. Better to have 100kt on target than 5mt hitting near it. Even our current 100kt bombs are all 'dial a yield' and they can be set to go from less than 1kt to a Hiroshima level (17kt) to 50kt to 75kt to the full 100kt or 320kt. Collateral damage and wiping out whole cities are just not a 'thing' today. I am not changing the original book. I am inserting UPDATE pages next to the original text. You can see the original method and suggestions I offer for 2022.

Acknowledgments

The author takes this opportunity to thank the following persons for their special contributions, without many of which it would have been impossible to have written this book:

L. Joe Deal, James L. Liverman, and W. W. Schroebel for the essential support they made possible over the years, first by the U.S. Atomic Energy Commission, next by the Energy Research and Development Administration, and then by the Department of Energy. This support was the basis of the laboratory work and field testing that produced most of the survival instructions developed between 1964 and 1979, given in this book. Mr. Schroebel also reviewed early and final drafts and made a number of improvements.

John A. Auxier, Ph.D., health physicist, who for years was Director of the Industrial Safety and Applied Health Physics Division, Oak Ridge National Laboratory (ORNL)—for manuscript review and especially for checking statements regarding the effects of radiation on people.

Conrad V. Chester, Ph.D., chemical engineer, civil defense researcher, developer of improved defenses against exotic weapons and unconventional attacks, nuclear strategist, and currently Group Leader, Emergency Planning Group, ORNL—for advice and many contributions, starting with the initial organization of material and continuing through all the drafts of the original and this edition.

William K. Chipman, LLD, Office of Civil Preparedness, Federal Emergency Management Agency—for review in 1979 of the final draft of the original ORNL edition.

George A. Cristy, M.S., who for many years was a chemical engineer and civil defense researcher at ORNL—for contributions to the planning of the original edition and editing of early drafts.

Kay B. Franz, Ph.D., nutritionist, Associate Professor, Food Science and Nutrition Department, Brigham Young University—for information and advice used extensively in the Food chapter.

Samuel Glasstone, Ph.D., physical chemist and the leading authority on the effects of nuclear weapons—for overall review and constructive recommendations, especially regarding simplified explanations of the effects of nuclear weapons.

Carsten M. Haaland, M.S., physicist and civil defense researcher at ORNL—for scientific advice and mathematical computations of complex nuclear phenomena.

Robert H. Kupperman, Ph.D., physicist, in 1979 the Chief Scientist, U.S. Arms Control and Disarmament Agency, Department of State—for review of the final draft of the 1979 edition.

David B. Nelson, Ph.D., electrical engineer and mathematician, for years a civil defense and thermonuclear energy researcher at ORNL, an authority on electromagnetic pulse (EMP) problems—for manuscript review and contributions to sections on electromagnetic pulse phenomena, fallout monitoring instruments, and communications.

Lewis V. Spencer, Ph.D., for many years a physicist with the Radiation Physics Division, Center for Radiation Research, National Bureau of Standards—for his calculations and advice regarding needed improvements in the design of blast shelters to assure adequate protection of occupants against excessive exposure to initial nuclear radiation.

Edward Teller, Ph.D., nuclear physicist, leading inventor of offensive and defensive weapons, a strong supporter of civil defense at Oak Ridge National Laboratory and worldwide—for contributing the Foreword, originally written for the American Security Council 1980 edition, and for his urging which motivated the author to work on this 1987 edition.

Eugene P. Wigner, Ph.D., physicist and mathematician, Nobel laureate, Professor Emeritus of Theoretical Physics, Princeton University, a principal initiator of the Nuclear Age and a prominent leader of the civil defense movement—for encouraging the writing of the original edition of this book, contributing the About the Author section, and improving drafts, especially of the appendix on expedient blast shelters.

Edwin N. York, M.S., nuclear physicist, Senior Research Engineer, Boeing Aerospace Company, designer of blast-protective structures—for overall review and recommendations, particularly those based on his extensive participation in nuclear and conventional blast tests, and for improving both the original and this edition.

Civil defense officials in Washington and several states for information concerning strengths and weaknesses of official civil defense preparations.

Helen C. Jernigan for editing the 1979 manuscript, and especially for helping to clarify technical details for non-technical readers.

May E. Kearny for her continuing help in editing, and for improving the index.

Ruby N. Thurmer for advice and assistance with editing the original edition.

Marjorie E. Fish for her work on the photographs and drawings.

Janet Sprouse for typing and typesetting the additions in the 1987 edition.

Introduction

SELF-HELP CIVIL DEFENSE

Your best hope of surviving a nuclear war in this century is self-help civil defense — knowing the basic facts about nuclear weapon effects and what you, your family, and small groups can do to protect yourselves. Our Government continues to downgrade war-related survival preparations and spends only a few cents a year to protect each American against possible war dangers. During the 10 years or more before the Strategic Defense Initiative (Star Wars) weapons can be invented, developed and deployed, self-help civil defense will continue to be your main hope of surviving if we suffer a nuclear attack.

Most Americans hope that Star Wars will lead to the deployment of new weapons capable of destroying attacking missiles and warheads in flight. However, no defensive system can be made leak-proof. If Star Wars, presently only a research project, leads to a deployed defensive system, then self-help civil defense will be a vital part of our hoped for, truly defensive system to prevent aggressions and to reduce losses if deterrence fails.

PURPOSE AND SCOPE OF THIS BOOK

This book is written for the majority of Americans who want to improve their chances of surviving a nuclear war. It brings together field-tested instructions that have enabled untrained Americans to make expedient fallout shelters, air pumps to ventilate and cool shelters, fallout meters, and other expedient life-support equipment. ("Expedient", as used in civil defense work, describes equipment that can be made by untrained citizens in 48 hours or less, while guided solely by field-tested, written instructions and using only widely available materials and tools.) Also described are expedient ways to remove even dissolved radioiodine from water, and to process and cook whole grains and soybeans, our main food reserves. Successive versions of these instructions have been used successfully by families working under simulated crisis conditions, and have been improved repeatedly by Oak Ridge National Laboratory civil defense researchers and others over a period of 14 years. These improved instructions are the heart of this updated 1987 edition of the original Oak Ridge National Laboratory survival book first published in 1979.

The average American has far too little information that would help him and his family and our country survive a nuclear attack, and many of his beliefs about nuclear war are both false and dangerous. Since the A-bomb blasted Hiroshima and hurled mankind into the Nuclear Age, only during a recognized crisis threatening nuclear war have most Americans been seriously interested in improving their chances of surviving a nuclear attack. Both during and following the Cuban Missile Crisis in 1962, millions of Americans built fallout shelters or tried to obtain survival information. At that time most of the available survival information was inadequate, and dangerously faulty in some respects — as it still is in 1987. Widespread recognition of these civil defense shortcomings has contributed to the acceptance by most Americans of one or both of two false beliefs:

One of these false beliefs is that nuclear war would be such a terrible catastrophe that it is an unthinkable impossibility. If this were true, there would be no logical reason to worry about nuclear war or to make preparations to survive a nuclear attack.

The second false belief is that, if a nuclear war were to break out, it would be the end of mankind. If this were true, a rational person would not try to improve his chances of surviving the unsurvivable.

This book gives facts that show these beliefs are false. History shows that once a weapon is invented it remains ready for use in the arsenals of some nations and in time will be used. Researchers who have spent much time and effort learning the facts about effects of nuclear weapons now know that all-out nuclear war would **not** be the end of mankind or of civilization. Even if our country remained unprepared and were to be subjected to an all-out nuclear attack, many millions of Americans would survive and could live through the difficult post-attack years.

Clarification on the Introduction

It's almost erroneous to just call this work of literary art Nuclear War Survival Skills. When a world nuclear war (as envisioned when this book was written) you lost all infrastructure. You lost your transportation, you lost your fuel, you lost your food, you lost your water, you lost your power, you lost your sanitation, you lost your medicine. It was all gone.

Cresson invented the term "Expedient Civil Denfse" because it was understood that the nuclear attack would be sudden and with little to no warning. You had what you had and you had what you could find.

So Cresson did not just have to teach you in this book how to make a fall-out shelter by digging a wide trench and covering it with cut trees and dirt but he had to tell you how to get and make emergency food. Plus how to cook it. How to purify your water. How to make infant formula from powdered milk, sugar, and cooking oil. How to make simple oil lamps from cooking oil and cotton string to provide light. How to make a device from 3 pipes to pound grain into flour to make some type of unleavened bread to eat.

This book could be retitled "EarthQuake Survival Skills". "Giant Hurricane Survival Skills", "Massive Blizzard just hit Survival Skills." and "The Electrical Grid got Hacked and the Power is Out Survival Skills.".

This is about the most all-encompassing "Family" and "Individual" Survival Skills book that has ever been written. Cresson was one of the smartest people you'd ever want to meet and when he was at Oak Ridge National Labs (ORNL) when he wrote the Nuclear War Survival Skills book; he had some of the smartest people in the country around him to ask questions and help him test things and more.

In the late 1970s when Cresson researched and tested and wrote this book, and it took him years to do this. Working at ORNL was about as close as having an "internet of genius IQ people" you could have.

THIS BOOK WILL NEVER BE OUT OF DATE.

This book is not 'dated', it's not 'out of date' and it won't be out of date. It's written on FUNDAMENTALS and those fundamentals do not change. Radiation is still radiation, no new types are being invented. It's still stopped by dirt and concrete and books and stuff.

There are some improved methods and tools available now that were not civilian off-the-shelf mass-manufactured at low prices then that we have now but even if you followed the instructions in the original 1979 or 1987 version, you'd still be alive and healthier than you would be without it.

Think about it. The nuclear technology that started the weapons race of the cold war started over 80 years ago. It's 80-year-old technology for a fission weapon. The only reason more people/countries do not have more weapons is that NOT in the difficulty of making atomic devices. Hell, the little boy was two specially shaped hunks of uranium 235 in a 6-inch naval gun barrel, sealed at both ends with the uranium split in half at each end of the barrel. It was literally a charge of black powder that violently shoved one half of the uranium into the other down the gun barrel that made the critical mass to get the first fission weapon dropped in war. It was so reliable, that they had to test the plutonium-based implosion device at Los Alamos before they deployed it. That was Fat Man. Little boy, the "gun-type" weapon. They knew it would work.

The only reason more entities on the planet do not have the weapon is because of the cost and the difficulty in making the source material for the weapon. Plutonium does not exist in nature, it's made in a nuclear reactor and that reactor currently runs on Uranium-238 with enriched Uranium-235 levels in it.

Making the U-235 is slow and it takes time and a lot of electricity. It was done in WW2 at ORNL because of its closeness to the Tennessee Valley Authority (TVA) and its massive hydroelectric dams. According to the late Ed York, more energy was used in the making of the U-235 with electricity than was released from the bomb when the little boy was detonated over Hiroshima in the form of heat, blast, light, and radiation combined.

I said to Ed York, "So, basically Hiroshima was a big water bomb?" and he replied, "You could look at it that way." Falling water, Hydroelectricity, made the U-235 from the U-238 to make the weapon capable of uncontrolled fission.

SO THIS BOOK IS NOT NEEDED?

If you extrapolate the past out into the future we will have more power, better technology, faster and more automated technology, and the ability to hide this process better and someone in the world who hates the USA, or someone else on the planet, will eventually make a device and you can bet they'll detonate it in Washinton DC, or New York City, or Atlanta, or Houston or Los Angeles. Distances and times to travel those distances are getting shorter, faster, quicker. Everyone in the world is closer to everyone else and the need for life-saving information in this book will only increase with each year.

This is why I plan on updating it every year and or if a major event happens in the middle of a year. Just as the March 2022 Ukraine conflict is making me make these updates.

I'm going to stick to updating you with technology and methods but like the above where I said take the past and extrapolate it into the future, I will be giving you a good dose of philosophy with the education. Like Cresson, I too will die someday and you'll have to use that thinking and philosophy to make future decisions for yourself. I hope to "Enable you" as much as Creason did. Also, NONE of the Original Text of the book is being changed. I'm only making these additional pages and inserting them next to the original text.

WHY YOU AND YOUR FAMILY AND ALMOST ALL OTHER AMERICANS ARE LEFT UNPROTECTED HOSTAGES TO THE SOVIET UNION

Unknown to most Americans, our Government lacks the defense capabilities that would enable the United States to stop being dependent on a uniquely American strategic policy called Mutual Assured Destruction (MAD). MAD maintains that if both the United States and Russia do not or can not adequately protect their people and essential industries, then neither will attack the other.

An influential minority of Americans still believe that protecting our citizens and our vital industries would accelerate the arms race and increase the risk of war. No wonder that President Reagan's advocacy of the Strategic Defense Initiative, derisively called Star Wars, is subjected to impassioned opposition by those who believe that peace is threatened even by research to develop new weapons designed to destroy weapons launched against us or our allies! No wonder that even a proposed small increase in funding for civil defense to save lives if deterrence fails arouses stronger opposition from MAD supporters than do most much larger expenditures for weapons to kill people!

RUSSIAN, SWISS, AND AMERICAN CIVIL DEFENSE

No nation other than the United States has advocated or adopted a strategy that purposely leaves its citizens unprotected hostages to its enemies. The rulers of the Soviet Union never have adopted a MAD strategy and continue to prepare the Russians to fight, survive, and win all types of wars. Almost all Russians have compulsory instruction to teach them about the effects of nuclear and other mass-destruction weapons, and what they can do to improve their chances of surviving. Comprehensive preparations have been made for the crisis evacuation of urban Russians to rural areas, where they and rural Russians would make high-protection-factor expedient fallout shelters. Blast shelters to protect millions have been built in the cities and near factories where essential workers would continue production during a crisis. Wheat reserves and other foods for war survivors have been stored outside target areas. About 100,000 civil defense troops are maintained for control, rescue, and post-attack recovery duties. The annual per capita cost of Russian civil defense preparations, if made at costs equivalent to those in the United States, is variously estimated to be between $8 and $20.

Switzerland has the best civil defense system, one that already includes blast shelters for over 85 percent of all its citizens. Swiss investment in this most effective kind of war-risk insurance has continued steadily for decades. According to Dr. Fritz Sager, the Vice Director of Switzerland's civil defense, in 1984 the cost was the equivalent of $12.60 per capita.

In contrast, our Federal Emergency Management Agency, that includes nuclear attack preparedness among its many responsibilities, will receive only about $126 million in fiscal 1987. This will amount to about 55 cents for each American. And only a small fraction of this pittance will be available for nuclear attack preparedness! Getting out better self-help survival instructions is about all that FEMA could afford to do to improve Americans' chances of surviving a nuclear war, unless FEMA's funding for war-related civil defense is greatly increased.

PRACTICALITY OF MAKING SURVIVAL PREPARATIONS DURING A CRISIS

The emphasis in this book is on survival preparations that can be made in the last few days of a worsening crisis. However, the measures put into effect during such a crisis can be very much more effective if plans and some preparations are completed well in advance. It is hoped that persons who read this book will be motivated at least to make the preparations outlined in Chapter 16, Minimum Pre-Crisis Preparations.

Well-informed persons realize that a nuclear attack by the Soviet Union is unlikely to be a Pearl-Harbor-type of attack, launched without warning. Strategists agree that a nuclear war most likely would begin after a period of days-to-months of worsening crisis. The most realistic of the extensive Russian plans and preparations to survive a nuclear war are based on using at least several days during an escalating crisis to get most urban dwellers out of the cities and other high risk areas, to build or improve shelters in all parts of the Soviet Union, and to protect essential machinery and the like. The Russians know that if they are able to complete evacuation and sheltering plans before the outbreak of nuclear war, the number of their people killed would be a small fraction of those who otherwise would die. Our satellites and other sources of intelligence would reveal such massive movements within a day; therefore, under the most likely circumstances Americans would have several days in which to make life-saving preparations.

The Russians have learned from the devastating wars they have survived that people are the most important asset to be saved. Russian civil defense publications emphasize Lenin's justly famous statement: "The primary productive factor of all humanity is the laboring man, the worker. If he survives, we can save everything and restore everything . . . but we shall perish if we are not able to save him." Strategists conclude that those in power in the Soviet Union are very unlikely to launch a nuclear attack until they have protected most of their people.

The reassurance of having at least a few days of pre-attack warning, however, is lessening. The increasing numbers of Soviet blast shelters and of first-strike offensive weapons capable of destroying our undefended retaliatory weapons will reduce the importance of pre-attack city evacuation as a means of saving Russian lives. These ongoing developments will make it less likely that Americans will have a few days' warning before a Soviet attack, and therefore should motivate our Government both to deploy truly defensive Star Wars weapons and to build blast shelters to protect urban Americans.

Nuclear weapons that could strike the United States continue to increase in accuracy as well as numbers; the most modern warheads usually can hit within a few hundred feet of their precise targets. The Soviet Union already has enough warheads to target all militarily important fixed-site objectives. These include our fixed-site weapons, command and control centers, military installations, oil refineries and other industrial plants that produce war essentials, long runways, and major electric generating plants. Many of these are either in or near cities. Because most Americans live in cities that contain strategically important targets, urban Americans' best chance of surviving a heavy nuclear attack is to get out of cities during a worsening crisis and into fallout shelters away from probable targets.

Most American civil defense advocates believe that it would be desirable for our Government to build and stock permanent blast shelters. However, such permanent shelters would cost many tens of billions of dollars and are not likely to be undertaken as a national objective. Therefore, field-tested instructions and plans are needed to enable both urban evacuees and rural Americans to build expedient shelters and life-support equipment during a crisis.

SMALLER NUCLEAR ATTACKS ON AMERICA

Many strategists believe that the United States is more likely to suffer a relatively small nuclear attack than an all-out Soviet onslaught. These possible smaller nuclear attacks include:

- A limited Soviet attack that might result if Russia's rulers were to conclude that an American President would be likely to capitulate rather than retaliate if a partially disarming first strike knocked out most of our fixed-site and retaliatory weapons, but spared the great majority of our cities. Then tens of millions of people living away from missile silos and Strategic Air Force bases would need only fallout protection. Even Americans who live in large metropolitan areas and doubt that they could successfully evacuate during a nuclear crisis should realize that in the event of such a limited attack they would have great need for nuclear war survival skills.

- An accidental or unauthorized launching of one or several nuclear weapons that would explode on America. Complex computerized weapon systems and/or their human operators are capable of making lethal errors.

- A small attack on the United States by the fanatical ruler of an unstable country that may acquire small nuclear weapons and a primitive delivery system.

- A terrorist attack, that will be a more likely possibility once nuclear weapons become available in unstable nations. Fallout dangers could extend clear across America. For example, a single small nuclear weapon exploded in a West Coast city would cause lethal fallout hazards to unsheltered persons for several miles downwind from the part of the city devastated by blast and fire. It also would result in deposition of fallout in downwind localities up to hundreds of miles away, with radiation dose rates hundreds of times higher than the normal background. Fallout would be especially heavy in areas of rainout; pregnant women and small children in those areas, following peacetime standards for radiation protection, might need to stay sheltered for weeks. Furthermore, in localities spotted across the United States, milk would be contaminated by radioiodine.

Surely in future years nuclear survival know-how will become an increasingly important part of every prudent person's education.

WHY THIS 1987 EDITION?

This updated and augmented edition is needed to give you:

- Information on how changes since 1979 in the Soviet nuclear arsenal — especially the great reductions in the sizes of Russian warheads and increases in their accuracy and number — both decrease and increase the dangers we all face. You need this information to make logical decisions regarding essentials of your survival planning, including whether you should evacuate during a worsening crisis or build or improvise shelter at or near your home.
- Instructions for making and using self-help survival items that have been re-discovered, invented or improved since 1979. These do-it-yourself items include: (1) Directional Fanning, the simplest way to ventilate shelters through large openings; (2) the Plywood Double-Action Piston Pump, to ventilate shelters through pipes; and (3) the improved KFM, the best homemakeable fallout meter.
- Facts that refute two demoralizing anti-defense myths that have been conceived and propagandized since 1979: the myth of blinding post-attack ultra-violet radiation and the myth of unsurvivable "nuclear winter".
- Current information on advantages and disadvantages, prices, and sources of some manufactured survival items for which there is greatest need.
- Updated facts on low cost survival foods and on expedient means for processing and cooking whole-kernel grains, soybeans, and other overproduced basic foods. Our Government stores no food as a war reserve and has not given even civil defense workers the instructions needed to enable survivors to make good use of America's unplanned, poorly distributed, large stocks of unprocessed foods.
- Updated information on how to obtain and use prophylactic potassium iodide to protect your thyroid against injury both from war fallout, and also from peacetime fallout if the United States suffers its first commercial nuclear power reactor accident releasing life-endangering radiation.
- Instructions for building, furnishing, and stocking economical, **permanent** home fallout shelters designed for dual use—in a new chapter.
- Information on what you can do to prevent sickness if fallout from an overseas nuclear war in which the United States is not a belligerent is blown across the Pacific and deposited on America — in a new chapter.

EXOTIC WEAPONS

Chemical and biological weapons and neutron warheads are called "exotic weapons". Protective measures against these weapons are not emphasized in this book, because its purpose is to help Americans improve their chances of surviving what is by far the most likely type of attack on the United States: a nuclear attack directed against war-related strategic targets.

Chemical Weapons are inefficient killing agents compared to typical nuclear warheads and bombs. Even if exterminating the unprepared population of a specified large area were an enemy's objective, this would require a delivered payload of deadly chemical weapons many hundreds of times heavier than if large nuclear weapons were employed.

Biological Weapons are more effective but less reliable than chemical weapons. They are more dependent on favorable meteorological conditions, and could destroy neither our retaliatory weapons nor our war-supporting installations. They could not kill or incapacitate well protected military personnel manning our retaliatory weapons. And a biological attack could not prevent, but would invite, U.S. nuclear retaliatory strikes.

Neutron Warheads are small, yet extremely expensive. A 1-kiloton neutron warhead costs about as much as a 1-megaton ordinary warhead, but the ordinary warhead not only has 1000 times the explosive power but also can be surface-burst to cover a very large area with deadly fallout.

REWARDS

My greatest reward for writing *Nuclear War Survival Skills* is the realization that the hundreds of thousands of copies of the original edition which have been sold since 1979 already have provided many thousands of people with survival information that may save their lives. Especially rewarding have been the thanks of readers — particularly mothers with small children — for having given them hope of surviving a nuclear war. Rekindled, realistic hope has caused some readers to work to improve their and their families' chances of surviving, ranging from making preparations to evacuate high risk areas during an all too possible worsening crisis, to building and stocking permanent shelters.

Because I wrote the original *Nuclear War Survival Skills* while working at Oak Ridge National Laboratory at the American taxpayers'

IT ALL CHANGED JUST A FEW YEARS LATER Cresson's last major update to the book was in 1987. There was a 1999 addition but his last major update was '87. In just 2 years from then the "Wall" of East and West would fall and just over 2 years later just before 1992 started the Union of Soviet Socialist Republics (Soviet Union) would officially dissolve.

1992 to the end of 2019 was a time of unheralded peace and prosperity that two entire generations grew up in it never knowing of the fears and forces that motivated the writing of this book. Cresson wrote this book because he knew the people needed it and he started it in the late 1970s. Cresson was an exploration geologist for Standard Oil in the 1930s. He was in the jungles of Venezuela and other South American locations and he went and joined the US Army in 1939 because he knew his country was going to war with Japan and it would be a jungle war and he wanted to help get his country ready.

HE WAS RIGHT IN 1987, HE IS RIGHT IN 2022 On the previous page, Cresson mentions the 1987 update to help inform you on possible radionuclide sickness from nuclear devices detonated on other continents going around the world and landing in the USA. Principally this type of radiation is going to affect you by entering the food chain and thus the increased need for Potassium Iodide (addressed later). However, that paragraph about that update in this book is probably the reason you are reading this book and its update right now because that is now a very strong likelihood. I've postulated and stated for some time that the year we have the first nuclear detonation in anger since 1945 will also be the year we have 6 to 12 more. Once the dam is broken no one will fear being 'the first one to use nuclear weapons."

PERMNAMENT HOME SHLELTER I will try to address it later in this update but as Cresson recommends I have a permanent fallout shelter in my basement. It's not a blast shelter, it's not under the ground, it's in the corner of my basement. It's been there since about 2000 and it's 4 feet wide by 4 feet tall by 8 feet long. Made of 2x4's and plywood. It's in the corner of the basement so those two sides have radiation shielding from the cement walls of the outside earth. My emergency food storage of flour, wheat, corn, rice, cooking oil, water, and other supplies are in buckets on top of and around the shelter on the top and other two sides. This is to provide me with a reduction in radiation from the fallout that is outside. I have several real and calibrated radiation meters so I know what I am receiving. I can come out of the shelter to eat, use the sanitation facilities, shower, etc....but while I am in the shelter my exposure to the radiation is much lower. Depending on the levels of radiation you do not need to hide in a cave for a month and never come out.

BIOLOGICAL WEAPONS All through all of my CBRN training (Chemical, Biological, Radiological, Nuclear) all of the focus was always on "Anthrax is about 35% lethal" or "Ebola could be 65% Lethal" or "Weaponized Smallpox would be over 85% lethal and higher." It was always about how lethal it was. Nuclear weapons are the 'big scarry'. The greatest threat to human life on the planet is one of two things. 1. The eventual asteroid hitting it in 10 minutes from now to 10's of millions of years from now or 2. A simple virus. We never thought in our wildest imagination of a concept that someone or a country would make a 0.5% - 1.0% lethal virus and release it on the whole world to destabilize countries for other purposes. Now whether you think this is a reality, conjecture, or fiction; a virus of low lethality has gone through the world population multiple times in multiple varients and killed a low percentage of the population since February of 2020. What can't be argued is those entire ways of life, entire ways of doing business, and entire economies have been transformed, destroyed, altered, or created. Because of a simple virus.

Fukashima showed the world what a nuclear reactor can do when it loses its primary cooling source and its multiple backup sources of cooling. COVID-19 showed the whole world, and everyone who wants to do evil to someone else, just what the power of even a very mild yet very contagious virus can do. It takes teams of scientists and a government to manufacture a detonating nuclear device along with many tens of billions of dollars or more. A very talented masters level college student can manipulate a virus where it can be the next pandemic. Its not easy, its not simple but a very talented person with a masters to Ph.D level of knowledge and the right lab tools (at a university) could do it.

REWARDS Cresson was paid by the US Government to write the original copy of this book. The 400,000 copies printed and sold by others over 9 years he did not get any royalty from nor wanted any. The people that printed and sold those 400,000 copies made a profit. Many did it to help others but the costs of paper and printing and binding and shipping and labor had to be covered. I, Steven Harris, do get a reward from this version of the book and I'm not paid by the government to do it. I have had the website NuclearWarSurvivalSkills.com up since before 2012. I paid to have it hosted in a high-speed cloud capable of tens of millions of unique hits and downloads a day. Those are monthly fees for the last 10+ years. The hosting provider guaranteed me the site would not crash, ever, from user traffic. They understood my mission. The 1987 version of Cresson's NWSS is up there for FREE Download. Without a fee, without condition, without signup or registration. Just free to download. I promised Cresson I'd make the book available to the whole world in a time of a crisis. That is what I have done for the last 10 years. The PDF file is hosted either on Amazon S3 or in the StorJ.io blockchain cloud. It costs about just under one-tenth of a penny for you to download the book from my hosted storage. Just in March 2022, I have had over 300,000 free downloads of the original NWSS PDF. I have kept the price for the book on Amazon low and available within a day to days for most of the modern world (US, Europe, Australia, Canada, Japan). Any funds my corporation gets from you buying a physical copy of the original book, or this 2022 updated copy that I have authored just goes to pay the bills to give the base version of NWSS away for free to all with no condition. I'm not driving a Bently, I drive a Dodge. Take that 0.1 US Cents per download and multiply it by 30 million if a nuke pops on the surface of the Earth in anger. Thank you for your support.

expense, I have no proprietory interest either in the original 1979 Government edition or in any of the privately printed reproductions. I have gotten nothing but satisfaction from the reported sales of over 400,000 copies privately printed and sold between 1979 and 1987. Nor will I receive any monetary reward in the future from my efforts to give better survival instructions to people who want to improve their chances of surviving a nuclear attack.

AVAILABILITY

None of the material that appeared in the original Oak Ridge National Laboratory uncopyrighted 1979 edition can be covered by a legitimate copyright; it can be reproduced by anyone, without receiving permission. Much new material, which I have written since my retirement in 1979 from Oak Ridge National Laboratory, has been added, and is printed in a different type. To assure that this new material also can be made widely available to the public at low cost, without getting permission from or paying anyone, I have copyrighted my new material in the unusual way specified by this 1987 edition's copyright notice.

RECOMMENDED ACTIONS

Work to persuade the President, your Congressmen, your Senators, and other leaders to support improved nuclear war survival preparations, starting with increased funding for war-related civil defense. Urge them to approve and fund the early deployment of truly defensive weapons that tests already have proven capable of destroying some warheads in flight. (Attempts to develop perfect defenses postpone or prevent the attainment of improved defenses.)

Obtain and study the best survival instructions available **long before** a crisis occurs. Better yet, also make preparations, such as the ones described in this book, to increase your and your family's chances of surviving.

During a crisis threatening nuclear attack, present uncertainties regarding the distribution of reliable survival information seem likely to continue. Thoroughly field-tested survival instructions are not likely to be available to most Americans. Furthermore, even a highly intelligent citizen, if given excellent instructions during a crisis, would not have time to learn basic facts about nuclear dangers and the reasons for various survival preparations. Without this understanding, no one can do his best at following any type of survival instructions.

By following the instructions in this book, you and your family can increase the odds favoring your survival. If such instructions were made widely available from official sources, and if our Government urged all Americans to follow them during a worsening crisis lasting at least several days, additional millions would survive an attack. And the danger of an attack, even the threat of an attack, could be decreased if an enemy nation knew that we had significantly improved our defenses in this way.

Chapter 1

The Dangers from Nuclear Weapons: Myths and Facts

An all-out nuclear war between Russia and the United States would be the worst catastrophe in history, a tragedy so huge it is difficult to comprehend. Even so, it would be far from the end of human life on earth. The dangers from nuclear weapons have been distorted and exaggerated, for varied reasons. These exaggerations have become demoralizing myths, believed by millions of Americans.

While working with hundreds of Americans building expedient shelters and life-support equipment, I have found that many people at first see no sense in talking about details of survival skills. Those who hold exaggerated beliefs about the dangers from nuclear weapons must first be convinced that nuclear war would not inevitably be the end of them and everything worthwhile. Only after they have begun to question the truth of these myths do they become interested, under normal peacetime conditions, in acquiring nuclear war survival skills. Therefore, before giving detailed instructions for making and using survival equipment, we will examine the most harmful of the myths about nuclear war dangers, along with some of the grim facts.

- **Myth**: Fallout radiation from a nuclear war would poison the air and all parts of the environment. It would kill everyone. (This is the demoralizing message of *On the Beach* and many similar pseudoscientific books and articles.)

- **Facts**: When a nuclear weapon explodes near enough to the ground for its fireball to touch the ground, it forms a crater. (See Fig. 1.1.) Many

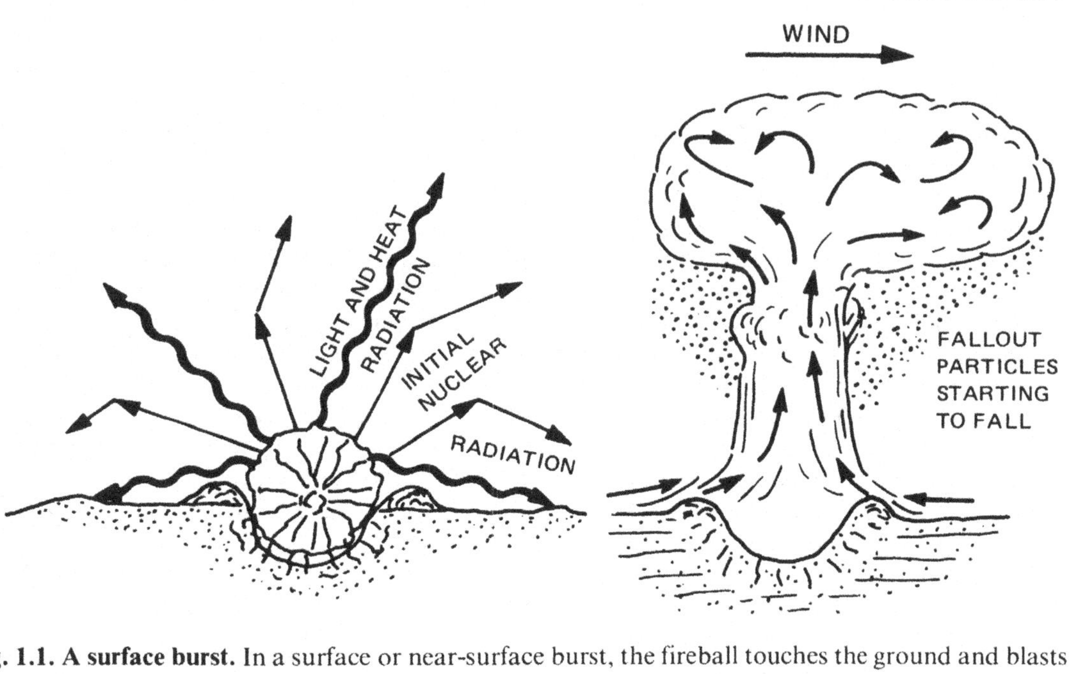

Fig. 1.1. A surface burst. In a surface or near-surface burst, the fireball touches the ground and blasts a crater.

Air Burst Nuclear Detonations vs Ground Burst Detonations

AIR BURST VS GROUND BURST

Pay particular attention to the previous page. When a nuclear device gets detonated people think of a bright light, a blast wave, and a mushroom cloud. I'm going to simplify this a bit but the nuclear reaction, the whole thing happens in less than one-millionth of a second. The blastwave, the light, the heat from the reaction, and the fireball all come from the massive energy release that happened in many forms. Part of this is the drastic heating of the air around the weapon and this goes to form what you see as the majority of the bright light and the fireball and the mushroom cloud. (yes, I'm simplifying it here)

This cloud, the heated air, is very hot, beyond comprehension hot and it expands out. When this fireball touches the ground, the earth, picks up, vaporizes, condenses, and also just plain melts soil, particles, buildings, cement, rocks, everything. Not all of the nuclear material in the bomb is used in the explosion, it literally blows itself apart before the whole reaction can use all of the nuclear material and that nuclear material gets mixed in with everything I just stated that got picked up from the ground and it goes up in the mushroom cloud. This goes up and then outward and away with the wind. The large particles start to fall out right away. Think of things the size of golf balls to a pea, then the smaller particles keep on staying in the air and go downwind. When normal material gets hit with neutrons it can become 'radioactive' as well. So along with all this material getting hit with neutrons as well as the radioactive elements of the weapon fusing with everything this travels and 'falls out' and those particles are radioactive for a period of time that decreases quickly.

DOING THE MOST DAMAGE.

If you are a foreign power or a terrorist and you want to detonate a nuclear device in the air, some single-digit thousands of feet above the ground. The shock wave (blast wave) extends outward and it also bounces off the ground and then reflects up and combines with the first wave to increase the blast wave pressure forming something called a Mach Y (or a mach stem). This increases the destructive radius of the device and makes more devastation. Weapons are ground burst near or at or in the ground to kill missile silos with our missiles in them. To destroy long airfields that bombers can use and blow up places like the previous NORAD command center at Cheyanne Mountain. If you want the most destruction on a population center you want the bomb to go off at a reasonable altitude to make a larger radius of destruction. Thus the weapons fireball probably will not hit the ground and pick up the earth. So the only thing that goes into the fallout from an air burst is the actual components of the bomb itself. The casing, the leftover radionuclides that did not react, the paint on the bomb, the wires, everything. I have some "Trinitite" from Ed York that he gave me. This is the sand under the first nuclear detonation in 1945 at Los Alamos. The bomb "the gadget" was on a tower. It melted the sand under it and turned it into green glass. Well, parts of the bomb, the tower, and even the minerals in the bodies of any ants walking under it along with the ground are all fused into the trinitite. Even minuscule amounts of the unreacted plutonium from the first weapon are in theory in the piece of trinitite that I have. So in theory I own plutonium even if it's billionths of a gram.

WHAT EVER HAPPENS IN 2022, RUSSIA GETS BLAMED.

So right now in the USA if there is a cyber attack and our power goes out, Russia gets blamed. If there is a nuclear detonation here then Russia gets blamed. Even if North Korea or Pakistan or (insert country name here) detonates a nuclear device in the USA, or anywhere, then Russia immediately gets the blame. So even if someone else does something here, Russia gets blamed. NOTE: the USA Nuclear NEST teams and the Department of Energy and the US Military can go into an area after a blast and they can read the exact components of the radiation and know where the bomb was made. What country, even what reactor. So the truth will come out but the first casualty of war is the truth.

MY POINT ?!! If Russia launches a missile at us over the North Pole then we pretty much know where it came from and it'd have to be many at once. If China or North Korea tries to send a bomber here, it's not going to make it. It's too long of a flight and our intelligence is too good. We'd know about it. Same with alone or a few missiles. It's a long flight across the "Pacific" and it'd probably be intercepted. The way a bad foreign actor could detonate a nuclear device in the USA is to smuggle it in (please do NOT say shipping container, there are many other ways to get stuff here). If it's smuggled in it will probably be delivered to the detonation location by ground vehicle (truck) and detonated on the ground. It's not impossible but putting in an airplane and flying it over LA would have a lot more difficulties than just driving a truck with it there. It would also probably be a fission device in the kiloton range and not a thermonuclear fusion device in the megaton range.

So my point is that if one did go off in the USA and it was not a full 1980's style USSR vs USA exchange of 10,000 devices then it would probably be a "Hiroshima" sized device (1kt to 200kt) and detonated on the ground. This would mean a much smaller radius of destruction and it would mean there would be very measurable fallout downwind from the device. You'd be able to measure the 'plume' and what was deposited all across the USA.

Even though there is Open Source Intelligence (OSINT) to allege that Russia, China already has nuclear devices hiding on continental USA soil this just goes to show that the theory that such a device would be detonated on the ground at a target location delivered by a ground vehicle is are probable scenario.

OSINT also will tell you about a Fractional Orbit Bombardment System (FOBS) but I want the addendum to deal with things that are more likely to happen than the things that are harder to achieve. Any future editions of this book will always address the more relevant threats presumed at that time to help you. One thing to remember is that history proves; that nothing happens the way you think it is going to.

thousands of tons of earth from the crater of a large explosion are pulverized into trillions of particles. These particles are contaminated by radioactive atoms produced by the nuclear explosion. Thousands of tons of the particles are carried up into a mushroom-shaped cloud, miles above the earth. These radioactive particles then fall out of the mushroom cloud, or out of the dispersing cloud of particles blown by the winds—thus becoming fallout.

Each contaminated particle continuously gives off invisible radiation, much like a tiny X-ray machine—while in the mushroom cloud, while descending, and after having fallen to earth. The descending radioactive particles are carried by the winds like the sand and dust particles of a miles-thick sandstorm cloud—except that they usually are blown at lower speeds and in many areas the particles are so far apart that no cloud is seen. The largest, heaviest fallout particles reach the ground first, in locations close to the explosion. Many smaller particles are carried by the winds for tens to thousands of miles before falling to earth. At any one place where fallout from a single explosion is being deposited on the ground in concentrations high enough to require the use of shelters, deposition will be completed within a few hours.

The smallest fallout particles—those tiny enough to be inhaled into a person's lungs—are invisible to the naked eye. These tiny particles would fall so slowly from the four-mile or greater heights to which they would be injected by currently deployed Soviet warheads that most would remain airborne for weeks to years before reaching the ground. By that time their extremely wide dispersal and radioactive decay would make them much less dangerous. Only where such tiny particles are promptly brought to earth by rain-outs or snow-outs in scattered "hot spots," and later dried and blown about by the winds, would these invisible particles constitute a long-term and relatively minor post-attack danger.

The air in properly designed fallout shelters, even those without air filters, is free of radioactive particles and safe to breathe except in a few rare environments—as will be explained later.

Fortunately for all living things, the danger from fallout radiation lessens with time. The radioactive decay, as this lessening is called, is rapid at first, then gets slower and slower. The dose rate (the amount of radiation received per hour) decreases accordingly. Figure 1.2 illustrates the rapidity of the decay of radiation from fallout during the first two days after the nuclear explosion that produced it. R stands for roentgen, a measurement unit often used to measure exposure to gamma rays and X rays. Fallout meters called dosimeters measure the *dose* received by recording the number of R. Fallout meters called survey meters, or dose-rate meters, measure the *dose rate* by recording the number of R being received per hour at the time of measurement. Notice that it takes about seven times as long for the dose rate to decay

ORNL-DWG 78-6265

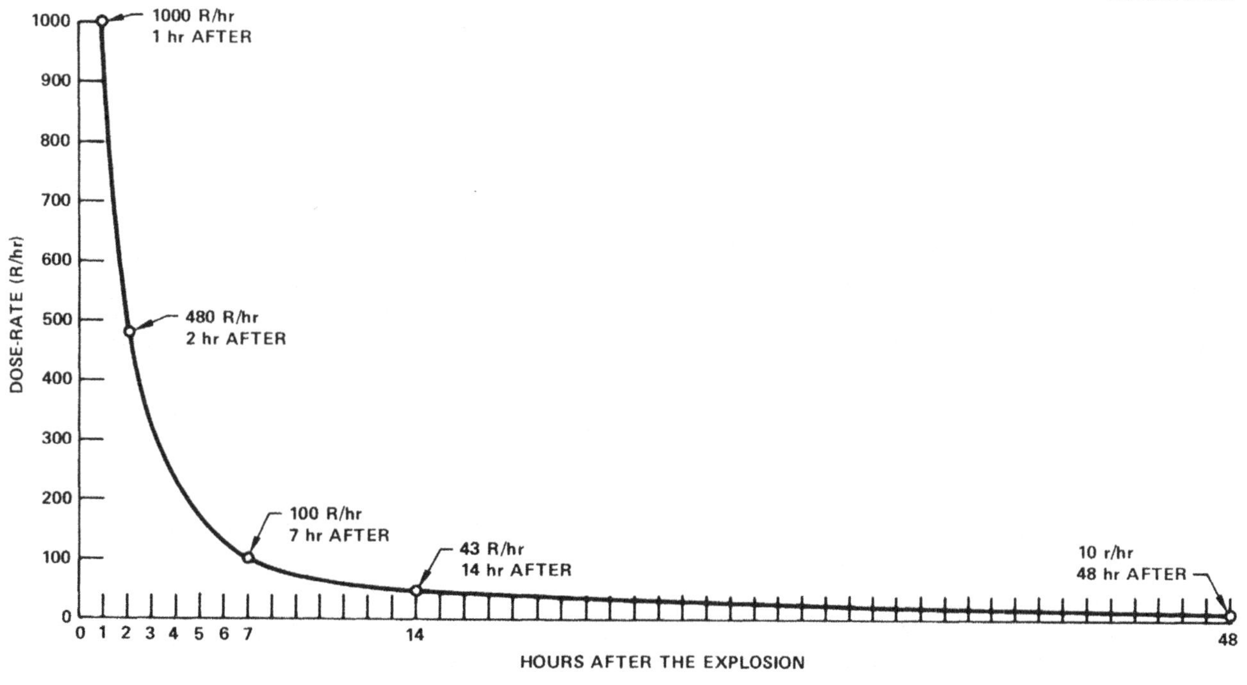

Fig. 1.2. Decay of the dose rate of radiation from fallout, from the time of the explosion, not from the time of fallout deposition.

from 1000 roentgens per hour (1000 R/hr) to 10 R/hr (48 hours) as to decay from 1000 R/hr to 100 R/hr (7 hours). (Only in high-fallout areas would the dose rate 1 hour after the explosion be as high as 1000 roentgens per hour.)

If the dose rate 1 hour after an explosion is 1000 R/hr, it would take about 2 weeks for the dose rate to be reduced to 1 R/hr solely as a result of radioactive decay. Weathering effects will reduce the dose rate further; for example, rain can wash fallout particles from plants and houses to lower positions on or closer to the ground. Surrounding objects would reduce the radiation dose from these low-lying particles.

Figure 1.2 also illustrates the fact that at a typical location where a given amount of fallout from an explosion is deposited later than 1 hour after the explosion, the highest dose rate and the total dose received at that location are less than at a location where the same amount of fallout is deposited 1 hour after the explosion. The longer fallout particles have been airborne before reaching the ground, the less dangerous is their radiation.

Within two weeks after an attack the occupants of most shelters could safely stop using them, or could work outside the shelters for an increasing number of hours each day. Exceptions would be in areas of extremely heavy fallout such as might occur downwind from important targets attacked with many weapons, especially missile sites and very large cities. To know when to come out safely, occupants either would need a reliable fallout meter to measure the changing radiation dangers, or must receive information based on measurements made nearby with a reliable instrument.

The radiation dose that will kill a person varies considerably with different people. A dose of 450 R resulting from exposure of the whole body to fallout radiation is often said to be the dose that will kill about half the persons receiving it, although most studies indicate that it would take somewhat less.[1] *(Note: A number written after a statement refers the reader to a source listed in the Selected References that follow Appendix D.)* Almost all persons confined to expedient shelters after a nuclear attack would be under stress and without clean surroundings or antibiotics to fight infections. Many also would lack adequate water and food. Under these unprecedented conditions, perhaps half the persons who received a whole-body dose of 350 R within a few days would die.[2]

Fortunately, the human body can repair most radiation damage if the daily radiation doses are not too large. As will be explained in Appendix B, a person who is healthy and has not been exposed in the past two weeks to a total radiation dose of more than 100 R can receive a dose of 6 R each day for at least two months without being incapacitated.

Only a very small fraction of Hiroshima and Nagasaki citizens who survived radiation doses—some of which were nearly fatal—have suffered serious delayed effects. The reader should realize that to do essential work after a massive nuclear attack, many survivors must be willing to receive much larger radiation doses than are normally permissible. Otherwise, too many workers would stay inside shelter too much of the time, and work that would be vital to national recovery could not be done. For example, if the great majority of truckers were so fearful of receiving even non-incapacitating radiation doses that they would refuse to transport food, additional millions would die from starvation alone.

- **Myth**: Fallout radiation penetrates everything; there is no escaping its deadly effects.

- **Facts**: Some gamma radiation from fallout will penetrate the shielding materials of even an excellent shelter and reach its occupants. However, the radiation dose that the occupants of an excellent shelter would receive while inside this shelter can be reduced to a dose smaller than the average American receives during his lifetime from X rays and other radiation exposures normal in America today. The design features of such a shelter include the use of a sufficient thickness of earth or other heavy shielding material. Gamma rays are like X rays, but more penetrating. Figure 1.3 shows how rapidly gamma rays are reduced in number (but not in their ability to penetrate) by layers of packed earth. Each of the layers shown is one halving-thickness of packed earth—about 3.6 inches (9 centimeters).[3] A halving-thickness is the thickness of a material which reduces by half the dose of radiation that passes through it.

The actual paths of gamma rays passing through shielding materials are much more complicated, due to scattering, etc., than are the straight-line paths shown in Fig. 1.3. But when averaged out, the effectiveness of a halving-thickness of any material is approximately as shown. The denser a substance, the better it serves for shielding material. Thus, a halving-thickness of concrete is only about 2.4 inches (6.1 cm).

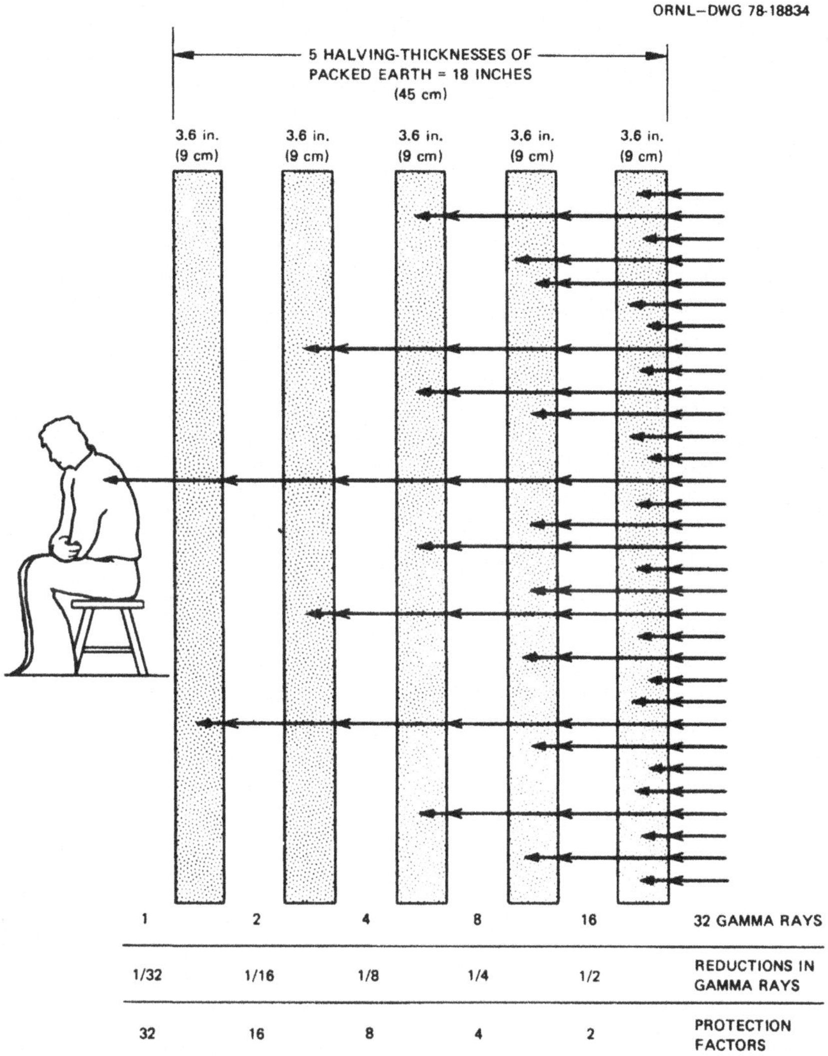

Fig. 1.3. Illustration of shielding against fallout radiation. Note the increasingly large improvements in the attenuation (reduction) factors that are attained as each additional halving-thickness of packed earth is added.

If additional halving-thicknesses of packed earth shielding are successively added to the five thicknesses shown in Fig. 1.3, the protection factor (PF) is successively increased from 32 to 64, to 128, to 256, to 512, to 1024, and so on.

- **Myth**: A heavy nuclear attack would set practically everything on fire, causing "firestorms" in cities that would exhaust the oxygen in the air. All shelter occupants would be killed by the intense heat.

- **Facts**: On a clear day, thermal pulses (heat radiation that travels at the speed of light) from an air burst can set fire to easily ignitable materials (such as window curtains, upholstery, dry newspaper, and dry grass) over about as large an area as is damaged by the blast. It can cause second-degree skin burns to exposed people who are as far as ten miles from a one-megaton (1 MT) explosion. (See Fig. 1.4.) (A 1-MT nuclear explosion is one that produces the same amount of energy as does one million tons of TNT.) If the weather is very clear and dry, the area of fire danger could be considerably larger. On a cloudy or smoggy day, however, particles in the air would absorb and scatter much of the heat radiation, and the area endangered by heat radiation from the fireball would be less than the area of severe blast damage.

The Most Important Drawing In This Book?

THE DRAWING OF THE RADIATION HALVING

The drawing on page 14 that shows that radiation is reduced in half with every 3.6 inches of dirt is one of the most important ones in this book that will save your life. So 5 layers of 3.6 inches of dirt which equals 18 inches of dirt will reduce the radiation of the people behind it by 32 times. So if you were going to get 3 Rads a day outside from some nuclear event, in your shelter in your house or outside that uses boxes of dirt, bricks and such to reduct the radition by 32 times would mean that youd be getting about 10miliRad a day. That is a lot better than getting 3 Rads a day. Note: in the full theoretically soviet exchange your outside radiation in very bad areas would not be 3 Rads per day but 600-1000 Rads per HOUR. That is a 100% letal does in an hour. If there was a ground detonation in Los Angeles of a small device and you were in Las Vegas and the fallout was 1 to 2 days away, with the knowledge in this book you could make a shelter in your home where the radiation would be not the 3 Rads per day in this hypothetical, but 10 milirads per day. Your radiation for a day could be 20 Rads, 3 Rads, 0.1 Rads or it could be 50 Rads or 50 millirads. Its too varible to guess at in these notes but it will be on all of your media what radiation levels are expected in what areas and for how long.

In the above theoretical example of getting 3 Rads a day outside and 1/32nd of that a day inside, if you were sheltering inside the house, you would have enough protection that you could leave your shelter in your house in Las Vegas and use the bathroom inside the house, get some food from the refrigerator or freezer, cook it, and take it back to your shelter. We are talking about you getting LESS radiation and not NO radiation.

3 NUMBERS REGARDING RADIATION

Cresson goes into this a bit more in his addendum on radiation hormesis but the 3 numbers that Ed York and Cresson and I decided on to remember are 3, 25 and 100. Despite OSHA radiation yearly limits for nuclear workers being a lot less you generally do not want to get more than 3 Rads per day. You want to keep it as far far far below this as possible. Keep in mind right now based on where you live in the USA your background radiation is from 3 microRads to 100 microRads per hour. A microRad is a millionth of a Rad. You can get 400 to 600 microRads an hour just flying in a jet across the country.

Ed York, at the time, was asked to set the maximum radiation an airforce pilot should receive before he has to abort his mission and return to base. This was probably the late 50's or early 60's, well Ed found out that at the time they could medically determine through blood work if you received 25 Rads or more at once so that became the limit. If you get 25 Rads from an event you really want to stay in your shelter and hide and get the lowest radiation dose possible for days or weeks but I can't advise on medical information in this book. At 100 Rads exposure that is the start of LD 1%. or Lethal Dose 1% where 1% of the people who recieve 100 Rads will die. Its also around the point where you will start to eventually loose your hair. So its highly varible, but if you get enough radiation to loose your hair there "MAY" be a 99% chance of survival. It does not mean you are going to die 100%. It does not mean you did not get more radiation or you are in that 1% and you are going to die.

So 5 Layers of 3.6" of dirt means you get 1/32nd the radiation. This is 2 to the 5th power or represented in text as 2^5. Which is 2 x 2 x 2 x 2 x2 = 32. 5 x 3.6" = 18" inches of dirt.

Instead of 5 layers of 3.6" of dirt you had 8 layers, it'd be 1/256th the radiation, if you had 10 layers, it would be 1/1024th the radiation.

LAYERS of 3.6" of Dirt and the Reduction

1 layers:	Reduction	2 times
2 layers:	Reduction	4 times
3 layers:	Reduction	8 times
4 layers:	Reduction	16 times
5 layers:	Reduction	32 times
6 layers:	Reduction	64 times
7 layers:	Reduction	128 times
8 layers:	Reduction	256 times
9 layers:	Reduction	512 times
10 layers:	Reduction	1024 times
11 layers:	Reduction	2048 times
12 layers:	Reduction	4096 times

Getting 600-1000 Rads quickly pretty much is LD 100. Lethal Dose 100% of the time. Although it might take you weeks or months to die. The radiation kills your bone marrow and your new red blood cells are made in your bone marrow. Red blood cells last about 120 days before they no longer work and are expelled from the body through fecal material. Since red blood cells are what transport oxygen all through your body from your lungs when you do not have enough of these you will die. This book is not a medical textbook on the effects of radiation but I wanted you to understand a few of the basics regarding the subject.

Its not just the radiation from the particles that is outside. What is very deterimental to the human body is having radioactdive particles on your cloths or skin and what is even worse is breathing them into your lungs or drinking or eathing the particles with your food. You do not want the particles inside your body radiating tissue with distance of millimeters or less. You want as much dirt and stuff and water and concrete between you and any source of radiation.

Cresson will disucuss in this book the rules of thumb in this book for decontamination of your clothing and making sure you do not eat or drink and even breath radionuclitides.

ORNL-DWG 78-6267

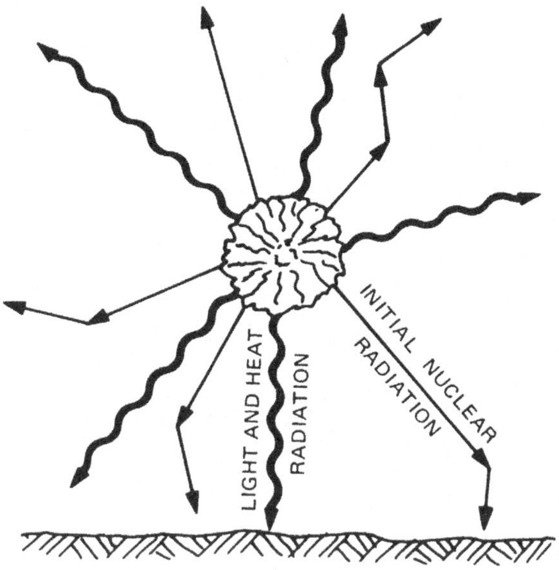

Fig. 1.4. An air burst. The fireball does not touch the ground. No crater. An air burst produces only extremely small radioactive particles—so small that they are airborne for days to years unless brought to earth by rain or snow. Wet deposition of fallout from both surface and air bursts can result in "hot spots" at, close to, or far from ground zero. However, such "hot spots" from air bursts are much less dangerous than the fallout produced by the surface or near-surface bursting of the same weapons.

The main dangers from an air burst are the blast effects, the thermal pulses of intense light and heat radiation, and the very penetrating initial nuclear radiation from the fireball.

"Firestorms" could occur only when the concentration of combustible structures is very high, as in the very dense centers of a few old American cities. At rural and suburban building densities, most people in earth-covered fallout shelters would not have their lives endangered by fires.

- **Myth:** In the worst-hit parts of Hiroshima and Nagasaki where all buildings were demolished, everyone was killed by blast, radiation, or fire.

- **Facts:** In Nagasaki, some people survived uninjured who were far inside tunnel shelters built for conventional air raids and located as close as one-third mile from ground zero (the point directly below the explosion). This was true even though these long, large shelters lacked blast doors and were deep inside the zone within which all buildings were destroyed. (People far inside long, large, open shelters are better protected than are those inside small, open shelters.)

Fig. 1.5. Undamaged earth-covered family shelter in Nagasaki.

Many earth-covered family shelters were essentially undamaged in areas where blast and fire destroyed all buildings. Figure 1.5 shows a typical earth-covered, backyard family shelter with a crude wooden frame. This shelter was essentially undamaged, although less than 100 yards from ground zero at Nagasaki.[4] The calculated maximum overpressure (pressure above the normal air pressure) was about 65 pounds per square inch (65 psi). Persons inside so small a shelter without a blast door would have been killed by blast pressure at this distance from the explosion. However, in a recent blast test,[5] an earth-covered, expedient Small-Pole Shelter equipped with blast doors was undamaged at 53 psi. The pressure rise inside was slight—not even enough to have damaged occupants' eardrums. If poles are available, field tests have indicated that many families can build such shelters in a few days.

The great life-saving potential of blast-protective shelters has been proven in war and confirmed by blast tests and calculations. For example, the area in which the air bursting of a 1-megaton weapon would wreck a 50-psi shelter with blast doors in about 2.7 square miles. Within this roughly circular area, practically all the occupants of wrecked shelters would be killed by blast, carbon monoxide from fires, or radiation. The same blast effects would kill most people who were using basements affording 5 psi protection, over an area of about 58 square miles.[6]

- **Myth:** Because some modern H-bombs are over 1000 times as powerful as the A-bomb that destroyed most of Hiroshima, these H-bombs are 1000 times as deadly and destructive.

- **Facts:** A nuclear weapon 1000 times as powerful as the one that blasted Hiroshima, if exploded under comparable conditions, produces equally serious blast damage to wood-frame houses over an area up to about 130 times as large, not 1000 times as large. For example, air bursting a 20-kiloton weapon at the optimum height to destroy most buildings will destroy or severely damage houses out to about 1.42 miles from ground zero.[6] The circular area of at least severe blast damage will be about 6.33 square miles. (The explosion of a 20 kiloton weapon releases the same amount of energy as 20 thousand tons of TNT.) One thousand 20-kiloton weapons thus air burst, well separated to avoid overlap of their blast areas, would destroy or severely damage houses over areas totaling approximately 6,330 square miles. In contrast, similar air bursting of one 20-megaton weapon (equivalent in explosive power to 20 million tons of TNT) would destroy or severely damage the great majority of houses out to a distance of 16 miles from ground zero.[6] The area of destruction would be about 800 square miles — not 6,330 square miles.

Today few if any of Russia's huge intercontinental ballistic missiles (ICBMs) are armed with a 20-megaton warhead. Now a huge Russian ICBM, the SS-18, typically carries 10 warheads, each having a yield of 500 kilotons, each programmed to hit a separate target. See *Jane's Weapon Systems, 1987-88.*

● **Myth:** A Russian nuclear attack on the United States would completely destroy all American cities.

● **Facts:** As long as Soviet leaders are rational they will continue to give first priority to knocking out our weapons and other military assets that can damage Russia and kill Russians. To explode enough nuclear weapons of any size to completely destroy American cities would be an irrational waste of warheads. The Soviets can make much better use of most of the warheads that would be required to completely destroy American cities; the majority of those warheads probably already are targeted to knock out our retaliatory missiles by being surface burst or near-surface burst on their hardened silos, located far from most cities and densely populated areas.

Unfortunately, many militarily significant targets — including naval vessels in port and port facilities, bombers and fighters on the ground, air base and airport facilities that can be used by bombers, Army installations, and key defense factories — are in or close to American cities. In the event of an all-out Soviet attack, most of these "soft" targets would be destroyed by air bursts. Air bursting (see Fig. 1.4) a given weapon subjects about twice as large an area to blast effects severe enough to destroy "soft" targets as does surface bursting (see Fig. 1.1) the same weapon. Fortunately for Americans living outside blast and fire areas, air bursts produce only very tiny particles. Most of these extremely small radioactive particles remain airborne for so long that their radioactive decay and wide dispersal before reaching the ground make them much less life-endangering than the promptly deposited larger fallout particles from surface and near-surface bursts. However, if you are a survival minded American you should prepare to survive heavy fallout wherever you are. Unpredictable winds may bring fallout from unexpected directions. Or your area may be in a "hot spot" of life-endangering fallout caused by a rain-out or snow-out of both small and tiny particles from distant explosions. Or the enemy may use surface or near-surface bursts in your part of the country to crater long runways or otherwise disrupt U.S. retaliatory actions by producing heavy local fallout.

Today few if any of Russia's largest intercontinental ballistic missiles (ICBMs) are armed with a 20-megaton warhead. A huge Russian ICBM, the SS-18, typically carries 10 warheads each having a yield of 500 kilotons, each programmed to hit a separate target. See *Jane's Weapon Systems,* 1987-1988. However, in March 1990 CIA Director William Webster told the U.S. Senate Armed Services Committee that "... The USSR's strategic modernization program continues unabated," and that the SS-18 Mod 5 can carry 14 to 20 nuclear warheads. The warheads are generally assumed to be smaller than those of the older SS-18s.

● **Myth:** So much food and water will be poisoned by fallout that people will starve and die even in fallout areas where there is enough food and water.

● **Facts:** If the fallout particles do not become mixed with the parts of food that are eaten, no harm is done. Food and water in dust-tight containers are not contaminated by fallout radiation. Peeling fruits and vegetables removes essentially all fallout, as does removing the uppermost several inches of stored grain onto which fallout particles have fallen. Water from many sources — such as deep wells and covered reservoirs, tanks, and containers — would not be contaminated. Even water containing dissolved radioactive elements and compounds can be made safe for drinking by simply filtering it through earth, as described later in this book.

● **Myth:** Most of the unborn children and grandchildren of people who have been exposed to radiation from nuclear explosions will be genetically damaged — will be malformed, delayed victims of nuclear war.

● **Facts:** The authoritative study by the National Academy of Sciences, *A Thirty Year Study of the Survivors of Hiroshima and Nagasaki,* was published in 1977. It concludes that the incidence of abnormalities is no higher among children later conceived by parents who were exposed to radiation during the attacks on Hiroshima and Nagasaki than is the incidence of abnormalities among Japanese children born to unexposed parents.

This is not to say that there would be no genetic damage, nor that some fetuses subjected to large radiation doses would not be damaged. But the overwhelming evidence does show that the exaggerated fears of radiation damage to future generations are not supported by scientific findings.

● **Myth:** Overkill would result if all the U.S. and U.S.S.R. nuclear weapons were used — meaning not only that the two superpowers have more than enough weapons to kill all of each other's people, but also that they have enough weapons to exterminate the human race.

• **Facts:** Statements that the U.S. and the Soviet Union have the power to kill the world's population several times over are based on misleading calculations. One such calculation is to multiply the deaths produced per kiloton exploded over Hiroshima or Nagasaki by an estimate of the number of kilotons in either side's arsenal. (A kiloton explosion is one that produces the same amount of energy as does 1000 tons of TNT.) The unstated assumption is that somehow the world's population could be gathered into circular crowds, each a few miles in diameter with a population density equal to downtown Hiroshima or Nagasaki, and then a small (Hiroshima-sized) weapon would be exploded over the center of each crowd. Other misleading calculations are based on exaggerations of the dangers from long-lasting radiation and other harmful effects of a nuclear war.

• **Myth:** Blindness and a disastrous increase of cancers would be the fate of survivors of a nuclear war, because the nuclear explosions would destroy so much of the protective ozone in the stratosphere that far too much ultraviolet light would reach the earth's surface. Even birds and insects would be blinded. People could not work outdoors in daytime for years without dark glasses, and would have to wear protective clothing to prevent incapacitating sunburn. Plants would be badly injured and food production greatly reduced.

• **Facts:** Large nuclear explosions do inject huge amounts of nitrogen oxides (gasses that destroy ozone) into the stratosphere. However, the percent of the stratospheric ozone destroyed by a given amount of nitrogen oxides has been greatly overestimated in almost all theoretical calculations and models. For example, the Soviet and U.S. atmospheric nuclear test explosions of large weapons in 1952-1962 were calculated by Foley and Ruderman to result in a reduction of more than 10 percent in total ozone. (See M. H. Foley and M. A. Ruderman, "Stratospheric NO from Past Nuclear Explosions", Journal of Geophysics, Res. 78, 4441-4450.) Yet observations that they cited showed no reductions in ozone. Nor did ultraviolet increase. Other theoreticians calculated sizeable reductions in total ozone, but interpreted the observational data to indicate either no reduction, or much smaller reductions than their calculated ones.

A realistic simplified estimate of the increased ultraviolet light dangers to American survivors of a large nuclear war equates these hazards to moving from San Francisco to sea level at the equator, where the sea level incidence of skin cancers (seldom fatal) is highest—about 10 times higher than the incidence at San Francisco. Many additional thousands of American survivors might get skin cancer, but little or no increase in skin cancers might result if in the post-attack world deliberate sun tanning and going around hatless went out of fashion. Furthermore, almost all of today's warheads are smaller than those exploded in the large-weapons tests mentioned above; most would inject much smaller amounts of ozone-destroying gasses, or no gasses, into the stratosphere, where ozone deficiencies may persist for years. And nuclear weapons smaller than 500 kilotons result in increases (due to smog reactions) in upper tropospheric ozone. In a nuclear war, these increases would partially compensate for the upper-level tropospheric decreases—as explained by Julius S. Chang and Donald J. Wuebbles of Lawrence Livermore National Laboratory.

• **Myth:** Unsurvivable "nuclear winter" surely will follow a nuclear war. The world will be frozen if only 100 megatons (less than one percent of all nuclear weapons) are used to ignite cities. World-enveloping smoke from fires and the dust from surface bursts will prevent almost all sunlight and solar heat from reaching the earth's surface. Universal darkness for weeks! Sub-zero temperatures, even in summertime! Frozen crops, even in the jungles of South America! Worldwide famine! Whole species of animals and plants exterminated! The survival of mankind in doubt!

• **Facts:** Unsurvivable "nuclear winter" is a discredited theory that, since its conception in 1982, has been used to frighten additional millions into believing that trying to survive a nuclear war is a waste of effort and resources, and that only by ridding the world of almost all nuclear weapons do we have a chance of surviving.

Non-propagandizing scientists recently have calculated that the climatic and other environmental effects of even an all-out nuclear war would be much less severe than the catastrophic effects repeatedly publicized by popular astronomer Carl Sagan and his fellow activist scientists, and by all the involved Soviet scientists. Conclusions reached from these recent, realistic calculations are summarized in an article, "Nuclear Winter Reappraised", featured in the 1986 summer issue of Foreign Affairs, the prestigious quarterly of the Council on Foreign Relations. The authors, Starley L. Thompson and Stephen H. Schneider, are atmospheric scientists with the National Center for Atmospheric Research. They showed " . . . that on scientific grounds the global apocalyptic conclusions of the initial nuclear winter hypothesis can now be relegated to a vanishing low level of probability." Their models indicate that in July (when the greatest temperature reductions would result) the average temperature in the United States would be reduced for a few days from about 70 degrees Fahrenheit to approximately 50 degrees. (In contrast, under the same conditions Carl Sagan, his associates, and the Russian scientists predicted a resulting average temperature of about 10 degrees below zero Fahrenheit, lasting for many weeks!)

Persons who want to learn more about possible post-attack climatic effects also should read the Fall 1986 issue of Foreign Affairs. This issue contains a long letter from Thompson and Schneider which further demolishes the theory of catastrophic "nuclear winter." Continuing studies indicate there will be even smaller reductions in temperature than those calculated by Thompson and Schneider.

Soviet propagandists promptly exploited belief in unsurvivable "nuclear winter" to increase fear of nuclear weapons and war, and to demoralize their enemies. Because raging city firestorms are needed to inject huge amounts of smoke into the stratosphere and thus, according to one discredited theory, prevent almost all solar heat from reaching the ground, the Soviets changed their descriptions of how a modern city will burn if blasted by a nuclear explosion.

Figure 1.6 pictures how Russian scientists and civil defense officials realistically described — before the invention of "nuclear winter" — the burning of a city hit by a nuclear weapon. Buildings in the blasted area for miles around ground zero will be reduced to scattered rubble — mostly of concrete, steel, and other nonflammable materials — that will not burn in blazing fires. Thus in the Oak Ridge National Laboratory translation (ORNL-TR-2793) of *Civil Defense,* Second Edition (500,000 copies), Moscow, 1970, by Egorov, Shlyakhov, and Alabin, we read: "Fires do not occur in zones of complete destruction . . . that are characterized by an overpressure exceeding 0.5 kg/cm² [~ 7 psi] . . . because rubble is scattered and covers the burning structures. As a result the rubble only smolders, and fires as such do not occur."

Translation: [Radioactive] contamination occurs in the area of the explosion and also along the trajectory of the cloud which forms a radioactive track.

Fig. 1.6. Drawing with Caption in a Russian Civil Defense Training Film Strip. The blazing fires ignited by a surface burst are shown in standing buildings outside the miles-wide "zone of complete destruction," where the blast-hurled "rubble only smolders."

Firestorms destroyed the centers of Hamburg, Dresden, and Tokyo. The old-fashioned buildings of those cities contained large amounts of flammable materials, were ignited by many thousands of small incendiaries, and burned quickly as standing structures well supplied with air. No firestorm has ever injected smoke into the stratosphere, or caused appreciable cooling below its smoke cloud.

The theory that smoke from burning cities and forests and dust from nuclear explosions would cause worldwide freezing temperatures was conceived in 1982 by the German atmospheric chemist and environmentalist Paul Crutzen, and continues to be promoted by a worldwide propaganda campaign. This well funded campaign began in 1983 with televised scientific-political meetings in Cambridge and Washington featuring American and Russian scientists. A barrage of newspaper and magazine articles followed, including a scare-mongering article by Carl Sagan in the October 30, 1983 issue of Parade, the Sunday tabloid read by millions. The most influential article was featured in the December 23, 1983 issue of Science (the weekly magazine of the American Association for the Advancement of Science): "Nuclear winter, global consequences of multiple nuclear explosions," by five scientists, R. P. Turco, O. B. Toon, T. P. Ackerman, J. B. Pollack, and C. Sagan. Significantly, these activists listed their names to spell TTAPS, pronounced "taps," the bugle call proclaiming "lights out" or the end of a military funeral.

Until 1985, non-propagandizing scientists did not begin to effectively refute the numerous errors, unrealistic assumptions, and computer modeling weaknesses of the TTAPS and related "nuclear winter" hypotheses. A principal reason is that government organizations, private corporations, and most scientists generally avoid getting involved in political controversies, or making statements likely to enable antinuclear activists to accuse them of minimizing nuclear war dangers, thus undermining hopes for peace. Stephen Schneider has been called a fascist by some disarmament supporters for having written "Nuclear Winter Reappraised," according to the Rocky Mountain News of July 6, 1986. Three days later, this paper, that until recently featured accounts of unsurvivable "nuclear winter," criticized Carl Sagan and defended Thompson and Schneider in its lead editorial, "In Study of Nuclear Winter, Let Scientists Be Scientists." In a free country, truth will out — although sometimes too late to effectively counter fast-hitting propaganda.

Effective refutation of "nuclear winter" also was delayed by the prestige of politicians and of politically motivated scientists and scientific organizations endorsing the TTAPS forecast of worldwide doom. Furthermore, the weaknesses in the TTAPS hypothesis could not be effectively explored until adequate Government funding was made available to cover costs of lengthy, expensive studies, including improved computer modeling of interrelated, poorly understood meteorological phenomena.

Serious climatic effects from a Soviet-U.S. nuclear war cannot be completely ruled out. However, possible deaths from uncertain climatic effects are a small danger compared to the uncalculable millions in many countries likely to die from starvation caused by disastrous shortages of essentials of modern agriculture sure to result from a Soviet-American nuclear war, and by the cessation of most international food shipments.

Chapter 2
Psychological Preparations

LEARNING WHAT TO EXPECT

The more one knows about the strange and fearful dangers from nuclear weapons and about the strengths and weaknesses of human beings when confronted with the dangers of war, the better chance one has of surviving. Terror, a self-destructive emotion, is almost always the result of unexpected danger. Some people would think the end of the world was upon them if they happened to be in an area downwind from surface bursts of nuclear weapons that sucked millions of tons of pulverized earth into the air. They might give up all hope if they did not understand what they saw. People are more likely to endure and survive if they learn in advance that such huge dust clouds, particularly if combined with smoke from great fires, may turn day into night—as have some volcanic eruptions and the largest forest fires.

People also should expect thunder to crash in strange clouds, and the earth to shake. The sky may be lit with the flickering purples and greens of "artificial auroras" caused by nuclear explosions, especially those that are miles above the earth.

FEAR

Fear often is a life-saving emotion. When we believe death is close at hand, fear can increase our ability to work harder and longer. Driven by fear, we can accomplish feats that would be impossible otherwise. Trembling hands, weak legs, and cold sweat do not mean that a person has become ineffective. Doing hard, necessary work is one of the best ways to keep one's fears under control.

Brave men and women who are self-confident admit their fears, even when the threat of death is remote. Then they plan and work to lessen the causes of their fears. (When the author helped Charles A. Lindbergh design a reinforced-concrete blast shelter for his family and neighbors, Lindbergh frankly admitted that he feared both nuclear attack and being trapped. He was able to lessen both of these fears by building an excellent blast shelter with two escape openings.)

TERROR

If the danger is unexpected enough or great enough, normal persons sometimes experience terror as well as fear. Terror prevents the mind from evaluating dangers and thinking logically. It develops in two stages, which have been described by Dr. Walo von Gregerz, a physician with much war experience, in his book *Psychology of Survival*. The first stage is apathy: people become indifferent to their own safety and are unable even to try to save themselves or their families. The second stage is a compulsion to flee.

Anxiety, fear, and terror can result in symptoms very similar to those caused by radiation injury: nausea, vomiting, extreme trembling, diarrhea. Dr. von Gregerz has described terror as being "explosively contagious." However, persons who learn to understand the nature of our inherent human traits and behavior and symptoms are less likely to become terrorized and ineffective in the event of a nuclear attack.

EMOTIONAL PARALYSIS

The most common reaction to great danger is not terror, but a kind of numbing of the emotions which actually may be helpful. Dr. von Gregerz calls this "emotional paralysis." This reaction allows many persons, when in the grip of great danger, to avoid being overwhelmed by compassionate emotions and

The 2022 Mental Attitude

FEAR IS THE WORST CANCER

I was always taught that "Fear and the inaction that comes from it is the worse cancer anyone can get." Everything in 2022 is promoted and advertised by fear. Usually by saying, "Stay Safe." all of the time. Its become a toxic poison running through our vernacular and culture in a post-2020 COVID global pandemic. I've started to detest the phrase, "Stay Safe" so much that I changed what I teach and tell people to, "Make it Safe." This is what this book and my addendums are going to try to enable you to do. Make it safe for yourself and those that you love.

"Stay Safe" implies no action. Do nothing. Literally, people are told to stay home, lock their doors and do nothing. This just makes you a hapless victim for anything that comes along. When you "Make it Safe" by loading yourself with information, knowledge, and practiced experience you are becoming prepared. Those who are prepared need not fear. This is mental preparedness too. The knowledge that you know what to do when and why and have confidence in yourself is one of the greatest things you can do to make sure you can "Make it Safe." for yourself and those that you love.

This preparedness can be in the form of food, water, medicine, and or the ability to measure radiation. To understand radiation and how it enters your body or will affect you from an event in the world.

Make you understand that if some small nukes pop off in the Ukraine theater that your exposure will probably be to radioactive iodine going around the world and depositing in certain areas and entering the food chain chiefly through dairy.

If you are in Phoenix Arizona and Los Angelos gets nuked you'll know how to look up the wind direction and estimate the time and direction of fallout. You can either shelter from the radiation by many of the methods in this book or you might be one of the immediate people leaving in a direction to take you out of the path of any fallout from the detonation.

Through this book, you may learn how to measure radiation with the Kearny Fallout Meter or more sensitive modern meters that are hopefully still available when you are reading this and be able to see the background radiation going up and know you are being affected. Note: Seeing an elevation in background radiation and measuring dangerous fallout radiation are 2 different things. Usually, a meter that measures one does not read the other.

In 2011 I used a sensitive Geiger counter to measure the fallout from the Fukushima nuclear accident when it eventually reached Pittsburgh PA. There was heavy rain and it came down on a large industrial facility. This ran down the gutters in a few places and left puddles. When the puddles started to evaporate the minor radiation got contracted and I could read an elevation of about 3x the normal background radiation that could have only come from Fukushima. A few weeks later there was no extra radiation in this area. Note: I measured about 21 microRads of radiation and I know the background radiation in the facility was about 6 to 9 microRads. Do not think this is scary, because if you flew on a commercial airliner you'd get over 400 microRads of radiation while at altitude. What did this mean? Well, I'd not be drinking from the puddle of water.

So the reading of an elevated from a background level of radiation may not be of harm to you in the least as far as the radiation goes but it might mean, you check what you eat and drink to make sure there are no radioactive particles in it. The alpha radiation from the Americium in your ionizing smoke detector is so weak that a sheet of paper can block the alpha particle yet you would not want to eat that and put it inside your body where there is nothing to block it.

When Cresson wrote this update in 1987 there was a great deal more rugged individualism in the United States. There were no trigger warnings and safe spaces or content warnings. I fear that an insignificant event of a nuclear nature will put plenty of people into abject fear and panic that is more harmful than anything from the event itself.

When COVID started I said the virus is not the danger. The fear of the virus is the danger and how correct I was. The fear of a nuclear device going off, even a small one will be Earth-shattering to the minds of many.

Fear will lead to panic and paralysis and that will lead to death.

In the teaching of military and other technical subjects when you are taught critical skills before you go on a mission or get into an environment of danger the education you receive beforehand is called "Front Loading". It's a more technical term than "Preparedness" but I like to use it. This book and the addendums I'm adding to it are trying to Front-Load you with knowledge and skills that you can use.

I'm getting well known for a saying to people when they start bringing up reasons of this and that and blah blah. My statement is, "Shut up and start finding reasons to NOT do something and start finding reasons TO do it."

If you want to do anything in this book for the protection of yourself and your family and those that you love you just do it. If you start to tell others about it and ask for their input you'll get a never-ending list of reasons to not do it. "Oh, that is paranoid, oh that is stupid. Why would you want to do that? That won't help you." and this will be from a litany of people who are not nuclear experts but people who have done nothing in their life and their goal is to get you to do nothing as well. You want to do something for the protection of those you love, then do it.

horrible sights. It permits them to think clearly and act effectively.

ATOM BOMB SURVIVORS

The atomic explosions that destroyed most of Hiroshima and Nagasaki were air bursts and therefore produced no deadly local fallout. So we cannot be sure how people would behave in areas subjected to both blast and fallout from surface bursts. However, the reactions of the Japanese survivors are encouraging, especially in view of the fact that among them the relative number of horribly burned people was greater than is likely to be found among a population that expects a nuclear attack and takes any sort of shelter. Dr. von Gregerz summarizes: "In most cases the victims were, of course, apathetic and often incapable of rational action, but open panic or extremely disorganized behavior occurred only in exceptional cases among the hundreds of thousands of survivors of the two atomic bombing attacks." Also encouraging: ". . . serious permanent psychological derangements were rare after the atomic bomb attacks, just as they were after the large-scale conventional bombings."

HELP FROM FELLOW AMERICANS

Some maintain that after an atomic attack America would degenerate into anarchy—an every-man-for-himself struggle for existence. They forget the history of great human catastrophes and the self-sacrificing strengths most human beings are capable of displaying. After a massive nuclear attack starvation would afflict some areas, but America's grain-producing regions still would have an abundance of uncontaminated food. History indicates that Americans in the food-rich areas would help the starving. Like the heroic Russians who drove food trucks to starving Leningrad through bursting Nazi bombs and shells,[7] many Americans would risk radiation and other dangers to bring truckloads of grain and other necessities to their starving countrymen. Surely, an essential part of psychological preparations for surviving a modern war is a well-founded assurance that many citizens of a strong society will struggle to help each other and will work together with little regard for danger and loss.

Chapter 3
Warnings and Communications

IMPORTANCE OF ADEQUATE WARNING

When Hiroshima and Nagasaki were blasted by the first nuclear weapons ever to be used in war, very few of the tens of thousands of Japanese killed or injured were inside their numerous air raid shelters. The single-plane attacks caught them by surprise. People are not saved by having shelters nearby unless they receive warning in time to reach their shelters— and unless they heed that warning.

TYPES OF WARNINGS

Warnings are of two types, strategic and tactical.

- **Strategic warning** is based on observed enemy actions that are believed to be preparations for an attack. For example, we would have strategic warning if powerful Russian armies were advancing into western Europe and Soviet leaders were threatening massive nuclear destruction if the resisting nations should begin to use tactical nuclear weapons. With strategic warning being given by news broadcasts and newspapers over a period of days, Americans in areas that are probably targeted would have time to evacuate. Given a day or more of warning, tens of millions of us could build or improve shelters and in other ways improve our chances of surviving the feared attack. By doing so, we also would help decrease the risk of attack.

- **Tactical warning** of a nuclear attack on the United States would be received by our highest officials a few minutes after missiles or other nuclear weapons had been launched against our country. Radar, satellites, and other sophisticated means of detection would begin to feed information into our military warning systems almost at once. This raw information would have to be evaluated, and top-level decisions would have to be made. Then attack warnings would have to be transmitted down to communities all over America.

Tactical warning (attack warning) of an out-of-the-blue, Pearl-Harbor-type attack would be less likely to be received by the average American than would an attack warning given after recognized strategic warning. However, the short time (only 15 to 40 minutes) that would elapse between missile launchings and the resultant first explosions on targets in the United States would make it difficult for even an excellent warning system to alert the majority of Americans in time for them to reach the best available nearby shelter.

Strengths and weaknesses of the present official warning system are summarized in the following two sections. Then the life-saving warnings that the first nuclear explosions would give, especially to informed people, are described.

OFFICIAL WARNING SYSTEM

The U.S. official warning system is designed to give civilians timely warning by means of siren signals and radio and television announcements. The National Warning System (NAWAS) is a wire-line network which is to provide attack information to official warning points nationwide. **NAWAS is not protected against electromagnetic pulse (EMP) effects from nuclear explosions.** When the information is received at warning points by the officials who are responsible, they will sound local sirens and initiate radio and TV emergency broadcasts — if power has not failed. Officials at NAWAS warning points include many local civil defense directors. NAWAS receives information from our constantly improving military warning and communications systems.

SIREN WARNINGS

The Attack Warning Signal is a wavering, wailing sound on the sirens lasting three to five minutes, or a series of short blasts on whistles or horns. After a brief pause, it is repeated. This signal means only one thing: take protective action—go promptly to the best available shelter. Do not try to telephone for information; get information from a radio broadcast after you reach shelter. It is Federal policy that the Attack Warning Signal will not be sounded unless an enemy attack on the United States has been detected. However, since local authorities may not follow this policy, the reader is advised to check the plans in his community before a crisis arises.

The following limitations of attack warnings given by sirens and broadcasting stations should be recognized:

- Only a relatively small fraction of urban Americans could hear the sirens in the present city systems, especially if most urban citizens had evacuated during a crisis.
- Except in a crisis threatening the outbreak of nuclear war at any moment, most people who would hear the attack warning signal either would not recognize it or would not believe it was a warning of actual attack.
- A coordinated enemy attack may include the detonation of a few submarine-launched ballistic missiles (SLBMs) at high altitudes over the United States within a few minutes of the launching of hundreds of SLBMs and intercontinental ballistic missiles (ICBMs). Such high-altitude bursts would produce electromagnetic pulse (EMP) effects primarily intended to knock out or disrupt U.S. military communications. These EMP effects also could knock out the public power necessary to sound sirens and could put most unprotected broadcasting stations off the air.

Radio warnings and emergency communications to the general public will be broadcast by the Emergency Broadcast System (EBS). This system uses AM broadcasting stations as the primary means to reach the public; selected FM and TV stations are included for backup. All stations during a crisis plan to use their normal broadcast frequencies.

EBS stations that are not put off the air by EMP or other effects of early explosions will attempt to confirm the siren warnings of a nuclear attack. They will try to give information to listeners in the extensive areas where sirens and whistles cannot be heard. However, EMP effects on telephones are likely to limit the information available to the stations. The functioning EBS stations should be able to warn listeners to seek the best available nearby shelter in time for most of these listeners to reach such shelter before ICBMs begin to explode. Limitations of the Emergency Broadcasting System in February 1986 included the fact that EMP protection had been completed for only 125 of the approximately 2,771 radio stations in the Emergency Broadcast System. One hundred and ten of 3,000 existing Emergency Operating Centers also had been protected against EMP effects. Many of the protected stations would be knocked out by blast; most do not afford their operating personnel fallout protection that is adequate for continuing broadcasts for long in areas subjected to heavy fallout.

WARNINGS GIVEN BY THE ATTACK ITSELF

The great majority of Americans would not be injured by the first explosions of a nuclear attack. In an all-out attack, the early explosions would give sufficient warning for most people to reach nearby shelter in time. Fifteen minutes or more before big intercontinental ballistic missiles (ICBMs) blasted our cities, missile sites, and other extensive areas, most citizens would see the sky lit up to an astounding brightness, would hear the thunderous sounds of distant explosions, or would note the sudden outage of electric power and most communications. These reliable attack warnings would result from the explosion of submarine-launched ballistic missiles (SLBMs). These are smaller than many ICBMs. The SLBM warheads would explode on Strategic Air Command bases and on many civilian airport runways that are long enough to be used by our big bombers. Some naval bases and high-priority military command and communication centers would also be targeted.

The vast majority of Americans do not know how to use these warnings from explosions to help them save their lives. Neither are they informed about the probable strategies of an enemy nuclear attack.

One of the first objectives of a coordinated enemy attack would be to destroy our long-range bombers, because each surviving U.S. bomber would be one of our most deadly retaliatory weapons. Once bombers are airborne and well away from their runways, they are difficult to destroy. To destroy our bombers before they could get away, the first SLBMs would be launched at the same time that ICBMs would be fired from their silos in Europe and Asia. U.S. surveillance systems would detect launchings and transmit warnings within a very few minutes. Since some enemy submarines would be only a few hundred miles from their targets, some SLBMs would explode on American targets about 15 or 20 minutes before the first ICBMs would hit.

Some SLBMs would strike civilian airport runways that are at least 7000 ft long. This is the minimum length required by B-52s; there were 210 such runways in the U.S. in 1977. During a crisis, big bombers would be dispersed to many of these long runways, and enemy SLBMs would be likely to target and hit these runways in an effort to destroy the maximum number of bombers.

Today most Soviet SLBMs have warheads between 100 kilotons and one megaton. See *Jane's Weapon Systems, 1987-88.* Within 10 to 15 minutes of the beginning of an attack, runways 7000 feet or longer are likely to be hit by airbursts, to destroy U.S. aircraft and airport facilities. Later cratering explosions may be used to destroy surviving long runways, or at least to produce local fallout so heavy that they could not be used for several days for re-arming and re-fueling our bombers. Therefore, homes within about 4 miles of a runway at least 7000 ft long are likely to be destroyed before residents receive warning or have time to reach blast shelters away from their homes. Homes six miles away could be lightly damaged by such a warhead, with the blast wave **from a 1-megaton explosion arriving about 22 seconds** after the warning light. Some windows would be broken 40 miles away. But the large majority of citizens would not be injured by these early SLBM attacks. These explosions would be life-saving "take cover" warnings to most Americans, if they have been properly informed.

Sudden power and communications failures caused by the electromagnetic pulse (EMP) effects of nuclear explosions also could serve as attack warnings in extensive areas. An EMP is an intense burst of radio-frequency radiation generated by a nuclear explosion. The strong, quick-rising surges of electric current induced by EMP in power transmission lines and long antennas could burn out most unprotected electrical and electronic equipment. **Also likely to be damaged or destroyed would be unprotected computers. The solid state electrical components of some aircraft and of some motors of modern autos, trucks, and tractors may be put out of commission. Metal bodies give some protection, whereas plastic bodies give little.**

The usual means of protecting electrical equipment against surges of current produced by lightning are generally ineffective against EMP. The protective measures are known, but to date all too few civilian installations have been protected against EMP effects. Three or four nuclear weapons skillfully spaced and detonated at high altitudes over the United States would produce EMP effects that might knock out most public power, most radio and TV broadcasting stations lacking special protection against these effects, and most radios connected to long antennas. Nuclear explosions on or near the ground may produce damaging EMP effects over areas somewhat larger than those in which such equipment and buildings would be damaged by the blast effects.

HOW TO RESPOND TO UNEXPECTED ATTACK WARNINGS

Although a Pearl-Harbor-type of attack is unlikely, citizens should be prepared to respond effectively to unexpected warnings.

These warnings include:

- Extremely bright lights—more light than has been seen before. The dazzling, bright lights of the first SLBM explosions on targets in many parts of the United States would be seen by most Americans. One should not look to determine the source of light and heat, because there is danger of the viewer's eyes being damaged by the heat and light from a large explosion at distances as far as a hundred miles away, in clear weather. Look down and away from the probable source, and quickly get behind anything that will shield you from most of the thermal pulse's burning heat and intense light. A thermal pulse delivers its heat and light for several seconds—for more than 11 seconds if it is from a 1-megaton surface burst and for approximately 44 seconds if from a 20-megaton surface burst.

If you are at home when you see the amazingly bright light, run out of rooms with windows. Hurry to a windowless hallway or down into the basement. If you have a shelter close to your house, but separate from it, do not leave the best cover in your home to run outdoors to reach the shelter; wait until about two minutes after first seeing the light.

If outdoors when you see the bright light, get behind the best available cover.

It would be impossible to estimate the distance to an explosion from its light or appearance, so you should stay under cover for about two minutes. A blast wave initially travels much faster than the normal speed of sound (about 1 mile in 5 seconds). But by the time its overpressure has decreased to 1 pound per square inch (psi), a blast wave and its thunderous sound have slowed down and are moving only about 3% faster than the normal speed of sound.

Warnings and Communications Update

When Cresson wrote this in 1987, CNN had just begun in 1980. Cable TV and over-the-air TV with AM and FM radio were the primary methods of communication. Cell phones were still 'car or bag phones' and cost at least $1399 at Radio Shack. Air time was around $1 / minute. You might have had email if you were on a Unix box (not Linux, Unix) at a university. There were no text messages, SMS, instant messages, or the worldwide websites. No signal, telegram, WhatsApp, Instagram, Facebook, Twitter and there were no mass-manufactured smartphones, let alone cell phones, which you could get for free or $30 or even $300. No one could call or message you. Unless it was on a landline phone. Many people are a member of a chat group on telegram, WhatsApp or Facebook (now on the downturn).

Basically, the moment a nuke goes off anywhere in the world with everyone having a camera and a communications device that image and mushroom cloud is going to go around the world quickly. You might even know before the president does. You've heard of the shot heard around the world, this will be the bright light and bang heard around the world.

The "Prompt Light" from a nuclear detonation and then the light from the 'fire ball' can literally be seen for 100, 200 or more miles. Depending on if it was a ground or a surface burst and the size of the weapon. You'll hear the boom and the rumble for up to 600 miles or more away (again depending). It'll be a sound like you've never heard before.

The video from people who see the light, but are not in blast range, will hit all forms of digital communications and media and then the ring doorbell cam video will start to show up more and more.

EMP AND YOUR CELL PHONE

In an all-out Soviet attack sending 10,000 to 20,000 nuclear warheads over the north pole to attack the USA in the 1980's threat model, it would be preceded by multiple nuclear EMP devices above the Earth's atmosphere. A friend of Cresson's, Ed Yorks, and myself, Sharron Packer, who at the time sold underground shelters much like Atlas does today, had an EMP alarm in her bedroom. It was a motorcycle horn and a 12-volt car battery with a relay that prevented it from 'honking'. The relay was energized by power from the wall outlet. When the power failed, the relay dropped and the motorcycle horn would go off and it could be heard anywhere in the home. She commented that thunderstorms killed her power quite a few times and her and her husband about hit the ceiling every time that horn went off in their bedrooms. In a real soviet attack, the EMP attack would precede the incoming missiles and thus this was their warning to get to the blast shelter.

THIS IS NOT WHAT WE ARE TALKING ABOUT HERE

The threat model we are talking about in this update is a nuclear device going off in Ukraine, or the EU, or even one smuggled into the USA. It goes off in downtown Los Angeles and maybe one in Las Vegas, DC, and New York. Devices in a truck and not falling from a bomber or an incoming ICBM. In this case, there is going to be no EMP attack to threaten you or kill your cell phone and the internet, and the cell system. If you are not near the blast, thermal damage (huge fires), and the immediate fallout (literally falling like solid rain) you can easily have hours to a day to days to prepare for any radiation that might fall out if you are in the right wind area. Believe me, there will be plenty of private videos from experts, non-experts, meteorologists, and the government on TV, all news outlets, and online videos that tell you where the radiation is going and how strong. The communications that could never have been imagined in 1987 will be near-instantaneous in 2022 and 2023.

THE NEW BOOGY MAN

The threat of EMP on the USA and killing all electronics and power from some rogue nation has become the boogyman. More myths surround this than facts and these myths are usually propagated by the same charlatans trying to sell out a solution in the form of an "EMP bag" or a "Faraday Bag" or a "Mylar Bag" or some other such nonsense. It takes a fusion class weapon (megatons) and not a simple fission device (kilotons) to produce a large crippling EMP and then it has to be at about 250 miles altitude. That is the altitude of the international space station. Currently, only the major powers have true full-scale large fusion weapons because as Edwin York taught, a fusion device (hydrogen bomb, thermonuclear device) is/was literally a million times harder to design and a million times more expensive per device to make than a fission device. Now, you have to do what SpaceX does and put that size of a device at the altitude of the international space station. That device and putting it there is not easy. It's not being done any decade soon by North Korea or Iran or any other Boogy Man. Russia can, China can, but for major hostile powers, that is about it. Is there a threat? Yes. Is it large? No. Will it change and get larger? History would say, "Probably Yes." The fallacies you have been sold are sold by the people selling the false devices to alleviate the false fears they filled you with. There is a kernel of truth but the corn stalk and the new ears of corn are the lie.

THE TEST. Take a portable FM radio, and turn it to a radio station as close to 108mhz as you can. Now go find the transmitter tower for that radio station and walk up to the fence that is around the tower, you are in the shadow of the tower. If you can still hear your FM radio playing through the bag then consider this. The amplitude of the "pulse" from the soviet class EMP device that would have killed that radio would be over a million times stronger than the strength of the signal of that radio station tower you are standing under. The other fallacy regarding soviet level EMP attack is people put their electronics wrapped in aluminum foil, in a candy tin, put that inside a popcorn tin and put that inside a metal garbage can. The big bad soviet scale EMP goes off and they go, "Yeah!! We were protected." They get their electronics out and then 2 days later, they go dead. Russia threw another EMP device. Then a week later, another one, then a month later, another one. It's not one EMP attack, it's a series of EMP attacks.

If no blast or sound reaches you in two minutes, you would know that the explosion was over 25 miles away and you would not be hurt by blast effects, unless cut by shattered window glass. After two minutes you can safely leave the best cover in your home and get a radio. Turn the dial to the stations to which you normally listen and try to find information. Meanwhile, quickly make preparations to go to the best shelter you and your family can reach within 15 minutes—the probable time interval before the first ICBMs start to explode.

At no time after an attack begins should you look out of a window or stay near a window. Under certain atmospheric conditions, windows can be shattered by a multimegaton explosion a hundred miles away.

- The sound of explosions. The thunderous booms of the initial SLBM explosions would be heard over almost all parts of the United States. Persons one hundred miles away from a nuclear explosion may receive their first warning by hearing it about $7^1/_2$ minutes later. Most would have time to reach nearby shelter before the ICBMs begin to explode.
- Loss of electric power and communications. If the lights go out and you find that many radio and TV stations are suddenly off the air, continue to dial if you have a battery-powered radio, and try to find a station that is still broadcasting.

HOW TO RESPOND TO ATTACK WARNINGS DURING A WORSENING CRISIS

If an attack takes place during a worsening crisis, the effectiveness of warnings would be greater. Even if our government did not order an evacuation of high-risk areas, millions of Americans would already have moved to safer areas if they had learned that the enemy's urban civilians were evacuating or that tactical nuclear weapons were being employed overseas. Many prudent citizens would sleep inside the best available shelter and stay in or near shelter most of their waking hours. Many people would have made or improved family or small-group shelters and would have supplied them with most essentials. The official warning systems would have been fully alerted and improved.

During such a tense crisis period, neighbors or people sheltered near each other should have someone listen to radio stations at all times of the day and night. If the situation worsened or an attack warning were broadcast, the listener could alert the others.

One disadvantage of waiting to build expedient shelters until there is a crisis is that many of the builders are likely to be outdoors improving their shelters when the first SLBMs are launched. The SLBM warheads may arrive so soon that the civilian warning systems cannot respond in time. To reduce the risk of being burned, persons working outdoors when expecting an attack should wear shirts, hats, and gloves. They should jump into a shelter or behind a nearby shielding object at the first warning, which may be the sudden cut-off of some radio broadcasts.

REMAINING INSIDE SHELTER

Curiosity and ignorance probably will cause many people to come out of shelters a few hours after an attack warning, if no blast or obvious fallout has endangered their area. This is dangerous, because several hours after almost all missiles have been launched the first enemy bombers may strike. Cities and other targets that have been spared because missiles malfunctioned or missed are likely to be destroyed by nuclear bombs dropped during the first several days after the first attack.

Most people should stay inside their shelters for at least two or three days, even if they are in a locality far from a probable target and even if fallout meter readings prove there is no dangerous fallout. Exceptions would include some of the people who would need to improve shelters or move to better shelters. Such persons could do so at relatively small risk during the interval between the ICBM explosions and the arrival of enemy bombers and/or the start of fallout deposition a few hours later.

Fallout would cover most of the United States within 12 hours after a massive attack. People could rarely depend on information received from distant radio stations regarding changing fallout dangers and advising when and for how long they could go outside their shelters. Weather conditions such as wind speed would cause fallout dangers to vary with distance. If not forced by thirst or hunger to leave shelter, they should depend on their own fallout meter readings or on radiation measurements made by neighbors or local civil defense workers.

HOW TO KEEP RADIOS OPERATING

Having a radio to receive emergency broadcasts would be a great advantage. The stations that would still be on the air after an attack would probably be too distant from most survivors to give them reliable information concerning local, constantly changing fallout dangers. However, both morale and the prospects of long-range survival would be improved in shelters with a radio bringing word of the large-area fallout situation, food-relief measures, practical survival skills, and what the government and other organizations were doing to help. Radio contact with the outside world probably can be maintained after an attack if you remember to:

- Bring all of your family's battery-powered, portable radios with you to shelter, along with all fresh batteries on hand.
- Protect AM radios by using only their built-in short loop antennas. The built-in antennas of small portable radios are too short for EMP to induce damaging surges of current in them.
- Keep antennas of FM, CB, and amateur radios as short as practical, preferably less than 10 inches. When threatened by EMP, a danger that may continue for weeks after the initial attack because of repeated, high-altitude explosions, do not add a wire antenna or connect a short radio antenna to a pipe. Remember that a surge of current resulting from EMP especially can damage diodes and transistors, thus ending a radio's usefulness or reducing its range of reception.
- Keep all unshielded radios at least six feet away from any long piece of metal, such as pipes, metal ducts, or wires found in many basements and other shelters. Long metal conductors can pick up and carry large EMP surges, causing induced current to surge in nearby radios and damage them.
- Shield each radio against EMP when not in use by completely surrounding it with conducting metal if it is kept within six feet of a long conductor through which powerful currents produced by EMP might surge. A radio may be shielded against EMP by placing it inside a metal cake box or metal storage can, or by completely surrounding it with aluminum foil or metallic window screen.
- Disconnect the antenna cable of your car radio at the receiver—or at least ground the antenna when not in use by connecting it with a wire to the car frame. Use tape or clothespins to assure good metal-to-metal contact. The metal of an outside mirror is a convenient grounding-point. Park your car as near to your shelter as practical, so that after fallout has decayed sufficiently you may be able to use the car radio to get distant stations that are still broadcasting.
- Prevent possible damage to a radio from extreme dampness (which may result from long occupancy of some belowground shelters) by keeping it sealed in a clear plastic bag large enough so the radio can be operated while inside. An additional precaution is to keep a plastic-covered radio in an air-tight container with some anhydrite made from wallboard gypsum, as described in Appendix C.
- Conserve batteries, because after an attack you may not be able to get replacements for months. Listen only periodically, to the stations you find give the most useful information. The batteries of transistor radios will last up to twice as long if the radios are played at reduced volume.

Chapter 4
Evacuation

CHANGED EVACUATION REQUIREMENTS

The most threatening Soviet nuclear warheads in the mid-1970s were multi-megaton, such as single warheads of approximately 20 megatons carried by each of over 250 SS-18s. About half of these huge Russian warheads would have hit within a quarter of a mile or less of their intended targets — close enough to destroy a missile in its hardened silo. Today's improved Russian warheads have a 50-50 probability of hitting within a few hundred feet of their aiming points. With such accuracy, multi-megaton warheads are not needed to destroy very hard targets, especially missiles in their blast-protective silos.

Soviet strategy continues to stress the destruction of military targets, in order to minimize Russian losses from retaliatory strikes. This logical, long-established Soviet strategy is emphasized in numerous authoritative Russian books, including the three editions of *Soviet Military Strategy,* by Marshall of the Soviet Union V. D. Sokolovskiy.

One result of this logical strategy has been the replacement of huge Soviet warheads by numerous, much smaller, much more accurate warheads. In 1990 almost all large missiles have several Multiple Independently-targetted Reentry Vehicles (MIRVed) warheads. Soviet warheads — especially the 10 warheads of 500 kilotons each carried by most SS-18s — could destroy almost all important U.S. fixed military installations, and also almost all U.S. command and control facilities, airport runways longer than 7,000 feet, major seaports, and the factories and refineries that are the basis of our military power. (Although an all-out Soviet attack could destroy almost all missile silos and missiles in them, a first-strike attack is deterred in part by the possibility that most U.S. missiles in silos would be launched on warning and would be in space, on their trajectories toward Russian targets, before Soviet warheads could reach their silos.)

How should your plans either to evacuate during a worsening crisis, or to remain in your home area, be influenced by the dramatic changes in the Soviet nuclear arsenal? Some of these changes are indicated by Fig. 4.1, that incorporates information on the dimensions of the stabilized clouds of one megaton and 200 kiloton explosions, from reference 6, *The Effects of Nuclear Weapons, 1977,* and similar information on a 20-megaton cloud derived from a graph on page 20 of *The Effects on the Atmosphere of a Major Nuclear Exchange,* by the Committee on the Atmospheric Effects of Nuclear Explosions, National Research Council, National Academy Press, Washington, D.C. 1985. (This NRC graph is based on Ballistic Missile Organization 83-5 Part 1, dated 29 September 1983, a report that is not generally available.)

The air bursting of one of the probably few 20-megaton warheads carried by Soviet ICBMs would destroy typical American homes up to about 16 miles from ground zero. In contrast, the air bursting of an approximately 1-megaton warhead — one of the large warheads in today's Soviet arsenal — would destroy most homes within a roughly circular area having a radius of "only" about 5 miles. So, if you take into consideration the advantages to Soviets of arming their largest ICBMs with several very accurate smaller warheads, each capable of destroying a militarily important target, you may logically conclude that unless your home is closer than 10 miles from the nearest probable target, you need not evacuate to avoid blast and fire dangers.

Your planning to avoid incapacitating or fatal exposure to fallout radiation will involve more uncertainties than will your plans to avoid blast and fire dangers. The high altitude winds that carry fallout farthest before deposition usually blow from west to east. Therefore, in most areas your chances of avoiding extremely dangerous radiation dangers are improved if

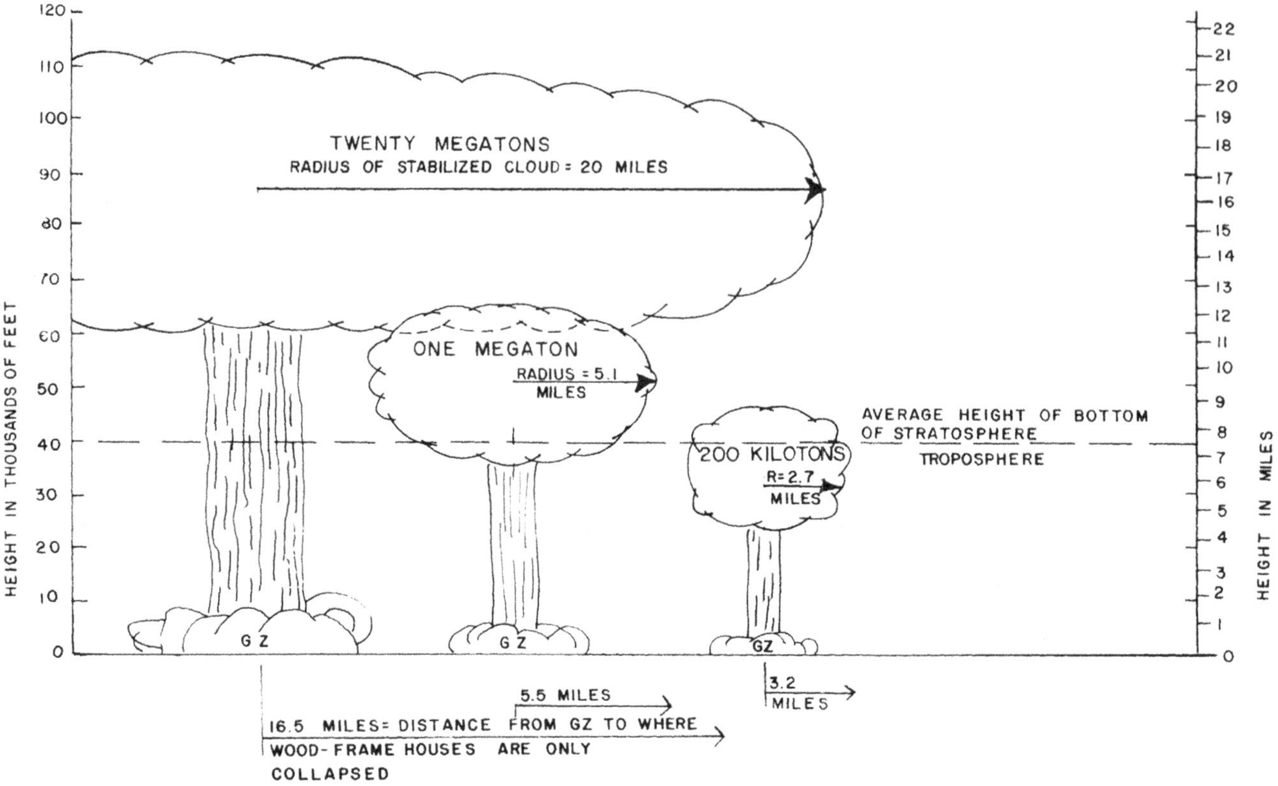

Fig. 4.1. Stabilized radioactive fallout clouds shown a few minutes after air-burst explosions, with distances from Ground Zeros at which the wood frames of typical homes are almost completely collapsed. The clouds from surface or near-surface bursts are almost as large, but the distances of blast damage are reduced by around 38 percent.

you evacuate westward to an area away from likely nearby targets. However, since no one can foretell with certainty in what directions future winds will blow, your plans to remain where you live, or your crisis evacuation plans should include building, improving, or utilizing high-protection-factor shelter, as explained in following chapters.

If you live near a target the destruction of which has high priority in Soviet war-winning strategy, then a decade or so ago it quite likely was targetted by a 20-MT warhead. Fig. 4.1 shows the awesome size of the stabilized radioactive cloud from a **20-MT air burst.** This cloud would expand in minutes to this huge size in the thin air of the stratosphere, would contain only extremely small particles almost all of which would remain airborne for weeks to years, and would result in no fallout deposition that would promptly incapacitate exposed people.

A **20-MT surface burst** or **near-surface burst** would produce a stabilized radioactive cloud extending almost as far in all directions from GZ as would a 20-MT air burst. Its tremendous fireball would "suck up" millions of tons of pulverized rock and would contaminate those particles with its radioactive material. Fallout particles as big as marbles[6] would fall from the stabilized cloud to the ground in minutes. Very heavy fallout could be deposited as far as 18 miles upwind from such a 20-MT explosion, with heavy fallout, capable of causing fatalities within days to weeks, extending downwind for several hundred miles.

A **1-MT surface burst,** Fig. 4.1, would produce a stabilized fallout cloud unlikely to result in fallout being deposited in the upwind or crosswind directions from GZ beyond the range of the explosion's home-destroying blast effects. Clearly, the risk of your being endangered by very heavy fallout if you remain 6 miles from GZ of a 1-MT surface burst, and happen to be upwind or crosswind from GZ, is less than the risk you would have run a decade ago if you had stayed 18 miles upwind or crosswind from the same target, which had been destroyed by a 20-MT surface or near-surface burst.

HIGHEST-RISK AND HIGH-RISK AREAS

Highest-risk areas are those in which buildings are likely to be destroyed by blast and/or fire, and/or where a person in the open for the first two weeks after fallout deposition would receive a total radiation dose of 10,000 R or more. The largest highest-risk areas would be those within our five Minuteman missile fields, within a few miles all around them, and for up to about 150 miles downwind. These huge highest-risk areas are indicated by five of the largest black fallout patterns on Fig. 4.2.

Fig. 4.2 is an oudated, computer-drawn fallout map based on a multi-megaton attack considered credible 10 years ago. (An updated, unclassified fallout map of the United States, showing radiation doses to persons in the open, is not available.) This outdated attack included 113 **surface bursts** of 20 megatons each on urban and industrial targets, an unlikely assumption similar to those used in making some official civil defense risk-area maps that assumed surface bursts on all targets nationwide. Employing all surface bursts makes little sense to the military, because air bursting the same weapons would destroy most military installations, as well as factories and other urban and industrial assets, over approximately twice as large an area.

As will be explained later, to survive in such areas people would have to stay inside very good shelters for several weeks, or, after two weeks or more, leave very good shelters and drive in a few hours to an area relatively free of fallout dangers. A "very good" fallout shelter is one that reduces the radiation dose received by its occupants to less than 1/200th of the dose they would have received outdoors during the same period. If the two-week dose outdoors were 20,000 R, such a shelter with a protection factor of 200 (PF 200) would prevent each occupant from receiving a dose greater than 100 R — not enough to incapacitate. Even a completely belowground home basement, unless greatly improved as described in Chapter 5, would give entirely inadequate protection.

High-risk fallout areas are those where the two-week dose outdoors is between 5,000 and 10,000 R. In such areas, good fallout shelters would be essential, supplied at least with adequate water and baby food for two weeks. Furthermore, survivors would have to remain inside shelters for most of each day for several additional weeks.

The radiation dangers in the shaded areas of the map are shown decreasing as the distances from the explosions increase. This generally is the case, although sometimes rain or snow carries radioactive particles to the ground, producing "rainouts" of exceptionally heavy fallout farther downwind. Furthermore, this computer-drawn map made at Oak Ridge National Laboratory does not indicate the very dangerous fallout near the isolated surface bursts. Although the most dangerous fallout would be carried by high-altitude winds that usually blow from west to east, such simplified fallout patterns as those shown should be used only as rough guides to help improve chances of evacuating a probable blast area or very heavy fallout area and going to a less dangerous area. Wind directions are undependable; an enemy's targeting can be unexpected; weapons can miss. A prudent citizen, no matter where he is, should try to build a shelter that gives excellent protection against fallout radiation.

A major disadvantage of all types of risk-area maps is the fact that poorly informed people often misinterpret them and conclude that if they are outside a mapped risk area, they are relatively safe from blast, fire, and even deadly fallout dangers.

Another reason for not placing much reliance on risk-area maps like Fig. 4.2 is that such unclassified maps available in 1986 are based on the largest attacks considered possible a decade ago. In 1986 the sizes of Soviet warheads are much smaller, their numbers are much larger, and their total megatonage and capability to produce fallout remain about the same as 10 years ago.

The outdated attack scenario used in producing Fig. 4.2 also involved the surface bursting of multi-megaton warheads totaling 3,190 megatons on military targets, including over 2,000 megatons logically surface bursted on our five Minuteman missile fields. Such an attack on our missile fields would produce about the same amount of fallout as is shown in Fig. 4.2. Today, however, heavy fallout from our missile fields would extend somewhat shorter distances downwind, because of the lower heights of the stabilized radioactive clouds from one-megaton and smaller surface and near-surface bursts, as compared to those of multi-megaton warheads that would have been exploded 10 years ago, at a time when a 20-megaton warhead was typical of the Soviet nuclear ICBM arsenal.

In 1986 hundreds of targets besides those indicated in Fig. 4.2 might be hit, but the total area of the United States subjected to lethal fallout probably would be less than is shown in Fig. 4.2. To maximize areas of destruction by blast and fire, most targets in urban and/or industrial areas would be attacked with **air bursts,** which would produce little or no promptly lethal or incapacitating fallout — except perhaps in scattered "hot spots" where rain-outs or snow-outs could bring huge numbers of tiny, very radioactive particles to earth within hours after the air bursting of today's kiloton-range Soviet warheads. And since most Americans live far away from "hard" targets — especially far from missile silos, downwind from which extremely heavy fallout is likely — most of us living in or near high-risk areas probably would be endangered primarily by blast and fire, not fallout, in the event of a Soviet attack.

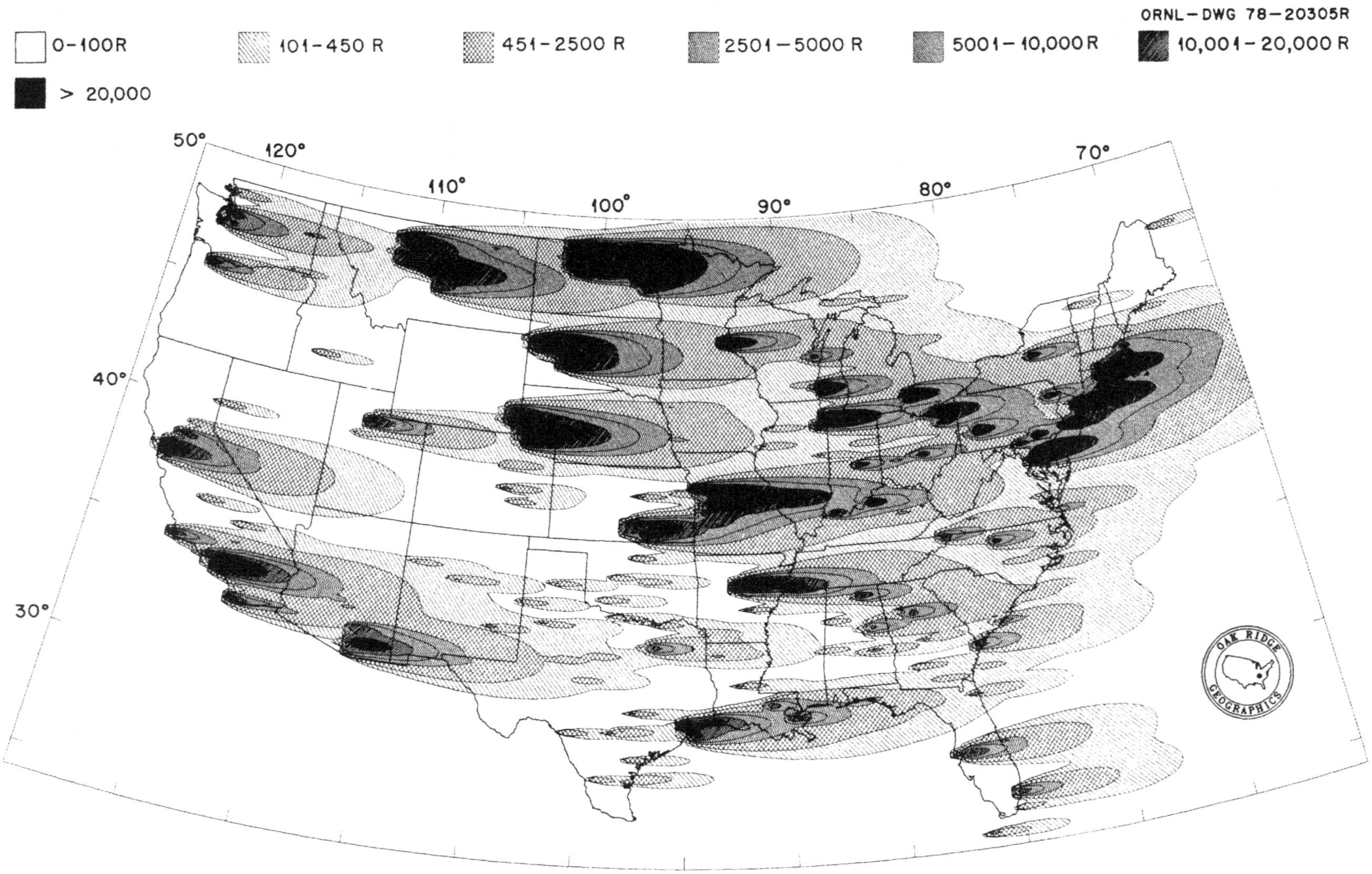

Fig. 4.2. Simplified, **outdated** fallout patterns showing total radiation doses that would be received by persons on the surface and in the open for the entire 14 days following the surface bursting of 5050 megatons on the targets indicated, if the winds at all elevations blew continuously from the west at 25 mph.

WHETHER TO EVACUATE

Let's assume that Russian cities were being evacuated, or that tactical nuclear weapons were beginning to be used in what had been an overseas conventional war involving the United States. In such a worsening crisis, most Americans could improve their survival chances by getting out of the highest-risk and high-risk areas.

U.S. capabilities for war-crisis evacuation are poor and tending to worsen. Several years ago, out of the approximately 3,100 evacuation plans required nationwide, about 1,500 had been made, and these involved only about one third of Americans living in risk areas. By 1986 some cities and states had abandoned their war-crisis evacuation plans; most still have plans that would save millions if ordered in time during a crisis lasting at least a few days and completed before the attack. Who would order an evacuation under threat of attack, and under what circumstances, remain unanswered questions. Furthermore, compulsory evacuation during a war crisis was not and is not part of any official American evacuation plan. So, if you believe that a nuclear attack on the United States is possible and want to improve your chances of surviving, then well before a desperate crisis arises you had better either make preparations to improve your and your family's survival chances at or near where you live, or plan and prepare to evacuate.

Spontaneous evacuations, in which Americans would make their own decisions without the authorities having recommended any movement, probably would occur during a worsening war crisis. Traffic jams and other complications are less likely to occur if citizens start leaving high-risk areas on their own, over a period of several hours to a few days, rather than if almost everyone, on receiving recommendations from officials, at once begins a poorly controlled evacuation. (Spontaneous evacuation by Gulf Coast residents, begun under threat of an approaching hurricane, have lessened subsequent traffic problems in the evacuations ordered or recommended by officials several hours later.)

Except in areas where the local civil defense war-crisis evacuation plans are well developed, most Americans living farther than 10 miles from the nearest probable separate target probably can best improve their chances of surviving a nuclear attack by preparing to remain at or near their homes and there to make or improve good shelters. Exceptions include those living in the vicinity of targets of great military importance to the Soviets — especially our missile fields, on which many warheads would be surface or near-surface bursted, producing extremely heavy fallout for up to 150 miles downwind. Americans living in these greatly endangered areas would do well to make their plans in keeping with the local official civil defense evacuation plans, at least regarding directions and distances to localities not likely to be endangered by heavy fallout.

Nuclear submarine ports, Strategic Air Command bases, and Air Force installations with long runways also would be destroyed by even a limited Soviet counterforce or disarming attack. These prime strategic assets are likely to be blasted by Submarine Launched Ballistic Missiles (SLBMs) in the first 15 or 20 minutes of the war. SLBM warheads are not as accurate as ICBM warheads, and air bursts can destroy bombers and submarines in port over about twice as large areas as if these same weapons are exploded at or near the surface. Therefore, SLBM warheads probably would be air bursted on these prime "soft" targets, with little or no local fallout. (In an all-out Soviet attack, hours later long runways are likely to be cratered by accurate ICBM warheads and by bombs, to make sure our returning bombers could not use them.)

On the following page are listed considerations, favorable and unfavorable, to evacuation. These comparative lists may help you and your family make a more logical decision regarding evacuation:

Favorable to Evacuation:	Unfavorable to Evacuation:
* You live in a highest-risk or high-risk area.	* You live outside a highest-risk or high-risk area and could build an expedient fallout shelter and make other survival preparations where you live.
* You have transportation (this means a car and enough gasoline), and roads are open to a considerably lower-risk area.	* You have no means of transportation or you believe that roads are likely to be blocked by the time you make your decision.
* You are in fairly good health or can evacuate with someone capable of taking care of you.	* You are sick, decrepit, or lack the will to try to survive if things get tough.
* Your work is not of the kind that your community depends on (such as a policeman, fireman, or telephone operator).	* You cannot suddenly leave your home area for several days without hurting others.
* You have some tools with which to build or improve a fallout shelter. You also have water containers, food, clothing, etc., adequate for life in the area to which you would go.	* You lack the tools, etc., that would be helpful—but not necessarily essential—to successful evacuation.

Instructions for building expedient fallout and blast shelters and for making expedient life-support equipment are given in following chapters. The reader is advised to study all of this book carefully before making up his mind regarding basic survival action.

THE NEED FOR AN EVACUATION CHECKLIST

A good flyer, no matter how many years he has flown, runs through a checklist covering his plane before taking off. Similarly, a citizen preparing under crisis pressures to do something he has never done before—evacuate—should use a checklist to be sure that he takes with him the most useful of his available possessions.

A family planning to use an expedient shelter or basement at or near home also should use the Evacuation Checklist on the following page to make sure needed survival items are not overlooked.

The family of six pictured in Fig. 4.3 used the Evacuation Checklist given below to select the most useful things that could be carried in and on their small car. They assembled categories of items in separate piles, then selected some items to take with them from each pile. They were able to leave their home 76 minutes after receiving the Evacuation Checklist. (Following chapters of this book include descriptions of this family's success in evacuating, building a Pole-Covered Trench Shelter, and living in it continuously for 77 hours.)

EVACUATION CHECKLIST

(Includes items for building or improving shelters)

Loading Procedure: Make separate piles for each category (except categories 1 and 5). Then load the car with **some items from each category**, taking as much as can be safely carried and being careful to leave room for all passengers.

A. THE MOST NEEDED ITEMS

Category 1. **Survival Information:** Shelter-building and other nuclear survival instructions, maps, all available small battery-powered radios and extra batteries, a fallout meter such as a homemade KFM (see Appendix C), and writing materials.

Category 2. **Tools:** Shovel, pick, saw (a bow-saw is best), ax or hatchet, file, knife, pliers, and *any other tools specified in the building instructions for the shelter planned.* Also take work gloves.

Category 3. **Shelter-Building Materials:** Rain-proofing materials (plastic, shower curtains, cloth, etc.) as specified in the instructions for the type of shelter planned. Also, unless the weather is very cold, a homemade shelter-ventilating pump such as a KAP, or the materials to build one (see Appendix B).

Category 4. **Water:** Small, filled containers plus all available large polyethylene trash bags, smaller plastic bags and pillow cases, water-purifying material such as Clorox, and a teaspoon for measuring.

Category 5. **Peacetime valuables:** Money, credit cards, negotiable securities, valuable jewelry, checkbooks, and the most important documents kept at home. (Evacuation may be followed not by nuclear war, but by continuing unstable nuclear peace.)

Category 6. **Light:** Flashlights, candles, materials to improvise cooking-oil lamps (2 clear glass jars of about 1-pint size, cooking oil, cotton string for wicks (see Chapter 11, Light), kitchen matches, and a moisture-proof jar for storing matches.

Category 7. **Clothing:** Cold-weather boots, overshoes, and warm outdoor clothing (even in summer, since after an attack these would be unobtainable), raincoats and ponchos. Wear work clothes and work shoes.

Category 8. **Sleeping Gear:** A compact sleeping bag or two blankets per person.

Category 9. **Food:** Food for babies (including milk powder, cooking oil, and sugar) has the highest priority. Compact foods that require no cooking are preferred. Include at least one pound of salt, available vitamins, a can and bottle opener, a knife, and 2 cooking pots with lids (4-qt size preferred). For each person: one cup, bowl, and large spoon. Also, a bucket stove, or minimum materials for making a bucket stove: a metal bucket, 10 all-wire coat hangers, a nail, and a cold chisel or screwdriver (see Chapter 9, Food).

Category 10. **Sanitation Items:** Plastic film or plastic bags in which to collect and contain excrement; a bucket or plastic container for urine; toilet paper, tampons, diapers, and soap.

Category 11. **Medical Items:** Aspirin, a first-aid kit, all available antibiotics and disinfectants, special prescription medicines (if essential to a member of the family), potassium iodide (for protection against radioactive iodine, see Chapter 13), spare eyeglasses, and contact lenses.

Category 12. **Miscellaneous:** Two square yards of mosquito netting or insect screen with which to screen the shelter openings if insects are a problem, insect repellents, a favorite book or two.

B. SOME USEFUL ITEMS (To take if car space is available):

1. Additional tools.

2. A tent, a small camp stove, and some additional kitchen utensils.

Just Give Me a List...

The Legendary Preparedness Instructor Jim Phillips taught me the "Just give me a list" subject and as I taught more preparedness it became true. People just asked me for a list, "Just give me a list of what I need." and I said, no, there is no list. It created frustration. I was doing an interview on a large podcast last year and someone asked for a list and I just sighed, I was frustrated... and I said, "you want a list?" They said, "Yes." I said, "My list might not be your list..." and they said, "Tell me your list." so I said Ok and I said the following, "1. Cat food, 2. Cat Toys, 3. Cat Litter, 4. Cat Nip...." and I get interrupted and they say, "wait, what is with the cat stuff?". I say, "Well you asked me for a list of what is important to me didn't you? that is what is important to me. Is it not the same for you?" They got my point. So, the following took about 50 hours of thought and conversation but I made a list from which YOU can make YOUR list. You might have a grandma to take care of, you might be diabetic or have very bad blood pressure or some other medical or physical or psychological needs than I do. So get paper and start here with YOUR LIST.

Human Needs for Life, Comfort, and Safety

1. Breathing and protection for the airway. Death in seconds.

If you can't breathe you'll start to suffer in about 3 seconds and be unsconscense in 7 to 8 seconds or dead in 3 minutes. This means you need to breathe. This has nothing to do with COVID masks. It has to do with you running from a forest fire through flame and smoke on the road. If you are coughing from smoke or dust from destruction or something else you need to be able to breathe. This also includes those of you with anaphylactic reactions to stuff like bee stings. No breath, no life. If you are an asthmatic you better have your medicine.

2. Protection from things making holes in your body so you do not bleed out and die. Death in Minutes

This means do not get shot. Do not let bullets make holes in your body. Do not get stabbed or have your arm ripped off by a Wookie and you bleed out in seconds and minutes and are dead. This means not only do not get hurt like this but if you do get a lesser wound that makes you bleed have the knowledge and the tools to stop the bleed such that you can get to medical assistance.

3. Fix too hot or too cold. Death in 10's of minutes to an hour

If I take you in your fall jacket and pants and clothing and its winter time and I throw you out of the nice warm car in Montana in a Blizzard with 35mph winds and its 5F outside and you are miles from anything and with no cell service well you can be rendered helpless and heading towards death in 30 minutes or less. You can't even walk a mile in those clothes and conditions. You can't even make it to the next exit and you are dead. Being too cold can kill you faster than being too hot in general but if you are going to be too hot or too cold you need to fix that problem. As Jim Phillips says CLOTHING is your "Mobile Personal Shelter". You do NOT need fire or shelter right that second to save your life in the above Montana blizzard, you need clothing.

4. Treatment of severe pain and injury or dire illness (like dysentery) Death in 1/2 a day to a few days.

If you become wounded with such pain that you are no longer mobile you are stuck right there. Broken bone pain. Worse pain you ever had, you cannot move pain. If you can't evacuate your house the hurricane or the flood or the radiation is going to get you. Dysentery comes from drinking or eating contaminated foods and you can have vomiting and diarrhea so bad you can dehydrate and die in as short of a period of time as 1/2 a day. 8 to 12 hours. Especially with children.

5. Hydration (and all that goes with it) Death in 1/2 to 4 days.

Yes, we are all the way down to number 5 before I tell you that you need water. Having water means methods of getting water, purification or treatment of water, storage of water, consumption, and use of water, and the transportation of water.

6. Daily Medications you must have. Death in Days to weeks.

Severe diabetics and those with chronic high blood pressure and other medical issues may require medication or treatments multiple times a day or they can die.

7. Illumination which includes Navigation

If you have 1 to 6 taken care of then you are not going to die of bleeding, freezing, lack of medication, or lack of water. Now we need to make sure that you can use the other half of the day for your benefit which we call night or darkness. Having illumination means you can see in the darkness, work in the darkness, fix in the darkness, eat and drink in the darkness and navigate and go places in the darkness. Getting away from danger might be a high priority for you. If on foot or bike and you do not have a light you will only be traveling when it's day light. Pure darkness means you stop moving. Navigation can just mean you are going this way or that way. The way you know you need to go. Follow the road. It can also mean maps and compass use and it can mean using a GPS or other device like this. Either way, it's lumped in with Illumination because you need light to see where you are going as well as to see the map or GPS. Yes, I know your phone or GPS is lit up. That is called illumination. Just don't trip over the aligator.

8. Food (and all that goes with it)

Cresson covers food very well in this book so read it and study it. Saying "FOOD" means the food, the stuff to cook it with, to eat it on, to eat it with, to protect it, seal it, and to transport it.

Just Give Me a List...page 2

9. Shelter (see #2)
Your mobile personal shelter (clothing) usually is going to need "Maintainece" as Jim Phillips calls it. That helps if you are inside or under something. Your body perspires and the water vapor from your skin can get trapped and frozen in your clothing, yes, even your 'precious wool' does this. So the ability to take off your clothing and wash them, shake them out, dry them out, fix or sew holes and such is a lot easier if you are in some type of shelter. Being able to be outside and in the elements in just your clothing is awesome. Being inside out of the elements and nice and cool or nice and warm with a place to cook, eat, washup, and sleep is even better.

10. Communications
10, 11, and 12 are hard because any of these could be either other one in priority or potential benefit for you. So you judge as you see fit. Communication does not mean cell phone or two-way radio it can mean an AM/FM radio for listening to news and what is happening. This might determine if you move one way, go the other way, or stay put. (See #11, transportation below). Obviously working and charged cell phone with signal and data (and a working internet) makes communications so much better. So if you have one of those working your first priority is to be able to charge and power it so you can use it. From CB to Ham Radio to Iridium Satellites and StarLink by SpaceX, there are many forms of communications. You pick the ones that are important or needed by YOU. I cannot do that.

11. Transportation and everything related to that form of transportation.
Walking, Bike, Motorcycle, Car, SUV, Truck, SemiRig, Boat, and Plane are all methods of transportation. Note: Walking on a smooth surface is a lot easier with your gear and supplies in a wagon or a cart. You might have to evacuate, or leave or flea or go, help grandma. If you are using some form of these transportation methods you need spare shoes, tire patch kit, fuel, jack, barter material, money, etc...

12. Radiological and Bacterial and Viral Protection and detection. |
If you have a biological disaster you'll need something to protect you from, detect, or disinfect this method of danger. If it's a nuclear incident you'll need something to measure radiation with and Cresson will cover that well in this book.

This is the Harris List from which you make your OWN List for yourself and those you care about. Your list can be pages long. You are you, you are not me. You can add more than the 12 I have here, you can delete items. This is just a GUIDE POST to guide you in your thinking of what is important to you for pre-disaster preparedness and for what you might need to take in a disaster when you are evacuating. If you can't take care of #1 and #2 then the rest of them kind of does not matter.

Fig. 4.3. Six members of a Utah family arriving at a rural shelter-building site 64 miles from their urban home.

EVACUATING BY CAR

The small car shown in Fig. 4.3 was skillfully loaded for a safe evacuation trip. To make room for supplies, the back seat was left at home. The load on top of the car included blankets, a small rug, and a small tent—all made of springy materials which kept the load from becoming compacted and working loose under the 1/4-inch nylon ropes tightened around it. The two loop-ended ropes went over the load and around the top of the car, passing over the tops of the closed doors.

USING MUSCLE POWER

Hazards of evacuation would include highways blocked by wrecks and stalled vehicles. If leadership and know-how were provided, the muscle power of people usually could quickly clear a highway. During a major Chinese evacuation before advancing Japanese armies in World War II, I observed Chinese, using only muscle power, quickly clear a mountain road of wrecks and other obstructions. Americans can do the same, if someone convinces them that they can do it, as proved by a wintertime episode on Monarch Pass over the Continental Divide in Colorado. At least 100 vehicles were held up after a large wrecking truck overturned on the icy highway. The patrolmen were doing nothing until I told them how the Chinese handled such a situation. The patrolmen then called for volunteers from among the delayed motorists to lift the overturned truck back onto its wheels. In less than 15 minutes, about 50 people had combined their muscle power and opened Monarch Pass to traffic.

Citizens should take direct action to keep traffic moving during a crisis evacuation.

MAKING AN EXPEDIENT OR PERMANENT SHELTER INSTEAD OF EVACUATING

Millions of Americans have homes within very large urban-industrial areas, probably not all of which would be subjected to blast and fire dangers. Many, whose homes are in the suburbs or adjacent towns in these metropolitan areas, could logically decide not to evacuate, but to build earth-covered shelters at or very near their homes and to supply them with life-support essentials. Likewise, people living even as close as 5 miles from an isolated probable target may decide to build a good shelter near their supplies, rather than to evacuate. This is a good idea, provided that (1) their homes are far enough away from probable aiming points to make such shelters practical, and (2) enough time, space, tools, materials, and supplies are available.

The photo (Fig. 4.4) shows a family with no adult male that built an expedient shelter that would give far better fallout, blast, and fire protection than almost any home. They succeeded, despite the necessity of working on cold November days with snow flurries. The top two inches of earth were frozen and the next two feet so dry that most of it had to be loosened with their dull pick. No member of this family had done any serious digging before, yet they built a shelter that would have given about 100 times as much protection against fallout radiation as would a typical small frame house and at least 25 times as much as a typical home basement.

(Fallout shelters are designed for protection against radiation from fallout particles. Although fallout shelters lack blast doors and other means for keeping out blast, the better types would prevent their occupants from being killed by blast effects in extensive areas where people in houses would have little chance of surviving. In this book, an "expedient shelter" generally means an expedient fallout shelter.)

Fig. 4.4. This family completed their Protection Factor 200 (PF 200) **fallout** shelter, a Door-Covered Trench Shelter with 2 feet of earth on its roof, 34 hours after receiving the building instructions at their home.

Even as simple an earth-covered fallout shelter as this Door-Covered Trench Shelter, if built well separated from flammable buildings, usually would save its occupants' lives in extensive areas devastated by blast and/or fire. The area of probable survival in a good **earth-covered** fallout shelter would extend from where blast damage would be light but fires likely to be numerous, inward toward GZ to where most homes would be collapsed by blast and/or destroyed by fire. This ring-shaped area of probable survival from blast and/or fire effects of a 1-MT air burst would extend from about 8 miles from GZ inward to approximately 5.5 miles. Its area would be about 105 square miles, more than the 95 square miles in the circular area with a radius of 5.5 miles centered on GZ and within which this simple a shelter probably would be collapsed by the blast overpressure of a 1-MT air burst. (Door-Covered Trench Shelters and most of the other types of **earth-covered** expedient shelters described in this book have been proven dependable in test explosions conducted by the Defense Nuclear Agency.)

In many areas, this and even better types of expedient fallout shelters affording considerable blast protection could be built by untrained families, following the written, field-tested instructions in this book. Furthermore (as shown in Appendix D, Expedient Blast Shelters) within a few days a small but significant fraction of the population could build expedient blast shelters complete with expedient blast doors and providing at least 15-psi blast protection.

Chapter 5
Shelter, the Greatest Need

ADEQUATE SHELTER

To improve your chances of surviving a nuclear attack, your primary need would be an adequate shelter equipped for many days of occupancy. A shelter that affords good protection against fallout radiation and weather would be adequate in more than 95% of the *area* of the United States. However, even in almost all areas not endangered by blast and fire during a massive nuclear attack, the fallout protection provided by most existing buildings would not be adequate if the winds blew from the wrong direction during the time of fallout deposition.

To remain in or near cities or other probable target areas, one would need better protection against blast, fire, and fallout than is provided by most shelters in buildings. Blast tests have proved that the earth-covered expedient fallout shelters described in this book can survive blast effects severe enough to demolish most homes.[5]

This chapter is concerned primarily with expedient shelters that give excellent protection against fallout radiation. These earth-covered fallout shelters could be built in 48 hours or less by tens of millions of Americans following field-tested, written instructions.[8] Expedient blast shelters are discussed in Appendix D. The special blast doors and other design features needed for effective blast protection require more work, materials, and skill than are needed for expedient fallout shelters.

If average Americans are to do their best when building expedient shelters and life-support equipment for themselves, they need detailed information about *what* to do and about *why* it is to their advantage to do it. We are not a people accustomed to blindly following orders. Unfortunately, during a crisis threatening nuclear war, it would take too long to read instructions explaining why each important feature was designed as specified. Therefore, only a few reasons are included in the step-by-step, illustrated instructions given in Appendix A for building 6 types of earth-covered expedient shelters during a crisis.

In this chapter, reasons will be given for designing a Pole-Covered Trench Shelter as specified in the Oak Ridge National Laboratory instructions given in Appendix A.2. The two pages of drawings and plans given at the end of Appendix A.2 show the parts of this shelter, except for the essential shelter-ventilating pump installed in its entrance trench. The following account of how an urban family, after evacuating, used these instructions to build such a shelter in less than 36 hours also includes explanations of various radiation dangers and of simple means to build protection against these dangers.

This family, like scores of other families recruited to build shelters or life-support equipment, was offered a sum about equivalent to laborers' wages if its members completed the experiment within a specified time. The test period began the moment the family received the written, illustrated instructions preparatory to evacuating by car, as mentioned in the preceding chapter. Like the other test families, this family was paid for all of its materials used. If a family worked hard and completed the project in half the specified time, it was paid a cash bonus. Throughout such tests workers were guided only by the written instructions, which were improved after each successive test.

The successful outcome of almost all the shelter-building experiments indicates that tens of millions of Americans in a nuclear war crisis would work hard and successfully to build earth-covered expedient shelters that would give them better protection against fallout, blast, and fire than would all but a very small fraction of existing buildings. However, this belief is dependent on two conditions: (1) that in a desperate, worsening crisis our country's highest officials would supply strong, motivating leadership; and (2) that Americans would have received—well in advance—shelter-building and other practical, tested survival instructions.

SHELTER AGAINST RADIATION

The family previously pictured evacuating by car (Fig. 4.3) drove 64 miles to build a shelter at the site shown in Fig. 5.1. Although the August sun was very hot in this irrigated Utah valley, the family members did not build in the shade of nearby trees. To avoid digging through roots, they carried the poles about 150 feet and dug their trench near the edge of the cornfield.

The father and the oldest son did most of the work of making the shelter. The mother and second son had health problems; the two youngest children were not accustomed to work.

The family followed an earlier version of the plans and instructions given in Appendix A for building a Pole-Covered Trench Shelter. Because the earth was firm and stable, the trenches were dug with vertical walls. If the earth had been less stable, it would have been necessary to slope the walls—increasing the width at the top of the main trench from 3½ to 5 feet.

Before placing the roof poles, the workers assured themselves a more comfortable shelter by covering the trench walls. They had brought a large number of the plastic garbage bags required in their home community and split some bags open to make wall coverings. Bed sheets or other cloth could have been used.

The room of this 6-person shelter was 3½ feet wide, 4½ feet high, and 16½ feet long. A small stand-up hole was dug at one end, so each tall occupant could stand up and stretch several times a day.

The trenches for entry and emergency exit were dug only 22 inches wide, to minimize radiation entering the shelter through these openings. One wall of these two narrow trenches was an extension of the

Fig. 5.1. Placing 9-foot poles for the roof of a Pole-Covered Trench Shelter.

room wall shown on the right in Fig. 5.1. The family sat and slept along the left wall, to be better shielded from radiation coming through the openings.

This shelter was designed so that its main trench could be enlarged to make a much more livable room without disturbing its completed roof. For this reason, the 9-foot roofing poles were placed off-center, with the two extra feet resting on the ground to the right of the main room.

Whenever practical, expedient shelters should be built so that they can be readily enlarged to make semi-permanent living quarters. After it becomes safe to emerge for limited periods, occupants could sleep and spend much of their waking time in such a rainproof dugout that affords excellent protection against continuing radiation. In cold weather, living in a dugout like this is more comfortable than living in a tent or shack. After the fallout radiation dose rate outdoors has decayed to less than about 2 R per hour, the small vertical entry could be enlarged and converted to a steeply inclined stairway.

The importance of giving inexperienced shelter builders detailed instructions is illustrated by the unnecessary work done by the young women shown in Fig. 5.2. They had agreed to try to build a Pole-Covered Trench Shelter, working unassisted and using only hand tools. Because the summer sun in Utah was hot, they selected a shady site under a large tree. The brief instructions they received included no advice on the selection of a building site. Cutting and digging out the numerous roots was very difficult for them and required several of the 22 hours they spent actually working.

Another disadvantage of making a shelter under trees is that more of the gamma rays from fallout particles on the leaves and branches would reach and penetrate the shelter than if these same particles were on the ground. Many gamma rays from fallout particles on the ground would be scattered or absorbed by striking rocks, clods of earth, tree trunks, or houses before reaching a belowground shelter.

Fig. 5.2. Two non-athletic college girls who completed a 4-person Pole-Covered Trench Shelter in $35^{1}/_{2}$ hours, despite tree roots.

TYPES OF SHIELDING

Shelters provide protection against radiation by utilizing two types of shielding: **barrier shielding** and **geometry shielding.**

- **Barrier shielding** is shown by Fig. 5.3, a simplified illustration. (In a real fallout area, a man in an open trench would have fallout particles all over and around him.) The 3-foot thickness of earth shown (or a 2-foot thickness of concrete) will provide an effective barrier, attenuating (absorbing) about 99.9% of all gamma rays from *fallout*. (In the illustration, only a single fallout particle 3 feet from the edge of the trench is considered.) Only one gamma ray out of 1000 could penetrate the 3 feet of earth shown and strike the person in the trench. Rays from particles farther away than 3 feet would be negligible; rays from particles closer than 3 feet would be attenuated according to the thickness of earth between the fallout particle and the man in the trench.

However, the man in the trench would not be protected from "skyshine," which is caused by gamma rays scattering after striking the nitrogen, oxygen, and other atoms of the air. The man's exposed head, which is just below ground level, would be hit by about one-tenth as many gamma rays as if it were 3 feet above ground (Fig. 5.3). Even if all fallout could be kept out of the trench and off the man and every part of the ground within 3 feet of the edges of the trench, skyshine from heavy fallout on the surrounding ground could deliver a fatal radiation dose to the man in the open trench.

Skyshine reaches the ground from all directions. If the man were sitting in a deeper trench, he would escape more of this scattered radiation, but not all of it. For good protection he must be protected overhead and on all sides by barrier shielding.

The barrier shielding of the Pole-Covered Trench Shelter shown in Fig. 5.4 was increased by shoveling additional earth onto its "buried roof." After father and son had mounded earth about 18 inches deep over the centerline of the roof poles, a large piece of 4-mil-thick polyethylene was placed over the mound. This waterproof material served as a "buried roof" after it was covered with more earth. Any rainwater trickling through the earth above the plastic would have run off the sloping sides of the "buried roof" and away from the shelter.

- **Geometry shielding** reduces the radiation dose received by shelter occupants by increasing the distances between them and fallout particles, and by

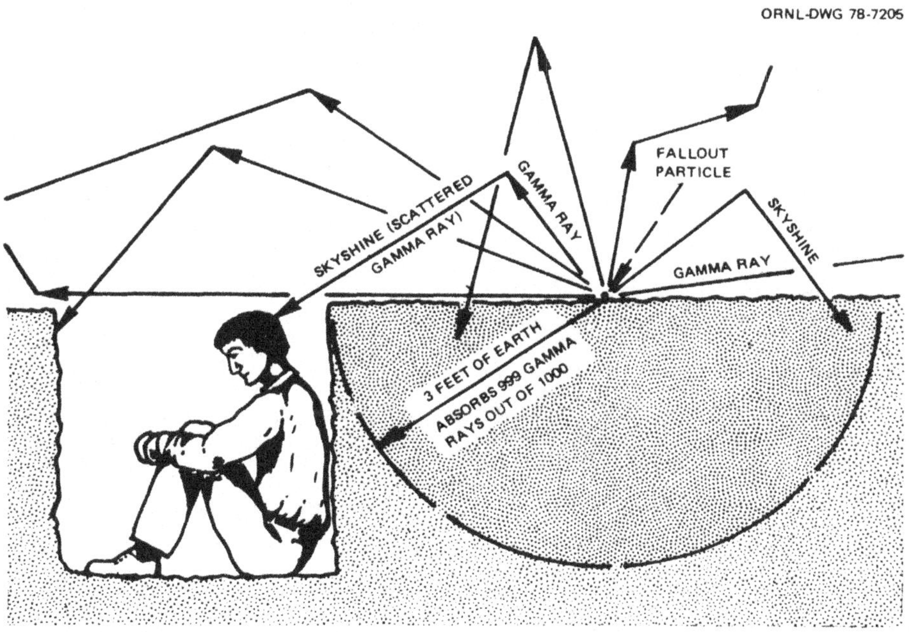

Fig. 5.3. Simplified illustration of barrier shielding and skyshine (scattered gamma radiation). An open trench provides poor protection.

Fig. 5.4. Increasing the barrier shielding over a Pole-Covered Trench Shelter.

providing turns in the openings leading into the shelter. Figure 5.5 is a sectional drawing of the shelter entry built by the Utah family.

The farther you can keep away from a source either of light or of harmful radiation, the less light or other radiation will reach you. If fallout particles are on the roof of a tall building and you are in the basement, you will receive a much smaller radiation dose from those particles than if they were on the floor just above you. Likewise, if either visible light or gamma rays are coming through an opening at the far end of a passageway, less will reach you at the other end if the passageway is long than if it is short.

Turns in passageways are very effective in reducing the amount of radiation entering a shelter through them. A right-angle turn, either from a vertical or horizontal entry, causes a reduction of about 90%.

Note: *Fallout* shelters need not provide additional shielding to protect occupants against initial nuclear radiation that is emitted from the fireballs of nuclear explosions. (See Figs. 1.1 and 1.4.) Large nuclear weapons would be employed in an attack on the United States. The initial nuclear radiation from the sizes of explosions that may endanger Americans would be greatly reduced in passing through the miles of air between the fireballs and those fallout shelters far enough away to survive the blast effects. The smaller an explosion, the larger the dose of initial nuclear radiation it delivers at a given blast overpressure distance from ground zero. (For a discussion of the more difficult shielding requirements of blast shelters that would enable occupants to survive blast effects much closer to explosions and therefore would be subjected to much larger exposures of initial nuclear radiation, see Appendix D, Expedient Blast Shelters.)

Figure 5.6 shows the completed shelter after it was occupied by the family of six just $32\frac{1}{2}$ hours after receiving the shelter-building instructions and beginning preparations to evacuate. (This family won a bonus for completion within 36 hours and also a larger bonus given if all members then stayed inside continuously for at least 72 hours.) To get a better idea of how six people can live in such a small shelter, look at the drawings at the end of Appendix A.2. In warm or hot weather, shelters, especially crowded ones, must be well ventilated and cooled by an adequate volume of outdoor air pumped through them. This family had built an efficient homemade air pump (a KAP) and used it as described in Chapter 6 and Appendix B.

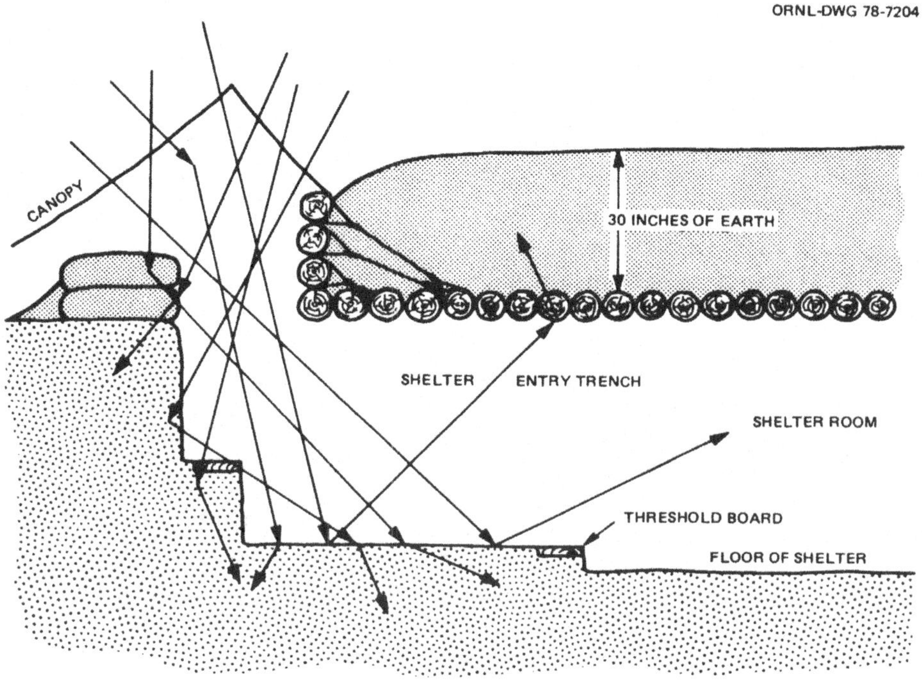

Fig. 5.5. Skyshine coming into a shelter through a vertical entry would be mostly absorbed while turning into and traveling down the entryway trench.

Fig. 5.6. Earth mounded over a $3^1/_2$-foot-wide Pole-Covered Trench Shelter. The canvas canopy would protect the vertical entry against both fallout and rain. (A smaller canopy over the air duct-emergency exit at the other end is obscured by the mounded earth.)

All of the earth excavated in digging the trenches was mounded over the roof poles, making a covering 30 inches deep. This shelter had a protection factor (PF) of over 300; that is, persons inside would receive less than 1/300th of the gamma-ray dose of fallout radiation that they would receive if they were standing outside in the open.

To have made the roof covering more than 36 inches thick would not have increased the protection against radiation very much, unless the entry trench and the air duct-emergency exit trench had been dug considerably longer. Field tests have shown that some families, given only 48 hours, cannot dig the longer trenches, cut the additional poles, and shovel on the additional earth necessary for a shelter that would offer significantly better protection than the shelter shown here. The Pole-Covered Trench Shelter and the other shelters described in Appendix A all have been built by untrained families within 48 hours, the minimum time assumed to be available to Americans before a possible attack if the Russians should begin to evacuate their cities.

EARTH ARCHING USED TO STRENGTHEN SHELTERS

Several types of expedient shelters can be made to withstand greater pressures if their roofs are built of *yielding* materials and covered with enough earth to attain "earth arching." This arching results when the yielding of the roof causes part of the load carried by the roof to be shifted to the overlying earth particles, which become rearranged in such a way that an arch is formed. This arch carries the load to surrounding supports that are less yielding. These supports often include adjacent earth that has not been disturbed.

To attain earth arching, the earth covering the yielding roof must be at least as deep as half the width of the roof between its supports. Then the resultant earth arch above the roof carries most of the load.

(A familiar example of effective earth arching is its use with sheet metal culverts under roads. The arching in a few feet of earth over a thin-walled culvert prevents it from being crushed by the weight of heavy vehicles.)

Figure 5.7 shows how a flexible roof yields under the weight of 30 inches of earth mounded over it and how earth arching develops. After the arch is formed, the only weight that the yielding roof supports is the weight of the small thickness of earth between the roof and the bottom of the arch.

Protective earth arching also results if a shelter is covered with a material that compresses when loaded, or if the whole roof or the whole shelter can be pushed down a little without being broken.

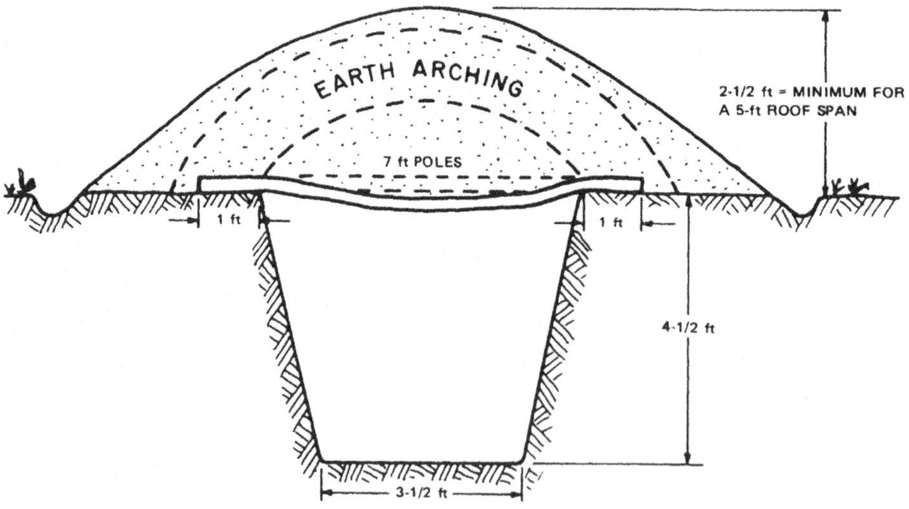

Fig. 5.7. Earth arching over a yielding roof enables a shelter to withstand much greater pressures.

SHELTER AGAINST BETA AND ALPHA PARTICLES

In addition to the invisible, light-like gamma *rays,* fallout particles radiate two types of hazardous invisible *particles:* beta and alpha particles. These radiations would be minor dangers to informed people in fallout areas, especially to those who had entered almost any kind of shelter before the fallout began to be deposited in their area.

- Beta particles are high-speed electrons given off by some of the radioactive atoms in fallout. Only the highest-energy beta particles can penetrate more than about 10 feet of air or about 1/8 inch of water, wood, or human body tissue. Any building that keeps out fallout particles will prevent injury from beta radiation.

The only frequently serious dangers are from (1) internal beta-radiation doses from fallout-contaminated food or drink, and (2) beta burns from **fresh** fallout particles. **Fresh** fallout particles are no more than a few days old and therefore very radioactive. If **fresh** particles remain for at least several tens of minutes in contact with the skin, beta burns are likely to result. If only thin clothing separates **fresh** fallout particles from the skin, a considerably longer time will elapse before their radiation causes beta burns.

In dry, windy weather, **fresh** fallout particles might get inside one's nose and ears, along with dust and sand, and could cause beta burns if not promptly washed off or otherwise removed.

Prompt washing will prevent beta burns. If water is not available, brushing and rubbing the fallout particles off the skin will help.

If a person is exposed outdoors where there is heavy, **fresh** fallout for a long enough time to receive a large dose of gamma radiation, the highest-energy beta radiation given off by **fresh** fallout particles on the ground may be a relatively minor danger to his eyes and skin. Even ordinary glasses give good protection to the eyes against such beta radiation, and ordinary clothing gives good protection to the skin.

Ordinary clothing will shield and protect the body quite well from all but the highest-energy beta particles given off by **fresh** fallout deposited on the clothing. Fallout-contaminated clothing should be removed as soon as practical, or at least brushed and beaten before entering a shelter room, to rid it of as many fallout particles as possible. (Fallout particles that are many days old will not cause beta burns unless large quantities are on the body for hours.)

Most of the knowledge about beta burns on human skin was gathered as a result of an accident during the largest U.S. H-bomb test in the tropical Pacific.[6] Winds blew the fallout in a direction not anticipated by the meteorologists. Five hours after the multimegaton surface burst, some natives of the Marshall Islands noticed a white powder beginning to be deposited on everything exposed, including their bare, moist skin. Unknown to them, the very small particles were fresh fallout. (Most fallout is sand-like, but fallout from bursts that have cratered calcareous rock, such as coral reefs and limestone, is powdery or flakey, and white.) Since the natives knew nothing about fallout, they thought the white dust was ashes from a distant volcanic eruption. For two days, until they were removed from their island homes and cared for by doctors, they paid practically no attention to the white dust. Living in the open and in lightly constructed homes, they received from the fallout all around them a calculated gamma-ray dose of about 175 R in the two days they were exposed.

The children played in the fallout-contaminated sand. The fallout on these islanders' scalps, bare necks, and the tops of their bare feet caused itching and burning sensations after a time. Days later, beta burns resulted, along with extreme discoloration of the skin. Beta burns are not deep burns; however, it took weeks to heal them. Some, in spite of proper medical attention, developed into ulcers. (No serious permanent skin injury resulted, however.)

For survivors confined inside crowded, unsanitary shelters by heavy fallout, and without medicines, beta burns could be a worse problem than were similar burns to the Marshall Islanders.

All of the Marshall Islanders unknowingly ate fallout-contaminated food and drank fallout-contaminated water for two days. Mainly as a result of this, radioactive iodine was concentrated in their thyroid glands, and thyroid abnormalities developed years later. (There is a simple, very low-cost means of attaining almost complete protection against this delayed hazard: taking minute prophylactic doses of a salt, potassium iodide. This will be discussed in Chapter 13.)

In dry, dusty, windy areas the human nasal passages usually filter out much dust. A large part of it is swallowed and may be hazardous if the dust is contaminated with fallout. Under such dry, windy conditions, beta burns also could be caused by large amounts of dust lodged inside the nasal passages. Breathing through a dust mask, towel, or other cloth would give good protection against this localized hazard. In conclusion: persons under nuclear attack should make considerable effort to protect themselves from beta radiation.

- **Alpha particles,** identical to the nuclei of helium atoms, are given off by some of the radioactive atoms in fallout. These particles have very little penetrating power: 1 to 3 inches of air will stop them. It is doubtful that alpha particles can get through unbroken skin; they cannot penetrate even a thin fabric.[6] Alpha particles are hazardous only if materials that emit them (such as the radioactive element plutonium) enter the body and are retained in bone, lung tissue, or other parts of the body. Any shelter that excludes fallout particles affords excellent protection against this radiation danger. Unless survivors eat or drink fallout-contaminated food or water in considerably larger quantities than did the completely uninformed natives of the Marshall Islands, danger from alpha particles would be minor.

PROTECTION AGAINST OTHER NUCLEAR WEAPONS EFFECTS

- **Flash burns** are caused by the intense rays of heat emitted from the fireball within the first minute following an explosion.[6] This thermal radiation travels at the speed of light and starts to heat or burn exposed people and materials before the arrival of the blast wave. Thermal radiation is reduced—but not eliminated—if it passes through rain, dense clouds, or thick smoke. On a clear day, serious flash burns on a person's exposed skin can be caused by a 20-megaton explosion that is 25 miles away.

A covering of clothing—preferably of white cloth that reflects light—can reduce or prevent flash burns on those who are in a large part of an area in which thermal radiation is a hazard. However, in areas close enough to ground zero for severe blast damage, the clothing of exposed people could be set on fire and their bodies badly burned.

- **Fires** ignited by thermal radiation and those resulting from blast and other causes especially would endanger people pinned down by fallout while in or near flammable buildings. Protective measures against the multiple dangers from fire, carbon monoxide, and toxic smokes are discussed in Chapter 7.

- **Flash blindness** can be caused by the intense light from an explosion tens of miles away in clear weather. Although very disturbing, the blindness is not permanent; most victims recover within seconds to minutes. Among the Hiroshima and Nagasaki survivors (people who had been in the open more than persons expecting a nuclear attack would be), there were a number of instances of temporary blindness that lasted as long as 2 or 3 hours, but only one case of permanent retinal injury was reported.[6]

Flash blindness may be produced by scattered light; the victim of this temporary affliction usually has not looked directly at the fireball. Flash blindness would be more severe at night, when the pupils are larger. Retinal burns, a permanent injury, can result at great distances if the eye is focused on the fireball.

People inside any shelter with no openings through which light can shine directly would be protected from flash burns and eye damage. Persons in the open with adequate warning of a nuclear explosion can protect themselves from both flash blindness and retinal burns by closing or shielding their eyes. They should get behind anything casting a shadow— quickly.

SKIN BURNS FROM HEATED DUST (THE POPCORNING EFFECT)

When exposed grains of sand and particles of earth are heated very rapidly by intense thermal radiation, they explode like popcorn and pop up into the air.[6] While this dust is airborne, the continuing thermal radiation heats it to temperatures that may be as high as several thousand degrees Fahrenheit on a clear day in areas of severe blast. Then the shock wave and blast winds arrive and can carry the burning-hot air and dust into an open shelter.[6,9] Animals inside open shelters have been singed and seriously burned in some of the nuclear air-burst tests in Nevada.[9]

Thus Japanese working inside an open tunnel-shelter at Nagasaki within about 100 yards of ground zero were burned on the portion of their skin that was exposed to the entering blast wind, even though they were protected by one or two turns in the tunnel.[4] (None of these Japanese workers who survived the blast-wave effects had fatal burns or suffered serious radiation injuries, which they certainly would have suffered had they been outside and subjected to the thermal pulse and the intense initial nuclear radiation from the fireball.)

Experiments conducted during several nuclear test explosions have established the amount of thermal radiation that must be delivered to exposed earth to produce the popcorning effect.[6] Large air bursts may result in exposed skin being burned by hot

Yes, I Have a Basement Fallout Shelter

Yes, I the author of these updates, DO have a basement fallout shelter as described by Cresson in this book. It's because I spent so much time with Cresson and this book and our discussion of it and testing of different things that I did it. First of all, I live in Michigan and in Michigan we have basements. This is not true for all of the USA and the world. So I put the shelter in the corner of the basement and my walls are poured concrete and my basement floor is a good 7 to 8 feet below the grade of the earth outside. So the corner has great radiation protection on the two sides of the corner. I built the corner shelter with 2x4s and plywood and it's 4 feet wide, 4 feet tall by 8 feet long in the corner of the basement. I put plywood on all sides that are not against the walls and then I put my food and water storage on the top, and around the 2 sides of it. I have plenty of boxes and milk creates to which I can add more dirt from outside to increase the protection from radiation. This is a radiation shelter NOT a blast shelter. So with my food, water, and addition of some dirt here and there it could offer a protection factor (PF) of 32 to about 100 times less than what is being received outside. As Cresson points out, these in-building radiation shelters will not provide enough radiation shielding in a large Russian nuclear exchange that has high radiation fallout. If outside fallout is 600 rads per hour and I'm getting 6 rads per hour in my shelter with a PF of 100 in about 16 hours I'm going to be at the LD 1% level of radiation exposure and that is going to be climbing. See the previous graph on the decay rate of dangerous fallout. However, if Chicago is nuked with a ground detonated nuclear device in the 20kt to 100kt range and the wind brings the fallout over me, I might be ok. Of course, I might die, there are a lot of variables but that would be about the worse case for me in the scenarios we are talking about in this 2022 update. Of course, Detroit getting nuked would be worse, but you understand my example. New York or DC or Atlanta or Miami or Houston getting nuked would blow the fallout with the prevailing wind mostly eastward and since I'm well west and north of those, my fallout shelter would not be needed. If Los Angeles, Las Vegas, San Francisco, Portland, Seattle all got hit at the same time, with half a dozen nukes on the ground in all of the major west coast cities there would be radiation that is measurable reaching me in Detroit and thus I might end up spending time in my shelter and this is where the PF (protection factor) of 32x to 100x reduction would be quite helpful.

INSTRUCTORS SHOULD SET THE EXAMPLE

I believe that instructors should set the example for the students and have actually done a great deal of what they are teaching. I've done everything in here over the last 30 years and much more when it comes to food, power, water, sanitation, and all of the other subjects but I have also made a basement fallout shelter over 20 years ago. I decided 'why not' and I needed a better way to organize and store the food storage I had anyway. We are talking about a year of food storage in volume for 2 people. So it's hundreds of pounds of white flour, beans, rice, some wheat, corn (treated for wevils), baking powder, baking soda, cooking oil, salt, water, and other supplies. The entrance of the shelter is about 2 feet wide and 3 feet tall and it's next to the wall. I have a 55-gallon barrel of water on a rolling dolly that I can roll in front of the entrance to reduce the radiation. I can stack things to make the entrance more narrow and then move the water up to the door when I'm inside to increase the protection factor of an opening in the shape of the entrance. It's expedient, it's simple, it works. Is it the most ideal and perfect? No, but it will work easily. Back in the day when I had a landline phone line, I even had my landline phone run into the shelter. I have a battery bank in the basement for emergency power. The battery bank does not need radiation shielding so its power can run into the small radiation shelter. Even my toilet can be outside the shelter as long as I'm in the shelter to shield myself from non-extreme levels of radiation. If the outside radiation is 5 rads per day and I'm in the shelter to get 1/50th the radiation (PF of 50) so I'm getting 20 millirads per day in the shelter then I can out of it for 5 minutes to use my improvised bucket toilet and keep the stench out of the shelter. If this was a full underground shelter and the radiation outside was 600 rads per hour or even 600 rads per day, you'd never do this. Not all the people reading this are going to be in a worst-case scenario. NWSS deals with the worst-case scenario. I'm trying to help you with the more moderate scenarios we are likely to face in the year 2022 etc...

IMPROVING THE RADIATION SHEILDING.

I should note, that I have 5-gallon buckets of wheat and flour and corn and other items on top of the shelter which is 4 feet by 8 feet, and it's heavily supported by the walls and a center support beam I put down the center of the shelter. Buckets are round, if I want to put dirt from outside in between the buckets to 'fill in the holes' between the buckets then I can do that. I have milk crates I can put a trash bag in and fill those up with dirt from outside to put around the shelter to provide more radiation shielding. I can literally just bring in and dump about a foot of dirt on the floor of the bedroom above the shelter to provide another layer of radiation shielding to the shelter below it.

These improvements might get me to a protection factor (PF) of 100 times less radiation than outside. A Cresson Pole Covered Trench shelter as described in this book will still provide higher levels of radiation protection. At least this one in the basement is here and ready to go right now.

If I had to make a pole covered trench shelter right now, or a door covered trench shelter I already know where there is a back howe I can borrow or acquire and my chain saw and all of my neighbor's wood fences around plus the doors from the house will allow me to make a long thin covered trench shelter for situations worse than what my in house shelter can handle.

dust and heated air produced at overpressure ranges as low as 3 or 4 psi. However, calculations indicate that the large surface bursts most likely to endanger Americans would not result in the occupants of small, open shelters being burned by these effects—except at somewhat higher overpressures.

Protection is simple against the heated dust and very hot air that may be blown into an open shelter by the blast. When expecting an attack, occupants of an *open* shelter should keep towels or other cloths in hand. When they see the bright light from an explosion, they should cover their heads and exposed skin. If time and materials are available, much better protection is given by making expedient blast doors, as described in Appendix D. When occupants see the very bright light from a large explosion miles away, they can close and secure such doors before the arrival of the blast wave several seconds later.

ESSENTIAL LIFE-SUPPORT EQUIPMENT

Shelters can be built to give excellent protection against all nuclear weapon effects, except in places within or very close to cratered areas. But most shelters would be of little use in areas of heavy fallout unless supplied with enough life-support equipment to enable occupants to stay in the shelters until conditions outside become endurable. In heavy fallout areas most high-protection-factor shelters would be crowded; except in cold weather, most would need a ventilating pump to remove warmed air and bring in enough cooler outdoor air to maintain survivable temperature-humidity conditions. Means for storing adequate water is another essential life-support requirement. These and other essential or highly desirable life-support needs are covered in following chapters.

BASEMENT SHELTERS

The blast and fire effects of a massive, all-out attack of the magnitude possible in 1987 would destroy or damage most American homes and other buildings and endanger the occupants of shelters inside them. Outside the blast and/or fire areas, the use of shelters inside buildings would not be nearly as hazardous. However, an enemy might also target some areas into which large numbers of urban Americans had evacuated before the attack, although such targetting is not believed to be included in Soviet strategy.

Earth-covered expedient shelters in a blast area give better protection against injury from blast, fire, or fallout than do almost all basements. But during the more likely kinds of crises threatening nuclear war most urban Americans, including those who would evacuate into areas outside probable blast areas, probably would lack the tools, materials, space, determination, physical strength, or time required to build good expedient shelters that are separate from buildings and covered with earth. As a result, most unprepared urban citizens would have to use basements and other shelters in existing structures, for want of better protection.

Shelters in buildings, including basement shelters, have essentially the same requirements as expedient shelters: adequate shielding against fallout radiation, strength, adequate ventilation-cooling, water, fallout radiation meters, food, hygiene, etc. Sketches and short descriptions of ways to improve the fallout protection afforded by home basements are to be found in widely distributed civil defense pamphlets, including two entitled "In Time of Emergency," and "Protection in the Nulear Age." In 1987, millions of copies of these pamphlets are stockpiled for possible distribution during a crisis. Unfortunately, most of such official instructions were written years ago, when the deliverable megatonnage and the number of Soviet warheads were small fractions of what they are today. Official civil defense instructions now available to average Americans do not inform the reader as to what degree of protection against fallout radiation (what protection factor) is given by the different types of do-it-yourself shelters pictured. There is no mention of dependable ways to provide adequate cooling-ventilation, an essential requirement if even a home basement is to be occupied by several families in warm or hot weather. Outdated or inadequate information is given about water, food, the improvement of shelter in one's home, and other survival essentials.

No field-tested instructions at present are available to guide householders who may want to strengthen the floor over a home basement so that it can safely support 2 feet of shielding earth piled on it. In areas of heavy fallout, such strengthening often would be needed to safely support adequate overhead shielding, especially if the house were to be jarred by a light shock from a distant explosion. In the following paragraphs, a way to greatly improve the fallout protection afforded by a typical home basement is outlined. If improved in this manner, a basement would provide excellent fallout protection for several families.

First, earth should be placed on the floor above to a depth of about one foot. Earth can be carried efficiently by using sacks or pillowcases, using the techniques described in Chapter 8 for carrying water. If earth is not available because the ground is frozen or because of the lack of digging tools, other heavy materials (containers of water, heavy furniture, books, etc.) should be placed on the floor above. These materials should weigh enough to produce a loading of about 90 pounds per square foot—about the same weight as earth one foot thick. This initial loading of the floor joists causes them to carry some of the weight that otherwise would be supported by the posts that then are to be installed.

Next, a horizontal beam is installed so as to support all of the floor joists under their centers. Figure 5.8 shows a beam and one of its supporting posts. Such a supporting beam preferably is made by nailing three 2×6s securely together. (Three 2×4s would serve quite well.)

ORNL–DWG 78-18368

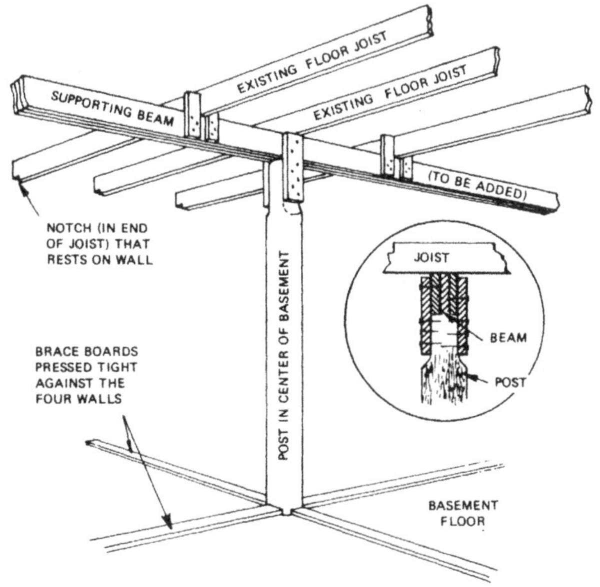

Fig. 5.8. Supporting beam and one of its posts installed to increase the load of shielding material that can be carried safely by the floor above a home basement.

Cut posts to fit exactly under the beam. If trees at least 4 inches in diameter are not available, make posts by nailing boards together. Position the two outermost posts within 2 feet of the ends of the beam. Space the posts at even intervals, with each post under a floor joist. A post under every third joist is ideal; this usually means a spacing between posts of about $4^1/_2$ feet. If the basement is 20 feet long, 5 posts are enough. Nail each post to the beam, and secure the bases of each with brace boards laid on the basement floor, as illustrated.

Finally, place a second 1-foot-thick layer of earth on the floor above. If the basement windows are protected with boards and if all but a part of one window and all the aboveground parts of the basement walls are covered with earth 2 feet thick, the basement shelter will have a protection factor of several hundred against fallout radiation.

Adequate ventilation and cooling should be assured by using a homemade air pump (a KAP), made and installed as described in Appendix B. Forced ventilation is especially necessary if more than one family occupies the basement in warm or hot weather.

More work and materials are required to improve a home basement in this manner than are needed to build a covered-trench shelter for one family. An earth-covered shelter separate from buildings will provide equally good protection against radiation, better protection against blast, and much better protection against fire.

If a family cannot build a separate, earth-covered shelter outdoors, often it would be advisable to make a very small shelter in the most protected corner of the basement. Such an indoor shelter should be of situp height (about 40 inches for tall people) and no wider than 3 feet. Its walls can readily be built of chairs, benches, boxes, and bureau drawers. Interior doors make an adequately strong roof. Expedient shielding materials, to be placed on the roof and the two exposed sides, can be ordinary water containers and bureau drawers, boxes, and pillow cases filled with earth or other heavy materials. Or, if heavy-duty plastic trash bags or 4-mil polyethylene film are available, make expedient water containers and use them for shielding. To do so, first line bureau drawers, boxes, pillow cases, trash cans, etc. with plastic. Place the lined containers in position to shield your shelter, then fill these expedient water containers with drinkable water (see Chapter 8).

As demonstrated by hot-weather occupancy tests of such very small indoor shelters, a small KAP or other air pump must be operated to maintain a forced flow of air through such a crowded shelter, to prevent intolerable temperature-humidity conditions. (See Chapter 6 for ventilation-cooling requirements, including the provision of an adequately large opening in each end of a shelter.) In some basements a second small KAP would be needed in hot weather to pump outdoor air through the basement. This KAP could be operated by pulling a cord from within the small shelter, using an improvised "pulley" as described in Appendix B.

PUBLIC SHELTERS

In the event of an unexpected attack, many unprepared Americans should and would take refuge in nearby marked public shelters. Throughout the populated areas that would not be subjected to blast, fire, or heavy fallout, the use of public shelters could save millions of lives. All persons concerned with survival should remember that the large majority of officially surveyed and marked shelters give better protection against radiation than most unimproved home basements.

Persons preparing to go to public shelters should be aware that many lack forced ventilation and that the blowers and fans of most forced ventilation systems would be stopped by loss of electric power due to electromagnetic pulse effects or by other effects of nuclear explosions on electrical systems. A blast wave at an overpressure range as low as 1 psi (144 pounds per square foot) would wreck most shelter-ventilating fans. In 1987, no water or food normally is stocked. A person who brought to a public shelter 10 large plastic trash bags and 10 pillow slips, to make 10 expedient water bags in which 60 gallons of water could be stored (as described in Chapter 8), would help both himself and dozens of other shelter occupants. If he hoped to share the basement in a strange family's home, his chances of being welcomed would be improved if he brought a small homemade shelter-ventilating pump and other survival items. The same small pump would be impractical in a large public shelter. An Oak Ridge National Laboratory study completed in 1978 found that if all citizens were to go to National Shelter Survey (NSS) shelters within one mile of their homes, 69% of those who found space would be in shelters rated for 1000 or more occupants.[10] The average number of shelter spaces in this largest class of public shelters was 3179. The prospect of living in an unequipped shelter crowded with this many unprepared people—each of whom would have only 10 square feet of floor space—is a strong motivation to work hard to build and equip a small, earth-covered shelter.

DECIDING WHAT KIND OF SHELTER TO BUILD OR USE

Before deciding what kind of shelter you and your family should build or use, it is best to read all of this book. Your final decision should include consideration of ways to provide life-support equipment discussed in following chapters. At this stage, however, the reader will find it helpful to review important reasons why different types of shelters offer the best hope of survival to different people, in different areas, and under different conditions.

This book is written primarily to improve the survival chances of people who cannot or do not build permanent shelters. The information which follows will help you select the best expedient or available shelter for your family.

SHELTER NEAR OR IN YOUR HOME

If your home is 10 or more miles from an average target such as a major airport with long runways, or is 20 or more miles from a great city with several strategic targets, you are fortunate: you can prudently build or use a shelter close to home. No one can foretell accurately which way the winds will blow or where weapons will explode, so, if practical, you should build a shelter that gives better protection against fallout, blast, and fire than shelters in buildings. Most people living outside targeted areas could build such a shelter in two days or less, using one of the designs of earth-covered expedient shelters detailed in Appendix A.

Even if you plan to evacuate, you should decide where you would take shelter nearby in case you were unable to do so. There is always a chance that an attack may be launched without warning, giving insufficient time to evacuate. Or the missile aimed at the area in which you live may miss its target. If your targeted home area were not hit, moderately heavy fallout might be the only danger; even an improved basement shelter would be adequate in that case.

EARTH-COVERED EXPEDIENT FAMILY SHELTERS

Advantages of earth-covered, expedient family shelters:

* Better protection against heavy fallout, blast, and fire than afforded by the great majority of shelters in buildings.

* The possibility of building in favorable locations, including places far removed from target areas, and places where it is impractical to build or to improve large group-shelters giving good protection.

Never Ever Use the Phrase, "Its Better Than Nothing."

THE WORDS YOU USE ARE CRITICAL TO YOUR SUCCESS OR FAILURE.
How you think and the words you choose to put in your head define the options that you consider. The options you consider are the actions that you'll make decisions on and implement. Your words that you and others use thus define what your final actions will be that may be actions to protect your life.

When you say, "It's better than nothing" then you have given up you've quit your search for something that will work and you have settled on something you hope and pray might work when you need it. You've just completed lazy thinking and complacency.

I have eliminated that phrase from the communities and groups that I work in and consult and advise. If you use that term you'll be berated and corrected. Yes, it's a group of people I work with that has very high standards of excellence.

WHAT DO WE SAY?
If I look at a guy and ask him, "Will that thing work?" and it has been a long search and a bunch of testing to make sure it will function then he'll tell me, "it's barely adequate." This means it will work when he needs it to work and it will work for at least the requisite number of times he'll need it and he's tested it to make sure. He might need it 10 times but he's tested it and every time it's broken at 15 or 20 uses. Ok. 10 is the max he needs, so, the item has been tested as being barely adequate for his function. He'd of found something better if he had the time and resources but for a "Hasty Solution" this selection has been declared as barely adequate. This is a world away from better than nothing and it's been tested. It's not a hope and a prayer. Your emergency reserve parachute only needs to work once. It working that once is pretty critical. Yes, I have parachuted from an aircraft.

Remember: Better than Nothing is WORSE than nothing. It's a real fine line of philosophy but what is the worse that can happen here? Do you die? We're only talking about nuclear detonations and war and fallout and radiation falling from the sky and radioactive particles in food and water and your child dying. So it's not like the stakes are life and death. <heavy sarcasm> Do not apply the standards you use as to what TV show to watch tonight to your decisions that are life and death.

WHAT ARE THE STAKES? WHAT IS THE WORSE THAT CAN HAPPEN?Here is something as a modern American in 2022 you are NOT used to making. You are NOT used to making life and death decisions. You always have a safety net. If you made a bad decision there is always 911 and the ambulance and the hospital trauma center and emergency surgery or the fire department. It's hard to screw up. Well, get used to this idea. When we are talking about preparedness for a disaster we are talking about life and death. We are talking about the difference between your child being alive and healthy or your childing having dysentery so bad you are holding them in your arms as they are vomiting and having constant diarrhea and you cannot get fluids into them fast enough and there is no 911 and ambulance and hospital and your child and you are covered in a mess of vomit and fecal material and they stop moving and die in your arms and now you have to bury them in the backyard and live with that memory for the rest of your life.

ATTEMPTED INVOLUNTARY MAN SLAUGHTER
I have been advising and consulting families that want to be better prepared. The basics, are some power, keeping their phones alive, food, water, medicine, sanitation, and the ability to leave.

At one time some family member came in and started with, "I don't know why you are doing this, this is stupid and a waste of your time and money, nothing is going to happen..." blah blah blah. I got very belligerent and in their face and told them in no uncertain terms to leave the room, the house, and to get out. Leave now!

When someone is trying to do basic common sense preparedness for their family and those that they love and thus keep them alive in a mild to severe disaster. Even in the 2021 Texas freeze out and power failure over 1000 people died from the effects of that. When they are trying to stop you from protecting your family from death I consider their words of ignorance trying to get you to do nothing Attempted Involuntary Man Slaughter. If they talked you out of it, and you did nothing, and the big Texas freeze happened and one of your children died because they talked you into not being prepared. That death is on them. That death in my observation criminal. Its negligence.

It's like you are taking sky diving instructions and someone is telling you, "oh, you do not need a parachute, gravity is not real and the earth is flat. You'll stop falling 3 feet above the ground and you can just put your feet down. Jump out of the airplane at 5000 feet with no parachute and enjoy the ride. Nothing is going to happen."

Its Attempted Involuntary Man Slaughter. The reaction to this is not politeness but nothing less than, "Shut up, go away, get out. We are learning to protect ourselves and stop trying to kill us."

* The opportunity for men, women, and children to work together to provide good protection in minimum time.

* A better chance to benefit from thoughtful preparations made in advance than would be the case in public shelters where water, food, etc. must be shared.

* Less risk of personality clashes, hysteria under stress, exposure to infectious diseases, and other problems that arise when strangers are crowded together for days or weeks.

Disadvantages of earth-covered, expedient shelters:

* It may be difficult to meet the requirement for time, space, people able to work hard, materials, and tools—and to get all these together at the building site.

* Building is difficult if heavy rain or snow is falling or if the ground is deeply frozen. (However, untrained Americans have built good fallout shelters with shielding provided by 5 or more feet of packed snow,[11] including a winter version of the Crib-Walled Pole Shelter described in Appendix A. The practicality of several Russian designs of snow-covered expedient shelters also has been demonstrated by winter construction tests in Colorado.[12])

* The fewer occupants of family shelters could not provide as many helpful skills as would be found in most public shelters, with tens-to-thousands of occupants.

* The lack of instruments for measuring changing radiation dangers. However, the occupants could make a homemade fallout meter by following the instructions in Appendix C, or buy a commercial instrument *before* a rapidly worsening crisis arises.

PUBLIC AND OTHER EXISTING SHELTERS

Advantages of the great majority of public and other existing shelters, most of which are in buildings:

* Their immediate availability in many localities, without work or the need to supply materials and tools.

* The provision of fair-to-excellent fallout protection—generally much better than citizens have available in their homes.

* The availability in some shelters of fallout meters and occupants who know how to use them and who can provide other needed skills.

* The chance for persons who are not able to carry food or water to a public shelter to share some brought by the more provident occupants.

Disadvantages of the great majority of public and other existing shelters available to large numbers of people:

* The location of most of them in targeted areas.

* Poor protection against blast, fire and carbon monoxide.

* Lack of water and means for storing it, and lack of stocked food.

* No reliable air pumps, which are essential in warm or hot weather for supplying adequate ventilating-cooling air to maintain endurable conditions in fully occupied shelters—especially belowground.

* Uncertainties regarding the availability of fallout meters and occupants who know how to use them.

* No dependable lights, sanitary facilities, or other life-support equipment, with few exceptions.

* The crowding together of large numbers of people who are strangers to each other. Under frightening conditions that might continue for weeks, the greater the number of people, the greater would be the risks of the spread of infectious diseases and of hysteria, personality clashes, and the development of other conflicts.

BELOWGROUND EXPEDIENT EARTH-COVERED FALLOUT SHELTERS

(Appendix A details two designs of belowground shelters, three designs of aboveground shelters, and one design that affords excellent protection built either below or aboveground).

Advantages of belowground, earth-covered expedient fallout shelters:

* They afford better protection than do aboveground, earth-covered types.

* Less time, work, and materials are required to build them than to build equally protective aboveground designs.

* If built sufficiently separated from houses and flammable woods, they provide much better protection against fire hazards than do shelters in buildings.

* If dug in stable earth, even types with unshored earth walls give quite good blast protection up to overpressure ranges of at least 5 psi — where most homes and buildings would be destroyed by blast or fire.

Disadvantages of belowground expedient fallout shelters:

* They are not practical in areas where the water table or rock is very near the surface.

* It is impractical to build them in deep-frozen ground.

* They are usually more crowded and uncomfortable than improved basement shelters.

EXPEDIENT BLAST SHELTERS

Advantages of expedient blast shelters:

* Occupants of expedient blast shelters described in Appendix D could survive uninjured in extensive blast areas where fallout shelters would not prevent death or injury.

* Blast doors would protect occupants from shock waves, dangerous overpressures, blast winds, and burns on exposed skin caused by the popcorning effect and heated air.

* The expedient blast shelters described in Appendix D of this book were built and blast tested in Defense Nuclear Agency blast tests. Their air-supply systems were not damaged by blast effects that would have bent over or broken off the aboveground, vertical air-supply pipes typical of even expensive imported Swiss and Finnish permanent family blast shelters. (Notwithstanding this weakness, such permanent blast shelters will save many lives.) The horizontal blast doors of these tested expedient blast shelters were not damaged because they were protected on all sides by spiked-together blast-protector logs surrounded by ramped earth. (In contrast, the horizontal blast door of the most expensive blast shelter described in a widely distributed Federal Emergency Management Agency pamphlet (number H-12-3) is unprotected on its sides. This untested blast door probably would be torn off and blown away if struck by a strong blast wave, following blast winds, and pieces of houses and trees that would be hurled hundreds of feet.)

* The blast-tested expedient blast valve described in Appendix D will prevent entry of blast waves through a shelter's ventilation pipes and resultant destruction of the ventilation pump and possible injury of occupants.

Disadvantages of expedient blast shelters:

* They require more time, materials, tools, skill, and work than are needed for building expedient fallout shelters.

* Especially expedient blast shelters should be well separated from buildings and woods that if burned are likely to produce dangerous quantities of carbon monoxide and toxic smoke.

* Their ventilation openings permit the entry of many more fallout particles than do the ventilation pipes with goosenecks and filters of typical permanent blast shelters. (However, deadly local fallout probably will not be a major danger in the blast areas where the great majority of Americans live, because a rational enemy will employ air bursts to destroy the mostly "soft" targets found in those areas. Air bursts can destroy most militarily significant "soft" targets over about twice as many square miles as can the surface or near-surface bursting of the same weapons. Fortunately, air bursts produce only tiny particles, and only a small fraction of these, while they still are very radioactive, are likely to be promptly brought to earth in scattered "hot spots" by rain-outs and snow-outs. Thus relatively few prompt fatalities or delayed cancer cases from air-burst fallout are likely to result—even from the air bursting of today's smaller Soviet warheads that would inject most of their particles into the troposphere at altitudes from which wet deposition can take place.

WARNING: Permanent home fallout and blast shelters described in widely available FEMA pamphlets have protection factors in line with the PF 40 minimum standard for public shelters in buildings. In heavy fallout areas a sizeable fraction of the occupants of PF 40 shelters will receive radiation doses large enough to incapacitate or kill them later. Permanent shelters built specifically to protect against nuclear weapon effects should have PFs much higher than PF 40.

None of the permanent home or family shelters described in official OCD, DCPA, or FEMA free shelter-building instruction pamphlets have been built for evaluation and/or testing — a finding confirmed to the author in 1987 by a retired shelter specialist who for some 20 years served in Washington with FEMA and its predecessors.

Chapter 6

Ventilation and Cooling of Shelters

CRITICAL IMPORTANCE

If high-protection-factor shelters or most other shelters that lack adequate forced ventilation were fully occupied for several days in warm or hot weather, they would become so hot and humid that the occupants would collapse from the heat if they were to remain inside. It is important to understand that the heat and water vapor given off by the bodies of people in a crowded, long-occupied shelter could be deadly if fallout prevents leaving the shelter.

When people enter an underground shelter or basement in the summertime, at first the air feels cool. However, if most shelters are fully occupied for a few days without adequate ventilation, the floors, walls, and ceilings, originally cool, will have absorbed about all the body heat of which they are capable. Some shelters will become dangerously hot in a few hours. Unless most of the occupants' body heat and water vapor from sweat are removed by air circulated through a typical shelter, the heat-humidity conditions will become increasingly dangerous in warm or hot weather. One of the most important nuclear war survival skills people should learn is how to keep occupied shelters adequately ventilated in all seasons and cool enough for many days of occupancy in warm or hot weather. Methods **for ventilating with homemade devices and for keeping ventilating air from carrying fallout particles into shelters are described in Appendices A and B. Instructions for Directional Fanning, the simplest means for forcing adequate volumes of air to flow through shelters, are given at the end of this chapter.**

MAKING AND USING AN EXPEDIENT AIR PUMP

The best expedient way to maintain livable conditions in a shelter, especially in hot weather, is to make and use a large-volume shelter-ventilating pump. Field tests have proved that average Americans can build the expedient air pump described in Appendix B in a few hours, with inexpensive materials found in most households.

This simple pump was invented in 1962 by the author. I called it a Punkah-Pump, because its hand-pulled operation is somewhat like that of an ancient fan called a "punkah", still used by some primitive peoples in hot countries. (Unlike the punkah, however, this air pump can force air to move in a desired direction and is a true pump.) It was named the Kearny Air Pump (KAP) by the Office of Civil Defense following tests of various models by Stanford Research Institute, the Protective Structures Development Center, and General American Transportation Company. These tests confirmed findings first made at Oak Ridge National Laboratory regarding the advantages of the KAP both as a manually operated pump for forcing large volumes of outdoor air through shelters and as a device for distributing air within shelters and fanning the occupants. See Fig. 6.1.

The air pump instructions given in Appendix B are the result of having scores of families and pairs of untrained individuals, including children, build and use this air pump. They were guided by successively improved versions of these detailed, written instructions, that include many illustrations (see Appendix B). Some people who are experienced at building things will find these instructions unnecessarily long and detailed. However, shelter-building experiments have shown that the physically stronger individuals, usually the more experienced builders, should do more of the hard, manual work when shelters are built, and that those less experienced at building should do the lighter work—including making shelter-ventilating pumps. These detailed, step-by-step instructions have enabled people who never

Fig. 6.1. A 6-foot KAP tested for durability at Oak Ridge. After 1000 hours of operation during which it pumped air through a room at a rate of 4000 cubic feet per minute (4000 cfm), there were only minor tears in the plastic flaps.

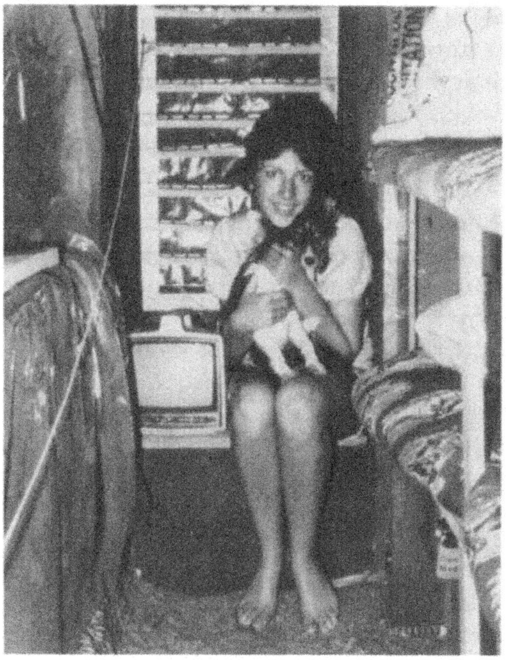

Fig. 6.2. Behind the girl is the homemade air pump that made it possible for a family of six to live in a crowded trench shelter for more than three days. Outside the temperature rose to 93° F.

before had attempted to build a novel device of any kind to make serviceable air pumps.

(The air pump instructions given in Appendix B repeat some information in this chapter. This repetition is included both to help the reader when he starts to build an air pump and to increase the chances of the best available complete instructions being given to local newspapers during some future crisis. The instructions given in this book could be photographed, reproduced, and mass-distributed by newspapers.)

Figure 6.2 shows (behind the girl) a 20-inch-wide by 36-inch-high KAP installed in the entry trench of a trench shelter. The father of the Utah family described earlier had made this simple pump at home, using only materials and tools found in many homes—as described in Appendix B. He carried the pump on top of his car to the shelter-building site. The pendulum-like, flap-valve pump was swung from two cabinet hinges (not shown) screwed onto a board. The board was nailed to roof poles of the narrow entry trench extending behind the girl in the photograph. The pull-cord was attached to the pump frame below its hinged top and extended along one trench wall for the whole length of the shelter. Any one of the six occupants could pull this cord and easily pump as much as 300 cubic feet per minute of outdoor air through the shelter and through the insect screens over both its entrances. (Without these screens, the numerous mosquitoes in this irrigated area would have made the family's shelter stay very unpleasant.)

During the 77 hours that the family continuously occupied their narrow, covered trench, the temperatures outside rose as high as 93° F. Without the air pump, the six occupants would have been driven from their shelter by unbearable temperature-humidity conditions during the day.[8]

The photo in Fig. 6.2 also shows how the air pump hung when not being operated, partially blocking the entry trench and causing a "chimney effect" flow of air at night. There was a 10-inch space between the air pump and the trench floor, and the resulting flow of air maintained adequate ventilation in the cool of the desert night, when outdoor temperatures dropped as low as 45° F. Cool outdoor air flowed down into the entry and under the motionless air pump, replacing the body-warmed air inside the shelter. The entering cool air continuously forced the warm air out of the shelter room at ceiling height through the emergency crawlway-exhaust trench at the other end. When the weather is cool, a piece of plastic or tightly woven cloth could be hung in the doorway of a well designed, narrow shelter, to cause a flow of fresh air in the same manner.

Numerous shelter occupancy tests have proved that modern Americans can live for weeks in an adequately cooled shelter with only 10 square feet of floor space per person.[13] Other tests, such as one conducted by the Navy near Washington, D.C. during an abnormally cool two weeks in August, 1962, have shown that conditions can become difficult even when summertime outdoor air is being pumped through a long-occupied shelter at the rate of 12 cubic feet per minute, per person.[14,15] This is four times the *minimum* ventilation rate for each occupant specified by the Federal Emergency Management Agency (FEMA) for American shelters: 3 cubic feet per minute (3 cfm). Three cfm is about three times the supply of outdoor air needed to keep healthy people from having headaches as a result of exhaled carbon dioxide. In hot, humid weather, much more outdoor air than 12 cfm per person must be supplied to a crowded, long-occupied shelter, as will be described in the following section and in Appendix B.

MAINTAINING ENDURABLE SHELTER CONDITIONS IN HOT WEATHER

The Navy test mentioned above showed how much modern Americans who are accustomed to air conditioning could learn from jungle natives about keeping cool and healthy by skillfully using hot, humid, outdoor air. While working in jungles from the Amazon to Burma, I observed the methods used by the natives to avoid unhealthful conditions like those experienced in the Navy shelter, which was ventilated in a conventional American manner. These jungle methods include the first five of the six cooling methods listed in this section. During 24 years of civil defense research, my colleagues and I have improved upon the cooling methods of jungle people, primarily by the invention and thorough field-testing of the homemade KAP described in Appendix B, and of the Directional Fans covered by the instructions at the end of this chapter.

Even during a heat wave in a hot part of the United States, endurable conditions can be maintained in a fully occupied, belowground shelter with this simple pump, if the test-proven requirements listed below are ALL met.

Most basement shelters and many aboveground shelters also can be kept at livable temperatures in hot weather if the cooling methods listed below are ALL followed:

- Supply enough air to carry away all the shelter occupants' body heat without raising the "effective temperature" of the air at the exhaust end of the shelter by more than 2°F. The "effective temperature" of the air to which a person is exposed is equivalent to the temperature of air at 100% relative humidity that causes the same sensation of warmth or cold. "Effective temperature" combines the effects of the temperature of the air, its relative humidity, and its movement. An ordinary thermometer does not measure effective temperature. In occupancy tests of crowded shelters when the supply of outdoor air was hot and dry, shelter occupants have been surprised to find that they felt hottest at the air-exhaust end of their shelter, where the temperature reading was lower than at the air-intake end. Their sweaty bodies had acted as evaporative air coolers, but their body heat had raised the effective temperature, a reliable indicator of heat stress. If 40 cubic feet per minute (40 cfm) per person of outdoor air is supplied and properly distributed, then (even if the outdoor air is at a temperature which is typical of the hottest hours during a heat wave in a hot, humid area of the United States) the effective temperature of the shelter air will be increased no more than 2°F by the shelter occupants' body heat and water vapor. Except for a relatively few sick people dependent on air conditioning, anyone could endure air that has an effective temperature only 2°F higher than that of the air outdoors.

(There are exceptions to this ventilation requirement when the ceiling or walls of basement or aboveground shelters in buildings are heated by the sun to levels higher than skin temperature. In such shelters, more than 40 cfm of outdoor air per occupant must be supplied. However, if a shelter is covered by at least two feet of earth, it will be so well insulated that its ceiling and walls will not get hot enough to heat the occupants.)

- Move the air gently, so as not to raise its temperature. In the aforementioned Navy test, a high speed, electric ventilating pump and the frictional resistance of pipes and filters raised the temperature of the air supplied to the shelter by 3°F. Under extreme heat wave conditions, an air supply 3°F hotter than outdoor air could be disastrous—especially if considerably less than 40 cfm per occupant is supplied, and body heat raises the air temperature several additional degrees.

● Distribute the air quite evenly throughout the shelter. In a trench shelter, where air is pumped in at one end and flows out the other, good distribution is assured. In larger shelters, such as basements, ventilating air will move from the air-supply opening straight to the air-exhaust opening. Persons out of this air stream will not be adequately cooled. By using one or more additional, smaller KAPs (also described in Appendix B), fresh air can be distributed easily throughout large shelter rooms, and the occupants will be gently fanned.

● Provide occupants with adequate drinking water and salt. In extremely hot weather, this means 4 quarts of water per day per person and 1 tablespoon (10 grams) of salt, including the salt in food.

● Wear as few clothes as practical. When the skin is bare, moving air can evaporate sweat more efficiently for effective cooling. Air movement can keep bare skin drier, and therefore less susceptible to heat rash and skin infections. In the inadequately ventilated Navy test shelter, 34 of the 99 initially healthy young men had heat rash and 23 had more serious skin complaints at the end of their sweaty two-week confinement, although their overall physical condition had not deteriorated.[15] However, at sick call every day all of these Navy test subjects with skin complaints were treated by medical corpsmen. In a nuclear war, very few shelter occupants would have medicines to treat skin diseases and infections, that if not taken care of usually worsen rapidly under continuously hot, humid conditions. Simple means for preventing skin diseases and infections—means proved very effective by jungle natives and by our best trained jungle infantrymen in World War II — are described in the Prevention of Skin Diseases section of Chapter 12.

● Keep pumping about 40 cfm of air per person through the shelter both day and night during hot weather, so that the occupants and the shelter itself will be cooled off at night. In the Navy test, the ventilation rate of 7 to 12 cfm was not high enough to give occupants the partial relief from heat and sweating that people normally get at night.[15] In a National Academy of Sciences meeting on protective shelters, an authority stated: "Laboratory experiments and field investigations have shown that healthy persons at rest can tolerate daily exposures to ETs [effective temperatures] up to 90° F, provided they can get a good night's sleep in a cooler environment."[14] An effective temperature 90° F is higher than the highest outdoor effective temperature during a heatwave in the South or in American deserts.

ADEQUATE VENTILATION IN COLD WEATHER

In freezing weather, a belowground shelter covered with damp earth may continue to absorb almost all of its occupants' body heat for many days and stay unpleasantly cold. In one winter test of such a fully occupied shelter, the temperature of the humid air in the shelter remained around 50° F.[16] Under such conditions, shelter occupants should continue to ventilate their shelter adequately, to avoid the following conditions:

● A dangerous buildup of carbon dioxide from exhaled breath, the first symptoms of which are headaches and deeper breathing.

● Headaches from the carbon monoxide produced by smoking. When the ventilation rate is low, smoking should not be permitted, even near the exhaust opening.

● Headaches, collapse, or death due to carbon monoxide from open fires or gasoline lanterns that release gases into the shelter air.

NATURAL VENTILATION

Enough air usually will be blown through an aboveground shelter if sufficiently large openings are provided on opposite sides and if there is any breeze. But if the weather is warm and still and the shelter crowded, the temperature-humidity conditions soon can become unbearable.

Adequate natural ventilation for belowground shelters is more difficult. Even if there is a light breeze, not much air will make a right-angle turn and go down a vertical entry, make another right-angle turn, and then flow through a trench or other shelter partially obscured by people and supplies.

In cool weather, occupants' body heat will warm the shelter air and make it lighter than the outdoor air. If a chimney-like opening or vent-duct is provided in the ceiling, the warmed, lighter air will flow upward and out of the shelter, provided an adequate air-intake vent is open near the floor. An Eskimo igloo is an excellent example of how very small ventilation openings, skillfully located in the ceiling and at floor level, make it possible in cold weather for chimney-type natural ventilation to supply the 1 cfm per person of outdoor air needed to prevent exhaled carbon dioxide from becoming dangerously concentrated.

In warm weather, chimney-type natural ventilation usually is inadequate for most high-protection-factor shelters that are fully occupied for days. And in hot weather, when as much as 40 cfm per occupant is required, body-warmed shelter air is no lighter than the outdoor air. Chimney-type ventilation fails completely under these conditions.

SHELTER VENTILATION WITHOUT FILTERS

Numerous tests have shown that the hazards from fallout particles carried into shelters by unfiltered ventilating air are minor compared to the dangers from inadequate ventilation. A 1962 summary of the official standards for ventilating systems of fallout shelters stated: "Air filters are not essential for small (family size) shelters . . . "[17] More recent findings have led to the same conclusion for large fallout shelters. A 1973 report by the Subcommittee on Fallout of the National Academy of Sciences on the radioiodine inhalation problem stated this conclusion: "The opinion of the Subcommittee is that inhalation is far less of a threat than ingestion [eating or drinking], and does not justify countermeasures such as filters in the ventilating systems of shelters."[18]

Recommendations such as those above realistically face the fact that, if we suffer a nuclear attack, the vast majority of Americans will have only the fallout protection given by buildings and some expedient shelters. Consequently, how best to use available resources must be the primary consideration when planning for protection against the worst dangers of a nuclear attack; relatively minor hazards may have to be accepted. For unprepared people, inhalation of fallout particles would be a minor danger compared to being forced out of a shelter because of dangerously inadequate ventilation.

The most dangerous fallout particles are those deposited on the ground within the first few hours after the explosion that produces them. Typically, these "hot" particles would be so large and fast-falling that they would not be carried into expedient shelters equipped with low-velocity air intake openings, such as those described in this book. Nor would these most dangerous "hot" fallout particles be "sucked" into gooseneck air-intake pipes, or other properly designed air-intake openings of a permanent shelter.

For most shelters built or improved hurriedly during a crisis it will be impractical to provide filtered air. The Car-Over-Trench Shelter pictured in Fig. 6.3 points up the overriding need for pumped air for occupants of crowded shelters during warm or hot weather. This simple shelter provides fallout protection about four times as effective as that given by a typical home basement. After the car was driven over the trench, earth was shoveled into the car and its trunk and on top of its hood. At one end was a combined crawlway entrance/air intake opening, at the other end, a 1-foot-square air exhaust opening. Each opening was covered by a small awning. To keep loose shielding earth from running under the car and into the trench, the upper edges of 5-foot-wide strips of polyethylene film first were attached with duct tape to the sides and ends of the car, about 2 feet above the ground. Then earth was piled onto the parts of the film strips that were lying on the ground, to secure them. Finally, earth was piled against the vertical parts of the attached film strips.

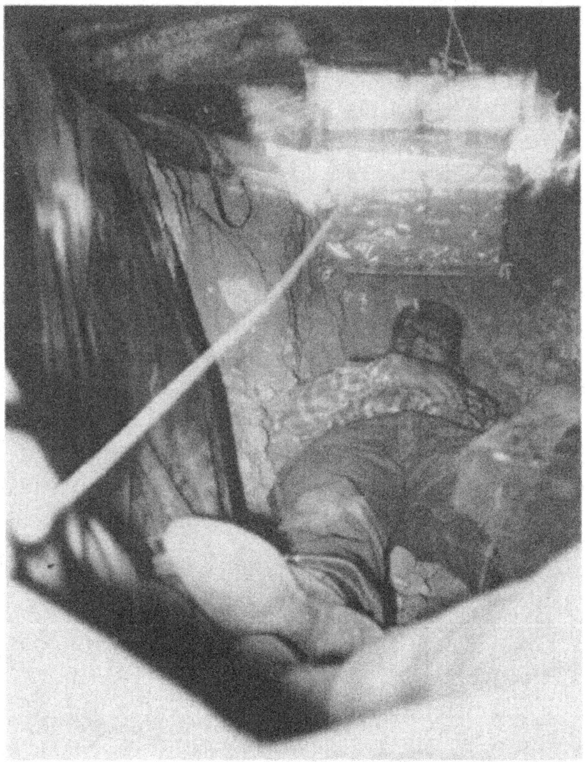

Fig. 6.3. Pulling a Small, Stick-Frame KAP to Keep Temperatures Endurable for Occupants of a Car-Over-Trench Shelter in Warm Weather. Enough air also can be supplied with a small Directional Fan, although more laboriously.

(Placing earth rolls — see page 150 — around the sides of an earth-loaded car provides better, more secure side shielding, but requires more materials and work.)

INHALATION DANGERS

Only extremely small fallout particles can reach the lungs. The human nose and other air passages " . . . can filter out almost all particles 10 micrometers [10 microns] [or larger] in diameter, and about 95 percent of those exceeding 5 micrometers." (See reference 6, page 599.) Five micrometers equal 5 millionths of a meter, or 5 thousandths of a millimeter.

Using a dust mask or breathing through cloth would be helpful to keep from inhaling larger "hot" fallout particles which may cause beta burns in noses, sinuses, and bronchial tubes. Many such retained particles may be swallowed when cleared from one's air passageways by the body's natural protective processes.

As shown below in Fig. 6.4, a relatively "large" particle — 40 microns (40 μ m) in diameter, spherical, and with the sand-like density of most fallout particles — falls about 1300 feet in 8 hours. (A dark-colored particle 40 microns in diameter is about as small a speck as most people can see with the naked eye.) Most 40-μ m-diameter fallout particles would take a

Better Preparedness - Moving Air

NWSS ASSUMES YOU HAVE NOTHING.
Further down in the book, Cresson has an entire section called pre-Disaster preparedness. I think this is a very important subject and it helps put you miles ahead of everyone else caught by surprise and having to use expedient methods and improvised methods.

For example, there are solar panels that can be found online. Solar panels that have a simple USB output on them. These solar panels with a USB output can go one or two USB-based batteries and charge the batteries at the same time. The same panel or other panels can go directly to us be lights and fans that may be in the shelter and being used while the sun is shining during the daytime. So it is entirely conceivable to have a 25 to 50 Watt USB solar panel charging up one or more USB batteries during the daytime, while another panel is running USB-based fans and lights inside of your dark shelter, even though there is some sunlight coming in through the opening. This will provide you with light and ventilation in a pole-covered trench shelter that is very minimal. A pre-disaster blast-resistant shelter will be a better and more complicated solar panel setup.

At the time of this writing in May 2022, a 30-watt USB solar panel is about $50.00 or $1.66 a watt. When Cresson wrote this update the price of solar panels was well over $10.00 per watt and those are for the rigid panels that still need the voltage and power regulator that is already in the USB solar panel. So that would be well over $300 instead of $50 and the easy-to-use USB battery and the LED lights, did not exist. Let alone the lithium-ion core technology of the USB battery. On a larger scale, I purchased a pallet of solar panels for a friend at $0.37 per watt and it was delivered by pallet on an LTL truck for less than $0.42 per watt total. That is panels and shipping. The use of solar power on that scale (by the pallet) is beyond the scope of this book and its update. Yet, what I mention above is an option for the average person today.

I'd suggest 3 of the 25-30 watt solar panels with a USB output on it. 2 of the 30,000MAH USB Batteries with a 3 digit display of the capacity on it and NOT 4 'dumb lights' on it to tell you the battery state of charge. Add to this some USB lights and USB-based fans and you're comfort and illumination will be greatly enhanced.

This will help with small shelter ventilation for comfort as well as exhausting some of your breath and moisture byproducts out of the shelter at night when you're trying to get some sleep. This can be done on a keep it simple basis. Trying to run a normal solar panel with a normal charge controller to a larger car-sized or RV sized battery inside the shelter with an inverter to run a fan and then to run a light and the amount of power coming in versus the amount of power being used can be a more of a complicated subject. However, the USB solar panels with USB batteries and the USB fans, and the USB lights make this subject a lot more simple and easy to implement for the non-electrical non-power experienced person. Note. You're going to want to have low-power USB fans and low-power USB lights. You're going to want to have not bright USB lights, but lights that are bright enough. So look for lights with the lumens or lowest power or current rating on them. USB Fans of 4 to 8 inches in diameter are desirable. You'd be amazon at how good a little 4" USB Fan just blowing on your face and your face alone make one person feel so much better. Yes. I have extensive experience with these USB fans. The one I use the most is an OPOLOR brand 8" USB fan. It sits no more than about 14 inches from me and when it's warm or I am in a warm area it's usually on the lowest or 2nd lowest setting.

These fans can be used to move air INTO or OUT of the shelter. Near the entrance or exit and these can be used to blow air directly on your face to make you feel cooler. I suggest getting some of these and experimenting with them pre-crisis. Your first-hand experience will relate directly to what I am saying.

How to Power You Shelter From Your Car

HOW TO POWER YOUR SHETER FROM YOUR CAR
When Cresson did the update to this book in 1987 vehicle Inverters that transformed 12 volts D. C from the vehicle into 120 volts AC (like what your house uses) did not exist yet. I know this because I bought one of the first digital-based modified sine wave inverters on the market when I was in the scientific labs of Chrysler Corporation in 1991, and a cost $300 for 300 Watt inverter in 1991 dollars.

Today an inverter that can do this is very easily available for $20 to $30, even at Walmart or Amazon. This can be clamped directly into the car battery or be plugged into the power outlet on the inside of the car and can provide 120 volts AC that could be run down into the shelter with about any thickness of an extension cable. This is to provide a low wattage amount of 120 volts AC to the occupants of the shelter. This is not to run your coffeemaker which takes about 1200 watts. It is only 120 watts or more, and I'm advocating that you run at a much lower wattage as low as possible such as 10 to 40 watts. You are only running a small radio and some very small watt led lights that are single-digit wattage. I mean like LED night lights. 120 volt AC LED lights that take between 0.5 watts and 5 watts max. Note: this is real wattage drawn not the "equivalent to" wattage as if it was an incandescent bulb. And you can also run some small 120 Volt fans. If you have the traditional box fan, you're going to be running this on the lowest setting to move air in and the shelter, and one will be more than enough.

This can run off of the vehicle battery for hours at least, depending upon how much power you are drawing. Then when you need to, you can push the automatic start on your key FOB and the vehicle automatically start and idles, thus providing more power into the shelter as well as recharging the vehicle battery at the same time. You do not want the vehicle battery to go dead or so low that you cannot restart the car again. That would not be productive. Many vehicles will automatically stop the idle after 20 minutes because it's for a cold morning warm-up idle. Other vehicles will stop the vehicle idle after one or two hours and others will have key FOBs which you can turn the vehicle off with. They won't run continually until the fuel runs out.

Having a remote start on the vehicle, where it will idle for 20 minutes at a time would be very convenient. In fact, it would be very conceivable to do this about once every two or three hours. From inside of the shelter. If you're just running a couple of led lights, and some small fans and the radio is so low power that it can just be on all the time.

This is something that was not thought of or addressed in the original 1987 version of this book because those items didn't exist and everything in the shelter would have to be 12 volts based.

If you arrive at a shelter location, you can fill up before you get there or have as full of a tank as you can. It can work in conjunction or instead of the solar that I mentioned in the previous paragraphs. Will run for two weeks. Probably not. Will it definitely provide you with more energy and more comfort during the initial parts of the sheltering? Yes, it will. An average American fuel tank when it's full will idle the vehicle for about 24 hours total. A small car having a small engine uses less fuel, but it has a smaller field tank. A larger Pickup Truck has a much larger fuel tank, and it has a larger engine so at idle a larger amount of fuel is consumed. Either way in my personal experimentation and testing both of which will idle for around 24 hours total before the fuel is exhausted on a full tank.

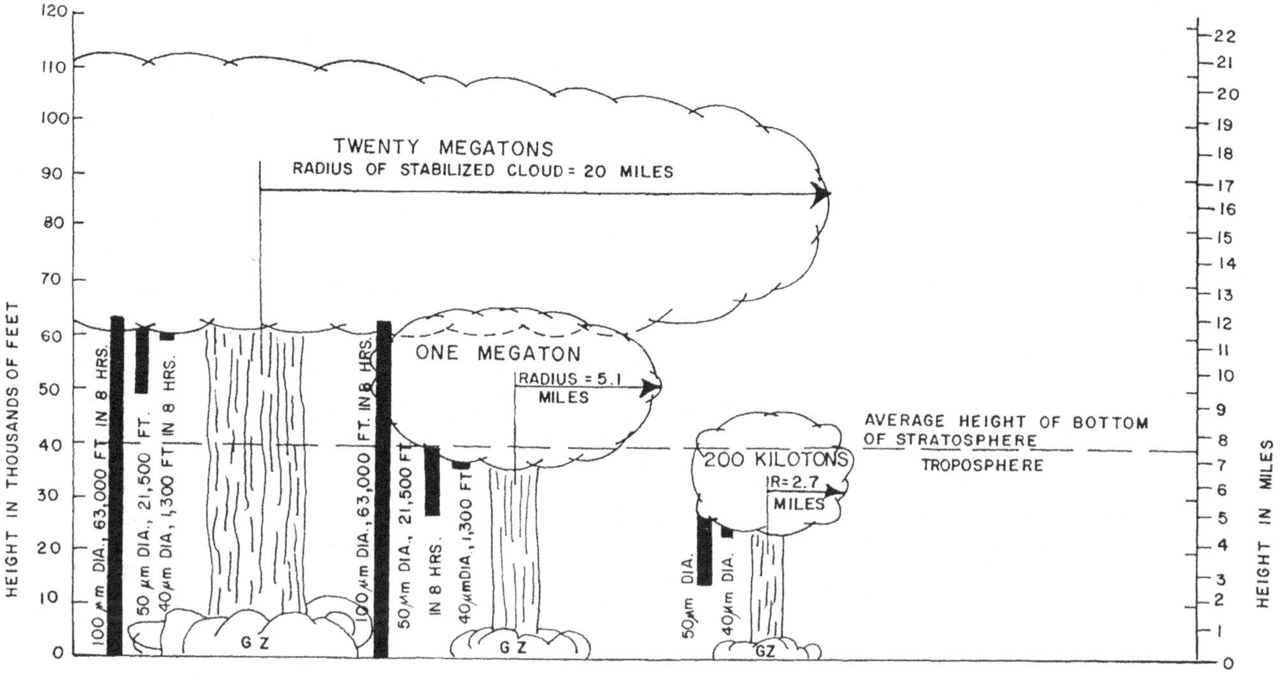

Fig. 6.4. Stabilized Radioactive Fallout Clouds Shown a Few Minutes After the Explosions, with distances that spherical fallout particles having diameters of 40, 50, and 100 microns fall in 8 hours.[6]

few days to fall from the cloud of a one-megaton explosion down far enough into the troposphere to be occasionally scavenged and promptly brought to earth by rain or snow while still very radioactive. In 1987, however, most of the thousands of deployed Soviet ICBM warheads are 550 kilotons or smaller. (See *Jane's Weapon Systems, 1987-88.*) The stabilized clouds of such explosions would be mostly in the troposphere, and some of even the tiniest particles — those small enough to be breathed into one's lungs — would be promptly scavenged and deposited in scattered "hot spots." Fortunately, most of the very small and tiniest fallout particles would not be deposited for days to months, by which time radioactive decay would have made them much less dangerous. Breathing tiny radioactive particles into one's lungs would constitute a minor health hazard compared to other dangers that would afflict an unprepared people subjected to a large scale nuclear attack.

SCAVENGING OF RADIOACTIVE PARTICLES

Scavenging is most effective below about 30,000 feet, the maximum height of most rain and snow clouds. See Fig. 6.4. Because the Soviets have deployed thousands of ICBMs with warheads of "only" 100 to 550 kilotons, Americans face increased dangers from very radioactive particles scavenged by rain-outs or snow-outs. The resultant "hot spots" of fallout heavy enough to kill unsheltered people in a few weeks could be scattered even hundreds of miles downwind from areas of multiple explosions, especially missile fields. Prudent Americans, even those living several hundred miles from important targets, whenever practical should equip their shelters with adequate ventilating pumps and dust filters.

This potential danger from extremely small fallout particles will be worsened if the United States deploys mobile ICBMs such as Midgetman, probably on large military reservations in the West. (The Soviet Union already has mobile ICBMs in its nuclear forces.) In the event of a Soviet attack, our hard-to-target mobile missiles probably would be subjected to a barrage of relatively small warheads air-bursted so as to blanket their deployment areas. The resultant large clouds of extremely small radioactive particles in the troposphere usually would be blown eastward, and resultant life-endangering "hot spots" from rain-outs and/or snow-outs could be scattered clear to the Atlantic coast.

Fortunately, even in many expedient shelters completed in a few days, filtered air can be provided by using a homemade KAP to pump air through furnace or air-conditioner filters, as described in the last section of Appendix B. To learn how you can supply a shelter at low cost with air so well filtered that essentially all extremely small fallout particles and infective aerosols are removed, see Appendix E, How To Make a Homemade Plywood Double-Action Piston Pump and Filter.

These worsening potential dangers from extremely small "hot" fallout particles brought promptly to earth by scavenging are not likely to endanger nearly as many Americans' lives as would 24-hour fallout of much larger particles from surface and near-surface explosions. Providing enough outdoor air to shelters, rather than filtered air, will continue to deserve first priority.

STOPPING OR RESTRICTING SHELTER VENTILATION

When instrument readings or observations show that heavy fallout has begun to be deposited, shelter occupants should decide whether to restrict or stop ventilation. If it is windy outside, even some sand-like fallout particles may be blown into a shelter with large ventilation openings. However, ventilation should not be restricted long enough to cause weaker occupants to be on the verge of collapse from overheating, or to result in headaches from exhaled carbon dioxide.

If a house is burning dangerously close to a separate, earth-covered shelter, closing the shelter's ventilation openings for an hour or two usually will prevent the entry of dangerous concentrations of carbon monoxide, carbon dioxide, or smoke. (Most houses will burn to the ground in less than two hours.)

When an attack is expected, a shelter, occupied or soon to be occupied, should be kept as cool as practical by pumping large volumes of outdoor air through it when the outdoor air is cooler than the shelter air. This also will assure that the air is fresh and low in exhaled carbon dioxide. Then, if a need arises to stop or restrict ventilation, the shelter can be closed for longer than could be done safely otherwise.

VENTILATION/COOLING OF PERMANENT SHELTERS

A permanent family fallout shelter, built at moderate cost before a crisis, should have a ventilation system that can supply adequate volumes of either filtered or unfiltered air, pumped in through an air-intake pipe and out through an air-exhaust pipe. Provision also should be made for the grim possibility that fallout could be so heavy that a shelter might have to be occupied for weeks, or even part-time for months. A small or medium-sized permanent shelter should be designed so that most of the time after an attack it can have adequate natural ventilation through its entryway and emergency exit. During hot spells, forced ventilation through these same large air passageways should be provided by using a homemade KAP. This manual air pump, described in Appendix B, can force large volumes of air through low-resistance openings with minimum effort.

Ways to ventilate and cool permanent shelters are described in Chapter 17, "Permanent Family Fallout Shelters for Dual Use," and in Appendix E, "How to Make and Use a Homemade Plywood Double-Action Piston Pump and Filter."

WARNING: MANY OFFICIAL INSTRUCTIONS FOR BUILDING AND VENTILATING SHELTERS ARE LIFE-ENDANGERING

The reader is advised not to read this section if pressed for time during a crisis, unless he is considering building an expedient or permanent shelter described in an official civil defense publication.

Because of the worldwide extreme fear of radiation, civil defense specialists who prepare official self-help instructions for building shelters have made radiation protection their overriding objective. Apparently the men in Moscow and Washington who decide what shelter-building and shelter-ventilating instructions their fellow citizens receive — especially instructions for building and improving expedient shelters—do not understand the ventilation requirements for maintaining endurable temperature/humidity conditions in crowded shelters. It must be remembered that shelters may have to be occupied continuously for days in warm or hot weather.

Russian small expedient shelters are even more dangerously under-ventilated than are most of their American counterparts, and can serve to illustrate similar ventilation deficiencies of American shelters. Figure 6.5 is a Russian drawing (with its caption translated) of a "Wood-Earth Shelter" in a Soviet self-help civil defense booklet, "Anti-Radiation Shelters in Rural Areas." This booklet, published in a 200,000-copy edition, includes illustrated instructions for building 20 different types of expedient shelters. All 20 of these shelters have dangerously inadequate natural ventilation, and none of them have air pumps. Note that this high-protection-factor, covered-trench shelter depends on air flowing down through its "Dust Filter with Straw Packing (hay)" and out through its small "Exhaust Duct with Damper."

As part of Oak Ridge National Laboratory's participation in Defense Nuclear Agency's "Dice Throw" 1978 blast test, I built two Russian Pole-Covered Trench Shelters. These were like the shelter shown in Fig. 6.5, except that each lacked a trapdoor and filter. As anticipated, so little air flowed through these essentially dead-ended test shelters that temperatures soon became unbearable.

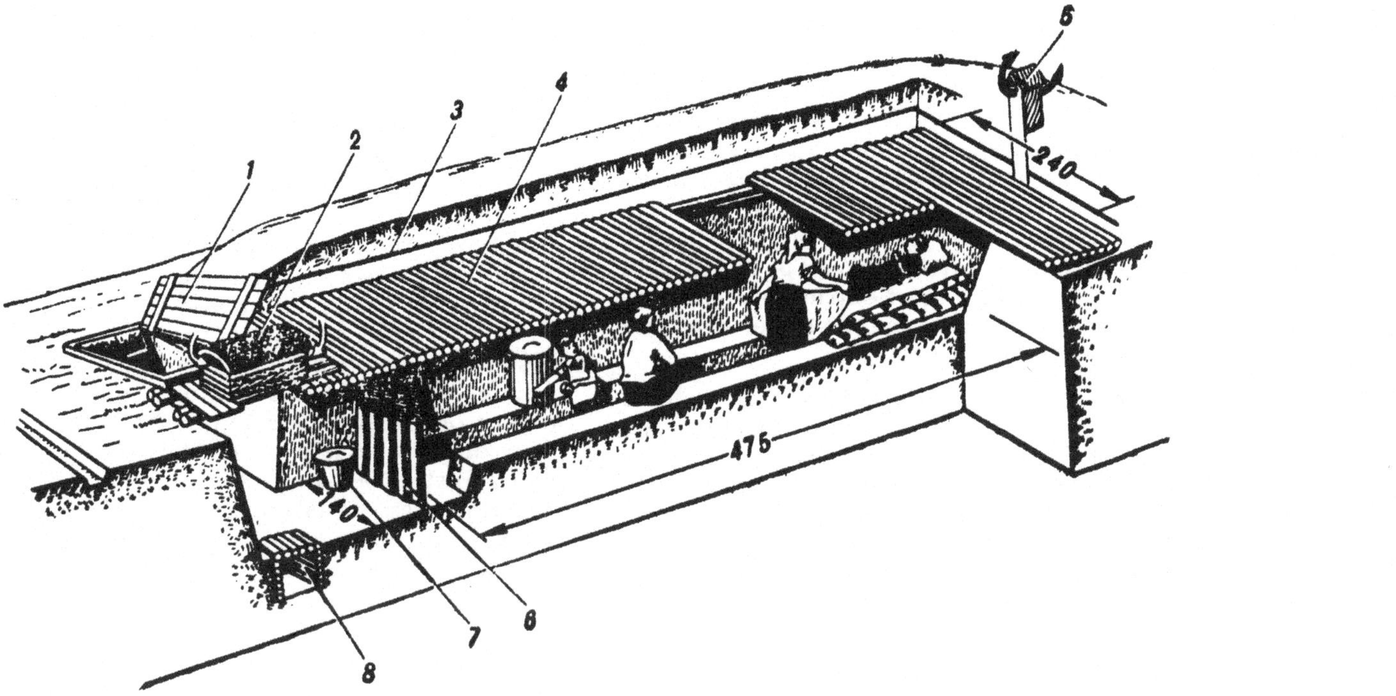

Fig. 6.5. Figure 20. Wood-Earth Shelter without Lining of the Walls for Clay Soils, 10 Occupants: 1 - Trap Door; 2 - Dust Filter with a Straw Packing (hay); 3 - Earth Cover 60-80 cm thick; 4 - Roofing made of Poles; 5 -Exhaust Duct with Damper; 6 - Curtain made of Tightly Woven Cloth; 7 - Removable Container for Wastes; 8 - Water Collecting Sump.

NOTE: Bill of materials is: Rough Lumber, 2.7 cubic meters; Nails, 0.12 kilogram; Wire, 0.64 kilogram; Work Requirement, 90-110 man-hours; Shielding Coefficient, 250-300.

Russian earth-covered expedient fallout shelters are based on military dugouts designed for brief occupancy during a conventional attack. Subsequently, they were improved for fallout protection but were made much less habitable by Soviet civil defense specialists. Apparently these specialists were ignorant of ventilation requirements, and almost certainly they did not field-test small expedient fallout shelters for habitability. Tens of millions of Russians have been taught to build such shelters.

Once any bureaucracy issues dangerously faulty equipment or instructions, it rarely corrects them except under pressure. I have experienced this reluctance even during wartime, when trying to improve faulty combat equipment that was causing American soldiers to lose their lives. Continuing proofs of such bureaucratic reluctance to correct dangerous errors are hundreds of thousands of potentially life-endangering civil defense pamphlets and booklets — especially the several editions of *In Time of Emergency* — kept nationwide in hundreds of communities, primarily for crisis distribution.

Some American official instructions for building expedient shelters have been slowly improved over the decades; the best are given in the June 1985 edition of *Protection in the Nuclear Age,* one of the Federal Emergency Management Agency's widely available free booklets. Yet even in this improved edition no mention is made of the crucial need for forced ventilation during warm weather, nor for expedient, simple means for providing pumped air. Also, in the June 1985 edition of *Protection in the Nuclear Age,* the second crawlway entry/exit of the Above-Ground, Door-Covered Shelter (see Appendix A.4) is replaced by a "4-6" DIA. PIPE FOR VENTILATION," which makes this very small shelter essentially dead-ended and thereby eliminates adequate ventilation in warm weather. With only a 6-inch-diameter air-exhaust opening, not nearly enough air can flow naturally in warm weather through this crowded shelter's room (only about 39 inches wide by 34 inches high). As proved by habitability tests in Florida and elsewhere, a KAP or Directional Fan must be used, even with two crawlway entry/exits.

The essential second crawlway entry/exit of the Aboveground Door-Covered Shelter was eliminated as the result of a recommendation by a contractor for FEMA charged with field testing and evaluating expedient shelters, and improving abbreviated shelter-building instructions. No habitability tests were required. So the contractor concluded in his 1978 report to FEMA that the second entry/exit should be eliminated because "The building of entries is time consuming and with this small a shelter a second entry is really not justified."

In peacetime, bureaucracies of all nations tend to divide up responsibilities between specialists and to promote means by which non-prestigious wartime problems can apparently be solved with the least expense and work.

DIRECTIONAL FANNING TO VENTILATE SHELTERS

The Directional Fanning instructions on the following two pages may save more lives than any other instructions given in this book for a homemakeable survival item. I regret that no one rediscovered this premechanization, simple, yet effective way of manually pumping air until after the original *Nuclear War Survival Skills* was published.

In 1980, Dr. William Olsen, a NASA research engineer long concerned with improving self-help civil defense, rediscovered one kind of Directional Fanning. Since then, with the assistance of able Americans and others, I have designed and tested several types of Directional Fans. I have field-tested and repeatedly improved the instructions to enable average people to quickly learn how to make and use such fans effectively.

The great advantage of Directional Fanning is that almost anyone who is given the field-tested instructions can quickly make and use one of these simple fans. Only very widely available materials are needed. The main disadvantage is that Directional Fanning is a more laborious way to ventilate a shelter than using KAPs, as described in detail in Appendix B.

Americans are not likely to receive Directional Fanning instructions from the Federal Emergency Management Agency. FEMA's predecessors, the Office of Civil Defense and the Defense Civil Preparedness Agency, were unable to get the millions of dollars necessary to buy factory-made KAPs and other manual air pumps to ventilate officially designated fallout shelters, and FEMA has avoided shelter ventilating controversies. No widely available official American publication includes instructions for making and using any expedient air-pumping device.

Thanks to Congressman Ike Skelton, Democrat of Missouri and strong civil defense advocate, in 1981 I was able to demonstrate Directional Fanning to Louis Giuffrida, at that time the Director of FEMA. I gave Directional Fans to the FEMA specialists concerned with shelter ventilation, all of whom have since left FEMA. To date, although Directional Fanning instructions have been reproduced in three private civil defense publications, and some 600 copies of a metric version of the instructions were distributed to British civil defense professionals at the 1984 Annual Study of Civil Defence and Emergency Planning Officers, FEMA has not even evaluated Directional Fanning.

In contrast, in 1981 I gave copies of instructions for both KAPs and Directional Fans to Dr. Yin Zhi-shu, the Director of the People's Republic of China's National Research and Design Institute of Civil Defense — and the next day he started evaluating these simple devices. (At that time I was traveling extensively in China as an official guest, exchanging civil defense information.) Dr. Yin, who heads all Chinese civil defense research and development, went with his top ventilation and shelter design specialists to a furniture factory in Beijing. There I watched workmen quickly build both a large and a small KAP, and also Directional Fans. Then Dr. Yin and his specialists began using their air-velocity meters to measure the volumes of air that these simple devices could pump. On the following days I participated in more ventilation tests using KAPs and Directional Fans in tunnel blast shelters in Beijing and in the port city of Dalien.

While watching these top Chinese civil defense professionals make and test KAPs and Directional Fans, I kept thinking: "This is the way Thomas Edison and Henry Ford would have evaluated simple devices of possible great importance to millions."

The reader is urged to keep the following two pages of Directional Fanning instructions ready for reproduction in a crisis. The sections on the small 2-handled Directional Fan and the large 1-Man Fan will be the most useful to unprepared people. Ventilation by pairs of men using Bedsheet Fans is an effective method for forcing very large volumes of outdoor air through tunnels, corridors and mines with ceilings at least 9 feet high — provided they have two large openings. However, this method requires organization and discipline.

DIRECTIONAL FANNING TO VENTILATE SHELTERS

Directional Fanning is the simplest way to force enough outdoor air through typical basement, trench, and other expedient shelters to maintain endurable conditions, even in extremely hot, humid weather.

During a worsening nuclear crisis most unprepared citizens probably will not have the time and/or materials needed to make a KAP or other efficient shelter-ventilating pump — even if they have the instructions. In contrast, tests with average citizens have indicated that if they have instructions for making and using Directional Fans and if there are a few hours of warning time before the attack, then the majority will be able to ventilate all of their expedient shelters, except some of the largest.

The principal disadvantage of Directional Fans is that they are more laborious to operate than are KAPs, that are manually powered, pendulum-like air pumps that conserve energy.

A. DIRECTIONAL FANNING TO VENTILATE AND COOL SMALLER SHELTERS

A **2-Handled** Directional Fan of the size illustrated is less tiring to use and requires less manual dexterity than does a 1-handled fan with the same size blade. With this small 2-handled fan you quite easily can force about 300 cubic feet per minute (300 cfm) of outdoor air through a crowded trench or basement shelter. This is enough air for up to 9 adults crowded into a small shelter in extremely hot, humid weather, and enough for about 100 people in cold weather. By fanning vigorously, 500 to 600 cubic feet per minute have been forced through a small covered-trench shelter.

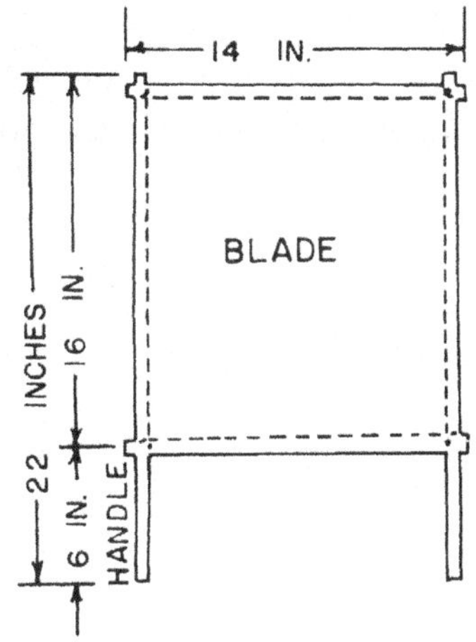

To make a durable 2-handled fan, first make its frame out of 2 sticks each 14 inches long and 2 sticks each 22 inches long. See sketch. To strengthen the corners, overlap the sticks about one-half inch, as shown.

When using sticks cut from a tree, select ones with diameters of about ¾ inch, and make shallow notches in all 4 sticks before tying together the 4 corners of the blade. If you do not have strong string, use ¾-inch-wide strips of bedsheet cloth, or other strong cloth, slightly twisted.

If using sawed sticks, be sure to use none smaller than ⅜ x ¾ inch in cross section. If you have very small nails or brads, use only one to connect each corner; then tie each corner securely. To prevent possible blistering of hands, wrap cloth around the fan handles, or wear gloves.

To cover the fan's blade, any strong, light fabric, such as bedsheet cloth, serves well. If you are going to sew on the cloth, first cut a 26 x 30-inch piece. Wrap the 30-inch width smoothly crosswise around the frame, after cutting 4 notches in the cloth's corners, so that the tied-together parts of the sticks will not be covered. Pin or tape the cloth to make a smooth blade; finally sew securely. (If waterproof construction adhesive is available, a smaller piece of cloth can be used and the blade can be covered in a very few minutes.)

If time and/or materials are very limited, **make a fan with its blade merely a piece of cloth connecting two 22-inch-long sticks.** This very simple fan is reasonably effective, although tiring to use.

Cardboard covering a blade is likely to become damp and fragile in the humid air of a crowded shelter. Very light sheetmetal makes a good fan blade and requires only 2 sticks. A blade of ¼-inch plywood is too heavy.

If no sticks are available, a double thickness of heavy, stiff cardboard 22 inches long by 14 inches wide will pump almost as much air if used as a handleless fan. The pieces should be securely tied or taped together. If waterproof tape is available, cover the parts that you will grip with sweaty hands, thus preventing dampening and softening the cardboard.

For maximum ventilation, the air-intake opening of a shelter should be at least as large as its air-exhaust opening. (If the air-exhaust opening of your small shelter is much larger than that shown in the sketches, block part of it off to reduce it to approximately this 24-inch-high by 20-inch-wide size, for more effective use with this fan.) The air should be fanned out of the shelter in the direction in which the air is naturally flowing. For maximum ventilation rate, fan about 40 strokes per minute.

With one or more Directional Fans, air inside a shelter can be distributed effectively and the occupants cooled. Also, if during the time of maximum fallout dose rate the occupants get close together in the most protective part of the shelter, they often will get unbearably hot unless fanned.

To fan air out through an air-exhaust opening, sit facing the opening with your elbows about 4 inches lower than the bottom of the opening. Then count 1, 2, 3 while you:

[1] **Quickly** raise the fan to a vertical position close in front of your face and **immediately** fan (push) a slug of air into the opening — ending the power stroke with your arms fully extended and with the fan almost horizontal and out of the way of air that was "sucked" behind the fan and is still flowing out through the opening.

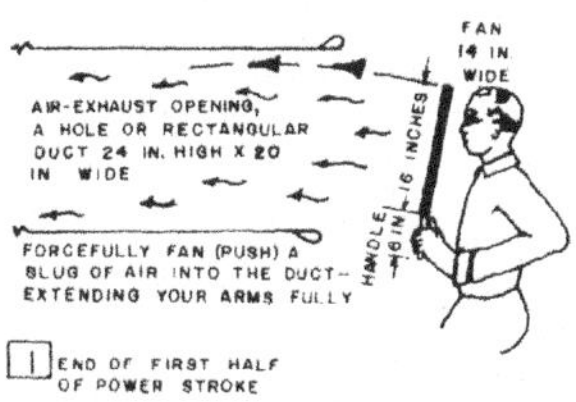

[2], [3] After a slight pause, leisurely withdraw the almost horizontal fan until the bottom of its blade almost touches your stomach — preparatory to the next power stroke.

To increase the flow of air through a shelter, while fanning the occupants:

Have two or more occupants sitting inside the shelter each use a fan of the size described above to fan the air so as to increase its velocity in the direction in which air already is flowing through the shelter. Such Directional Fanning is especially effective in increasing the air flow through small, narrow shelters.

To avoid higher radiation exposures near openings, build an essentially airtight partition across the shelter room, with a 24-inch-high x 20-inch-wide hole in it through which to fan. By fanning through a 24 x 20-inch hole in a cardboard partition built across a doorway inside a U-shaped permanent trench shelter 76 feet long, the air flow was increased by an average of 327 cubic feet per minute.

B. DIRECTIONAL FANNING TO VENTILATE AND COOL LARGER SHELTERS

1. With a Large 1-Man Fan

To ventilate larger basements, big covered trenches, and other large shelters lacking adequate ventilation, use one or more large 1-man fans. See sketch. Note that the 20 x 30-inch fan blade is made like a 2-stick kite, and that the upper end of the longer diagonal stick serves as a 10-inch handle. The model illustrated is made of 2 nominal 1 x 2-inch boards, one 46 inches long and the other 35 inches long. These boards are connected at a point 17½ inches from their lower ends, first with a single clinched nail, and then by being tied securely. The edges of the handle are rounded smooth.

The blade frame is covered on both sides with strong bedsheet cloth, that is wrapped around and secured to the strong cords or wires tied to notches cut in the boards (or sticks) near the 4 corners of the blade. (If cord or wire is not available, 4 2-inch-wide strips of strong cloth, slightly twisted, serve well.)

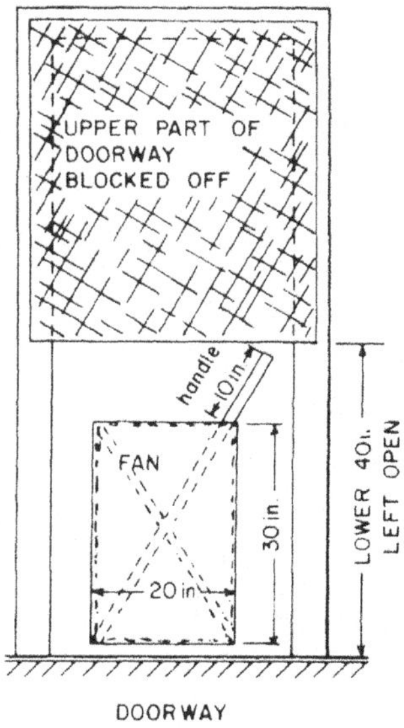

A durable but laboriously heavy fan can be made in a few minutes using a 20 x 30-inch piece of ¼-inch plywood nailed to a single 46-inch-long, 1 x 2-inch board. Or use a single round stick about 1¼ inches in diameter, flattened on one side.

A fan with its blade made of two sheets of very heavy cardboard tied on both sides of a 1 x 2-inch board is decidedly effective when dry. However, typical cardboard will become soft and worthless in most crowded, long-occupied, humid shelters.

To fan directionally, it is best to stand just outside and to one side of a doorway, so that your body does not obstruct the air flow. Preferably stand opposite and facing the open door, which should be secured open and perpendicular to its doorway. Hold the fan like a golf club and swing it with your arms extended. Then slowly count 1, 2 while you:

[1] Make the power stroke with the fan blade broadside until the end of the stroke, when you quickly turn it 90 degrees.

[2] Make the pendulum-like return stroke with the fan blade kept edgewise ("feathered") to the air flow until the end, when you quickly turn it 90 degrees, preparatory to making the next power stroke.

To pump more air, block off the upper part of the doorway with cloth, cardboard, plywood, etc., to prevent air from flowing back in the wrong direction through the upper part of the doorway. See sketch on preceding page.

Whenever practical, directionally fan the air in the same direction that the air is naturally flowing through the shelter. More air usually can be pumped through a shelter if the fan is used to force air out through the air-exhaust opening. This reduces the air pressure inside the shelter and causes fresh outdoor air to be "sucked" into the shelter through the air-intake doorway, or through other large air-intake openings. Thus with one fan 1,000 cubic feet per minute can be pumped through a fully occupied shelter. This is enough outdoor air — if it is properly distributed within the shelter — to maintain tolerable conditions for weeks for 25 occupants during extremely hot weather, and for up to about 300 occupants during cold weather.

To ventilate and cool a room having only one doorway and no other opening, do not block off any part of the doorway. If air is fanned into such a room through the lower part of its completely open doorway, then air will flow back out of the room through the upper part of the doorway. However, this pumps much less air than when a separate, large air-exhaust opening is provided.

To increase the flow of outdoor air through a tunnel-shelter, several fanners equally spaced along its length should each fan in the direction of the natural air flow. This procedure was first proved practical during a 1981 ventilation test that Cresson H. Kearny participated in with Chinese civil defense officials in the port city of Dalien. In this test 5 fanners, each with a fan of approximately the size illustrated, forced air from the outdoors through a 395-foot section between two opened entrances of a typical Chinese tunnel-shelter. The air flow was increased from a natural flow of 290 cubic feet per minute to 3,680 cubic feet per minute. The 5 excellent Chinese fans each had a blade made of a piece of 3 mm (approx. ⅛ inch) plywood nailed to a single board.

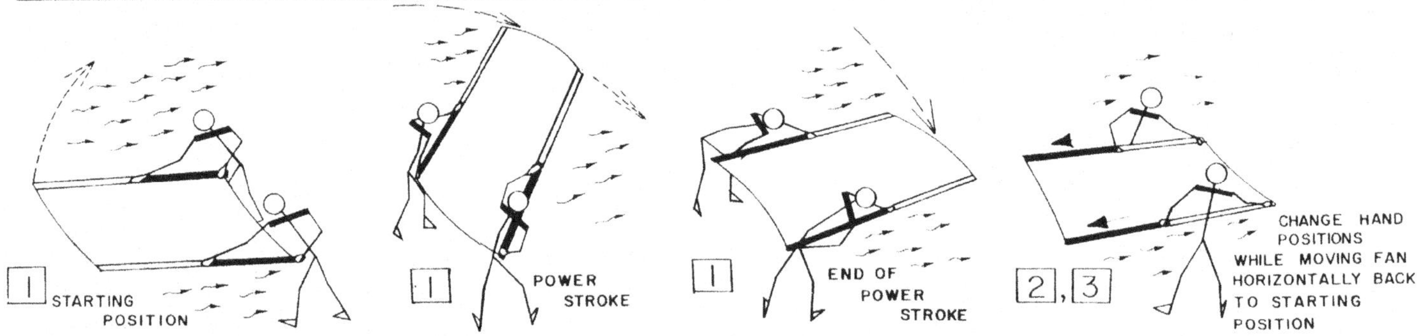

2. With a Bedsheet Fan

Use a 2-man Bedsheet Fan to force thousands of cubic feet per minute of outdoor air through a tunnel or long corridor having at least a 9-foot ceiling and a large opening at each end. The most practical design tested was made from a strong double bedsheet cut down to 6-foot width, with the wide hem at its head-end left unchanged and with a similar-sized hem sewn in its opposite end, to give a finished length of 6 feet. A 6-foot-long, nominal 1 x 2-inch board (or an approximately 1½ inch diameter stick) was secured inside each end hem of various models with waterproof construction adhesive, or with tacks, or by tying. Before a board was inserted, its edges were rounded. Round sticks were smoothed.

Two persons preparing to use a Bedsheet Fan (see sketch) should stand facing each other, at right angles to the desired direction of air flow, with the cloth extended horizontally between them. Each fanner should grip his stick with one hand near its "downwind" end and with his other hand near its center.

A pair of Directional Fanners get ready to make a power stroke by leaning in the upwind direction, as illustrated. Then the pair of fanners should count 1, 2, 3 while they:

[1] Make the power stroke by rapidly sweeping their sticks and the attached cloth in an arc, until they are leaning in the downwind direction and the sticks and cloth are again horizontal. See sketch.

[2], [3] Hold the sticks and cloth horizontal (to permit air that was "sucked" behind the cloth to continue flowing in the desired direction) while leisurely moving the Bedsheet Fan back to the starting position. During this move the fanners change hands, as illustrated. (Note that what was the upper side of the fan at the beginning of the power stroke now has become the lower side.)

Two men thus fanning vigorously produced a net air flow of 5,500 cubic feet per minute through an empty school corridor that is 8 feet wide, has a 9-foot ceiling, and is 194 feet long. The doors at both ends were open. To adequately ventilate and cool people crowded into a long tunnel in hot weather, a pair of Bedsheet Fanners should be positioned about every 100 feet along its length.

The practicality of using Bedsheet Fans to ventilate some very large mines or caves having 2 or more large openings was proved by tests with members of the Citizens Preparedness Group of Greater Kansas City. These tests were conducted in 1982 near Kansas City in a huge limestone mine that has a ceiling averaging about 17 feet high, corridors about 35 feet wide, columns of unexcavated rock about 15 feet square, and over 1,000,000 square feet of level, dry floor space. The air inside is "dead", remarkably still, because the only openings are two truck-sized portals on one side of the mine. Five pairs of Bedsheet Fanners, spaced about 75 feet apart down a corridor, after fanning for several minutes produced a measured air flow of approximately 100,000 cubic feet per minute through this part of this corridor!

With many more pairs of Bedsheet Fanners working, enough air for at least 10,000 occupants could be "sucked" into this mine through one of its 17 x 20-foot portals, fanned down a corridor to the far "dead end" of the mine, then fanned through a cross corridor, and finally fanned back out through the corridor that has the second truck-sized portal at its outer end.

A pair of pre-mechanization coal miners produced a directed airflow by holding a piece of canvas **vertically** between them while they quickly walked a short ways in the direction of the desired airflow; they walked back with the canvas held **horizontally** between them. Then they repeated.

C. ADDITIONAL ADVANTAGES OF DIRECTIONAL FANS

1. No installation is needed, thus saving working time and materials for making habitable shelters hurriedly built or upgraded during a crisis.

2. Directional Fans enable shelter occupants to quickly reverse the direction of air flow through their shelter when outdoor wind changes cause the direction of natural air flow to be reversed.

3. Four or more Directional Fans when used to circulate air within a shelter room can serve like air ducts, while simultaneously fanning occupants.

4. Directional Fans are very unlikely to be damaged by blast effects severe enough to wreck bladed fans or other fixed ventilation devices placed at or near air-intake or air-exhaust openings, but not severe enough to injure shelter occupants.

Chapter 7

Protection Against Fires and Carbon Monoxide

RELATIVE DANGERS

Fire and its consequences probably would be the third-ranking danger to unprepared Americans subjected to a massive nuclear attack. Direct blast effects would be first, covering a large fraction of densely populated areas and killing far more people. Considerably fewer fatalities seem likely to result from the second-ranking danger, fallout radiation.

THE FACTS ABOUT FIRE HAZARDS

Firestorms would endanger relatively few Americans; only the older parts of a few American cities have buildings close enough together, over a large enough area, to fuel this type of conflagration. Such fires have not occurred in cities where less than about 30% of a large area was covered with buildings.[19]

In the blast area of Hiroshima, a terrifying fire storm that burned almost all buildings within an area of about 4.4 square miles resulted from many fires being ignited almost simultaneously. Many were caused by heat radiation from the fireball. Even more fires were due to secondary effects of the blast, such as the overturning of stoves. The buildings contained much wood and other combustible materials. The whole area burned like a tremendous bonfire; strong winds that blew in from all directions replaced the huge volumes of hot air that rose skyward from the intense fires.

Lack of oxygen is not a hazard to occupants of shelters in or near burning buildings or to those in shelters that are closed tightly to prevent the entry of smoke or fallout. Carbon monoxide, toxic smoke from fires, or high concentrations of carbon dioxide from shelter occupants' exhaled breaths would kill occupants before they suffered seriously from lack of oxygen.

FIRES IGNITED BY HEAT RADIATION

Figure 7.1 shows a wood-frame house after it was heated for one second by heat radiation from a small nuclear weapon exploded in a Nevada test. This test house had no furnishings, but the heat was intense enough to have ignited exposed upholstery, curtains, bedding, papers, etc. in a typical home.

Heat radiation will set fire to easily ignitable materials (dry newspapers, thin dark fabrics, dry leaves and dry grass) in about the same extensive areas over which blast causes moderate damage to frame houses. The blast wave and high-speed blast winds will blow out many flames. However, tests have shown that fire will continue to smolder within some materials such as upholstery and dry rotted wood, and after a while it often will burst into flame and will spread. The burning automobile pictured in Fig. 7.2 is an example of such ignition beyond the range of severe blast damage.

The number of fires started by heat radiation in areas where blast is not severe can be reduced by whitewashing the insides of window panes and by removing flammable materials from places in and around houses where heat radiation could reach them. Also, occupants of shelters in some homes that would be only slightly damaged by blast could move quickly to extinguish small fires and throw out smoldering upholstered articles before fallout is deposited.

Fig. 7.1. Heat radiation charred the paint on this house, which had been painted white to reflect heat rays. The charring instantaneously produced the smoke. However, precautions had been taken to prevent this typical U.S. house from being destroyed by fire, because the test was made to enable engineers to study the effects of blast, rather than fire. The house was demolished by the 5-psi overpressure blast that struck seconds later, but it did not burn.

Fig. 7.2. Thermal radiation from a nuclear explosion entered the car above through its closed windows and ignited the upholstery. The windows were blown out by the blast a few seconds later. However, the explosion was at such a distance that the blast wave was not severe enough to dent the car body.

Earth-covered shelters can be protected against heat radiation from nuclear explosions and other causes by painting any exposed wood and other combustible materials at shelter openings with a thick coating of slaked lime (old-fashioned white-wash). The World War II firebombing of Kassel was less effective than were similar raids on other German cities because the roof timbers of buildings had been so treated.[20]

Figure 7.3 illustrates the effectiveness of a thick coating of slaked lime in protecting a rough pine board against ignition by heat radiation. No flames from the burning logs touched the board. (Before this photograph was taken, the uppermost burning logs of a vertical-sided pile were removed so that the board could be seen clearly.)

Chinese civil defense instructions recommend coating exposed wood with both slaked lime and mud.[21] If only mud is available, a coating of it protects wood quite well. If kept damp, a mud coating is even more effective. (Simply keeping all exposed flammable materials damp is helpful.)

In blast areas, cloth or plastic canopies over the openings of expedient shelters usually would be ignited by the heat and certainly would be blown away by even moderate blast winds. If extra canopies and stakes could be made and kept inside the shelter, these replacements could be quickly erected after blast winds subside and before fallout begins—at least 15 minutes after the explosion. If no spare canopies were available, it would be best to keep the available canopies and their stakes inside the shelter, if it were not raining.

FOREST AND BRUSH FIRES

Unless forests or brushy areas are dry, it is difficult to start even scattered fires. Dangerous mass fires would be unlikely, except in blast areas where the heat radiation would be very intense. However, people building a shelter would do well to select a shelter site at least as far away from trees as the height of the tallest tree that could fall on the shelter—because of fire and smoke hazards in dry weather, and because digging a shelter among tree roots is difficult.

Fig. 7.3. Heat radiation had ignited the flaming half of the board on the ground, while the half near the shovel—painted white with a thick coating of slaked lime—had not even begun to smoke.

Fires in the 2022 Threat Model Theory

CALIFORNIA FOREST FIRES SMELT AND SEEN IN MICHIGAN AS HAZE AND SUNSETS
Cresson is talking about forests and cities burning from 1000's or 10'000's of thousands of nuclear devices going off.

The threat of Carbon Monoixde (CO) poisening is a lot higher if your shelter is in a field and the forest behind you is on fire.

However with the theory put forth that the current situation with Ukraine would only involve nuclear detonations in that 'theater' and even if we had 'don't mess with us' detonations on the USA soil from Russia and there were a handful of these, say, 10. Then what Cresson is talking about is not as relavant unless you are near that detonation.

Make no mistake about it, a nuclear device going off in the atmosphere (air burst) or on or in the ground (ground burst) is going to start a lot of fires in cities or anything below and around it for many square miles. 16 square miles of fire (10,000+ acres) instantly ignited type of fire is possible.

There are fires smaller than that in California and 'out west' that have made so much smoke that it make the sun 'not visible' in Michigan a few days later. You could see where the sun was but the upper atmosphere haze was so bad the sun was just a blur. There were air quality alerts and people senesative to particles in the air (like smoke) were affected and peoples eyes were scratchy and itchy and some people had constant nasel drainage. Others could say they could smell the smoke in the air from 2000 miles away.

If a nuke gets detonated on the west coat everyone and their brother will be tracking the radiation as it moves across parts of America but its safe to say that if the smoke from the fires from the detonation have reached you that the amount of fall-out generated is now also at your position. Please follow the other instructions in this book about making your environment safe from fallout. A single device on the west coast might have fallout that people in Las Vegas need to shelter from (agian...depending) but those of us days away will be of more concerned about tracking it in the house, eating or drinking something contamined with the micro amounts of fall out. Cresson addresses this well in the book.

SAFE TO SAY that your medical preperations should include perscription or over the countery alergy medications that you normally use when smoke from 1000 miles away and or seasonal alergies affect you. You know what affects your nose, eyes and lungs and how bad. Have extra for what works for you. Consult with your doctor long before an incident and obtain extra. If your insurance won't cover it and limits you to only a 30 day supply on a month to month basis. Consider asking your doctor for a generic (which is cheaper) and or using www.GoodRX.com for free, no sign up needed, discount codes to use at your pharmacy.

I personally have asked my doctor for well over 15 years for extra perscriptions of certain antibiotics for times of emergency or when I travel. I don't buy these on insurance I just use GoodRx.com and get them cheap. In April of 2022 100mg of Doxycycline for a 10 day supply (20 capsules) is about $5.49 on GoodRX.com I tell my doctor, and he agrees with me, "Hey Doc, I don't want to have to run to an all night pharmacy or call you at 3am for an emergency perscription. I want to have it on hand. Give me the perscription (for what I'm asking him for) and I promise to call you if something happens before I take it.

I've done this. I had a tick stuck in my hip, that could not reach, and it died in there and it got infected. I called my doctor, he got back to me some 20 minutes later. I told him what was up and he asked where I was, I told him over 1000 miles away and over a mile from the closest house and near a small town that rolls up the sidewalks at 5pm and has one pharmacy. He told me to take 1 of the 100mg doxycline a day for 3 days and to have someone remove it. It was hard to reach on my left hip and a bit towards my back. I did send him a photo of it. I went to the pharmacy (small town) the next day and asked if anyone there as a medical asssistant or a nurse in their past. Older lady said, "I was honey, for 20 years" and I showed the spot to her and I had a set of tweezers, hemostats, a small short scalpel (like an exacto knife) and had alcohol to clean the wound and the instruments (disinfect them) and she just looked at me. She used the alcohol wipe on the tweezers, on the bite and tick location and took it out in about 5 seconds. I used my phone on super zoom to take a close up photo and we both could see that there were no dead body parts stuck behind.

She looks at me and says, "You need a perscription. That's slightly infected and our ticks have lime disease around here." I showed her my bottle, told her what my doctor said (this was day 2) and she goes, "Your mama was like me, she did not raise any stupid children. Good job."

This is not medical advice, its a personal story. I'm using my experience as an example to you of what I did fo myself. Consult with your own personal physician about what you can do for yourself.

If I did not find the nurse, I'd of gone to the local volunteer fire fighter location (where the fire trucks are), found a fire fighter and asked where can I find the EMT or the Medic who rides in the Boo Boo Bus (Fire Ambulance). Again, small town, rural North Carolina. This is just an example of how I got a small medical problem solved for myself in a small town. If I was in town I'd of just gone to my PCP (Doctor) and had him take care of it...but... in a nuclear incident you doctor might not be available. Again, not medical advice. Just me thinking outside of the box. There was no emergency but I was 'practising' on solving the medical issue without a doctor or an ER or a Hospital etc... I'm serious. That was practise. Notice how much easier it was by having my doctor entrust me with medication and I had the needed tools and disinfectants ready for anyone I found with talent.

CAUSES OF FIRE

Figure 7.4 pictures the same house shown in Fig. 7.1 after it had been struck by the blast effects of a small nuclear test explosion at the 5-psi overpressure range. (If the house had been hit by the blast effects of a multimegaton weapon, with longer-lasting blast winds, it would have been wrecked about as completely at the 3-psi overpressure range. At the 3-psi overpressure range, the blast winds from an explosion 1000 times as powerful as the Nevada test explosion that wrecked this house would blow 10 times as long. This longer-duration, 100-mph blast wind would increase the damage done by the blast wave. The 3-psi overpressure range from a 20-megaton surface burst is about 10 miles from the center of the crater, and from a one-megaton surface burst, about 4 miles.[6])

If the blast-wrecked house shown in the illustration had had a furnace in operation when it was demolished, the chances of its being set on fire would have been high. In Hiroshima many of the first fires resulted from secondary effects of blast, especially the overturning of stoves, and not from heat radiation. Although the air burst produced no fallout, firefighters from undamaged, nearby communities were unable to reach most of the burning areas because of blast debris blocking the roads. Later they were kept from burning areas by the intense heat. Some water mains were broken, which made water unavailable for firefighting in certain areas.

In the event of an attack on the United States employing many surface bursts, fallout would prevent firefighting for days to weeks in a large part of the most populated regions.

The basements of many substantial buildings will withstand 5-psi blast effects and can prevent occupants from suffering serious injuries from blast. Most home basements can be reinforced with stout boards and posts so as to give good protection against blast effects up to considerably higher than 5 psi. But considering the dangers of fires in probable blast areas, it is safer to build an earth-covered shelter well removed from buildings than it is to seek protection in shelters inside buildings.

CARBON MONOXIDE AND TOXIC SMOKE

If an undamaged building is burning, people inside may be killed by carbon monoxide, toxic smoke, or fiery-hot air. Tests have shown that even fast-burning, rubble-free fires produce very high concentrations of carbon monoxide. If large-scale fires are burning near a shelter, the dangers from both carbon dioxide and carbon monoxide may continue for as long as 1½ hours after ignition.[22] Therefore, the ventilation pipes or openings of a shelter should not be placed close to a building that might be expected to burn.

In the smoldering rubble of a large test fire, after 24 hours the carbon monoxide concentration was still more than 1% and the air temperature was

Fig. 7.4. Unburned wreckage of the same two-story, wood-frame house pictured in Fig. 7.1 after being wrecked by the 5-psi blast effects of a small nuclear test explosion.

1900°F. A carbon monoxide concentration of only 0.08% (8 parts CO in 10,000 parts of air) will cause headache, dizziness, and nausea in 45 minutes, and total collapse in 2 hours.

Realization of carbon monoxide dangers to persons in simple fallout shelters and basements may have led the writers of Soviet civil defense publications to define the "zone of total destruction" as the blast areas where the overpressure exceeds 7 psi and "residential and industrial buildings are completely destroyed ... the rubble is scattered and covers the burning structures," and "As a result the rubble only smolders, and fires as such do not occur."[23] Smoldering fires produce more carbon monoxide than do fiercely burning fires. Whether or not the occupants of basement shelters survive the direct blast effects is of little practical importance in those blast areas where the rubble overhead burns or smolders. So in the "zone of complete destruction," Russian rescue brigades plan to concentrate on saving persons trapped inside excellent blast shelters by the rubble.

About 135,000 Germans lost their lives in the tragic city of Dresden during three days of firebomb raids. Most casualties were caused by the inhalation of hot gases and by carbon monoxide and smoke poisoning.[20] Germans learned that when these dangers were threatening an air raid shelter, the occupants' best chance of survival was to run outside, even if the bombs were still falling. But in a nuclear war the fallout dose rate may be so high that the occupants of a shelter threatened by smoke and carbon monoxide might suffer a more certain and worse death by going outside. Instead, if they know from instrument readings and their calculations that they probably would receive a fatal dose before they could reach another shelter, the occupants should close all openings as tightly as possible. With luck, carbon monoxide in deadly concentrations would not reach them, nor would they be overcome by heat or their own respiratory carbon dioxide before the fire dangers ended.

Dr. A.Broido, a leading experimenter with fires and their associated dangers, reached this conclusion: "If I were building a fallout shelter I would spend a few extra dollars to build it in my backyard rather than in my basement, locating the intake vent as far as possible from any combustible material. In such a shelter I would expect to survive anything except the close-in blast effects."[22]

This advice also applies to expedient shelters built during a crisis.

Chapter 8
Water

WATER AND SALT REQUIREMENTS

Painful thirst has been experienced by very few Americans. We take for granted that we will always have enough water to drink. Most of us think of "food and water" in that order, when we think of survival essentials that should be stored. But if unprepared citizens were confined in a shelter by heavy fallout, they soon would realize that they should have given first priority to storing adequate water.

For the kidneys to eliminate waste products effectively, the average person needs to drink enough water so that he urinates at least one pint each day. (When water is not limited, most people drink enough to urinate 2 pints. Additional water is lost in perspiration, exhaled breath, and excrement.) Under cool conditions, a person could survive for weeks on 3 pints of water a day—if he eats but little food and if that food is low in protein. Cool conditions, however, would be the exception in crowded belowground shelters occupied for many days. Under such circumstances four or five quarts of drinking water per day are essential in very hot weather, with none allowed for washing. For a two-week shelter stay, 15 gallons per person should be stored in or close to a shelter. This amount usually would provide for some water remaining after two weeks, to prevent thirst in case fallout dangers were to continue.

In a 1962 Navy shelter occupancy test lasting two weeks, 99 sailors each consumed an average of 2.4 quarts (2.3 liters) of water per day.[15] The test was conducted in August near Washington, D.C.; the weather was unseasonably cool. The shelter was not air-conditioned except during the last two days of the test.

When one is sweating heavily and not eating salty food, salt deficiency symptoms—especially cramping—are likely to develop within a few days. To prevent this, 6 or 8 grams of salt (about $^{1}/_{4}$ oz, or $^{1}/_{2}$ tablespoon) should be consumed daily in food and drink. If little or no food is eaten, this small daily salt ration should be added to drinking water. Under hot conditions, a little salt makes water taste better.

CARRYING WATER

Most families have only a few large containers that could be used for carrying water to a shelter and storing it in adequate amounts for several weeks. Polyethylene trash bags make practical expedient water containers when used as waterproof liners *inside* smaller fabric bags or pillowcases. (Plastic bags labeled as being treated with insecticides or odor-controlling chemicals should not be used.) Figure 8.1 shows a teenage boy carrying over 10 gallons (more than 80 pounds) of water, well balanced front and back for efficient packing. Each of his two burlap bags is lined with two 20-gallon polyethylene trash bags, one inside the other. (To avoid possible pinhole leakage it is best to put one waterproof bag inside another.)

To close a plastic bag of water so that hardly any will leak out, first spread the top of the bag until the two inner sides of the opening are together. Then fold in the center so that the folded opening is 4 thicknesses, and smooth (see Fig. 8.2). Continue smoothly folding in the middle until the whole folded-up opening is only about $1^{1}/_{2}$ inches wide. Then fold the top of the bag over on itself so the folded-up opening points down. With a strip of cloth or a soft cord, bind and tie the folded-over part with a bow knot, as illustrated.

Fig. 8.1. Carrying 80 pounds of water in two burlap bags, each lined with two larger plastic trash bags, one inside the other.

ORNL-DWG 78-7106

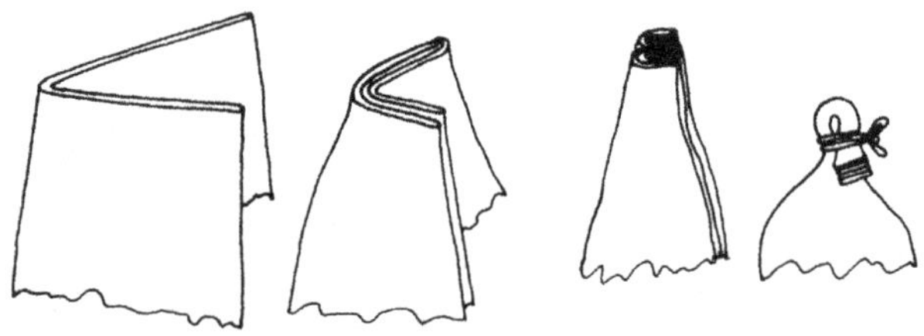

Fig. 8.2. Folding and tying the mouth of a water-filled plastic bag.

For long hikes, it is best to tie the water-holding plastic bags so that the openings are higher than the water levels inside.

To transport this type of expedient water bag in a vehicle, tie a rope around the fabric outer bag near its opening, so that the rope also encircles and holds the plastic liner-bags just below their tied-shut openings. The other end of this rope should then be tied to some support, to keep the openings higher than the water level.

To use two fabric bags or pillowcases to carry a heavy load of water contained in *larger* plastic liner-bags, connect the two fabric bags as shown in Fig. 8.1.

A small pebble, a lump of earth, or a similar object should be tied inside the opening of each bag before the two are tied together, to hold them securely. The bag that is to be carried in front should have the pebble tied about 4 inches further down from the edge of its opening than the pebble tied in the bag to be carried in back. This keeps the pebbles from being pressed against the carrier's shoulder by a heavy load.

A pair of trousers with both legs tied shut at the bottoms can be used to carry a balanced load if pillowcases or other fabric bags are not at hand. Such a balanced load can be slung over the shoulder with the body erect and less strained than if the same weight were carried in a single bag-like pack on the back. However, trouser legs are quite narrow and do not provide room to carry more than a few gallons.

To prevent water from slowly leaking through the tied-shut openings of plastic bags, the water levels inside should be kept below the openings.

STORING WATER

When storing expedient water bags in a shelter, the water levels inside should be kept below the openings.

Not many expedient shelters would be large enough to store an adequate volume of water for an occupancy lasting two or more weeks. Plastic-lined storage pits, dug in the earth close to the shelter, are dependable for storing large volumes of water using cheap, compact materials. Figure 8.3 shows a cylindrical water-storage pit dug so as to have a diameter about two inches smaller than the inflated

ORNL-DWG 77-10423R

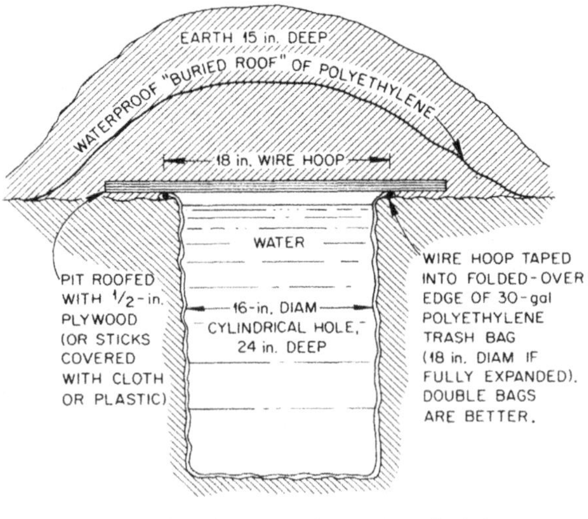

Fig. 8.3. Vertical section of cylindrical water-storage pit lined with two 30-gallon waterproof plastic bags. This pit held about 20 gallons.

Want to Look Smart? Use Figure 8.2 on Page 67

TRASH BAG IN A PILLOW CASE, GENIUS THAT DOES MANY THINGS.

Look at Fig 8.2 on the previous page, page 67. DO NOT forget this. In fact, STOP what you are doing, go grab a regular trash bag, not a 'drawstring one', and DO THIS. Right now. Do it now. Learn this right now. Learn to fold a trash bag top like this. You pull it tight apart with your fingers, fold it in half tightly, and you do it again and again until it's about the width of 2 or 3 of your fingers then you fold it over as shown in the figure and you can use string, duct tape, a zip tie, anything to tie it shut. Trash bags are fragile, and I've done this with the thinnest of trash bags (0.7mm ones), so you put this in a pillowcase or other cloth sack for strength. A reusable cloth shopping bag will work, and a pillowcase works fantastic.

The fabric case is the strength to hold whatever is in the sealed trash bag. The trash bag can be broken easily, and the cloth around it takes the stress of what is in the trash bag (usually water or air).

If you read Jungle Snafus and Remedies also written by Cresson Kearny (available at www.RobinsonBooks.com click on OTHER) you'll see Cresson would use this in several ways.

1. He'd use the trash bag as a 'Pack Liner' for a combat backpack for his Jungle Troops. That way, if it rained, nothing in the pack got wet. The fabric of the pack got wet, but the stuff in the pack did not get wet. So a trash bag in a pillowcase in your duffle bag or anything else will prevent anything you don't want to get wet (like this book) or electronics from getting wet from rain, or worse.

2. The pack liner in the backpack had 'trapped air' in it and his troops could march into a lake or river, float across, walk out on the other side and keep going. All was dry and the pack did not sink. I had a small 26-pound emergency backpack at a meeting I was at with Cresson. I bet everyone around us $1 as to if I would sink or swim if I jumped into the swimming pool. Everyone felt the pack and I had a scale there. They all knew it was 26 pounds. I had one of Cresson's pack liners (from a trash bag) in there and about 20 people bet I'd sink. Cresson did not take the bet but he just smiled at me. I jumped into the deep end and I shot up like a cork and paddled around like a dog with the pack on my back.

3. You can put the trash bag full of air in a pillowcase (make sure it's smaller than the pillowcase when 'inflated') and tie it off with some rope and you can hold onto this when trying to cross water. It's your floatation method. Your expedient floaties. Or tie it to something heavy and you'll make sure it won't sink if (when) you drop it.

4. Do the same as #3 but do as Cresson suggests on the previous page and put water into it. Water is heavy. 8.3 pounds per gallon. So you are probably not putting in all you want but all that you can carry. You can also take a milk crate or an open 5-gallon pail and put this in there and fill it up and yes, it's heavy, but if you are traveling by truck or car you now have plenty of water to take with you.

FUN FACT: I showed this to a person that became a very close and dear friend of mine in 2003. He was a former US Navy Seal and I told him, "I bet I can show you some stuff you've not seen..." "Try!" was all he said. So, I put a 30-gallon trash bag with air in it inside of a pillowcase. The trick is, that the volume of the trash bag with the air has to be LESS than the volume of the pillowcase. I tied off the plastic bag and then tied off the pillowcase so the plastic bag would not come out. I had it on the floor and I said "floatation" and he looks at me as if he was going to hit me. I was about 215lbs at that time and I stood on the pillowcase with the slightly inflated trash bag on the inside with both feet off the floor and balanced on it. I bounced up and down on it a bit and it flexed in and out. He looked at me and it and says, "I like that, the way you did that, is something new." and that is how I got him and a good portion of the Seal Team community in the area (Virginia Beach) introduced to Cresson's documented best practices going back to before WW2 through his book Jungle Snafus and Remedies.

diameter of the two 30-gallon polyethylene trash bags lining it (one bag inside the other). Before a plastic bag is placed in such a pit, the ends of roots should be cut off flush to the wall with a sharp knife, and sharp rocks should be carefully removed.

The best way to keep the upper edges of the pit-lining bags from slipping into the pit is shown in Fig. 8.3: Make a circular wire hoop the size of the opening of the bag, and tape it inside the top. In firm ground, the upper edges of double bags have been satisfactorily held in place simply by sticking six large nails through the turned-under edges of the bags and into the firm earth.

Figure 8.3 shows how to roof and cover a water storage pit so as to protect the water. The "buried roof" of waterproof material prevents any contamination of the stored water by downward-percolating rainwater, which could contain bacteria or small amounts of radioactive substances from fallout. The thick earth cover over the flexible roofing gives excellent blast protection, due to the earth arching that develops under blast pressure. In a large Defense Nuclear Agency blast test, a filled water-storage pit of the size illustrated was undamaged by blast effects at an overpressure range which could demolish the strongest aboveground buildings (53 psi).

Fig. 8.4. These two 30-gallon polyethylene trash bags, one inside the other, held 16 gallons of water. They were undamaged by 50-psi blast effects while buried in dry, very light soil. The plywood roof and the earth placed over the water bag were removed before this picture was taken.

A simpler way to store water is illustrated in Fig. 8.4. If the soil is so unstable that an unshored water storage pit with vertical sides cannot be dug, the opening of the bag (or of one bag placed inside another) can simply be tied shut so as to minimize leakage (see Fig. 8.4). Fill the bag with water, tie it, and place it in the pit. Then bury it with earth to the level of the water inside. A disadvantage of this method is leakage through the tied-shut openings due to pressure of loose earth on the bag. To lessen leakage, leave an air space between the filled bag and a roofing of board or sticks, so that the weight of earth piled on top of the roofing will not squeeze the bag. This storage method has another disadvantage: after the earth covering and the roof are removed, it is difficult to bail out the water for use—because as water is bailed out, the loose surrounding earth moves inward and squeezes the bag above the lowered water level.

Fig. 8.5. Post-blast view of plastic-lined water-storage pit undamaged at a 6.7-psi overpressure range. This pit held about 200 gallons.

Large volumes of water can be stored in plastic-lined rectangular pits. In order to roof them with widely available materials such as ordinary ¾-inch plywood or small poles, the pits should be dug no wider than 3 feet. Figure 8.5 pictures such a pit: 8 feet long, 27 inches wide, and 30 inches deep. It was lined with a 10-foot-wide sheet of 4-mil polyethylene. The edges of this plastic sheet were held in place by placing them in shallow trenches dug near the sides of the pit and covering them with earth. Earth was mounded over the plywood roof to a depth of about 30 inches, with a "buried roof" of polyethylene. The earth cover and its "buried roof" were similar to the pit covering illustrated by Fig. 8.3. This rectangular pit contained about 200 gallons of water. No water leaked out after the pit had been subjected to blast effects severe enough to have flattened most substantial buildings. However, rectangular pits at higher overpressures failed, due to sidewall caving that caused leaks.

In a subsequent blast test by Boeing Aerospace Company, a plastic-lined water pit was undamaged at the 200-psi overpressure range. First a rectangular pit 4 ft. wide, 12 ft. long, and 2 ft. deep was dug. Then inside this pit a 2 x 10 x 2-ft. water-storage pit was dug, and lined with plastic film. After being filled full of water, the storage pit was covered with plywood, on which was shoveled 2 ft. of earth.

Plastic garbage cans are usually watertight; most used metal garbage cans are not. If thoroughly cleaned and disinfected with a strong chlorine bleach solution, watertight garbage cans can serve for emergency water storage, as can some wastebaskets. If new plastic film is available, it can be used as a lining to waterproof any strong box. To lessen the chances of the plastic being punctured, rough containers first should be lined with fabric.

If shelter is to be taken in or near a building, water trapped in hot water heaters and toilet flush tanks or stored in tubs might be available after an attack.

SIPHONING

Pouring water out of a heavy water-storage bag is inconvenient and often results in spillage. Dipping it out can result in contamination. If a tube or piece of flexible garden hose is available, siphoning (see Fig. 8.6) is the best way. A field-tested method is described below. To prevent the suction end of the tube from being obstructed by contact with the plastic liner of the bag, tape or tie a wire "protector" to the end, as pictured later in this section.

To start siphoning, suck on the tube until water reaches your mouth. Next fold over the tube near its end, to keep the tube full. Lower its closed end until it is near its position shown in Fig. 8.6. Then release your hold on the tube, to start siphoning.

To cut off the water, fold over the tube and secure it shut with a rubber band or string.

Water can be siphoned from a covered water storage pit into a belowground shelter so that the siphon will deliver running water for weeks, if necessary. The Utah family mentioned earlier siphoned all they needed of the 120 gallons of water stored in a nearby lined pit. A field-tested method of siphoning follows:

ORNL-DWG 78-14676

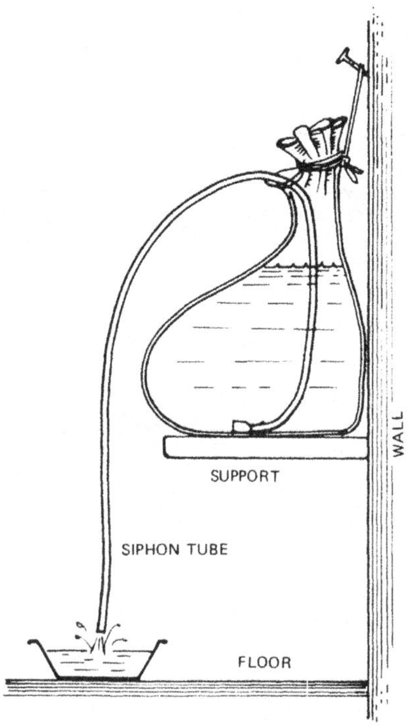

Fig. 8.6. Using a tube to siphon water from a fabric bag lined with a larger plastic bag.

1. Dig the water storage pit far enough away from the shelter so that the covering mounds will not interfere with drainage ditches.

2. Use a flexible tube or hose which is no more than 25 feet long. For a single family, a flexible rubber tube with an inside diameter of 1/4 inch (such as surgical tubing) would be best. A flexible 1/2-inch hose of the type used with mobile homes and boats serves well. As indicated by Fig. 8.7, the tube should be long enough to extend from the bottom of the water pit to within about a foot of the shelter floor.

3. Make sure that the end in the water pit will not press against plastic and block the flow of water. This can be avoided by (1) making and attaching a wire "protector" to the end of the tube, as shown in Fig. 8.8, or (2) taping or tying the end to a rock or other object, to keep the end in the desired position.

4. Protect the tube by placing it in a trench about 4 inches deep. This small trench is best dug before roofing either the storage pit or the shelter. Be sure a roof pole or board does not crush the tube. Cover the tube with earth and tie it so that the end in

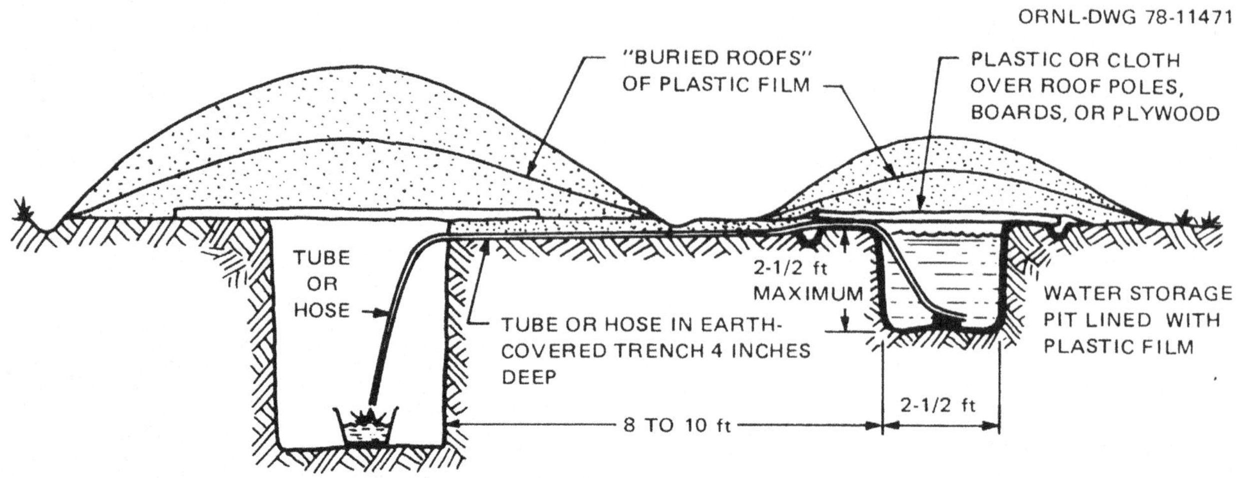

Fig. 8.7. Water siphoned into a belowground shelter.

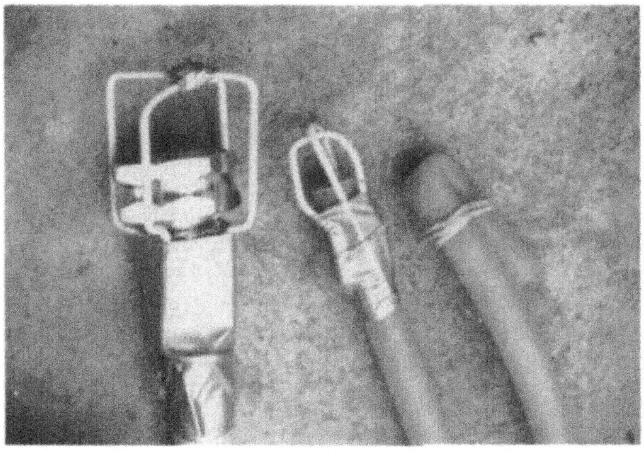

Fig. 8.8. Two wire "protectors," each made of two pieces of coathanger wire taped to a ½-inch flexible hose and a rubber tube. Shown on the right is a tube closed with a rubber band to stop a siphoned flow of water.

the storage pit cannot be accidentally pulled out of position.

5. To start the flow of water into the shelter, hold the free end of the tube at about the height of the surface of the water in the storage pit, while pulling gently on the tube so that the part in the shelter is practically straight. Exhale as much breath as you can, then place the end of the tube in your mouth, and suck hard and long. (The longer the tube or hose and the larger its diameter, the more times you will have to suck to start the flow of water.)

6. Without taking the tube out of your mouth, shut it off airtight by bending it double near the end.

7. Exhale, straighten the tube, and suck again, repeating until you feel a good flow of water into your mouth while still sucking. Shut off the flow by bending the tube double before taking it out of your mouth.

8. Quickly lower the end of the tube (which is now full of water) and place the closed end in a container on the shelter floor. Finally, open the end to start the siphoned flow.

9. When you have siphoned enough water, stop the flow by bending the tube double. Keep it closed in the doubled-over, air-tight position with a strong rubber band or string, as shown in Fig. 8.8. To prevent loss of water by accidental siphoning, suspend the end of the tube a couple of inches higher than the surface of the water in the storage pit outside and close to where the tube comes into the shelter. (Despite precautions, air may accumulate in the highest part of the tube, blocking a siphoned flow and making it necessary to re-start the siphoning by repeating the sucking.)

DISINFECTING WATER

Water-borne diseases probably would kill more survivors of a nuclear attack than would fallout-contaminated water. Before an attack, if water from a municipal source is stored in expedient containers that could be unclean, it should be disinfected. For long storage, it is best to disinfect all water, since even a few organisms may multiply rapidly and give stored water a bad taste or odor. Properly disinfected water remains safe for many years if stored in thick plastic or glass containers sealed airtight. For multi-year storage do not use thin plastic containers, such as milk jugs, which in time often develop leaks.

Any household bleach solution, such as Clorox, that contains sodium hypochlorite as its only active ingredient may be used as a source of chlorine for disinfecting. The amount of sodium hypochlorite, usually 5.25%, is printed on the label. (In recent years, perhaps as a precaution against drinking undiluted chlorine bleach solution, some household bleach containers show a warning such as "Not For Personal Use." This warning can be safely disregarded if the label states that the bleach contains only sodium hypochlorite as its active ingredient, and if only the small quantities specified in these and other instructions are used to disinfect water.) Add 1 scant teaspoonful to each 10 gallons of clear water, and stir. Add 2 scant teaspoonfuls if the water is muddy or colored. Wait at least 30 minutes before drinking, to allow enough time for the chlorine to kill all the microorganisms.[24] Properly disinfected water should have a slight chlorine odor.

To disinfect small quantities of water, put 2 drops of household bleach containing 5.25% sodium hypochlorite in each quart of clear water. Use 4 drops if the water is muddy or colored.[24] If a dropper is not available, use a spoon and a square-ended strip of paper or thin cloth about 1/4 inch wide by 2 inches long. Put the strip in the spoon with an end hanging down about 1/2 inch beyond the end of the spoon. Then when bleach is placed in the spoon and the spoon is carefully tipped, drops the size of those from a medicine dropper will drip off the end of the strip.

As a second choice, 2% tincture of iodine can be used. Add 5 drops to each quart of clear water, and let stand 30 minutes.[24] If the water is cloudy, add 10 drops to each quart. Commercial water purification tablets should be used as directed.

If neither safe water nor chemicals for disinfecting it are available during a crisis, store plenty of the best water at hand—even muddy river water. Most mud settles to the bottom in a few days; even in a crowded shelter ways often could be found to boil water. Bringing water to a boil for one minute kills all types of disease-causing bacteria.[24] Boiling for 10 to 20 minutes is required to kill some rarer infective organisms.

SOURCES OF WATER IN FALLOUT AREAS

Survivors of a nuclear attack should realize that neither fallout particles nor dissolved radioactive elements or compounds can be removed from water by chemical disinfection or boiling. Therefore, water should be obtained from the least radioactive sources available. Before a supply of stored drinking water has been exhausted, other sources should be located. The main water sources are given below, with the safest source listed first and the other sources listed in decreasing order of safety.

1. Water from deep wells and from water tanks and covered reservoirs into which no fallout particles or fallout-contaminated water has been introduced. (Caution: Although most spring water would be safe, some spring water is surface water that has flowed into and through underground channels without having been filtered.)

2. Water from covered seepage pits or shallow, hand-dug wells. This water is usually safe IF fallout or fallout-contaminated surface water has been prevented from entering by the use of waterproof coverings and by waterproofing the surrounding ground to keep water from running down outside the well casing. Figure 8.9 is taken from a Chinese civil defense manual.[21] It shows a well dug to obtain safe water from a fallout-contaminated source. If the earth is not sandy, gravelly, or too porous, filtration through earth is very effective.

3. Contaminated water from deep lakes. Water from a deep lake would be much less contaminated by dissolved radioactive material and fallout particles than water from a shallow pond would be, if both had the same amount of fallout per square foot of surface area deposited in them. Furthermore, fallout particles settle to the bottom more rapidly in deep lakes than in shallow ponds, which are agitated more by wind.

4. Contaminated water from shallow ponds and other shallow, still water.

5. Contaminated water from streams, which would be especially dangerous if the stream is muddy from the first heavy rains after fallout is deposited.

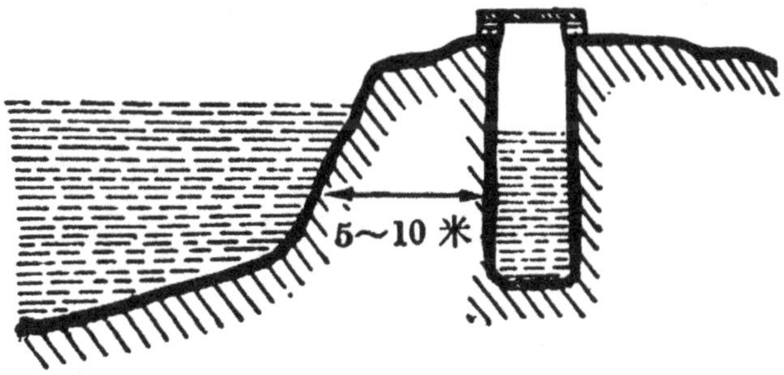

Fig. 8.9. A water-filtering well. This Chinese drawing specifies that this well should be dug 5 to 10 meters (roughly 5 to 10 yards) from a pond or stream.

The first runoff will contain most of the radioactive material that can be dissolved from fallout particles deposited on the drainage area.[25] Runoff after the first few heavy rains following the deposit of fallout is not likely to contain much dissolved radioactive material, or fallout.

6. Water collected from fallout-contaminated roofs. This would contain more fallout particles than would the runoff from the ground.

7. Water obtained by melting snow that has fallen through air containing fallout particles, or from snow lying on the ground onto which fallout has fallen. Avoid using such water for drinking or cooking, if possible.

WATER FROM WELLS

The wells of farms and rural homes would be the best sources of water for millions of survivors. Following a massive nuclear attack, the electric pumps and the pipes in wells usually would be useless. Electric power in most areas would be eliminated by the effects of electromagnetic pulse (EMP) from high-altitude bursts and by the effects of blast and fire on power stations, transformers, and transmission lines. However, enough people would know how to remove these pipes and pumps from wells so that bail-cans could be used to reach water and bring up enough for drinking and basic hygiene.

How to make a simple bail-can is illustrated in Fig. 8.10. An ordinary large fruit-juice can will serve, if its diameter is at least 1 inch smaller than the diameter of the well-casing pipe. A hole about 1 inch in diameter should be cut in the center of the can's bottom. The hole should be cut from the inside of the can: this keeps the inside of the bottom smooth, so it will serve as a smooth seat for a practically watertight valve. To cut the hole, stand the can on a flat wood surface and press down repeatedly with the point of a sheath knife, a butcher knife, or a sharpened screwdriver.

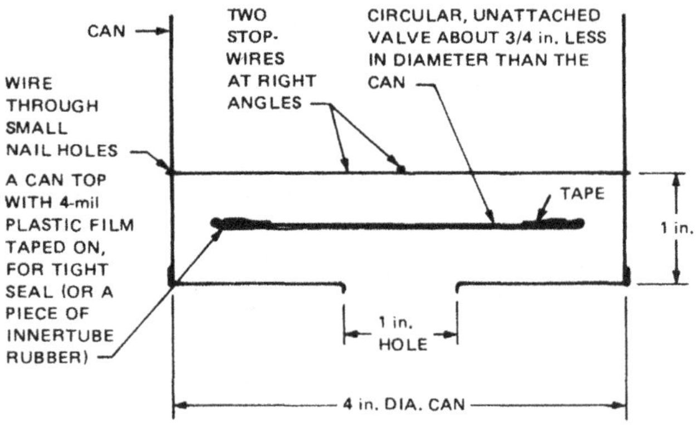

Fig. 8.10. Lower part of an expedient bail-can. The unattached, "caged" valve can be made of a material that does not have the springiness of soft rubber.

The best material for the circular, unattached valve shown in Fig. 8.10 is soft rubber, smooth and thin, such as inner-tube rubber. Alternately, the lid of a can about $^{3}/_{4}$ inch smaller in diameter than the bail-can may be used, with several thicknesses of plastic film taped to its smooth lower side. Plastic film about 4 mils thick is best. The bail (handle) of a bail-can should be made of wire, with a loop at the top to which a rope or strong cord should be attached.

Filling-time can be reduced by taping half-a-pound of rocks or metal to the bottom of the bail-can.

REMOVING FALLOUT PARTICLES AND DISSOLVED RADIOACTIVE MATERIAL FROM WATER

The dangers from drinking fallout-contaminated water could be greatly lessened by using expedient settling and filtration methods to remove fallout particles and most of the dissolved radioactive material. Fortunately, in areas of heavy fallout, less than 2% of the radioactivity of the fallout particles contained in the water would become dissolved in water.[25] If nearly all the radioactive fallout particles could be removed by filtering or settling methods, few casualties would be likely to result from drinking and cooking with most fallout-contaminated water.

- **Filtering**

Filtering through earth removes essentially all of the fallout particles and more of the dissolved radioactive material than does boiling-water distillation, a generally impractical purification method that does not eliminate dangerous radioactive iodines. Earth filters are also more effective in removing radioactive iodines than are ordinary ion-exchange water softeners or charcoal filters. In areas of heavy fallout, about 99% of the radioactivity in water could be removed by filtering it through ordinary earth. To make the simple, effective filter shown in Fig. 8.11, the only materials needed are those found in and

ORNL DWG 77-18431

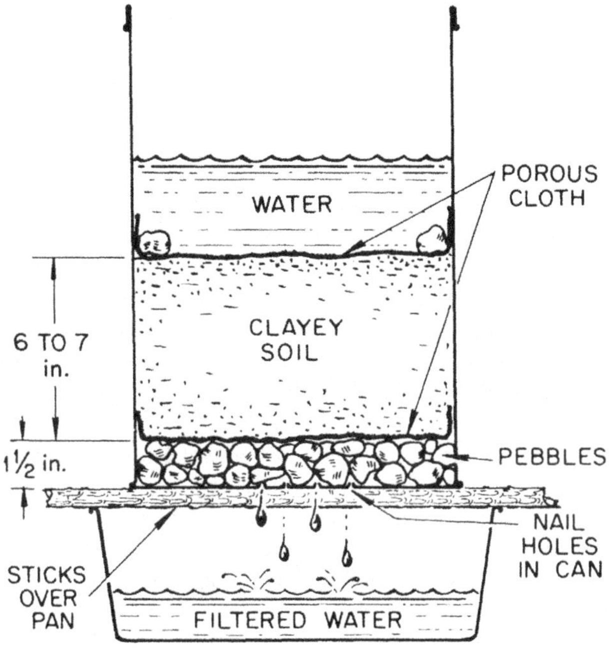

EXPEDIENT FILTRATION

Fig. 8.11. Expedient filter to remove radioactivity from water.

around the home. This expedient filter can be built easily by proceeding as follows:

1. Perforate the bottom of a 5-gallon can, a large bucket, a watertight wastebasket, or a similar container with about a dozen nail holes. Punch the holes from the bottom upward, staying within about 2 inches of the center.

2. Place a layer about 1½ inches thick of washed pebbles or small stones on the bottom of the can. If pebbles are not available, twisted coat-hanger wires or small sticks can be used.

3. Cover the pebbles with one thickness of terrycloth towel, burlap sackcloth, or other quite porous cloth. Cut the cloth in a roughly circular shape about 3 inches larger than the diameter of the can.

4. Take soil containing some clay—almost any soil will do—from at least 4 inches below the surface of the ground. (Nearly all fallout particles remain near the surface except after deposition on sand or gravel.)

5. Pulverize the soil, then gently press it in layers over the cloth that covers the pebbles, so that the cloth is held snugly against the sides of the can. Do not use pure clay (not porous enough) or sand (too porous). The soil in the can should be 6 to 7 inches thick.

6. Completely cover the surface of the soil layer with one thickness of fabric as porous as a bath towel. This is to keep the soil from being eroded as water is poured into the filtering can. The cloth also will remove some of the particles from the water. A dozen small stones placed on the cloth near its edges will secure it adequately.

7. Support the filter can on rods or sticks placed across the top of a container that is larger in diameter than the filter can. (A dishpan will do.)

The contaminated water should be poured into the filter can, preferably after allowing it to settle as described below. The filtered water should be disinfected by one of the previously described methods.

If the 6 or 7 inches of filtering soil is a sandy clay loam, the filter initially will deliver about 6 quarts of clear water per hour. (If the filtration rate is faster than about 1 quart in 10 minutes, remove the upper fabric and recompress the soil.) After several hours, the rate will be reduced to about 2 quarts per hour.

When the filtering rate becomes too slow, it can be increased by removing and rinsing the surface fabric, removing about ½ inch of soil, and then replacing the fabric. The life of a filter is extended and its efficiency increased if muddy water is first allowed to settle for several hours in a separate container, as described below. After about 50 quarts have been filtered, rebuild the filter by replacing the used soil with fresh soil.

- **Settling**

Settling is one of the easiest methods to remove most fallout particles from water. Furthermore, if the water to be used is muddy or murky, settling it before filtering will extend the life of the filter. The procedure is as follows:

1. Fill a bucket or other deep container three-quarters full of the contaminated water.

2. Dig pulverized clay or clayey soil from a depth of four or more inches below ground surface, and stir it into the water. Use about a 1-inch depth of

Remember that Water Filtration Method

THE GRAVITY FILTER, THE SOIL FILTER.
Rain falls on the earth and the water goes through the ground and into the water table (from 3 feet to 3000 feet below the surface) and that is where people will sink a water well to get well water. The water gets 'cleaned' of particles and stuff as it goes through the earth and into the water table. This is the same principle but only done in about a foot or two instead of 10s, 100s, or 1000s of feet.

Whereas the clay soil is best for removing particles that may be slightly radioactive this example is not just for nuclear emergencies but almost any disaster where you have to clean up the water before you treat it (do not forget to treat it) and drink it.

Clay is used here but if you look on youtube and other online educational places you'll see people doing this to 'clean up the water with sand and other materials. Many swimming pools have a 'sand filter' like this to clean stuff out of the pool before it goes to the pump.

Personally, I put a cut piece of a thick bath towel on the bottom of the bucket over the hole but under the pebbles, and then I put the layers of clay and or sand (or both) and or dirt in the bucket and then I put another piece of a bath towel on the top. Then I pour in the water and let it "percolate" down through the earth in the bucket and such. It's NOT fast. But it will get all of the particles floating around in the water out of the water and trapped in the bucket. This does NOT (repeat NOT) remove harmful bacteria and viruses in the water.

This removes rocks, twigs, grass, ants, floating and suspended particles in 'cloudy' water, and generally, it comes out perfectly clear (but NOT disinfected) out the bottom.

Please follow Cresson's instructions in the water section (Page 70 DISINFECTING WATER) in this book on the treatment of the water for infectious microbes by heating (or boiling) and with bleach and other methods and the amount of time for each method before you can assume the water is safe to drink.

On page 70 Cresson states that the water treated with bleach should still have a slight beach odor to it. This is unappealing to many people. You can run this water through an activated carbon filter to remove the chlorine.

A "Britta Brand Pitcher" or a "Zero Water Pitcher" or "Britta 26 oz water bottle with filter" which has an activated carbon filter that goes down the center. These will remove bad 'tastes' from the water like chlorine or iodine. Note: People with 'shellfish allergies may have an adverse reaction to iodine-based water treatment and should consult with a doctor before a disaster. Note: Chlorine Bleach (sodium hypochlorite) does NOT contain iodine.

STOP THE STUPIDITY WITH SOMETHTING THAT HAS A NAME.
Why do people in professional marketing give products new and unique names? Because it no longer becomes what it is but this special thing with a special name. Then, its no longer what it really is but "blah blah" cures cancer, "blah blah" helps me lose weight, "blah blah" can change the orbit of the moon if I hold it up at the right angle for 5 minutes but only when I can face due north. It takes on a life and a world of its own. This can be used to demonize and destroy something as well. Look at 5G. It's no longer a multiband spread-spectrum method of frequency modulation .... it's "5G". It 'causes this' or 'causes that' or 'blah blah.' when in reality it's the same as 4G LTE but on different, yet close, frequencies and some new ones. It has become the Boogy Man.

In preparedness, I'll ask someone what they have for water purification and they'll say, "Oh, I'm fine. I got a BLAH BLAH. I'm all good, I'm perfect, I invested in one." In this case "BLAH BLAH" is an expensive stainless steel water filtration system, mostly based on activated carbon, that has the same name as a university in California. People think that because they have this "Blah Blah" they are fine.

It does a great job of making your tap water into 'drinking bottle water' tasting good. It does that.... but so will most good quality activated carbon filters. This blah blah has taken on a life of its own. It removes this, it removes that. It's safe to drink when it goes through the blah blah and really it's not. There are 7 main methods of water 'treatment' for disinfection that Jim Phillips teaches and most good ones involve at least 2 of them. Blah blah does not. It does one of these 7 main methods really good, carbon filtration. You really need the filter as shown in this book for removing radioactive particles that are not dissolved in the water. You then need to chemically treat it as Cresson describes on page 70 and then, and then, you can run it through your blah blah filter to make it taste better. Your expensive blah blah filter is NOT proven to remove all bacteria, all viruses, and all things biological that might harm you. It might remove some of the dominant ones but not all of the ones you'll find in ponds, puddles, lakes, or ditch water.

You're best off filtering (bucket filter), treating with chemicals, and then filtering again (carbon filter) to get the chemical taste out. That is your best quality and probably the safest water to drink. Cresson has instructions on page 70 on just treating cloudy water with bleach and then waiting and drinking it with no filtration.

Like Cresson says, more people will die from lack of water, or people getting sick from water with regular wild biological contamination (bacteria) than will die from drinking any radiological material in the water. Cresson saw a lot of Chinese civilians die from water-borne illness when they were running from the invading Japanese Army in China when he was there in World War II. He talked to me about that experience in his life. I would not say that it haunted him, but it stuck with him and the need to help the average civilian in times of war. It made him determined to protect American Civilians.

dry clay or dry clayey soil for every 4-inch depth of water. Stir until practically all the clay particles are suspended in the water.

3. Let the clay settle for at least 6 hours. The settling clay particles will carry most of the suspended fallout particles to the bottom and cover them.

4. Carefully dip out or siphon the clear water, and disinfect it.

- **Settling and Filtering**

Although dissolved radioactive material usually is only a minor danger in fallout-contaminated water, it is safest to filter even the clear water produced by settling, if an earth filter is available. Finally—as always—the water should be disinfected.

POST-FALLOUT REPLENISHMENT OF STORED WATER

When fallout decays enough to permit shelter occupants to go out of their shelters for short periods, they should try to replenish their stored water. An enemy may make scattered nuclear strikes for weeks after an initial massive attack. Some survivors may be forced back into their shelters by the resultant fallout. Therefore, all available water containers should be used to store the least contaminated water within reach. Even without filtering, water collected and stored shortly after the occurrence of fallout will become increasingly safer with time, due particularly to the rapid decay of radioactive iodines. These would be the most dangerous contaminants of water during the first few weeks after an attack.

Chapter 9
Food

MINIMUM NEEDS

The average American is accustomed to eating regularly and abundantly. He may not realize that for most people food would not be essential for survival during the first two or three weeks following a nuclear attack. Exceptions would be infants, small children, and the aged and sick, some of whom might die within a week without proper nourishment. Other things are more important for short-term survival: adequate shelter against the dangers from blast and fallout, an adequate supply of air, and enough water.

The average American also may not realize that small daily amounts of a few unprocessed staple foods would enable him to survive for many months, or even for years. A healthy person—if he is determined to live and if he learns how to prepare and use whole-grain wheat or corn—can maintain his health for several months. If beans are also available and are substituted for some of the grain, the ration would be improved and could maintain health for many months.

The nutritional information given in this chapter is taken from a July, 1979 publication, *Maintaining Nutritional Adequacy During a Prolonged Food Crisis.*[26] This book brings together from worldwide sources the nutritional facts needed to help unprepared people use unaccustomed foods advantageously during the prolonged crisis that would follow a heavy nuclear attack. The practical know-how which will be given in this chapter regarding the expedient processing and cooking of basic grains and beans is based on old ways which are mostly unknown to modern Americans. These methods have been improved and field-tested by civil defense researchers at Oak Ridge National Laboratory.

LOSS OF HIGH-PROTEIN ANIMAL FOODS

A massive nuclear attack would eliminate the luxurious, complicated American system of food production, processing, and distribution. Extensive, heavy fallout and the inability of farmers to feed their animals would kill most of the cattle, hogs, and chickens that are the basis of our high-protein diet. The livestock most likely to survive despite their owners' inability to care for them would be cattle on pasture. However, these grazing animals would swallow large numbers of fallout particles along with grass, and many would drink contaminated water. Their digestive tracts would suffer severe radiation damage.[27] Also, they would suffer radiation burns from fallout particles. Thus in an outdoor area where the total dose from gamma radiation emitted within a few days from fallout particles on the ground might be only 150 R, most grazing animals probably would be killed by the combined effects of external gamma-ray radiation, beta burns, and internal radiation.[27]

PRECAUTIONS WHEN EATING MEAT

In areas where the fallout would not be enough to sicken animals, their meat would be safe food. In fallout areas, however, animals that have eaten or drunk fallout-contaminated food or water will have concentrated radioactive atoms and molecules in their internal organs. The thyroid gland, kidneys, and liver especially should not be eaten.

If an animal appears to be sick, it should not be eaten. The animal might be suffering from a sickening or fatal radiation dose and might have developed a bacterial infection as a result of this dose. Meat contaminated with the toxins produced by some kinds of bacteria could cause severe illness or death if eaten, even if thoroughly cooked.

Under crisis conditions, all meat should be cooked until it is extremely well done—cooked long past the time when it loses the last of its pink color. To be sure that the center of each piece of meat is raised to boiling temperature, the meat should be cut into pieces that are less than ½-inch thick before cooking. This precaution also reduces cooking time and saves fuel.

SURVIVAL OF BREEDING STOCK

Extensive areas of the United States would not receive fallout heavy enough to kill grazing animals. The millions of surviving animals would provide some food and the fertile breeding stock needed for national recovery. The loss of fertility caused by severe radiation doses is rarely permanent. Extensive experiments with animals have shown that the offspring of severely irradiated animals are healthy and fertile.[27]

LIVING ON BASIC PLANT FOODS

Even if almost all food-producing animals were lost, most surviving Americans should be able to live on the foods that enable most of the world's population to live and multiply: grains, beans, and vegetables. And because of the remarkable productivity of American agriculture, there usually would be enough grain and beans in storage to supply surviving Americans with sufficient food for at least a year following a heavy nuclear attack.[28] The problem would be to get the unprocessed foods, which are stored in food-producing regions, to the majority of survivors who would be outside these regions.

Surprisingly little transportation would be needed to carry adequate quantities of these unprocessed foods to survivors in famine areas. A single large trailer truck can haul 40,000 pounds of wheat—enough to keep 40,000 people from feeling hunger pains for a day. More than enough such trucks and the fuel needed to carry basic foods to food-short areas would survive a massive nuclear attack.[28] It is likely that reasonably strong American leadership and morale would prevail so that, after the first few weeks, millions of the survivors in starving areas should receive basic unprocessed foods.

Eating food produced in the years after a large attack would cause an increase in the cancer rate, due primarily to its content of radioactive strontium and cesium from fallout-contaminated soil. Over the first 30 years following an attack, this increase would be a small fraction of the number of additional cancer deaths that would result from external radiation.[29] Cancer deaths would be one of the tragic, delayed costs of a nuclear war, but all together would not be numerous enough to endanger the long-term survival of the population.

LIVE OFF THE LAND?

Very few survivors of a heavy attack would be in areas where they could live off the land like primitive hunters and gatherers. In extensive areas where fallout would not be heavy enough to kill human beings, wild creatures would die from the combined effects of external gamma radiation, swallowed fallout particles, and beta burns on their bodies. Survival plans should not include dependence on hunting, fishing, or gathering wild plants.

FOOD FOR SHELTER OCCUPANTS

Most people would need very little food to live several weeks; however, the time when survivors of blast and fallout would leave their shelters would mark the beginning of a much longer period of privation and hard manual labor. Therefore, to maintain physical strength and morale, persons in shelters ideally should have enough healthful food to provide well-balanced, adequate meals for many weeks.

In most American homes there are only enough ready-to-eat, concentrated foods to last a few days. Obviously, it would be an important survival advantage to keep on hand a two-week supply of easily transportable foods. In any case, occupants of shelters would be uncertain about when they could get more food and would have to make hard decisions about how much to eat each day. (Those persons who have a fallout meter, such as the homemade instrument described in Chapter 10, could estimate when and for how long they could emerge from shelter to find food. As a result, these persons could ration their limited foods more effectively.)

During the first few weeks of a food crisis, lack of vitamins and other essentials of a well-balanced diet would not be of primary importance to previously well-nourished people. Healthful foods with enough calories to provide adequate energy would meet short-term needs. If water is in short supply, high-protein foods such as meat are best eaten only in moderation, since a person eating high-protein foods requires more water than is needed when consuming an equal number of calories from foods high in carbohydrates.

EXPEDIENT PROCESSING OF GRAINS AND SOYBEANS

Whole-kernel grains or soybeans cannot be eaten in sufficient quantities to maintain vigor and health if merely boiled or parched. A little boiled whole-kernel wheat is a pleasantly chewy breakfast cereal, but experimenters at Oak Ridge got sore tongues and very loose bowels when they tried to eat enough boiled whole-kernel wheat to supply even half of their daily energy needs. Some pioneers, however, ate large quantities of whole-kernel wheat without harmful results after boiling and simmering it for many hours. Even the most primitive peoples who subsist primarily on grains grind or pound them into a meal or paste before cooking. (Rice is the only important exception.) Few Americans know how to process whole-kernel grains and soybeans (our largest food reserves) into meal. This ignorance could be fatal to survivors of a nuclear attack.

Making an expedient metate, the hollowed-out grinding stone of Mexican Indians, proved impractical under simulated post-attack conditions. Pounding grain into meal with a rock or a capped, solid-ended piece of pipe is extremely slow work. The best expedient means developed and field-tested for pounding grain or beans into meal and flour is an improvised 3-pipe grain mill. Instructions for making and using this effective grain-pounding device follow.

Improvised Grain Mill

The grain mill described can efficiently pound whole-grain wheat, corn, etc., into meal and flour—thereby greatly improving digestibility and avoiding the diarrhea and sore mouths that would result from eating large quantities of unground grain.

TO BUILD:

(1) Cut 3 lengths of pipe, each 30 inches long; $^3/_4$-inch-diameter steel pipe (such as ordinary water pipe) is best.

(2) Cut the working ends of the pipe off squarely. Remove all roughness, leaving the full-wall thickness. Each working end should have the full diameter of the pipe.

(3) In preparation for binding the three pieces of pipe together into a firm bundle, encircle each piece of pipe with cushioning, slip-preventing tape, string or cloth—in the locations illustrated.

(4) Tape or otherwise bind the 3 pipes into a secure bundle so that their working ends are as even as possible and are in the same plane—resting evenly on a flat surface.

(5) Cut the top smoothly out of a large can. A 4-inch-diameter, 7-inch-high fruit-juice can is ideal. If you do not have a can, improvise something to keep grain together while pounding it.

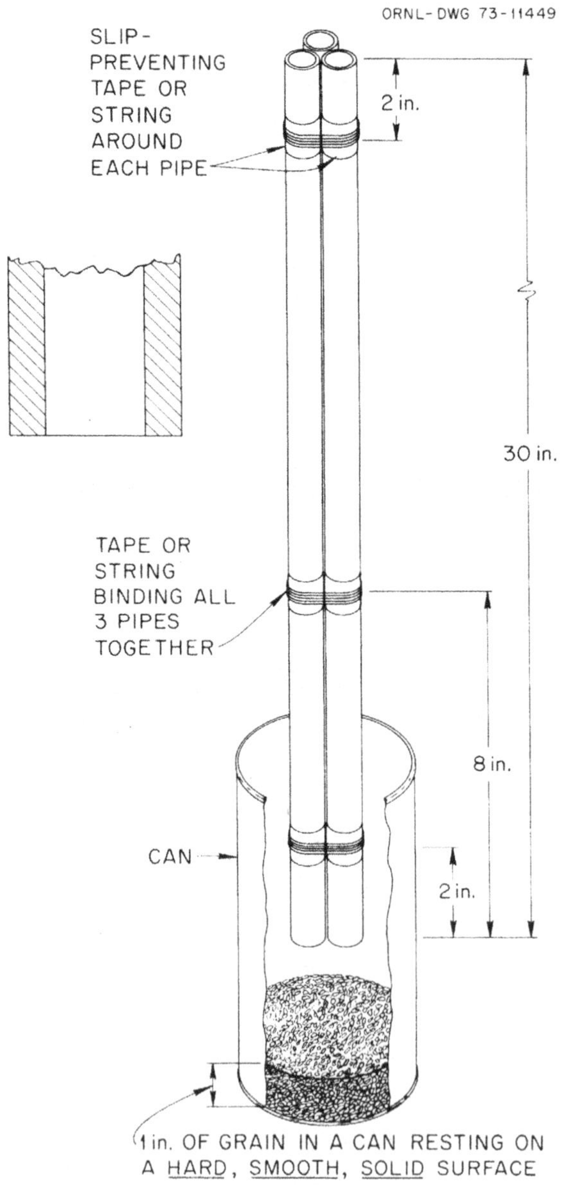

TO MAKE MEAL AND FLOUR:

(1) Put clean, dry grain ONE INCH DEEP in the can.

(2) To prevent blistering your hands, wear gloves, or wrap cloth around the upper part of the bundle of pipes.

(3) Place the can (or open-ended cylinder) on a *hard, smooth, solid* surface, such as concrete.

(4) To pound the grain, sit with the can held between your feet. Move the bundle of pipes straight up and down about 3 inches, with a rapid stroke.

(5) If the can is 4 inches in diameter, in 4 minutes you should be able to pound $^1/_2$ lb (one cup) of whole-kernel wheat into $^1/_5$ lb of fine meal and flour, and $^3/_{10}$ lb of coarse meal and fine-cracked wheat.

(6) To separate the pounded grain into fine meal, flour, coarse meal, and fine-cracked wheat, use a sieve made of window screen.

(7) To separate flour for feeding small children, place some pounded grain in an 18 × 18-inch piece of fine nylon net, gather the edges of the net together so as to hold the grain, and shake this bag-like container.

(8) To make flour fine enough for babies, pound fine meal and coarse flour still finer, and sieve it through a piece of cheesecloth or similar material.

As soon as fallout decay permits travel, the grain-grinding machines on tens of thousands of hog and cattle farms should be used for milling grain for survivors. It is vitally important to national recovery and individual survival to get back as soon as possible to labor-saving, mechanized ways of doing essential work.

In an ORNL experiment, a farmer used a John Deere Grinder-Mixer powered by a 100-hp tractor to grind large samples of wheat and barley. When it is used to grind rather coarse meal for hogs, this machine is rated at 12 tons per hour. Set to grind a finer meal-flour mixture for human consumption, it ground both hard wheat and feed barley at a rate of about 9 tons per hour. This is 2400 times as fast as using muscle power to operate even the best expedient grain mill. With its finest screen installed, this large machine can produce about 3 tons of whole wheat flour per hour.

Unlike wheat and corn, the kernels of barley, grain sorghums, and oats have rough, fibrous hulls that must be removed from the digestible parts to produce an acceptable food. Moistening the grain will toughen such hulls and make them easier to remove. If the grain is promptly pounded or ground into meal, the toughened hulls will break into larger pieces than will the hulls of undampened grain. A small amount of water, weighing about 2% of the weight of the grain, should be used to dampen the grain. For 3 pounds of grain (about 6 cups), sprinkle with about one ounce (28 grams, or about 2 tablespoons) of water, while stirring constantly to moisten all the kernels. After about 5 minutes of stirring, the grain will appear dry. The small amount of water will have dampened and toughened the hulls, but the edible parts inside will have remained dry. Larger pieces of hull are easier to remove after grinding than smaller pieces.

One way to remove ground-up hulls from meal is by flotation. Put some of the meal-hulls mixture about 1 inch deep in a pan or pot, cover the mixture with water, and stir. Skim off the floating hulls, then pour off the water and more hulls. Sunken pieces of hulls that settle on top of the heavier meal can be removed with one's fingers as the last of the water is poured off. To produce a barley meal good for very small children, the small pieces of hulls must again be separated by flotation.

Figure 9.1 illustrates sieving fine, dry barley-meal and the smaller pieces of hulls from the coarser

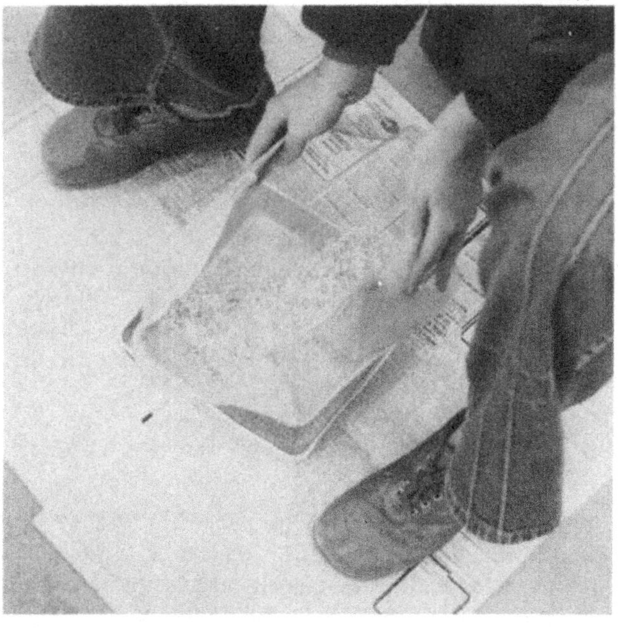

Fig. 9.1. Sieving ground barley through a window-screen sieve.

meal and the larger pieces. The sieve was made of a piece of window screen that measured 20 × 20 inches before its sides were folded up and wired to form an open-topped box.

To lessen their laxative effects, all grains should be ground as finely as possible, and most of the hulls should be removed. Grains also will be digested more easily if they are finely ground. The occupants of crowded shelters should be especially careful to avoid foods that cause diarrhea.

COOKING WITH MINIMUM FUEL

In areas of heavy fallout, people would have to remain continuously in crowded shelters for many days. Then they would have to stay in the shelters most of each 24 hours for weeks. Most shelter occupants soon would consume all of their ready-to-eat foods; therefore, they should have portable, efficient cook stoves. A cook stove is important for another reason: to help maintain morale. Even in warm weather, people need some hot food and drink for the comforting effect and to promote a sense of well-being. This is particularly true when people are under stress. The Bucket Stove pictured on the following pages (Figs. 9.2 and 9.3) was the most satisfactory of several models of expedient stoves developed at Oak Ridge and later field-tested.

• Bucket Stove

If operated properly, this stove burns only about $^1/_2$ pound of dry wood or newspaper to heat 3 quarts of water from 60° F to boiling.

Materials required for the stove:

* A metal bucket or can, 12- to 16-quart sizes preferred. The illustrations show a 14-quart bucket and a 6-quart pot.

* Nine all-metal coat hangers for the parts made of wire. (To secure the separate parts of the movable coat-hanger wire grate, 2 feet of finer wire is helpful.)

* A 6 × 10-inch piece of a large fruit-juice can, for a damper.

Construction:

With a chisel (or a sharpened screw driver) and a hammer, cut a $4^1/_2 \times 4^1/_2$-inch hole in the side of the bucket about $1^1/_2$ inches above its bottom. To avoid denting the side of the bucket when chiseling out the hole, place the bucket over the end of a log or similar solid object.

To make the damper, cut a 6-inch-wide by 10-inch-high piece out of a large fruit-juice can or from similar light metal. Then make the two coat-hanger-wire springs illustrated, and attach them to the piece of metal by bending and hammering the outer 1 inch of the two 6-inch-long sides over and around the two spring wires. This damper can be slid up and down, to open and close the hole in the bucket. The springs hold it in any desired position. (If materials for making this damper are not available, the air supply can be regulated fairly well by placing a brick, rock, or piece of metal so that it will block off part of the hole in the side of the bucket.)

To make a support for the pot, punch 4 holes in the sides of the bucket, equally spaced around it and about $3^1/_2$ inches below the bucket's top. Then run a coat-hanger wire through each of the two pairs of holes on opposite sides of the bucket. Bend these two wires over the top of the bucket, as illustrated, so that their four ends form free-ended springs to hold the cooking pot centered in the bucket. Pressure on the pot from these four free-ended, sliding springs does not hinder putting it into the stove or taking it out.

Bend and twist 4 or 5 coat hangers to make the movable grate, best made with the approximate dimensions given in Fig. 9.2.

For adjusting the burning pieces of fuel on the grate, make a pair of 12-inch-long tongs of coat-hanger wire, as illustrated by Fig. 9.3.

To lessen heat losses through the sides and bottom of the bucket, cover the bottom with about 1 inch of dry sand or earth. Then line part of the inside and bottom with two thicknesses of heavy-duty aluminum foil, if available.

To make it easier to place the pot in the stove or take it out without spilling its contents, replace the original bucket handle with a longer piece of strong wire.

Operation:

The Bucket Stove owes its efficiency to: (1) the adjustable air supply that flows up through the burning fuel, (2) the movable grate that lets the operator keep the maximum amount of flame in contact with the bottom of the cooking pot, and (3) the space between the sides of the pot and the inside of the bucket that keeps the rising hot gases in close contact with the sides of the pot.

In a shelter, a Bucket Stove should be placed as near as practical to an air exhaust opening before a fire is started in it.

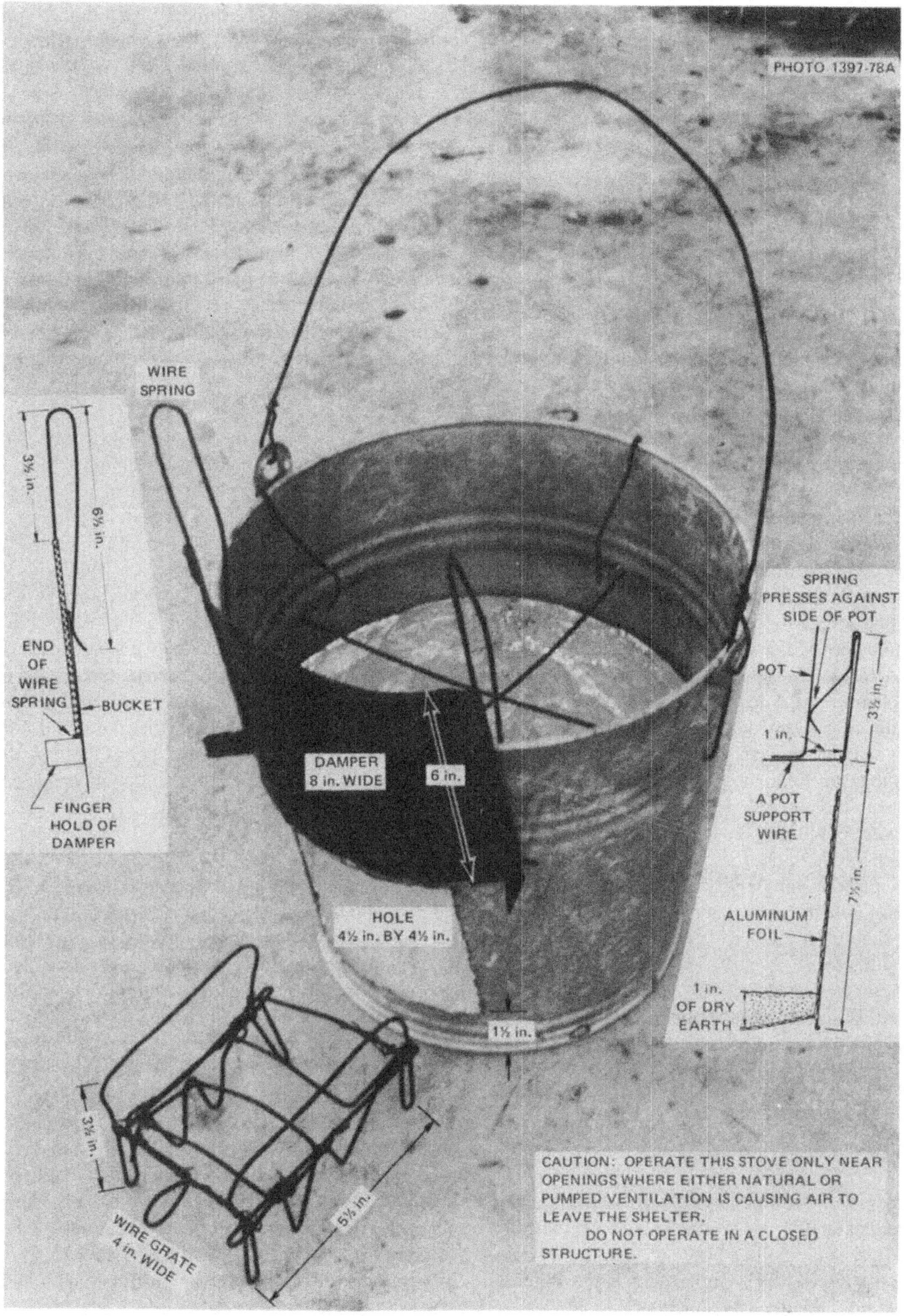

Fig. 9.2. Bucket-stove with adjustable damper and movable wire grate.

What is a Newspaper ?

WHAT WAS WIDELY AVAILABLE IS NOT NOW

The improvised bucket stove on the following page has three things that have almost or completely disappeared from modern 2022 culture. One is the pieces of newspaper, which used to be very abundant everywhere in a home and a neighborhood, are basically no longer in existence let alone in bountiful existence. As a child. I used to pick up newspapers in the early seventies and take them back for recycling for a penny a pound from all my neighbors. The Wall Street Journal when I had delivered it to my house in the mid-1990s was one thick and heavy newspaper. Now it's smaller than many magazines. If you can even find a magazine or have it delivered. Magazines are also not purchased and or delivered to people's house homes like they used to be in 1987.

So the idea of using a twisted piece of newspaper as a fuel that you continue to add to the bucket stove to heat up what you want to cook is not as prevalent today as it was in 1987. We might not have newspapers today in abundance but a lot of homes have Amazon boxes in abundance. Either people throw these out or they save them and re-use them for lots of little things or for when they have to ship something to someone else. If you need fuel for your bucket stove and you are going to evacuate, raid your neighbor's recycle bin. You can use ripped-up box pieces you can twist or just put them into the bucket stove the same way you would the pieces of newspaper. You can use this as a fuel source for heating water, pasteurizing water, cooking grains or food, and warming food or water up.

One of the things that's nice to do is if you have cans of food that you would rather eat warm and would rather eat directly from the can, you can put about an inch or two of water into a pot that goes into this stove and the fire is lit underneath. Warming the water in the pot with the cans in the water will heat up the cans without burning the food. It's a little less fuel-efficient, but it certainly is the lesson of simplicity and ease. As Cresson taught in his book Jungle Snafus and Remedies, Americans like eating their food hot and this can help improve the morale in the shelter. If you have an abundance of fuel then eat warm food and beverage.

The other thing in this diagram that might be hard to get is the metal bucket in itself. More and more pails and bucks are made from plastic. As of this writing in April of 2022 Lowes and Home Depot in the USA still have metal 2.5-gallon metal buckets as went and personally verified 2 days ago. However, these may increasingly disappear as time and change march on.

The other thing that is hard to find is metal coat hangers, whereas they were abundant in 1989 most of us today have plastic coat hangers of one type or another, but you can still find the metal coat hangers. I believe the best place to find them today is a dry-cleaning store. Metal coat hangers of all thicknesses are still available on Amazon. However, Cresson was using the thinner smaller ones for the bucket stove because those were the ones considered most 'expendable' in the days of the past when you picked up your dry cleaning.

Either you'll have these available or you will have to obtain them or you'll have to improvise when needed. The fuel support and some of the other stuff could be done with copper wire that is ripped out of the wall of the house (Obviously with no power on stripped and then bent into shape.) For the purposes of the stove. It won't be as rigid as a metal coat hanger, but you will have plenty of time to find a configuration that works.

ROCKET STOVE - PRE-DISASTER PREPAREDNESS

On the subject of pre-disaster preparedness is the subject of a rocket stove. Rocket stoves are widely available today for purchase online. You want to get one that is as insulated around the vertical part of the stove as possible. Rocket stoves are very mislabeled and misunderstood by almost everyone. Most people call any stove that is in a J tube configuration, a rocket stove, and this is not correct. A rocket stove is a J tube configuration but it needs to be very well insulated with either clay or ceramic or perlite or other refractory installation rather than just being naked metal.

A rocket stove works the way it does by preheating the fuel in proximity to the flame and by its 'chimney' that directs the flame onto the bottom of the pot being insulated. Thus it does not lose heat to the surrounding air and the flame wants to shoot straight up. Doing so pulls in the fresh air in abundance and makes for very efficient combustion without the smoke of a traditional twig or stick stove. A rocket stove is designed to be fed fuel as you need it literally one or two twigs at a time. Much the same as Cresson's bucket stove is intended to be fed pieces of newspaper (or ripped up Amazon boxes) as you need to. Keep the flame slow and steady and constant under the pot. Do not feed in a lot of fuel and just let it go wild. Fuel conservation will be critical. Combine any of these methods of cooking with the fireless cooker in the following pages and you will have something that works very well.

HARRIS FUEL FOR US SPECIAL FORCES.

There are elements of US Special Forces (SoF) that I have taught about food, fuel, cooking, batteries, power, and more. A 12-man squad would usually have 2 or 3 guys that carried a Primus Omnifuel Stove that burned gasoline, diesel, Jet-A, kerosene, white gas, etc... It would burn every liquid fuel except for alcohol fuel. The rest of the ODA would all carry an alcohol stove about the size of a hockey puck and about a pint of marine stove alcohol fuel. There are no moving parts to this stove and its simplicity itself. This was the backup in case the Omnifuel stoves had to get ditched or damaged. Marine Alcohol fuel is pure ethanol but it's denatured (usually with methanol) so you cannot drink it. Methanol is poisenous. As soon as I found this out I had them all switch their pint of Marine Alcohol Fuel over to “Everclear brand 190 Proof Ethanol” Everclear still works as a stove fuel but it could be used to disinfect wounds, skin, medical instruments, and it could be used as trading material to locals as well as consumed as a hasty aesthetic in an emergency in the event of severe, debilitating pain and they had to be on the move to exfiltration or CASEVAC.

Fig. 9.3. Bucket-stove with its sliding damper partly closed. Foot-long tongs of coat hanger wire are especially useful when burning twisted half-pages of newspaper.

If wood is to be burned, cut and split dry wood into small pieces approximately 1/2 inch square and 6 inches long. Start the fire with paper and small slivers of wood, placing some under the wire grate. To keep fuel from getting damp in a humid shelter, keep it in a large plastic bag.

If newspaper is to be burned, use half-pages folded and twisted into 5-inch-long "sticks," as illustrated. Using the wire tongs, feed a paper "stick" into the fire about every half-minute.

Add fuel and adjust the damper to keep the flame high enough to reach the bottom of the pot, but not so high as to go up the sides of the pot.

To use the Bucket Stove for heating in very cold weather, remove the pot and any insulation around the sides of the bucket; burn somewhat more fuel per minute.

If used with the Fireless Cooker described on the following pages, a Bucket Stove can be used to thoroughly cook beans, grain, or tough meat in water. Three quarts of such food can be cooked with less fuel than is required to soft-boil an egg over a small campfire.

- **Fireless Cooker**

A Fireless Cooker cooks by keeping a lidded pot of boiling-hot food so well insulated all around that it loses heat very slowly. Figure 9.4 shows one of these simple fuel-saving devices made from a bushel basket filled with insulating newspapers, with a towel-lined cavity in the center. The cavity is the size of the 6-quart pot. A towel in this cavity goes all around the pot and will be placed over it to restrict air circulation. If the boiling-hot pot of food is then covered with newspapers about 4 inches thick, the temperature will remain for hours so near boiling that in 4 or 5 hours even slow-cooking food will be ready to eat.

The essential materials for making an effective Fireless Cooker are enough of any good insulating materials (blankets, coats, paper, hay that is dry and pliable) to cover the boiling-hot pot all over with at least 3 or 4 inches of insulation. A container to keep the insulating materials in place around the pot is useful.

Wheat, other grains, and small pieces of tough meat can be thoroughly cooked by boiling them briskly for only about 5 minutes, then insulating the pot in a Fireless Cooker for 4 or 5 hours, or overnight. Whole beans should be boiled for 10 to 15 minutes before they are placed in a Fireless Cooker.

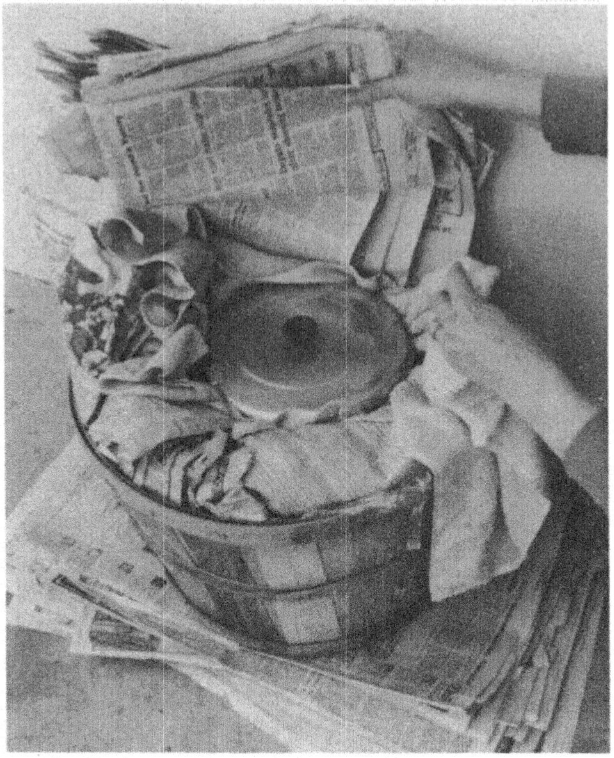

Fig. 9.4. Boiling-hot pot of food being placed in an expedient Fireless Cooker.

COOKING GRAIN AND BEANS WHEN SHORT OF FUEL OR POTS

- **Cooking Grain Alone**

When whole grains are pounded or ground by expedient means, the result usually is a mixture of coarse meal, fine meal, and a little flour. Under shelter conditions, the best way to cook such meal is first to bring the water to a boil (3 parts of water for 1 part of meal). Add 1 teaspoon (5 grams) of salt per pound of dry meal. Remove the pot from the fire (or stop adding fuel to a Bucket Stove) and quickly stir the meal into the hot water. (If the meal is stirred into briskly boiling water, lumping becomes a worse problem.) Then, while stirring constantly, again bring the pot to a rolling boil. Since the meal is just beginning to swell, more unabsorbed water remains, so there is less sticking and scorching than if the meal were added to cold water and then brought to a boil.

The Fireless Cooker is a Preparedness Hardskill

THE FIRELESS COOKER IS AUTOMATED COOKING

The fireless cooker as shown on the next page is a lesson that is not to be forgotten and used in an emergency.

Heating up food in hot water, either to boiling or near-boiling, and then putting the pot into a highly insulated surrounding, allowing the food to cook on its remaining sensible heat, is very much a best practice in the preparedness field. In the photo, you see a wooden bushel basket filled with the newspaper being used to insulate the metal pot full of hot water and food. Today you are going to substitute the newspaper for clothing, blankets, pillowcases, and anything else that you can find that is light and fluffy to replace the newspaper. You'll end up using something other than a wooden-based bushel basket but you will find something. The principal is still entirely able to be used today. Not only can you improvise this stuff around the house, you can also pre-purchase these items in advance. And if you're going to pre-purchase these, I would suggest you buy either a 64 or 128-ounce double-wall stainless steel vacuum insulated bottle. Commonly known by the brand named Thermos.

Other companies not called thermos make these as well. The keywords to remember are, "double-wall vacuum insulated stainless steel bottle." These are off the shelf at local big box stores and I personally own a 64-ounce bottle and they are available online at 128 ounces of volume, which is one gallon in size.

One gallon of food and water cooks a lot of food without you doing anything other than just heating it up to start with. These will work very well, if not better than a fireless cooker described in this book. The double-wall vacuum bottle is purchased ahead of time. The fireless cooker in this book is immediately improvised with what you own. You do not need to put anything around the vacuum bottles. They are already incredibly insulated. The bottles already keep beverages hot for 24 to 48 hours.

This is more than enough time as described in the fire list cooker documentation. To cook things that take a fair amount of time to be cooked without having a constant fire underneath them by just heating it all up and putting it in a "Thermos" is simplicity itself. For example, you can heat up beans and water. You can put these into the thermos. Let the food self cook.

If the food is not hot enough after a few hours, and, it probably will be, put the food back into the pot and put a small fire under it to bring it up to the desired eating temperature. It is the concept of highly insulated self-cooking of food that has already been brought up to temperature and allowing it to cook at that temperature for a significant period of time measured in hours is the best practice that I want you to remember and use it.

PREPARENESS IS NOT STUFF IT IS PRACTICE, PRACTICE, PRACTICE.

It would be extremely beneficial to your personal emergency skillset if you tried this before the disaster even happens. When everything is fine and normal and then you'll know how well it will work in times of trouble. Preparedness is not just getting stuff. Its Practice, Practice, Practice.

MAIL ORDER PREPAREDNESS

When Cresson wrote this version of NWSS in 1987 the idea of mail-order took a week or weeks for the order to arrive. That is if you bought it from a catalog by calling the 800 number and using a credit card. You might have it in a week if you were lucky.

The idea of going to Amazon.com did not even exist and that the item would show up in an hour or two, or the same day or early the next day or just the next day period was a very foreign and unimaginable concept.

If there is a hurricane 3 days away and you need emergency supplies because you are going to be stuck in a strong structure taking care of a family member that cannot leave the idea of ordering your needed emergency supplies and food and having them delivered is entirely possible. In one day no less. I commonly have my groceries delivered in a few hours after ordering and Amazon commonly delivers in 12 hours or less for common items and in the next 1 to 2 days for most items but I live in a major metropolitan area. My friends who live more rural are happy to get Amazon or online orders in 1 week.

If any type of Fireless Cooker is available, the hot cereal only has to be boiled and stirred long enough so that no thin, watery part remains. This usually takes about 5 minutes. Continue to cook, either in the Fireless Cooker for at least 4 or 5 hours, or by boiling for an additional 15 or 20 minutes.

When it is necessary to boil grain meal for many minutes, minimize sticking and scorching by cooking 1 part of dry meal with at least 4 parts of water. However, cooking a thinner hot cereal has a disadvantage during a food crisis: an increased volume of food must be eaten to satisfy one's energy needs.

If grain were the only food available, few Americans doing physical work could eat enough of it to maintain their weight at first, until their digestive tracts enlarged from eating the very bulky foods. This adaptation could take a few months. Small children could not adjust adequately to an all-grain diet; for them, concentrated foods such as fats also are needed to provide enough calories to maintain growth and health.

• Cooking Grain and Beans Together

When soybeans are being used to supplement the lower quality proteins of grain and when fuel or pots are in short supply, first grind or pound the beans into a fine meal. To further reduce cooking time, soak the bean meal for a couple of hours, keeping it covered with water as it swells. Next put the soaked bean meal into a pot containing about 3 times as much water as the combined volume of a mixture of 1 part of dry bean meal and 3 or 4 parts of dry grain meal. Gently boil the bean meal for about 15 minutes, stirring frequently, before adding the grain meal and completing the cooking.

Stop boiling and add the grain meal while stirring constantly. Again bring the pot to a boil, stirring to prevent sticking and scorching, and boil until the meal has swelled enough to have absorbed all the water. After salting, boil the grain-bean mush for another 15 minutes or more before eating, or put it in a fireless cooker for at least 4 or 5 hours.

Soybeans boiled alone have a taste that most people find objectionable. Also, whole soybeans must be boiled for a couple of hours to soften them sufficiently. But if soybeans are pounded or ground into a fine meal, and then 1 part of the soybean meal is boiled with 4 parts of meal made from corn or another grain, the soybeans give a pleasant sweetish taste to the resulting mush. The unpleasant soybean taste is eliminated. If cooked as described above, soybeans and other beans or dried peas can be made digestible and palatable with minimum cooking.

100% GRAIN AND 100% BEAN DIETS

A diet consisting solely of wheat, corn, or rice, and salt has most of the essential nutrients. The critical deficiencies would be vitamins A, C, and D. Such a grain-based diet can serve adults and older children as their "staff of life" for months. Table 9.1 shows how less than 1¾ pounds of whole wheat or dry yellow corn satisfies most of the essential nutritional requirements of a long-term emergency ration. [The nutritional values that are deficient are printed in bold type, to make an easier comparison with the Emergency Recommendations, also printed in bold type. Food energy is given in kilocalories (kcal), commonly called calories (Cal).] Expedient ways of supplying the nutrients missing from these rations are described in a following section of this chapter.

Other common whole grains would serve about as well as wheat and yellow corn. At least ⅙ oz of salt per day (about 5 grams) is essential for any ration that is to be eaten for more than a few days, but ⅓ oz (about 10 g or ¾ tablespoon) should be available to allow for increased salt needs and to make grain and beans more palatable. This additional salt would be consumed as needed.

To repeat: few Americans at first would be able to eat the 3 or 4 quarts of thick mush that would be necessary with a ration consisting solely of whole-kernel wheat or corn. Only healthy Americans determined to survive would be likely to fare well for months on such unaccustomed and monotonous food as an all-grain diet. Eating two or more different kinds of grain and cooking in different ways would make an all-grain diet both more acceptable and more nourishing.

Not many people would be able to eat 27 oz (dry weight before cooking) of beans in a day, and fewer yet could eat a daily ration of almost 23 oz of soybeans. Beans as single-food diets are not recommended because their large protein content requires the drinking of more fluids. Roasted peanuts would provide a better single-food ration.

GRAIN SUPPLEMENTED WITH BEANS

People who live on essentially vegetarian diets eat a little of their higher-quality protein food *at every meal,* along with the grain that is their main source of nutrition. Thus Mexicans eat some beans along with their corn tortillas, and Chinese eat a little fermented soybean food or a bit of meat or fish with a bowl of rice. Nutritionists have found that grains

Table 9.1. Daily rations of 100% grain, beans, or peanuts[a]

	Wheat (dry)	Yellow Field Corn[b] (dry)	Emergency Recommendations	Soybeans (dry)	Red Beans (dry)	Peanuts (roasted)
Weight	790g (27.8 oz)	750g (26.4 oz)		645g (22.7 oz)	760g (26.8 oz)	447g (15.8 oz)
Energy, kcal	2600	2600	2600	2600	2600	2600
Protein, g	103	67	55[c]	220	171	117
Fat, g	15	29	30	114	11	218
Calcium, mg	324	165	400	1458	836	322
Magnesium, mg	1260	1100	200-300	1710	1240	782
Iron, mg	26	15.7	10	54.2	52.4	9.8
Potassium, mg	2920	2130	1500-2000	10800	7420	3132
Vitamin A, RE	0	368	555	52	15	0
Thiamin, mg	4.3	2.8	1.0	7.1	3.9	1.3
Riboflavin, mg	1.0	0.9	1.4	2.0	1.5	0.6
Niacin, mg	34.0	16.5[d]	17.0	14.2	17.5	76.4
Vitamin C, mg	0	0	15-30	0	0	0
Vitamin D, μg	0	0	0[e]	0	0	0

[a]Salt (1/3 oz, or 10 g, or 3/4 tablespoon) should be available. This would be consumed as needed.

[b]White corn supplies no Vitamin A, whereas yellow corn supplies 49 RE (retinol equivalent, a measure of Vitamin A value) per 100 g dry weight. Most corn in the United States is yellow corn.

[c]If a diet contains some animal protein such as meat, eggs, or milk, the recommended protein would be less than 55 g per day. If most of the protein is from milk or eggs, only 41 g per day is recommended.

[d]The niacin in corn is not fully available unless the corn is treated with an alkali, such as the lime or ashes Mexicans (and many Americans) add to the water in which corn kernels are soaked or boiled.

[e]Infants, children, and pregnant and lactating women should receive 10μg (10 micrograms, or 400 IU) of vitamin D. For others, the current recommended daily allowance (RDA) for vitamin D is 200 IU (5μg).

are low in some of the essential amino acids that the human body needs to build its proteins. For long-term good health, the essential amino acids must be supplied in the right proportions *with each meal* by eating some foods with more complete proteins than grains have. Therefore, in a prolonged food crisis one should strive to eat *at every meal* at least a little of any higher-quality protein foods that are available. These include ordinary beans, soybeans, milk powder, meat, and eggs.

Table 9.2 shows that by adding 7.0 oz (200 g) of red beans (or other common dried beans) to 21.1 oz (600 g) of either whole wheat or yellow corn, with salt added, you can produce rations that contain adequate amounts of all the important nutrients except vitamin C, vitamin A, vitamin D, and fat. If 5.3 oz (150 g) of soybeans are substituted for the red beans, the fat requirement is satisfied. The 600 g of yellow corn contains enough carotene to enable the body to produce more than half the emergency recommendation of vitamin A. The small deficiencies in riboflavin would not cause sickness.

Other abundant grains, such as grain sorghums or barley, may be used instead of the wheat or corn shown in Table 9.2 to produce fairly well-balanced rations. Other legumes would serve to supplement grain about as well as red beans. (Peanuts are the exception: although higher in energy (fat) than any other unprocessed food, the quality of their protein is not as high as that of other legumes.)

EXPEDIENT WAYS TO SUPPLY DEFICIENT ESSENTIAL NUTRIENTS

• Vitamin C

A deficiency of vitamin C (ascorbic acid) causes scurvy. This deadly scourge would be the first nutritional disease to afflict people having only grain and/or beans and lacking the know-how needed to sprout them and produce enough vitamin C. Within only 4 to 6 weeks of eating a ration containing no vitamin C, the first symptom of scurvy would appear: swollen and bleeding gums. This would be followed by weakness, then large bruises, hemorrhages, and wounds that would not heal. Finally, death from hemorrhages and heart failure would result.

The simplest and least expensive way to make sure that you, your family and neighbors do not suffer or die post-attack from scurvy is to buy one kilogram (1,000,000 milligrams) of pure vitamin C, which is the crystalline "ascorbic acid" form. Unlike vitamin C tablets, pure vitamin C crystals do not deteriorate. An inexpensive mailorder source is Bronson Pharmaceutical, 4526 Rinetti Lane, La Canada, California 91011;

Table 9.2. Daily rations of whole wheat or yellow corn supplemented with soybeans or red beans. Recommended daily salt ration, including salt in food: ¾ tablespoon (⅓ oz, or 10 g).

	600g (21.1 oz) Whole wheat plus 200g (7.0 oz) Red beans (dry wt)	600g (21.1 oz) Whole wheat plus 150g (5.3 oz) Soybeans (dry wt)	Emergency Recommendations	600g (21.1 oz) Yellow corn[a] plus 150g (5.3 oz) Soybeans (dry wt)	600g (21.1 oz) Yellow corn plus 200g (7.0 oz) Red beans (dry wt)
Energy, kcal	2,666	2,585	2,600	2,693	2,774
Protein, g	123	129	55[b]	105	98
Fat, g	15	39	30	50	26
Calcium, mg	466	585	400	471	352
Magnesium, mg	1,286	1,358	200 300	1,280	1,208
Iron, mg	33.6	32.4	10	25.2	26.4
Potassium, mg	4,188	4,736	1,500 2,000	4,220	3,672
Vitamin A, RE	4	12	555	306	298
Thiamin, mg	4.3	5.0	1.0	3.9	3.2
Riboflavin, mg	1.1	1.2	1.4	1.2	1.1
Niacin, mg	30.4	29.1	17.0	16.5[c]	17.8
Vitamin C, mg	0	0	15 30	0	0
Vitamin D, μg	0	0	0[d]	0	0

[a]White corn supplies no vitamin A, whereas yellow corn supplies 49RE (retinol equivalent, a measure of vitamin A value) per 100g dry weight. Most corn in the United States is yellow corn.

[b]If a diet contains animal protein such as meat, eggs or milk, the recommended protein would be less than 55g per day. If all the protein is from milk or eggs, only 41g per day is required.

[c]The niacin in corn is not fully available unless corn is treated with an alkali, such as the lime or ashes added by Mexicans and Americans in the South and Southwest to the water in which they soak or boil corn kernels.

[d]Infants, children, and pregnant and lactating women should receive 10μg (10 micrograms, or 400 IU) of vitamin D. For others, the current recommended daily allowance (RDA) for vitamin D is 200 IU (5 μg).

in 1988 I bought one kilogram for $18.75, postage paid. An ample daily dose is 25 milligrams, about 0.0009 ounce. Ten grams (about one third ounce) is enough for a whole year for one person who is eating only unsprouted grain and/or other foods providing **no** vitamin C. One gram (1,000 mg) of crystalline ascorbic acid is ¼ teaspoonful. If you do not have a ¼ teaspoon, put one **level** teaspoonful of the crystals on a piece of paper, and divide the little pile into 4 equal parts; each will be approximately 1,000 mg. One of these 1,000 mg piles can easily be divided into 4 tiny piles, each 250 mg. A 250 mg pile provides 10 ample daily doses of 25 mg each. If your family has a 1,000,000 mg supply, taking a 50 mg daily dose of pure crystalline ascorbic acid may be preferred, either sprinkled on food or dissolved in water.

One good expedient way to prevent or cure scurvy is to eat sprouted seeds — not just the sprouts. Sprouted beans prevented scurvy during a famine in India. Captain James Cook was able to keep his sailors from developing scurvy during a three-year voyage by having them drink an unfermented beer made from dried, sprouted barley. For centuries the Chinese have prevented scurvy during the long winters of northern China by consuming sprouted beans.

Only 10 mg of vitamin C taken each day (1/5 of the smallest vitamin C tablet) is enough to prevent scurvy. If a little over an ounce (about 30 grams) of dry beans or dry wheat is sprouted until the sprouts are a little longer than the seeds, the sprouted seeds will supply 10 to 15 mg of vitamin C. Such sprouting, if done at normal room temperature, requires about 48 hours. To prevent sickness and to make sprouted beans more digestible, the sprouted seeds should be boiled in water for not longer than 2 minutes. Longer cooking will destroy too much vitamin C.

Usual sprouting methods produce longer sprouts than are necessary when production of enough vitamin C is the objective. These methods involve rinsing the sprouting seeds several times a day in safe water. Since even survivors not confined to shelters are likely to be short of water, the method illustrated in Fig. 9.5 should be used. First the seeds to be sprouted are picked clean of trash and broken seeds. Then the seeds are covered with water and soaked for about 12 hours. Next, the water is drained off and the soaked, swollen seeds are placed on the inside of a plastic bag or a jar, in a layer no more than an inch deep. If a plastic bag is used, you should make two loose rolls of paper, crumple them a little, dampen them, and place them inside the bag, along its sides. As shown in Fig. 9.5, these two dampened paper rolls keep the plastic from resting on the seeds and form an air passage down the center of the bag. Wet paper should be placed in the mouth of the bag or jar so as to leave an air opening of only about 1 square inch. If this paper is kept moist, the seeds will remain sufficiently damp while receiving enough circulating air to prevent molding. They will sprout sufficiently after about 48 hours at normal room temperature.

Fig. 9.5. Sprouting with minimum water.

Sprouting seeds also increases their content of riboflavin, niacin, and folic acid. Sprouted beans are more digestible than raw, unsprouted beans, but not as easily digested or nourishing as are sprouted beans that have been boiled or sauteed for a couple of minutes. Sprouting is not a substitute for cooking. Contrary to the claims of some health food publications, sprouting does not increase the protein content of seeds, nor does it improve protein quality. Furthermore, sprouting reduces the caloric value of seeds. The warmth generated by germinating seeds reduces their energy value somewhat, as compared to unsprouted seeds.

- **Vitamin A**

Well-nourished adults have enough vitamin A stored in their livers to prevent vitamin A deficiency problems for several months, even if their diet during that time contains none of this essential vitamin. Children would be affected by deficiencies sooner than adults. The first symptom is an inability to see well in dim light. Continuing deficiency causes changes in body tissues. In infants and children, lack of vitamin A can result in stunted growth and serious eye problems—even blindness. Therefore, a survival diet should be balanced with respect to vitamin A as soon as possible, with children having priority.

Milk, butter, and margarine are common vitamin A sources that would not be available to most survivors. If these were no longer available, yellow corn, carrots, and green, leafy vegetables (including dandelion greens) would be the best sources. If these foods were not obtainable, the next best source would be sprouted whole-kernel wheat or other grains—if seeds could be sprouted for three days *in the light,* so that the sprouts are green. Although better than no source, sprouting is not a very satisfactory way to meet vitamin A requirements. The development of fibrous roots makes 3-day sprouted wheat kernels difficult to eat. And one must eat a large amount of seeds with green sprouts and roots to satisfy the recommended daily emergency requirements—up to 5½ cups of 5-day sprouted alfalfa seeds. Survivors of a nuclear attack would wish they had kept an emergency store of multivitamin pills.

- **Vitamin D**

Without vitamin D, calcium is not adequately absorbed. As a result, infants and children would develop rickets (a disease of defective bone mineralization). A massive nuclear attack would cut off the vast majority of Americans from their main source of vitamin D, fortified milk.

Vitamin D can be formed in the body if the skin is exposed to the ultraviolet rays of the sun. Infants should be exposed to sunlight very cautiously, initially for only a few minutes—especially after a massive nuclear attack. Such an attack possibly could cause atmospheric changes that would permit more ultraviolet light to reach the earth's surface, causing sunburn in the U.S. as severe as on the equator today. In cold weather, maximum exposure of skin to sunlight is best done in a shallow pit shielded from the wind. Exposure in a shallow pit would give about 90 percent protection from gamma radiation from fallout particles on the surrounding ground.

- **Niacin and Calcium**

Niacin deficiency causes pellagra, a disease that results in weakness, a rash on skin exposed to the sun, severe diarrhea, and mental deterioration. If a typical modern American had a diet primarily of corn and lacked the foods that normally supply niacin, symptoms of pellagra would first appear in about 6 months. Since corn is by far our largest crop—the U.S. production in 1985 was about 425 billion pounds—the skillful treatment of corn would be important to post-attack survival and recovery.

During the first part of this century, pellagra killed thousands of Americans in the South each year. These people had corn for their principal staple and ate few animal protein foods or beans. Yet

Mexicans, who eat even more corn than did those Southerners—and have even fewer foods of animal origin—do not suffer from pellagra.

The Mexicans' freedom from pellagra is mainly due to their traditional method of soaking and boiling their dried corn in a lime-water solution. They use either dry, unslaked lime (calcium oxide, a dangerously corrosive substance made by roasting limestone) or dry, slaked lime (calcium hydroxide, made by adding water to unslaked lime). Dry lime weighing about 1% as much as the dry corn is added to the soak water, producing an alkaline solution. Wood ashes also can be used instead of lime to make an alkali solution. The alkali treatment of corn makes the niacin available to the human body. Tables 9.1 and 9.2 show corn as having adequate niacin. However, the niacin in dried corn is not readily available to the body unless the corn has received an alkali treatment.

Treating corn with lime has another nutritional advantage: the low calcium content of corn is significantly increased.

- **Fat**

The emergency recommendation for fat is slightly over 1 ounce per day (30 g) of fat or cooking oil. This amount of fat provides only 10% of the calories in the emergency diet, which does not specify a greater amount because fats would be in very short supply after a nuclear attack. This amount is very low when compared to the average diet eaten in this country, in which fat provides about 40% of the calories. It would be difficult for many Americans to consume sufficient calories to maintain normal weight and morale without a higher fat intake; more fat should be made available as soon as possible. Increased fat intake is especially important for young children, to provide calories needed for normal growth and development. Oak Ridge National Laboratory field tests have shown that toddlers and old people, especially, prefer considerably more oil added to grain mush than the emergency recommendation of 10%.

- **Vitamin B-12 and Animal Protein**

Vitamin B-12 is the only essential nutrient that is available in nature solely from animal sources. Since a normal person has a 2 to 4-year supply of vitamin B-12 stored in his liver, a deficiency should not develop before enough food of animal origin would again be available.

Many adults who are strict vegetarians keep in good health for years without any animal sources of food by using grains and beans together. It is more difficult to maintain normal growth and development in young children on vegetarian diets. When sufficient animal sources of food are available, enough should be provided to supply 7 grams of animal protein daily. This could be provided by about 1.4 ounces (38 g) of lean meat, 0.7 ounce (20 g) of nonfat dry milk, or one medium-sized egg. When supplies are limited, young children should be given priority. Again: a little of these high-grade supplementary protein foods should be eaten with every meal.

- **Iron**

Most people live out their lives without benefit of an iron supplement. However, many pregnant and nursing women and some children need supplemental iron to prevent anemia. One tested expedient way to make more iron available is to use iron pots and pans, especially for cooking acid foods such as tomatoes. Another is to place plain iron nails (not galvanized nails) in vinegar until small amounts of iron begin to float to the surface. This usually takes 2 to 4 weeks. Then a teaspoon of iron-vinegar solution will contain about 30 to 60 mg of iron, enough for a daily supplement. The emergency recommendation is 10 mg per day. A teaspoon of the iron-vinegar solution is best taken in a glass of water. The iron content of fruit, such as an apple, can be increased by placing iron nails in it for a few days.

FOOD RESERVES

Russia, China, and other countries that make serious preparations to survive disasters store large quantities of food—primarily grain—both in farming areas and near population centers. In contrast, the usually large U.S. stocks of grain and soybeans are an unplanned survival resource resulting from the production of more food than Americans can eat or sell abroad. The high productivity of U.S. agriculture is another unplanned survival asset. Providing enough calories and other essential nutrients for 100 million surviving Americans would necessitate the annual raising of only about 12% of our 1985 crop of corn, wheat, grain sorghum, and soybeans — if nothing else were produced. In 1985, the U.S.

production of corn, wheat, soybeans, and grain sorghum totalled about 625 billion pounds — about 7 pounds per day for one year for every American. A total of 2 pounds per person per day of these basic staples, in the proportions shown in Table 9.2, would be sufficient to provide the essentials of an adequate vegetarian diet weighing about 27 ounces. (Grain sorghum is not listed in Table 9.2; it has approximately the same food value as corn.) The remaining 5 ounces of the 2 pounds would feed enough chickens to meet a survivor's minimum long-term requirement for animal protein.

If corn, wheat, grain sorghum, and soybeans were the only crops raised, the annual production would need to be only 730 pounds per person. Our 1985 annual production would have supplied every adult, child, and infant in a population of 100 million with 6250 pounds of these four staples. This is more than 8 times enough to maintain good nutrition by Chinese standards.

Recovery from a massive nuclear attack would depend largely on sufficient food reserves being available to enable survivors to concentrate on restoring the essentials of mechanized farming. Enough housing would remain intact or could be built to provide adequate shelter for the first few crucial years; enough clothing and fabrics would be available. But if survivors were forced by hunger to expend their energies attempting primitive subsistence farming, many deaths from starvation would occur and the prospects for national recovery would be greatly reduced.

Americans' greatest survival asset at the end of 1985 was about 17 billion bushels (about 850 billion pounds) of wheat, corn, grain sorghums, and soybeans **in storage,** mostly on farms. If 200 million Americans were to survive a limited nuclear attack and if only half of this stored food reserve could be delivered to the needy, each survivor would have adequate food for over 3 years, by Chinese nutritional standards.

In view of the crucial importance of large food reserves to the prospects for individual and national survival, it is to be hoped that U.S. food surpluses and large annual carry-overs will continue.

A BASIC SURVIVAL RATION TO STORE

A ration composed of the basic foods listed below in Table 9.3 provides about 2600 calories per day and is nutritionally balanced. It keeps better than a ration of typical American foods, requires much less space to store or transport, and is much less expensive. The author and some friends have stored enough of these basic foods to last their families several months during a crisis, and have eaten large quantities of these foods with satisfaction over the past 20 years. (A different emergency ration should be stored for infants and very small children, as will be explained in the following section.) Field tests have indicated that the majority of Americans would find these basic foods acceptable under crisis conditions. In normal times, however, no one should store this or any other emergency food supply until after he has prepared, eaten, and found its components satisfactory.

Unprocessed grains and beans provide adequate nourishment for many millions of the world's people who have little else to eat. Dry grains and beans are very compact: a 5-gallon can holds about 38 pounds of hard wheat. Yet when cooked, dry whole grains become bulky and give a well-fed feeling — a distinct advantage if it is necessary to go on short rations during a prolonged crisis.

This basic ration has two disadvantages: (1) it requires cooking, and (2) Americans are unaccustomed to such a diet. Cooking difficulties can be minimized by having a grain-grinding device, a

Table 9.3. A basic survival ration for multi-year storage

	Ounces per day	Grams per day	Pounds for 30 days full ration	Kilograms for 30 days full ration
Whole-kernel hard wheat	16	454	30.0	13.6
Beans	5	142	9.4	4.3
Non-fat milk powder	2	57	3.8	1.7
Vegetable oil	1	28	1.9	0.9
Sugar	2	57	3.8	1.7
Salt (iodized)	$^{1}/_{3}$	10	0.63	0.3
Total Weights	$26^{1}/_{3}$	748	49.5	22.5
Multi-vitamin pills:		1 pill each day		

bucket stove with a few pounds of dry wood or newspapers for fuel, and the know-how to make a "fireless cooker" by using available insulating materials such as extra clothing. The disadvantage of starting to eat unaccustomed foods at a stressful time can be lessened by eating more whole grains and beans in normal times—thereby, incidentally, saving money and improving a typical American diet by reducing fat and increasing bulk and fiber.

When storing enough of this ration to last for several months or a year, it is best to select several kinds of beans for variety and improved nutrition. If soybeans are included, take into account the differences between soybeans and common beans, as noted earlier in this chapter.

In many areas it is difficult to buy wheat and beans at prices nearly as low as the farmer receives for these commodities. However, in an increasing number of communities, at least one store sells whole-grain wheat and beans in large sacks at reasonable prices. Mormons, who store food for a range of possible personal and national disasters, are often the best sources of information about where to get basic foods in quantity, at reasonable cost. Soon after purchase, bulk foods should be removed from sacks (but not necessarily from sealed-plastic liner-bags) and sealed in metal containers or in thick-walled plastic containers for storage. Especially in the more humid parts of the United States, grain and beans should be frequently checked for moisture. If necessary, these foods should be dried out and rid of insects as described later in this chapter.

Vegetable oil stores as well in plastic bottles as in glass ones. The toughness and lightness of plastic bottles make them better than glass for carrying when evacuating or for using in a shelter. Since a pound of oil provides about 2¼ times as much energy as does a pound of sugar, dry grain, or milk powder, storing additional vegetable oil is an efficient way to improve a grain diet and make it more like the 40%-fat diet of typical Americans.

All multivitamin pills providing 5000 International Units (1500 mg retinol equivalent) vitamin A, 400 IU (10 mg) of vitamin D, and 50 to 100 mg of vitamin C, must meet U.S. Government standards, so the least expensive usually are quite adequate. Storage in a refrigerator greatly lengthens the time before vitamin pills must be replaced with fresh ones. Because vitamin C is so essential, yet very inexpensive and long-lasting, it is prudent to store a large bottle.

It would be wise to have on hand ready-to-eat, compact foods for use during a week or two in a shelter, in addition to those normally kept in the kitchen. It is not necessary to buy expensive "survival foods" or the special dehydrated foods carried by many backpackers. All large food stores sell the following concentrated foods: non-fat milk powder, canned peanuts, compact ready-to-eat dry cereals such as Grape Nuts, canned meat and fish, white sugar, vegetable oil in plastic bottles, iodized salt, and daily multivitamin pills. If shelter occupants have a way to boil water (see Figs. 9.2 and 9.3, Bucket Stove), it is advisable to include rice, noodles, and an "instant" cooked cereal such as oatmeal or wheat—along with coffee and tea for those who habitually drink these beverages.

Parched grain is a ready-to-eat food that has been used for thousands of years. Whole-kernel wheat, corn, and rice can be parched by the following method: Place the kernels about ¼-inch deep in a pan, a skillet, or a tin can while shaking it over a flame, hot coals, or a red hot electric burner. The kernels will puff and brown slightly when parched. These parched grains are not difficult to chew and can be pounded to a meal more easily than can the raw kernels. Parched grain stores well if kept dry and free of insects.

EMERGENCY FOOD FOR BABIES

Infants and very small children would be the first victims of starvation after a heavy nuclear attack, unless special preparations are made on their behalf. Our huge stocks of unprocessed foods, which could prevent the majority of unprepared survivors from dying of hunger, would not be suitable for the very young. They need foods that are more concentrated and less rough. Most American mothers do not nurse their infants, and if a family's supply of baby foods were exhausted the parents might experience the agony of seeing their baby slowly starve.

Few Americans have watched babies starving. In China, I saw anguish on starving mothers' faces as they patted and squeezed their flat breasts, trying to get a little more milk into their weak babies' mouths. I saw this unforgettable tragedy in the midst of tens of thousands of Chinese evacuating on foot before a ruthless Japanese army during World War II. Years later, my wife and I stored several hundred pounds of milk powder while our five children were small. I believe that parents who fear the use of nuclear weapons will be glad to bear the small expense of keeping on hand the emergency baby foods listed in Table 9.4, below. (More detailed descriptions of these and many other foods, with instructions for their use, are given in an Oak Ridge National Laboratory report, *Maintaining Nutritional Adequacy During A Prolonged Food Crisis,* ORNL-5352, 1979. This report may be purchased for $6.50 from National Technical Information Service, U.S. Department of Commerce, 5385 Port Royal Road, Springfield, Virginia 22161.)

To make a formula adequate for a 24-hour period, the quantities of instant non-fat dry milk, vegetable cooking oil, and sugar listed in the "Per Day" column of Table 9.4 should be added to 4 cups of safe water. This formula can be prepared daily in cool weather or when a refrigerator is available. In warm or hot weather, or under unsanitary conditions, it is safer to make a formula 3 times a day. To do so, add $^1/_3$ cup plus 2 teaspoons (a little less than one ounce) of instant non-fat milk powder to $1^1/_3$ cups ($^2/_3$ pint) of boiled water, and stir thoroughly. Then add 1 tablespoon (about $^1/_3$ ounce, or 9 grams) of vegetable oil and 2 teaspoons of sugar, and stir. (If regular bakers' milk powder is used, $^1/_4$ cup is enough when making one-third of the daily formula, 3 times a day.) If baby bottles are not at hand, milk can be spoon-fed to an infant.

Especially during a war crisis, the best and most dependable food for an infant is mother's milk—provided the mother is assured an adequate diet. The possibility of disaster is one more reason why a mother should nurse her baby for a full year. Storing additional high-protein foods and fats for a nursing mother usually will be better insurance against her infant getting sick or starving than keeping adequate stocks of baby foods and the equipment necessary for sanitary feeding after evacuation or an attack.

To give a daily vitamin supplement to a baby, a multivitamin pill should be crushed to a fine powder between two spoons and dissolved in a small amount of fluid, so that the baby can easily swallow it. If an infant does not receive adequate amounts of vitamins A, D, and C, he will develop deficiency symptoms in 1 to 3 months, depending on the amounts stored in his body. Vitamin C deficiency, the first to appear, can be prevented by giving an infant 15 mg of vitamin C each day (about $^1/_3$ of a 50-mg vitamin C tablet, pulverized) or customary foods containing vitamin C, such as orange juice. Lacking these sources, the juice squeezed from sprouted grains or legumes can be used. If no vitamin pills or foods rich in vitamin D are available, exposure of the baby's skin to sunlight will cause his body to produce vitamin D. It would be wise to wait about 30 days after an attack before exposing the baby to sunlight. After that, short exposures would be safe except in areas of extremely heavy fallout. As a further precaution, the baby can be placed in an open, shallow pit that will provide shielding from radiation given off by fallout particles on the ground. Initial exposure should be very short, no more than 10 minutes.

If sufficient milk is not obtainable, even infants younger than six months should be given solid food. Solid foods for babies must be pureed to a fine

Table 9.4. Emergency food supply for one baby.

Ingredients	Per Day		Per Month		Per 6 Months	
	Volumes and Ounces	Grams	Pounds	Kilograms	Pounds	Kilograms
Instant non-fat dry milk	1 cup + 2 tablespoons ($2^3/_4$ oz)	8	6	2.72	32	15
Vegetable cooking oil	3 tablespoons (1 oz)	30	2	0.90	12	5.5
Sugar	2 tablespoons (0.7 oz)	20	1.3	0.60	8	3.6
Standard daily multi-vitamin pills	$^1/_3$ pill		10 pills		60 pills	

Baby Food Works for Adults as Well

INSTANT PUDDING AND MORE WITH OIL
When Cresson was alive he and I experimented with many variants of the Water, Powdered Milk, Sugar, and Cooking Oil mixture for adult food as well as babies. He already perfected what could be used for children so he and I mostly focused on adults.

One of the combinations I came up with that he liked the most and I have taught further into military circles is taking instant powdered pudding mix. This is the just add water type, not the stove cooktop type. If the mixture called for 1.5 cups of water I'd add 3 cups of water. Double what was called for. This would not make pudding but more of a 'thick shake type drink' that was vanilla or chocolate flavored. Then to this mixture, we'd add the number of calories in the form of sugar and oil desired. The sugar was added for immediate calories, protein powder might be added for mid-term delayed calories and the cooking oil or melted butter was added for a longer-term high-calorie addition. One tablespoon (TBS) of corn oil or most other cooking oils is 120 calories. 8 Tablespoons, or 1/2 cup (4oz), of oil and or butter would be nearly 1000 calories in one drink. Typically these were made to be at least 16 ounces or more in size. You did not guzzle it all at once, but you could, but most people drank it over 15 to 30 minutes as there were in the classroom and we were talking. You can add more or less sugar to taste and for immediate energy and more or less oil for the desired calories needed. One full stick of butter (or 1/4 of a pound) is just over 800 calories. Melting a full stick, or a half a stick of butter, in a cup of hot chocolate makes it an incredibly rich and divine drink to consume. We also used "non-dairy powdered creamer" to substitute for butter. This is basically powdered margarine which is hydrogenated oil. We did not care about the health issues most of the popular culture talk about with hydrogenated oils. We were after the extreme amount of easy-to-carry calories for a colder environment they would be operating in as a warfighter. This was a diet supplement when deployed on an operation and it was not an extensive daily diet for months.

SOUTH POLE EXAMPLES Robert Scott's attempt to reach the south pole consisted of a variety of high-calorie foods but among these were hot cocoa and butter. They would melt about an entire stick of butter into a cup of hot cocoa and drink it. They did this to keep up the number of daily calories they needed for the energy expended in their daily travel and in keeping their body warm.

Roland Amundson not only took very high-fat meat and foods but he also ate his dogs. Mostly the slower dogs were slaughtered and fed to the other more hearty dogs but the men would slice off a filet of dog meat and eat it and enjoy it as much as beef. In the last economic and electrical grid disaster to hit Venezuela most of the people left there that did not flea ended up eating their pets out of sheer desperation for food. This is what hungry people will do. If the idea of eating a variety of improvised baby food is not one you can see yourself doing imagine the mental changes and desperation needed to kill and eat your pet.

Scott made it to the south pole, only to find Amundson had beat him there by 5 weeks. Scott's planning and experience were not as good as Amundson and he and his remaining men froze to death on the way back. Amundson not only made it to the South Pole and back but on his Artic Expeditions (North Pole) when his ship got stuck in the ice and he had to winter over, he and his men got a little fat.

Planning for your next situation where food is not in abundance and planning it smartly and practicing with those foods before the disaster happens is a very important part of surviving the disaster.

texture. Using a modern baby food grinder makes pureeing quick and easy work. Under crisis conditions, a grinder should be cleaned and disinfected like other baby-feeding utensils, as described later in this section.

Several expedient methods are available: the food can be pressed through a sieve, mashed with a fork or spoon, or squeezed through a porous cloth. Good sanitation must be maintained; all foods should be brought to a boil after pureeing to insure that the food is safe from bacteria.

A pureed solid baby food can be made by first boiling together 3 parts of a cereal grain and 1 part of beans until they are soft. Then the mixture should be pressed through a sieve. The sieve catches the tough hulls from the grain kernels and the skins from the beans. The grain-beans combination will provide needed calories and a well-supplemented protein. The beans also supply the additional iron that a baby needs by the time he is 6 months old. Flours made from whole grains or beans, as previously described, also can be used; however, these may contain more rough material.

Some grains are preferable to others. It is easier to sieve cooked corn kernels than cooked wheat kernels. Since wheat is the grain most likely to cause allergies, it should not be fed to an infant until he is 6 to 7 months old if other grains, such as rice or corn, are available.

Small children also need more protein than can be supplied by grains alone. As a substitute for milk, some bean food should be provided at every meal. If the available diet is deficient in a concentrated energy source such as fat or sugar, a child's feedings should be increased to 4 or 5 times a day, to enable him to assimilate more. Whenever possible, a small child should have a daily diet that contains at least one ounce of fat (3 tablespoons, without scraping the spoon). This would provide more than 10% of a young child's calories in the form of fat, which would be beneficial.

If under emergency conditions it is not practical to boil infant feeding utensils, they can be sterilized with a bleach solution. Add one teaspoon of ordinary household bleach to a quart of water. (Ordinary household bleach contains 5.25% sodium hypochlorite as its only active ingredient and supplies approximately 5% available chlorine. If the strength of the bleach is unknown, add 3 teaspoons per quart.) Directions for safe feeding without boiling follow:

The Utensils (Include at least one 1-quart and one 1-pint mason jar, for keeping prepared formula sterile until used.)

1. Immediately after feeding, wash the inside and outside of all utensils used to prepare the formula and to feed the infant.

2. Fill a covered container with clean, cold water and add the appropriate amount of chlorine bleach.

3. Totally immerse all utensils until the next feeding (3 or 4 hours). Be sure that the bottle, if used, is filled with bleach solution. Keep container covered.

At Feeding Time

1. Wash hands before preparing food.

2. Remove utensils from the disinfectant chlorine solution and drain, but do not rinse or dry.

3. Prepare formula; feed the baby.

4. Immediately after feeding, wash utensils in clean water and immerse again in the disinfectant solution.

5. Prepare fresh chlorine solution each day.

STORAGE OF FOODS

Whole grains and white sugar can be stored successfully for decades; dried beans, non-fat milk powder, and vegetable oil can be stored for several years. Some rules for good storage follow:

• **Keep food dry.** The most dependable way to assure continuing dryness is to store dry grain in metal containers, such as ordinary 5-gallon metal storage cans or 55-gallon metal drums with gasketed lids. Filled 5-gallon cans are light enough to be easily carried in an automobile when evacuating.

Particularly in humid areas, grain which seems to be dry often is not dry enough to store for a long period. To be sure that grain is dry enough to store for years, use a drying agent. The best drying agent for this purpose is silica gel with color indicator. The gel is blue when it is capable of absorbing water and pink when it needs to be heated to become an effective drying agent again. Silica gel is inexpensive if bought from chemical supply firms located in most cities. By heating it in a hot oven or in a can over a fire until it turns blue again, silica gel can be used repeatedly for years.

The best containers for the silica gel used to dry grain (or to determine its dryness) are homemade cloth envelopes large enough for a heaping cupful of the gel. A clear plastic window should be stitched in, through which color changes can be observed. Put an evelope of silica gel on top of the grain in a 5-gallon can filled to within a couple of inches of its top. Then close the can tightly. Even a rather loose-fitting lid can be sealed tightly with tape. If after a few days the silica gel is still blue, the grain is dry enough. If the silica gel has turned pink, repeat the process with fresh envelopes until it can be seen that the grain is dry.

● **Keep grains and beans free of weevils, other insects, and rodents.** Dry ice (carbon dioxide) is the safest means still widely available to the public for ridding grain and beans of insects. Place about 4 inches of dry ice on top of the grain in a 5-gallon metal container. Put the lid on somewhat loosely, so that air in the grain can be driven out of the can. (This will happen as the dry ice vaporizes and the heavy carbon dioxide gas sinks into the grain and displaces the air around the kernels.) After an hour or two, tighten the lid and seal it with tape. After one month, all insects in this carbon-dioxide atmosphere will have died from lack of oxygen.

● **Store foods in the coolest available place, out of the light.** Remember that the storage life of most foods is cut in half by an increase of 18° F (10° C) in storage temperature.[30] Thus 48 months of storage at 52° F is equivalent to 24 months at 70° F, and to 12 months at 88° F.

Illustrative of the importance of cool storage are my experiences in storing non-fat milk powder in an earth-covered, cool shelter. In steel drums I stored unopened 100-pound bags of compact, non-fat milk powder that I bought from bakeries. The cost per pound was much less than I would have paid for the largest packages sold in supermarkets. After 7 years storage at temperatures of about 50° F the year around, my milk powder was still good — as good as it would have been if stored in a normally air-conditioned and heated home for about 3 years.

● **Do not place stored metal containers directly on the floor.** To avoid possible condensation of moisture and the rusting that results, place containers on spaced boards. For long-term storage in damp permanent shelters or damp basements, use solid-plastic containers with thick walls.

● **Rotate stored foods.** Eat the oldest food of each type and replace it with fresh food. Although cooking oil and non-fat milk powder remain edible after several years of storage at room temperature, these and most other dry foods are more nourishing and taste better if stored for no more than 2 years. Most canned foods taste better if kept no more than one year. Exceptions are whole grains and white sugar, which stay good for decades if stored properly.

● **Store plenty of salt.** In our modern world salt is so abundant and cheap that most Americans do not realize that in many areas soon after a major nuclear attack salt would become a hard-to-get essential nutrient. Persons working hard without salt would suffer cramps and feel exhausted within a few days. Most famine relief shipments of grain probably would not include salt. So store enough salt both to salt your family's food for months and to trade for other necessities.

SEEDS

For thousands of years storing seeds has been an essential part of the survival preparations made by millions of prudent people fearing attack. Seeds are hopes for future food and the defeat of famine, that lethal follower of disastrous wars.

Among the most impressive sounds I ever heard were faint, distant rattles of small stones, heard on a quiet, black, freezing night in 1944. An air raid was expected before dawn. I was standing on one of the bare hills outside Kunming, China, trying to pinpoint the sources of lights that Japanese agents had used just before previous air raids to guide attacking bombers to blacked-out Kunming. Puzzled by sounds of cautious digging starting at about 2:00 AM, I asked my interpreter if he knew what was going on. He told me that farmers walked most of the night to make sure that no one was following them, and were burying sealed jars of seeds in secret places, far enough from homes so that probably no one would hear them digging. My interpreter did not need to tell me that if the advancing Japanese troops succeeded in taking Kunming they would ruthlessly strip the surrounding countryside of all food they could find. Then those prudent farmers would have seeds and hope in a starving land.

If you doubt that enough of our current "oversupply" of stored whole grains, soybeans, milk powder, etc. would reach you after a nuclear attack, you should store seeds known to grow well in your area.

When getting your supply of survival seeds, remember:

- Grains and beans are the best plant sources of energy and protein.
- Even if you have enough vitamins for several months, you may not be able to buy more until long after a nuclear war.
- The deadly curses of scurvy, vitamin A deficiencies, and pellagra can be prevented by eating the plants, seeds, and sprouted seeds described earlier in this chapter.
- Plants grown from hybrid seeds give larger yields, but do not produce as productive seeds as do plants grown from good non-hybrid seeds.
- Seeds of proven productivity in your locality may be more valuable than money after a major nuclear attack.
- You should get and store mostly non-hybrid seeds, after learning from experienced local gardeners which are best.

Chapter 10
Fallout Radiation Meters

THE CRITICAL NEED

A survivor in a shelter that does not have a dependable meter to measure fallout radiation—or that has one but lacks someone who knows how to use it—will face a prolonged nightmare of uncertainties. Human beings cannot feel, smell, taste, hear, or see fallout radiation. A heavy attack would put most radio stations off the air, due to the effects of electromagnetic pulse, blast, fire, or fallout from explosions. Because fallout intensities often vary greatly over short distances, those stations still broadcasting would rarely be able to give reliable information concerning the constantly changing radiation dangers around a survivor's shelter.

Which parts of the shelter give the best protection? How large is the radiation dose being received by each person? When is it safe to leave the shelter for a few minutes? When can one leave for an hour's walk to get desperately needed water? As the fallout continues to decay, how long can one safely work each day outside the shelter? When can the shelter be left for good? Only an accurate, dependable fallout meter will enable survivors to answer these life-or-death questions.

Gamma radiation is by far the most dangerous radiation given off by fallout particles. Gamma rays are like X rays, only more penetrating and harmful. The roentgen (R) is the unit most commonly used to measure exposures to gamma rays, or to X rays, and most American civil defense instruments give readings in roentgens (R) or roentgens per hour (R/hr). Therefore, for simplicity's sake, in this book almost all radiation **doses** are given in roentgens (R), and radiation **dose rates** are given in roentgens per hour (R/hr). This simplification is justified because, for external whole-body gamma radiation from fallout, the numerical value of an exposure or dose given in roentgens is approximately the same as the numerical value given in rems or rads. (For information on the rem and the rad, and on the seriousness and probability of injuries likely to be suffered as a result of receiving different sized doses of gamma radiation, see "Lifetime Risks from Radiation", a section of Chapter 13.)

The dose (the quantity) of radiation that a person receives, along with the length of time during which the dose is received, determine what injuries, if any, will be suffered as a result of the dose. Of people who, in a few days, each receive a dose of 350 roentgens under nuclear war conditions, about half will die. Doses are measured with small instruments called **dosimeters,** either by directly reading the dose between the time at which a dosimeter is charged to read zero and the time of a subsequent reading, or by calculating by subtraction the dose between two readings. However, to avoid receiving a lethal or sickening dose, the most useful instrument is a **dose rate meter.** The National Academy of Sciences' Advisory Committee on Civil Defense in 1953 concluded: "The final effectiveness of shelter depends upon the occupants of any shelter having simple, rugged, and reliable dose rate meters to measure the fallout dose rate outside the shelter."

With a reliable dose rate meter you can quite quickly determine how great the radiation dangers are in different places, and then promptly act to reduce your exposure to these unseen, unfelt dangers. For example, if you go outside an excellent fallout shelter and learn by reading your dose rate meter that you are being exposed to 30 R/hr, you know that if you stay there for one hour you will receive a **dose** of 30 R. But if you go back inside your excellent shelter after 2 minutes, then while outside you will have received a **dose** of only 1 R. (2 minutes = 2/60 of an hour = 1/30 hr; and receiving a dose at the rate of 30 R/hr for 1/30 hr results in a dose of 30 R/hr x 1/30 hr = 1R.) Under nuclear war conditions, receiving an occasional dose of 1R (1,000 milliroentgens) would be of little concern, as explained in Chapter 13 and 18.

WARNINGS FOR BUYERS OF FALLOUT METERS

You are "on your own" when buying a dose rate meter or dosimeter because:

- No U.S. Government agency or other Government facility advises the public regarding sources of the best available radiation-measuring instruments for use in time of war, or warns concerned individuals that certain instruments are either incapable of measuring adequately high dose rates or doses for wartime use, or are dangerously inaccurate. For example, a dose rate meter that in 1982 sold nationwide was tested in that year at Oak Ridge National Laboratory to determine its accuracy for measuring gamma radiation. This instrument was reasonably accurate at low dose rates, but at the high dose rates of life or death importance in a nuclear war its readings were dangerously low: When it should have read 150 R/hr, it read 13.9 R/hr. Another dose rate meter of this same model, tested in California by Dr. Bruce Clayton, read only 16 R/hr when it should have read 400 R/hr. Obviously, if this model were used and trusted by a person doing rescue work for hours outdoors in heavy fallout, while believing that he was receiving a non-incapacitating dose he actually would be getting a fatal dose!

- Instruments that measure only milliroentgen-range dose rates are sold for war use by some companies. Since most Americans have no idea what size of radiation doses would incapacitate or kill them, and do not even know that a milliroentgen is 1/1000 of a roentgen, some people buy instruments that are capable of measuring maximum dose rates of only one roentgen or less per hour. For example, an American company advertised and sold for $370.00 in 1986 its dose rate meter that has a maximum range of "0 - 1000 mR/hr." It is the only dose rate meter in that company's listing of "Radiation Detection Products for the General Public", described as " . . . applicable for use in case of nuclear war." The highest dose rate that it can measure, one roentgen per hour, is far too low to be of much use in a nuclear war.

- Used and surplus dose rate meters and dosimeters are likely to be inaccurate or otherwise unreliable. Very few buyers have access to a radiation source powerful enough to check instruments for accuracy over their full ranges of measurements. My education regarding bargain fallout meters began in 1961, after I bought two dosimeters of a model then being produced by a leading manufacturing company and purchased in quantity by the Office of Civil Defense. Within a week after receiving these instruments, one of them could not be charged. The other was found to be inaccuate. Later I learned that the manufacturing company sold to the public its instruments that did not pass Government quality tests.

Most Federal and State organizations do not criticize faulty civil defense products, apparently because they are not charged with this responsibility and want to avoid angering manufacturers and sellers who may go to their Congressmen or Legislators to seek redress for lost sales.

In this book I am not giving the names of any of the companies that sell or have sold potentially life-endangering survival items. To do so would reduce the chances of this book being distributed or advocated by Government agencies.

WAR RESERVES OF FALLOUT METERS

One of Americans' most important assets for surviving a nuclear war is the Federal Emergency Management Agency's (FEMA's) supply of fallout meters. These instruments include approximately 600,000 dose rate meters and about 3,300,000 dosimeters, all suitable for wartime use. In 1986 almost all of these old instruments—that can be found—reportedly still are in good working condition. Because of continuing inadequate funding for civil defense, in recent years most of FEMA's instruments have been serviced, calibrated, and, if necessary, repaired only once every four years. In a few localities these instruments are no longer being serviced.

Most of these critically important instruments are kept in cities, in buildings likely to be destroyed by blast or fire in the event of a massive Soviet attack. If there were a sufficiently long, officially recognized period of warning before an attack, it might be possible during such a worsening crisis to move a large fraction of these fallout meters outside the areas of probable blast or fire damage, and to place them in officially designated fallout shelters. However, this unlikely development would not provide private family shelters with instruments.

Most families need their own fallout meters. This need is greatest for families living in localities not likely to be damaged by blast or fire, and for those planning to evacuate to such less hazardous localities during a worsening crisis.

COMMERCIALLY AVAILABLE FALLOUT METERS

In 1987 an American does not have many choices if he wants to buy an off-the-shelf dose rate meter suitable for measuring the high levels of fallout radiation that would result from a nuclear attack. Although inexpensive dose rate meters and dosimeters have been under development by the military services and civil defense researchers for the past 15 years, they have not been produced commercially for sale to the public. Field tests of factory-produced models have not been completed at this writing.

Dose Rate Meters

The best radiation-measuring instrument for wartime use available in the United States in 1987 is the Universal Survey Meter RD-10, manufactured in Finland by Alnor Oy. It is sold in the United States by a subsidiary, Alnor Nuclear, 2585 Washington Road, Suite 120, Pittsburg, Pennsylvania 15241. In 1988 the FOB price, pre-paid, is $1,100.00. The RD-10 accurately measures gamma and X rays from very close to natural background radiation up to 300 R/hr, in two ranges (0.03 - 300 mR/hr, and 0.03 - 300 R/hr). It meets Finnish Army standards for ruggedness and accurate operation in sub-zero cold (down to -25°C, or -13°F); it has an illuminated scale for night use and an audible pulse rate signal, and is built to withstand electromagnetic pulse (EMP) effects. (A few of my friends and I for years have owned Finnish instruments of an earlier model, the RD-8; they still are in excellent working condition.)

A less expensive dose rate meter designed for rugged wartime use is the Portable Radiological Dose Rate Meter PDRM 82, manufactured in England by Plessey Controls Limited, Sopers Lane, Poole, Dorset BH17 7ER, England. This instrument is the current standard issue of the British armed forces and civil defense, is designed for a storage life of at least 20 years, is microcomputer controlled, EMP-proof, and displays "FAIL" if a fault exists. (Like all instruments, occasionally a PDRM 82 does fail. One bought by a friend in 1987 and tested by a radiation laboratory in Utah read 86 centigrays per hour when it should have read 300, and failed to display "FAIL." Mailed back to England, Plessey Controls finally replaced it with another new PDRM 82.) The only consequential disadvantages of the PDRM 82, compared to more expensive dose rate meters, are that it reads in centigrays per hour (cGy/hr is equivalent to Rads/hr, or R/hr) and does not measure dose rates lower than 0.1 cGy/hr (100 mR/hr). In 1987 this portable, four-digit-liquid-display dose rate meter is sold by Plessey Controls for 250 British pounds plus air shipment charges — all pre-paid. To learn the latest delivery date and the latest price delivered direct by air, write Plessey Controls. However, in a nuclear war 100 mR/hr will be a low dose rate in most life-threatening fallout areas. (I bought a PDRM 82 direct from England in 1984, my objective being to have it tested at Oak Ridge National Laboratory. I later learned that such testing was unnecessary, since U.S. Army specialists already had tested the PDRM 82 and had found it excellent.)

Technical Note. Conversion of readings of most foreign and scientific radiation-monitoring instruments to the radiation units usually given by American civil defense instruments, or used in the U.S. in regulations and articles concerning radiation hazards:

ABSORBED RADIATION DOSE

1 gray (1 Gy) = 100 Rads
1 centigray (1 cGy) = 1 Rad
(As explained in the first section of this chapter, for practical civil defense work 1 Rad = 1 roentgen = 1 Rem.)

DOSE EQUIVALENT

1 sievert (1 Sv) = 100 Rems
1 millisievert (1 mSv) = 0.1 Rem

ACTIVITY

1 bequerel (1 Bq) = 27 picocuries
(Radiation contamination of milk and water are given in picocuries per liter, or bequerels per liter. One picocurie is one millionth of one millionth of a curie; 1 curie is 37,000,000,000 bequerels.)

No wonder that most newspaper and television accounts of radiation accidents and hazards are confused!

I have not been able to find an American-made, modern dose rate meter that is designed for wartime use and is being sold in 1987. Among those designed for peacetime use that may be satisfactory in wartime is the RO-2A manufactured by Eberline, P.O. Box 2108, Santa Fe, New Mexico 87504-2108. The RO-2A is a portable air ionization-chamber instrument used to measure beta, gamma, and X-ray radiation from 50 mR/hr to 50 R/hr. The price in 1987 is $950.00. In Eberline's summary specifications and in the specifications that I have read of other U.S. manufacturers of dose rate meters, no mention is made of the instruments' being EMP-proof.

Dosimeters

Several reliable dosimeters and dosimeter-chargers are sold in the United States. Among the established retail sources is Dosimeter Corporation, P.O. Box 42377, Cincinnati, Ohio 45242. Its DCA Model No. 686 measures accumulated doses from 0 to 600 R, and in January of 1986 sold for $59.95. The battery powered charger, DCA Model No. 909, cost $90.00; one charger can be used to charge several dosimeters.

A more expensive direct reading 600 R dosimeter is model 019-006 of Atomic Products Corporation, P.O. Box 1157, Center Moriches, New York 11934. It sells for $120.00; dosimeter charger 020-001, " . . . used to 'zero' all Direct-Reading Dosimeters", costs $98.00.

To keep them dependable, all commercially available dosimeters and dose rate meters should be (1) kept supplied with fresh batteries for charging or operating, (2) checked with a strong enough radiation source (at no longer than 3-year intervals) to see if they still are measuring radiation accurately, and (3) repaired if necessary. (To learn whether a dose rate meter still is functioning, use a radioactive check source such as Dosimeter Corporation's Check Source (Model 3001), that contains 5 microcuries cesium-137 and sells for $35.00. This type of check test will prove only that your instrument measures dose rates slightly above normal background radiation; it will not prove that your instrument could accurately measure the much higher dose rates that will be of vital concern in a nuclear war. Some instrument companies will properly calibrate a radiation measuring instrument that is sent to them. For example, Dosimeter Corporation charges $50.00 to calibrate a dose rate meter or dosimeter, and makes needed repairs at an additional cost.)

The reader is advised to buy at least a good commercial dose rate meter, with which to quickly measure high levels of fallout radiation —if he can afford one. A family that has a reliable dose rate meter, and that remains in a shelter almost all of the time during which fallout dose rates outdoors are dangerously high, can calculate with sufficient accuracy the accumulated doses received by its members. To do this, a continuous record must be kept of dose rates and the times at which those measurements are made. (Having a reliable dosimeter eliminates the need for keeping such detailed records and making these calculations, but if only one instrument can be afforded it should be a dose rate meter.) A good commercial instrument, if properly maintained and periodically calibrated with a radiation source to check its accuracy, probably will be serviceable for years.

A prudent owner of even an excellent dose rate meter would do well to make and learn to use a KFM, the dependable homemakeable fallout meter briefly described later in this chapter, with complete instructions for making and using it given in Appendix C. Then during a period of heavy war fallout you can check the readings of your complex instrument by comparing them with those of your KFM, and, if the complex instrument is giving inaccurate readings, your KFM will meet your basic need.

A HOMEMAKEABLE DOSE RATE METER, THE KFM

- **What is a KFM?**

The only do-it-yourself fallout meter that is accurate and dependable was invented in 1977. It is called the KFM (Kearny Fallout Meter); one is pictured in Fig. 10.1.

Fig. 10.1. A homemade KFM, an accurate dose rate meter for measuring dose rates from 30 mR/hr (0.03 R/hr) up to 43 R/hr.

This simple instrument has undergone rigorous scientific testing in several laboratories, including Oak Ridge National Laboratory; its accuracy and dependability were confirmed. Many hundreds of KFMs have been made by untrained people, ranging from members of junior high school science classes to grandmothers making them for their children and grandchildren. These successful makers have been guided only by thoroughly field-tested instructions and patterns not quite as good as the improved ones given in Appendix C of this updated book.

Only common materials found in millions of homes are needed to build a KFM. (If all of the materials, including those for a dry-bucket, have to be purchased, their total cost in 1986 is less than seventeen dollars.) The KFM serves as an accurate dose rate meter when used in conjunction with a watch and the KFM's attached table relating changes in readings in listed time intervals to dose rates. No radiation source is needed either to initially calibrate a KFM or subsequently to check its accuracy. (Calibrations for accuracy were completed at Oak Ridge National Laboratory and are the basis of the KFM's attached table.) A KFM is more accurate than most civil defense instruments, and its accuracy is **permanently** established by the laws of physics applicable to the specified dimensions and other characteristics of its parts, and to their positioning relative to each other— **provided that it is made and maintained according to the instructions.** Unlike all factory-made radiation measuring civil defense instruments that are reliable and available today, a KFM is charged electrostatically. No battery is needed.

- **Additional Advantages of KFMs**

* A KFM combines the provenly practical radiation measuring functions of an electroscope and of an ionization chamber having a specified volume. Electroscopes were the basic radiation measuring instruments used by scientists, including Nobel Laureate Lord Rutherford, who pioneered studies of atomic nuclei and radiations. The author is indebted to another Nobel Laureate physicist, Dr. Luis W. Alvarez, for the idea of making a homemade electroscope with two thread-suspended, aluminum-foil leaves, to measure fallout radiation. Many excellent and unavoidably expensive dose rate meters, including civil defense instruments, are ionization chamber devices.

* A KFM, used in conjunction with a watch, does not have to be charged to any specified initial reading, or discharged by exposure to radiation to any specified final reading, to accurately measure the dose rate during a time interval specified on its attached table. Fig. 10.2 illustrates this operational advantage of KFMs.

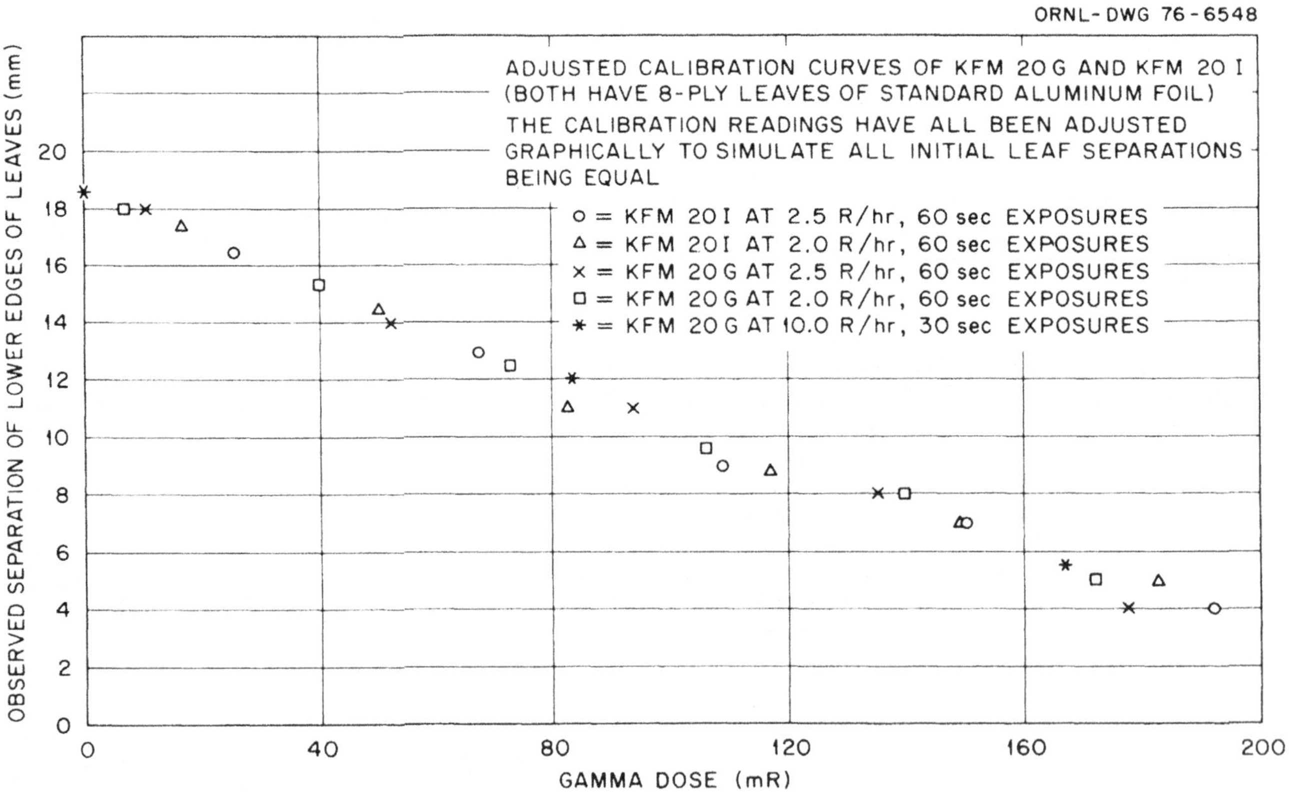

Fig. 10.2 Normalized Calibration Points for Two KFMs, Showing the Straight-Line Relationship Between Milliroentgen Radiation DOSES and Resultant Readings. The complete instructions for making and using a KFM (see Appendix C) explain how an operator with a watch can use this instrument to accurately measure DOSE RATES.

• Additional Information on Accuracy and Dependability

* Readers who want additional technical information on the KFM are advised to buy a copy of the original Oak Ridge National Laboratory report on this instrument, *The KFM, A Homemade Yet Accurate and Dependable Fallout Meter* (ORNL-5040, CORRECTED), by Cresson H. Kearny, Paul R. Barnes, Conrad V. Chester, and Margaret W. Cortner. Date published: January 1978. Copies are sold by the National Technical Information Service, U.S. Department of Commerce, 5285 Port Royal Road, Springfield, Virginia 22161. Since the price continues to increase, it is best to write first, to learn the postage-paid cost.

* Civil defense professionals of foreign countries also have concluded that KFMs have lifesaving potential. The June 1978 Special Issue of The Journal of the Institute of Civil Defence ("The Premier Society of Disaster Studies", with headquarters in London) was entirely devoted to the KFM, and gave international distribution to the original complete instructions and cut-out paper patterns. The interest of Chinese civil defense officials in the KFM and my other low cost survival inventions led to my making, with White House approval, two long trips in China as an official guest. In eight Chinese cities I acquired survival know-how by exchanging civil defense information with top civil defense officials.

• A Major Disadvantage: A KFM Looks Like a Toy

* This instrument appears too simple to be trusted to measure deadly radiation, a frightening mystery to most people. Typical moderns are accustomed to pushing buttons and twisting dials to get information instantly from instruments they do not understand. Most feel that a dependable radiation-monitoring instrument has to be complex. However, especially during a worsening nuclear crisis many typical Americans would build KFMs if they become convinced of the accuracy and dependability of this homemakeable instrument that they can understand, use intelligently, and repair if necessary.

• **Caution:** Earlier versions of KFM-making instructions, written when common sewing threads were good insulators, recommend sewing threads for suspending a KFM's leaves. Now most sewing threads are anti-static treated, are poor insulators, and are unsatisfactory for use in KFMs. Makers of KFMs should use the instructions in this updated edition, that recommend widely available, excellent insulators for suspending a KFM's leaves, and that incorporate several field-tested design improvements.

• Instructions for Making and Using KFMs

Appendix C gives the latest field-tested instructions (with patterns) to enable you to make a KFM and to learn how to use it.

The great need for civil defense instruments is likely to be fully recognized only during a worsening nuclear crisis. Therefore, in this edition the KFM instructions and patterns are printed on only one side of a sheet, with extra patterns at the end of the text, and with two pages at the very end to expedite the rapid reproduction of the KFM instructions. Timed printing tests by two newspapers have proved that, with the help of these two pages of special instructions, a newspaper can paste up and photograph all pages of the KFM instructions, print a 12-page tabloid giving them, and start distributing the tabloid—all in less than one hour. Thus, if you have a copy of this book during an all-too-possible nuclear crisis, you may be able to give these instructions to a newspaper and help thousands of your fellow citizens obtain the information that they need to make fallout meters for themselves.

• Advice on Building a KFM

The reader is urged to set aside several hours in the near future for making a KFM and for mastering its use. During field tests, average American families have needed about 6 hours to study the instructions given in Appendix C, to make this simple instrument, and to learn how to use it. These several hours may not be available in the midst of a crisis. Higher priority work would be the building of a high-protection-factor shelter, the making of a shelter ventilating pump, and the storing of adequate water. In a crisis it might not be possible to obtain some needed materials for a KFM.

It is very difficult to concentrate on unfamiliar details during a nerve-racking crisis, or to do delicate work with hands that may become unsteady. The best time to build and learn to use a KFM is in peacetime, long before a crisis. Then this long-lasting instrument should be stored for possible future need.

• Primary Source of Materials

To get the materials needed to make both an excellent KFM and also a low-range instrument of the same design and size, write to Stephen Jones, 1402 South, 1000 West, Salt Lake City, Utah 84104. He sells inexpensive Kits for making KFMs of two types, and is the most experienced Kit developer, selling a large number of Kits per month in 1999.

To best keep your KFM very dry and always ready for crisis use, keep it stored in a 1-quart metal paint can, along with at least 2 ounces of color-indicator silica gel, sold by chemical supply firms. Seal the can with waterproof tape or non-hardening caulking.

Chapter 11
Light

THE NEED FOR MINIMUM LIGHT

Numerous disasters have proved that many people can remain calm for several days in total darkness. But some occupants of a shelter full of fearful people probably would go to pieces if they could see nothing and could not get out. It is easy to imagine the impact of a few hysterical people on the other occupants of a pitch-dark shelter. Under wartime conditions, even a faint light that shows only the shapes of nearby people and things can make the difference between an endurable situation and a black ordeal.

Figure 11.1 shows what members of the Utah family saw in their shelter on the third night of occupancy. All of the family's flashlights and other electric lights had been used until the batteries were almost exhausted. They had no candles at home and failed to bring the cooking oil, glass jar, and cotton string included in the Evacuation Checklist. These materials would have enabled them to make an expedient lamp and to keep a small light burning continuously for weeks, if necessary.

Fig. 11.1. Night scene in a trench shelter without light.

At 2 AM on the third night, the inky blackness caused the mother, a stable woman who had never feared the dark, to experience her first claustrophobia. In a controlled but tense voice she suddenly awoke everyone by stating: "I have to get out of here. I can't orient myself." Fortunately for the shelter-occupancy experiment, when she reached the entry trench she overcame her fears and lay down to sleep on the floor near the entrance.

Conclusion: In a crisis, it is especially bad not to be able to see at all.

ELECTRIC LIGHTS

Even in communities outside areas of blast, fire, or fallout, electric lights dependent on the public power system probably would fail. Electromagnetic pulse effects produced by the nuclear explosions, plus the destruction of power stations and transmission lines, would knock out most public power.

No emergency lights are included in the supplies stocked in official shelters. The flashlights and candles that some people would bring to shelters probably would be insufficient to provide minimum light for more than a very few days.

A low-amperage light bulb used with a large dry cell battery or a car battery is an excellent source of low-level continuous light. One of the small 12-volt bulbs in the instrument panels of cars with 12-volt batteries will give enough light for 10 to 15 nights,

You Are Too Stupid To Use a Candle

FEMA, REDCROSS AND READY.GOV

Despite the proven history of candles dating back from 5000 to 7000 years ago and variations of an oil lamp that used a plant oil or rendered animal fat with a wick. Along with a plant like a rush soaked in plant oil going back 12,000 to 15,000 years ago. Somehow, the American Red Cross and the Federal Emergency Management Authority (FEMA) declared about 10 years ago that the American people are too stupid to use something as dangerous as the candle and they stopped recommending candles for emergency preparedness and all cases. This is not something I can condone. Nor is it something Cresson would condone. I actually have a variation of one of his oil lamps sitting all of about 1 ft from me right now that I was taking pictures of and demonstrating to a preparedness group. His simple oil lamp using a single thread from a multi-thread cotton string in a clear mason jar of cooking oil is sheer brilliance. Literally and figuratively. It will make enough light that you can see what you're doing in a completely dark shelter, especially once your eyes have dark-adapted to the environment. The human eyeball goes through adaptations and darkness in several stages, but they generally occur after about 30 seconds, 3 to 5 minutes, and at 40 minutes.

If you're in a completely dark environment for 40 minutes, you have your maximum level of night vision available. Your eyes are very sensitive to any amount of light. One of my favorite types of candles to purchase before an emergency is real church candles, which you normally get from a Catholic supply store. These are not the Jesus candles that you get for a dollar at the dollar store. Typically those burned very poorly and they burned down the middle, wasting a great deal of wax and not putting out a great deal of light. The professional church candles have a wax that melts at a much lower temperature. They will have a pure melted liquid wax layer that the wick goes through. Then you are getting pure candlelight through the clear glass that is illuminating the shelter and the dark environment.

Among my favorites are the three-day and the seven-day candles. Which they do, indeed burned for three days straight or seven days straight 24 hours a day, but at most you'll need yours for 8 hours a day so a 7-day candle (based on 24 hours) would really last you over 21 days of use at night. There are also smaller votive candles that also come with glass holders. These can burn from 8 to 24 hours, and they are simple and easy, and convenient to use. The "tea light" candles you buy at the big box store by the 100 in a bag last about 4 hours.

However, when you're faced with an extraordinary situation the design here for both the simple candle in the soda can as a reflector and hanging mount as well as the simple oil lamp using a clear Mason jar and a piece of a cotton string that you unravel provides a very small and usable amount of light works exceptionally well and lasts a long time. Note: you have to use a natural fiber like cotton for the wick. Whereas jute and sisal will work the flame will be better with the cotton string. Any synthetic string like a nylon string will just melt and not bring up the oil by the capillary action of the natural fiber wick. If you had a fiberglass 'wick' that would work exceptionally well as well, but it will not 'burn down' as the oil level gets lower. You need to use a fiberglass wick in a lamp type device that inserts the wick into the oil and pulls the oil up by capillary action and not one where the string is in the oil and burns down as the oil is used up.

I, Steven Harris, the update author for Nuclear War Survival skills, am very critical and very derogatory of not only Red Cross but FEMA as well as ready.gov. I do not consider anyone that thinks you are too stupid to use the candle worthy of giving out other credible information in time of a disaster. It is faith and trust in each other, your family, your friends and neighbors, and even stranger that will help get you through a disaster. Not having trust in even an individual to use something as historic as a candle overrides all of the faith and trust that needs to be instilled in one's self as well as those you are with to make it through the disaster. You are in a life and death disaster with possible nuclear detonations burning tens of square miles per event with radioactive fallout, radionuclides in the food and water that you might drink and all of the other horrors that come with a nuclear detonation and someone lawyer behind the ready.gov website is worried about you starting a fire with matches and a candle.

I believe in you. I have trust in you. I know you can do it. Please follow what myself and Cresson are telling you in this book. Please practice it before a disaster, as often as possible, you might actually have some fun. When something really happens you'll know that you know how to do it and it will be an easy day. This is no different than an athlete or a musician practicing for the game or the performance they have to give. You really do need to practice preparedness. It's not as if your life depends on it. If you lose the football game, you've lost a game. At worst you've had an athletic injury. When you screw up your preparedness practice during a disaster people die. You see them swept away in the rushing water. The house falls in on them. They burn to death (but not from a candle) or they have uncontrolled diarrhea and vomiting from water that was not treated and they can die in your arms in as little as 12 hours from dysentery. The sounds of the pangs of hunger in your crying children are not something you want in your permanent memory. Cuts and scrapes can become infected and become septic and fatal. Right now you are living with a 911 system with a legion of police officers, firefighters, EMTs, Paramedics, and Hospitals with Level 1 Trauma centers standing at the ready to work miracles and multiple lifetimes of experience and expertise all to save your life.

FUN FACT: Figure 11.1 on the previous page. Night scene in a trench shelter without light. Cresson told me he used a square piece of black felt to make that image. His fellow scientists at ORNL told him he should have taken a photo in a 100% no-light shelter with a film camera and then printed that 100% black photo.

When there is a light brighter than you've ever seen in your life and a bang so loud and rumbles for longer than you've ever heard the worst thunder in your life then all of that legion of experience and expertise to save your life goes away and you are in the end. You are the 911. You are the help. No one is coming to help you. You are it. Cowboy up. No pressure.

This might be a hyper or Critical attitude. However, in my professional experience, I have not seen that much credibility coming out of any of these three organizations. Nor would I advise you to seek their counsel in the time of disaster. Indeed the content of Cresson's original book is by far more detailed, in-depth, and actually tested on volunteers and those experiences were used to change the instructions and documentation until it was as easy to follow as you can see in this current book. I am not just updating this book for tools and methods in 2022, but I'm giving you the pep talk and the "you can do it" that you very much need. You do not need to "stay safe", you need "make it safe" and you do that with information, knowledge, and the experience you gain in trying that information and experience.

The book Nuclear War Survival Skills was produced by the US government, Oakridge National Laboratories. However, it was Cresson Kearny that was the author and the main focus behind this book. It's not a fantastic book by the government it's a fantastic book by Cresson that the US Government published. It was his brilliance and insight and experience over his lifetime from being a geologist in the jungles of Venezuela for the standard oil company in the 1930s. Cresson volunteered to join the US Army in 1939 because he knew his country was going to war, and it was going to be a tropical war with the Japanese. And that he had critical jungle experience from being a long-duration exploration geologist. His experience and expertise were going to be beneficial to the warfighter at that time for the theaters they were going to have to fight in. Cresson never ever stopped helping the military, the warfighter, and the American public at large with his life of dedication to the protection, and assisting of those people and soldiers in need of something just a bit better. He had no politics that clouded his judgment or got in his way of coming up with the best practice and the best methods to help people in need. Cresson jumped off a bridge into the Potomac River in Washinton DC, in the winter, to prove to a general how effective his flotation methods were for the average soldier. Remember in the movie Saving Private Ryan when they were going towards Omaha beach in the landing crafts and their rifles were in clear plastic bags? Those were Cresson's bags for the M1 Garand Rifle. They were designed to make the rifle buoyant and float and not to keep the rifle dry. Unfortunately, the US Army did NOT adapt his 5-liter collapsable canteen bladder. Usually, a soldier with a full combat load would have 2 of those strapped to him and filled with air when in a water environment. When on the land he'd fill them with drinking water. Between those bladders and his rifle bag, his pack liner, he was fully buoyant. Men in the landing craft on D-Day went over the side of the boat to escape the german machine guns slicing through them when the ramp dropped and they ended up drowning under the weight of their equipment on D-Day. That is the dedication and depth of history of the man that made this book. When I was an engineer in the scientific labs at Chrysler Corporation we called this "Role Model Quality." Words and deeds like this are all too often not used in the current safe space culture.

The idea that you need a 72-hour kit or a three-day kit to get through a disaster is absolutely ludicrous. As we have seen all through the covid situation, as well as the food shortages and the majority of other disasters that have happened in the last 10 years. The U. S government is nowhere to be found within three days and they are not coming to your rescue. Over 1000 people died in Texas in 2021 when Texas had the great freeze-up. Everyone's heat and power failed due to natural gas line failures and wind turbine failures. The US Government was not there handing out hot beverages, food, blankets, warm places to sleep, and the other things that were needed. People were sleeping in their cars with the heater on to stay warm and there were scrounging for almost everything that they could find and the stores were soon emptied.

One of my favorite news reports was of a father that had just spent the night sleeping in his car with his family waiting for the grocery store to open and he was complaining that the store was out of bottled water to drink and he did not know what to do. In the meantime he motioned around at all of the snow and ice and asked the reporter what was he supposed to do for his thirsty children. It never occurred to him to take the snow and especially the ice and to put it in Ziploc bags or other enclosures such as buckets and to put them in a warm environment like the inside of the car or under the hood of the car (which is quite warm) and to melt the snow and ice to make water for his family to drink. I guess that drinking water only comes from a bottle these days with a label and a date on it. The underhood ambient of a car at idle is easily above 160F which is the temperature at which you pasteurize water and kill most if not all of the possible pathogens in it and it's safe to drink once you let it cool. If he kept the water hot he could have made tea.

You do not need a three-day kit. You need a good week, plus and I mean a good solid week of food and water. I would highly recommend that you have totes or whatever other container you desire like milk crates with your emergency supplies in them for both home protection and having to evacuate. I would suggest you have a solid month of food and water and medicine and sanitary supplies and everything that is needed. I don't mean you can get by for a month. I mean, you can do well for a month. This means you might really have six weeks of supplies instead of four weeks of supplies. Other people will need assistance There are underestimations you will make and how much you will eat or drink. That is why I say you over-prepare for a month. There is no way Cresson would tolerate this sheer mediocrity of ready.gov, The Red Cross, or the Federal Emergency Management Association and the dearth of information that they put out today. I will admit that I am very professionally biased in my statement but as a lifetime professional in the field the only thing that allows mediocrity and substandardness to exist is the silence of the experts. ***I will not be silent.***

without discharging a car battery so much that it cannot be used to start a car.

Making an efficient battery-powered lighting system for your shelter is work best done before a crisis arises. During a crisis you should give higher priority to many other needs.

Things to remember about using small bulbs with big batteries:

- Always use a bulb of the same voltage as the battery.
- Use a small, high-resistance wire, such as bell wire, with a car battery.
- Connect the battery after the rest of the improvised light circuit has been completed.
- Use reflective material such as aluminum foil, mirrors, or white boards to concentrate a weak light where it is needed.
- If preparations are made before a crisis, small 12-volt bulbs (0.1 to 0.25 amps) with sockets and wire can be bought at a radio parts store. Electric test clips for connecting thin wire to a car battery can be purchased at an auto parts store.

CANDLES AND COMMERCIAL LAMPS

Persons going to a shelter should take all their candles with them, along with plenty of matches in a waterproof container such as a Mason jar. Fully occupied shelters can become so humid that matches not kept in moisture-proof containers cannot be lighted after a single day.

Lighted candles and other fires should be placed near the shelter opening through which air is leaving the shelter, to avoid buildup of slight amounts of carbon monoxide and other headache-causing gases. If the shelter is completely closed for a time for any reason, such as to keep out smoke from a burning house nearby, all candles and other fires in the shelter should be extinguished.

Gasoline and kerosene lamps should not be taken inside a shelter. They produce gases that can cause headaches or even death. If gasoline or kerosene lamps are knocked over, as by blast winds that would rush into shelters over extensive areas, the results would be disastrous.

SAFE EXPEDIENT LAMPS FOR SHELTERS

The simple expedient lamps described below are the results of Oak Ridge National Laboratory experiments which started with oil lamps of the kinds used by Eskimos and the ancient Greeks. Our objective was to develop safe, dependable, long-lasting shelter lights that can be made quickly, using only common household materials. Numerous field tests have proved that average Americans can build good lamps by following the instructions given below (Fig. 11.2).

These expedient lamps have the following advantages:

- They are safe. Even if a burning lamp is knocked over onto a dry paper, the flame is so small that it will be extinguished if the lamp fuel being burned is a cooking oil or fat commonly used in the kitchen, and if the lamp wick is not much larger than $^{1}/_{16}$ inch in diameter.
- Since the flame is inside a jar, it is not likely to set fire to a careless person's clothing or to be blown out by a breeze.
- With the smallest practical wick and flame, a lamp burns only about 1 ounce of edible oil or fat in eight hours.
- Even with a flame smaller than that of a birthday candle, there is enough light for reading. To read easily by such a small flame, attach aluminum foil to three sides and the bottom of the lamp, and suspend it between you and your book, just high enough not to block your vision. (During the long, anxious days and nights spent waiting for fallout to decay, shelter occupants will appreciate having someone read aloud to them.)
- A lamp with aluminum foil attached is an excellent trap for mosquitoes and other insects that can cause problems in an unscreened shelter. They are attracted to the glittering light and fall into the oil.
- Two of these lamps can be made in less than an hour, once the materials have been assembled, so there is no reason to wait until a crisis arises to make them. Oil exposed to the air deteriorates, so it is best not to store lamps filled with oil or to keep oil-soaked wicks for months.

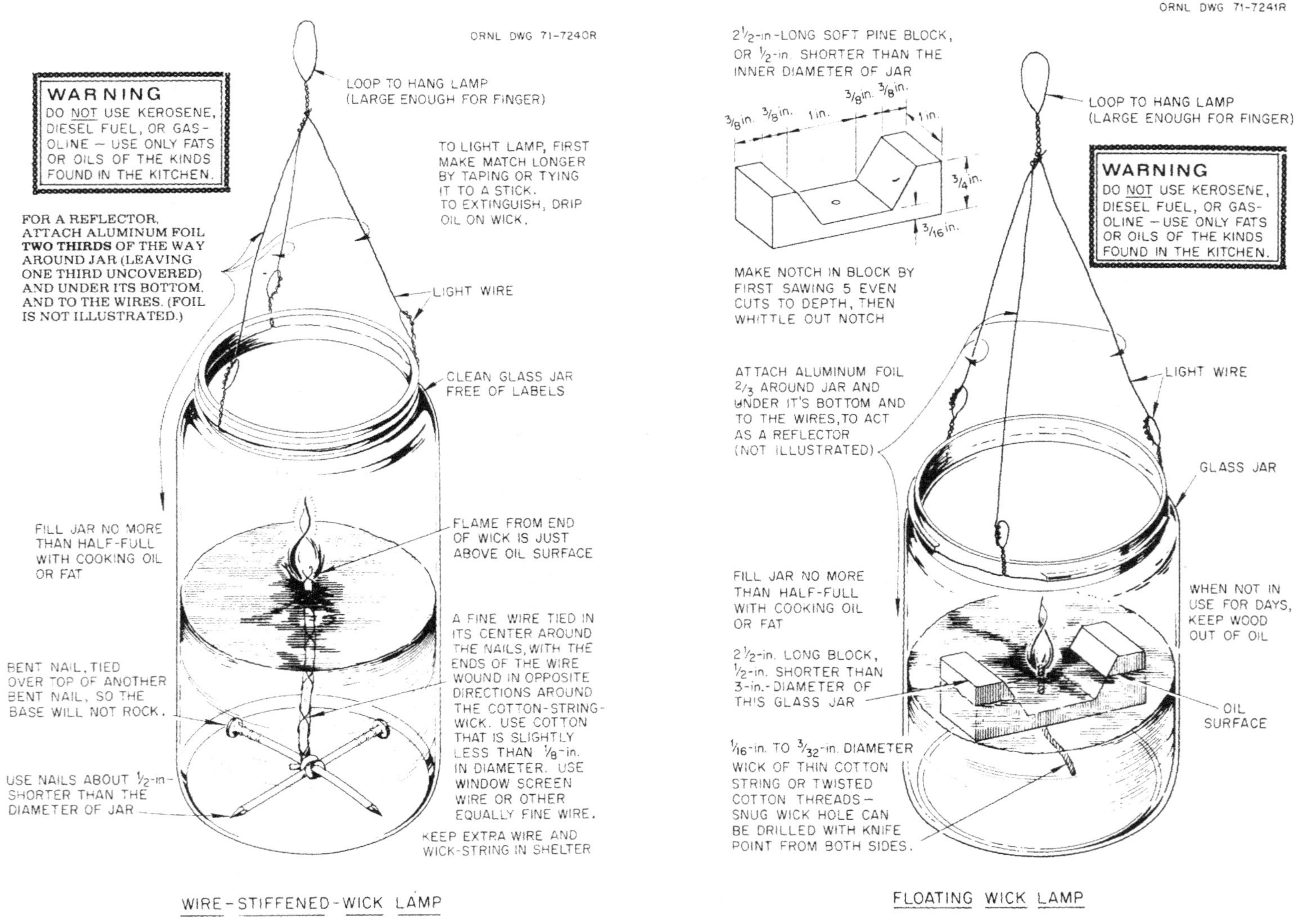

Fig. 11.2. Safe expedient lamps.

Chapter 12
Shelter Sanitation and Preventive Medicine

AN OUNCE OF PREVENTION

Should fallout force Americans to stay crowded into basements and expedient shelters for days or weeks, they should protect themselves against the spread of infectious diseases by taking both accustomed and unaccustomed preventive measures. Thousands of our jungle infantrymen in World War II learned to practice many of the health-preserving techniques described in this chapter. If modern medical facilities were temporarily unavailable, the prevention of diseases would become much more important to all of us.

The following infection-preventing measures are simple, practical, and require some self-discipline. The author has observed their practice and has used them while exploring and soldiering in a number of jungle, desert, and mountain regions. I also have used these measures while field-testing nuclear war survival skills in several states.

Basic first aid also would be of increased importance during a major confrontation or war. Good first aid booklets and instructions are available in practically all communities, so most first aid information will not be repeated here.

DISPOSAL OF HUMAN WASTES

To preserve health and morale in a shelter without a toilet or special chemicals for treatment of excrement and urine, human wastes should be removed before they produce much gas. A garbage can with a lid or a bucket covered with plastic will not hold the pressurized gas produced by rotting excrement. The following expedient means of disposal are listed in *increasing* order of effectiveness.

- Use a 5-gallon paint can, a bucket, or a large waterproof wastebasket to collect both urine and excrement. Use and keep it near the air-exhaust end of the shelter. Keep it tightly covered when not in use; a piece of plastic tied over the top keeps out insects and reduces odors. When such waste containers are full or begin to stink badly while covered, put them outside the shelter—still covered to keep out flies.

For some people, especially the aged, bringing a toilet seat from home would be justified. Padding on the edge of the bucket also helps those who have to sit down. An improvised seat of plywood or board serves well.

If only one container is available and is almost filled, periodically dump the wastes outside—unless fallout is still being deposited. Before an anticipated attack, people who plan to stay in a shelter should dig a waste-disposal pit if they do not have sufficient waste containers for weeks of shelter occupancy. The pit should be located about 3 feet from the shelter in the down-wind direction. This usually will be the air exhaust end of an earth-covered shelter. The pit should be surrounded by a ring of mounded, packed earth about 6 inches high, to keep surface water from heavy rains from running into it.

Quickly putting or dumping wastes outside is not hazardous once fallout is no longer being deposited. For example, assume the shelter is in an area of heavy fallout and the dose rate outside is 400 R/hr—enough to give a potentially fatal dose in about an hour to a person exposed in the open. If a person needs to be exposed for only 10 seconds to dump a bucket, in this 1/360th of an hour he will receive a dose of only about 1 R. Under war conditions, an additional 1-R dose is of little concern. If the shelter design does not permit an occupant to dispose of wastes without running outside, he can tie cloth or plastic over his shoes before going out, and remove these coverings in the entry before going back inside the shelter room. This precaution will eliminate the chance of tracking "hot" fallout particles into the shelter, and the small chance of someone getting a tiny beta burn in this way.

- Have all occupants only urinate in the bucket, and defecate into a piece of plastic. Urine contains few harmful organisms and can be safely dumped outside.

Two thicknesses of the thin plastic used to cover freshly drycleaned clothes will serve to hold bowel movements of several persons. Gather the plastic around the excrement to form a bag-like container. Tie the plastic closed near its upper edges with a string or narrow strip of cloth. Do not tie it so tightly as to be gas-tight. Each day's collection should be gently tossed outside. As the excrement rots, the gas will leak out of the tied end of the plastic covering. Flies will be attracted in swarms, but they will not be able to get into the plastic to contaminate their feet or to lay eggs. And because rotting excrement is so attractive to flies, shelter occupants will be bothered less by these dangerous pests.

If you have prudently kept a can of modern fly bait in your survival supplies, a little sprinkled on top of the plastic covering can kill literally thousands of flies. The most effective fly baits, such as Die Fly and Improved Golden Malrin, are sold in farm supply stores.

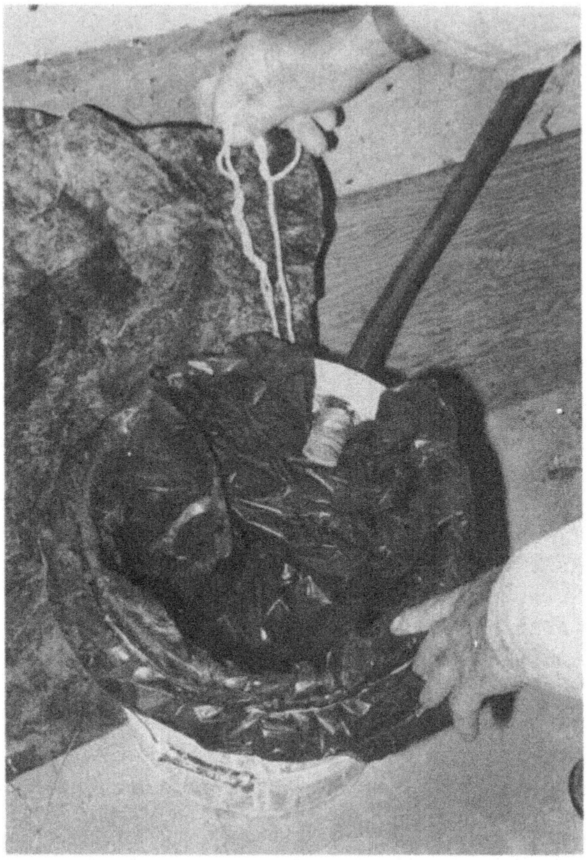

Fig. 12.1. A 5-gallon paint can used for a hose-vented toilet-can, **with a plastic trash bag for its removable liner.**

- Use a hose-vented, 5-gallon can or bucket lined with a heavy plastic bag; cover tightly with plastic when not in use. Figure 12.1 shows this type of expedient toilet.

The vent-hose runs through a hole near the top of the paint can shown and is taped to seal it to the can. Such a hole can be quite easily cut with a chisel or a sharpened screwdriver. The hose is long enough to extend outside the shelter. Its outer end should be secured about 6 inches above ground level, to prevent water from running into it during a heavy rain. When a toilet-can is tightly covered, foul gases can escape through the hose to the outdoors.

With its opening tied shut, a large plastic trash bag containing as much as 30 pounds of wastes can be lifted out of a toilet-can and disposed of outside the shelter.

The 6-member Utah family described in preceding chapters used a home-like expedient toilet during their 77-hour shelter stay. Figure 12.2 pictures the toilet seat they took with them, placed on a hose-vented container in a hole in the ground. The toilet was at one end of the shelter. A person sitting on this toilet could put his feet in the adjacent "stand-up hole" and be more comfortable.

The blanket shown hanging on the left in Fig. 12.2 could be drawn in front of the toilet for privacy. Behind the girl's head was the emergency crawlway-ventilation trench. When the toilet was being used, the shelter-ventilating KAP pumped air under the blanket-curtain and out the ventilation trench, resulting in very little odor in the rest of the shelter.

Vomiting is certain to cause both morale and health problems, especially for unprepared shelter occupants fearing this first dramatic symptom of radiation sickness. Nervousness, combined with the effects of unaccustomed food and water, will cause even some healthy persons to vomit. In a crowded shelter, the sight and smell of vomit will make others throw up. Plastic bags, well distributed throughout a shelter, are the best means to catch vomit and keep it

Fig. 12.2. The hose-vented expedient toilet used by the Utah family for over 3 days. (The unconnected telephone was brought along as a joke.)

off the floor. Buckets, pots, or a newspaper folded into a cone also will serve.

DISPOSAL OF DEAD BODIES

In large shelters which are occupied for many days, someone may die even when no occupants have been injured by blast, fire, or radiation. The sight or the sickly-sweet stink of a decaying human body is greatly disturbing. Some civil defense workers have theorized that the best way to take care of a corpse in a shelter until the fallout dose-rate outdoors is low enough to allow burial is to seal it in a large plastic bag. A simple test with a dead dog proved this idea impractical: gas pressure caused the bag to burst. One solution is to put the corpse outside as soon as the odor is evident. First, if possible, place it in a bag made of large plastic trash bags taped together and perforated with a few pinholes.

CLEAN WATER AND FOOD

Disinfecting water by boiling (preferably for at least 10 minutes) or by treating it with chlorine or iodine has been described in Chapter 8, Water.

When water is first stored, it should be disinfected by the addition of 1 scant teaspoon of ordinary household bleach for each 10 gallons.

To avoid contaminating water when removing small quantities from a container such as a waterproof bag, the simplest way is first to pour some into a pot or other medium-sized container, from which small amounts can be poured into individual cups. Dipping water with a cup runs more risk of contamination. The cleanest way to take small quantities of water out of a container is to siphon it with a flexible tube, as described in Chapter 8, Water.

Sanitary storage of food in expedient shelters is often difficult. Although almost any paper or plastic covering will keep fallout particles from food, shelter dampness can cause paper containers to break. Ants, roaches, and weevils can cut through paper or plastic coverings to reach food inside. Placing paper containers of food in plastic bags and suspending the bags from the ceiling of the shelter entryway gives good protection against bugs, and quite good protection against moisture for a few weeks. (Do not obstruct the air flow through an entryway if heat is a problem.) A small amount of insect repellent or grease smeared on the suspending string or wire will stop all crawlers. Metal and strong plastic containers with tight lids protect food best.

The hygienic preparation and serving of food in a shelter, especially in hot weather, require that all cooked food be eaten promptly. It is best to eat within half-an-hour after cooking. Canned foods should be consumed shortly after opening. The cleaning and disinfecting of utensils, bowls, etc., should be done promptly, to prevent bacteria from multiplying and to lessen the chances of ants and other insects being attracted into the shelter. Sugar should be mixed with cereals in the cooking pot, to avoid spilling.

In Oak Ridge National Laboratory shelter tests, only a few infants and toddlers have been included among the occupants. Feeding infants and small children over a piece of plastic would be one good way to keep the inevitable spillage from complicating shelter life.

To avoid using dishes, most foods can be served on squares of plastic. Spoons and such plastic "dishes" can be licked clean after eating, then disinfected by boiling or by dipping them into chlorine bleach solution containing one tablespoon of Clorox-type bleach to a quart of water.

A shelter occupant without a spoon can eat very thick grain mush in a sanitary manner by placing it on a piece of plastic held in his hand, forming it into a ball, and taking bites. Although Chinese peasants often eat wet-rice balls held in their bare hands, experiments have indicated — not unexpectedly — that Americans do not like to eat this way.

Cooking without oil or fat makes disinfecting utensils much easier when water and fuel are being conserved. Cereals and sugar are easy to wash off with a little water, without soap.

CONTROL OF INSECTS

Insect sprays used in high-protection-factor shelters are likely to cause more problems than they eliminate. Poisonous insecticides should be used with caution. Insect repellents on the skin and clothing are generally helpful, but not likely to be in sufficient supply to last for weeks or months. Some insect problems and simple means of controlling them are described below.

Mosquitoes would multiply rapidly after an attack, because normal control measures would not be in effect. Using insect screen or mosquito netting to cover the ventilation openings of a shelter is the best way to keep out mosquitoes, flies, and all larger insects. The **lack of insect screening—when it would be too late to obtain any—could result in more harrassment, discomfort and possible disease than most people accustomed to modern living are likely to imagine.** However, if the shelter has no air pump, it is impractical to use screens that obstruct the free movement of vital air—except in cold weather.

The fly population would explode after a nuclear attack. Radiation doses several times larger than doses that would kill people do not sterilize insects. In extensive rural areas where almost all people could have adequate shelter to be safe from fallout, most domestic animals and wild creatures would be killed. Trillions of flies would breed in the dead bodies.

If you have prudently kept a can of modern fly bait in your survival supplies, a little sprinkled on top of the plastic covering can kill literally thousands of flies.

Shelter occupants should make every effort to prevent flies from reaching disease-spreading human wastes.

Ants, especially in the warmer parts of the country, could drive people out of expedient shelters. The best prevention is to try to find a shelter-building site that is not near an ant nest. If shelter occupants are careful in storing food and eating, ants are less likely to become a problem.

Ticks and chiggers are usually found on grass and low bushes. To avoid carrying these pests into the shelter, do not bring grass or dead leaves into your shelter for bedding except in freezing weather. Cut leafy branches high above the ground: few pests live in tall vegetation.

PERSONAL POSSESSIONS

Toothbrushes are not boiled or otherwise disinfected after being used, because we all develop considerable resistance to our own infective organisms. For the same reason, each individual should have his own personal drinking cup, bowl, and spoon. They should be cleaned as well as possible and kept covered when not in use.

PREVENTION OF SKIN DISEASES

In crowded shelters, especially during hot weather, skin diseases are likely to be a more serious problem than is generally recognized. The importance of learning how to prevent skin diseases was made apparent by one of the very few shelter-occupancy tests to be conducted in the summer without air conditioning. This was a Navy test in which 99 men lived for 12 days in an underground shelter cooled only with outdoor summer air.[15] The incidence of skin complaints was high, even though medical treatment was available on a daily basis. The total number of reports to sick call was 560; 34 of these 99 healthy young men contracted heat rash and 23 had other skin complaints such as fungus infections. However, these sailors lived in an inadequately ventilated shelter and did not cleanse their sweaty skins or use the other methods listed below for preventing skin troubles.

Even in shelters that are skillfully ventilated with adequate outdoor air, skin diseases will be a serious problem — especially in hot weather — unless special hygiene measures are followed. Humid heat and heat rash increase susceptibility to skin diseases. Most of the following measures for preventing skin diseases have been practiced by jungle natives for thousands of years.

- Wash off sweat and dead skin. (When it is hot and humid, dead skin is continuously rubbing and flaking off and starting to decay.) Many jungle natives rinse their bodies several times a day. Bathing several times a day with soap is harmful in humid heat; the rapid loss of normal skin oils is one of the causes of skin diseases. Your skin can be kept fairly clean by rinsing off each day with just a cup of water, while rubbing gently with a very small cloth. A 6-inch square of bedsheet cloth serves well. So that you can dispose of the dirty water afterwards, wash yourself while standing on a piece of plastic with its edges held up slightly. (Place sticks or narrow boards under the edges.) Use about two-thirds of the precious water for the first rinse, starting from the face down and gently rubbing neck, armpits, stomach, groin, buttocks, and feet with a washcloth. Then use the remaining water to rinse off again, using bare fingers. If boiling water is available, sterilize washcloths every day by boiling them for a few minutes.

- Sleep as cool and bare as practical, to dry the maximum skin area.

- If practical, sit and sleep only where other members of your family do and avoid use of bedding by more than one family.

- Avoid infection from toilet seats by disinfecting with a strong chlorine solution and then rinsing, by covering with paper, or by not sitting down.

- Wash or disinfect clothing as often as practical, especially underwear and socks. Disinfecting clothing, not laundering it, is the most important health objective under difficult shelter conditions. Dipping clothing into boiling water disinfects it. Unless plenty of water is available for rinsing, do not disinfect clothing by putting it in a chlorine bleach solution.

- Wear shoes or sandals when walking about, to prevent fungus infections of the feet.

RESPIRATORY DISEASES

The spread of respiratory and other diseases transmitted by coughing and sneezing would be difficult to control in long-occupied shelters. Adequate ventilation would help in disease prevention. In small shelters, it would be better if persons who are sneezing or coughing could stay near the opening being used for air exhaust. In large shelters with many occupants, the risk of one or more of them having a disease that is easily spread obviously will be higher than in a small shelter.

Chapter 13
Surviving Without Doctors

A TEMPORARY RETURN TO SELF-HELP

Most doctors, hospital facilities, and medical supplies are located in cities. An all-out attack would destroy most of these modern blessings. Even if medical assistance were nearby, only a few of the survivors confined to shelters in areas of heavy fallout would be able to get needed medicines or the help of a doctor. For periods ranging from days to months, most unprepared survivors would be forced to live under medical conditions almost as primitive as those experienced by the majority of mankind for all but the past few decades of human history.

BENIGN NEGLECT

Life without modern medical help would be less painful and hazardous for those survivors who have some practical knowledge of what should be done—or not done—under primitive, unsanitary conditions. Information about first aid and hygienic precautions can be obtained from widely available Red Cross and civil defense booklets and courses. This knowledge, with a stock of basic first aid supplies, would reduce suffering and prevent many dangerous illnesses. However, first aid instructions do not include advice about what to do for serious injuries and sicknesses if no doctors or effective medicines are available.

Where There Is No Doctor,[32] the excellent self-help handbook recommended by Volunteers in Technical Assistance, gives much information that goes far beyond the scope of first aid. But even this handbook repeatedly recommends getting professional medical help whenever possible for serious injuries and illnesses.

Fortunately, the human body has remarkable capabilities for healing itself, especially if the injured or sick person and his companions practice intelligent "benign neglect." Such purposeful non-interference with the body's recuperative processes was called "masterful inactivity" by Colonel C. Blanchard Henry, M.D., a widely recognized authority on mass casualty evacuation and treatment. Colonel Henry was one of the first medical officers to visit Hiroshima and Nagasaki after their destruction and was an experienced analyzer of civil defense preparations in several countries.

The following is a brief summary of Colonel Henry's medical advice for nuclear war survivors living under primitive conditions and unable to get the help of a doctor or effective medicines.[33] (Additional advice, enclosed in brackets, is from a medical publication.[34])

- **Wounds:** Apply only pressure dressings to stop bleeding—unless an artery has been cut, as by a blast-hurled piece of glass. If blood is spurting from a wound, apply both a pressure dressing and a windlass-type tourniquet. Loosen the tourniquet pressure about every 15 minutes, to allow enough blood to reach the flesh beyond the tourniquet and keep it alive. There is a fair chance that clotting under the pressure dressing will stop blood loss before it becomes fatal.

- **Infected wounds:** Do not change dressings frequently. The formation of white pus shows that white corpuscles are mobilizing to combat the infection. In World War I, wounded soldiers in hospitals suffered agonies having their wounds cleaned and dressed frequently; many died as a result of such harmful care. In contrast, before antibiotics became available late in World War II, casts and dressings on infected wounds sometimes were not changed for weeks. (The author saw this treatment in China and India and smelled the stench resulting from such "benign neglect" of American soldiers' wounds — neglect that helped save limbs and lives.)

- **Pieces of glass deeply embedded in flesh**: Do not probe with tweezers or a knife in an attempt to extract them. Most glass will come out when the wounds discharge pus.

- **Burns**: Do not apply grease, oil or any other medicine to the burned area. Cover the area securely with a clean, dry dressing or folded cloth. Do not change the dressing frequently. [For most burns, the bandage need not be removed until the tenth to fourteenth day. Give plenty of slightly salted water: about 1 teaspoon (4.5 gm) of salt per quart (or liter), preferably chilled, in amounts of 1 to 3 liters daily.[34]]

- **Broken bones**: Apply simple splints to keep the bones from moving. Do not worry about deformities; most can be corrected later by a doctor. Do not attempt traction setting of broken bones.

- **Shock**: Keep the victim warm. Place blankets or other insulation material under him. Do not cover him with so many blankets that he sweats and suffers harmful fluid losses. Give him plenty of slightly salted water [about a teaspoon of salt in a liter (or quart) of water].

- **Heat prostration**: Give adequate fluids, including slightly salty water.

- **Simple childbirth**: Keep hands off. Wait until the mother has given birth. Do not tie and cut the cord unless a potent disinfectant is available. Instead, use the primitive practice of wrapping the cord and the placenta around the infant until they dry. Avoid the risk of infecting the mother by removing the rest of the afterbirth; urge the mother to work to expel it.

- **Toothache**: Do not attempt to pull an aching tooth. Decaying teeth will abscess and fall out. This is a painful but seldom fatal process — one which was endured by most of our remote ancestors who reached maturity.

VETERINARIAN ANTIBIOTICS

People who for decades have used antibiotics to combat their infections have not produced normal quantities of antibodies, and have subnormal resistance to many infections. People who have not been dependent on antibiotics have these antibodies. In the aftermath of a massive nuclear attack, most surviving Americans would be in rural areas; many would need antibiotics. A large part of their need could be met by the supplies of veterinarian antibiotics kept on livestock and chicken farms, at feed mills, and in small towns. Many animals are given more antibiotics in their short lives than most Americans receive in theirs. Hogs, for example, are given antibiotics and or other disease-controlling medicines in their feed each day. In many farming areas, veterinary antibiotics and other medicines are in larger supply than are those for people. Realistic preparations to survive an all-out attack should include utilizing these supplies.

RADIATION SICKNESS

For the vast majority of Americans who would receive radiation doses from a massive attack, the help of doctors, antibiotics, blood transfusions, etc., would not be of life-or-death importance. Very few of those receiving acute doses (received within 24 hours) of less than 100 R would become sick, even briefly. All of those exposed to acute doses between 100 R and 200 R should recover from radiation effects.[6] However, under post-attack conditions of multiple stresses and privations, some who receive acute radiation doses of 100 R to 200 R may die of infectious diseases because of their reduced resistance. If total doses this size or even several times larger are received over a period of a few months in small doses of around 6 R per day, no incapacitating symptoms should result. The human body usually can repair almost all radiation damage if the daily doses are not too large.

The majority of those with acute doses of less than about 350 R will recover without medical treatment. Almost all of those receiving acute doses of over 600 R would die within a few weeks, even if they were to receive treatment in a typical hospital during peacetime. If all doctors and the equipment and drugs needed for heroic treatments magically were to survive an attack — and persons suffering from radiation sickness could reach them — relatively few additional lives could be saved.

The most effective way to reduce losses of health and life from radiation sickness is to prevent excessive exposure to radiation. Adequate shelter and essential life-support items are the best means of saving lives in a nuclear war. The following information on radiation sickness is given to help the reader understand the importance of building a good shelter and to help him distinguish between symptoms of common illnesses and first symptoms of radiation sickness.

The first symptoms of radiation sickness are nausea, vomiting, headache, dizziness, and a general feeling of illness.[6] These symptoms begin several hours after exposure to acute doses of 100 R to 200 R, and within 30 minutes or less after receiving a fatal dose. A source of probable confusion is the fact that one or more of these symptoms is experienced by many people when they are first exposed to great danger, as in an air raid shelter during a conventional bombardment.

The occupants of a shelter might worry unnecessarily for weeks, mistaking their early emotional reactions for the initial phase of radiation sickness. This would be particularly true if they had no dependable instrument for measuring radiation, or if none of them knew how to use such an instrument.

The initial symptoms end within a day or two. Then follows the latent phase of radiation sickness, during which the patient experiences few, if any, symptoms. If the dose received was in the non-fatal range, the latent phase may last as long as 2 weeks.

In the final phase, the victim of serious or fatal radiation sickness will have reduced resistance to infections and is likely to suffer diarrhea, loss of hair, and small hemorrhages of the skin, mouth, and/or intestinal tract. Diarrhea from common causes may be confused with the onset of radiation sickness, but hemorrhages and loss of much hair are clear indications of having received serious, but not necessarily fatal, radiation exposure. The final phase usually lasts for one to two months. Any available antibiotics should be reserved for this critical phase of the illness.

Doses of 1000 R to 5000 R result in bloody diarrhea, fever, and blood circulation abnormalities, with the initial symptoms beginning within less than 30 minutes after exposure and the final phase occurring less than a day thereafter. Death results within 2 to 14 days. The victim of a dose of over 5000 R dies a hard death within 48 hours, due to radiation damage to the central nervous system.

Recovery from most cases of radiation sickness will be more likely for patients who receive a well balanced diet, rest, freedom from stress, and clean surroundings. But most patients, even without these advantages, will survive—as proved by the survival of thousands of Hiroshima and Nagasaki citizens who suffered serious radiation sickness. Nursing radiation victims is not hazardous. Even persons dying from a dose of 5000 R are not sources of dangerous radiation by wartime standards, and radiation sickness is not contagious.

LIFETIME RISKS FROM RADIATION

The large radiation doses that many survivors of a nuclear attack would receive would result in serious long-term risks of death from cancer, but the lifetime risks from even large wartime radiation doses are not as bad as many people believe. Significantly, no official U.S. estimates have been made available to the public regarding excess cancer deaths to be expected if America is subjected to a nuclear attack. However, reliable statistics are available on the numbers of additional fatal cancers suffered by persons who received large whole-body radiation doses at Hiroshima and in other disasters, and who lived for months to decades before dying. Dr. John N. Auxier—who for years was a leading health physicist at Oak Ridge National Laboratory, was one of the American scientists working in Japan with Japanese scientists studying the Hiroshima and Nagasaki survivors, and currently is working on radiation problems with International Technology Corporation—in 1986 summarized for me the risk of excess fatal cancers from **large** whole-body radiation doses: "If 1,000 people each receive a whole-body radiation dose of 100 rems [or 100 rads, or 100 R], about 10 additional fatal cancers will result." These 10 fatal cancers will be in addition to about 150 fatal cancers that normally will develop among these 1,000 people during their lifetimes. This risk is proportional to large doses; thus, if 1,000 people each receive a dose of 200 rems, about 20 additional lethal cancer cases would be expected.

"Rem" is an abbreviation for "roentgen equivalent (in) man."[6] The rem takes into account the biological effects of different kinds of radiation. For external gamma-ray radiation from fallout, the numerical value of an exposure or dose given in roentgens is approximately the same as the numerical value given in rems or in rads. The rad is the unit of radiation energy absorption in any material and applies to all kinds of nuclear radiations. Therefore, for simplicity's sake, this book gives both instrument readings (exposures) and doses in roentgens (R).

The reader desiring good information on the long-term and worldwide effects of radiation is referred to two authoritative reports of the National Academy of Sciences, Washington, D.C. 20006: *The Effects on Populations of Exposures to Low Levels of Ionizing Radiation* (The BEIR Report made by the NAS Committee on the Biological Effects of Ionizing

Radiation) (November 1972); and *Long-Term World-wide Effects of Multiple Nuclear-Weapons Detonations* (1975).

From the standpoint of basic survival know-how, these and other complicated scientific studies show that **to minimize lifetime risks from radiation**, after a nuclear attack people should:

- Provide the best protection against radiation for pregnant women and young children, since fetuses and the very young are the most likely to be hurt by radiation.
- **Realize that, with the exception of lung cancer, older people are no more susceptible to radiation injury than are those in the prime of life. Also, a 65-year-old probably will not live long enough to die of a cancer that takes 20 years or more to develop. Many older people, if they know realistic risk estimates, will choose to do essential outdoor work and take non-incapacitating radiation doses in order to spare younger members of their families the risk of getting cancer decades later.**

PREVENTION OF THYROID DAMAGE FROM RADIOACTIVE IODINES

There is no medicine that will effectively prevent nuclear radiations from damaging the human body cells that they strike. However, a salt of the elements potassium and iodine, taken orally even in very small quantities ½ hour to 1 day before radioactive iodines are swallowed or inhaled, prevents about 99% of the damage to the thyroid gland that otherwise would result. The thyroid gland readily absorbs both non-radioactive and radioactive iodine, and normally it retains much of this element in either or both forms. When ordinary, non-radioactive iodine is made available in the blood for absorption by the thyroid gland before any radioactive iodine is made available, the gland will absorb and retain so much that it becomes saturated with non-radioactive iodine. When saturated, the thyroid can absorb only about 1% as much additional iodine, including radioactive forms that later may become available in the blood; then it is said to be blocked. (Excess iodine in the blood is rapidly eliminated by the action of the kidneys.)

An excess of ordinary iodine retained in the thyroid gland is harmless, but quite small amounts of radioactive iodine retained in the thyroid eventually will give such a large radiation dose to thyroid cells that abnormalities are likely to result. These would include loss of thyroid function, nodules in the thyroid, or thyroid cancer. Sixty-four Marshall Islanders on Rongelap Atoll were accidentally exposed to radioactive fallout produced by a large H-bomb test explosion on Bikini Atoll, about 100 miles away. Twenty-two of them developed thyroid abnormalities beginning nine years later.[6] In the two days before they were taken out of the fallout area, these completely uninformed natives, living essentially outdoors, had received estimated whole-body gamma-ray doses of about 175 R from the fallout all around them. They absorbed most of the radioactive iodine retained by their thyroid glands as a result of eating and drinking fallout-contaminated food and water during their two days of exposure. (Because of unusual environmental conditions at the time of fallout deposition, some of the retained radioactive iodine may have come from the air they breathed.)

An extremely small and inexpensive daily dose of the preferred non-radioactive potassium salt, potassium iodide (KI), if taken ½ hour to 1 day before exposure to radioactive iodine, will reduce later absorption of radioactive iodine by the thyroid to only about 1% of what the absorption would be without this preventive measure. Extensive experimentation and study have led to the Federal Drug Administration's approval of 130-milligram (130-mg) tablets for this preventive (prophylactic) use only.[36,37] A 130-mg dose provides the same daily amount of iodine as does each tablet that English authorities for years have placed in the hands of the police near nuclear power plants, for distribution to the surrounding population in the very unlikely event of a major nuclear accident. It is quite likely that a similar-sized dose is in the Russian "individual, standard first-aid packet." According to a comprehensive Soviet 1969 civil defense handbook,[38] this first-aid packet contains "anti-radiation tablets and anti-vomiting tablets (potassium iodide and etaperain)."

- **Prophylactic use of potassium iodide in peacetime nuclear accidents.**

When the Three Mile Island nuclear reactor accident was worsening and it appeared that the reactor's containment structure might rupture and release dangerous amounts of radioactive iodines and other radioactive material into the atmosphere, the Government rushed preparation of small bottles of a saturated solution of potassium iodide. The reactor's containment structure did not rupture. The 237,013 bottles of saturated KI solution that were delivered to Harrisburg, Pennsylvania—mostly too late to

have been effective if the Three Mile Island accident had become an uncontained meltdown —were stored in secret in a warehouse, and were never used.

Since this famous 1979 accident, that injured no one, the Governors of the 50 states have been given the responsibility for protecting Americans against radioiodines by providing prophylactic potassium iodide. By May of 1986, only in Tennessee have Americans, other than some specialists, been given potassium iodide tablets; around one nuclear reactor some 7,500 residents have been given the officially approved KI tablets, to assure their having this protection if a nuclear accident occurs.

In April of 1982 the Bureau of Radiological Health and Bureau of Drugs, Food and Drug Administration, Department of Health and Human Services released "FINAL RECOMMENDATIONS, Potassium Iodide As A Thyroid-Blocking Agent In A Radiation Emergency: Recommendations On Use". These lengthy recommendations are summarized in the FDA's "mandated patient product insert". (See a complete copy in the following section.) This insert is packed with every bottle of non-prescription KI tablets sold. However, the lengthy FDA recommendations contain many facts not mentioned in this required insert, including the following: "Based on the FDA adverse reaction reports and an estimated 48 x 10^6 [48 million] 300-mg doses of potassium iodide administered each year [in the United States], the NCRP [National Council on Radiation Protection and Measurements] estimated an adverse reaction rate of from 1 in a million to 1 in 10 million doses." (Note that this extremely low adverse reaction rate is for doses over twice as large as the 130-mg prophylactic dose.)

FDA PATIENT INFORMATION USE OF 130-MG SCORED TABLETS OF POTASSIUM IODIDE FOR THYROID BLOCKING

(Potassium Iodide Tablets, U.S.P.)
(Pronounced poe-TASS-e-um EYE-oh-dyed)
(Abbreviated KI)

TAKE POTASSIUM IODIDE ONLY WHEN PUBLIC HEALTH OFFICIALS TELL YOU. IN A RADIATION EMERGENCY, RADIOACTIVE IODINE COULD BE RELEASED INTO THE AIR. POTASSIUM IODIDE (A FORM OF IODINE) CAN HELP PROTECT YOU.

IF YOU ARE TOLD TO TAKE THIS MEDICINE, TAKE IT ONE TIME EVERY 24 HOURS. DO NOT TAKE IT MORE OFTEN. MORE WILL NOT HELP YOU AND MAY INCREASE THE RISK OF SIDE EFFECTS. **DO NOT TAKE THIS DRUG IF YOU KNOW YOU ARE ALLERGIC TO IODINE** (SEE SIDE EFFECTS BELOW).

INDICATIONS

THYROID BLOCKING IN A RADIATION EMERGENCY ONLY

DIRECTIONS FOR USE

Use only as directed by State or local public health authorities in the event of a radiation emergency.

DOSE

ADULTS AND CHILDREN ONE YEAR OF AGE OR OLDER: One (1) tablet once a day. Crush for small children.
BABIES UNDER ONE YEAR OF AGE: One-half (½) tablet once a day. Crush first.
DOSAGE: Take for 10 days unless directed otherwise by State or local public health authorities.
Store at controlled room temperature between 15° and 30°C (59° to 86°F). Keep bottle tightly closed and protect from light.

WARNING

POTASSIUM IODIDE SHOULD NOT BE USED BY PEOPLE ALLERGIC TO IODIDE. Keep out of the reach of children. In case of overdose or allergic reaction, contact a physician or public health authority.

DESCRIPTION

Each iOSAT™ Tablet contains 130 mg. of potassium iodide.

HOW POTASSIUM IODIDE WORKS

Certain forms of iodine help your thyroid gland work right. Most people get the iodine they need from foods like iodized salt or fish. The thyroid can "store" or hold only a certain amount of iodine.

In a radiation emergency, radioactive iodine may be released in the air. This material may be breathed or swallowed. It may enter the thyroid gland and damage it. The damage would probably not show itself for years. Children are most likely to have thyroid damage.

If you take potassium iodide, it will fill up your thyroid gland. This reduces the chance that harmful radioactive iodine will enter the thyroid gland.

WHO SHOULD NOT TAKE POTASSIUM IODIDE

The only people who should not take potassium iodide are people who know they are allergic to iodide. You may take potassium iodide even if you are taking medicines for a thyroid problem (for example, a thyroid hormone or antithyroid drug). Pregnant and nursing women and babies and children may also take this drug.

HOW AND WHEN TO TAKE POTASSIUM IODIDE

Potassium iodide should be taken as soon as possible after public health officials tell you. You should take one dose every 24 hours. More will not help you because the thyroid can "hold" only limited amounts of iodine. Larger doses will increase the risk of side effects. You will probably be told not to take the drug for more than 10 days.

SIDE EFFECTS

Usually, side effects of potassium iodide happen when people take higher doses for a long time. You should be careful not to take more than the recommended dose or take it for longer than you are told. Side effects are unlikely because of the low dose and the short time you will be taking the drug.

Possible side effects include skin rashes, swelling of the salivary glands, and "iodism" (metallic taste, burning mouth and throat, sore teeth and gums, symptoms of a head cold, and sometimes stomach upset and diarrhea).

A few people have an allergic reaction with more serious symptoms. These could be fever and joint pains, or swelling of parts of the face and body and at times severe shortness of breath requiring immediate medical attention.

Taking iodide may rarely cause overactivity of the thyroid gland, underactivity of the thyroid gland, or enlargement of the thyroid gland (goiter).

WHAT TO DO IF SIDE EFFECTS OCCUR

If the side effects are severe or if you have an allergic reaction, stop taking potassium iodide. Then, if possible, call a doctor or public health authority for instructions.

HOW SUPPLIED

Tablets (Potassium Iodide Tablets, U.S.P.): bottles of [number of tablets in a bottle] tablets ( ). Each white, round, scored tablet contains 130 mg. potassium iodide.

Note that this official FDA required insert given above prudently stresses the name, the pronunciation, and the chemical formula (KI) of these Government-approved 130-mg potassium iodide tablets. Perhaps this emphasized information will keep some alarmed Americans (misinformed in a future crisis by the media that typically stated during the Chernobyl nuclear accident that "iodine tablets" were being given to people endangered by radioactive iodine from the burning reactor) from getting and taking iodine tablets, widely sold for water purification, or tincture of iodine.

Strangely, neither in official information available to the general public on the prophylactic use of KI nor in the above-mentioned FDA "Final Recommendations" is any mention made of the much greater need for KI in a nuclear war—even for Americans during an overseas nuclear war in which the United States would not be a belligerent.

Also note that this official insert contains no instructions for giving a crushed KI tablet to infants and small children. Nor is there any mention of the fact that the KI under the tablet's coating is a more painful-tasting drug than any that most people ever have taken. This omitted information is given in the next to last section of this chapter.

- **Protection against radioactive iodine in fallout from a nuclear war fought outside the United States.**

Most strategists believe that a nuclear war fought by nations other than the United States is a more likely catastrophe than a nuclear attack on America. Several of the Soviet and Chinese nuclear test explosions have resulted in very light fallout deposition and some contamination of milk by radioactive iodine in many of the 50 states. However, serious contamination of milk, fruits, and vegetables could result if war fallout from many overseas nuclear explosions were carried to an America at peace. These potential dangers and effective countermeasures are included in Chapter 18, Trans-Pacific Fallout.

If a nuclear war were to be fought in northern parts of Asia, or in Europe, or in the Middle East, a very small fraction of the fallout would come to earth on parts or all of the United States.[40] This fallout would not result in an overwhelming catastrophe to Americans, although the long-term health hazards would be serious by peacetime standards and the economic losses would be great.[40] The dangers from radioactive iodine in milk produced by cows that ate fallout-contaminated feeds or drank fallout-contaminated water would be minimized if Americans did not consume dairy products for several weeks after the arrival of war fallout. Safe milk and other baby foods would be the only essential foods that soon would be in very short supply. The parents of babies and young children who had stored potassium iodide would be especially thankful they had made this very inexpensive preparation, that can give 99%-effective protection to the thyroid. All members of families with a supply of potassium iodide could safely eat a normal diet long before those without it could do so.

The most dangerous type of radioactive iodine decays rapidly. At the end of each 8-day period it gives off only half as much radiation as at the start of that period. So at the end of 80 days it emits only about 1/1000 as much radiation per hour as at the beginning of these 80 days. Because of this rapid decay, a 100-day supply of potassium iodide should be sufficient if a nuclear war, either overseas or within the United States, were to last no more than a week or two.

KI In 2022, What, Where, How

POTASSIUM IODIDE ONLINE AND TYPES AND PRICES. Ebay, Amazon, KI4U.com
There are 2 main "name" brands of KI on the market right now in 2022. Thyrosafe and IOSAT are the 2 main brands. Both are (KI) which is potassium iodide (often misspoken as potassium iodine). There is also Potassium IODATE which when you follow the instructions will perform the same function.

Thyrosafe has the advantage that it is one 65mg pill per day per adult and thus it's one 65 mg pill per day for a child. The IOSAT pills are 130mg and they have to be broken in half for a child's dose which is not always easy.

The 3 largest online suppliers of KI and these brand names are Amazon.com, Ebay.com, and KI4U.com

In March of 2022 when there were nuclear fears in Russia - Ukraine Invasion 14 day supplies of the above pills were selling for up to $200 per pack. Those are sold and completed prices on eBay. Amazon was sold out. Dozens of people paid that price according to completed auction records. It was not a one-off thing. We saw the prices go from $29 to $35 to $50 to $99 to $149 to $199 per pack over the course of a little more than a week. Some people bought the 5-pack of these pills for $999.

When a crisis of a nuclear nature happens, people will RUSH to get KI and they will pay any price to get it when they are scared.

Buy it BEFORE the crisis and get it a lot cheaper. There are other suppliers of KI in capsules on Amazon and right now their prices are less than $30 for quantity 60 of the 65 mg capsules. This is more than enough for 2 adults to take 2 pills a day for 14 days.

The bottles MUST SAY "Potassium Iodide" or "Potassium Iodate" on them. THEY CAN NOT say Potassium with iodine. That is NOT the same thing. Not even close. Will not help you even a little bit. Eating salt with iodine is NOT a solution either. The amount of salt you'd have to eat to get enough iodine would be lethal to a human (yes, too much NaCl is lethal). Also, "Lugols Iodine" is NEVER a solution or a substitute either no matter how much stupidity you read or watch on the web.

Also on Amazon and eBay, you will see a white bottle with a red diamond logo on it that says AZ LABORATORIES and they will sell you the raw KI crystalline powder. Follow Cresson's instructions in this book on how to make a saturated solution of KI and water and then dispense it to adults and children. An eyedropper bottle helps with this if you want to buy some empty ones. Bottles need to either be opaque (do not let light in) or they need to be brown transparent (like a beer bottle) and not clear glass or clear plastic transparent.

THERE IS NO DATE, POTASSIUM IODIDE NEVER EXPIRES. EVER. PERIOD. NO EXCEPTIONS.
The amount of stupidity in the public surrounding this subject is astounding so I will try to make it straightforward and simple and erase all of the fallacies from your mind.

In inorganic chemistry (like the type you were supposed to have in high school) every chemical is one of three things. It's an acid, a base, or a salt. What you call salt, table salt, is Sodium Chloride or NaCl. Sea Salt is a mixture of about 25% Potassium Chloride (KCl) and 75% NaCl. It's called salt because chemically it's a salt. Kind of how Xerox became generic for a copy machine. Kleenex became generic for nasal tissue.

Marketing in an effort does a lot of stupid things to play on your ignorance of a subject to get you to buy their item over the same item from the competition. Like, we sell the 'freshest ground salt' for your dining pleasure.

That freshly ground salt came from salt mines and the ones under Michigan were formed about 400 MILLION years ago. That is when the salt deposits formed. The salt already existed before that only it was in an ancient sea. So that freshly ground NaCl is hundreds of millions to a billion years old. Do you think the date on the canister of salt means anything if it's over 400 million years old? No. It means nothing.

The same goes for Potassium Iodide (KI). It's a salt very similar to NaCl or KCl in that it's a tightly bound compound of potassium and Iodine. It's not going anywhere. It's not changing, it's not going out of date. It's NOT a "Medicine" in the traditional sense like an aspirin or a Tylenol or an antibiotic. It's not a complex organic molecule it's a very stable inorganic molecule. Despite the law that says there has to be a date on the package, just like there has to be an expiration date on a bottle of water, and water can be as old as salt, it will never go out of date for any reason.

Now if you open up a package from in 50 years and it's in pill form and in a blister pack, will the binder that holds the salt together in a tablet form of been degraded and you have a packet of powder? Yes. That might be true. Can you just take that same powder and it will be exactly the same as taking that pill on the day it was pressed into pill form? Yes. Exactly the same. The date on the KI pill packets is meaningless when it comes to the effectiveness of ingesting the KI active ingredient.

Here is the article from the NRC (Nuclear Regulatory Commission) of the US Government that tells you what I just said is true.

`https://www.nrc.gov/about-nrc/emerg-preparedness/about-emerg-prepared-ness/potassium-iodide/ki-faq.html#kiexpired`

There are no spaces in the above link, type it in exactly as you see it as one line.

The probability of most Americans being supplied with prophylactic potassium iodide during a major nuclear disaster appears low. Under present regulations the decision concerning whether to stockpile and dispense potassium iodide tablets rests solely with each state's governor.[41]

● Need for thyroid protection after a nuclear attack on the United States.

After a nuclear attack, very few of the survivors would be able to obtain potassium iodide or to get advice about when to start taking it or stop taking it. In areas of heavy fallout, some survivors without potassium iodide would receive radiation doses large enough to destroy thyroid function before modern medical treatments would again become available. Even those injuries to the thyroid that result in its complete failure to function cause few deaths in normal times, but under post-attack conditions thyroid damage would be much more hazardous.

● Ways to obtain potassium iodide for prophylactic use.

* *By prescription.*

With a prescription from a doctor, a U.S.P. saturated solution of potassium iodide can be bought at many pharmacies today. (In a crisis, the present local supplies would be entirely inadequate.) The saturated solution contains a very small amount of a compound that prevents it from deteriorating significantly for a few years. It is best stored in a dark glass bottle with a solid, non-metallic cap that screws on liquid-tight. A separate medicine dropper should be kept in the same place. An authoritative publication[36] of the National Committee on Radiation Protection and Measurements states: "Supplies of potassium iodide can be stored in a variety of places, including homes, . . . "

In 1990 the price of a 2-ounce bottle of U.S.P. saturated solution of potassium iodide, which is sold by prescription only, ranges from about $7.00 to $11.00 in Colorado. A 2-ounce bottle contains about 500 drops. Four drops provide the daily dose of 130 mg for adults and for children older than one year. For babies less than one year old, the daily dose of a saturated solution is two drops (65 mg). Thus approximately 99% effective protection against the subsequent uptake of radioactive iodine by the thyroid can be gotten by taking saturated potassium iodide solution. If bought by prescription, today the recommended daily dose costs 6 to 9 cents.

* *Without prescription.*

In 1990 the leading company selling **130-mg potassium iodide tablets** without prescription and by mail order in the United States is ANBEX, Inc., P.O. Box 861, Cooper Station, New York, N.Y. 10276. Two bottles, each containing fourteen 130-mg potassium iodide tablets, cost $10.00. Thus the cost per 24-hour dose is 36 cents. To the best of my knowledge, the company in the U.S. that in July of 1990 is selling 130-mg KI tablets without prescription at the lowest price is Preparedness Products, 3855 South 500 West, Bldg. G, Salt Lake City, Utah 84115. This company sells 14 tablets, in a brown, screw-cap glass bottle, for $3.50, postpaid, including shipping charges. For three or more bottles, the price is $2.50 per bottle.

After the disastrous Russian nuclear power reactor accident at Chernobyl in May of 1986, pharmacies in Sweden soon sold all of their 130-mg potassium iodide tablets and Poland limited its inadequate supplies of prophylactic iodide salts to the protection of children. In California, pharmacists reported abnormally large sales of iodine tablets, and also of tincture of iodine—apparently due to the buyers' having been misinformed by the media's reports that Europeans were taking "iodine" for protection.

Individuals can buy **chemical reagent grade potassium iodide,** that is purer than the pharmaceutical grade, from some chemical supply firms. No prescription or other authorization is necessary. In 1990 the least expensive source of which I am aware is NASCO, 901 Jamesville Avenue, Fort Atkinson, Wisconsin 53538. The price for 100 grams (100,000 mg) in 1990 is $10.50, plus $2.00 to $4.00 for shipping costs. Thus the cost in 1990 for a 130-mg daily dose is less than 2 cents. NASCO sells 500 grams (500,000 mg—about one pound) for $35.50, plus $2.00 to $4.00 for shipping—making the cost per standard daily dose only one cent.

For years of storage, crystalline or granular potassium iodide is better than a saturated solution. Dry potassium iodide should be stored in a dark bottle with a gasketed, non-metallic cap that screws on tightly. Two-fluid-ounce bottles, filled with dry potassium iodide as described below, are good sizes for a family. Separate medicine droppers should be kept with stored bottles.

Thus at low cost you can buy and store enough potassium iodide for your family and large numbers of your friends and neighbors—as I did years ago.

● Practical expedient ways to prepare and take daily prophylactic doses of a saturated solution of potassium iodide.

To prepare a saturated solution of potassium iodide, fill a bottle about 60% full of crystalline or granular potassium iodide. (A 2-fluid-ounce bottle, made of dark glass and having a solid, non-metallic, screwcap top, is a good size for a family. About 2 ounces of crystalline or granular potassium iodide is needed to fill a 2-fluid-ounce bottle about 60% full.) Next, pour safe, room-temperature water into the bottle until it is about 90% full. Then close the bottle tightly and shake it vigorously for at least 2 minutes. Some of the solid potassium iodide should remain permanently undissolved at the bottom of the bottle; this is proof that the solution is saturated.

Experiments with a variety of ordinary household medicine droppers determined that 1 drop of a saturated solution of potassium iodide contains from 28 to 36 mg of potassium iodide. The recommended expedient daily doses of a saturated solution (approximately 130 mg for adults and children older than one year, and 65 mg for babies younger than one year) are as follows:

* For adults and children older than one year, 4 drops of a saturated solution of potassium iodide each 24 hours.

* For babies younger than one year, 2 drops of a saturated solution of potassium iodide each 24 hours.

Potassium iodide has a painfully bad taste, so bad that a single crystal or 1 drop of the saturated solution in a small child's mouth would make him cry. (A small child would be screaming in pain before he could eat enough granular or crystalline KI to make him sick. Some KI tablets are coated and tasteless.) Since many persons will not take a bad-tasting medication, especially if no short-term health hazards are likely to result from not taking it, the following two methods of taking a saturated solution are recommended:

* Put 4 drops of the solution into a glass of milk or other beverage, stir, and drink quickly. Then drink some of the beverage with nothing added. If only water is available, use it in the same manner.

* If bread is available, place 4 drops of the solution on a small piece of it; dampen and mold it into a firm ball the size of a large pea, about ⅜ inch in diameter. There is almost no taste if this "pill" is swallowed quickly with water. (If the pill is coated with margarine, there is no taste.)

As stated before, 4 drops of the saturated solution provide a dose approximately equal to 130 mg of potassium iodide.

● Preparing potassium iodide tablets to give to infants and small children.

The official FDA instructions for using KI tablets state that one half of a 130-mg tablet, "first crushed", should be given every 24 hours to "babies under one year of age", and that a whole tablet should be crushed "for small children."

Putting even a small fraction of a crushed or pulverized potassium iodide tablet on one's tongue is a startling experience, with a burning sensation. A slightly burnt sensation continues for hours. Therefore, a mother is advised to make this experiment where her children cannot see her.

To eliminate the painfully bad taste of a crushed or pulverized KI tablet, first **pulverize it thoroughly.** Next stir it for a minute into at least 2 ounces of milk, orange juice, or cold drink, to make sure that the KI (a salt) is completely dissolved. Then the taste is not objectionable. If only water is available, stir the pulverized tablet into more than 2 ounces of water.

KI is a corrosive salt, more injurious than aspirin to tissue with which it is in direct contact. Some doctors advise taking KI tablets after meals, except when so doing would delay taking the initial dose during an emergency. All recognize that taking a dilute solution of KI is easier on the stomach than taking the same dose in tablet form. This may be a consequential consideration when taking KI for weeks during a prolonged nuclear war emergency.

● WARNINGS

* Elemental (free) iodine is poisonous, except in the very small amounts in water disinfected with iodine tablets or a few drops of tincture of iodine. Furthermore, elemental iodine supplied by iodine tablets and released by tincture of iodine dropped into water is not effective as a blocking agent to prevent thyroid damage. If you do not have any potassium iodide, DO NOT TAKE IODINE TABLETS OR TINCTURE OF IODINE.

* DO NOT MAKE A FUTILE, HARMFUL ATTEMPT TO EAT ENOUGH IODIZED SALT TO RESULT IN THYROID BLOCKING. Iodized salt contains potassium iodide, but in such a low concentration that it is impossible to eat enough iodized salt to be helpful as a blocking agent.

OTHER WAYS TO PREVENT THYROID DAMAGE

Besides the prophylactic use of potassium iodide, the following are ways to prevent or reduce thyroid damage under peacetime or war-time conditions:

* Do not drink or otherwise use fresh milk produced by cows that have consumed feed or

water consequentially contaminated with fall-out or other radioactive material resulting from a peacetime accident or from nuclear explosions in a war.

* As a general rule, do not eat fresh vegetables until advised it is safe to do so. If under wartime conditions no official advice is obtainable, avoid eating fresh leafy vegetables that were growing or exposed at the time of fallout deposition; thoroughly wash all vegetables and fruits.

* If a dangerously radioactive air mass is being blown toward your area and is relatively small (as from some possible nuclear power facility accidents), and if there is time, an ordered evacuation of your area may make it unnecessary even to take potassium iodide.

* For protection against **inhaled** radioactive iodine, the FDA Final Recommendations (which are mentioned in the preceding section) state that the following measures "should be considered": "... sheltering [merely staying indoors can significantly reduce inhaled doses], evacuation, respiratory protection, and/or the use of stable iodide."

Research has been carried out in an effort to develop a thyroid protection procedure based on the ordinary iodine solutions which are used as disinfectants. Since iodine solutions such as tincture of iodine and povidone-iodine are dangerous poisons if taken orally, these experiments have utilized absorption through the skin after topical application on bare skin.

All reported experimental topical applications on human skin have given less thyroid protection than does proper oral administration of potassium iodide. Moreover, undesirable side effects of skin application can be serious. For these reasons researchers to date have not recommended a procedure for the use of ordinary iodine solutions for thyroid protection.

Potassium iodide, when obtained in the crystalline reagent form and used as recommended above on pages 114 and 115, is safe, inexpensive, and easy to administer. Prudent individuals should obtain and keep ready for use an adequate supply of potassium iodide well in advance of a crisis.

Chapter 14

Expedient Shelter Furnishings

IMPORTANCE OF ADEQUATE FURNISHINGS

Throughout history, people have endured being crowded together while living and sleeping on hard surfaces. In times of war and privation, people have lived in such conditions for much longer periods than would be necessary for shelter occupancy due to fallout.[42] Realistic basement-shelter-occupancy tests conducted by research contractors for the U.S. Office of Civil Defense (now the **Federal Emergency Management Agency**) have shown that modern Americans can live and sleep for two weeks on a concrete floor. In some of these tests, only 8 square feet of floor space was provided for each person; only pieces of corrugated cardboard 3/16-inch thick lessened the hardship of sleeping and sitting on concrete.[13]

Nevertheless, shelters should be adequately furnished whenever possible, for these reasons:

- More people can occupy a properly furnished shelter—for weeks, if necessary—if adequate additional ventilation is supplied for the additional occupants.
- Cleanliness, health, and morale are better if well-designed furnishings are used. More serious complications than discomfort are likely to result if occupants have to huddle together on a bare floor—especially if the floor is damp earth.
- Persons occupying a shelter made relatively comfortable by its furnishings are more likely to stay in the shelter long enough to avoid dangerous exposure to fallout radiation.

CHAIRS, BENCHES, AND BUNKS

The father of the previously described Utah family of six knew that the members of his family would be most uncomfortable and probably would have sore backs if they spent the required 72 hours of continuous shelter occupancy huddled on the floor. (Their shelter room was only 3½ feet wide and 16½ feet long.) So this family took with them from home four folding chairs and two pieces of plywood (each 21 inches wide by 6 feet long) tied as part of the load on top of the family car. Four small wooden boxes served as food containers during the drive to the shelter-building site. In the shelter, the boxes were used to support the ends of two narrow plywood bunks (Fig. 14.1).

The family's system of sleeping and sitting in shifts worked reasonably well. There were discomforts: the adults found the two plywood bunks too narrow, and the plywood was so hard that all the family members used their sleeping bags for padding rather than for needed warmth on chilly nights. The father and oldest son, whose turn to sleep was during normal waking hours, had trouble sleeping in such a small shelter while the lively 4-year-old son was awake.

Note that in the shelter pictured in Fig. 14.1 the earth walls are covered with plastic from trash bags. Covering earth walls with plastic or bed sheets makes for a cleaner shelter, with less earth falling in the faces of people who sleep on the floor. Bedsheets on the walls make a shelter brighter, but are flammable and a potential fire hazard. The plastic film prevented the

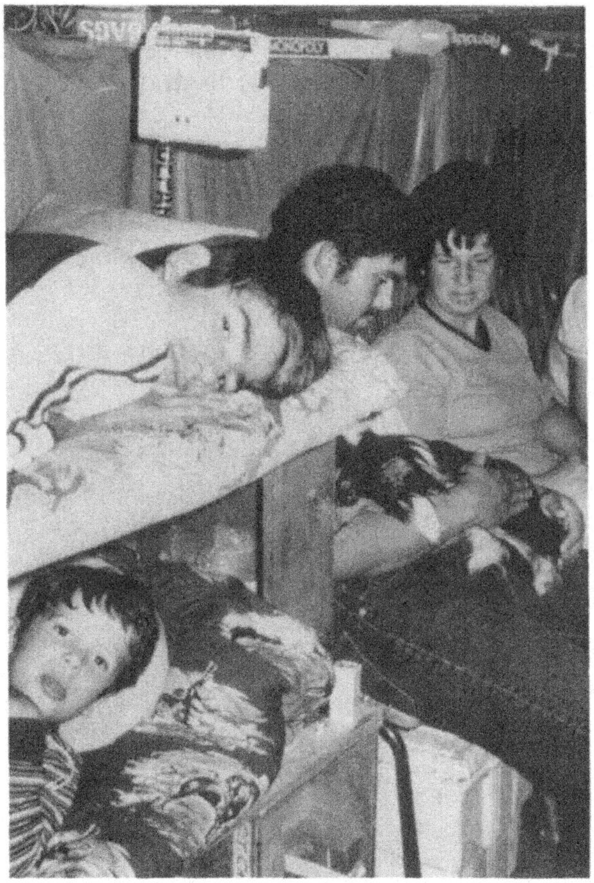

Fig. 14.1. Bunks and folding chairs furnished this Pole-Covered Trench Shelter. (Note the suspended transistor radio. Reception is good in all types of expedient shelters tested to date.)

Fig. 14.2. Benches with overhead bunks in a skillfully designed Small-Pole Shelter of Russian design. Three rural families in a wooded area of Tennessee built this expedient blast shelter in 48 hours, including the time spent felling trees and making furnishings.

earth walls from drying and crumbling as a result of the hot, dry desert air pumped through the shelter during the day.

Benches with overhead wooden bunks are shown in Fig. 14.2. These were installed in a Small-Pole Shelter 6 feet wide with a ceiling almost 7 feet high.

A well-designed expedient shelter should be as small as practical, with all space used very efficiently. The builders should make the heights and widths of benches and bunks as specified in the detailed shelter drawings, such as those for the Small-Pole Shelter given in Appendix A.3.

Serious difficulties can result from failure to use specific dimensions that may appear unimportant. For example, in field tests at Fort Bragg, N.C., 48 airborne infantrymen, working only with hand tools, cut pine trees and built two 24-man Small-Pole Shelters in less than 24 hours.[43] The men did not think it necessary to use the specific dimensions when they made the furnishings. As a result, they built the benches too high and the overhead bunks too far below the ceilings. This error forced the men to sit for hours in hunched positions. Even these able-bodied young men would have developed very sore backs and would have wanted very much to leave their shelters if they had been forced to sit in a bent-over position for days.

Figure 14.2 shows a good example of the importance of using dimensions which have been thoroughly field-tested when building essential parts of a shelter. Note the small air-exhaust opening above the girl lying on the overhead bunk at one end of the shelter. This opening led to a small, chimney-like, air-exhaust duct made of boards, with its cross-sectional area as specified in Russian civil defense handbooks for natural ventilation of small expedient shelters. With such a small air-exhaust opening—only 4 square inches (10 square centimeters) per person—a fully occupied shelter of this size would soon become dangerously overheated in warm or hot weather, even though a good low-pressure expedient shelter-ventilating pump (a KAP or a Directional Fan) were to be used. A much larger air-exhaust opening is needed. See Appendix A.3.

BEDSHEET-HAMMOCK AND CHAIR

On the last night of the Utah family's shelter stay it was clear that the six members would win the cash bonus offered them for their 72-hour occupancy of the shelter starting immediately after they completed building it. Therefore, the author showed them that night how to make boat-shaped hammocks out of bedsheets. (Any strong cloth of the right size can be used.) They were shown how to hang these short, yet stable, hammocks securely from poles of the shelter roof. With three members sleeping in hammocks, two on the plywood bunks, and one on the floor, all six could sleep at the same time. Figure 14.3 shows part of this sleeping arrangement.

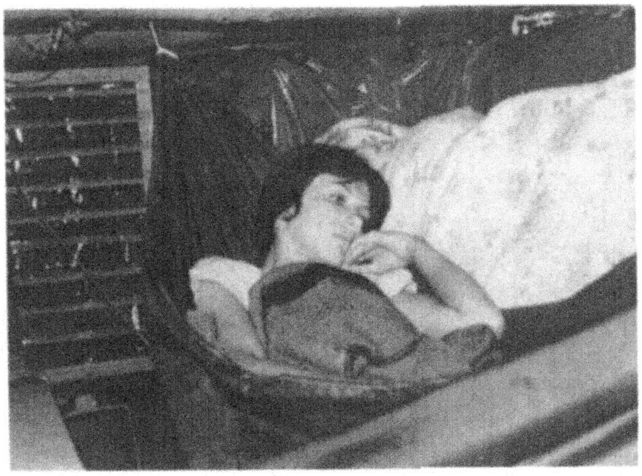

Fig. 14.3. Girl resting in a boat-shaped hammock. Her brother slept on the upper bunk of their 3½-ft-wide trench shelter.

In a shelter this size without bunks, hanging four short hammocks at slight angles to the length of the trench would permit four occupants to sleep comfortably. An additional two persons could sleep on the floor. In the Utah family's shelter, the floor was made comfortable by covering the damp earth with pieces of polyethylene cut from trash bags, then placing strips of shag rug over the plastic.

In shelters with ceilings at least 6 feet high, one hammock can be hung above another. In a Small-Pole Shelter that is 6 feet wide, a greater number of people can sleep or sit comfortably at the same time if Bedsheet-Hammocks and Bedsheet-Chairs are used rather than benches or a combination of benches and overhead bunks. Figure 14.4 shows how Bedsheet-Hammocks can be used like double-deck bunks.

Fig. 14.4. Bedsheet-Hammocks hung one above the other across the room of a Russian-type Small-Pole Shelter made of lumber.

Detailed instructions for making a Bedsheet-Hammock and a Bedsheet-Chair are given at the end of this chapter.

In an evacuation during a real crisis, carrying comfortable folding chairs and the materials to make wooden bunks would not be advisable. If the family car were loaded instead with an equivalent weight of additional food and clothing, the members' prospects of surviving would be improved. But in an actual crisis evacuation, a family planning to occupy a shelter with a strong roof should take along a bedsheet for each member. The other lightweight items described in the instructions for making a Bedsheet-Hammock and a Bedsheet-Chair also should be carried. By following the instructions at the end of this chapter, a comfortable hammock can be made and quickly converted to a comfortable suspended chair when not needed for sleeping.

Hammocks hung high off the floor and above other sleepers must be strong, securely suspended, and cupped so that it is impossible to fall out accidentally. This is why the instructions emphasize using a double thickness of bedsheet and folding the cloth so as to make the hammock boat-like, with high sides.

In a cold shelter, keeping warm in a hammock is somewhat difficult. Easily compressible materials, such as those used in a sleeping bag, are squeezed so thin under a person's body that they lose most of their insulating value. Pads of newspapers about an inch thick, protected by cloth coverings, will reduce heat losses. The best insulation is a quilt, fastened to the underside of a hammock by attaching it with rows of stitches every few inches and at right angles to each other.

Figure 14.5 shows a Bedsheet-Hammock that had been quickly converted into a Bedsheet-Chair and hung near a shelter wall. It occupies less than half the floor space used by the two hammocks shown in the preceding illustration. If a reclining seat is desired, the two support-points on the ceiling to which the chair-arm cords are attached can be located farther out from the wall.

Enough padding material should be placed in the bowl-shaped seat of a Bedsheet-Chair to make it rather flat. Extra clothing or a folded blanket can be used. The three cords suspending the chair should be adjusted for length so that the sitter's feet can rest on the floor and the edge of the chair seat does not press on the undersides of his thighs. (Such pressure cuts off circulation. During the London Blitz of World War II, many of the people who sat night after night in shelters on folding chairs with canvas seats developed serious leg conditions. Authorities later prohibited bringing such chairs into shelters.)

Fig. 14.5. A Bedsheet-Hammock converted into a comfortable suspended Bedsheet-Chair.

> CAUTION: To prevent skin infections and other diseases from spreading, a person's hammock or chair should not be used by others. This precaution is particularly important if the shelter is hot and its occupants are sweaty.

HOW TO MAKE A BEDSHEET-HAMMOCK AND CONVERT IT TO A SUSPENDED BEDSHEET-CHAIR

1. PURPOSE: To enable more people to occupy a shelter more comfortably.

2. ADVANTAGES:

* The hammock can be made in a few minutes, once you have the materials and the know-how.
* The only materials required are a strong double-bed sheet (or an equally large piece of

any strong fabric), a few feet of rope (or a piece of strong fabric from which expedient "rope" can be made quickly), a few large nails, and some wire.

* It is difficult to fall out of the hammock because its sides are each made about 8 inches shorter than its lengthwise mid-section, so as to produce a boat-like shape.
* It provides room for head and shoulders close to either end; thus it is practical to hang this hammock between supports that are as close together as 6 feet. See Fig. 14.6.

Before beginning work, someone should read aloud all of the instructions for making the hammock. This will help to avoid mistakes.

Fig. 14.6. The author lying in a Bedsheet-Hammock. (Note that he is pulling the operating cord of a homemade shelter-ventilating pump, a KAP.)

MAKING A BEDSHEET-HAMMOCK

A. How to fold and tie the bedsheet:

1. Select a strong double-bed sheet (one containing polyester is best) and use a ruler or tape measure to avoid guessing at measurements.
2. Fold the bedsheet lengthwise down its center line, so that pairs of corners are together.
3. With the sheet folded, mark the center of each of the two folded ends; then hold one end up.
4. Starting at one corner of one end of the folded bedsheet, make accordion-like pleats.

Make each pleat about 2 inches wide; make the left corner of each pleat about 1 inch lower than the left corner of the preceding pleat, when the sheet is being held as illustrated. Use your left hand to hold the completed pleats in place, while making new pleats with your right hand.

ORNL-DWG 77-17387

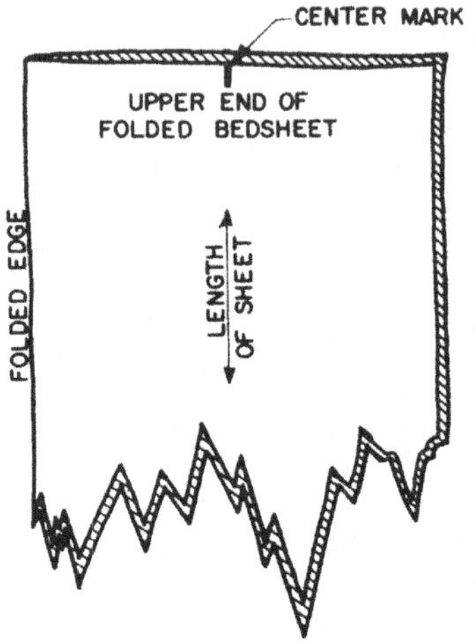

ORNL-DWG 77-17388

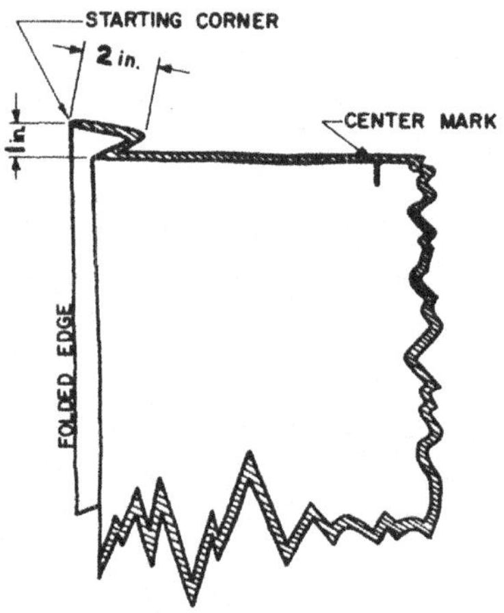

ORNL-DWG 77-17389

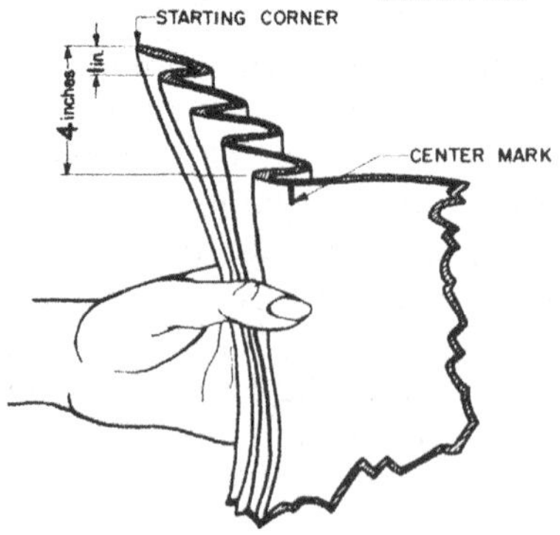

5. When one-half of the upper end of the sheet has been folded into pleats almost to the CENTER MARK, adjust the pleats so that the CENTER MARK is about 4 inches below the STARTING CORNER.

6. Continue making 2-inch pleats on past the CENTER MARK, but make the right corner of each pleat about 1 inch higher than the right corner of the preceding pleat. When the pleat-folding is completed, the STARTING CORNER and the other corner should be at the same height (4 inches) above the CENTER MARK.

7. Tie the hammock-supporting rope tightly around the end of the sheet about 3 inches below the edge with the CENTER MARK. (If a rope strong enough to support at least the weight of two men is not available, make an expedient "rope" by tearing a 16-inch-wide strip from a sheet or other strong cloth and then rolling this strip crosswise to its length to make a tight roll several feet long. Then tie string or small strips of cloth about 1 inch wide around it, spaced 4 to 6 inches apart, to keep the rolled-up cloth from unrolling.)

8. Bend the pleat-folded end of the sheet downward around the hammock rope, so that the knot of the hammock rope is uppermost.

9. To keep the sheet from being pulled through the encircling hammock rope, bind the doubled-over end of the sheet with cord (or with narrow strips of cloth) about 1 inch below the rope. Tie the binding cord at least four times around, knotting it each time around.

10. Repeat the procedure (4 through 9) with the other end of the double-folded sheet, thus producing a boat-shaped hammock with its two sides each about 8 inches shorter than its lengthwise center section.

ORNL-DWG 77-17390

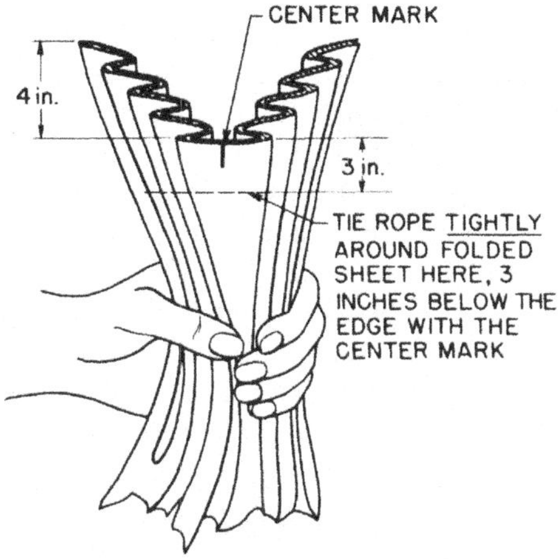

ORNL-DWG 77-17391

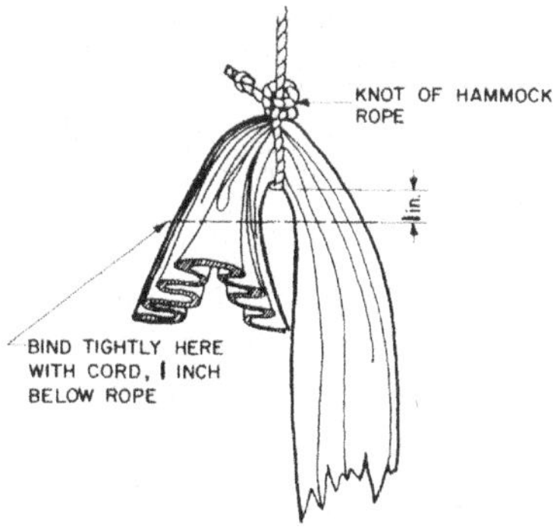

ORNL-DWG 77-17392

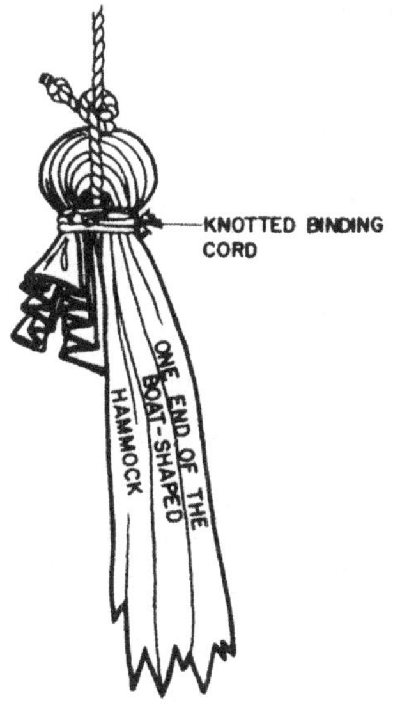

B. How to hang the hammock:

1. To suspend a hammock from a strong wooden roof such as the poles of a Pole-Covered Trench Shelter, drive two strong nails (at least $3^1/_2$ inches long) into the wood at approximately 45° angles, crossing and touching each other. Bind the two nails together with wire. To prevent a hammock rope from being rubbed directly against fixed metal, make a loose loop of strong wire (best if doubled) through the crossed nails; tie the hammock rope to this free-moving wire loop.

2. To suspend the hammock from a wooden wall, use the same type of crossed-nails supports, with the nails driven in one above the other.

3. For comfort and safety, hang the hammock with the head end 18 inches higher than the center and with the foot end 24 inches higher than the center.

4. To make sure that the hammock is strong enough, two persons should place their open hands on its centerline and put all of their weight on the hammock.

5. To suspend hammocks and hammock-chairs from a pole roof that is not being built under fear of immediate attack, use loops of strong wire around the poles at the planned support points. (The correct placement of wire loops takes considerable time and delays completion of the shelter.) To reduce stresses and possible breakage, the loops should be loose, as illustrated.

ORNL-DWG 77-17394

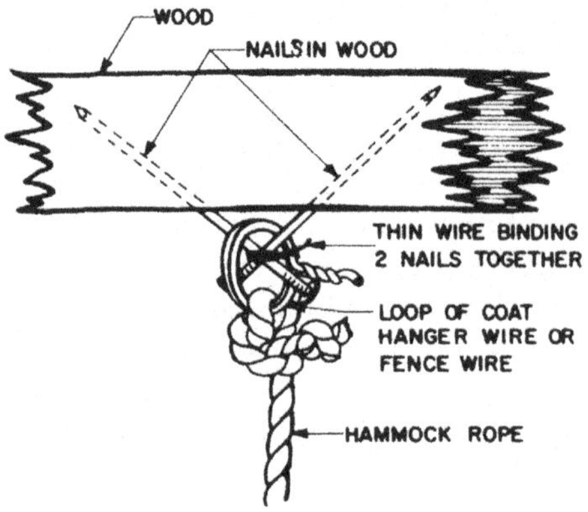

ORNL-DWG 78-6321

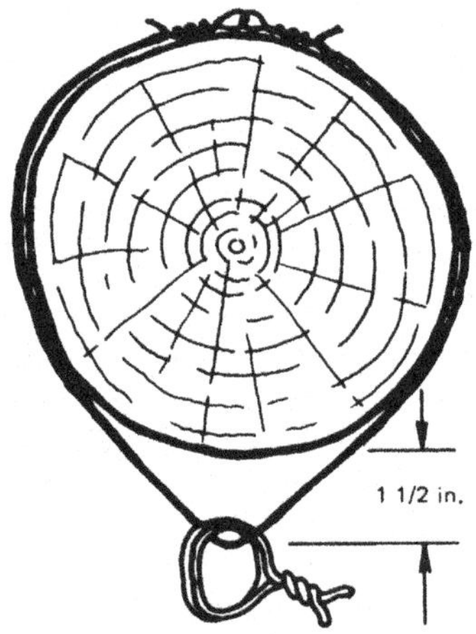

MAKING A SUSPENDED BEDSHEET-CHAIR

A Bedsheet-Hammock may be quickly converted into a comfortable Suspended Bedsheet-Chair so that a shelter occupant can sit comfortably, yet occupy less floor space during the daytime. Follow these steps:

1. Select one end of the hammock to be the top of the back of the chair.
2. From this end, measure 52 inches (4 ft 4 in.) along each side-edge of the hammock (see sketch), and mark these two spots.
3. About $2^1/_2$ inches in from these two marks (toward the centerline of the hammock), make two more marks.
4. To make an attachment point for a chair "arm", hold a pebble (or a lump of earth) under one of these last marks, pull the double-thickness cloth tight around the pebble, and tie it in place. (See illustration.) Repeat on the other side-edge of the hammock.
5. Tie the end of one rope (or "rope" made of 10-inch-wide strip of strong cloth) to one attachment point, and the end of another rope to the other attachment point.
6. Suspend the top of the back of the chair to a suspension point on the ceiling at least 4 inches out from the wall, and adjust the length of this suspending rope so that the chair arms will be about the same height from the floor as the arms of an easy chair (see sketch).
7. Suspend the arms of the chair from two suspension points 20 inches apart and 20 inches farther out from the wall than the suspension point of the back of the chair. (Study the illustration.)
8. Fold the unused end of the hammock up and back into the "seat" of the chair; fill the hollow of the seat with coats, a blanket, or anything else soft, to make it comfortable.
9. Adjust the lengths of all three suspending ropes so that the chair seat is the right height for the person sitting in it. When both feet are flat on the floor, the front edge of the seat should not press against the undersides of the thighs.
10. To simplify repeated conversion of the hammock to a chair, mark the spot on each of the 3 suspending ropes where each is tied to its suspension point on the ceiling; also mark the spot on each suspending rope for a chair arm where each is tied to its suspension point on a chair arm. If enough light rope or strong cord is available, the easiest and quickest way to connect and disconnect the arm supports is to suspend each arm with a double strand of rope, looped around an attachment point as illustrated by the sketch of the attachment point.

ORNL DWG 77-18432

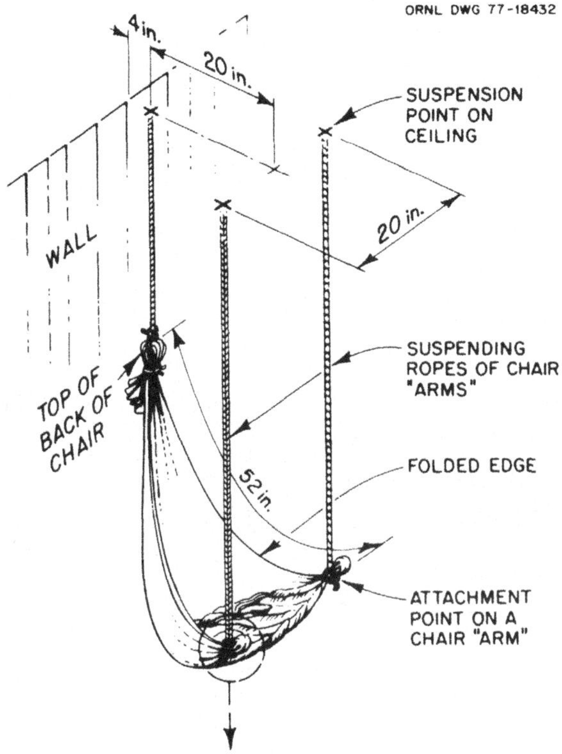

ORNL-DWG 77-17395

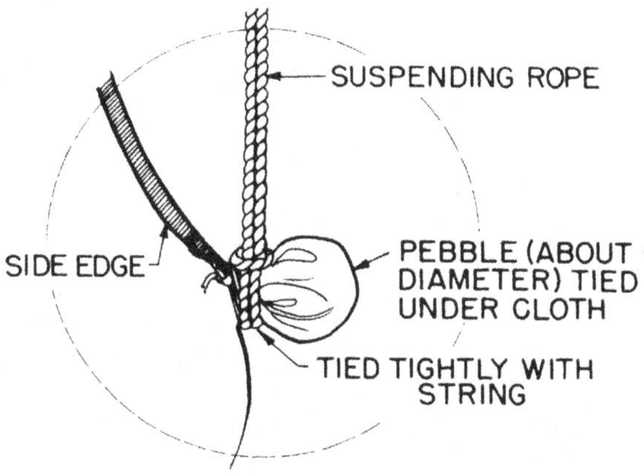

ATTACHMENT POINT

Chapter 15

Improvised Clothing and Protective Items

BASIC PRINCIPLES OF COLD WEATHER CLOTHING

If Americans would learn to use skillfully the ordinary clothing, towels, cloth, newspapers, and paper bags in their homes, they could keep warm enough to stay healthy—even under much colder conditions than they believe endurable without specialized outdoor winter clothing. Efficient cold-weather clothing can be improvised if the following ways of conserving body heat are understood and used:

- **Trap "dead" air.** Covering enough of your body with a thick layer of trapped "dead" air is the basic requirement for keeping warm. Figure 15.1 shows how efficient body insulation works: Both the air warmed by close contact with the skin and the water vapor from evaporated perspiration flow outward into the insulating material. Any material that breaks up and separates air into spaces no more than $^1/_8$ inch across has efficient cells of "dead" air. Air that is within $^1/_{16}$ inch of any surface—whether that of a filament of goose down or of a piece of paper—is slowed down by "sticking" to that surface and becoming hard to move. Trapped "dead" air moves outward very slowly, carrying heat away from the body at a slow rate—thus minimizing heat losses by convection.

ORNL-DWG 77-18426

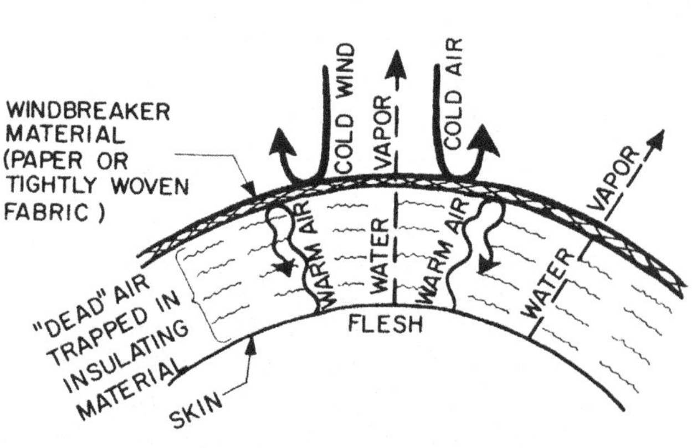

Fig. 15.1. Efficient body insulation.

- **Use windbreaker materials.** An outer windbreaker layer of clothing that is essentially air-tight, such as a brown paper bag worn over a knit wool cap, prevents the escape of warmed air and results in an insulating layer of trapped "dead" air. A single layer of good windbreaker material also prevents cold outside air from being blown into the insulating material and displacing warmed air (Fig. 15.1).

The best windbreaker materials permit very little air to pass through them, while at the same time they allow water vapor to escape. Perspiration that cannot be felt or seen on cool skin continually evaporates, forming warm water vapor close to the skin. This moisture escapes outward through good insulating and windbreaker materials; as a result, underlying body insulation remains dry and efficient. Water vapor can pass readily through many sheets of newspaper or unglazed brown paper, although not enough wind can flow through a single sheet to be felt.

- **Prevent excessive heat losses by conduction.** Body heat also is lost by conduction—the direct flow of heat into a colder material. For example, if one sleeps in an excellent goose-down sleeping bag laid directly on cold ground, body weight will compress the down to a small fraction of an inch. This barrier to heat flow is too thin and will cause the body to lose heat rapidly to the cold earth. Likewise, the soles of ordinary shoes are such poor insulators that standing or walking on frozen ground sometimes results in frozen feet.

MINIMIZING HEAT LOSSES FROM HEAD AND NECK

The head and neck of the girl pictured in Fig. 15.2 are insulated almost as well as if she were wearing the hood of a skin-side-out Eskimo parka. She folded a large, fluffy bath towel and placed it over her head, neck, and the upper part of her body. A brown paper bag was worn over the towel. The edges of the face hole cut in the bag were taped to prevent tearing. A strip of cloth was tied around the part of the bag over her neck. Such a parka-like covering not only is the most efficient way to insulate the head and neck but also prevents air warmed by the body from escaping upward around the neck. The girl also is wearing a man's shirt large enough to cover and hold thick newspaper insulation around her body and arms.

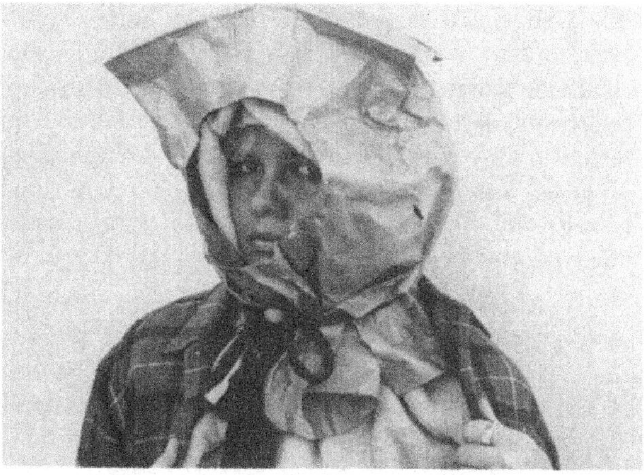

Fig. 15.2. A bath towel and a paper bag used to efficiently insulate head, neck, and shoulders.

It is very important to prevent heat losses from the head and neck, which have many blood vessels near the skin surface. Heat losses from these vital parts cannot be sensed nearly as well as heat losses from other parts of the body. Furthermore, blood vessels near the surface in the head and neck do not automatically constrict to reduce heat losses, as they do in other parts of the body when heat is being lost faster than it can be supplied by metabolism. So when a person is in the cold—particularly when inactive—he should keep his hands, feet, and whole body warmer by insulating his head and neck very well. (One difficulty in following this advice is that a well-covered head often will feel unpleasantly warm—even sweaty—before one's body temperature rises enough to increase the warming flow of blood to hands and feet.)

INSULATING THE WHOLE BODY

Occupants of freezing-cold shelters can keep warm enough to sleep without blankets by skillfully using ordinary indoor clothing plus paper and pieces of cloth to insulate their whole bodies. The girls pictured in Fig. 15.3 slept without a blanket in a frozen Door-Covered Trench Shelter while the night temperature outdoors dropped to 10° F. The shelter's ventilation openings were adjusted so that the inside temperature remained a few degrees below freezing, to prevent frozen earth from melting into icy mud. These girls had insulated themselves well. First, they covered their cotton shirts and pants with 10 thicknesses of newspaper wrapped around their bodies and tied with strips of cloth. Then around each arm and leg they wrapped and tied 8 sheets of newspaper, thus insulating their limbs with at least 16

Fig. 15.3. Girls wearing expedient clothing are prepared for sleeping in the freezing-cold trench shelter.

thicknesses. As an outer covering over their legs, they wrapped wide strips torn from a bedsheet. Their expedient foot coverings were of the type described in a following paragraph. Their heads and necks were insulated with towels covered with brown paper bags. Old cotton raincoats allowed water vapor to pass through and helped hold in place the insulating newspapers, which extended to cover the girls' bare hands.

The girls slept on newspapers spread about an inch thick over the gravel floor of the trench. When sleeping on cold or frozen ground, it is best to place newspapers or other insulation on top of a layer of small limb-tips or brush, so that drying air can circulate under the bedding. A sheet of plastic under bedding will keep it from being dampened by a wet floor but will not prevent it from being dampened after a few days by condensed water vapor from the sleeper's body.

Newspaper and other paper through which water vapor can pass are such good windbreaker materials that they can be used under any loose-fitting outer garment—even one through which air can pass quite readily. They also provide good insulation. Figure 15.4 shows the author coming out of an icy shelter at sunup. Many thicknesses of newspaper covered my body and arms and extended like cuffs from my sleeves. A porous cotton bathrobe covered the newspapers and helped hold them in place. Because so little heat was lost through this clothing, plenty of warm blood continued to flow to my bare hands, ridding my body of excess heat by radiation.

IMPROVISED WINTER FOOTWEAR

Cold-weather footwear that is warmer than all but the best-insulated winter boots can be improvised readily. The trick is learning how to tie the several insulating layers securely in place, so that you could hike for miles in the snow if necessary.

For use in dry snow, first tie a porous insulating layer—such as two bath towels or 10 big sheets of newspaper—over each shoe. If you have no low-heeled shoes, make a paper sole by folding 3 large newspaper sheets to make a sole that has 72 thicknesses of paper. Then proceed in the following manner:

1. Place your foot and the sole on 10 newspaper sheets, as pictured in Fig. 15.5.

Fig. 15.4. The author emerges after a night's sleep in freezing-cold temperatures inside a Car-Over-Trench Shelter. Expedient clothing, primarily newspaper insulation, kept him warm without a blanket.

A Paper Bag and a Newspaper?

NO PAPER GROCERY BAGS AND NO NEWSPAPERS
Other things can be used. Any notebook paper can be used but also, take a knife to the cushions to your outdoor patio furniture cushions, couches, chairs, and car seats (front and back).

The open-cell foam can be cut and sculpted and held together with needle and thread (I know) as well as duct tape, to replace the newspaper insulation Cresson is showing. This was made very popular by the preparedness legend and world-class cold-weather expert Jim Phillips. I have done it, I've used it, and it works. Get that foam and shape it so it goes around your foot, over and around your head, around your body and you'll be quite a warm person.

You'll want the foam to be about 1 inch (25.4mm) thick on average for very cold areas. If your foam is a lot thicker then cut it like a cake layer so it's about an inch or so in thickness. In warmer climates where it's only slightly cold you can experiment with thinner layers like 1/2" or 12.7mm

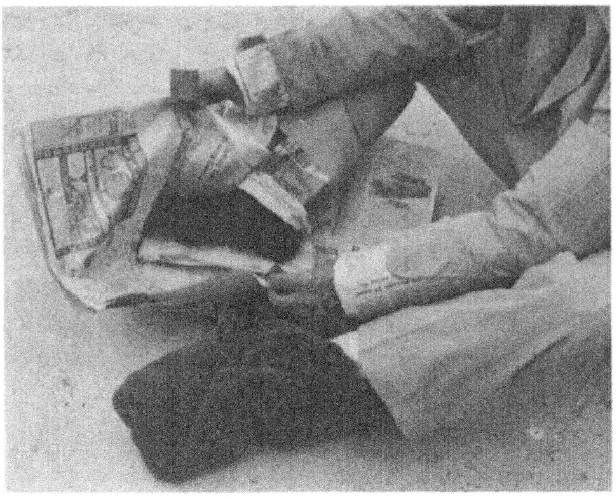

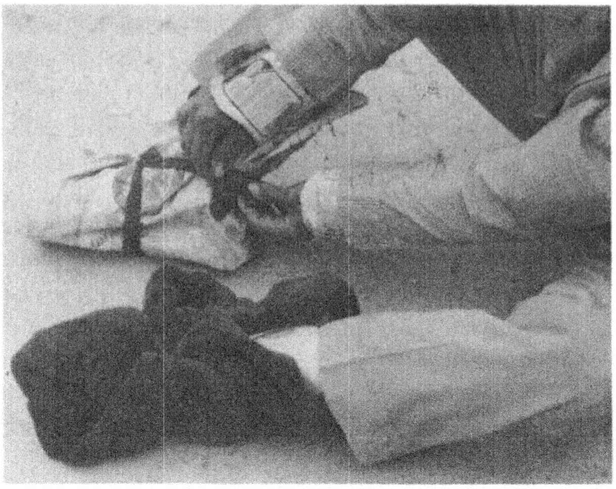

Fig. 15.5. Insulating a foot with a folded newspaper sole and 10 sheets of newspaper.

2. Fold all the sheets over the top of your foot while keeping the sole in the proper place, as indicated in Fig. 15.5.
3. Use a strip of cloth about 3 inches wide and 5 feet long to tie the papers in front of your ankle with a single overhand knot (half of a square knot). With the same strip, tie another single overhand knot over the tendon behind the ankle. Finally, tie a bow knot in front of the ankle.
4. Cover the insulating layer with a tough fabric, such as canvas or burlap sack material; secure with a second strip of cloth and tie as described above.

If the snow is wet, place a piece of strong plastic film or coated fabric outside the insulating layer, after securing it with the first strip of cloth. The outer protective covering should be tied over the waterproofing, with the second strip of cloth securing both it and the waterproofing. (When resting or sleeping in a dry place, remove any moistureproof layer in the foot coverings, to let your feet dry.) Figure 15.6 shows a test subject's waterproofed expedient foot-covering, held in place as described above, after a 2-mile hike in wet snow. His feet were warm, and he had not stopped to tighten or adjust the cloth strips.

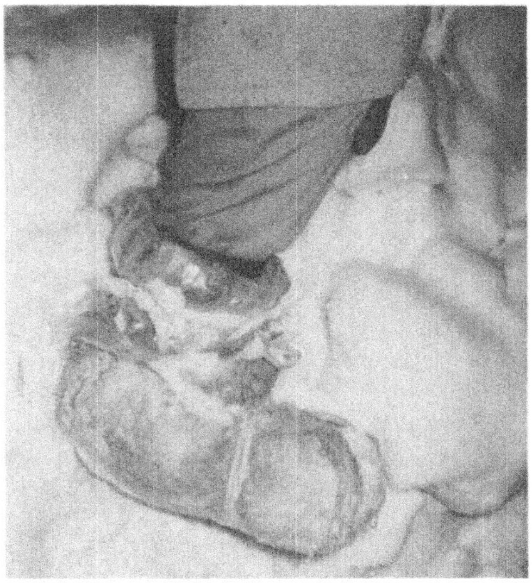

Fig. 15.6. Expedient water-proofed foot-covering, over a newspaper sole and other newspaper insulation.

Persons who have not worked outdoors in icy weather seldom realize the importance of warm footwear for winter. Russian civil defense manuals direct urban citizens to take winter boots with them when they evacuate, even in summer.

KEEPING WARM WITHOUT FIRE

- If occupants of a cold room or shelter lack adequate clothing and bedding, all should lie close together.
- Always place some insulating material between your body and a cold floor. (Pieces of shag rug are excellent.) Plastic film should be placed under the insulating material if the ground is damp.
- Go to bed or put on all your body insulation before you begin to feel cold. Once the loss of body heat causes blood vessels in your hands and feet to constrict, it often is hard to get these vessels to return to normal dilation again.
- Do not jump up and down or wave your arms to get or to keep warm. The windchill factor is a measure of air movement over your skin; rapid body movements always cause some such air movement. If practical, lie down and cover up; then do muscular tension exercises by repeatedly tightening all your muscles so tight that you tremble.
- Prevent sweating and the dampening of insulation by taking off or opening up clothing as you begin to exercise, before you begin to sweat.
- If you are getting cold, don't smoke. Nicotine causes blood vessels to constrict and the flow of blood to hands and feet to be reduced.
- Don't drink an alcoholic beverage to warm yourself. Alcohol causes increased blood flow close to the skin surface, resulting in rapid loss of body heat. It is impossible for alcohol to make up for such loss for very long.

RAINWEAR

All that is needed to make serviceable, improvised rainwear is waterproof material and waterproof tape. Plastic film from large trash bags will do; 4-mil polyethylene is better; tough, lightweight, coated fabric is best. Fabric duct tape is the best widely available tape.

Figure 15.7 shows a pair of improvised rain chaps. Rain chaps are separate leg coverings, each with a loop to suspend it from one's belt and usually made large enough to be pulled on and off over the shoes and trousers. Rain chaps are better than waterproof trousers for working or walking while wearing a poncho or raincoat, because body movements cause drying air to be literally pumped under the chaps. This air keeps trousers and legs dry, and therefore warmer.

Fig. 15.7. Improvised rain chaps made of trash-bag polyethylene and freezer tape.

In the same way, a poncho or rain cape will allow plenty of air to reach the garments under them while one is working. When exercise is stopped, clothing underneath will stay dry and warm for some time.

SANDALS

Shoes are almost always in short supply for years following a disastrous war. Except in very cold weather, sandals can be made to serve quite well. The best sandal designs for hard work and serious walking have a strap around the heel and in front of the ankle, with no thong between the toes (Fig. 15.8).

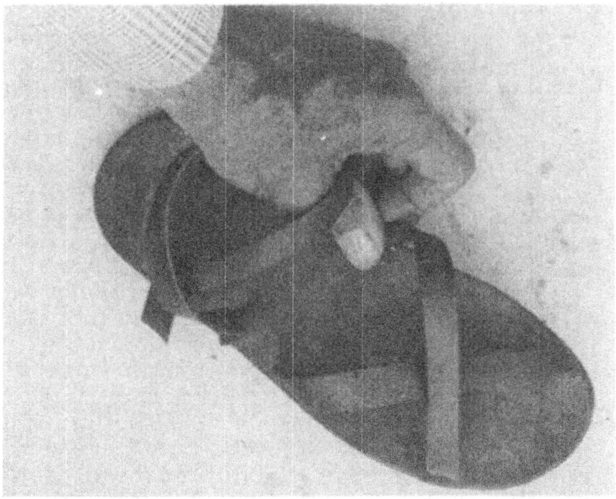

Fig. 15.8. A Ho Chi Minh Sandal, excellent Vietnamese expedient footwear. Rubber bands cut from an inner tube have been inserted into a sole of auto-tire tread.

Such sandals also have the advantage of enabling one to wear socks and other foot insulation inside the straps.

CLOTHING TO PROTECT AGAINST BETA BURNS

If fresh and very radioactive fallout particles remain for long on the skin or extremely close to the skin, beta burns result. Any clothing that keeps fallout off the skin helps greatly. The best expedient protection is given by an outer layer of easily removable clothing similar to the improvised rainwear previously described, but fully covering the hair and neck and providing plastic trousers instead of chaps. Removable shoe coverings are highly advisable. All such protective coverings should be removed before entering a shelter, or removed in the entryway before going into the shelter room.

If a person has fallout particles on clothing that he must continue to wear, he should vigorously brush his outer clothing before entering a shelter room. If fallout particles are washed off, rinsed off, or otherwise removed from the skin within a few minutes, no beta burns will result.

A few days after a nuclear explosion, fallout particles are not radioactive enough to cause beta burns. In areas of heavy fallout, the danger from external doses of gamma radiation from fallout on the ground will continue much longer than will the risk of beta burns from some of these same fallout particles.

The gamma rays given off by fallout particles brought into a shelter on clothing or bodies would subject shelter occupants to gamma doses so small as to be of no significance by wartime standards. Nor would shelter occupants be endangered by radiation from the body of a person who, before reaching shelter, had received a gamma dose large enough to kill him many times over. Except in science fiction stories, the body of such a person does not become "radioactive."

FALLOUT MASKS

For the majority of Americans in most fallout areas, means for filtering fallout particles out of the air they breathe would not be essential survival equipment.[18] Most fallout particles tiny enough to enter one's lungs would fall to earth so slowly that they would reach ground thousands of miles away from the explosions. By then, radioactive decay would make them much less dangerous, and their deposition would be spread out over much of the earth.

In past years American-endangering Soviet warheads typically were between 20 and one megaton. Explosions this large would inject almost all fallout particles into the stratosphere, high above rain clouds. Today thousands of deployed Soviet ICBM warheads are between 550 and 100 kilotons. (See *Jane's Weapon Systems, 1987-88.*) Both surface bursts and air bursts of today's smaller warheads would inject most of their radioactive particles into the troposphere, from whence rain-outs and snow-outs would bring huge numbers of even tiny particles to earth in "hot spots" scattered across America.

Persons living in dry, windy areas often wear dust masks and goggles to protect their noses and eyes from dust and sand particles. If fallout particles are mixed with dust and sand that is being blown into a shelter, then persons in windy areas who occupy small below-ground expedient shelters should cover their noses and mouths with several thicknesses of towels or other cloth. Those who have dust masks should wear them, especially when working outside in dry, windy weather soon after fallout deposition. Other than whole-body exposure to gamma rays, the main danger to well informed people would be from possible beta burns caused by fresh, "hot" fallout particles that would collect in nasal passageways, and from swallowed fallout particles. (Much of the material continually eliminated from the nose and throat is swallowed.) In some fallout "hot spots" a secondary danger would be breathing extremely small, "hot" fallout particles into one's lungs, after a rain-out of tiny fallout particles from fallout clouds produced by today's typical kiloton-range Soviet warheads. In some areas "hot" particles would be dried and blown about by the winds within hours of their deposition in rain showers.

Making a homemade dust and fallout mask is still not a high priority survival project. In normal times, it is better to buy and store good masks and goggles. The following instructions for making a homemade mask are an improved design based on a Russian design (Fig. 15.9). This mask is the best of several

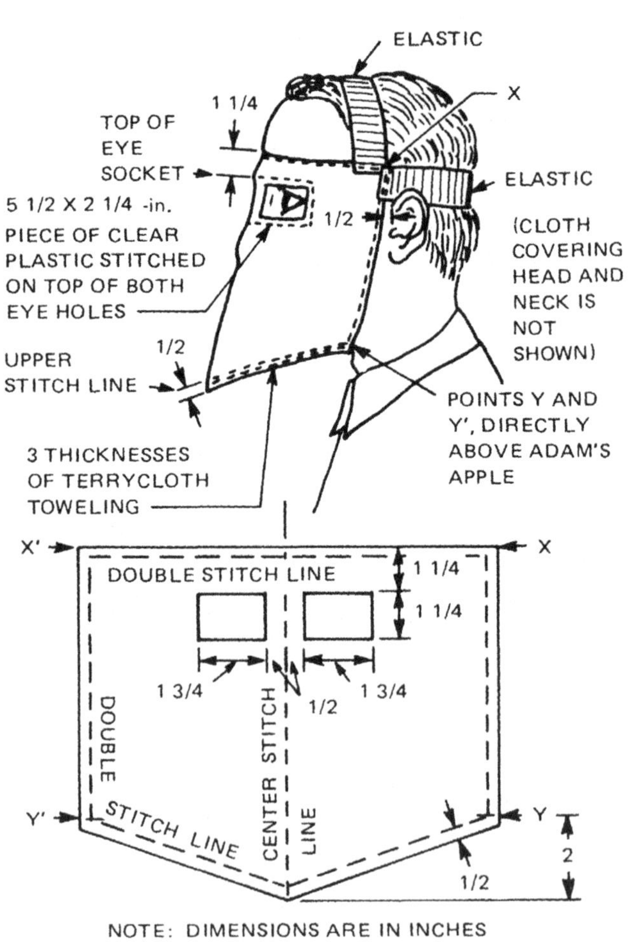

Fig. 15.9. A Russian-type homemade fallout mask. For most Americans this will continue to be a low-priority item as long as Russian warheads are large.

homemade types, and the following instructions for making and using it have been field-tested.

AN INDIVIDUALLY-FITTED FALLOUT MASK

Materials Needed:

1. Three rectangular pieces of fluffy toweling (terry cloth preferred), each piece approximately 12×15 inches (or use 10 men's handkerchiefs).
2. Elastic. (The best expedient elastic is from the waistband of a man's undershorts.)
3. Clear plastic (from a photo album, billfold, plastic storm window, etc.).
4. Sewing materials.

Measurements:

1. Tie a string vertically around your head and face, passing it 1/2 inch in front of each of your ears and making it quite tight.
2. Tie a second string horizontally around your head, crossing your forehead 1 1/4 inches above the top of your eye sockets. These two strings should cross each other at points X and X^1, over your temples.
3. Measure the distance X-to-X^1 across your forehead and the distance X-to-X^1 going under your chin (around your lower jaw and next to your throat), as indicated by Fig. 15.9.

Construction:

1. Cut out 3 pieces of terry cloth, making the width of each piece equal to X-to-X^1 (the curved distance across your forehead), and the height of each piece equal to the distance X-to-Y plus 1/2 inch—that is, equal to half the distance X-to-X^1 (measured under your chin) plus 1/2 inch. See Fig. 15.9.
2. Cut the lower edge of each piece as illustrated.
3. Stitch the 3 pieces of terry cloth together, one on top of the other, thus making the mask three layers thick. Stitch around all four edges of the cloth rectangle and down the centerline.
4. Mark and cut out the eye holes, as illustrated. Make the mask's dimensions smaller for children.
5. Cut one rectangle of clear plastic measuring 5 1/2 × 2 1/4 inches, and sew this plastic over the outside of the eye holes, stitching the plastic around its edges and down the centerline.
6. Fold the three pieces along their vertical centerline and stitch the lower side together, along the upper stitch line Y-to-Y^1. Stitch 1/2 inch from the lower edge. Then sew a second row of stitches.
7. Sew on the elastic head bands, making them short enough to hold the mask tightly around your face. If the elastic is from the waistband of a man's undershorts, use a doubled elastic both over the top of your head and around the back of your head. Make these elastic pieces so short that you can just put all your fingers comfortably between the elastic and your head when the pieces are fully stretched. If using a weaker elastic, be sure to adjust the lengths to a tight fit, to prevent air leaks under the edges of the mask. Because of the thickness of material where the elastics are connected to the upper corners of the mask, it may be necessary to do this stitching by hand.
8. To keep fallout particles off your head and neck, sew a loose-fitting piece of bedsheet cloth (not illustrated) to the edges of the mask that fit around your face. This cloth should extend back over your head and down over your collar, over which it can be tied.

Use:

Put on the mask by first placing it over your chin, then pulling the back elastic down to fit around the back of your head.

CAUTION:

To avoid spreading infections, each mask should be labeled and worn by only one person.

Chapter 16
Minimum Pre-Crisis Preparations

Your chances of surviving a nuclear attack will be improved if you make the following low-cost preparations before a serious crisis arises. Once many Americans become convinced that a nuclear attack is a near certainty, they will rush to stores and buy all available survival supplies. If you wait to prepare until a crisis does arise, you are likely to be among the majority who will have to make-do with inadequate supplies of water containers, food, and materials. Furthermore, even if you have the necessary materials and instructions to make the most needed survival items, you and your family are not likely to have time to make all of them during a few days of tense crisis.

The following recommendations are intended primarily for the majority who live in areas likely to be subjected to blast, fire, or extremely heavy fallout. These people should plan to evacuate to a safer area. (Many citizens living outside high-risk areas, especially homeowners with yards, can and should make better pre-crisis preparations. These would include building high-protection-factor permanent shelters covered with earth.)

SHELTER

Keep on hand the tools and materials your family or group will need to build or improve a high-protection-factor expedient shelter: One or more shovels, a pick (if in a hard-soil area), a bow-saw with an extra blade, a hammer, and 4-mil polyethylene film for rainproofing your planned shelter. Also store the necessary nails, wire, etc. needed for the kind of shelter you plan to build.

Keep instructions for shelter-building and other survival essentials in a safe and convenient place.

VENTILATION-COOLING

Make a homemade shelter-ventilating pump, a KAP, of the size required for the shelter you plan to build or use.

WATER

Keep on hand water containers (including at least four 30-gallon untreated polyethylene trash bags and two sacks or pillowcases for each person), a pliable garden hose or other tube for siphoning, and a plastic bottle of sodium hypochlorite bleach (such as Clorox) for disinfecting water and utensils.

FALLOUT METER

Make one or two KFMs and learn how to use this simple instrument.

FOOD

Store at least a 2-week supply of compact, non-perishable food. The balanced ration of basic dry foods described in Chapter 9, Food, satisfies requirements for adults and larger children at minimum cost. If your family includes babies or small children, be sure to store more milk powder, vegetable oil, and sugar.

Continuing to breast-feed babies born during an impending crisis would greatly simplify their care should the crisis develop and worsen.

For preparing and cooking basic foods:

- Make a 3-Pipe Grain Mill like the one described in Chapter 9, Food, or buy a small hand-cranked grain mill, which grinds more efficiently than other expedient devices.

- Make a Bucket-Stove as described in Chapter 9. During evacuation, the stove can be used as a container. Store some kitchen-type wooden matches in a waterproof container.
- Keep essential containers and utensils on hand for storing and transporting food and for cooking and serving in a shelter.

SANITATION

A hose-vented 5-gallon can, with heavy plastic bags for liners, for use as a toilet. Include some smaller plastic bags and toilet paper with these supplies. Tampons.

Insect screen or mosquito netting, and fly bait. See Chapter 12.

MEDICINES

- Any special medications needed by family members.
- Potassium iodide, a 2-oz bottle, and a medicine-dropper, for prophylactic protection of the thyroid gland against radioactive iodines. (Described in the last section of Chapter 13, Survival Without Doctors.)
- A first-aid kit and a tube of antibiotic ointment.

LIGHT

- Long-burning candles (with small wicks) sufficient for at least 14 nights.
- An expedient lamp, with extra cotton-string, wicks, and cooking oil as described in Chapter 11.
- A flashlight and extra batteries.

RADIO

A transistor radio with extra batteries and a metal box in which to protect it.

OTHER ESSENTIALS

Review the EVACUATION CHECKLIST (developed primarily for persons who make no preparations before a crisis) and add items that are special requirements of your family.

Harris PreCrisis Preparedness

OMG THIS IS ENDLESS.

I cannot emphasize pre-crisis preparedness more than anything else. You are 100% going to be affected in your life by power failures, hurricanes, blizzards, storms, earthquakes, floods, forest fires, etc... Something is going to happen to change your world for a period of time whether it's man-made or natural. You should have a minimum level of preparedness for yourself and those that you care for and love. The Toxic Positivity of "Oh, it will all be fine, I don't need to do anything." is a form of self-induced complacency that kills people.

I have an endless number of classes given by me in both audio and video format for food, water, energy, power, illumination, and communications. It is so beyond numerous I would be a fool to think could even enter a smattering of it here on this page. No matter what year you are reading this I will try to keep links to this content up and available at either www.NuclearWarSurvivalSkills.com or www.Harris1234.com

If you do anything, get the food and water items in this book and practice with them. Make the meals, try them. You might find you really enjoy your beans and cornmeal if you add a certain spice to it that you enjoy or someone suggested. By a bunch of that spice with your other pre-crisis preparations.

Try the Harris double water instant pudding with sugar, protein powder, and cooking oil (or butter) added. Try it, change it, make it your own, put your name on it, and tell others about it. Show them.

Please, listen to this advice carefully. There are a lot of people who will tell you to NOT do something. I have become unapologetic in telling people, "Shut up, stop finding reasons to NOT do it, and start finding a reason TO DO it."

Do NOT tell people what you are going to do. Only show them what you have done. It's hard to talk you out of doing something when you've already done it and you are showing them the results.

Using yourself as an example is a great way of saying, "Look, I did this, it's easy. You can do this too. I'll help you."

Chapter 17
Permanent Family Fallout Shelters for Dual Use

THE NEED

Having a permanent, ready-to-use, well supplied fallout shelter would greatly improve millions of American families' chances of surviving a nuclear attack. Dual use family shelters — shelters that also are useful in peacetime — are the ones that Americans are most likely to build in normal peacetime and to maintain for years in good condition for use in a nuclear war.

The longer nuclear peace lasts, the more difficult it will be, even during a recognized crisis, to believe that the unthinkable war is about to strike us and that we should build expedient shelters and immediately take other protective actions. The lifesaving potential of permanent, ready-to-use family shelters will increase with the years.

Americans who decide to build permanent shelters need better instructions than can be obtained from official sources or from most contractors. This chapter brings together fallout shelter requirements, based on shelters and shelter components that have been built and tested in several states and nations. The emphasis is on permanent fallout shelters that many Americans can build for themselves. The author believes that millions of Americans can build good permanent fallout shelters or have local contractors build them — if they learn the shelter requirements outlined in the following sections of this chapter and the facts about nuclear weapon effects and protective measures given in preceding chapters. Builders can use their skills and available local resources to construct permanent, dependable fallout shelters at affordable cost.

Requirements for a permanent, dual-use family fallout shelter follow.

A HIGH PROTECTION FACTOR, AT AFFORDABLE COST

A permanent fallout shelter should be built — and can easily be built — to have a high enough protection factor to prevent its occupants from receiving fatal or incapacitating radiation doses, and also from receiving doses large enough to seriously worsen their risks of developing cancer in the years following an attack. Shelters with a protection factor of 40 (PF 40) meet the minimum standard of protection for public shelters throughout the United States, and permanent family fallout shelters described in official pamphlets provide at least PF 40 protection. In almost all fallout areas, PF-40 shelters would prevent occupants from receiving fatal or incapacitating radiation doses while inside these shelters. However, in areas of heavy fallout the occupants of PF-40 shelters could receive radiation doses large enough to significantly contribute to the risk of contracting cancer years later. Furthermore, the larger the dose you receive while in a shelter, the smaller the dose you can receive after you leave shelter without being incapacitated or killed by your total dose.

If you build a permanent shelter, you would be foolish to build a shelter with a PF of only 40 when additional protection is so easy to obtain. By making a shelter with a 6-inch-thick concrete roof covered by 30 inches of shielding earth, and with other easily attained design features shown in Figs. 17.1 and 17.2, you can have a shelter with a protection factor of about 1000. (An occupant of a PF 1000 shelter will receive a radiation dose only 1/1000th as large as he would receive if he were standing outside in an open field during the same time interval.) To attain PF 1000 protection near the inner door of the illustrated

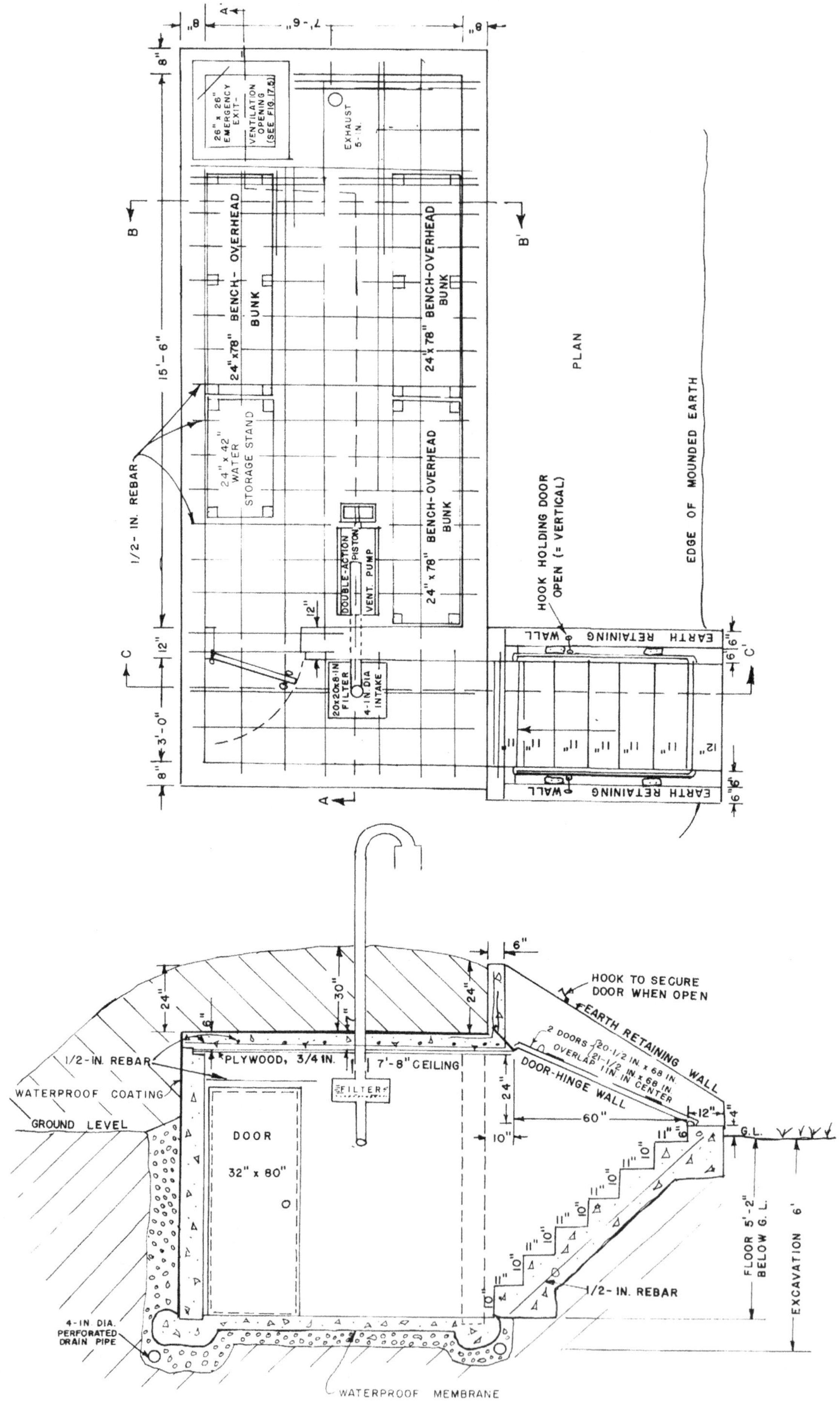

Fig. 17.1. Permanent Family Fallout Shelter for Dual Use.

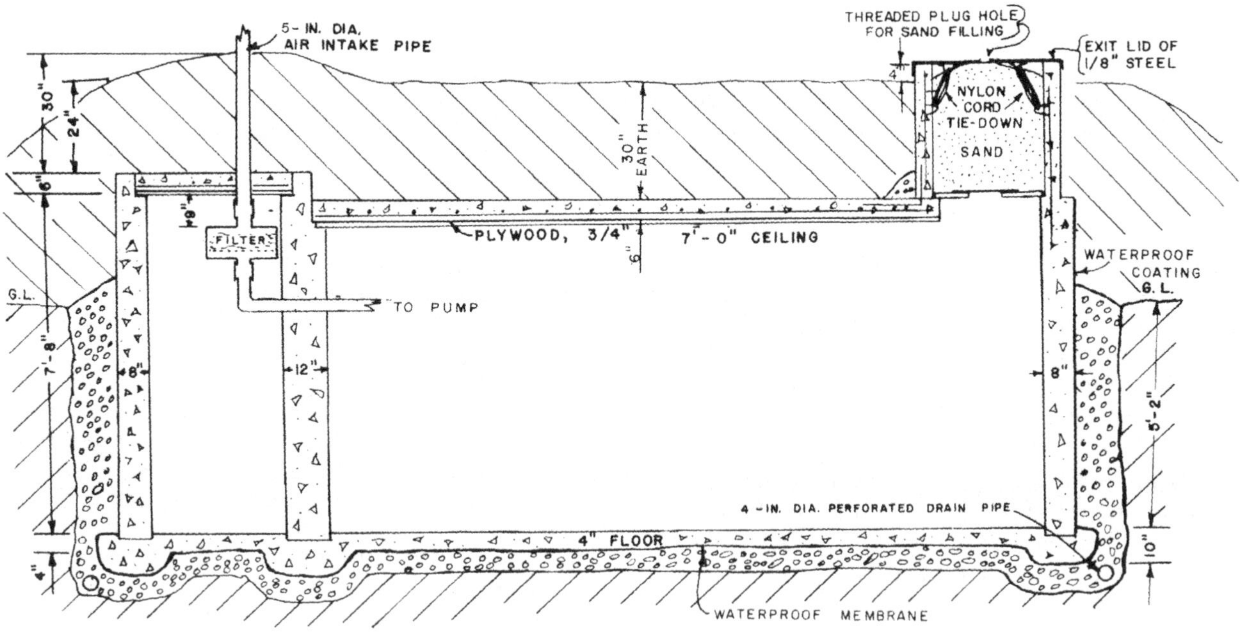

SECTION A-A'

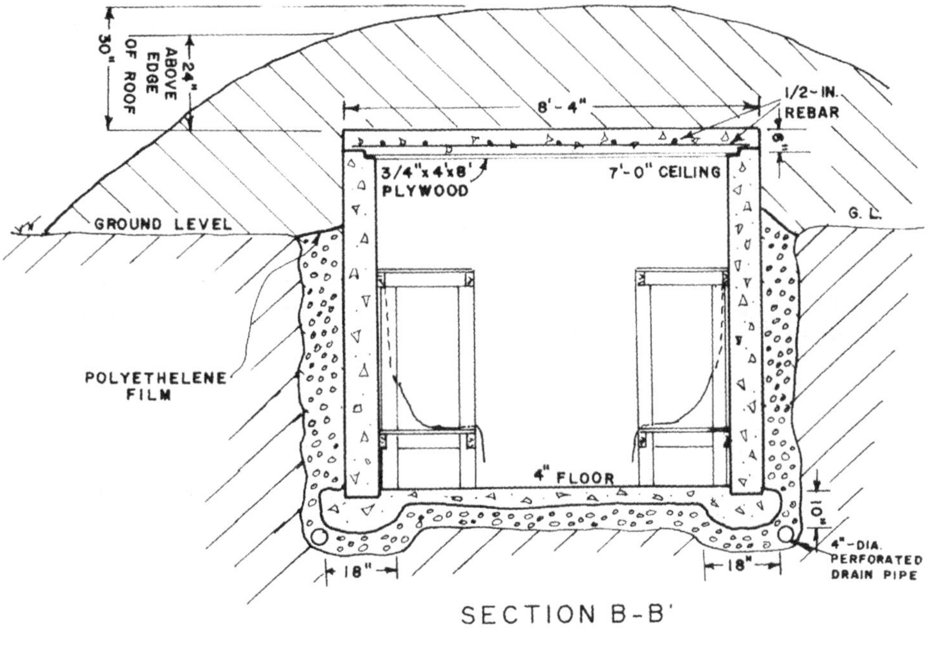

SECTION B-B'

Fig. 17.2. Permanent Family Fallout Shelter for Dual Use.

shelter, its occupants must place containers full of water and/or other good shielding material against the door. They can do this easily and quickly if the shelter is supplied with filled water containers such as described in the Water section of this chapter.

The illustrated shelter room has 106 square feet of floor space — room enough for 5 adults and the survival essentials they will need for long occupancy, if shelter furnishings like those described in this chapter are provided. For each additional occupant, increase this shelter's length by 2 feet. To increase room size, increase length and not width. This retains maximum roof strength at minimum cost.

Note in Figs. 17.1 and 17.2 the 12-inch-thick concrete wall between the landing at the foot of the stairs and the end of the shelter room. Only a very small fraction of the radiation coming through the outer doors and down the stairs will make the 90 degree turn through the inner door, and most of this radiation will not strike shelter occupants if they place containers filled with water and other shielding material against the door.

Also note the homemakeable, low cost Double-Action Piston Pump and filter, shown in Fig. 17.1, that even in a heat wave will supply adequate air through the 5-inch-diameter air-intake pipe — all described in Appendix E.

Few survival-minded Americans, before a recognized international crisis arises, either can afford or believe that they can afford to build a permanent family fallout shelter costing around $10,000 in 1987. A small reinforced concrete, below-ground shelter of the type specified in official Federal Emergency Management Agency pamphlets costs about $100 per square foot of floor space, if built by a contractor in a typical suburban area. Those with the needed skills and time can save about half of this cost by doing their own work. Also, at many building sites where gravity drainage of the earth around a shelter's walls can be assured and hydrostatic earth pressure against the walls thus prevented, no steel reinforcement in the poured concrete or concrete block walls is needed — unless required by the local building code.

Caution: Steel reinforcement in the walls and floor is needed in some clay soils that swell when wet and exert sufficient inward and upward pressure to crack unreinforced walls and floor slabs. Consult local builders who have learned from experience whether wall and floor reinforcement is needed in the type of soil where you plan to build. If needed, a grid of ½-inch rebars, spaced at 12 inches, usually is adequate. To save money on steel reinforcement, check prices in salvage yards for used rebars and substitute reinforcing materials such as junked cable and small pipes.

How to safely pour a shelter's concrete roof slab without using a contractor's usual forms and equipment is indicated by Figs. 17.1 and 17.2. These drawings show 8-ft.-long sheets of ¾-inch plywood supported at their ends on shelter walls 7 feet-6 inches apart. Preparatory to pouring the concrete, the plywood sheets should be supported along the centerline of the shelter by 4"x4"s and other lumber, which can be used later to build seats and overhead bunks. Plywood left on the ceiling reduces condensation and heating problems in cold weather, but increases the volume of outdoor air that must be pumped through the shelter to maintain tolerable temperatures when it is occupied in hot weather. This was clearly demonstrated in the summer of 1963 when the author used SIMOCS (simulated occupants that produce heat and water vapor like people) to determine the habitability of a six-roomlet below ground group shelter, with a reinforced concrete roof that had been built in this manner by six New Jersey farm families. They had left ordinary ¾-inch exterior plywood on the ceiling. Because the hollow concrete wall-blocks and the well drained gravel under the floor also kept heat from escaping into the surrounding soil, and because only natural ventilation was provided, the temperature/humidity became dangerously high within a few hours.

Insulating a shelter's walls and ceiling can be disadvantageous, because insulation makes unavailable the "heat sink" of the shelter and its surrounding earth. In hot weather insulation reduces the time during which ventilation can be stopped or restricted without disastrously overheating the occupants.

Today, for such a shelter it would be better to use pressure-treated, rot-proof plywood and lumber, approved by leading building codes. For information, write to the American Plywood Association, P.O. Box 11700, Tacoma, WA 98411, enquiring about rot-proof plywood, dimensional lumber, and other material used in building the All-Weather Wood Foundation. Most lumber yards will obtain treated plywood on order, and sell it for about 50% more than ordinary exterior grade plywood.

Big savings in shelter construction costs are made by using salvaged and/or used materials. Manufacturers of pre-cast reinforced concrete beams and floor sections often sell rejects for very little. Most salvage yards have steel beams and other material that make excellent roofing for earth-covered shelters. (Shortly before the Cuban Missile Crisis, when living near New York, I built for myself at modest cost a very small shelter on a well drained hillside. I made it almost entirely of steel channels bought and cut to order at a salvage yard.) Used cylindrical steel tanks with closed ends often make good low-cost permanent shelters. One of the best low-cost family shelters that I ever went into was on a hillside overlooking San Francisco Bay. It was made of a salvaged steel brewing tank that had been installed after a vertical cylindrical entrance with a door had been welded on it. The tank's exterior had been protected with a bituminous coating. Its survival-minded owner was a brilliant Hungarian refugee who, as a boy, had survived in a deep wine cellar throughout the Russian siege and shelling of Budapest. Nothing equals war experience to teach the lifesaving value of shelters.

MINIMIZATION OF FIRE AND CARBON MONOXIDE DANGERS

Many shelter designers and builders do not realize the probable extent of fires after a major nuclear attack. Nor do the big majority of them provide shelters built under or close to a house with adequate protection against the entry of deadly amounts of carbon monoxide if the house burns. Although the areas of fires resulting from a nuclear explosion generally will be about as extensive as the areas of significant blast damage,[6] on a clear day a house up to about 8 miles from ground zero can be ignited by the thermal pulse of a 1-megaton airburst.[6] Figure 7.2 in Chapter 7 is a photograph of a car set on fire by a nuclear explosion so far away that the car was not even dented by the blast. This photograph indicates how a thermal pulse can go through window glass and ignite curtains, upholstery, or dry paper, even if flammable material outdoors is too damp to be ignited. Furthermore, fires from any cause can spread, especially in fallout areas following a nuclear attack when firefighters may be unable or unwilling to expose themselves outdoors to radiation.

Good protection against carbon monoxide is provided by a permanent earth-covered shelter, built with its entry outdoors and well separated from a house and other flammable structures, and constructed so that it can be closed gas-tight. Both the air-intake and the air-exhaust pipes should be installed so that they can be quickly closed air-tight, as with screw-on fittings. Such closures should be kept well greased and securely attached close to where they would be used. If a shelter's entry is through a passageway from a house, a gasketted steel firedoor, insulated on the shelter side, should be installed near the house end of the passageway. The shelter should be further protected by a second gas-tight door, to prevent the entry of carbon monoxide and smoke if heat from the burning house destroys the gasket on the firedoor. If special firedoor gaskets are not available, rubber weatherstripping will serve. To lessen the risk of carbon monoxide being pumped into the shelter if the house burns and air must be pumped into the shelter while the fire still is smoldering, the air-intake and pump should be at the far end of the shelter, and the air-exhaust pipe and emergency exit should be near the passageway from the house.

Be sure to seal electrical conduits leading from a basement to a connected shelter, so that if the house burns carbon monoxide can not flow through the conduits into the shelter when fresh outdoor air is not being pumped into the shelter. The author, while conducting ventilation and habitability tests of an earth-covered blast shelter connected through a tunnel to a house's basement, observed air flowing out through unsealed conduits, the reverse of such a possible life-endangering flow of carbon monoxide. When the shelter was being maintained at a slight overpressure by cranking its blower to pump in outdoor air, a little air flowed through the unsealed conduit into the basement.

For ways to minimize carbon monoxide dangers arising from cooking, heating, lighting, and smoking, see following sections in this chapter.

Remember that air contaminated with only 0.16% carbon monoxide can kill you in 2 to 3 hours, and 0.04% carbon monoxide causes frontal headaches and nausea in 2 to 3 hours. The Navy sets its safe allowable carbon monoxide concentration in air at 0.01%. (*Shelter Habitability Studies — The Effect of Oxygen Depletion and Fire Gasses on Occupants of Shelters,* by J. S. Muraoka, Report NCEL-TR-144, July 1961.)

PREVENTION OF CRACKS AND WET SHELTER PROBLEMS

If wet basements are a problem in your locality, below ground shelters are likely to be wet and unsatisfactory unless appropriate preventative measures are taken during their design and construction. When making plans, you should consult local builders of satisfactory basements. You also should question persons who at various times of the year have observed excavations, holes, and/or basements in your immediate vicinity, or have noted seasonal swampy places or springs.

The most difficult type of shelter to keep dry for decades is one that is wholly or partially below the water table for part or all of the year. Concrete is not completely watertight. Waterproof coatings and coverings often are damaged during construction, or deteriorate with age.

Shelter walls sometimes crack due to settling and earth movements. Metal shelters usually develop small leaks long before they become dangerously weakened.

A 100-occupant, below ground shelter, built in 1984 near Dallas, Texas as a prototype blast shelter for industrial workers, was flooded when the water table rose. The poorly sealed opening of this shelter's emergency exit was below ground level, and after heavy rains was below the water table. A prudently designed shelter has the top of its emergency exit slightly above the surface of the surrounding earth, as illustrated in Fig. 17.2. All underground electric conduits leading down into a shelter must be well sealed to prevent entry of water.

To prevent a wholly or partially below-water-table shelter from becoming wet inside sooner or later, it should have a sump and an automatic sump pump to discharge water to the ground outside. If at any time you find that the sump pump is discharging an appreciable amount of water, you may have a serious wet-shelter problem if electric power fails after an attack.

A manually operated bilge pump and a sufficiently long discharge hose can be bought for about $20.00 from marine supply mail order firms, including West Marine Products, Box 5189, Santa Cruz, California 95063, and Defender Industries, Inc., P.O. Box 820, New Rochelle, New York 10802-0820. (Long established marine supply companies also are good sources of use-proven chemical toilets, first aid kits, lights, rope, etc.)

Shelter roof surfaces should be gently sloped, no matter how good a waterproof coating is to be applied. By making a concrete shelter roof as little as 1 inch thicker along its centerline than along its sides, so that it slopes to both sides, the prospects are improved for having an earth-covered coated roof that will not leak for decades.

Figures 17.1 and 17.2 illustrate the following ways to prevent having a wet shelter:

* Put a layer of gravel or crushed rock in the bottom of the excavation, and install perforated drainage pipes if gravity drainage is practical.

* Cover the gravel or crushed rock in the floor area with a plastic vapor barrier before pouring a concrete floor.

* Coat the outer surfaces of roof and walls with bituminous waterproofing or other coating that has proved to be most effective in your locality.

* Backfill with gravel or crushed rock against the walls, to keep the soil from possibly becoming saturated. Saturated soil exerts hydrostatic pressure against walls, and may crack them and cause them to leak. In some areas it is more economical to cover a shelter's coated walls with a subsurface drainage matting (such as Enkadrain, manufactured and sold by BASF Corporation, Fibers Division, Enka, North Carolina 28728). This will eliminate the costs of backfilling with gravel or crushed rock.

NON-FLOATABLE SHELTERS

In most localities the water table usually is below the depth of excavation needed to build or install a belowground shelter. In some areas, however, after rainy periods the water table may rise until it is only a foot or two below the surface. Then a watertight shelter may float upward through the surrounding saturated soil, unless its weight plus the weight of its covering earth is sufficient to withstand its buoyancy. (In many places swimming pools are kept full to prevent them from being cracked by uneven buoyant forces if the water table rises.)

Dramatic examples of floating shelters were steel blast shelters, guaranteed by contractors to be watertight, that were installed under the lawns of some Houston, Texas homes shortly after the Cuban Missile Crisis. When the water table rose after heavy rains, these shelters came up to the surface like giant mushrooms, to the frustrated dismay of their owners and the satisfaction of anti-defense newspaper feature writers.

The most expensive permanent family fallout shelter described in a Federal Emergency Management Agency free handout (pamphlet H-12-1) is floatable. It is designed to be built of reinforced concrete covered by a flagstone patio only about 3 inches above the ground. Its 6-inch-thick concrete roof is covered by a total thickness of only 6 inches of sand and flagstone. Like the rest of FEMA's permanent shelters, no prototype of this approximately PF-40 shelter was built, nor is there any record of anyone actually having built this shelter. In contrast, the belowground shelter illustrated by Figs. 17.1 and 17.2 would not float even if it did not have assured gravity drainage of the surrounding soil through the perforated drain pipes in the gravel on which it rests, because this shelter is weighted down by the thick earth berm on its roof.

ADEQUATE, DEPENDABLE VENTILATION/COOLING

Basic facts that you need to provide adequate, dependable ventilation for a small or medium sized shelter are given in Chapter 6, **Ventilation and Cooling of Shelters.** A good permanent shelter has two ventilation systems:

- The **primary ventilation system** of a small permanent shelter should utilize a manually operated centrifugal blower, or a homemade Plywood Double-Action Piston Pump. (See Appendix E.) A satisfactory air pump must be capable of supplying adequate outdoor air through an air-intake pipe, a filter, and an air-exhaust pipe. (See Figs. 17.1 and 17.2.) "Adequate outdoor air" for a small shelter means at least 15 cubic feet per minute per occupant for the cooler parts of the United States, and at least 30 cfm per occupant in most of the country. Most permanent shelters have centrifugal blowers that can not deliver an adequate volume of air in hot weather for each planned occupant.

For a medium sized permanent shelter, installing two or more manually powered air pumps is both more dependable and more economical than providing an emergency generator and its engine to supply power to an electric blower. The Swiss, who have made the world's best and most expensive per capita preparations to survive a war, use one or more hand-cranked centrifugal blowers to ventilate most of their shelters.

- The **multi-week and/or emergency ventilation system** of a permanent shelter that has an emergency exit should depend on a homemade KAP, made before a crisis and kept ready to use. (See Appendix B, **How to Make and Use a Homemade Shelter-Ventilating Pump, the KAP.**) By opening both the entrance and the emergency exit, the shelter is provided with two large, low-resistance openings through which a KAP can pump large volumes of air with minimum work.

Warning: Keep screen doors and/or screen panels ready to protect all openings against the swarms of flies and mosquitoes likely to become dangerous pests in fallout areas. Use your KAP to pump adequate air through screens. Insect screens greatly reduce natural ventilation, as the author first noted in Calcutta while a bed-ridden patient in a stifling hot ward of a hastily constructed Army hospital. Because there were no fans or blowers to pump in outdoor air or circulate the air inside, window screens were opened in the daytime when malaria mosquitoes were not flying. The doctors correctly concluded that the temperature reduction when the screens were opened helped the patients more than they were endangered by the entering filthy flies. Adequate ventilation is more important than protection from flies, but with a KAP and insect screens you can have both. Flies, mosquitoes, and other insects can be killed very effectively by occasionally spraying or painting screens and other alighting surfaces with water solutions of insecticides containing permithin and sold in many farm stores.

ADVICE ON VENTILATION OPENINGS AND FITTINGS

- Install ventilation pipes large enough to reduce resistance to airflow, thus increasing the volume of air that the shelter's pump can deliver. A shelter with a 200-cfm pump (such as the homemakeable Plywood Double-Action Piston Pump described in Appendix E) should have 5-inch galvanized steel pipe. The pumps that are installed in most family shelters deliver only about 100 cfm or less. Four-inch pipe is adequate for use with pumps this small, provided that the pipes have no more than two right-angle turns below each gooseneck. (A 90-degree L gives about as much resistance to airflow as 12 feet of straight pipe.)

- Make and install a gooseneck with its mouth about twice the diameter of the pipe, as indicated in Fig. 17.1. The purpose of such a gooseneck is to prevent more of the larger descending fallout particles from being pumped or blown into the shelter. For example, if 200 cfm of air is being pumped into a shelter through a gooseneck of 5-inch-diameter pipe with its mouth also 5 inches in diameter, the velocity of the air up into the mouth of the gooseneck is about 1,440 feet per minute, and sand-like spherical particles smaller than approximately 500 microns in diameter also are "sucked" up.[6] But if the 5-inch gooseneck's mouth is 10 inches across, then the upward air velocity is reduced to about 360 feet per minute, and only particles smaller than approximately 180 microns across are "sucked" up. Particles in the 180 to 500 micron-diameter range are relatively large and fall to earth in about 40 to 70 minutes from 35,000 feet, the base of the mushroom cloud of a 1-megaton explosion. (See Fig. 6.4.) These particles are very dangerous because their radioactivity has had little time to decay, and should be kept out of a shelter's ventilation system. Furthermore, large particles retained in a shelter's filter restrict airflow sooner than do small ones. (If an appropriately curved piece of 5-inch steel pipe cannot be found in a salvage yard or elsewhere, a good welder can use 5-inch steel pipe to make a substitute gooseneck with two 90-degree turns.)

- Do not use air intake hoods on a permanent shelter's pipes, because hoods are not as effective as goosenecks in preventing fallout particles from entering ventilation pipes. Also, pumping a given volume of air through a hood is more work than pumping the same volume through a gooseneck with equal cross-sectional areas.

- Never install any screen inside a gooseneck or air intake hood, because spider webs and the debris that sticks to webs will greatly reduce airflow. The author saw a gooseneck with a blast valve built inside it; spider webs and attached trash on this blast valve had consequentially reduced the volume of air that this shelter's pump could deliver. Of course a screen is much more easily obstructed than a blast valve. Yet FEMA's widely distributed pamphlets on a permanent Home Fallout Shelter (H-12-1) and on a Home Blast Shelter (H-12-3) continue in successive editions to give detailed instructions for making an air intake hood with a screen soldered inside it. But these shelters that never have been built have much more serious weaknesses, including the likelihood that the aboveground parts of the ventilation pipes of the blast shelter would be bent over or broken off by blast-wind-hurled parts of buildings and trees, even in suburbia. (350 mph is the maximum velocity of the blast wind where the blast overpressure is 15 psi from a 1-megaton air burst.[6] The ventilation openings of the blast-tested expedient blast shelters described in Appendix D are much more likely to remain serviceable after being subjected to severe blast effects, because blast-protector logs are placed around their openings, that are only a few inches above ground level.)

PREVENTION AND CONTROL OF CONDENSATION

A shelter can be watertight, yet at certain seasons of the year its walls, ceiling, and floor can be dripping wet with water condensed from entering outdoor air. (This is a serious problem, except in arid parts of the West.) During the winter months a shelter and its surrounding earth get cold; then especially on some spring days the dew point of entering outdoor air is higher than the temperature of the shelter's interior surfaces. As a result, condensation occurs on those surfaces that are cooler than the dew point of the pumped-through air.

The most dramatic example that I have observed of the seriousness of this condensation problem was the dripping ceiling and wet walls of a reinforced-concrete, family-sized shelter that I inspected on an early spring day at the Civil Defence College in Yorkshire, England.

Such condensation also can occur in aboveground structures. Before World War II I had a 600-year-old bedroom in Queen's College, Oxford University. My bedroom's outer wall was made of solid limestone blocks about 15 inches thick, simply plastered and painted on the inside. On some spring days moisture condensed on the inside of the cold outer wall, ran down, and collected in little puddles on the floor. The occasional small coal fire in my adjacent study was barely sufficient to gradually evaporate the water and reduce my bedroom's humidity enough to prevent mold from forming. This often-repeated occurrence proves the inadequacy of merely keeping an electric light turned on for heat to prevent condensation inside an uninsulated shelter built in a cool, frequently humid locality.

Condensation and resultant 100 percent humid air can rust and eat away most steel pipes. Ventilation pipes should be made of galvanized steel or other materials that are undamaged by seasonal condensation and 100 percent humidity. In Connecticut I saw shelter ventilation pipes made of steel protected with two coats of marine paint; they were badly rusted only two years after installation.

Operating a dehumidifier with automatic controls is the most practical way for most people to prevent condensation and other dampness problems in a shelter during peacetime. Almost all of the Chinese shelters that I inspected in six cities are dual-use shelters and typically are equipped with large dehumidifiers. A small dehumidifier adequate for a family shelter can be bought from a dependable mail order company, such as Sears, for about $250 in 1987.

To save floor space and facilitate removal of water, a dehumidifier should be installed near a shelter's ceiling. Then water from the dehumidifier can be disposed of most easily through a pipe or tube providing gravity drainage, best to the outdoors, second best to the sewer. (After a nuclear attack the sewer system may become clogged and sewage may back up and flow into a belowground room having pipes that normally discharge into the sewer, and that lack check valves.) If the above mentioned ways of removing water are not possible, a sump and an automatic sump pump discharging water to the ground outdoors can solve the peacetime water disposal problem.

After an attack, electric power can be expected to fail and shelter humidity will have to be controlled as much as possible by ventilation with outdoor air. A simple way to learn when to ventilate a shelter to dry it was described in a Russian article on shelter management: Keep several small cans of water in the shelter. They will be at about the same temperature as the shelter walls when the shelter is closed and is not being ventilated. If a filled can is exposed to outdoor air for about 10 minutes and moisture condenses on it (as a glass filled with an iced drink "sweats" on a humid summer day), do not ventilate the shelter. If no moisture condenses on the can, ventilate.

A WALK-IN ENTRANCE

Only a small fraction of permanent family shelters without a walk-in entrance have been kept in good condition for many years. Permanent family shelters with vertical or crawl-in entrances are found so inconvenient that the big majority of owners do not use them even for rotated food storage. In normal peacetime, most well informed Americans concerned with protecting their families conclude that only a shelter skillfully designed for dual use justifies the cost of building and maintaining it. Significantly, Chinese civil defense has come to the same conclusion regarding Chinese permanent public shelters: those that have been built, and that still are being built, are almost all useful both in peacetime and in wartime.

If a family can use its shelter without having to go outside and be exposed to rain, snow, cold, or night problems, its dual use shelter will be a more valuable peacetime asset than a shelter not directly connected to the house. Furthermore, a directly connected shelter can be entered more quickly in a crisis, and probably will reduce post-attack exposures to fallout radiation received by persons carrying things into the shelter, or by those moving about post-attack to protect the home. The main disadvantages of a directly connected shelter are that it usually provides poorer protection against heat, smoke and carbon monoxide if the house burns and that it is more expensive to build than an earth-covered shelter with an outdoor walk-in entrance, such as the one illustrated in Figs. 17.1 and 17.2.

AN EMERGENCY EXIT THAT ALSO PROVIDES A SECOND LARGE VENTILATION OPENING

Having an emergency exit in a fallout shelter is not as important as having one in a blast shelter, unless the fallout shelter is under or connected to a building. (Since buildings are likely to burn, it is important to have a means of escape.) However, an emergency exit makes any shelter more practical to live in than a shelter with only one large opening — especially in a heavy fallout area where it may be necessary to stay inside most of the time for weeks or months. Occupants of a shelter with only one large opening will not have adequate natural ventilation and will have to keep laboriously pumping air — at least intermittently — through the air-supply pipes to maintain liveable temperature and/or humidity conditions.

By opening both a shelter's entrance and its emergency exit, and taking measures to prevent the entry of rain, snow, and all but the smallest fallout particles (see Appendix F), natural ventilation will be adequate most of the time, except in hot, calm weather. With two large openings, a homemade KAP (see Appendix B) can be used to pump enough outdoor air through the shelter, with much less work than is required to pump less air with a relatively high-pressure pump through typical ventilation pipes.

A DEPENDABLE, HIGH-PROTECTION-FACTOR EMERGENCY EXIT

Occupants of a shelter with a dependable emergency exit will have less fear of being trapped if the main entry is blocked. If they open the exit, they also will be able to ventilate the shelter with natural ventilation through the entry and the exit, or with forced ventilation by operating a KAP.

To provide excellent radiation protection, a typical high-PF emergency exit is filled with sand. Such an exit has a bolted-on steel plate on its bottom inside the shelter, and an easily cut, waterproof, plastic-film covering over its top, which is a few inches below ground level. Obvious disadvantages of this typical sand-filled emergency exit include the difficulty of safely removing the bottom plate while sand is pressing down on it, and the impossibility of cutting the plastic film over the top of the exit without having fallout-contaminated earth fall on the person who does the cutting, and into the shelter room. Furthermore, if the earth covering the top of an emergency exit is frozen, occupants may be unable to break through it and get out.

An improved design of sand-filled emergency exit was conceived by Dr. Conrad V. Chester of Oak Ridge National Laboratory and in 1986 was further improved, built, and tested in a full-scale model by the author. As shown in Fig. 17.2, the sand in this 26 x 26-inch square vertical exit was supported by a piece of 3/4-inch exterior plywood, that should be of the previously mentioned rot-proof type, pressure impregnated with wood preservative.

In the center of this 25½ x 25½-inch plywood sand-support was an 8-inch-diameter hole covered with two thicknesses of strong nylon cloth.

The double thickness of cloth was firmly attached to the plywood by being folded over four 3/16-inch galvanized steel rods, that were stapled to the plywood with galvanized poultry-netting staples. (See Figs. 17.2 and 17.3.) The nylon cloth covering the hole can be easily and quickly cut with a knife, permitting sand to fall harmlessly into the shelter room.

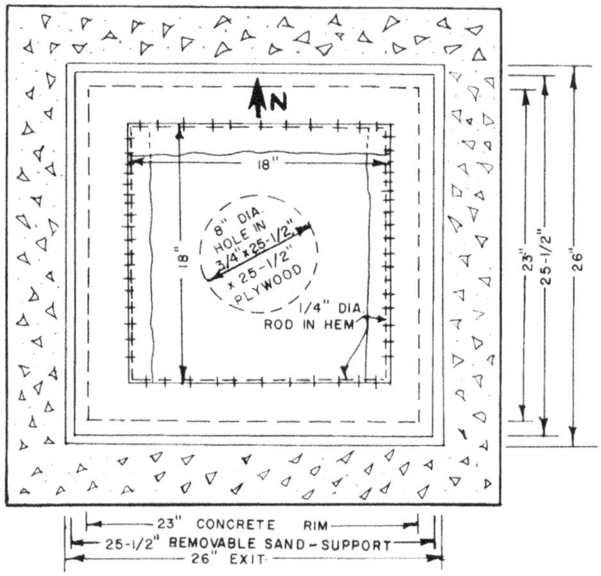

Fig. 17.3. Plan of Vertical Emergency Exit, Before Filling with Sand.

As shown in Figs. 17.2 and 17.3, the square 26 x 26-inch plywood sand-support rests on a 1½-inch-wide rim or ledge around the 23 x 23-inch square hole in the shelter's reinforced concrete roof slab. After a shelter occupant has cut out the nylon cloth covering the hole and all but about 30 lbs of sand has fallen or been pushed by his hand down into the shelter room, he can tilt the plywood sand-support up into a vertical position, and then turn it 45 degrees. The 26-inch width of the sand-support permits it to be easily lifted down through the 32.5-inch-long diagonal of the 23 x 23-inch square hole in the shelter's roof slab.

Note the North-pointing arrow on the plywood sand-support shown in Fig. 17.3. Because the exit of this shelter was not made perfectly square, the sand-support could be tilted most easily from its horizontal position into the vertical position if it was oriented so that its side marked "N" was to the north. A similar "N" arrow on the lower side of this sand-support enabled a man below it, after the exit's lid was tied down and before the exit was filled with sand, to position the sand-support for easy tilting and removal when the last of the sand was being cleared from this exit. The sand-support should be cut to fit the exit **after** the exit is completed, because it is difficult to build an exit exactly to specified dimensions.

The top of the emergency exit should be a few inches above the earth around it, to prevent rainwater on the ground from possibly running in. Securely cover the exit's top with a lid of 1/8-inch galvanized steel having a threaded plug-hole (cut from a steel barrel) welded over a hole cut in the lid's center. Such a lid can be closely fitted to the top of a concrete exit by oiling it and pressing it against the concrete before the concrete begins to set.

Before filling the exit with sand, while inside the exit tie the lid down on each of its four sides with nine loops of 3/32-inch nylon cord repeatedly tightened between four galvanized steel "Ʊ's" welded to the lower side of the lid, and four "Ʊ's" set in the shelter's walls and roof slab, as indicated in Fig. 17.2. Use pliers to tighten, stretch, and hold the nylon cord while making the loops. Then after the plywood sand-support is positioned in the bottom of the exit, the exit can be filled by pouring dry sand through the plug-hold in the steel lid. Finally, the plug-hole should be closed so that it cannot be opened, and then made waterproof. To make doubly sure that the lid will not rust, paint it with a cement paint, and then with whatever color outdoor paint you want.

A shelter occupant can cut out the nylon cloth covering the hole in the sand-support, remove all sand and the plywood sand-support from this exit, cut the four tightened nylon-cord multiple loops holding down the lid, push off the lid, and then climb up and step outside — all in less than 5 minutes, even if damp sand has been used to fill the exit. (To make removal of the sand more difficult, in his tests the author used damp sand that does not flow freely and makes it necessary to loosen it repeatedly, with one's hand and arm thrust up through the 8-inch hole in the plywood sand-support.)

In a well designed **blast** shelter this sand-filled emergency exit will provide excellent protection against severe blast. Blast tests have proved that a 1/8-inch steel lid (the equivalent of a blast door) the size of this exit's lid will withstand blast effects of at least 50 psi. Furthermore, sand arching will transfer blast loadings on the sand outward from the slightly downward deflecting plywood sand-support to its edges, and thence to the supporting reinforced concrete rim or ledge around the 23 x 23-inch hole in the shelter's roof slab. (See Fig. 17.2.)

A small shelter with an emergency exit near its far end has additional advantages: It can be supplied with adequate natural ventilation most of the time, with easy forced ventilation by a KAP when forced ventilation is needed, and with daylight illumination. Means for attaining these advantages are described in Appendix F.

ADEQUATE STORAGE SPACE FOR ESSENTIALS

As will be shown in the following sections of this chapter, about 20 square feet of shelter floor area per family member is needed for shelter furnishings and to store adequate water for a month, a year's supply of compact dry foods, cooking and sanitary equipment, blankets, tools, and other post-attack essentials. Twenty square feet per family member also provides enough space per person to store winter clothing and footwear, camping equipment, and foods normally kept on hand and rotated as consumed in the course of ordinary family living. Additional space is needed if you plan to use your shelter as a workshop, or as a fallout shelter to save a few of your unprepared friends without endangering your own family.

SEATS/BUNKS/SHELVES

Seats and overhead bunks built like those specified in Fig. 17.4 and pictured in Fig. 17.5 enable more shelter occupants to sit and sleep more comfortably in less space than when using any other shelter furnishings known to the author. Note that the seat has an adjustable backrest. This backrest is similar to the fine-mesh nylon fishnet backrests tested in a prototype of an expensive blast shelter designed and furnished at Oak Ridge National Laboratory.

Shelter habitability tests have proved the need for backrests. Even some young German soldiers had painfully sore backs after sitting on ordinary benches during a 2-week shelter occupancy test.

Backrests should be installed in peacetime and kept ready for crisis use, rolled up against their upper attachments and covered. Then easily removeable storage shelves, if needed, can be installed between benches and overhead bunks.

To sit or sleep comfortably, pull the bedsheet forward and then sit on about the outer foot of the 2-foot-wide seat.

Although this 5-occupant shelter is illustrated with a bunk for each family member, it is

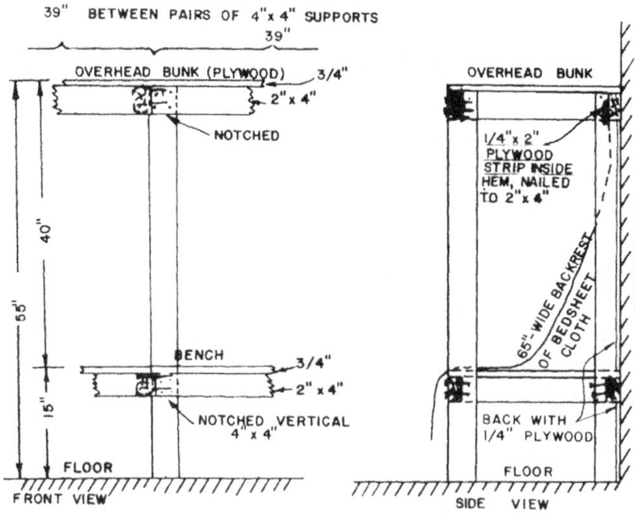

Fig. 17.4. Seat with Overhead Bunk Proportioned for a Shelter Room with a 7-Ft. or Higher Ceiling. A seat with a backrest should be 24 inches wide.

Fig. 17.5. Backrests of Bedsheet Cloth and 2-Inch-Thick Pads Make Sitting and Sleeping Comfortable.

prudent to count on stored supplies making some bunks unusable, and to realize that in a desperate crisis it might be hard to refuse shelter to an unprepared good neighbor. Note that with four persons seated on a 6.5-foot-long seat and one person on the overhead bunk, five persons can be quite comfortably accommodated on 25 square feet of floorspace, including plenty of room for the sitters' legs.

To store the most supplies in a shelter, you should install shelves after you know the heights of the items to be stored. Often the space between an overhead bunk and the ceiling can best be used by making easily removeable additional shelves.

WATER

- **Water needs:** Even most well-maintained shelters do not have enough water for prolonged occupancy. A permanent shelter should provide each occupant with at least 30 gallons of safe water — enough for an austere month, except in very hot weather.
- **Containers:** The most practical water container for shelter storage is a 5-gallon rigid plastic water can with a handle, a large diameter opening for quick filling and emptying, and a small spout for pouring small quantities. A 5-gallon water can of this type sells for about $5 in discount stores.

The plastic bottles that household chlorine bleach is sold in also are good for multi-year storage of drinking water, as are glass jugs. Plastic milk jugs are not satisfactory, because after a few years they often become brittle and crack.

Some shelter owners do not realize that, although a shelter can be kept dry in peacetime, except in the arid West its air is likely to become extremely humid after a few days of crowded occupancy. Very humid air soon softens and weakens cardboard containers of food and flexible water bags.

- **Disinfecting for multi-year storage:** To store safe water and keep it safe for years, first disinfect the container by rinsing it with a strong solution of chlorine bleach. Then rinse it with safe water before filling it with the clear, safe water to be stored. Next, disinfect by adding household bleach that contains 5.25% sodium hypochlorite as its only active ingredient, in the quantities specified in this book's Water chapter for disinfecting muddy or cloudy water. To 5 gallons, add 1 scant teaspoon of bleach. Finally, to prevent possible entry of air containing infective organisms through faulty closures, seal the container's closures with duct tape.
- **Making efficient use of storage space:** A 5-gallon rigid plastic water container typically measures 7 x 12 x 21 inches, including the height of its spout. Nine such 5-gallon containers can be placed on a 2 x 3-foot floor area. Twenty-seven 5-gallon containers, holding 135 gallons of water, can be stored on and over 6 square feet of floor if you make a water storage stand 24 x 42 x 48 inches high, built quite like the seat with overhead bunk described in the Seats/Bunks/Shelves section of this chapter. This easily moveable storage stand should have two plywood shelves, one 24 inches and the other 48 inches from the floor.
- **Using filled containers for shielding:** Filled 5-gallon water containers can be moved quickly to provide additional shielding where needed to increase the protection factor of all or part of a shelter. For example, near the inner door of the shelter illustrated by Figs. 17.1 and 17.2 the protection factor is less than 1000. But if enough filled water containers are placed so as to cover the door with almost the equivalent of an 18-inch-thick "wall" of shielding water, the PF of the part of the shelter room near the door can be raised to about PF 1000.

If a shelter has twenty-seven 5-gallon cans of water stored on and under the above-described 2-shelf water storage stand, then in less than 3 minutes 2 men can shield the shelter door quite adequately. All they have to do is take the 18 cans off the shelves, put 9 of them on the floor against the door and doorway, move the storage stand over the 9 door-shielding cans, and place the remaining 18 cans on the stand's 2 shelves.

Equally good doorway shielding can be provided by placing at least a 24-inch thickness of containers full of dense food, such as whole-grain wheat or sugar, against the doorway. Two 55-gallon drums of wheat, each weighing about 400 pounds, can be quickly "walked" on a concrete floor and positioned so as to shield the lower part of a doorway. Heavy containers on the floor can provide a stable base on which to stack other shielding material.

- **A water well:** The best solution to the water problem quite often is a well inside the shelter. In many areas the water table is less than 50 feet below the surface, and a 50-foot well, cased with 6-inch steel pipe, can be drilled and completed for about $2000. Well drilling should be done after the shelter excavation has been dug and before the concrete shelter floor has been poured. An in-shelter well would be of vital importance not only to the occupants of a family shelter, but later on probably to nearby survivors. Even if only a gallon or so an hour could be bailed from a well too weak to be useful in peacetime, it would be a tremendous family asset post-attack. If infective organisms are found in water from a well drilled to provide water during and after an attack, safe water for months can be assured by merely storing a few gallons of household chlorine bleach.

If enough water for worthwhile peacetime use can be pumped from a well, install a submersible electric pump, with plastic pipe in the well. Then in an emergency the pipe and the attached pump can be pulled by hand out of the well, with only a saw being needed to cut off lengths of the plastic pipe as it is pulled. After the well casing has been cleared of pump, pipe and wires, a homemade 2-foot-long bail-bucket on a nylon rope can be used to draw plenty of water. (See Chapter 8, Water, for instructions.)

● **Local water sources:** Most Americans' normal piped water would not run for months after a large nuclear attack. A month's supply of water stored in your shelter should be adequate, because, even if your area has heavy fallout, in less than a month radioactive decay will make it safe to haul water from nearby sources.

An important part of your shelter preparations is to locate nearby wells, ponds, streams, and streambeds that when dry frequently have water a foot or two below the surface. The author has found that digging a water pit in an apparently dry streambed often supplies enough filtered water to satisfy several families' basic needs. To keep the sides of a water pit dug in unstable ground from caving in, you should drive a circle of side-by-side stakes around the outside of your planned pit before starting to dig. With more work and materials, you and other survivors needing filtered water could dig a well like the Chinese water source shown on page 71. If you are in a fallout area, before drinking water from a water pit you should filter it through clayey soil to remove fallout particles and dissolved radioactive isotopes, as described in the Water chapter. Of course it is prudent to chlorinate or boil all surface and near-surface water after it has been filtered.

FOOD

● **Advantages of a one-year supply:** A family that expends the money and work to build and provision its own shelter should store a year's supply of long-lasting foods. If post-attack conditions enable you to continue living and making a living near your home, having a year's food supply will be a tremendous advantage. And if your area is afflicted with such dangerous, continuing fallout radiation and/or other post-attack conditions that surviving unprepared residents are soon forced to evacuate to better areas, then your and your family's chances will be better if hunger does not force you to move during the chaotic first few months after a nuclear attack.

● **Costs of a one year food supply for a family shelter:** Table 17.1 shows the wide range of 1987 costs of the basic survival foods for multi-year storage that are listed and explained on page 88.

The delivered costs listed in the right hand column include UPS shipping charges in the nearest and least expensive of UPS's 8 zones. For UPS shipping costs to the most distant points in the 48 states, add 34 cents per pound delivered.

All the foods in this survival ration, if stored in moisture-proof and insect-proof containers (the non-fat milk powder should be in nitrogen-packed cans), will provide healthful nutrition for at least 10 years. The exception is the multi-vitamin tablets, which should be replaced every 2 or 3 years, depending on storage temperature. So a family that spends about $300 per member on such a one year survival ration can consider that each of its members has been covered by famine insurance for $30 a year.

Scurvy will be the first incapacitating, then lethal vitamin deficiency to afflict unprepared, uninformed Americans. A multi-vitamin tablet contains enough vitamin C to fully satisfy the daily requirement. However, a prudent shelter owner also should store vitamin C tablets, that keep for years. One hundred 500-mg generic vitamin C tablets — 50,000 mg of vitamin C — in 1987 typically cost about $1.20 in a discount store; a 10 mg daily dose prevents scurvy. After a nuclear war in some areas vitamin C will be worth many times its weight in gold.

● **Sources of the basic foods listed in Table 17.1:**

* **Wheat:** If you live in a wheat producing area, the least expensive sources of ready-to-store wheat usually are local seed-cleaning firms. A hundred pounds or more of hard wheat, dried, bagged, and ready to store in moisture proof containers, costs about 10 cents a pound. (Today the wheat farmer receives about 4.5 cents a pound for truckloads, usually straight out of the field, not dry enough to store except in well ventilated granaries, and containing trash that makes weevil infestations more likely.) In some communities a few stores sell big bags of dry, cleaned hard wheat for 20 to 35 cents a pound.

Shelter owners who are unable or unwilling to obtain wheat from such sources can buy high

Table 17.1. A basic one-year survival ration for one adult male.

Component	Ounces per day	Pounds per year	Range of 1987 retail prices in dollars per pound, FOB, or picked up	Range of 1987 costs in dollars for a one year supply, FOB, or picked up	Range of 1987 costs in dollars for a one year supply delivered and in containers for multi-year storage
Whole-kernel hard wheat	16	365	0.10 to 0.40	36.50 to 135.00	56 to 175
Beans, pinto	5	114	0.25 to 0.79	28.50 to 90.11	38 to 110
Non-fat milk powder	2	46	1.68 to 3.86	77.28 to 177.56	83 to 184
Vegetable oil	1	23	0.36 to 0.57	8.28 to 13.11	9 to 14
Sugar	2	46	0.25 to 0.30	11.50 to 13.80	16 to 20
Salt, iodized	1/3	8	0.17 to 0.20	1.36 to 1.60	2 to 3
Multi-vitamin tablets (low generic, and an expensive brand)	1 per day	365 per year	1.3 to 11.8 cents per tablet	4.75 to 43.07	6 to 44
Total $ costs					$210 to $550

protein hard wheat at higher prices from health food stores and a few mail order companies. The lowest mail order FOB price known to the author for hard western wheat in 1990 is $3.17 for 10 pounds, in a vacuum-packed metallized plastic bag similar to the containers used for some U.S. Army combat rations. This long-lasting wheat, as well as other grains and legumes, is sold by Preparedness Products, 3855 South 500 West, Salt Lake City, Utah 84115. Another reliable mail order source of wheat and other dry foods packaged for multi-year storage is The Survival Center, 5555 Newton Falls Rd., Ravenna, Ohio 44266.

* **Beans,** like wheat, in many communities can be purchased from local farmers' co-ops or local stores at much lower delivered cost than from mail order firms. In one small Colorado town the co-op sold 25 pounds of pinto beans in a polyethylene bag for $11.25—45 cents a pound. Local supermarkets sell bulk pinto beans for around 60 cents a pound.

* **Non-fat milk powder** in 1990 is sold nationwide in the larger cardboard packages for around $2.85 per pound. A better buy for multi-year storage is the instant non-fat milk powder sold by Preparedness Products. This Mormon-owned firm's 1990 FOB price is $57.95 for a case of 6 nitrogen-packed cans, containing a total of 22.5 pounds. The author bought a case three years ago and found this non-fat instant milk powder to be excellent. At $2.58 a pound, plus UPS shipping charges, the cost is considerably less than for comparable milk powder packaged for multi-year storage and sold by other companies.

* **Vegetable oil, sugar, salt,** and **multi-vitamin tablets** are best bought at discount supermarkets. In cities such stores often sell large plastic containers of vegetable oil as "loss leaders" to attract customers, at prices as low as wholesale. Vegetable oil prices in small communities typically are much higher. For an economical survival ration, buy the lowest priced vegetable oil. Remember that one of the worst post-attack nutritional deficiencies will result from chronic shortages of fats (including oils), and that babies and little children cannot survive for a year on a diet of only grains and beans, with no oil or fat. See the Food chapter.

● CAUTIONS: Typical health food stores and most firms that specialize in survival foods sell basic foods at high prices, especially grains, beans, and milk powder. Investigate several other sources before buying.

To make sure that an advertised "one year supply" of survival foods actually will keep an adult well nourished for a whole year, require the seller to inform you **by mail** what his "one year supply" provides a typical adult male in: (1) calories, k cal; (2) protein, g; and (3) fat, g. Then you can use the values in the "Emergency Recommendations" column in Table 9.1 on page 84 to determine whether the advertised "one year supply" is adequate.

● **Transitional foods:** The emotional shock of suddenly being forced by war to occupy your shelter will be even worse if you have to adapt suddenly to an unaccustomed diet. It would be a good idea to occasionally practice eating only your survival rations for a day or two, and to store in your shelter a two week supply of canned and dry foods similar to those your family normally eats. Then it will be easier if war forces you to make the changeover. Of course the transitional foods that you store should be rotated and replaced as needed, depending on their shelf lives.

● **A hand-cranked grain mill:** Whole kernel grains and soybeans must be processed into meal or flour for satisfactory use as principal components of a diet. If unprepared America suffers a nuclear attack, unplanned, local food reserves and/or famine relief shipments will consist mostly of unprocessed wheat, corn, and soybeans. Then a family with a manual grain mill will have a survival advantage and will be a neighborhood asset.

Many health food stores at least have sources of hand-cranked grain mills. Mills with steel grinding plates are more efficient and less expensive than "stone" mills. A mail order firm that still sells hand-cranked grain mills of a make that the author has bought and found to be well made and efficient is Moses Kountry Health Foods, 7115 W. 4th N.W., Albuquerque, New Mexico 87107. It sells a serviceable Polish mill (Model "OB" Hand Grain Mill) for $35.73 FOB, plus UPS shipping charges. This mill cranks easily and grinds wheat into coarse meal or fine flour more efficiently than any of the American manual grain mills that the author has bought and used over the decades. Apparently manual grain mills no longer are manufactured in the U.S. Before buying a grain mill be sure to learn whether it grinds corn, our largest food reserve. In 1987 the author bought an advertised West German mill. Only after receiving it by mail order did he learn by reading the accompanying directions that it is not made for grinding corn.

COOKING AND HEATING

● **Safety precautions:** The first rule for safe cooking and/or heating in a shelter is to do it as near as practical to the exhaust opening. If the fire is under an exhaust pipe, install a hood over the fire. Operate the shelter ventilating pump when cooking, unless a natural airflow out through the exhaust opening can be observed or felt. Keep flammable materials, especially clothing, well away from any open fire.

● **Hazardous fuels:** Charcoal is the most hazardous fuel to burn in confined spaces, because it gives off much carbon monoxide. In a crowded shelter there are obvious dangers in using the efficient little stoves carried by backpackers and in storing their easily vaporized and ignited fuels.

● **"Canned heat":** These convenient fuels are expensive. Sterno, widely used to heat small quantities of food and drink, typically retails in 7-ounce cans for what amounts to about $9.00 per pound.

● **Wood:** The safest fuel to burn in a shelter is wood, the most widely available and cheapest fuel. Furthermore, wood smoke is irritating enough to usually alert shelter occupants to sometimes accompanying carbon monoxide dangers. Scrap lumber cut into short lengths, made into bundles and stored in plastic bags, occupies minimum space and stays dry. Keep a saw and a hatchet in your shelter.

● **Bucket Stove:** The most efficient, practical and safe stove with which to cook or heat for weeks or months in a family shelter is a Bucket Stove, that burns either small pieces of wood or small "sticks" of twisted newspaper. (See the Food chapter.) Especially if you believe that you may have to live in your shelter for months or that your normal fuel will not be available after a nuclear attack, you should make and store at least two Bucket Stoves.

● **An improved Fireless Cooker:** To save a great deal of fuel and time, particularly with slow-cooking grains and beans, make a very well insulated Fireless Cooker similar to the expedient one described on page 82 of the Food chapter. Make a plywood box, first measuring carefully to insure that, when completely lined with 4 inches of styrofoam, the styrofoam will fit closely around a large, lidded pot wrapped in a bath towel. An excellent Fireless Cooker is a war survival asset that also is useful for peacetime cooking.

(To boil about twice as much wheat flour-meal in a given pot as can be boiled when making wheat mush, and to use the minimum amount of water and fuel, salt a batch of the flour-meal, add enough water while working it to make a stiff dough, then make dough balls about 1½ inches in diameter, and roll them in flour-meal. Drop the wheat balls into enough boiling water to cover them, and boil at a rolling boil for 10 minutes. Then put the boiling-hot pot in a well insulated Fireless Cooker for several hours. Corn balls can be made and boiled in this manner, also without the almost constant stirring required when boiling a mush made of home-ground flour-meal.)

● **A sturdy work bench:** In the corner under the emergency exit build a work bench, secured to a wall, on which to cook and to which you can attach your grain mill. A bench 36 inches high, 42 inches wide, and 30 inches deep will serve. (The other corner at the air-exhaust end of the shelter should be the curtained-off toilet and bathing area.)

● **Very warm clothing, footwear, and bedding:** Heating a **well ventilated** shelter usually is unnecessary even in freezing weather if the occupants have these essentials for living in the cold, or if they have the materials needed to make at least as good expedient means for retaining body heat as are described in Chapter 15. The author has felt the warm hands of little Chinese children wearing padded clothing while living in their below freezing homes, where there was scarcely enough straw, grass, and twigs to cook with. If you store plenty of strong thread and large needles in your shelter, you can make warm clothing out of blankets — as some frontier settlers did to survive the subzero winters of Montana.

LIGHT

● **White paint:** To make a little light go a long way, paint the walls, ceiling, floor, and furnishings pure white.

● **Candles:** The most dependable and economical lights for a family shelter are long-burning candles. The best candle tested by the author is the 15-hour candle manufactured by the Reed Candle Company of San Antonio, Texas and sold by the millions in New Mexico each Christmas season for use in outdoor decorative "luminarias". This votive-type, short candle is not perfumed and has a wick supported by a small piece of metal attached to its base, so that the wick remains upright and continues to burn if the wax melts and no longer supports it. If burned in one of the candle-lamps described below, this candle gives enough light to read by for 15 hours.

The author has been able to find only one mail order source of 15-hour candles like those sold by the millions in New Mexico: Preparedness Products, 3855 South 500 West, Salt Lake City, Utah 84115. A case of 144 candles sells for $49.00, FOB in 1990. When UPS shipping charges are added, the delivered cost is between 35 and 40 cents for each 15-hour candle, depending on the distance shipped.

Persons who stock a permanent shelter should realize that after a nuclear war fats, oils, paraffin, and all other sources of light will be in extremely short supply for at least many months. Light at a delivered cost of about two cents per hour will be a bargain blessing.

* The second-best shelter candle tested by the author is a standard Plumber's Candle, that retails for about 60 cents in many stores nationwide, and that burns for about 10 hours with a brighter flame than a votive-type candle.

Two types of expedient candle-lamps were proved by multi-day tests to be the most practical:

* The best expedient candle-lamp is made of a 1-pint Mason jar, identical to the cooking-oil lamp pictured on page 102 of the Light chapter except for the substitution of a short candle for the oil and wick. To make a stable candle base on a glass jar's rounded bottom, cover it with hot candle wax. To be able to light the candle and then put it inside the glass jar, make tongs out of an 18-inch length of coathanger wire bent in the middle, with each of its two ends bent inward 90 degrees and cut off to make 1/4-inch-long candle grippers.

* The second-best candle-lamp is made by cutting a standard aluminum pop or beer can, as illustrated. Use a **sharp** small knife. To make a stable base for a short candle, put enough sand across the can's rounded bottom to barely cover its center. The first candle burned will saturate and then harden the sand, making a permanent candle base or holder.

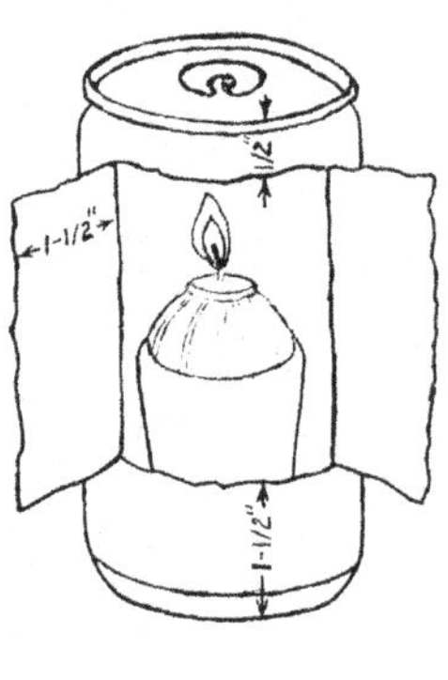

Caution: Although candles are the safest non-electric lights for shelter use, they produce enough carbon monoxide to cause headaches in a poorly ventilated, long-occupied shelter. In a 2-week habitability test of a family shelter in Princeton, the father and mother did not smoke, yet they had persistent headaches. Specialists later concluded that their headaches were caused by the small amounts of carbon monoxide produced by the candles used both for light and to heat food and drink.

● **Expedient lamps:** The very economical lamp that burns cooking oil in a 1-pint glass jar is the better of the two expedient lamps pictured on page 102. For use in a shelter, however, long-burning candles, that are serviceable after decades of storage, are more practical. Among the disadvantages of expedient lamps is the fact that untreated, soft cotton string needed to make excellent wicks is no longer available in some communities, and making wire-stiffened wicks is a time consuming chore.

- **Other light sources:** See the Light chapter.

NYLON HAMMOCK-CHAIRS

To enable the maximum number of additional people to occupy a shelter for days to months, nylon Hammock-Chairs should be made before a war crisis arises, and should be kept stored for emergency use. The best field-tested model for use in shelters that are at least 7 feet wide is similar to the expedient Hammock-Chair described on pages 120 through 124, is made of strong nylon cloth, and is 40 inches wide by 9 feet long along its center line, with each of its long sides being 8 feet-4 inches long. At each end is a curved hem 3½ inches wide, through which a loop-ended nylon hammock rope is run, to draw the slung hammock into a boat-like, secure shape with adequate head and shoulder room. The breaking strength of a hammock rope should be at least 600 pounds.

To attach the nylon ropes that support the suspended chair's two "arms," a loop of nylon webbing, or of folded and stitched nylon cloth, should be sewn to each side edge of the hammock 52 inches from the end of the hammock that will serve as the top of the back of the chair. See the illustrations on page 124. Especially in permanent family shelters, support points both for the hammocks, and for the hammocks when they are converted into suspended chairs, should be made when the shelter is being built.

OFTEN OVERLOOKED SANITATION AND OTHER SHELTER NEEDS

Store enough soap to last your family for at least a year. After a major nuclear attack the edible fats and oils, used in past generations to make soap, will almost all be eaten. Production of detergents is based on inter-dependent, vulnerable chemical industries not likely to be restored for years.

A chemical toilet would help bridge the gap between modern living and surviving in a crowded shelter. For months-long occupancy, however, a more practical toilet is likely to be a 5-gallon can with a seat, a plastic trash bag for its removable liner, a piece of plastic film for its tie-on cover, and a hose to vent gasses to the outdoors. See page 104. Store at least 200 large plastic trash bags.

The author knows from his experiences in primitive regions that using anything other than paper in place of toilet paper or cloth is hard to get accustomed to. A hundred pounds of newspaper, stored in plastic trash bags to prevent it from getting damp, takes up only about 3 cubic feet of storage space and would be useful for many purposes.

Keep several thousand matches, in Mason jars, so that they will be sure to stay dry even if your shelter becomes very humid post-attack.

Store most of your radiation monitoring instruments in your shelter, along with paper and pencils with which to keep records of radiation exposures, etc. A steel or reinforced concrete shelter should have a transistor radio with extra batteries, and a vertical pipe through which an antenna can be run up to improve reception.

No one can remember all the needed survival facts and instructions given even in this one book, so keep *Nuclear War Survival Skills* and other survival guidance in your shelter, and also other books that you believe may improve your family's morale and survival chances.

PRACTICE SHELTER LIVING

A family that spends a weekend living in its completed small shelter will learn more about unrecognized shelter needs — and more about each other — than members are likely to learn if they all read civil defense information for two whole days. Furthermore, after this educational experience family members old enough to have nuclear fears will know for sure that anti-defense activists are talking nonsense when they maintain that if most Americans had shelters they would become less heedful of nuclear war dangers and more likely to support aggressive leaders.

Chapter 18
Trans-Pacific Fallout

POTENTIAL DANGERS TO AMERICANS

Many strategists believe that if a nuclear war is fought in the next few decades it probably will not involve nuclear explosions on any of our 50 states. Perhaps the first nuclear war casualties in the United States will be caused by fallout from an overseas nuclear war in which our country is not a belligerent. As the number of nations with nuclear weapons increases — especially in the Middle East — this generally unrecognized danger to Americans will worsen. Trans-Pacific war fallout, carried to an America at peace by the prevailing west-to-east winds that blow around the world, could be several hundred times more dangerous to Americans than fallout from the worst possible overseas nuclear power reactor accident, and many times more dangerous than fallout from a very improbable U.S. nuclear power reactor accident as lethal as the disastrous Chernobyl accident was to Russians.

Fig. 1 is a map showing fallout from a single above ground Chinese nuclear test explosion ("a few hundred kilotons") on December

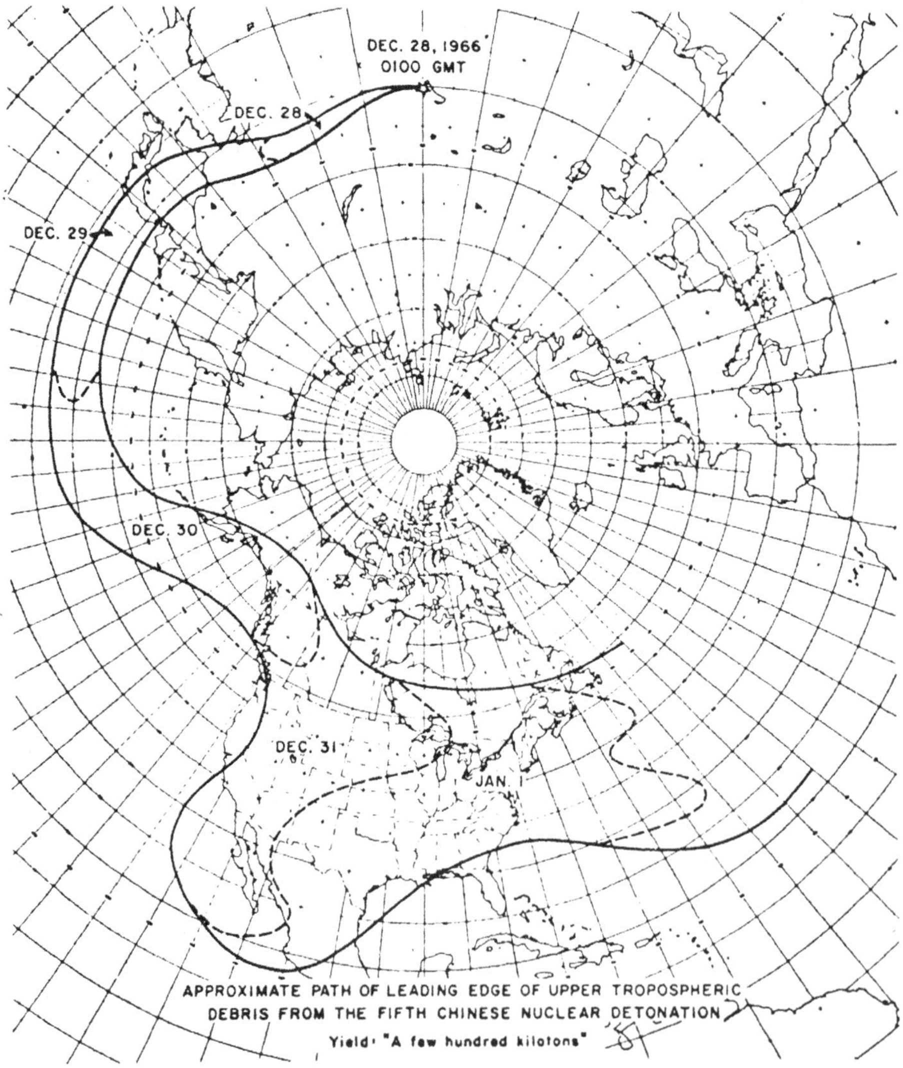

Fig. 1. The Fifth Chinese Nuclear Test was Detonated on Dec. 28, 1966. It "involved thermonuclear material," and, according to the AEC press release, was a "nuclear test in the atmosphere at their test site near Lop Nor." As indicated above, by the end of Dec. 31, 1966 the leading edge of its fallout cloud extended as far east as the dotted line shown running from Arizona to the Great Lakes.

28, 1966. It produced fallout that by January 1, 1967 resulted in the fallout cloud covering most of the United States. This one Chinese explosion produced about 15 million curies of iodine-131 — roughly the same amount as the total release of iodine-131 into the atmosphere from the Chernobyl nuclear power plant disaster. (The Lawrence Livermore National Laboratory's preliminary estimate is that 10-50 million curies of iodine-131 were released during the several days of the Chernobyl disaster; in contrast, its estimate of the iodine-131 released during the Three Mile Island nuclear power plant accident, the worst commercial nuclear power plant accident in American history, is about 20 curies.)

Fig. 1 is from an Oak Ridge National Laboratory report, *Trans-Pacific Fallout and Protective Countermeasures* (ORNL-4900), written by the author of this book in 1970, but not published until 1973. No classified information was used in any version of this report, that summarized findings of the unclassified Trans-Pacific Fallout Seminar funded by the U.S. Atomic Energy Commission. This seminar was attended by experts who came from several research organizations and deliberated at Oak Ridge National Laboratory for two days in March of 1970.

Later in 1970 a final draft of this report was submitted to Washington for approval before publication. It was promptly classified. Publication without censorship was not permitted until after it was declassified in its entirety in 1973. None of the recommendations in this pioneering report were acted upon, but many of them are given in this chapter.

The findings and conclusions of the above mentioned 1970 Oak Ridge National Laboratory Trans-Pacific Fallout Seminar, summarized in the 1973 report, were confirmed by a later, more comprehensive study, *Assessment and Control of the Transoceanic Fallout Threat*, by H. Lee and W. E. Strope (1974; 117 pages), Report EGU 2981 of Stanford Research Institute.

Fallout from the approximately 300 kiloton Chinese test explosion shown in Fig. 1 caused milk from cows that fed on pastures near Oak Ridge, Tennessee and elsewhere to be contaminated with radioiodine, although not with enough to be hazardous to health. However, this milk contamination (up to 900 picocuries of radioactive iodine per liter) and the measured dose rates from the gamma rays emitted from fallout particles deposited in different parts of the United States indicate that trans-Pacific fallout from even an overseas nuclear war in which "only" two or three hundred megatons would be exploded could result in tens of thousands of unprepared Americans suffering thyroid injury. Unprepared Americans do not have potassium iodide, the very effective prophylactic medication to prevent thyroid injury from radioiodine, and few could get it during the several days that it would take trans-Pacific war fallout to reach the United States. Fortunately, removal of even a cancerous thyroid rarely is fatal to people blessed with modern medical facilities.

Only about 7,500 Americans (people living within a few miles of a nuclear power plant in Tennessee) have been given prophylactic potassium iodide to keep in their homes. No government organization has advised even Americans living near other nuclear facilities to buy and keep any kind of prophylactic medicine to protect their thyroids in case of a peacetime nuclear accident. As expected, official warnings and advice to the public continue not even to mention preparations that individual Americans could make to protect themselves and their families against thyroid injury either from trans-Pacific war fallout deposited on an America at peace, or as a result of war fallout if our country is subjected to a nuclear attack.

The worst danger to Americans from trans-Pacific fallout from a large nuclear war would be the whole-body gamma radiation doses that millions would receive from fallout particles deposited on the ground, on streets, on and in buildings. Protective countermeasures would include both sheltering some pregnant women and small children living in "hot spot" areas of abnormally high rain-out of fallout, and evacuating others. Unless such unavoidably time-consuming and expensive countermeasures were taken, several thousand additional Americans might die from cancer in the following 20 or 30 years. The largest total doses would be received by people who would live normal unsheltered lives for the first month or so after fallout deposition, while the dose rates would be highest.

Several thousand additional cancer deaths would be extremely difficult to detect, if caused by whole-body gamma radiation from fallout deposited nationwide, with these scattered deaths occurring over the 20 or 30 years following a trans-Pacific war fallout disaster. For during these same decades about 15 million Americans normally would die from cancers indistinguishable from those caused by whole-body radiation from war fallout deposited on an America at peace.

An authoritative risk estimate of getting cancer from **low doses** of radiation is given in Report No. 77 (March 15, 1984) of the National Council on Radiation Protection and Measurement, "Exposures from the Uranium Series with Emphasis on Radon and Its Daughters":

> "The low dose model for total excess cancer mortality is one hundred cases per million people exposed to one rem uniform whole body radiation. This would make the overall risk of cancer to the average individual in the population about one in ten thousand per rem, i.e., if ten thousand persons are exposed to a dose of one rem (one thousand mrem), one excess [fatal] cancer would be expected within the lifetime of the group."

Many radiation specialists have concluded from studies of the effects of extremely low doses that the above and similar conservative estimates of excess cancer deaths overestimate the number of fatalities likely to result from low radiation doses, such as would be received by millions of Americans from trans-Pacific war fallout.

TO PROTECT YOURSELF AGAINST TRANS-PACIFIC FALLOUT, START BY REALIZING THAT:

• The dangers from trans-Pacific **war** fallout have been increased by the continuing trend toward deployment of more accurate, smaller, more numerous nuclear weapons, because:

* A large nuclear explosion (half a megaton, or more) injects most of its fallout particles and gases into the stratosphere, above the tops of clouds and above the altitudes at which quite prompt removal of contaminants from the atmosphere by scavenging takes place. Very small particles in the stratosphere do not reach the ground before they are blown at least several thousand miles. Most of these tiny particles remain airborne for weeks to years, are very widely dispersed, and are blown around the world several to many times before being deposited. By then the radioactivity of iodine-131 (that has a half life of only a little more than 8 days) is so greatly reduced that it is not nearly as dangerous as is radioactive iodine deposited much sooner with the fallout from smaller weapons of several hundred kilotons, or less, explosive power.

* Nuclear explosions smaller than about half a megaton (500 kilotons) inject all or most of their fallout to lower altitudes — within the troposphere, below the stratosphere. Most of such fallout is deposited during the radioactive cloud's first world-circling trip, when even quite rapidly decaying radioiodine still is dangerously radioactive. This greater danger from smaller nuclear weapons has been proved by numerous measurements of fallout from many nuclear test explosions, both foreign and American.

• The dangers from trans-Pacific fallout produced by peacetime nuclear accidents are not nearly as serious as many Americans have been led to believe. For example, the Chernobyl nuclear power reactor accident injected as much radioactive iodine into the atmosphere as would the explosions of several kiloton-range nuclear weapons totaling perhaps as much as half a megaton in explosive power. But not nearly as much of the radioactivity caused by this reactor accident reached the United States as would reach us from several nuclear explosions in the same area, capable of injecting an equal amount of radioactivity into the atmosphere, because:

* The cloud from the steam explosion that blew off the roof and otherwise damaged the Chernobyl reactor building, may have risen quite soon to 20,000 feet or more and was partially blown eastward clear across Asia and the Pacific Ocean. However, the top of the radioactive **smoke** cloud over the Chernobyl power plant, that burned for days, rose only about 3,000 feet above the ground. As a result, much of the airborne Chernobyl radiation stayed at relatively low altitudes where scavenging (removal) of smoke and fallout particles and gasses is most effective and rapid, due to aggregation on cloud droplets, rain-out, and dry deposition. In contrast, almost all of the fallout particles and radioactive gasses from a nuclear explosion are injected much higher, to altitudes where scavenging is less effective; there, the generally prevailing west-to-east winds promptly start transporting very small particles and radioactive gasses (that originate in the mid-latitudes of the northern hemisphere) around the world.

* Variable winds for days carried much of the Chernobyl radioactive material northward to Scandanavian countries, then westward and southward to other European countries. The resultant wide dispersal of this fallout allowed time for both scavenging and radioactive decay before a small fraction of these invisible radioactive clouds rose and also were blown eastward by the prevailing high-altitude winds. These west winds carried an extremely small fraction of the radioactive emissions from the burning Chernobyl plant clear across Asia and the Pacific to America.

• The media habitually exaggerate dangers from nuclear accidents, and exploited the Chernobyl disaster. For example, when Dr. Robert Gale, the leading bone marrow transplant specialist who helped save a few Chernobyl victims, first returned from Russia, an Associated Press article quoted him as saying: "I think we can say there are at least 50,000 to 100,000 people who have had some dose of radiation which might be of long-term concern. There will, unfortunately, be additional casualties. We hope the number will be small." The Rocky Mountain News headlined "100,000 SOVIETS TO SUFFER FROM RADIATION, DOCTOR SAYS". Mary McGrory, the syndicated liberal columnist, also misinterpreted Dr. Gale's risk estimate and misinformed her readers by writing: "He [Dr. Gale] estimated that there could be 100,000 cases of radiation sickness . . .". Such dramatic news items give the impression that 100,000 Russians — not just a small fraction of that number — are likely to suffer sickness or death from the Chernobyl radiation. So additional typical Americans, reading misinformation of this type and knowing very little about statistical evaluations of risks based on probabilities, have had their worst nuclear fears strengthened.

The public's exaggerated fears of extremely small amounts of radiation also are worsened by the media's use without explanations of very small units of radiation measurement, including the picocurie. (The picocurie is used to express the radioactive contamination of milk, water, etc., and is only **one millionth of a millionth** [1/1,000,000,000,000] of a curie.) One episode in which fears of radiation were thus worsened occurred shortly after the invisible fallout cloud from the Chernobyl disaster first reached the United States. Some listeners were frightened when a radio announcer merely stated that milk samples in northwest Oregon showed 118 picocuries per liter of radioactive iodine. Few Americans know that they will not be advised to stop using fresh milk unless its contamination is 15,000 picocuries or more per liter — as specified in the Food and Drug Administration's official, very cautious "Protective Action Guidance", published in the Federal Register of October 22, 1982.

The maximum measured radioactive contamination of milk in the United States by iodine-131 from the Chernobyl disaster was in milk produced by cows grazing on pasture in Washington: 560 picocuries per liter. The much greater potential danger from trans-Pacific **war** fallout is brought out by the fact that the approximately 300-kiloton Chinese test explosion of December 28, 1966 resulted in worse iodine-131 contamination of milk produced by a cow grazing on pasture near Oak Ridge, Tennessee: 900 picocuries per liter. Even a small overseas nuclear war with only 20 or so kiloton-range nuclear explosions could cause high enough contamination of milk to result in the Government's warning Americans to refrain from using fresh milk. Most Americans would heed this warning and would not drink or otherwise use fresh milk for weeks. In addition, a small overseas nuclear war possibly would cause a few American casualties years to decades later.

TWO SUMMARY CONCLUSIONS

1. Trans-Pacific war fallout deposited on an America at peace surely would be a disaster, but not an overwhelming one. The economic and psychological impact probably would be more damaging than the losses of health and life.

2. Prudent individuals should make preparations to enable them to use the low cost protective countermeasures described in this book, especially those in Chapter 13. Some of the most effective countermeasures, such as getting enough prophylactic potassium iodide to prevent thyroid damage even if war fallout dangers from explosions in the United States or overseas were to continue for a couple of months, cannot be accomplished after even an overseas nuclear war begins.

Appendix A
Instructions for Six Expedient Fallout Shelters

SHELTER-BUILDING INSTRUCTIONS

The following step-by-step instructions for building 6 types of earth-covered **expedient** shelters have enabled untrained families to build even the most difficult of these shelters in less than 2 days. The only families who took longer—up to 4 days—were the few who were delayed by very heavy rains. Each of these shelters has been built by several different families or groups of families. Only widely available materials and hand tools are required. They have been built under simulated crisis conditions in environments typical of large regions of the United States: covered-trench types have been built in forested clay hills of Tennessee, in a bare Colorado valley in snowy November, in an irrigated Utah valley in hot August. Most of the aboveground shelters were built by families in Florida, where the water table is within 18 inches of the surface.

All of these test families used instructions that contained general guidance to help inexperienced persons build almost any type of earth-covered shelter. In this appendix, general instructions which apply to all types of shelters will be given first, to avoid repetition. (However, if the instructions for building one type of shelter are reproduced separately, the pertinent parts of these general instructions should be given before the step-by-step instructions for building that shelter.

WARNING

Earth-covered shelters built of green poles can become unsafe within a few months, because of fungi and/or boring insects. In damper parts of the U.S., earth-covered shelters built of dry poles or untreated lumber can become unsafe after several months. An exception is very dry areas of the West, where some pioneers lived for years in earth-covered dugouts with pole roofs.

GENERAL INSTRUCTIONS FOR BUILDING AN EXPEDIENT SHELTER

1. Read all the instructions and study the drawings before beginning work. (Most families have found it helpful first to read the instructions aloud and then to discuss problems and work assignments.)
2. Sharpen all tools, including picks and shovels. Dull tools waste time and energy. If no file is available, tools can be sharpened by rubbing them hard on concrete or a rough stone.
3. Wear gloves from the start. Blisters can lead to serious infections, especially if antibiotics cannot be obtained.
4. Whenever practical, select a building site that:
   - Will not be flooded if heavy rains occur or if a large dam farther up a major valley is destroyed by a nuclear explosion.
   - Is in the open and at least 50 ft away from a building or woods that might be set afire by the thermal pulse from an explosion tens of miles away. (Keep well away from even a lone tree; it is hard to dig through roots.)
   - Has earth that is firm and stable, if the planned shelter is to be a trench type with unshored (unsupported) earth walls. To make sure that the earth is firm and stable enough so that the walls will not cave in, make a "thumb-test" by digging an 18-in.-deep hole and trying to push your bare thumb into the undisturbed earth at the bottom. If you can push your thumb no farther than 1 in., the earth should be safe enough. If the earth does not pass the thumb-test, move to another location and repeat the test. Or build a belowground shelter with shored walls, or an aboveground shelter.
   - Has a sufficient depth of earth above rock or the water table for a trench to be dug to the depth

required. (To find out, try to dig a pit to the required depth before excavating the whole trench. Or, if you are quite sure there is no water-table problem, try driving down a sharpened rod or pipe to the required depth in several places along the planned length of the trench.)

5. If the shelter must be built on sloping ground, locate it with its length crosswise to the direction of the slope.

6. Before staking out the shelter, clear the ground of brush, weeds and tall grass over an area extending about 10 ft beyond the planned edges of the excavation. (If loose earth is shoveled onto tall plants, the earth will be difficult to shovel the second time when covering the completed shelter roof.)

7. Stake out the complete shelter, and then dig by removing layers of earth.

8. When digging earth that is too firm to shovel without first breaking it up, start picking (or breaking with a shovel) in a line across the center of the trench. Next, shovel out a narrow trench 6 or 8 in. deep all the way across the width of the trench. Then with pick or shovel break off row after row of earth all the way across the width of the trench, as illustrated.

ORNL–DWG 78-16212

9. When digging a trench, to avoid having to move the excavated earth twice more to get it out of the way, first pile all earth about 8 ft away from the trench. Later, pile additional earth you are excavating at least 3 ft away.

10. Never risk a cave-in by digging into lower parts of an earth wall. It is dangerous to produce even a small overhanging section of wall or to dig a small, cave-like enlargement of a shelter.

11. When making a "sandbag" of a pillowcase or sack to hold earth shielding in place around the sides of shelter openings or along the edges of a shelter roof, fill it so that it will be only about two-thirds full after its opening is tied shut securely. Avoid dropping the sandbag.

12. If sufficient sandbags are not available, make earth-filled "rolls." Bed sheets or any reasonably strong fabric or plastic film can be used to make these rolls as described below. (To make a longer roll than the one illustrated below, several persons should make one together, standing side-by-side.)

To make an 8-in.-high earth-filled roll:

(1) Select a piece of cloth at least as strong as a new bed sheet, 2 ft longer than the side of the opening to be protected, and 5 ft wide.

(2) Place 2 ft of the width of the cloth on the ground, as illustrated.

ORNL–DWG 78-16213

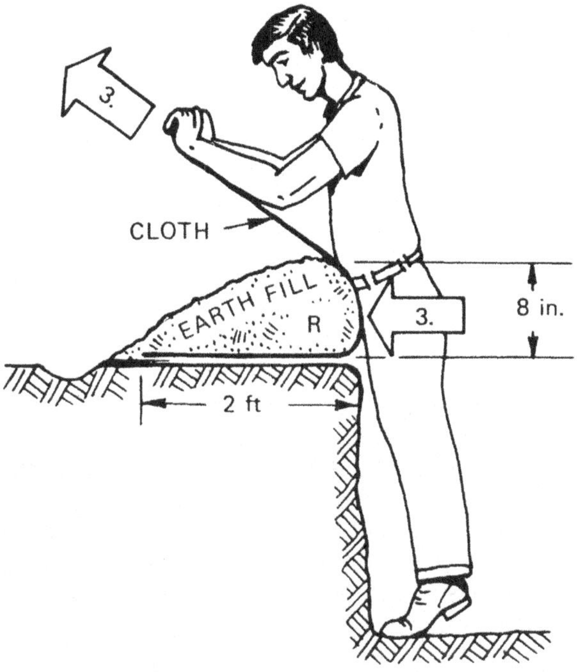

(3) While using both hands to hold up and pull on 3 ft of the width of the cloth and pressing against the cloth with your body, have another person shovel earth onto and against the cloth.

(4) While still pulling on the cloth, pull the upper part down over the earth that covers the lower part of the cloth.

(5) Cover the upper part of the cloth with earth so as to form an earth-filled "hook" near the upper edge, as illustrated.

ORNL–DWG 78-16214

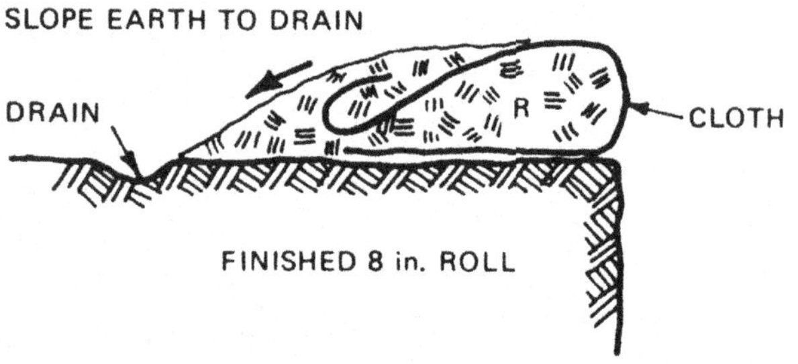

(6) If a greater thickness of rolls is needed, level the earth on top of a roll; then make anotner earth-filled roll on this level surface.

13. Cut and haul poles and logs more easily by doing the following:

(1) Take time to sharpen your tools before starting to work—no matter how rushed you feel.

(2) When sawing green trees that have gummy resin or sap, oil your saw with kerosene or diesel fuel. If you don't have these, use motor oil, grease, or even soap.

(3) When felling a small tree, the following method will help make a square cut, keep your saw from being pinched, and help make the tree fall in the desired direction: (a) Saw the tree about one-third through on the side toward which you want it to fall. (b) Then start sawing the opposite side, while another person pushes on the tree with a 10-ft push-pole, pressing the end of the push-pole against the tree about 10 ft above the ground. A push-pole with a forked end—or with a big nail on the end—is best.

(4) After a tree has been felled, trim off all limbs and knots so that the pole or log is smooth and will require no additional smoothing

ORNL–DWG 78-16210

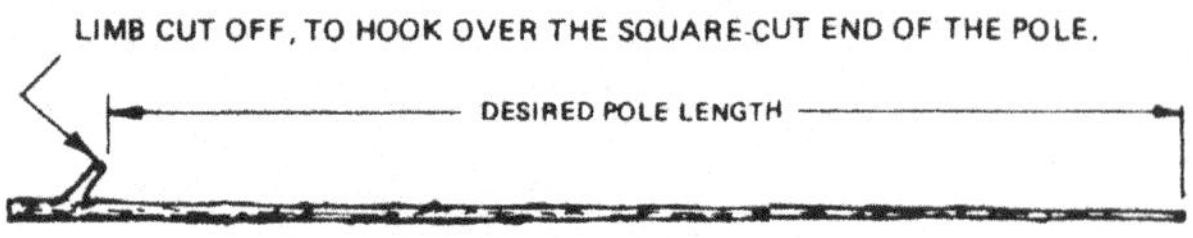

when you get ready to move it, or to use it for building your shelter. Make and use a measuring stick to speed up measuring and cutting poles and logs to the right lengths.

(5) It usually is best first to cut the poles exactly two or three times the final length of the poles to be used in the shelter.

(6) When you are ready to move the poles to the shelter site, drag them rather than trying to carry them on your shoulders. Shouldering them is more tiring, and you could injure yourself severely if you should trip.

To drag a log or several poles by hand: (a) Cut a stick 2 to $2\frac{1}{2}$ in. in diameter and about $3\frac{1}{3}$ ft long; (b) Tie a short piece of $\frac{1}{4}$-in. (or stronger) rope to the center of the stick; (c) Make a lasso-like loop at the free end of the rope, so that when it is looped around the log and two people are pulling (see illustration), the front end of the log is raised about 6 in. above the ground. The loop should be tightened around the log about 2 ft. from its end, so that the end of the log cannot hit the backs of the legs of the two people pulling it.

ORNL–DWG 78-16211

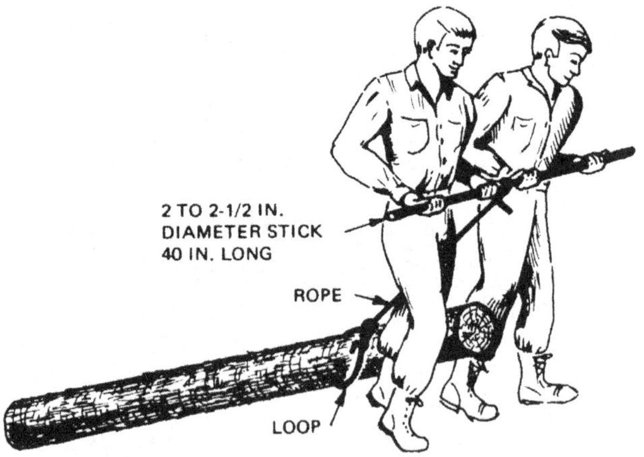

CAUTION: If you drag a log down a steep hill, one person should tie a rope to the rear end of the log, and then follow the dragger, ready to act as the brake if needed.

(7) When you get the poles or logs to the location where you will build the shelter, cut them to the desired minimum diameters and specified lengths, and put all those of one specified

type together. Be sure that the diameter of the small end of each pole of one type is at least as large as the minimum diameter specified for its type. Make and use a measuring stick, as previously described.

14. Use snow for shielding material for aboveground shelters if the earth is so deep-frozen that digging is impractical. For a Ridge-Pole Shelter (see Appendix A.5), cover the entire shelter with 5 ft of wetted or well-packed snow. For a Crib-Walled Shelter (see Appendix A.6), fill the cribs and then cover and surround the entire shelter with snow at least 5 ft thick. With wetted or well-packed snow 5 ft thick, the protection factor is about 50. Families have completed these winter shelters within 2 days.

    Several hundred pounds of snow can be moved at a time by sledding it on a piece of canvas or other strong material 6 to 8 ft wide. Attach a stick across one end of the material and tie a rope to the ends of the stick, so as to form a "Y" bridle on which a person can pull.

    To keep the occupants of a snow-covered expedient shelter dry and tolerably warm in sub-freezing weather, provide sufficient ventilation openings to maintain inside temperatures at a few degrees *below* freezing. (See Chapter 14, Expedient Clothing.)

15. Make a reliable canopy over the shelter entry. By following the instructions given in Fig. A on the following page, you can make a dependable canopy that ordinary winds will neither tear nor blow down and that will not catch rainwater—even if you have no waterproof material stronger than 4-mil polyethylene film.

16. Take to your shelter enough window screen or mosquito netting to cover its openings. Except in freezing-cold weather, flies and mosquitoes would soon become a problem in most localities soon after an attack.

17. Work to complete (1) an expedient ventilating-cooling pump (a KAP) and (2) the storage of at least 15 gallons of water per person. This work should be accomplished by the time your shelter is completed. Especially in an area of heavy fallout during warm or hot weather, an earth-covered, high-protection-factor shelter when full of people would be useless unless adequately ventilated and cooled and provided with enough water.

18. In cold weather, restrict air flow through the shelter by hanging curtains of plastic or tightly woven fabric, or by otherwise partially obstructing its two openings. Always be sure to leave at least a few square inches open at the floor level of one opening and at the ceiling height of the other, to provide enough ventilation to prevent a harmful concentration of exhaled carbon dioxide. To prevent exhaled water vapor from wetting clothing and bedding and reducing its insulating value, keep the ventilation openings as wide open as possible without causing shelter temperatures to be intolerably cold.

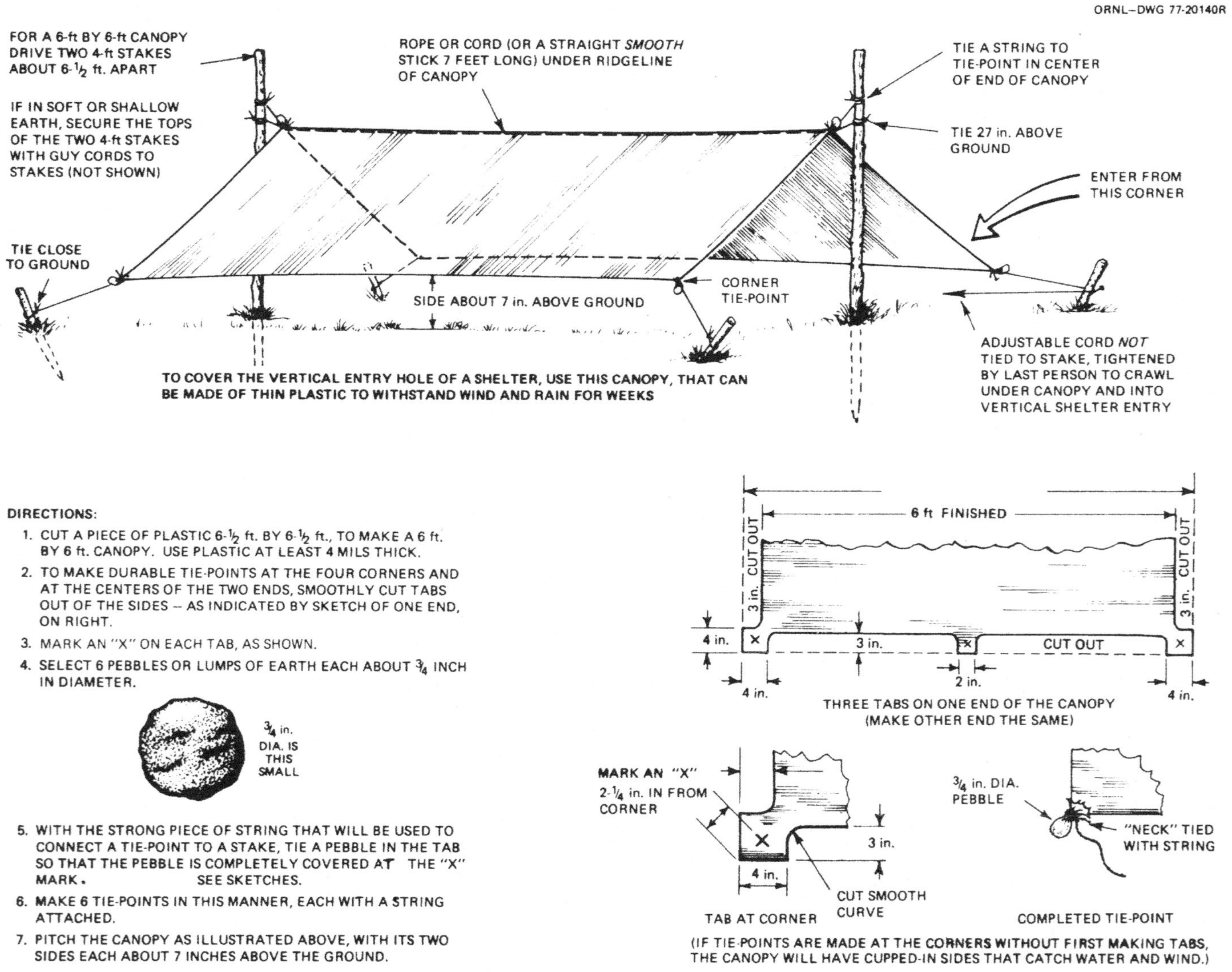

Fig. A. A dependable canopy to keep fallout and rain out of a vertical entry.

Appendix A.1
Door-Covered Trench Shelter

(See illustration at the end of Appendix A.1)

PROTECTION PROVIDED

Against fallout radiation: Protection Factor 250 (PF 250)—a person in the open outside this shelter would receive 250 times as much fallout radiation as he would if inside.

Against blast: Better protection than most homes, if built in very stable earth. Blast tests have indicated that this shelter would be undamaged up to at least the 5-psi overpressure range from large explosions. Without blast doors, the shelter's occupants could be injured at this overpressure range, although probably not fatally.

Against fire: Excellent, if sufficiently distant from fires producing carbon monoxide and toxic smoke.

WHERE PRACTICAL

In a location where at least one hollow-core door per occupant is available, and where the earth is very stable and a dry hole or trench 4½ feet deep can be dug without difficulty. (A family evacuating in a pickup truck or large station wagon can carry enough doors, with doorknobs removed. Strong boards at least 6 feet long and at least one full inch thick, or plywood at least ¾-inch thick, also can be used to roof this 36-inch-wide trench and to support its overhead earth shielding.)

Warning: Some doors with single-thickness panels if loaded with earth will break before they bend enough to result in protective earth arching.

FOR WHOM PRACTICAL

For a typical family or other group with two or more members able to work hard for most of 36 hours. (Stronger-than-average families with most members able to work hard have completed this type of shelter is less than 24 hours after receiving step-by-step, well illustrated instructions.)

CAPACITY

The shelter illustrated is roofed with **3 doors** and is the **minimum** length for **3 persons.** (If you have additional doors, or boards and sticks at least 3 ft long, make the entryway trenches 3 or 4 ft longer than illustrated—if not pressed for time.)

For each additional person, add an additional door. (If more than about 7 persons are to be sheltered, build two or more separate shelters.)

BUILDING INSTRUCTIONS

1. Before beginning work, study the drawings and read ALL of the following instructions.
2. Divide the work; CHECK OFF EACH STEP WHEN COMPLETED.
3. By the time the shelter is finished, plan to have completed (1) a ventilating pump (a KAP 16 in. wide and 28 in. high), essential for this shelter except in cool weather, and (2) the storage of at least 15 gallons of water per occupant (see Appendix B and Chapter 8).
4. Start to assemble materials and tools that are listed for the illustrated 3-person shelter.

A. Essential Materials and Tools for a 3-Person Shelter

- Three hollow-core doors.
- A shovel (and a pick, if the earth is very hard).
- Two to three square yards per person of waterproof materials for rainproofing the roof. Use materials such as 4-mil polyethylene film, shower curtains, plastic tablecloths, plastic mattress covers, or canvas.
- Two pieces of plastic or tightly woven cloth (each about 6½ × 6½ ft) to make canopies over the two shelter openings. Also sticks and cords or strips of cloth to support

the canopies—as described in Fig. A of the introductory section of this appendix.

- Materials and tools for building a simple shelter-ventilating pump, a KAP 16 in. wide and 28 in. high. (See Appendix B.) Only in cold or continuously breezy, cool weather can tolerable temperatures and humidities be maintained in a crowded underground shelter without an air pump.

- Containers for storing adequate water. (See Chapter 8.)

B. Useful Materials and Tools

- Large cans, buckets, and/or pots with bail handles—in which to carry earth and later to store drinking water or human wastes.

- Two pillowcases and one bedsheet per person—to make "sandbags" around shelter openings and to cover trench walls. (If available, large sheets of 4-mil polyethylene are better than bedsheets, because they keep earth walls damp and stable. They also help keep shelter occupants dry and clean and prevent earth from falling into their eyes.)

- File, knife, pliers, hammer.

- Measuring tape, yardstick, or ruler.

- Expedient life-support items.

5. To save time and work, SHARPEN ALL TOOLS AND KEEP THEM SHARP.

6. Wear gloves from the start—even tough hands can blister and become painful and infected after hours of digging.

7. Check to be sure the earth is stable and firm enough so that a trench shelter with unshored (unsupported), **vertical** earth walls will be safe from cave-ins. (Interior doors are not strong enough to roof an earth-covered trench wider than 3 ft.)

   As a test of the stability of earth, dig a small hole about 18 in. deep. Remove all loose earth from the bottom of the hole. Then make a "thumb test" by pushing your bare thumb into the undisturbed surface at the bottom of the hole. If you can push your thumb into the earth no farther than one inch, the earth should be suitable for this type of shelter. If the earth does not pass the "thumb test," move to another location and try the test again. Continue to relocate and repeat until suitable earth is found, or build a shored-trench or aboveground shelter.

8. Prepare to dig a vertical-walled trench $4^1/_2$ ft deep and 3 ft wide. To determine the length of the trench, add together the widths of all the doors to be used for roofing it, then subtract 8 in. from the sum. (To avoid arithmetical errors, it is best to lay all the doors side by side on the ground.)

9. Clear any brush, grass, or weeds that are more than a few inches high from the area where the trench will be dug. Also clear the ground around all sides of the trench, to a distance of about 8 ft from the sides and ends of the trench.

10. Stake out a rectangular trench 36 in. wide, with its length as determined above. Also stake out the entrance at one end, as illustrated in Fig. A.1 at the end of Appendix A.1, and the ventilation trench and opening at the other.

11. Dig the main trench, the entryway trench, and the ventilation trench. Place the excavated earth along both lengthwise sides of the trench, starting at the outside edges of the cleared space. Be sure that no earth is piled closer than 3 ft to the sides of the trench.

12. To be sure that unstable, unsafe earth is not encountered at depths below 18 in., repeat the "thumb test" each time the trench is deepened an additional foot. If the earth does not pass the test, do not dig the trench any deeper; try another location.

13. To keep each trench its full width as it is dug, cut a stick 36 in. long and another 18 in. long; **use them repeatedly from the start** to check the widths of the main trench and the entry trenches. Keeping the trenches full width will save much work and time later.

14. Carefully level and smooth the ground to a distance of $2^1/_2$ ft from the sides of the trench, so that the doors will lie flat on the ground up to the edges of the trench.

15. If plenty of sheets, bedspreads, plastic, and/or other materials are available, cover the trench walls with them. Wall coverings should stop one inch from the floor of the trench to prevent their being stepped on and pulled down. Plastic wall coverings keep some types of damp earth walls from drying out and crumbling.

16. To be able to place an adequate thickness of shielding earth all the way to and around the entryway and ventilation hole, stack improvised "sandbags" around these two openings before placing the earth on the roof. Or use cloth or plastic material to make "rolls" of earth, as illustrated in the introductory section of Appendix A.

17. Shovel earth around the rolls, sandbags, or other means used to raise the level of the earth around the two shelter openings. Slope this earth outward, and pack it, so that rainwater on the ground cannot run into the shelter.

18. To rainproof the shelter and to prevent the roofing doors from being dampened and weakened, use available waterproof materials as follows:

    a. If the earth is *dry*, the easiest and best way to make a rainproof roof is to place the doors directly on the ground, with each of the end doors overlapping an end of the main trench by 4 or 5 in. (Be sure again to level the ground surface as you place each door, so that each lies flat against the ground all the way to the edges of the trench.) Next, mound dry earth over the doors. First place a few inches of earth on the doors near their ends; then mound it about 12 in. deep above the centerline of the trench. Slope the earth to both sides so as to just cover the ends of the doors. Next, smooth off the earth mound, being careful to remove sharp stones that might puncture rainproof materials. Then place waterproof material over the smooth mound, making the "buried roof" shown in Fig. A.1. Finally, carefully mound an additional 12 to 15 in. of earth on top of the buried roof, again placing it first over the doors near their ends. The earth over the trench should be at least 2 ft thick, so that effective earth arching will support most of the weight of the earth covering and will provide considerable protection if struck by blast.

    b. If the earth is *wet*, place the waterproof material directly on top of the doors, to keep them dry and strong. To make water run off this waterproof covering and to keep water from collecting on a horizontal surface and leaking through, slope the doors toward one side of the trench by first making one side of the trench about 3 in. higher than the other side. A way to raise one side—without increasing the distance the doors must span—is to place an earth-filled "roll" of bedsheets or other material along one edge of the trench. To keep the waterproof material used to cover the doors from sliding down the slope of the doors when earth is shoveled on, tuck the upper edge of the material under the higher ends of the doors. Finally, mound earth over the doors, first placing it near their ends. The mound should be at least 2 ft deep above the centerline of the roof and about 3 or 4 in. deep over both ends of the doors.

    If more waterproof material is available than is required to make a buried roof (or to cover the doors) and to make the illustrated canopies over the two shelter openings, use this excess material to cover the wet ground on which the doors are placed.

19. Dig small drainage ditches around the completed shelter, to lead runoff water away.

20. To keep rain and/or sand-like fallout particles from falling into the shelter openings, build an open-sided canopy over each opening, as illustrated in Fig. A, shown in the introductory section of Appendix A.

21. Install the air pump (a KAP) in the shelter opening into which air is already naturally moving.

22. If the shelter has a KAP, protection against radiation can be increased by placing containers of water and of heavy foods, or bags of earth, so as to partially block the openings. This would still permit adequate air to be pumped through the shelter, except in very hot weather.

23. For seats, place water and food containers, bedding, etc., along the side of the trench that is farther from the off-center entry trenches. If the trench floor is damp, covering it with a waterproof material, tree limbs, or brush will help.

24. Fill all available water containers, including pits which have been dug and lined with plastic, then roofed with available materials. If possible, disinfect all water stored in expedient containers, using one scant teaspoon of a chlorine bleach, such as Clorox, for each 10 gallons of water. Even if only muddy water is available, store it. If

you do not have a disinfectant, it may be possible to boil water when needed.

25. Put at least your most useful emergency tools inside your shelter.

26. As time and materials permit, continue to improve your chances of surviving by doing as many of the following things as possible:
   (1) Make a homemade fallout meter, as described in Appendix C, and expedient lights. (Prudent people will have made these extremely useful items well ahead of time.)
   (2) Install screens or mosquito netting over the two openings, if mosquitoes or flies are a problem. Remember, however, that screen or netting reduces the air flow through a shelter — even when the air is pumped through with a KAP.
   (3) Dig a stand-up hole near the far end of the shelter. Make the hole about 15 in. in diameter and deep enough to permit the tallest of the shelter occupants to stand erect occasionally.

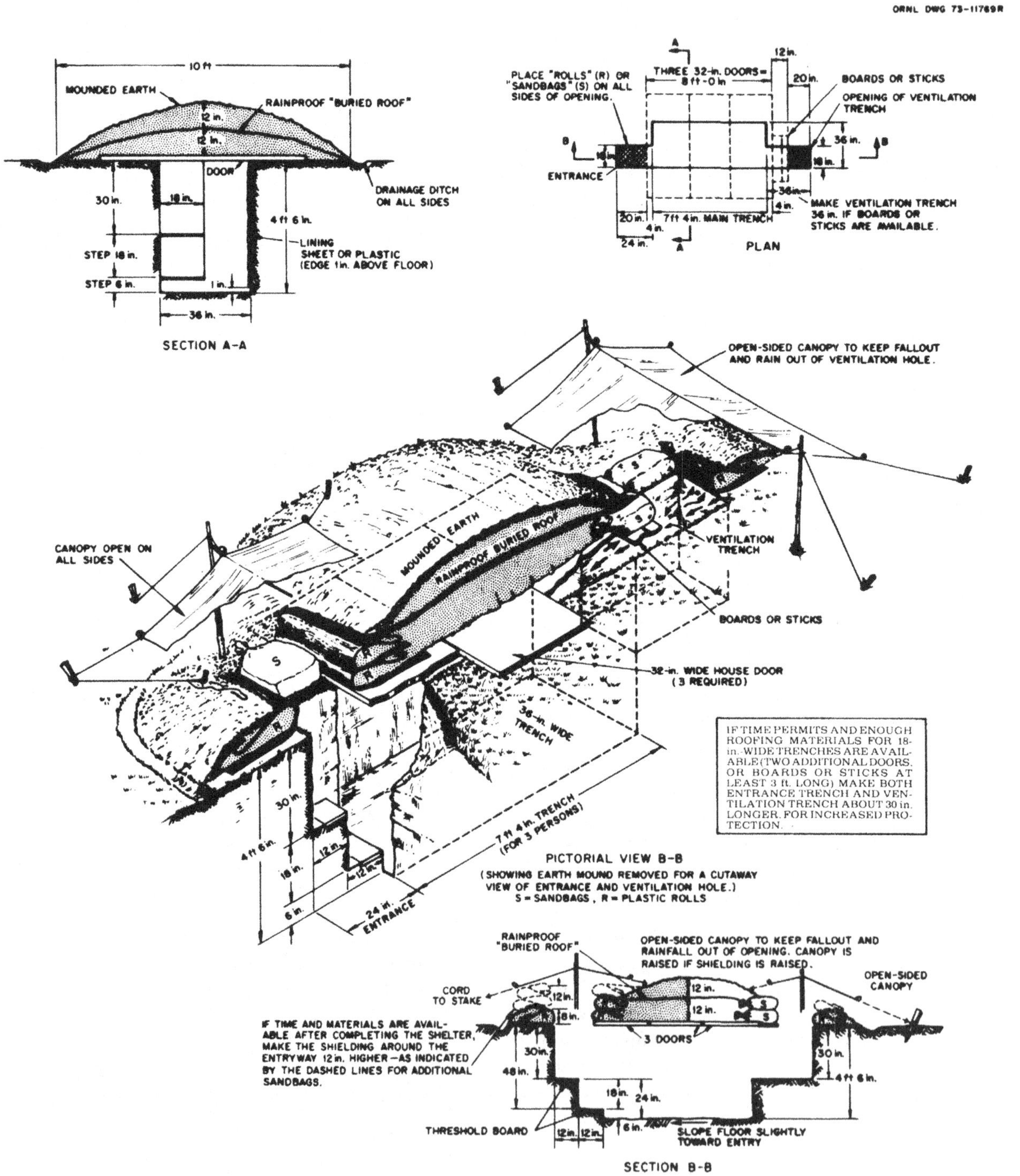

Fig. A.1. Door-Covered Trench Shelter.

Appendix A.2
Pole-Covered Trench Shelter

PROTECTION PROVIDED

Against fallout radiation: Protection Factor 300 (PF 300)— a person in the open outside this shelter would receive 300 times more fallout radiation than he would if he were inside.

Against blast: Quite good protection if built in stable earth. Blast tests have indicated that this shelter, if built in stable earth, would not be seriously damaged by blast effects of large explosions at least up to the 7-psi overpressure range. (At 7 psi, most buildings would be demolished.) Without blast doors, occupants of the shelter could be injured, although probably not fatally at this overpressure.

Against fire: Excellent, if sufficiently distant from fires producing carbon monoxide and toxic smoke.

WHERE PRACTICAL

In wooded areas with small trees, for builders who have an ax or a bow saw, crosscut or chain saw, and digging tools. Or in any location where the necessary poles may be obtained.

In stable earth, where the water table or rock is more than 4½ ft below the surface.

FOR WHOM PRACTICAL

For a typical family or other group with two or more members able to work hard for most of 48 hours. (Stronger-than-average families with almost all members able to work hard have completed this type of shelter is about 24 hours after receiving step-by-step, well illustrated instructions, before travelling to the wooded building site and beginning to cut trees and haul poles.)

CAPACITY

The shelter illustrated is the minimum length recommended for 4 persons. For each additional person, add at least 2¾ ft to the length of the shelter room. If more than about 10 persons are to be sheltered, build 2 or more separate shelters.

BUILDING INSTRUCTIONS

1. Before beginning work, study the drawings and read ALL of the following instructions. Divide the work so that some people will be digging while others are cutting and hauling poles. CHECK OFF EACH STEP WHEN COMPLETED.
2. By the time the shelter is finished, plan to have completed: (1) a ventilating pump, and (2) the storage of at least 15 gallons of drinking water per occupant (see Appendix B and Chapter 8).
3. Start to assemble materials and tools. Those listed are for the illustrated 4-person shelter with a room 11 ft long.

A. Essential Materials and Tools

- Saw (bow saw or crosscut preferred) and/or ax for cutting poles to the lengths and diameters illustrated.
- Shovels (one for each two workers).
- Pick (if the ground is hard).
- Rainproof roof materials (very important in rainy, cold weather). At least 2 square yards of such material per person would be required; 3 square yards per person would be better. Shower curtains, plastic tablecloths, plastic mattress covers, canvas, and the like can be used. Also needed are 2 pieces of plastic or tightly woven cloth, each about 6½ × 6½ ft, to make canopies over the two shelter openings.
- Materials and tools for building a simple shelter-ventilating pump, a KAP 22 in. wide and 36 in. long. (See Appendix B.) Only in cold or continuously breezy, cool weather

can tolerable temperatures and humidities be maintained for days in a crowded underground shelter that lacks an air pump.

- Containers for storing adequate water. (See Chapter 8.)

B. Useful Materials and Tools

- Large cans, buckets, and/or pots with bail handles—in which to carry earth and later to store drinking water and human wastes.
- Two bedsheets and two pillowcases per person for covering cracks between roofing logs, making "sandbags," and improvising bedsheet-hammocks and bedsheet-chairs.
- A file.
- A measuring tape, yardstick, or ruler.
- Rope, or strong wire (100 ft)—to make earth-retaining pole walls close to the shelter openings (as explained in step 19) and for hammock supports, etc.
- Chain saw, pick-mattock, hammer, hatchet, pliers.
- Kerosene, turpentine, or oil—to keep hand saws from sticking in gummy wood.
- Expedient life-support items recommended in this book.
- Mosquito netting or window screen to cover the openings, if mosquitoes or flies are likely to be a problem.

4. To save time and work, SHARPEN ALL TOOLS AND KEEP THEM SHARP.
5. Wear gloves from the start—even tough hands can blister after hours of chopping and digging, and become painful and infected.
6. If possible, select a location for the shelter that is in the open and at least 50 ft from a building or woods. Remember that on a clear day the thermal pulse (flash of heat rays) from a very large nuclear explosion may cause fires as far away as 25 miles.
7. If the site chosen is on a steep slope, locate the shelter with its length crosswise to the direction of the slope.
8. Stake out the outlines of the trench, driving stakes as indicated in Fig. A.2.1 at the end of Appendix A.2. If more than 4 persons are to be sheltered, increase the length of the shelter room by 2 ft 9 in. for each additional person.
9. Clear the ground of saplings and tall grass within 10 ft of the staked outlines so that later the excavated earth can be easily shoveled back onto the completed shelter roof.
10. Start digging, throwing the first earth about 10 ft beyond the staked outlines of the trench. Less able members of the family should do the easier digging, near the surface. Those members who can use an ax and saw should cut and haul poles. See the introductory section of this appendix for the know-how to make this hard work easier.
11. Pile all excavated earth at least 2 ft beyond the edges of the trench, so roofing poles can be laid directly on the ground. To make sure that the trenches are dug to the specified full widths at the bottoms, cut and use two sticks—one 42 in. long and the other 22 in. long—to check trench widths repeatedly.
12. At the far end of the shelter dig the ventilation trench-emergency exit, making it 22 in. wide and 40 in. deep. This will help provide essential ventilation and cooling. In cold weather or when fallout is descending, canvas or plastic curtains should be hung in the two openings to control the air flow.
13. Make and install threshold boards, to keep the edges of earth steps and earth ledges from being broken off. (In damp earth, it is best to install threshold boards before roofing the shelter.) If boards are lacking, use small poles.
14. Unless the weather is cold, build a shelter-ventilating pump—a KAP 20 in. wide × 36 in. high. (If the weather is *cold*, building a KAP can be safely delayed until after the shelter is completed.) A KAP should be made before a crisis, or, if possible, before leaving home.
15. Obtain fresh-cut green poles, or, as a second choice, sound, dry, untreated poles. Use no poles smaller in diameter than those specified in the accompanying drawings. For ease in hauling, select poles no more than 50% larger in diameter than those specified.

16. Lay the poles side by side over the trench. Alternate the large and small ends to keep the poles straight across the trench. If roof poles 9 ft long are being used to roof a 5-ft-wide trench, be sure to place the roof poles so that their ends extend 2 ft farther beyond one side of the trench than beyond the other side. This will enable shelter occupants, after the stoop-in shelter is completed, to widen the shelter room 2 ft on one side. First, it can be widened to provide a 2-ft-wide sleeping ledge. Later, it can be further deepened to make space for additional expedient hammocks or for double-bunk beds of poles or boards built on each side of the shelter.

17. For ease and safety later when hanging expedient bedsheet-hammocks and bedsheet-chairs in the completed shelter, place **loose** loops around roof poles in the approximate locations given by the diagram on the second shelter drawing, Fig. A.2.2. Make these loose loops of rope, or strong wire, or 16-in-wide strips of strong cloth, such as 50% polyester bedsheet rolled up to form a "rope". (For making hammocks and seats, see Chapter 14. These are not essential, although decidedly useful.)

18. Cover the cracks between the logs with cloth, leaves, clay, or any other material that will keep dirt from falling down between the cracks. CAUTION: DO NOT try to rainproof this flat roof, and then simply cover it with earth. Water will seep through the loose earth cover, puddle on the flat roofing material, and leak through the joints between pieces of roofing material or through small holes.

19. Place 6-ft-long poles, one on top of the other, next to the entrances. This will keep earth to be placed on top of the entryway trenches from falling into the openings. Secure these poles with wire or rope. (See View A-A[1] in Fig. A.2.1.) If wire or rope is not available, make earth-filled "rolls" to hold the earth nearly vertical on the trench roof next to each opening. (See the introductory section of this appendix.)

20. Mound earth to a center depth of about 18 in. over the shelter roof (as shown in View B-B[1] in Fig. A.2.1) to form the surface of the future "buried roof." Be sure to slope both sides of the mound. Then smooth its surface and remove sharp roots and stones that might puncture thin rainproofing materials to be placed upon it.

21. Place the waterproofing material on the "buried roof." If small pieces must be used, lay them in shingle-like fashion, starting at the lower sides of the mounded earth.

22. Cover the buried roof with another 18 in. of mounded earth, and smooth this final earth surface.

23. Finish the entrances by placing some shorter poles between the two longer poles next to each entryway. Bank and pack earth at least 6 in. deep around the sides of the entrances, so that rainwater on the ground cannot run into the shelter entrances.

24. Dig surface drainage ditches around the outside of the mounded earth and around the entrances.

25. Place a piece of water-shedding material over each of the entrances, forming an open-ended canopy to keep fallout and rain from the shelter openings. (See Fig. A in the introductory section of Appendix A.) Almost all fallout would settle on these suspended canopies, rather than falling into shelter openings—or would fall off their edges and onto the ground like sand.

26. Hang the KAP from the roof of the trench opening into which outdoor air can be felt flowing, so that air will be pumped in the direction of the natural flow of air. **(If you have no KAP, make and use a small Directional Fan.)**

27. Fill all available water containers, including pits which have been dug and lined with plastic, then roofed with available materials. If possible, disinfect all water stored in expedient containers, using one scant teaspoon of a chlorine bleach, such as Clorox, for each 10 gallons of water. Even if only muddy water is available, store it. If you do not have a disinfectant, it may be possible to boil water when needed.

28. **Put all of your emergency tools inside your shelter.**

29. As time and materials permit, continue to improve your chances of surviving by doing as many of the following things as possible:
    (1) Make a homemade fallout meter, as described in Appendix C, and expedient lights. **(Prudent people will have made these extremely useful items well ahead of time.)**
    (2) Make and hang expedient bedsheet-hammocks and bedsheet-chairs, following the installation diagram shown in Fig. A.2.2.
    (3) Install screens or mosquito netting over the two openings, if mosquitoes or flies are a problem. Remember, however, that screen or netting reduces the air flow through a shelter—even when the air is pumped through with a KAP.
    (4) Dig a stand-up hole near the far end of the shelter. Make the hole about 15 in. in diameter and deep enough to permit the tallest of the shelter occupants to stand erect occasionally.

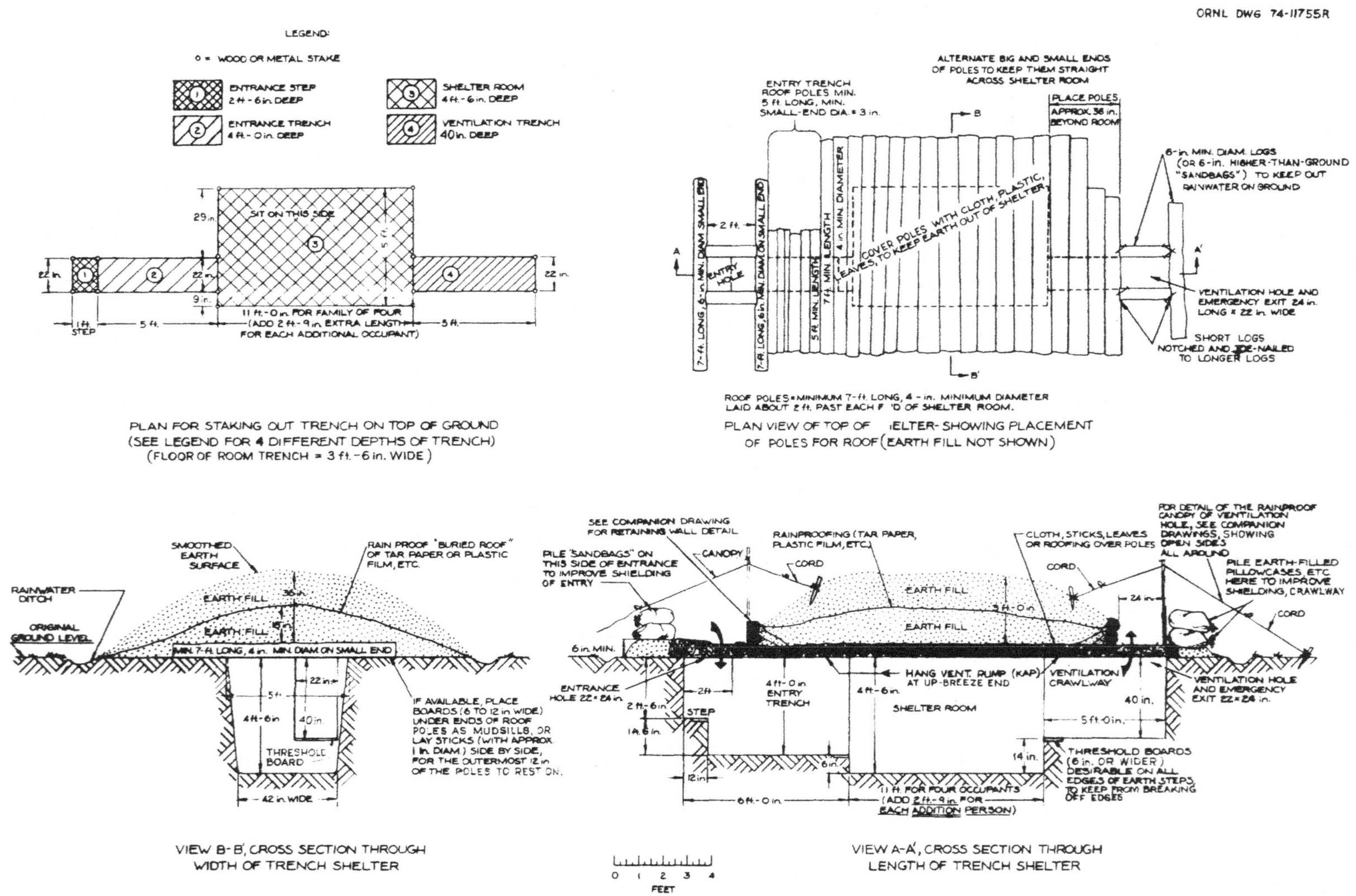

Pole-Covered Trench Shelter
(To be Built Only in Firm Ground, Such as a Strong, Stable Clay or Loam)
See Accompanying Drawing

Fig. A.2.1. Pole-Covered Trench Shelter.

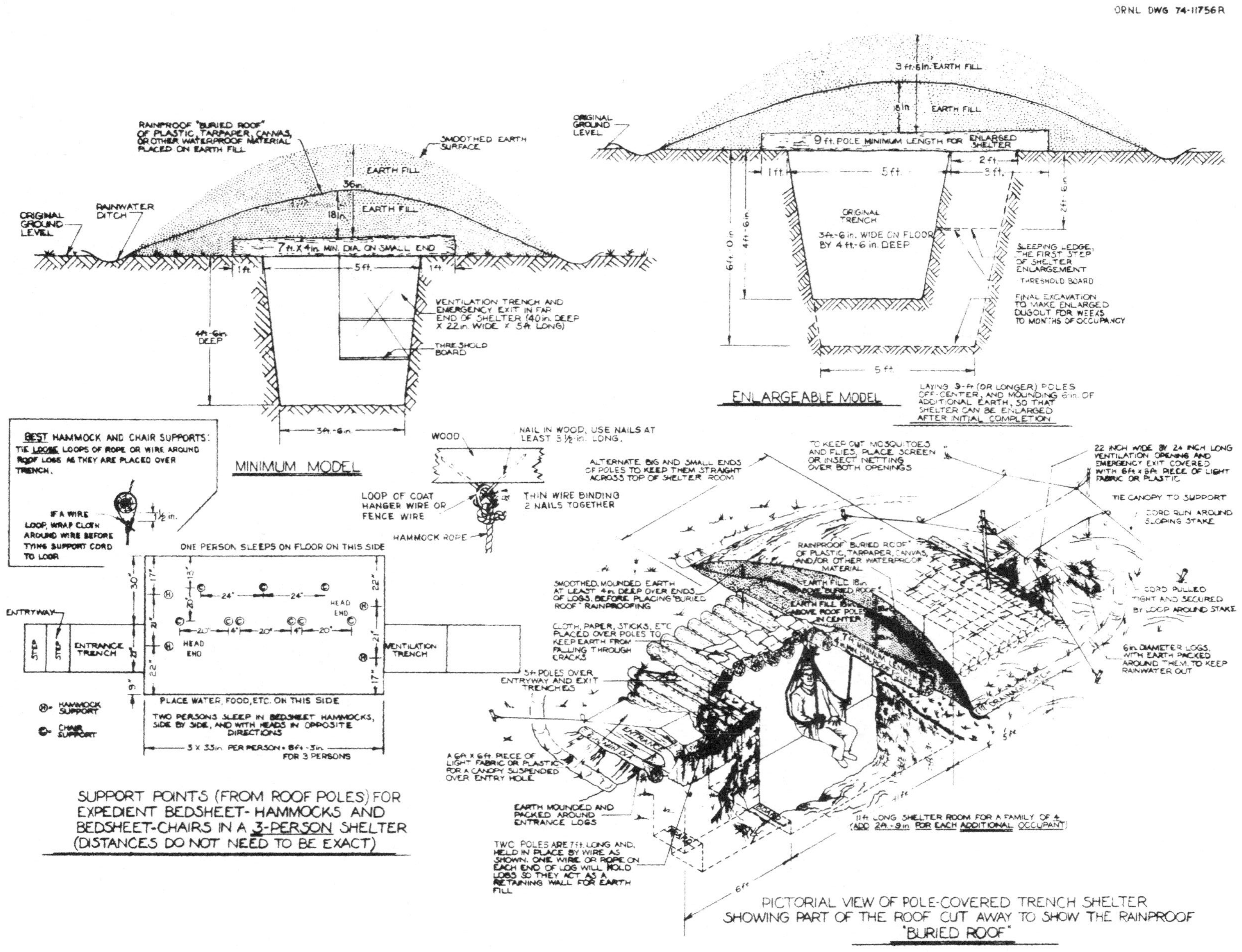

Fig. A.2.2. Pole-Covered Trench Shelter.

Appendix A.3
Small-Pole Shelter

PROTECTION PROVIDED

Against fallout radiation: Protection Factor 1000 (PF 1000), if the shelter is covered with at least 3 ft of earth. That is, a person in the open outside this shelter will receive a gamma ray dose 1000 times greater than he will receive inside the shelter. See drawings at the end of Appendix A.3.

Against blast: This shelter is excellent for preventing fatalities if it is built with strong expedient blast doors; it is still quite good if built without them. (These instructions are for fallout shelters. The instructions for making blast doors and other essentials for adequate blast protection are given in Appendix D. Without blast doors, occupants are likely to suffer serious injuries above 7 psi.)

Against fire: Excellent, if sufficiently distant from fires that produce carbon monoxide and toxic smoke.

WHERE PRACTICAL

In wooded areas with small trees, for builders who have a saw (bow saw, crosscut, or chain saw) and digging tools. Any location is suitable if the necessary poles may be obtained there. Try to avoid roots.

For belowground, semiburied, or aboveground construction. (However, aboveground construction requires the excavation and movement of so much earth that it is not practical for 2-day construction by families with only hand tools.)

FOR WHOM PRACTICAL

For families or other groups with most members able to work hard 12 hours a day for 2 days. (Most people do not realize how hard and long they can work if given a strong incentive.)

CAPACITY

The drawings and lists of materials given in these instructions are for a 12-person shelter. For each additional occupant beyond 12, add 1 ft to the length of the shelter room.

This shelter requires less work and materials per occupant if its room is sized for about 24 persons, because the entrances are the same regardless of the length of the room. (To make the shelter room twice as long, each of the horizontal, ladder-like braces on the floor and near the ceiling of the room can be made with two poles on a side, rather than one long pole on a side.)

If the room is sized for more than 24 people, management and hygiene problems become more difficult when it is occupied.

For 12 people to live for many days in this shelter without serious hardship, the benches and bunks must be built with the dimensions and spacings given in the illustration. Or, materials must be available for making and suspending 12 expedient bedsheet-hammocks that can be converted each day into 12 bedsheet-chairs.

BUILDING INSTRUCTIONS

1. Study both of the two drawings (Fig. A.3.1 and A.3.2 at the end of Appendix A.3) and read all of these instructions before beginning work. CHECK OFF EACH STEP WHEN COMPLETED.
2. By the time the shelter is finished, plan to have completed (1) a ventilating pump (a KAP 24 in. wide and 36 in. high), essential except in cold weather, and (2) the storage of at least 15 gallons of water per occupant.

3. Start to assemble the required materials. For building a **12-person** Small-Pole Shelter, the materials are:

• Green poles. No pole should have a small end of less diameter than the minimum diameter specified for its use by Figs. A.3.1 and A.3.2. The table below lists the number and sizes of poles needed to build a 12-person Small-Pole Shelter.

Pole Length	Minimum Diameter of Small End	Number of Poles Required	Width[b]
6 ft 2 in.	5 in.	2	–
3 ft 1 in.	5 in.	12	–
2 ft 4 in.[a]	5 in.	12	–
10 ft 8 in.	5 in.	–	7 ft
8 ft 8 in.	5 in.	–	7 ft
10 ft 6 in.	4 in.	4	–
7 ft 2 in.	4 in.	–	47 ft
5 ft 6 in.[a]	4 in.	12	–
6 ft 10 in.	4 in.	–	3 ft
6 ft 3 in.	4 in.	8	–
2 ft 6 in.[a]	4 in.	16	–
2 ft 3 in.	4 in.	4	–
5 ft 2 in.	3½ in.	–	8 ft
3 ft 10 in.	3½ in.		36 ft
10 ft[c]	2 in.	12	–

[a]To be shortened to fit for crossbraces.
[b]Width equals the distance measured across a single layer of poles when a sufficient number of poles are laid on the ground side by side and **touching**, to cover a rectangular area.
[c]For supports during construction.

NOTE: The above list does not include flooring materials, to be placed between the poles of the ladder-like braces on the earth floor.

• Rainproofing materials: Preferably one 100-ft roll, 12 ft wide, of 6-mil polyethylene. The minimum amount needed is 200 sq. ft. of 4-mil polyethylene, or 200 sq. ft of other waterproof plastic such as tablecloths, shower curtains, and/or vinyl floor covering. Also include 100 ft of sticks for use in drainage ditch drains (½-in. diameter, any lengths).

• Nails, wire, and/or cord: Ten pounds of 40-penny nails plus 4 pounds of 16-penny nails are ideal. However, 7 pounds of 16-penny nails can serve.

• Boards for benches and overhead bunks, if bedsheet-hammocks are not to be used. (Boards are desirable, but not essential; small poles can be used instead.) 2 × 4-in. boards—70 feet for frames (or use 3-in.-diameter poles). 1 × 8-in. boards—100 feet (or use 1- to 2-in.-diameter poles).

• Materials to build a homemade ventilating pump (a KAP 24 in. wide and 36 in. high—see Appendix B) and to store at least 15 gallons of water per occupant (see Chapter 8).

4. Desirable muscle-powered tools for building a 12-person, Small-Pole Shelter are listed below. (Most builders have succeeded without having this many tools. A backhoe, chain saws, and other mechanized equipment would be helpful, but not essential.)

Tools	Quantity
Ax, long-handle	2
Bow-saw, 28-in.	2
(or 2-man crosscut saw)	1
Pick	2
Shovel, long-handle	3
Claw hammer	2
File, 10-in.	1
Steel tape, 10-ft	1

(Also useful: a 50-ft steel tape and 2 hatchets)

5. To help drain the floor, locate the shelter so that the original ground level at the entrance is about 12 inches lower than the original ground level at the far end of the shelter—unless the location is in a very flat area.

6. Stake out the trench for the entire shelter. Even in very firm ground, if the illustrated 12-person shelter is being built, make the excavation at the surface 9 ft 8 in. wide and 18 ft long (3 ft longer than the entire length of the wooden shelter). The sloping sides of the excavation are necessary, even in very firm earth, to provide adequate space for backfilling and tamping. (The trench illustrated in Fig. A.3.1 is 6 ft 4 in. deep, to minimize work when providing only for excellent fallout protection. For improved **blast** protection, the trench should be **at least** 7 ft deep.)

7. Check the squareness of the staked trench outline by making its diagonals equal.

8. Clear all brush, tall grass, and the like from the ground, to a distance of 10 ft all around the staked location—so that later you can easily shovel loose earth back onto the roof.

9. If the ground is unstable, excavate with sides that are appropriately less steep.

10. When digging the trench for the shelter, use a measuring stick 7 ft 8 in. long (the minimum

bottom width) to repeatedly check the excavation width.

11. When digging with a shovel, pile the earth dug from near ground level about 10 ft away from the edges of the excavation. Earth dug from 5 or 6 ft below ground level then can easily be piled on the surface only 1 to 5 ft from the edge of the excavation.

12. Finish the bottom of the excavation so that it slopes vertically $^1/_2$ in. per foot of length toward the entrance, and also slopes toward the central drain ditch. (Later, sticks covered with porous fabric should be placed in the ditches, to serve like a crushed-rock drain leading to a sump.)

13. While some persons are excavating, others should be cutting **green** poles and hauling them to the site. Cut poles that have **tops no smaller than the specified diameters for each type of pole** (not including the bark).

14. For ease in handling poles, select wall and roof poles with top diameters no more than 50% larger than the specified minimum diameters.

15. Sort the poles by size and lay all poles of the same size together, near the excavation.

16. Before the excavation is completed, start building the ladder-like, horizontal braces of the shelter frame. Construct these braces on smooth ground near the excavation. Place two straight poles, each 10 ft 6 in. long (with small-end diameters of 4 in.), on smooth ground, parallel and 6 ft 2 in. apart. Hold these poles securely so that their outer sides are exactly 6 ft 2 in. apart, by driving two pairs of stakes into the ground so that they just touch the outsides of the two long poles. Each of the four stakes should be located about one foot from the end of a pole. To keep the 10 ft 6 in. poles from being rotated during the next step, nail two boards or small poles across them perpendicularly as temporary braces, about 4 ft apart.

    Then with an ax or hatchet, slightly flatten the inner sides of the two poles at the spots where the ends of the 6 cross-brace poles will be nailed. Next, saw each cross-brace pole to the length required to fit snugly into its place. Finally, toenail each cross-brace pole in place, preferably with two 40-penny nails in each end.

17. Place the lower, ladder-like horizontal brace of the main room on the floor of the completed excavation.

18. Build the frame of the main room. Near the four corners of the room, secure four of its wall poles in their final vertical positions by nailing, wiring, or tying temporary brace-poles to the inner sides of these 4 wall poles and to the inner sides of the two long poles of the ladder-like horizontal brace on the bottom of the excavation. To keep the two pairs of vertical wall poles exactly 6 ft 2 in. apart until the upper ladder-like horizontal brace is secured in its place, nail a temporary horizontal brace across each pair of vertical poles, about 1 ft below their tops.

19. To support the upper ladder-like horizontal brace, nail blocks to the inner sides of the four vertical wall poles, as shown in the lower right-hand corner of the pictorial view, Fig. A.3.2. If you have large nails, use a block about 3 in. thick and 6 in. long, preferably cut from a green, 4-in.-diameter pole.

20. In the finished shelter, DO NOT leave any vertical support poles under the long poles of the upper ladder-like horizontal brace; to do so would seriously reduce the usable space along the walls for benches, bunks, and occupants.

21. While some workers are building the frame of the main room, other workers should make the four ladder-like horizontal braces for the two entrances, then make the complete entrances. To keep the ladder-like horizontal braces square during construction and back-filling, nail a temporary diagonal brace across each one.

22. When the four wall poles and the two ladder-like horizontal braces of the main room are in place, put the remaining vertical wall poles in place, touching each other, until all walls are completed. When placing the wall poles, keep them vertical by alternately putting a butt and a top end uppermost. Wall poles can be held in position by backfilling and tamping about a foot of earth against their lower ends, or they can be wired in position until backfilled.

23. Be sure to use the two 5-in.-diameter poles (6 ft 2 in. long) by placing one next to the top and the other next to the bottom of each of the main doorways to the room. Study the drawings. Use braces, each 2 ft 3 in. long, to hold apart the top and bottom of each doorway—thus making sure that a 24-in.-wide air pump can swing in either doorway.

24. To prevent earth from coming through the cracks between wall poles, cover the walls with

cloth, plastic, rugs, roofing, or even cardboard. If none of these are available, use sticks, twigs, or grass to cover the wider cracks.

25. After all horizontal bracing and vertical wall poles are in place, begin backfilling, putting earth between the walls and trench sides. Pay particular attention to the order of filling. The earth fill behind all the walls must be brought up quite evenly, so that the earth fill behind one side is no more than 12 in. higher at any one time than the earth on the opposite side. Lightly **tamp the earth fill in 6-in. layers.** A pole makes a good tamper; do not use a mechanical tamper.

26. Next, lay the roof poles side by side, touching each other on top of the wall poles. Cover at least the larger cracks with plastic, roofing, boards, or sticks to keep earth from falling through. If the earth is sandy, cover the whole roof with some material such as bedsheets or plastic to keep sand from running through the cracks.

    CAUTION: Do not try to rainproof this flat roof and simply cover it with earth. If you do, water will seep straight through the loose earth cover, puddle on the flat roofing material, and leak through the joints between pieces of roofing material or through small holes.

27. Mound earth over the shelter, piling it about 15 in. deep along the centerline of the roof and sloping it toward the sides of the roof, so that the earth is only about 2 in. deep over the ends of the roof poles. (Preparatory to mounding earth onto the roof, place gradestakes in position so you will be able to know the locations and depths of roof poles as you cover them.) Continue these slopes to two side drainage ditches. Smooth this mounded earth with a rake or stick and remove any sticks or rocks likely to puncture the rainproof roofing material to be laid on it.

28. Place rainproofing material on top of the smooth, mounded earth—as shown in sections of the drawings in Fig. A.3.1—to make a "buried roof." Plastic film, such as 4-mil polyethylene, is preferable. Roofing material, plastic shower curtains and tablecloths, or canvas can also be used. Be sure to overlap adjoining pieces.

29. Place the rest of the earth cover over the shelter, being sure that the corners of the shelter have at least $2^1/_2$ ft of earth over them. Mound the dirt, smoothing its surface so that water will tend to run off to the surface drainage ditches which should be dug all around the edges of the mounded earth.

30. Build the benches and overhead bunks. If boards are available, use them; if not, use small, straight poles. On each side, build a row of benches and bunks 9 ft long, centered in the shelter. In order to use the shelter space to the greatest advantage, make the heights and widths of the benches and bunks the same as the thoroughly tested heights (14 in. and 4 ft 5 in.) and widths (16 in. and 24 in.) given by Fig. A.3.2. Also be sure to space their vertical supports 3 ft apart—so two adults can sit between each pair of vertical bunk supports.

31. Narrow the ends of the overhead bunks so that the aisle between them is about 28 in. wide for a distance of 38 in. from each doorway. This allows room for installation and operation of an expedient air pump (a KAP) for prevention of dangerous overheating in warm weather.

32. Place a canopy (open on all sides) over each entrance, to minimize the entry of sand-like fallout particles or rain.

33. To improve the floor, lay small poles between the lower brace poles, so that the floor is approximately level. Or, use sticks covered with scrap boards.

34. Fill all available water containers, including pits which have been dug and lined with plastic, then roofed with available materials. If possible, disinfect all water stored in expedient containers, using one scant teaspoon of a chlorine bleach, such as Clorox, for each 10 gallons of water. Even if only muddy water is available, store it. If you do not have a disinfectant, it may be possible to boil water when needed.

35. Put all of your emergency tools inside your shelter.

36. As time and materials permit, continue to improve your chances of surviving by doing as many of the following things as possible:
    (1) Make a homemade fallout meter, as described in Appendix C, and expedient lights. (Prudent people will have made these extremely useful items well ahead of time.)
    (2) Install screens or mosquito netting over the two openings, if mosquitoes or flies are a problem. Remember, however, that screen or netting reduces the air flow through a shelter—even when the air is pumped through with a KAP.

EXPEDIENT VENTILATION AND COOLING

(Those workers who are to work only on the shelter itself, if pushed for time, need not read this section before beginning their work.)

Install a KAP (one that is 24 in. wide and 36 in. high) near the top of the doorway through which you can feel air naturally flowing into the shelter room at that time. (If the direction of the natural air flow changes, move the KAP to the other opening.) To enable the KAP to efficiently pump fresh air from the outdoors all the way through the shelter, block the lower half of the doorway in which the KAP is installed with a quickly removable covering, such as a plastic-covered frame made of sticks. Be sure to connect the KAP's pullcord only 11 in. below its hinge line. This prevents excessive arm motions which would cause unnecessary fatigue.

If short of time or materials, make a small Directional Fan.

In windy or cold weather, control the natural flow of air through the shelter by hanging adjustable curtains in the doorways at both ends, and/or by making and using trapdoors on the tops of the vertical entryways. For adjustable curtains, use pieces of plastic, each with a supporting stick attached to its upper edge. This allows for different-sized openings in the doorways: (1) an opening under the lower edge of the adjustable curtain at the air-intake end of the room, and (2) an opening over the top of the curtain at the air-exhaust end of the room. In cold weather, this arrangement usually will provide adequate chimney-type ventilation for the shelter without using an air pump.

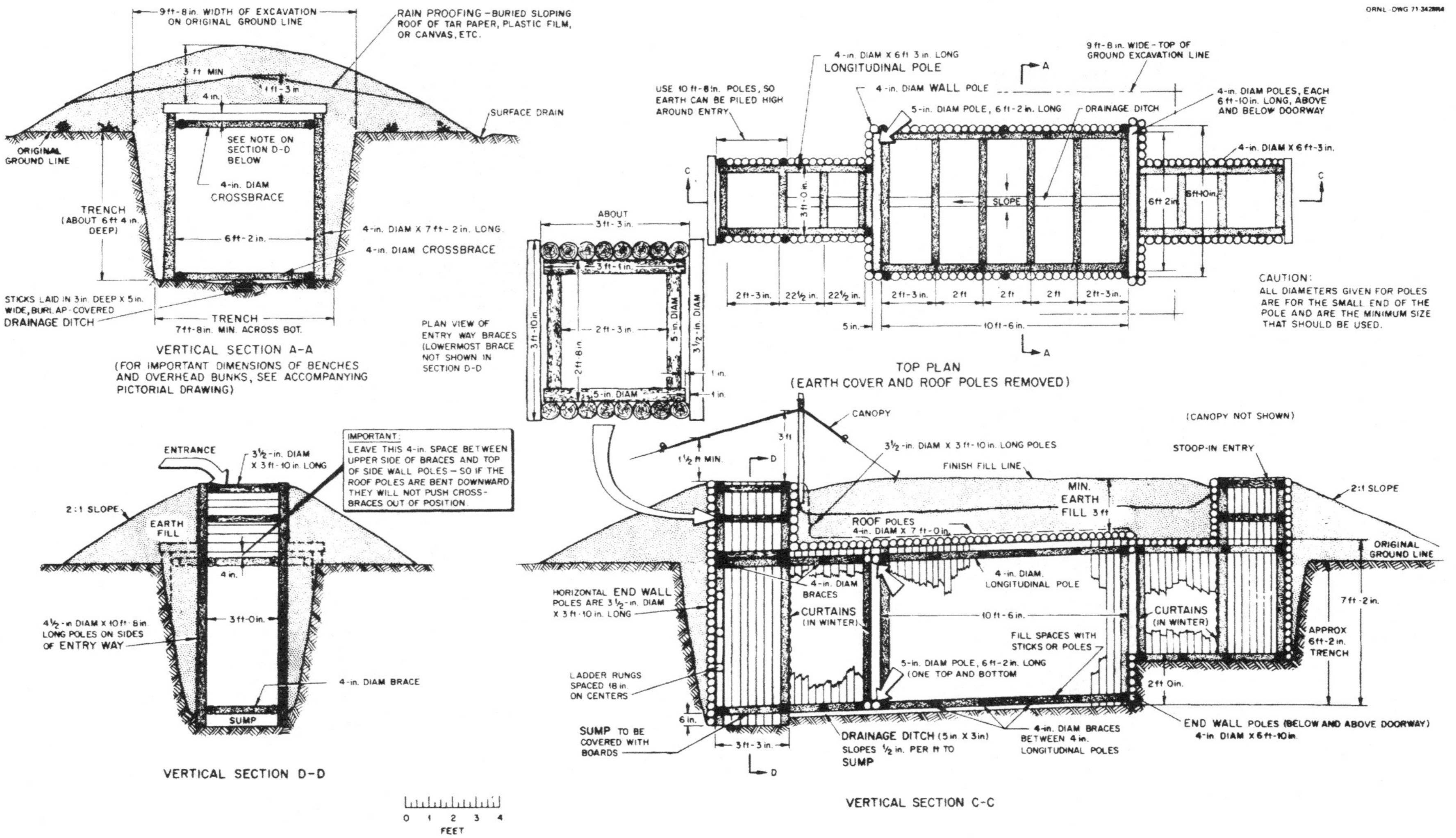

Fig. A.3.1. Plan and Elevation of Small-Pole Shelter.

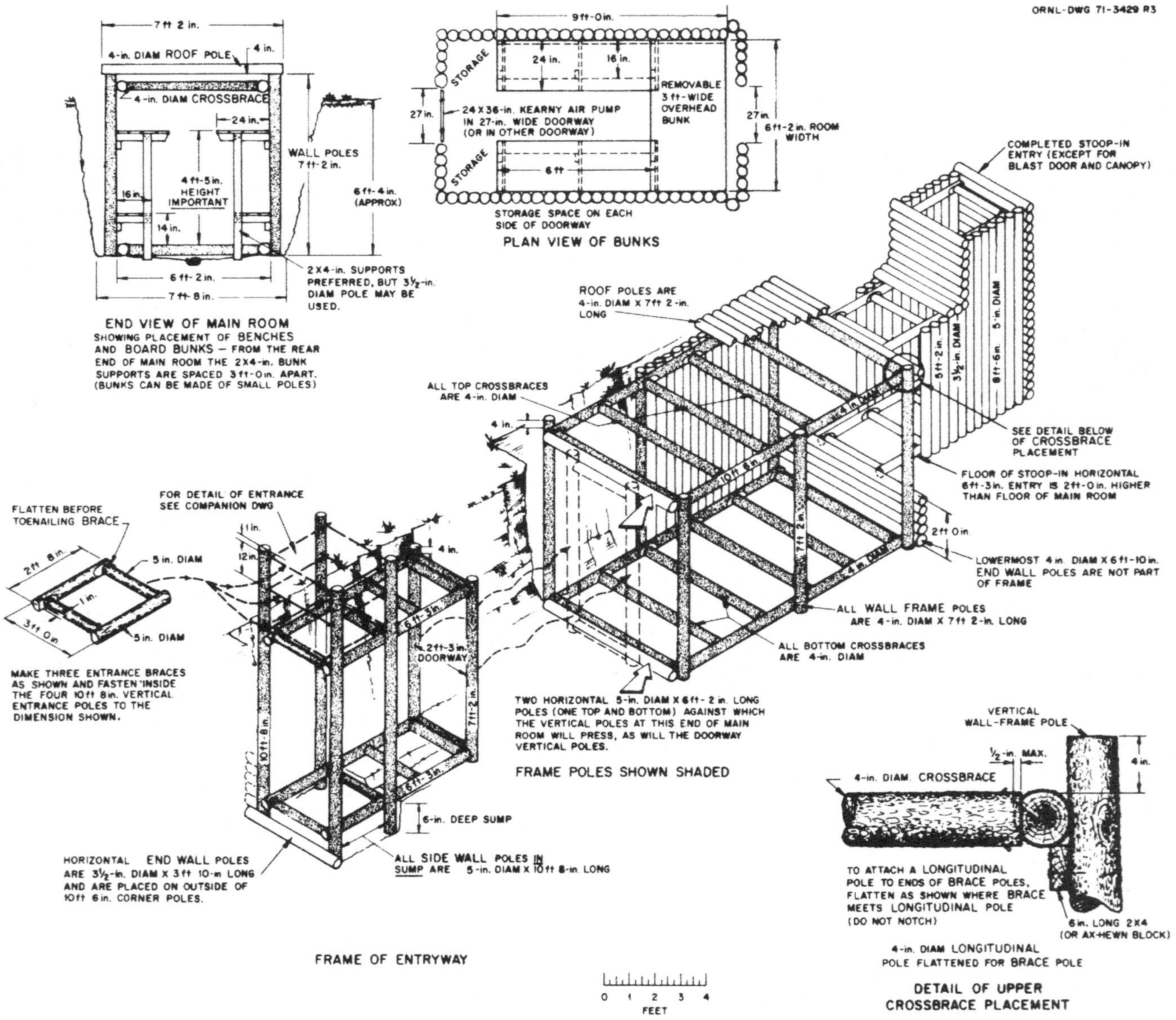

Fig. A.3.2. Pictorial View of Small-Pole Shelter.

Appendix A.4
Aboveground, Door-Covered Shelter

PROTECTION PROVIDED

Against fallout radiation: Protection Factor about 200 (PF 200) if covered with 30 in. of earth. (A person in the open outside this shelter would receive about 200 times more fallout radiation than if he were inside.) The drawing at the end of Appendix A.4 shows the earth cover only 20 in. thick, resulting in a PF of about 100.

Against blast: Better protection than most homes. Blast tests have indicated that this shelter would be undamaged at least up to the 5-psi overpressure range from large explosions. Without blast doors the shelter's occupants could be injured at this overpressure range, although probably not fatally.

Against fire: Fair, if the cloth in the entries is covered with mud and if the shelter is sufficiently distant from fires producing carbon monoxide and toxic smoke.

WHERE PRACTICAL

In a location where at least one hollow-core door per occupant is available, where a dry trench at least 14 inches deep can be dug without difficulty, but the water table or rock is too close to the surface for a covered-trench shelter to be practical. (A family evacuating in a pickup truck or large station wagon can carry enough doors, with doorknobs removed. Strong boards at least 6 feet long and at least one full inch thick, or plywood at least ¾-inch thick, also can be used to roof this shelter and to support its overhead earth shielding.

Warning: Some doors with single-thickness panels if loaded with earth will break before they bend enough to result in protective earth arching.

FOR WHOM PRACTICAL

For a typical family or other group with two or more members able to work hard for most of 36 hours. Very little building skill is needed. (An urban family of six, with 14- and 12-year-old sons and 13- and 9-year-old daughters, completed this shelter, sized for six persons, in one long working day: 13 hours and 43 minutes after receiving the step-by-step, will illustrated instructions at their Florida home 10 miles from the rural building site. This family used its pickup truck to carry them, the interior doors, and other survival items.)

CAPACITY

The shelter illustrated in Fig. A.4 is the minimum length for 4 persons. It is roofed with 6 doors.

For each additional person, add another door. (If more than about 7 persons are to be sheltered, build 2 or more separate shelters.)

BUILDING INSTRUCTIONS

1. Before beginning work, study the drawing and read ALL of the following instructions. Divide the work so that some will be digging while others are building an air pump, storing water, etc. CHECK OFF EACH STEP WHEN COMPLETED.

2. By the time the shelter is finished, plan to have completed a ventilating pump (a 16-in.-wide by 24-in.-high KAP—essential except in cold weather) and the storage of 15 gallons of water per occupant. (See Appendix B and Chapter 8.)

3. Start to assemble the materials and tools needed. For the illustrated 4-person shelter, these are:

A. Essential Materials and Tools

- Six doors. Boards or plywood at least ⅝-in. thick can be used to replace one or more of the doors.

- At least 4 double-bed sheets for each of the first four persons, and 3 double-bed sheets for each additional person to be sheltered—or enough pieces of fabric and/or of plastic to cover at least as large an area as the sheets would cover. (This material is for making aboveground shelter walls, to serve as sand bags.)

- Rainproofing materials (plastic film, shower curtains, plastic tablecloths, mattress protectors, etc.)—15 square yards for the first 4 persons and 2½ square yards for each additional person.

- A shovel (one shovel for each two workers is desirable). A pick or mattock if the ground is very hard.
- A knife (the only essential tool for making a small shelter-ventilating KAP) and materials for a KAP 16 in. wide and 24 in. high. (See Appendix B.)
- Containers for storing water. (See Chapter 8.)

B. Useful Materials and Tools

- Two or more buckets, large cans and/or large pots with bail handles—to carry earth, and later to store water or wastes.
- Saw (or ax or hatchet)—to cut a few boards or small poles.
- Hammer and at least 15 small nails (at least $2^1/_2$ in. long).
- Tape measure, yardstick, or ruler.
- Additional cloth and/or plastic—equivalent in size to 2 more double-bed sheets for each person.
- Additional waterproof material—2 more square yards per person.
- Pillowcases, or cloth or plastic bags—to serve as earth-filled sand bags. The more, the better.

4. To save time and work, sharpen all tools and keep them sharp.
5. Wear gloves from the start, to help prevent blisters and infections.
6. Select a building site where there is little or no chance of the ground being covered with water, and where the water table (groundwater level) is not likely to rise closer than 18 inches to the surface.
7. To avoid the extra work of digging among roots, select a site away from trees, if practical.
8. To lessen the dangers of fire and smoke from nearby houses or trees that might catch fire, locate your shelter as far as is practical from houses and flammable vegetation.
9. Before staking out your shelter, provide one door per person to roof the main room plus one additional door for each of the two entries. Be sure the door knobs have been removed. Use the two widest doors to roof the entries.
10. To be sure that all the walls will be in the proper positions to be roofed with the available doors, lay all the doors on the ground, touching each other and in the same relative positions they will have when used to roof the shelter. When all the roof doors are on the ground, side by side, determine the exact length of the shelter room. (Note that Fig. A.4 illustrates a shelter sized for only 4 persons.)
11. Stake out the shelter.
12. Make the earth-filled "rolls" that will form the aboveground walls of your shelter. To make walls out of the rolls:

    (1) Use doors as vertical forms to hold the earth-filled rolls in place until the walls are completed. (These are the same doors that you will use later to roof the shelter.)

    (2) Brace the door-forms with 36-in.-long braces (boards or sticks) that press against the doors, as shown in Fig. A.4. Nail only the upper braces, using only very small nails.

    (3) After the forms for the two inner sides of the shelter have been finished, put parts of the long sides of bedsheets on the ground, as illustrated. (Or use other equally wide, strong cloth or plastic material.) About a 2-ft width of cloth should be on the ground, and the rest of each sheet should be folded up out of the way, over the outsides of the door-forms. Adjacent sheets should overlap about 1 ft when making a roll than is longer than one sheet.

    (4) Shovel earth onto the parts of the sheet on the ground to the height of the rolls you are making, as shown. Note that the roll to be made on one side is 2 in. higher than the roll on the other side.

    (5) Shape the surface of the shoveled-on earth as illustrated, to hold the "hooks" of cloth to be formed when the exposed sides of the sheets are folded down.

    (6) Fold down the upper side of each sheet while pulling on it to keep it tight and without wrinkles. It should lie on the

prepared earth surface, including the small narrow trench, as illustrated in the first section of this appendix.

(7) Pack earth onto the part of the folded-down sheet that is in the narrow, shallow trench. Then, as shown in the sketches at the bottom of the accompanying drawing, fold back the loose edge over this small amount of packed earth to form a "hook." (The hook keeps the weight of the earth inside a roll from pulling the cloth out of its proper position.)

(8) Make a roll first on one side of the shelter, then on the other, to keep the heights of the earth **on both sides** of the shelter **about** equal. This will keep the unequal heights of earth from pushing the door-forms out of their vertical positions.

(9) Add additional earth on top of the rolls so that the height of the level earth surface, out to the full width of a roll, is the same as the height of the cloth-covered part of the roll that is against the door-form.

(10) When the roll walls have been raised to their planned heights on both sides of the shelter, remove the braces and the door-forms—being careful to keep the brace nails from damaging the doors.

(11) The door-forms of the side-walls of the shelter can be removed before building the end-walls.

13. When smoothing the earth surfaces of the final tops of the roll walls on both sides, check to see that they have the same slope as the lower sides of the roof doors will have after they are placed on the roll walls. (A slope is necessary so that rainwater reaching the waterproof covering to be placed over the doors will run off the lower side.) Study Fig. A.4.

14. After the side-walls have been completed (except for their ends that form the sides of an entry) and after the door-forms have been removed, use the same doors for forms to build the two 22-in.-wide entries.

15. Use earth-filled "sand bags" (made of pillowcases or sacks, and/or the tucked-in ends of earth-filled rolls) to make the outer ends of each entryway.

16. Make the two doorway frames if lumber, nails, and a saw are available. Make each frame as high as the wall on each side of it, and slope the top board of each frame so that it will press flat against the door to be supported. (If materials for a frame are lacking, place a single 2 by 4-in. board—or a pole about 6 ft. long—across the top of the entry, in the position shown in Fig. A.4 for the top of the doorway frame.)

17. After carefully removing all the temporary braces from the door-forms and the doors themselves, improve the slopes of the tops of all supporting walls so that the doors will be supported evenly and, without being twisted, will make contact with the smooth, sloping earth or cloth upon which they will rest.

18. If more than enough waterproof plastic or similar material is available to cover all the roof doors, also cover the tops of the walls on which the roof doors will rest. This will keep the doors from absorbing water from damp earth.

19. Dig the illustrated 14-in.-deep, 36-in.-wide trench inside the shelter. (If the water table is too high to dig down 14 in., in some locations the walls can be raised to a height of 38 in. by cutting turf sods and laying them on top of the walls. Another way the wall height can be increased is by making additional rolls.)

20. Place the roof doors in their final positions, and cover them with waterproof material (if available). Be sure the waterproof material is folded under the higher edges of the doors—to keep the material from slipping downward on the sloping doors as earth is shoveled onto the roof.

21. Extend the waterproof material on top of the doors a couple of feet beyond the lower ends of the doors—if enough material is available to cover all of the roof doors.

22. When shoveling the first layer of earth onto the rainproof material protecting the doors, avoid hitting and possibly puncturing it with rocks or sharp pointed roots in the earth.

23. To make earth arching more effective in supporting most of the earth to be placed on the roof doors, first mound earth on and near the ends of the doors.

24. Cover the roof with at least 20 in. of earth. Make sure that there also is a thickness of at least 20 in. of earth at the corners of both the room and entries.

25. To prevent surface water from running into the shelter if it rains hard, mound packed earth about 5 in. high just inside the two entries. Rain can be kept out by a small canopy or awning that extends 2 or 3 ft in front of the outermost edge of a doorway that roofs an entry.

26. If any waterproof material remains, use it to cover the floor of the shelter.

27. If the weather is warm or hot, install a 16-in.-wide by 24-in.-high air pump (a KAP). Attach its hinges to the board across the roof of the entry into which outside air is moving naturally at the time. (If short of time or materials for a KAP, make a small Directional Fan.)

28. Cover all exposed combustible material with mud, earth, or other fireproof material, to reduce the chance of exposed cloth being ignited from a nuclear explosion or heat from a nearby fire.

29. Fill all available water containers, including pits which have been dug and lined with plastic, then roofed with available materials. If possible, disinfect all water stored in expedient containers, using one scant teaspoon of a chlorine bleach, such as Clorox, for each 10 gallons of water. Even if only muddy water is available, store it. If you do not have a disinfectant, it may be possible to boil water when needed.

30. Put at least your most useful emergency tools inside your shelter.

31. As time and materials permit, continue to improve your chances of surviving by doing as many of the following things as possible:
    (1) Make a homemade fallout meter, as described in Appendix C, and expedient lights. (Prudent people will have made these extremely useful items well ahead of time.)
    (2) Install screens or mosquito netting over the two openings, if mosquitoes or flies are a problem. Remember, however, that screen or netting reduces the air flow through a shelter — even when the air is pumped through with a KAP.

ORNL DWG. 74-8132R

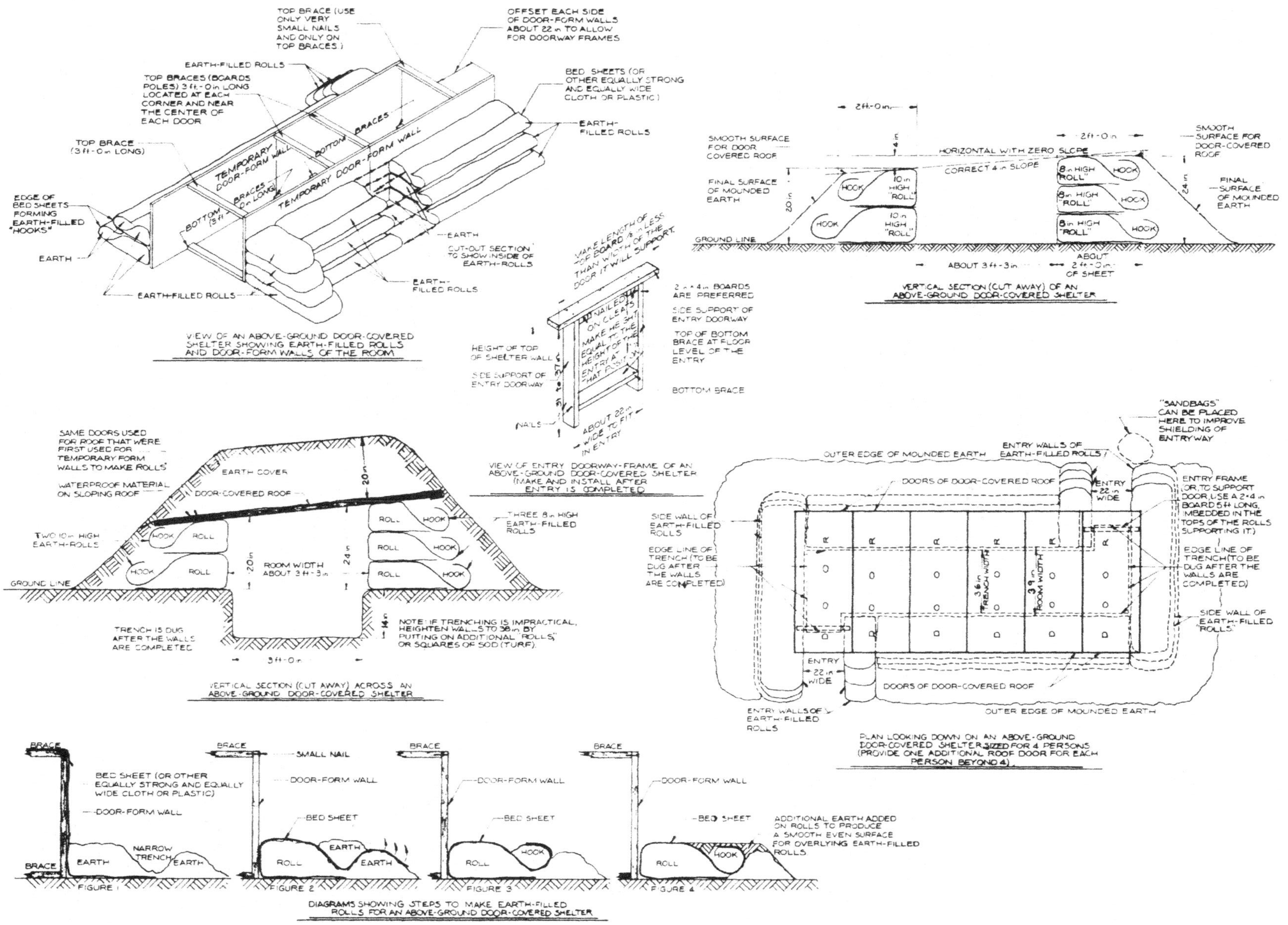

Fig. A.4. Aboveground, Door-Covered Shelter.

Appendix A.5
Aboveground, Ridgepole Shelter

PROTECTION PROVIDED

Against fallout radiation: Protection Factor 300 (PF 300) if covered with 24 in. of earth. (A person in the open outside this shelter would receive about 300 times more fallout radiation than if he were inside.) See the accompanying drawing at the end of Appendix A.5.

Against blast: Better protection than most homes. Blast tests have indicated that this shelter would be undamaged at least up to the 5-psi overpressure range from large explosions. Without blast doors, the shelter's occupants could be injured at this overpressure range, although probably not fatally.

Against fire: Good, if the shelter is sufficiently distant from fires producing carbon monoxide and toxic smoke.

WHERE PRACTICAL

In many wooded areas and wherever enough poles are available.

In locations where belowground expedient shelters are impractical because the water table or rock is too close to the surface for a covered-trench shelter.

FOR WHOM PRACTICAL

For a family or other group with five or more members able to work hard for most of 48 hours, with at least one member able to saw and fit poles and use the hand tools listed on the following page. (A group of rural Florida families, with 12 of the 15 members able to work, completed a shelter like this 23 hours and 40 minutes after receiving the step-by-step, well illustrated instructions 12 miles from the wooded building site. They used only muscle-powered tools, and moved over 50 tons of sandy shielding earth.)

CAPACITY

The shelter illustrated in Fig. A.5 is the minimum length for 5 persons. For each additional person, add 1 ft to the length of the ridgepole and shelter room. (If more than about 15 persons are to be sheltered, build 2 or more separate shelters.)

BUILDING INSTRUCTIONS

1. Before beginning work, study Fig. A.5 and read ALL of the following instructions.
2. Divide the work. CHECK OFF EACH STEP WHEN COMPLETED.
3. By the time the shelter is finished, plan to have completed a ventilating pump (a KAP 20 in. wide and 26 in high, essential for this shelter except in cool weather) and the storage of at least 15 gallons of water per occupant. (See Appendix B and Chapter 8.)
4. Start to assemble the materials. **For the illustrated 5-person shelter,** these are:

A. Essential Materials and Tools

- Poles. (Fresh-cut, green poles are best; sound, untreated poles are satisfactory.) See the following list for the number of poles required for a 5-person shelter.

Use	Pole Length	Minimum Diameter of Small End	Number of Poles Required	Width When All Are Laid on the Ground
For main room:				
Ridgepole	4 ft 9 in.	6 in.	1	
Column-posts	4 ft 3 in.	5 in.	2	
Footing log	8 ft 0 in.	6 in.	1	
Cross braces	6 ft 2 in.	3 in.	2	
Roof poles	9 ft 0 in.	4 in.	—	5 ft[a]
Vertical end-wall poles	5 ft 0 in.[c]	3½ in.	—	14 ft[b]
Slanting end-wall poles and extras	6 ft 6 in.[c]	3½ in.	—	18 ft[b]
For outer sections of entryways:				
Horizontal poles	8 ft 0 in.	3½ in.	4	
Cross braces (material for 16)	5 ft 0 in.[c]	3½ in.	6	
Wall poles	3 ft 4 in.	3 in.	—	32 ft[b]
Roof poles	2 ft 8 in.	2½ in.	—	12 ft[b]
For inner sections of entryways:				
Long, sloping poles	14 ft 0 in.	4 in.	4	
Cross braces	1 ft 8 in.[c]	4 in.	8	
Vertical support poles	4 ft 0 in.[c]	4 in.	8	
Roof poles	3 ft 0 in.	2½ in.	—	13 ft[b]

[a]This width equals the distance measured across the tops of a single layer of poles when a sufficient number of poles are laid on the ground side by side *with all the same ends in a straight line and touching*. (These poles will be placed butt-ends down to form the walls of the shelter room.)

[b]This width equals the distance measured across a single layer of poles when a sufficient number of poles are laid on the ground side by side and *touching, with large ends and small ends alternating so as to cover a rectangular area.*

[c]To be cut into the various lengths needed to close the ends of the main room and also to close a part of each entryway.

- A saw and an ax or hatchet, to cut green poles. (A bow saw or crosscut saw serves well and often is more dependable than a chain saw. Having an extra blade for a bow saw may be essential.)
- Two shovels (one shovel for each two workers is desirable). A pick will also be needed, if the earth is hard.
- Large buckets, cans, or pots with bail handles—in which to carry earth, and later to store water or wastes.
- A knife.
- A hammer and at least 80 nails (3 in. or longer). If these are not at hand, rope, wire, or strips of cloth can be used to lash poles together. At least 200 ft. of rope or strong wire will be needed, or two additional bedsheets for each person to be sheltered. (Other fabric of equal strength can be used.) The cloth can be cut or torn into foot-wide strips and twisted slightly to make "rope."
- Three double-bed sheets for the illustrated 5-person shelter or a piece of strong fabric or plastic of about the same size. One additional sheet for each additional 2 occupants. (If sufficient sheets or other material are not available, use many sticks and small poles, placed across the 9-ft side poles.)
- At least 2 square yards per person of rainproofing material (shower curtains, plastic tablecloths, plastic mattress covers, or the like)—essential in rainy, cold weather.
- Materials for building a ventilating pump, a KAP 20 in. wide and 26 in. high. (See Appendix B.)
- Containers for storing 15 gallons of water per occupant. (See Chapter 8.)

B. Useful Tools and Materials

- Additional saws, axes, hatchets, shovels, and large buckets or cans.

- A chain saw—if there is a person in the group who is skilled at operating one.
- Kerosene, turpentine, or oil—to keep a handsaw from sticking in green, gummy wood.
- A measuring tape, yardstick, or ruler.
- One bedsheet for each person to be sheltered, or a piece of strong fabric or plastic of about the same size.
- A total of 40 square yards of rainproofing materials for the illustrated 5-person shelter and $3^1/_2$ square yards for each additional person. (Even thin plastic will serve for the "buried roof.")

5. To save time and work, SHARPEN ALL TOOLS AND KEEP THEM SHARP.
6. Wear gloves from the start—even tough hands can blister after hours of digging and chopping and can become painful and infected.
7. Select a shelter location where there is little chance of the ground being covered with water if it rains hard. (If you are sure the water table will not rise to cover the floor of a shallow excavation, you can save work by first lowering the area of the planned main room by a foot or two. After the shelter is roofed, the excavated earth can be shoveled back to help cover the completed pole roof.) To avoid the extra work of cutting roots when excavating earth, select a site at least as far away from a tree as the tree is tall.
8. For a shelter that is completely aboveground, clear grass, weeds, etc. from the area where the shelter is to be built. (This reduces the possible problem of chiggers, ticks, etc.) Do not remove any earth at this stage.
9. Stake out the entire shelter. Check the squareness of the shelter room by making its diagonals equal. Then drive two lines of stakes to mark the outside edges of the completed earth covering. Place these stakes 4 ft outside the future positions of the lower ends of the roof poles.
10. Check the squareness of the future floor area inside the two lines marking where the two V-shaped, 4-in.-deep trenches will be dug, to secure the lower ends of the sloping side-poles of the room. These two parallel lines are 14 ft 6 in. apart. When the two diagonals joining the ends of these two parallel lines are equal in length, the area between them has square corners.
11. While some persons are staking out the shelters, others should be cutting green poles and hauling them to the site. Cut poles that have tops with diameters (excluding bark) no smaller than the diameters specified on the illustration for each type of pole.
12. To make the hauling and handling of the longer poles easier, select poles with top diameters no more than 50% larger than the specified minimum diameters.
13. Sort the poles by length and diameter and lay all poles of each size together, near the excavation.
14. AS SOON AS POLES ARE BROUGHT TO THE SITE, SOME WORKERS SHOULD START BUILDING THE FOUR LADDER-LIKE HORIZONTAL BRACES FOR THE ENTRYWAYS—TO AVOID DELAYS LATER. Study the drawing. Then construct these braces on smooth ground near the excavation. Place two straight poles, each 8 ft long (with small-end diameters of $3^1/_2$ in.), on smooth ground, parallel and so that their outer sides are 3 ft apart. Hold these poles securely so that their outer sides are exactly 3 ft apart, by driving two pairs of stakes into the ground so that they just touch the outsides of the two long poles. Each of the four stakes should be located about one foot from the end of a pole. To keep the 8-ft poles from being rotated during the next step, nail two boards or small poles across them perpendicularly, as temporary braces, about 4 ft apart.

    Then with an ax or hatchet, slightly flatten the inner sides of the two poles at the spots where the ends of the 4 cross-brace poles will be nailed. Next, saw each cross-brace pole to the length required to fit snugly into its place. Finally, toenail each cross-brace pole in place, preferably with two large nails in each end.
15. If more than 5 persons are to be sheltered, use 3 column-posts for 6 to 9 persons, and 4 column-posts for 10 to 14 persons.
16. For each additional person beyond 5, make the ridgepole and the footing log each 1 foot longer than shown in Fig. A.5.

17. After notching the footing log (see drawing), place it in a trench dug deep enough so that the bottoms of its notches are about 4 inches below the surface of the ground.

18. Carefully dig the 4-in.-deep, V-shaped, straight trenches in which the lower ends of the 9-ft wall poles will rest. Dig each of these two parallel trenches 7 ft. 3 in. from the center line of the footing log.

19. Carefully notch a "V" only about 1/2-in. deep in the top of each of the two outer column-posts. Then saw off the other ends so that each is 4 ft. 3 in. long. (When they are placed on the notched footing log and the ridgepole is placed on them, the upper side of the ridgepole will be about 4 ft. 4 in. above the ground.)

20. Place the two **outer** column-posts in their notches in the footing log, and secure the base of each column-post against sideways movement by placing two small-diameter, 4-ft horizontal poles just below the ground level on both sides, as illustrated. Then temporarily place and brace the ridgepole in position.

21. For shelters sized for more than 5 occupants, make and place the inner column-post, or posts. To avoid cutting a "V"-notched column-post too short, first carefully "V"-notch each remaining column-post, cut it about 1 in. too long, and trim it off to fit in its final position under the ridgepole.

22. If nails at least 4 in. long are available, nail sloping cross-braces to the inner sides of the column-posts. If nails are not available, notch slightly bowed cross-braces and the column-post as illustrated; then lash or wire them in position. (Strips of ordinary bedsheets, torn about a foot wide and twisted together slightly, can be made to serve as lashing "rope.") To hold the tops of the column-posts securely against the upper ends of the cross-braces, a tightened "rope" loop that encircles the tops of the column-posts can be used.

23. Next put four of the larger-diameter, 9-ft roof-poles in position, with the outsides of the outermost two roof poles each only about 1 in. from an end of the ridge pole.

24. Place the rest of the 9-ft roof-poles in position, making sure that all their small ends are uppermost, and that they are pressed together and overlap on the ridgepole at least as far as illustrated. Pack earth between their lower ends. If the earth is clay, put small spacers of wood between the ends.

25. At each end of the shelter room, build extra shelter space and an entryway. First position two 14-ft poles with their upper ends resting on the outermost wall poles. Study Fig. A.5. Place the two 14-ft poles 20 in. apart, parallel, and equally distant from the centerline of the ridgepole. Nail four 20-in.-long spacer-poles between each pair of 14-ft poles, as illustrated. To make sure that the upper ends do not move before earth pressure holds them in place, tie the upper ends of the 14-ft poles together. Drive a stake against the lower end of each 14-ft pole, to keep it from slipping outward. Under the center of each 14-ft pole, place two supporting, vertical posts.

26. Dig. 4-in.-deep trenches for the lower ends of the sloping end-wall poles of the main room. These poles must be cut to length so that their upper ends will be about 4 in. above the outermost 9-ft roof pole against which they lean. Dig narrow, vertical trenches, about 8 in. deep, for all vertical wall poles that do not press against horizontal brace poles near the ground.

27. Start placing the sloping end-wall poles. First place the longest pole, then the shorter poles—all touching.

28. Across the open spaces between the 9-ft roof poles, place limbs and/or sticks roughly horizontally, as shown in the lower left-hand drawing. Be sure to use limbs or sticks that have diameters of at least 1/2 in. and put them no farther apart than 6 in. Leave needles and leaves on the limbs. Do not leave sharp ends sticking upward. Do not place more than a 6-in.-thick mass of limbs and leaves over the side-poles. The thickness of the earth cover necessary for excellent fallout protection might be unintentionally reduced by making the limb cover too thick.

29. Place bedsheets (or 4-mil-thick polyethylene film or equally sturdy material) over the limbs and sticks to keep earth from falling through the roof.

30. To prevent sand or dry earth from falling between the cracks where the poles are side by side, cover these parts of the roof with cloth, plastic, or paper. If these materials are not

available, use sticks, leaves, and grass. (In tick or chigger season, avoid using grass or leaves from on or near the ground.)

31. After the entryways are completed, begin to cover the shelter with earth. **Starting from the ground up,** put on a full 1-ft thickness of earth cover. First raise its height about a foot on one side or end of the shelter, and then on the other—repeatedly. This is to prevent unequal loading from tipping the shelter or pushing it over. (Do not excavate any earth closer than 3 ft to the line of stakes marking the final outer edge of the completed, 2-ft-thick earth cover.)

32. Fill the spaces between the entryways and the main room only with earth. (An equal thickness of wood or other light material provides much less protection against radiation.)

33. Before placing the rainproofing material for the "buried roof," smooth the surface of the 1-ft-thick earth cover. This will prevent sharp rocks or sticks from puncturing the plastic or other rainproofing material. If you do not have sufficient waterproofing materials to cover the whole roof, use what is available to rainproof the central part, on both sides of the ridgepole.

34. To prevent rainwater on the ground outside from running into the entryways, make mounds of packed earth about 4 inches high across the entryway floors, about 2 ft from their outer ends. Dig a shallow drainage ditch completely around the earth mounded over the shelter.

35. Unless the weather is cold, install your shelter-ventilating KAP in the entry into which you can feel air moving naturally. (If short of time or materials, make a small Directional Fan.)

36. Complete the storage of water and other essentials.

37. To prevent fallout or rain from falling onto the floor of the outer entryways, place a small awning (not illustrated) over each opening.

38. Fill all available water containers, including pits which have been dug and lined with plastic, then roofed with available materials. If possible, disinfect all water stored in expedient containers, using one scant teaspoon of a chlorine bleach, such as Clorox, for each 10 gallons of water. Even if only muddy water is available, store it. If you do not have a disinfectant, it may be possible to boil water when needed.

39. Put all of your emergency tools inside your shelter.

40. As time and materials permit, continue to improve your chances of surviving by doing as many of the following things as possible:
    (1) Make a homemade fallout meter, as described in Appendix C, and expedient lights. (Prudent people will have made these extremely useful items well ahead of time.)
    (2) Make and hang expedient bedsheet-hammocks.
    (3) Install screens or mosquito netting over the two openings, if mosquitoes or flies are a problem. Remember, however, that screen or netting reduces the air flow through a shelter — even when the air is pumped through with a KAP.
    (4) Dig a stand-up hole near the far end of the shelter. Make the hole about 15 in. in diameter and deep enough to permit the tallest of the shelter occupants to stand erect occasionally.

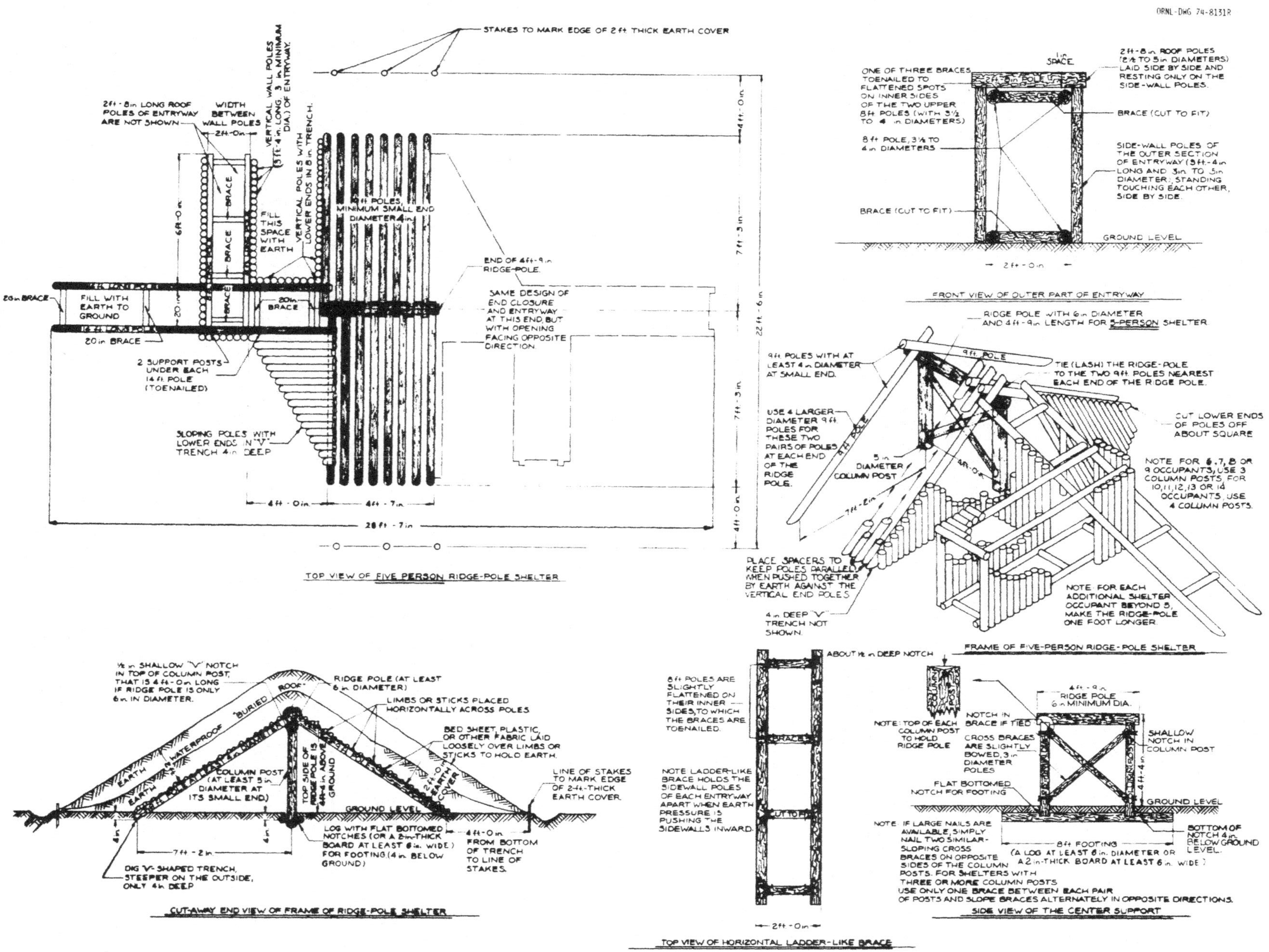

Fig. A.5. Aboveground, Ridgepole Shelter.

Appendix A.6
Aboveground, Crib-Walled Shelter

PROTECTION PROVIDED

Against fallout radiation: Protection Factor 200 (PF 200) if the earth-filled cribs are built to the full width of 3 ft, as illustrated in Fig. A.6 at the end of these instructions. (A person in the open outside this shelter would receive about 200 times as much fallout radiation as he would if inside.) If earth is mounded to the top of the walls and 3 ft deep over the roof, the protection factor can be raised to PF 500 or better. See the accompanying drawing at the end of Appendix A.6.

Against blast: Better protection than most homes. Without blast doors, occupants could be injured—although probably not fatally—at lower overpressure ranges than those that would destroy this shelter.

Against fire: Poor, if the shelter is built as illustrated. The cloth and outer poles would be unprotected from thermal pulse and other possible sources of intense heat. However, if earth is mounded around the walls so as to cover all exposed cloth and wood, good fire protection would be provided.

WHERE PRACTICAL

The crib-walled shelter is practical in many wooded areas and whenever enough poles are available, or in locations where belowground expedient shelters are impractical because the water table or rock is too close to the surface for a covered-trench shelter.

FOR WHOM PRACTICAL

For a family or group with three or more members able to work very hard for most of 48 hours. An unskilled family with an ax or saw and materials found in most American homes can build this shelter. No nails are required. (Groups with the nails, tools, skill, and the number of workers required to build a Ridgepole Shelter are advised to do so; a Crib-Walled Shelter requires almost twice the total length of poles and more work to provide shelter for a given number of persons.)

CAPACITY

The shelter illustrated in Fig. 6.1 is the minimum length for 5 persons. For each additional person, add $1\frac{1}{2}$ ft to the length of the room. (If more than about 12 persons are to be sheltered, build 2 or more separate shelters.)

BUILDING INSTRUCTIONS

1. Before beginning work, study the drawing and read ALL of the following instructions.
2. Divide the work. CHECK OFF EACH STEP WHEN COMPLETED.
3. By the time the shelter is finished, plan to have completed a ventilating pump (a KAP 20 in. wide and 26 in. high, essential for this shelter except in cool weather) and the storage of at least 15 gallons of water per occupant. (See Appendix B and Chapter 8.)
4. Start to assemble materials and tools.

A. Essential Materials and Tools

- Poles. (Fresh-cut, green poles are best; sound, untreated poles are satisfactory.) For the illustrated 5-person shelter, the required poles are listed on the following page.

Use	Pole Length	Minimum Diameter of Small End	Number of Poles Required	Width When All Are Laid on the Ground[a]
Sides of longest crib	12½ ft	3 in.		7 ft
Sides of middle-sized crib	10 ft	3 in.		7 ft
Sides of shortest crib	7 ft	3 in.		7 ft
Ends of all cribs	3½ ft	3 in.		21 ft
Vertical poles at the corners of all cribs	3½ ft	2 in.	56	
Main roof	9 ft	3½ in.		12 ft
Entryway roofs	5 ft.	2½ in.		22 ft

[a] This width is the distance measured across a single layer of poles when a sufficient number of them are laid on the ground side by side and touching, with large ends and small ends alternating so as to cover a rectangular area.

- A saw (preferably a bow saw with an extra blade, or a crosscut saw) and/or an ax—for cutting green poles.
- A shovel (one for each two workers is desirable).
- A pick (if the ground is very hard).
- Two to five large cans, buckets, and/or pots with bail handles, in which to carry earth and to store water or wastes later.
- A knife.
- A minimum of 300 ft of wire at least as strong as clothesline wire. Second choice would be 300 ft of rope, or (third choice) 8 double-bed sheets that could be torn into 1-ft-wide strips and twisted slightly to serve as rope. For each additional person beyond 5, supply 20 ft of wire or rope or half a double-bed sheet.
- Rainproof roofing materials—at least 2 square yards per person. Such materials as plastic film, shower curtains, plastic tablecloths or plastic mattress covers can be used. These materials are essential for prolonged shelter occupancy in rainy, cold weather.
- Fifteen double-bed sheets (or equal square-yardage of other strong cloth or plastic).
- Materials for building a ventilating pump, a KAP 20 inches wide and 30 in. high. (See Appendix B.)
- Containers for storing 15 gallons of water per occupant. (See Chapter 8.)

B. Useful Materials and Tools

- Additional saws and shovels, chain saw, pick-mattock, hammer, hatchet.
- Kerosene, turpentine, or oil—to keep a hand-saw from sticking in gummy wood.
- A file.
- Two additional double-bed sheets per person, or equivalent square-yardage of other equally strong fabric or plastic.
- A measuring tape, yardstick, or ruler.
- Old newspapers (about 15 pounds).
- A total of 30 square yards of rainproofing materials for the illustrated 5-person shelter, and 3 square yards for each additional person to be sheltered. (Even thin plastic will serve to make a rainproof "buried roof.")

5. To save time and work, SHARPEN ALL TOOLS AND KEEP THEM SHARP.
6. Wear gloves from the start. Even tough hands can blister and become painful and infected after hours of digging and chopping.
7. Select a shelter location where there is little or no chance of the ground being covered with water by a hard-rain.

8. If the building site is near the edge of a woods, pick a site at least 40 ft from the nearest trees—to avoid roots.

9. Clear off grass, weeds, etc., from the area where you plan to build the shelter—this also will help to avoid chiggers or ticks. Do not remove any earth.

10. Stake out the entire shelter, locating the 6 required cribs. BE SURE TO MAKE THE INSIDE LENGTH OF THE MAIN ROOM EQUAL TO THE NUMBER OF PERSONS TO BE SHELTERED MULTIPLIED BY $1^1/_2$ FT. The illustrated shelter is sized for 5 persons, and the poles listed are those required for this 5-person shelter.

11. While some persons are staking out the shelter, others should be cutting green poles and hauling them to the site. Cut poles with tops no smaller than the diameters specified. (Note: the specified diameters do not include bark.)

12. Select poles with small-end diameters no more than 50% larger than the specified minimum diameters, to make handling of the long wall and roof poles easier.

13. Sort the poles by length and diameter and lay all poles of each size together, near the excavation.

14. Use larger trees and poles, up to 6 in. in diameter, to make the $3^1/_2$-ft-long end-poles of the cribs (Fig. A.6). Do not use poles with small-end diameters of less than 3 in. for the side-wall poles of the cribs. For vertical brace-poles, use poles with diameters of at least 2 in., cut off at the height of the upper side of the uppermost horizontal poles against which they are tied.

15. Be sure to cut off all limbs so that the poles are quite smooth. Usually it is easier to drag smoothed poles to the building site before cutting them into the required lengths. Pull them by the small, lighter ends.

16. Determine if there are enough long poles to make the side-poles of the two cribs forming the sides of the shelter room without splicing two shorter poles together. If the shelter is being built for more than 7 persons, it will require side poles that are longer than $15^1/_2$ ft. Therefore, if a shelter for more than 7 persons is being built, it would be best to use 2 cribs placed end-to-end on each side of the shelter room, instead of a single crib as illustrated by Fig. A.6.

17. Place the lowermost four poles of each of the cribs in their final positions, so that all the bases of the crib-walls are in position on the ground. Use the thicker, heavier poles at and near the bottom of each crib. BE SURE THE ROOM IS LONG ENOUGH TO PROVIDE $1^1/_2$ FT OF ROOM LENGTH FOR EACH PERSON TO BE SHELTERED.

18. To build each crib:

    (1) Place two $3^1/_2$-ft end-poles on the ground. Put two of the side-poles on top of the two end-poles so that the ends of all four poles extend 3 in. (no more) beyond where they cross. The thicker poles should be used first to add stability.

    (2) Stack additional pairs of end-poles and side-poles to form the crib, keeping each wall of the crib vertical, until the tops of the uppermost side-poles are at least 42 in. above the ground. To keep the uppermost poles of the crib about level while the crib is being raised, alternate the large ends and small ends of poles.

    (3) Place a pair of small, vertical brace-poles in each of the four corners of the crib. The tops of the vertical brace-poles should be no higher above the ground than the upper sides of the crib's uppermost horizontal poles.

    (4) Tie each pair of vertical brace-poles together tightly at bottom, middle, and top. For tying, use 3-ft lengths of strong wire, rope, or slightly twisted, foot-wide strips of cloth at least as strong as cotton bed sheeting. Square knots with back-up overhand knots are best, but three overhand knots—one on top of the other—will hold.

    (5) If the crib is more than 8 ft long, place an additional pair of vertical brace-poles, with one in position at the outside center of each long crib-wall. Tie this pair of vertical brace-poles together permanently just above the ground, but not yet in the middle or near the top of the crib. Temporarily tie each of these center vertical brace-poles to the uppermost side-pole of the wall it touches.

    (6) Line the crib with cloth or plastic film, making sure that several inches of the lining hangs over the uppermost poles. So that the lining will not be pulled down when the crib is being filled with earth, tie the upper edge of

the lining to the uppermost wall pole about every 2 ft. First cut a small hole through which to thread a tie-string or a 2-in.-wide tie-strip of cloth. (If plenty of cloth and/or plastic is available for lining the cribs, secure the lining by simply wrapping a greater width of the upper edge of the lining around the uppermost crib wall-pole.)

(7) Permanently tie together the pair of vertical center brace-poles, using horizontal ties at their centers and just below the uppermost horizontal wall-poles of the crib. Use the strongest material you have for these horizontal ties across the center of the crib.

(8) Excavate earth 10 ft or so beyond the outer sides of the cribs. To save work, carry it in buckets and dump it inside the cribs. (Two children can carry a heavy bucket of earth by running a strong, 4-ft stick through the bail or handle of the bucket and tying the bail to the center of the stick before lifting.) Save earth closer to the cribs to put on the roof.

(9) Fill the lined crib with earth from which almost all grass, roots, and the like have been removed. Avoid placing hard lumps of earth in contact with the lining. Fill the crib so that the surface of the earth inside it is about 4 in. above the upper sides of the uppermost horizontal poles.

19. Line the narrow spaces between adjacent cribs with cloth or plastic; then fill these spaces with earth **a little at a time, tamping repeatedly so as to avoid leaving air spaces.**

20. Place the 9-ft roof poles over the main room. (If poles are unavailable and boards 1½ in. thick are available, use two thicknesses of boards.) Use the strongest roof poles (or double-thickness boards nailed together) nearest the entryways. Then put shorter, 5- or 6-ft poles or boards over the entryways.

21. To keep earth from falling through the cracks between the roof poles, put sticks in the larger cracks and cover the roof with two or more thicknesses of cloth, plastic, or other material. Newspapers will do, if better materials are lacking.

22. Put earth on the roof to the depths shown for the illustrated "buried roof." Be sure to slope all sides and smooth this gently mounded earth surface so that the buried roof will shed water.

23. So that the earth cover near the outer edges of the roof will be a full 2 ft thick, make the earth cover slope steeply near the edges. Steep earth slopes can be made and kept stable by using large lumps of turf to make a steep bank, or by using earth-filled "rolls" of cloth or other material along the edges of a roof.

24. Put in place the waterproof material of the buried roof.

25. Pile on the rest of the earth cover, as illustrated, to **at least** a full 2-ft thickness.

26. Smooth the surface of the earth cover, including the sides, so that rain will run off. Do not walk on the finished roof.

27. To prevent rainwater on the ground outside from running into the entryways, make mounds of packed earth about 4 in. high across the entryway floors. Make the mounds about 2 ft from the outer ends of the floors. Dig a shallow drainage ditch completely around the shelter.

28. Unless the weather is cold, install your shelter-ventilating KAP in the entry into which you can feel air moving naturally. (If short of time or materials, make a small Directional Fan.)

29. To prevent fallout or rain from falling onto the floor of the outer entryways, place small awnings (not illustrated) over the openings.

30. If time and energy are available, mound earth all around the shelter. Doing so will reduce fire hazards by covering flammable materials; it also will increase fallout protection.

31. Fill all available water containers, including pits which have been dug and lined with plastic, then roofed with available materials. If possible, disinfect all water stored in expedient containers, using one scant teaspoon of a chlorine bleach, such as Clorox, for each 10 gallons of water. Even if only muddy water is available, store it. If you do not have a disinfectant, it may be possible to boil water when needed.

32. Put all of your emergency tools inside your shelter.

33. As time and materials permit, continue to improve your chances of surviving by doing as many of the following things as possible:
    (1) Make a homemade fallout meter, as described in Appendix C, and expedient lights. (Prudent people will have made these extremely useful items well ahead of time.)
    (2) Make and hang expedient bedsheet-hammocks.
    (3) Install screens or mosquito netting over the two openings, if mosquitoes or flies are a problem. Remember, however, that screen or netting reduces the air flow through a shelter — even when the air is pumped through with a KAP.
    (4) Dig a stand-up hole near the far end of the shelter. Make the hole about 15 in. in diameter and deep enough to permit the tallest of the shelter occupants to stand erect occasionally.

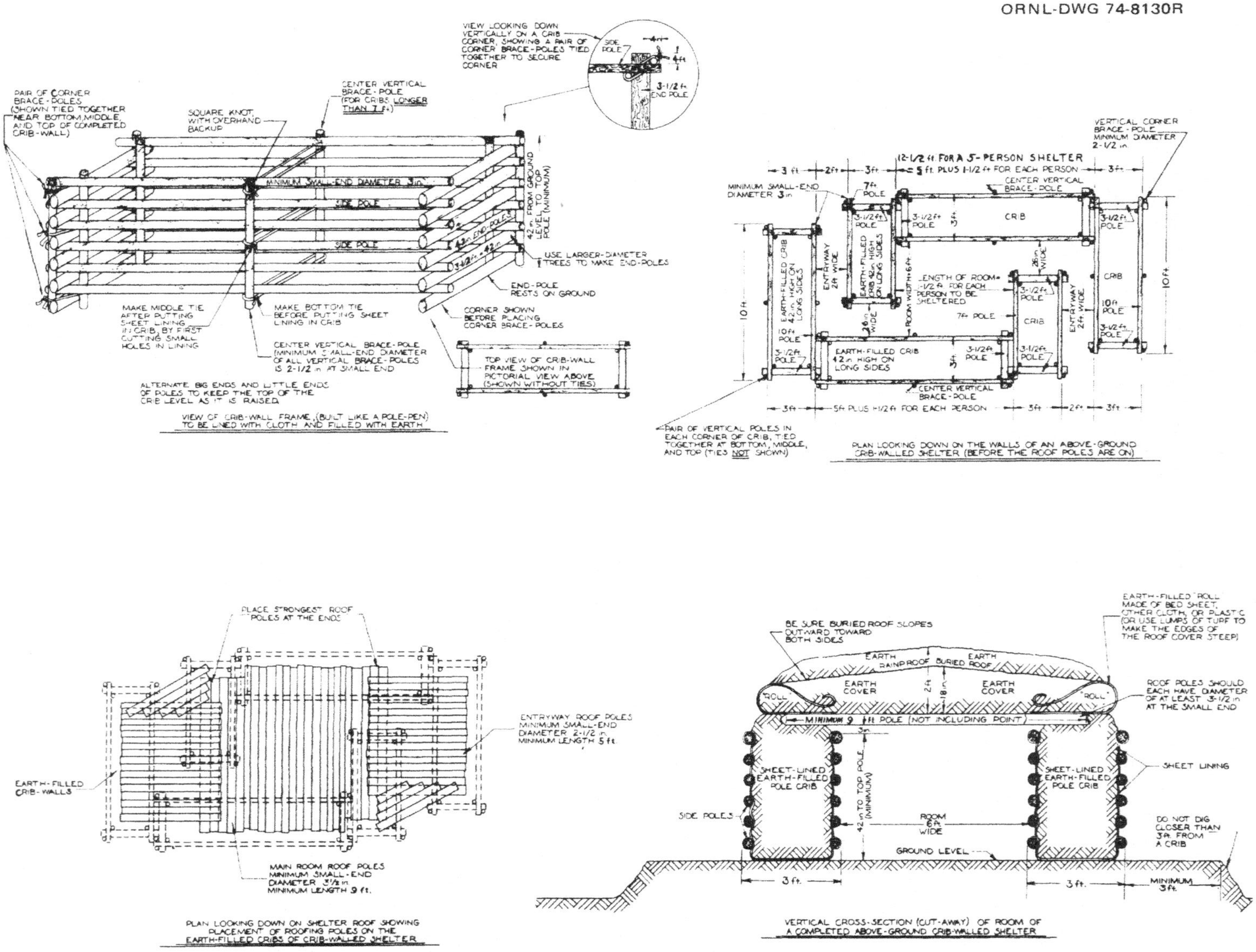

Fig. A.6. Aboveground, Crib-Walled Shelter.

Appendix B
How to Make and Use a Homemade Shelter-Ventilating Pump, the KAP

I. THE NEED FOR SHELTER AIR PUMPS

In warm weather, large volumes of outside air MUST be pumped through most fallout or blast shelters if they are crowded and occupied for a day or more. Otherwise, the shelter occupants' body heat and water vapor will raise the temperature-humidity conditions to DANGEROUSLY high levels. If adequate volumes of outdoor air are pumped through typical belowground shelters in hot weather, many times the number of persons could survive the heat than otherwise could survive in these same shelters without adequate forced ventilation. Even in cold weather, about 3 cubic feet per minute (3 cfm) of outdoor air usually should be pumped through shelters, primarily to keep the carbon dioxide exhaled by shelter occupants from rising to harmful concentrations.

The KAP (Kearny Air Pump) is a practical, do-it-yourself device for pumping adequate volumes of cooling air through shelters—with minimum work. The following instructions have been improved repeatedly after being used by dozens of small groups to build KAPs—including families, pairs of housewives, and children. None of these inexpert builders had previously heard of this kind of pump, yet almost all groups succeeded in making one in less than 4 hours after assembling the materials. Their successes prove that almost anyone, if given these detailed and thoroughly tested instructions, can build a serviceable, large-volume air pump of this simple type, using only materials and tools found in most American homes.

If possible, build a KAP large enough to pump through your shelter at least 40 cubic feet per minute (40 cfm) of outdoor air for each shelter occupant. If 40 cfm of outdoor air is pumped through a shelter and distributed within it as specified below, even under heat-wave conditions the effective temperature of the shelter air will not be more than 2° F higher than the effective temperature outdoors. (The effective temperature is a measure of air's effects on people due to its heat, humidity, and velocity.) The 36-inch-high by 29-inch-wide KAP described in these instructions, if used as specified, will pump at least 1000 cfm of outside air through a shelter that has the airflow characteristics outlined in these instructions.

If more than 25 persons might be expected to occupy a shelter during hot weather, then it is advisable to build a larger KAP. The 72-inch-high by 29-inch-wide model described can pump between 4000 and 5000 cfm.

To maintain tolerable temperature-humidity conditions for people in your shelter during hot weather, you **must**:

- Pump enough outdoor air all the way through the shelter (40 cfm for each occupant in very hot, humid weather).

- Distribute the air evenly within the shelter. If the KAP that pumps air through the shelter does not create air movement that can be felt in all parts of the shelter in hot weather, one or more additional KAPs will be needed to circulate the air and gently fan the occupants.

- Encourage the shelter occupants to wear as little clothing as practical when they are hot. (Sweat evaporates and cools best on bare skin.)

- Supply the occupants with adequate water and salt. For prolonged shelter occupancy under heat-wave conditions in a hot part of the country, about 4 quarts of drinking water and $^1/_3$ ounce (1 tablespoon) of salt per person are required every 24 hours, including salt in food that is eaten. Normal American meals supply about $^1/_4$ ounce of salt daily. Salt taken in addition to that in food should be dissolved in the drinking water.

- Pump outdoor air through your shelter day and night in warm weather, so that both the occupants and the shelter are cooled off at night.

Almost all of the danger from fallout is caused by radiation from visible fallout particles of heavy, sand-like or flakey material. The air does **not** become radioactive due to the radiation continuously given off by fallout particles.

The visible fallout particles rapidly "fall out" of slow moving air. The air that a KAP pumps through a shelter moves at a low speed and could carry into the shelter only a very small fraction of the fallout particles that cause the radiation hazard outside. This fraction, usually not dangerous, can be further reduced if occupants take the simple precautions described in these instructions.

CAUTION

Before anyone starts to build this unusual type of air pump, ALL WORKERS SHOULD READ THESE INSTRUCTIONS AT LEAST UP TO **SECTION V, INSTALLATION**. Otherwise, mistakes may be made and work may be divided inefficiently.

When getting ready to build this pump, all workers should spend the first half-hour studying these instructions and getting organized. Then, after materials are assembled, two inexperienced persons working together should be able to complete the 3-foot model described in the following pages in less than 4 hours. To speed up completion, divide the work; for example, one person can start making the flaps while another begins work on the pump frame.

II. HOW A KAP WORKS

As can be seen in Figs. 1 and 2, a KAP operates by being swung like a pendulum. It is hinged at the top of its swinging frame. When this air pump is pulled by a cord as illustrated, its flaps are closed by air pressure and it pushes air in front of it and "sucks"

ORNL-DWG 66-12320A

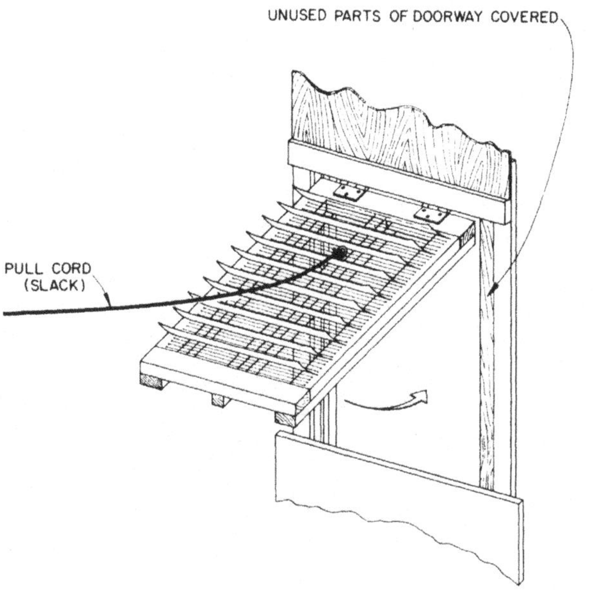

Fig. 1. Section through the upper part of a doorway, showing operation of a KAP.

ORNL-DWG 66-12319A

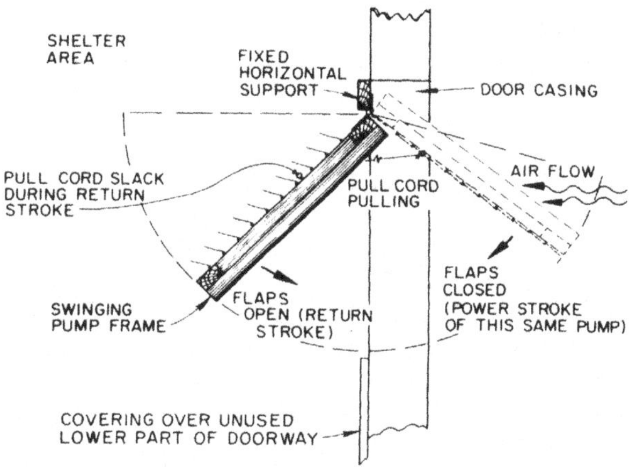

Fig. 2. KAP in doorway (with flaps open during its return stroke).

air in back of it. Thus a KAP pumps air through the opening in which it swings. This is the power stroke. During its power stroke, the pump's flaps are closed against its flap-stop wires or strings, which are fastened across the face of the frame.

When a KAP swings freely back as a pendulum on its return stroke, all its flaps are opened by air pressure. The pumped air stream continues to flow in the direction in which it has been accelerated by the power stroke, while the pump itself swings in the opposite direction (see Fig. 2). Thus the flaps are one-way valves that operate to force air to flow in one direction, where desired.

The KAP can be used: (1) to supply **outdoor** air to a shelter, (2) to distribute air within a shelter, and/or to fan the occupants.

1. To force **outdoor** air **through** a shelter, an **air-supply** KAP usually is operated as an air-intake pump by pulling it with a cord (see Fig. 1). (Only rarely is it necessary to operate a KAP as an air-exhaust pump by pushing it with a pole, as described in the last section of these instructions.)

2. To distribute air **within** a shelter and/or to fan the occupants, **air-distribution** KAPs may be hung overhead and operated as described later.

III. INSTRUCTIONS FOR BUILDING A KAP

In this section, instructions are given for making a KAP 36 inches high and 29 inches wide, to operate efficiently when swinging in a typical home basement doorway 30 inches wide. If your doorway or other ventilation opening is narrower or wider than 30 inches, you should make your KAP 1 inch narrower than the narrowest opening in which you plan to install it. Regardless of the size of the KAP you plan to build, first study the instructions for making the 36 × 29-inch model.

In Section VII you will find brief instructions for making a narrower and even simpler KAP, one more suitable for the narrow openings of small trench shelters and other small expedient shelters. Section VIII covers large KAPs, for large shelters.

A. Materials Needed for a KAP 36 inches High by 29 inches Wide

The preferred material is listed as first (1st) choice, and the less-preferred materials are listed as (2nd), (3rd), and (4th) choices. It is best to assemble, spread out, and check all your materials before beginning to build.

1. The pump frame and its fixed support:

- Boards for the frame:

  (1st) 22 ft of 1 × 2-in. boards. (A nominal 1 × 2-in. board actually measures about $^3/_4$ × 1-$^3/_4$ in., but the usual, nominal dimensions will be given throughout these instructions.) Also, 6 ft of 1 × 1-in. boards. Soft wood is better.

  (2nd) Boards of the same length that have approximately the same dimensions as 1 × 2-in. and 1 × 1-in. lumber.

  (3rd) Straight sticks or metal strips that can be cut and fitted to make a flat-faced KAP frame.

- Hinges: (1st) Door or cabinet butt-hinges; (2nd) metal strap-hinges; (3rd) improvised hinges made of leather, woven straps, cords, or 4 eyescrews which can be joined to make 2 hinges. (Screws are best for attaching hinges. If nails are used, they should go through the board and their ends should be bent over and clinched—flattened against the surface of the board.)

- A board for the fixed horizontal support: (1st) A 1 × 4-in. board that is at least 1 ft longer than the width of the opening in which you plan to swing your pump; (2nd) A wider board.

- Small nails (at least 24): (1st) No. 6 box nails, about $^1/_2$ in. longer than the thickness of the two boards, so their pointed ends can be bent over and clinched); (2nd) other small nails.

2. The flaps (See Figs. 1, 2, 6, 7, and 8):

- Plastic film or other **very light,** flexible material—12 square feet in pieces that can be cut into 9 rectangular strips, each 30 × 5$^1/_2$ in.: (1st) polyethylene film 3 or 4 mils thick (3 or 4 one-thousandths of an inch); (2nd) 2-mil polyethylene from large trash bags; (3rd) tough paper.

- Pressure-sensitive waterproof tape, enough to make 30 ft of tape $^3/_4$ in. to 1 in. wide, for securing the hem-tunnels of the flaps: (1st) cloth duct tape (silver tape); (2nd) glass tape; (3rd) scotch tape; (4th) freezer or masking tape, or sew the hem tunnels. (Do not use a tape that stretches: it may shrink afterward and cause the flaps to wrinkle.)

3. The flap pivot-wires:

(1st) 30 ft of smooth wire at least as heavy and springy as coat hanger wire, that can be made into **very straight** pieces each 29 in. long (nine all-wire coat hangers will supply enough); (2nd) 35 ft of somewhat thinner wire, including light, flexible insulated wire; (3rd) 35 ft of smooth string, preferably nylon string about the diameter of coat hanger wire.

4. The pull cord:

(1st) At least 10 ft of cord; (2nd) strong string; (3rd) flexible, light wire.

5. The flap-stops:

- (1st) 150 ft of light string; (2nd) 150 ft of light, smooth wire; (3rd) 150 ft of very strong thread; (4th) 600 ft of ordinary thread, to provide 4 threads for each stop-flap.
- (lst) 90 tacks (not thumbtacks); (2nd) 90 small nails. (Tacks or nails are desirable but not essential, since the flap-stops can be tied to the frame.)

B. Tools

A hammer, saw, wirecutter pliers, screwdriver, scissors, knife, yardstick, and pencil are desirable. However, only a strong, sharp knife is essential for making some models.

C. Building a KAP 36 inches High by 29 inches Wide

A 36×29-in. KAP is most effective if operated in an air-intake or exhaust opening about 40 in. high and 30 in. wide. (If your shelter might have more than 25 occupants in hot weather, read all these instructions so you will understand how to build a larger pump, briefly described in Section VIII.)

NOTE THAT THE WIDTHS AND THICKNESSES OF ALL FRAME PIECES ARE EXAGGERATED IN ALL ILLUSTRATIONS.

1. The frame

a. Cut two pieces of 1 × 2-in. boards, each 36 in. long, and two pieces of 1 × 2-in. boards, each 29 in. long; then nail them together(see Fig. 3). Use nails that do not split the wood, preferably long enough to go through the boards and stick out about 1/2 in. on the other side. (To nail in this manner, first put blocks under the frame so that the nail points will not strike the floor.) Bend over nail points which go through.

Next, cut and nail to the frame a piece of 1 × 1-in. lumber 36 in. long, for a center vertical brace. (If you lack time to make or to find a 1 × 1-in. board, use a 1 × 2-in. board.) Figure 3 shows the back side of the frame; the flap valves will be attached on the front (the opposite) side.

ORNL DWG 71-7003

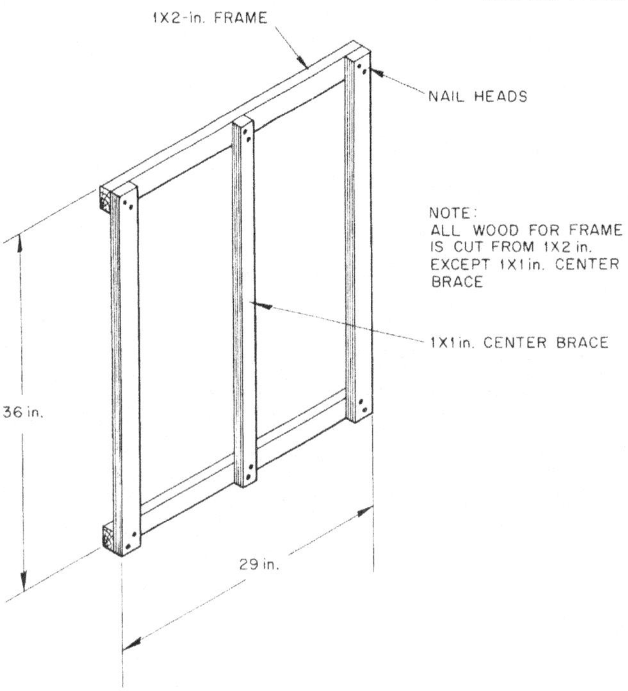

Fig. 3. KAP frame (looking at the back side of the frame).

b. To make the front side smooth and flat so that the flaps will close tightly, fill in the spaces as follows: Cut two pieces of 1 × 2-in. boards long enough to fill in the spaces on top of the 36-in. sides of the frame between the top and bottom horizontal boards, and nail these filler boards in place. Do the same thing with a 1 × 1-in. board (or a board the size of that used for the center brace) as a filler board for the center brace (see Fig. 4).

If the frame is made of only one thickness of board 3/4 in. to 1 in. thick, it will not be sufficiently heavy to swing back far enough on its free-swinging return stroke.

2. The hinges

Ordinary door butt-hinges are best. So that the pump can swing past the horizontal position, the hinges should be screwed onto the front of the frame, at its top, in the positions shown in Fig. 4. (Pick one of the 29-in. boards and call it the top.) If you do not have a drill for drilling a screw hole, you can make a hole by driving a nail and then pulling it out. Screw the screw into the nail hole.

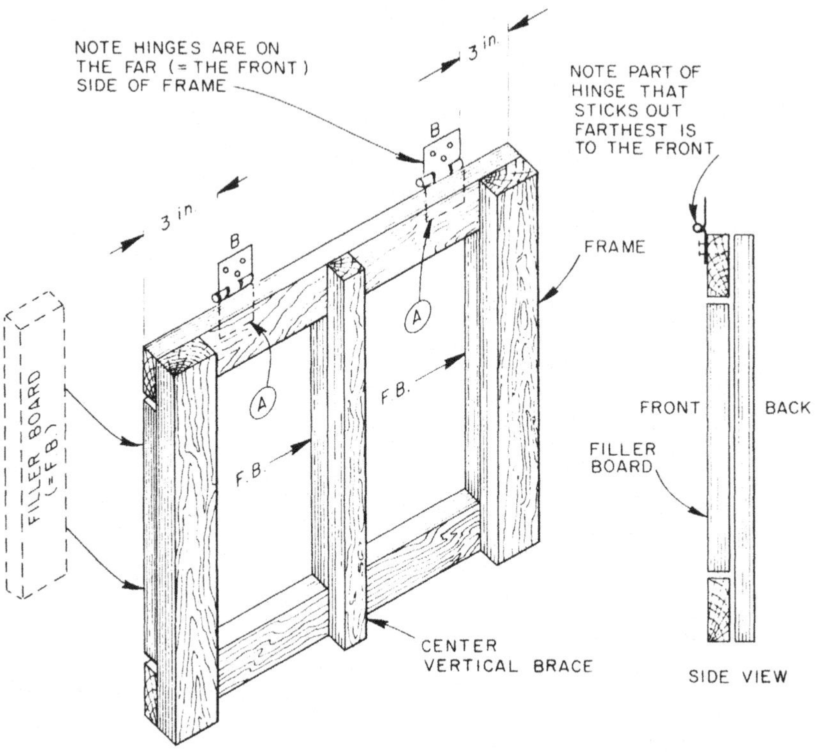

Fig. 4. Completing the frame.

3. The pivot-wires and flaps

a. Make 9 flap pivot-wires. If you have smooth, straight wire as springy and thick as coat hanger wire, use it to make **nine** 29-in.-long straight lengths of wire. If not, use wire from all-wire coat hangers or use strings. First, cut off all of the hook portion of each coat hanger, including the twisted part. If you have only ordinary pliers, use the cutter to "bite" the wire all around; it will break at this point if bent there. Next, **straighten** each wire **carefully.** Straighten all the bends so that each wire is straight within $^1/_4$ in., as compared to a straight line. Proper straightening takes 1 to 5 minutes per wire. To straighten, repeatedly grasp the bent part of the wire with pliers in slightly different spots, each time bending the wire a little with your other hand. Then cut each wire to a 29-in. length. Finally, bend no more than $^1/_2$ in. of each end at a right angle and in the same plane—that is, in directions so that all parts of the bent wire will lie flat against a smooth surface. The bent ends are for secure attachment later (see Fig. 8).

b. Make 9 polyethylene flaps that will be the hinged valves of the KAP. First cut 9 strips, making each strip 30 in. long by $5^1/_2$-in. wide (see Fig. 5). To cut plastic flaps quickly and accurately, cut a long strip of plastic 30 in. wide. Then cut off a flap in this way: (1) draw a cutting guideline on a wide board $5^1/_2$ in. from an edge; (2) place the 30-in.-wide plastic strip so that it lies on this board, with one of the strip's side edges just reaching the edge of the board; (3) place a second board over

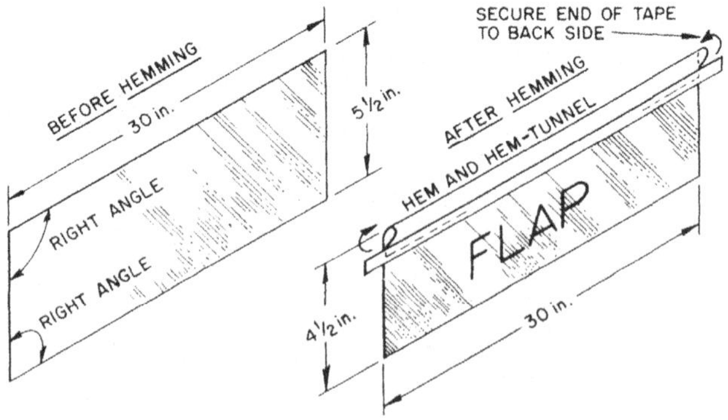

Fig. 5.

the plastic on the first board, with a straight edge of this second upper board over the guideline on the lower board; and finally (4) cut off a flap by running a **sharp** knife along the straight edge of the upper board.

To form a hem along one of the 30-in. sides of a $5^1/_2 \times 30$-in. rectangular strip, fold in a **1-in.** hem. This makes the finished flap $4^1/_2$ in. wide.

To hold the folded hem while taping it, paper clips or another pair of hands are helpful. For each hem, use two pieces of pressure-sensitive tape, each about 1 in. wide and 16 in. long. Or make the hem by sewing it very close to the cut edge to form a hem-tunnel (see Fig. 5).

After the hem has been made, cut a notch with scissors in each hemmed corner of the flap (Figs. 6 and 8). Avoid cutting the tape holding the hem. Each notch should extend downward about $^1/_2$ in. and should extend horizontally from the outer edge of the flap to $^1/_4$ in. inside the inner side of the frame, when the flap is positioned on the frames as shown in Fig. 6.

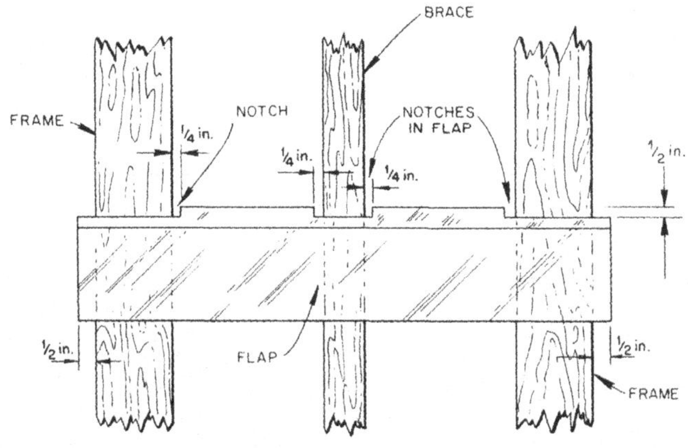

Fig. 6. Sizes of notches in flaps.

Also cut a notch in the center of the flap (along the hem line) extending $^1/_2$ in. downward and extending horizontally $^1/_4$ in. beyond each of the two sides of the vertical brace (see Fig. 6). The notch MUST be wider than the brace. [However, if you are building a pump using wire netting for flap-stops (see Fig. 13), then do NOT cut a notch in the center of each flap.]

c. Take the 9 pieces of straightened wire and insert one of them into and through the hem-tunnel of each flap, like a curtain rod running through the hem of a curtain. Check to see that each flap **swings freely** on its pivot-wire, as illustrated by Fig. 7. Also see Fig. 8.

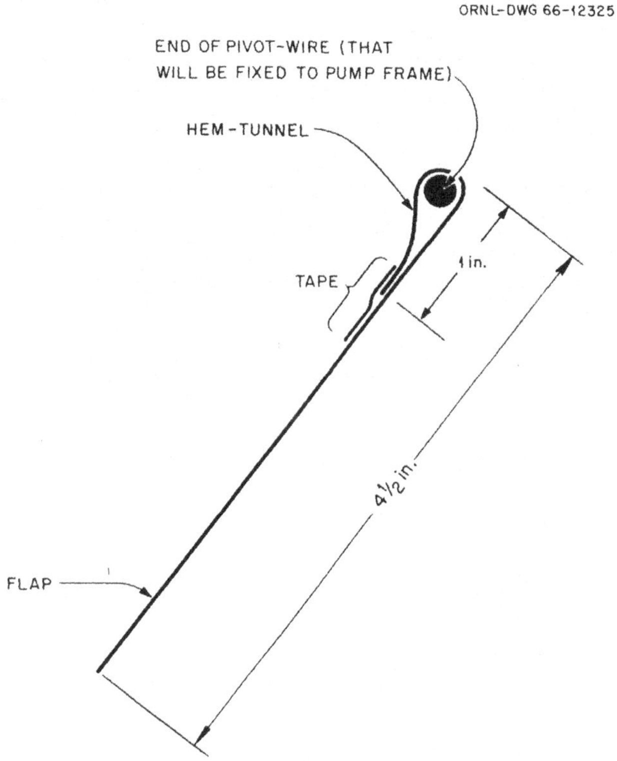

Fig. 7. End view.

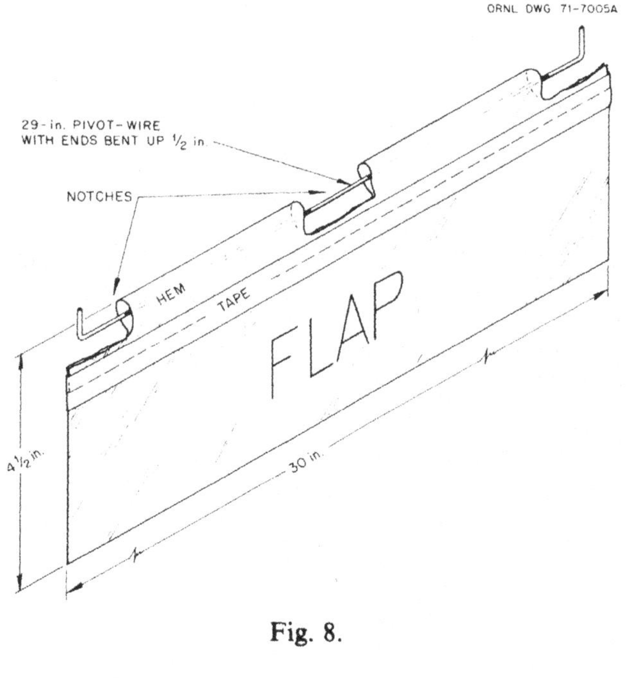

Fig. 8.

d. Put aside the flaps and their pivot-wires for use after you have attached the flap-stops and the hinges to the frame, as described below.

e. Using the ruler printed on the edge of this page, mark the positions of each pivot-wire (the arrowheads numbered 0, 3 5/8, 7 1/4 in.) and the position of each flap-stop (the four marks between each pair of numbered arrowheads on this ruler). All of these positions should be marked both on the vertical sides of the 36-in.-long boards of the frame and on the vertical brace. Mark the position of the uppermost pivot-wire (the "0" arrowhead on this ruler) 1/4 in. below the top board to which the hinges have been attached (see Figs. 9 and 10).

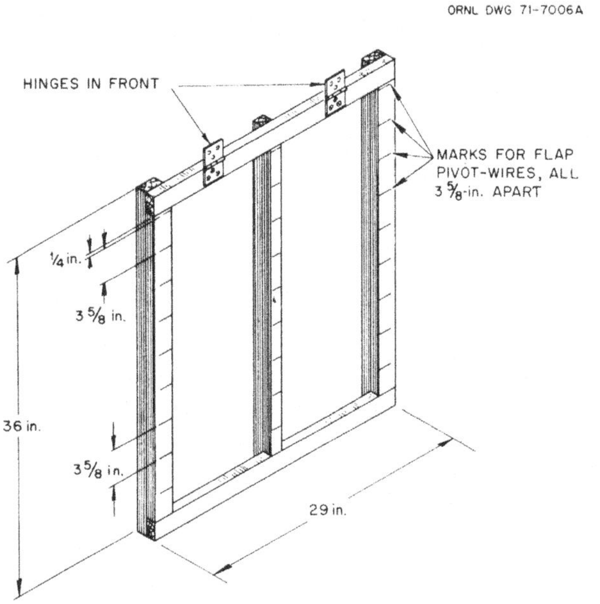

Fig. 9.

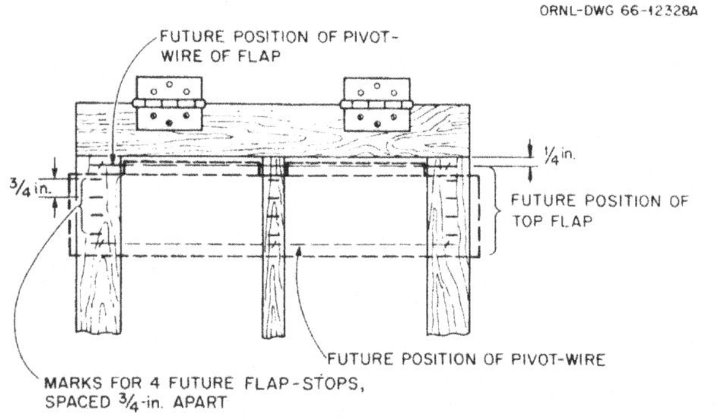

Fig. 10.

4. The flap-stops

So that the flaps may swing open on only one side of the frame (on its front, or face), you must attach horizontal flap-stops made of strings or wires across the face of the frame. (See Figs. 10 and 11.) Nail or tie four of these flap-stops between the marked points where each pair of the horizontal pivot-wires for the flaps will be placed. Be careful not to connect any flap-stops in such a way that they cross the horizontal open spaces in which you later will attach the flap pivot-wires.

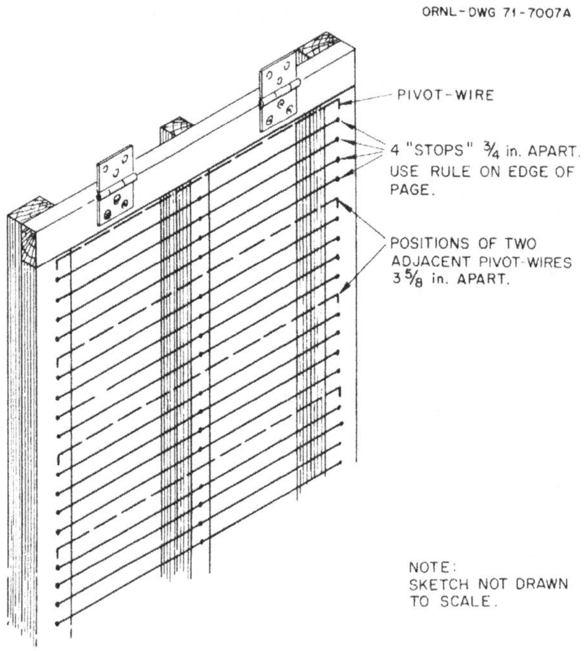

Fig. 11. Positions of pivot-wires and flap-stops.

If you have tacks (NOT thumbtacks) or very small nails, drive three in a horizontal line to attach each flap-stop—one in each of the two vertical 36-in. sides of the frame and one in the vertical center brace (see Fig. 11). First, drive all of these horizontal lines of tacks about three-quarters of the way into the boards. Then, to secure the flap-stop string or thin wire quickly to a tack, wind the string around the tack and immediately drive the tack tightly into the frame to grip the string (see Fig. 11).

If you have no tacks or nails, cut notches or slots where the flap-stops are to be attached. Cut these notches in the edges of the vertical sides of the frame and in an edge of the center brace. Next, secure the flap-stops (strings or wires) by tying each

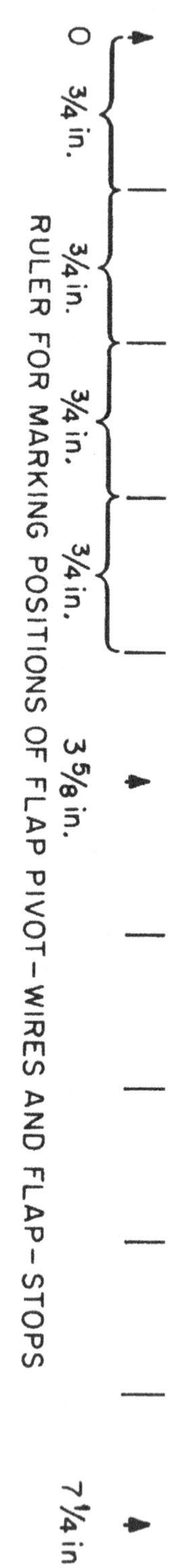

one in its notched position. This tying should include wrapping each horizontal flap-stop once around the vertical center brace. The stops should be in line with (in the same plane as) the front of the frame. Do not stretch flap-stops too tightly, or you may bend the frame.

5. Final assembly

a. Staple, nail, or tie the 9 flap pivot-wires or pivot-strings (each with its flap attached) in their positions at the marked $3^5/_8$-in. spacings. Start with the lowest flap and work upward (see Fig. 11). Connect each pivot-wire at both ends to the 36-in. vertical sides of the frame. **Also connect it to the vertical brace.** BE CAREFUL TO NAIL THE PIVOT-WIRES ONLY TO THE FRAME AND THE BRACE. DO NOT NAIL ANY PLASTIC DIRECTLY TO THE WOOD. All flaps must turn freely on their pivot-wires.

If any flap, when closed, overlaps the flap below it by more than 1 in., trim off the excess so that it overlaps by only 1 in.

b. Screw (or nail, if screws are not available) the upper halves of the hinges onto the horizontal support board on which the KAP will swing. (A 1-in.-thick board is best, $3^1/_2$ in. wide and at least 12 in. longer than the width of the doorway or other opening in which this KAP is to be installed.)

Be careful to attach the hinges in the UNusual, OUT-OF-LINE POSITION shown in Fig. 12.

CAUTIONS: Do NOT attach a KAP's hinges directly to the door frame. If you do, the hinges will be torn loose on its return stroke or on its power stroke.

If you are making a KAP to fit into a rectangular opening, make its frame 4 in. SHORTER than the height of its opening and 1 in. NARROWER than the width of the opening.

c. For this 3-ft model, tie the pull-cord to the center brace about **$12^1/_2$ in. below the hinge line,** as shown in Fig. 12. (If you tie it lower, your **arm movements will waste energy.**) Use small nails or wire to keep the tie end from slipping up or down on the center brace. (For a more durable connection, see Fig. 22.)

Cut a slot in the flap above the connection of the pull-cord to the vertical brace, deep enough so that this flap will close completely when the KAP is being pulled. Tape the end and edges of the slot.

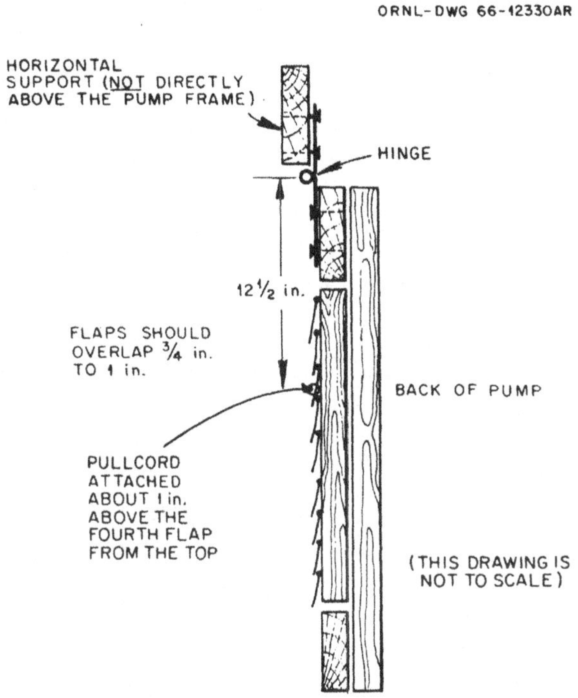

Fig. 12. Hinge is attached so pump can swing 180 degrees.

IV. MORE RAPID CONSTRUCTION

(Skip this section if you cannot easily get chicken wire and $^1/_4$-in.-thick boards.)

If chicken wire and boards about $^1/_4$ in. thick are available, use the chicken wire for flap-stops. By using these materials, the time required to build a given KAP can be reduced by about 40%. One-inch woven mesh is best. (Hardware cloth has sharp points and is unsatisfactory.)

Figure 13 illustrates how the mesh wire should be stapled to the KAP frame. Next, unless the KAP is wider than 3 ft, the front of the whole frame (except for the center brace) should be covered with thin boards approximately $^1/_2$ in. thick, such as laths. Then the pivot-wires, with their flaps on them, should be stapled onto the $^1/_4$-in.-thick boards. This construction permits the flaps to turn freely in front of the chicken-wire flap-stops.

With this design, the center of each pivot-wire should NOT be connected to the center brace, nor should the center of the flap be notched. However, pivot-wires that are attached this way must be made and held straighter than pivot-wires used with flap-stops made of straight strings or wires.

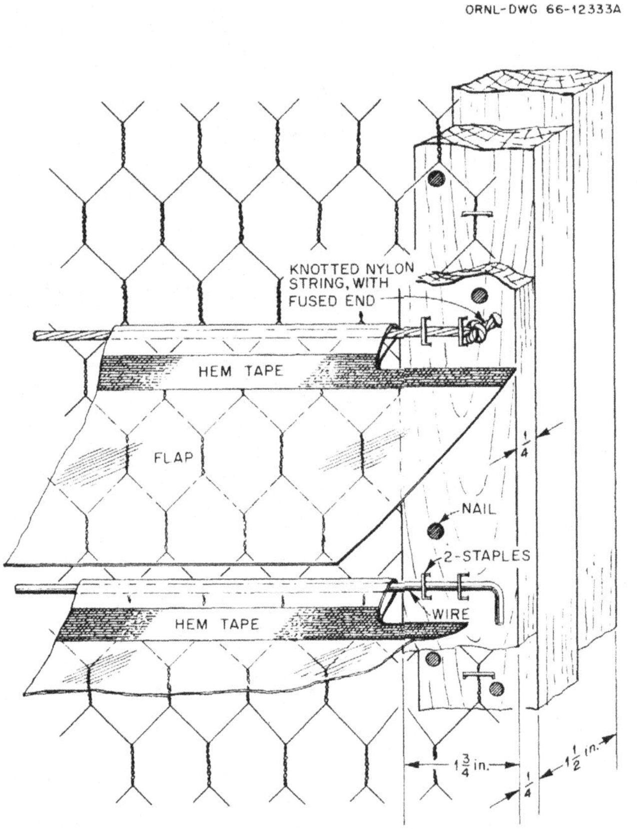

Fig. 13. Flaps attached $^1/_4$ inch in front of chicken wire used for flap-stops.

Note in Fig. 13 that each pivot-wire is held firm and straight by **2** staples securing each end. The wire used should be at least as springy as coat hanger wire. If string is used instead of wire, nylon cord about the diameter of coat hanger wire is best for the pivot-strings.

If the KAP is wider than 3 ft, its center vertical brace should also be covered with a $^1/_4$-in.-thick board, and each pivot-wire should be attached to it. Furthermore, the center of each flap should be notched.

V. INSTALLATION AND ACCESSORIES

A. Minimum Open Spaces Around a KAP

To pump its maximum volume, an air-supply KAP with good metal hinges should be installed in its opening so that it swings only about $^1/_2$ in. above the bottom of the opening and only $^1/_2$ in. to 1 in. from the sides of the opening.

B. Adequately Large Air Passageways

When using a KAP as an air-supply pump to force air through a shelter, it is essential to provide a **low-resistance** air passageway **all the way through** the shelter structure from an **outdoor** air-intake opening for **outdoor** air to a separate air-exhaust opening to the **outdoors** (see Fig. 14).

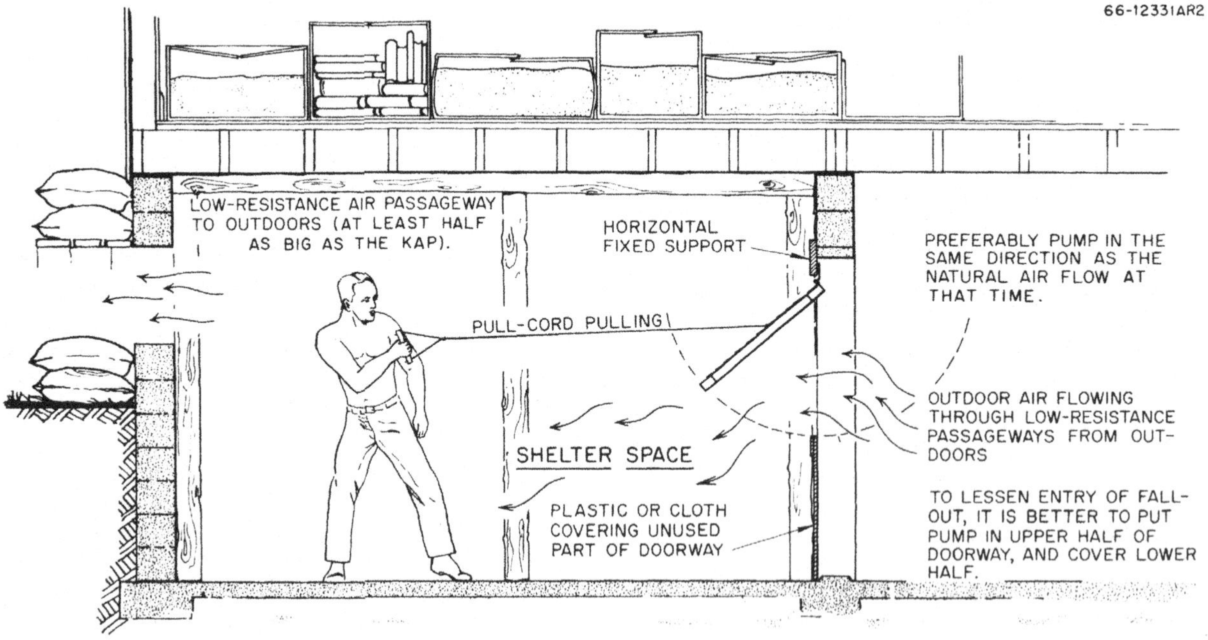

Fig. 14.

A low-resistance air passageway is one that is **no smaller** in cross-sectional area than half the size of the KAP pumping the air. For example, a 36 × 29-in. KAP should have a passageway no smaller than about 3½ sq. ft. An air-supply KAP of this size will force at least 1000 cubic feet per minute (1000 cfm) through a shelter having such openings, if it is installed as illustrated in Fig. 14.

If smaller air passageways or air-exhaust openings are provided, the volume of air pumped will be greatly reduced. For example, if the air-exhaust opening is only 1¾ sq. ft (¼ the size of this KAP), then this KAP will pump only about 500 cfm. And if the air-exhaust opening is only a 6 × 6-in. exhaust duct (¼ sq. ft), then this same 36 × 29-in. KAP will pump only about 50 cubic feet per minute. This would not provide enough outdoor air for more than one shelter occupant in a well-insulated shelter under heat-wave conditions in the hottest humid parts of the United States. In contrast, when the weather is freezing cold and the shelter itself is still cold enough to absorb the heat produced by the shelter occupants, this same 6 × 6-in. exhaust duct and the air-intake doorway will cause about 50 cfm of outdoor air to flow by itself through the shelter without using any pump. The reason: body heat warms the shelter air, and the warm air rises if cold air can flow in to replace it. Under these **cold** conditions—provided the air is distributed evenly throughout the shelter by KAP or otherwise—50 cfm is enough outdoor air for about 17 people.

To provide adequately large air passageways for air-supply KAPs used to ventilate shelters in buildings, in addition to opening and closing doors and windows, it may be necessary to build large ducts (as described below). Breaking holes in windows, ceilings, or walls is another way to make large, efficient air passageways.

Figure 15 illustrates how a 3-ft KAP can be used as a combined air-supply and air-distribution pump to adequately ventilate a small underground shelter that has an exhaust opening too small to provide enough ventilation in warm weather. (A similar installation can be used to ventilate a basement room having only one opening, its doorway.) Note how, by installing a "divider" in the doorway and entryway, the single entryway is converted into a large air-intake duct and a separate, large air-exhaust duct. To obtain the maximum increased volume of fresh outdoor air that can be pumped through the shelter—a total of about 1000 cfm for a 36 × 29-in. KAP—the divider should extend about 4 ft horizontally into the shelter room, as shown in Fig. 15. The 6 ft at the end of the divider (the almost-horizontal part under the KAP) can be made of plywood, provided it is installed so that it can be taken out of the way in a few seconds.

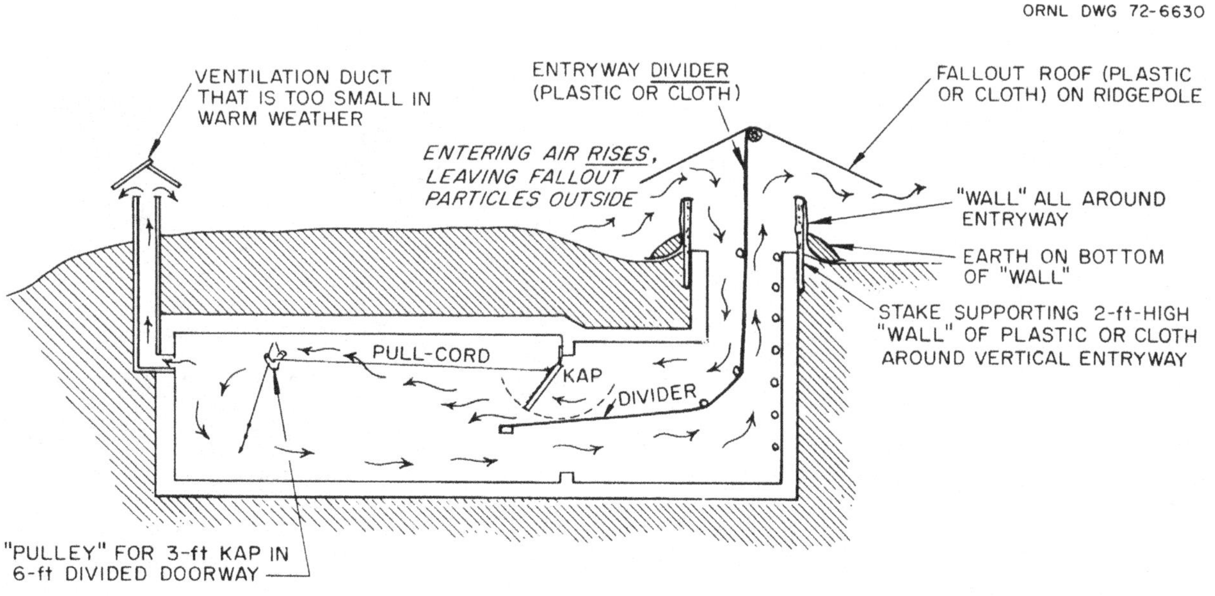

Fig. 15. Ventilating a shelter when the air-exhaust opening is too small.

Note how the entry of fallout into a shelter can be minimized by covering the entryway with a "roof" and by forcing the slow-moving entering air to rise over an obstruction (the "wall") before it flows into the shelter. The sand-like fallout particles fall to the ground outside the "wall."

C. Adequate Distribution of Air Within the Shelter

To make sure that each shelter occupant gets a fair share of the outdoor air pumped through the shelter, **air-distribution KAPs** should be used inside most large shelters. These KAPs are used within the shelter, separate from and in addition to air-supply KAPs (see Fig. 16). Air-distribution KAPs can serve in place of both air-distribution ducts and cooling fans. For these purposes, one or more 3-ft-high KAPs hung overhead from the shelter ceiling are usually most practical. If KAPs cannot readily be hung from the ceiling, they can be supported on light frames made of boards or metal, somewhat like those used for a small child's swing.

ORNL DWG 72-7547

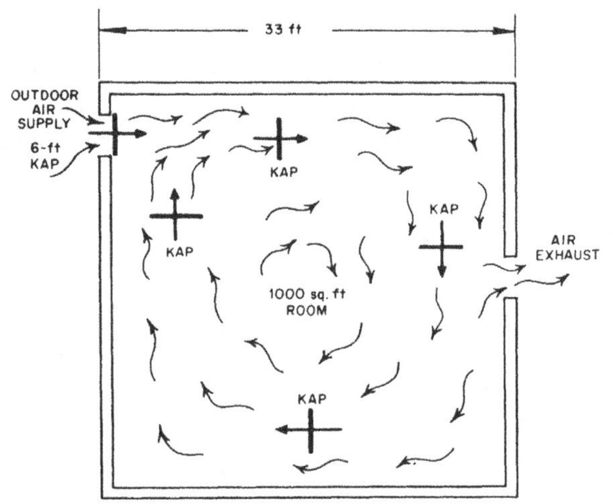

Fig. 16. The use of air-distribution KAPs.

You should make and use enough KAPs to cause air movement that can be felt in all parts of your shelter. Remember that if KAPs are installed near the floor and the shelter is fully occupied, the occupants' bodies will partially block the pumped airflow more than if the same KAPs were suspended overhead.

As a general rule, for shelters having more than about 20 occupants, provide one 3-ft air-distribution KAP for every 25 occupants. In relatively wide shelters, these interior KAPs should be positioned so that they produce an airflow that circulates around the shelter, preventing the air that is being pumped into the shelter from flowing directly to the exhaust opening. Figure 16 illustrates how four KAPs can be used in this way to distribute the air within a shelter and to fan the 100 occupants of a 1000-sq.-ft shelter room. Avoid positioning an air-distribution KAP so that it pumps air in a direction greater than a right angle turn from the direction of airflow to the location of the KAP.

D. Operation with a Pulley

A small KAP—especially one with improvised hinges or one installed at head-height or higher—can be pulled most efficiently by running its pull-cord over a pulley or over a greased homemade "pulley" such as described in Figs. 17 and 18. A pulley should be hung at approximately the same height as the hinges of the KAP, as illustrated in Fig. 15. To make

ORNL DWG 71-7242

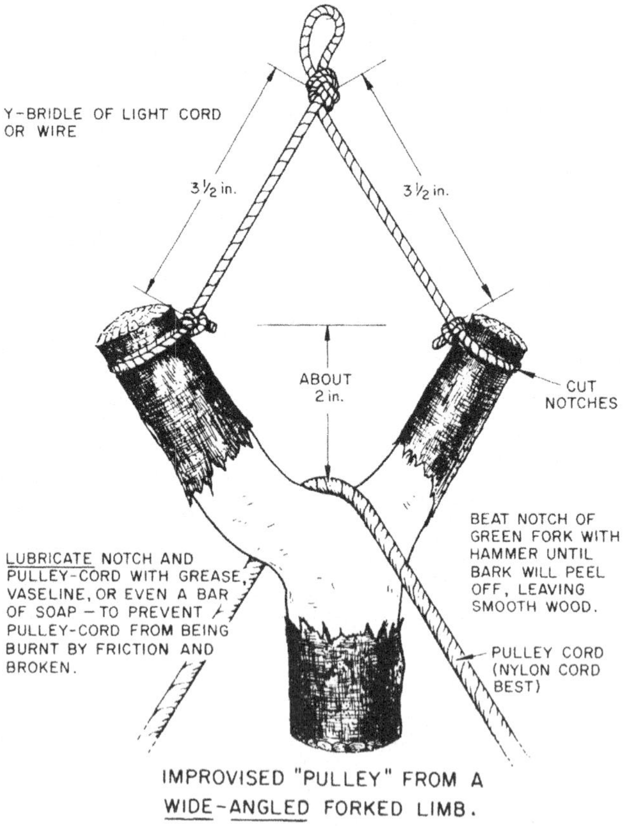

Fig. 17.

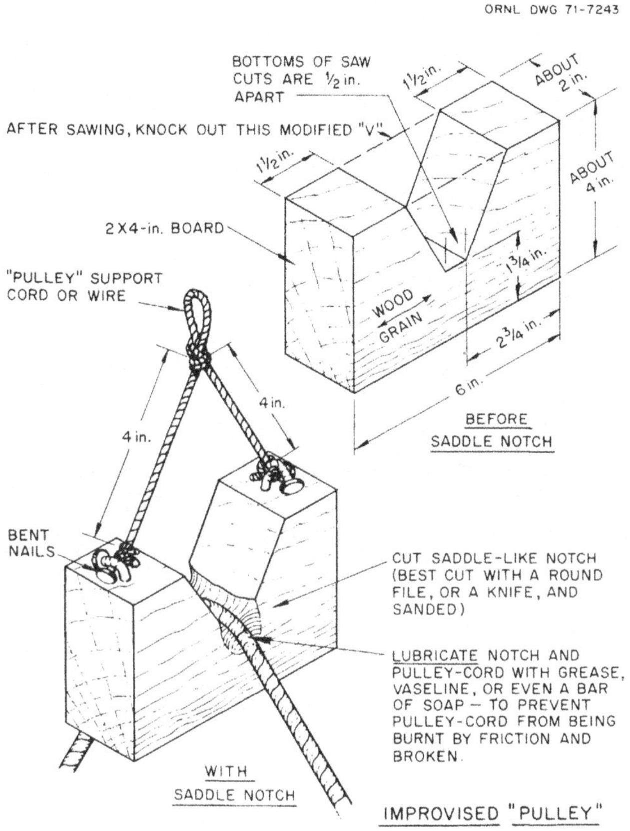

Fig. 18.

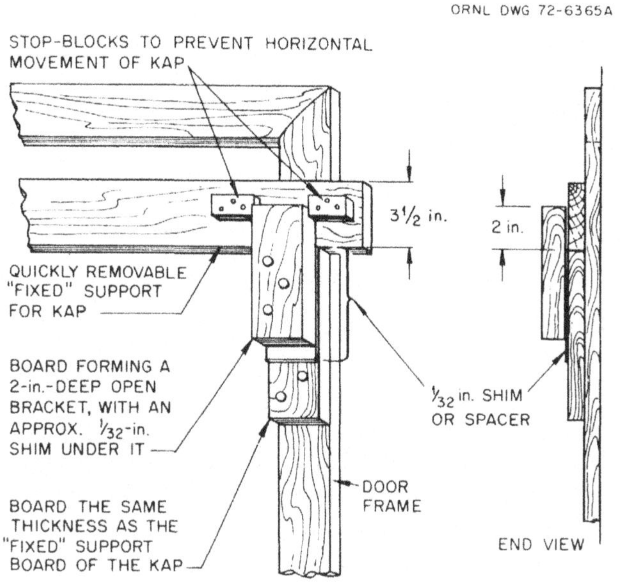

Fig. 19. Quick-removal bracket for KAP.

a comfortable hand-hold on which to pull downward, tie two or three overhand knots in a strip of cloth on the end of the pull-cord.

(Such a "pulley" can also be used to operate a bail-bucket to remove water or wastes from some shelters, without anyone having to go outside.)

E. Quick-Removal Brackets

The air-supply KAP that pumps air through your shelter is best held in its pumping position by mounting it in homemade quick-removal brackets (see Fig. 19) for the following reasons:

- A KAP provided with quick-removal brackets can be taken down easily and kept out of the way of persons passing through its doorway when it is not in use. It can be kept in a place where people are unlikely to damage it.
- By installing two sets of quick-removal brackets in opposite shelter openings, you can quickly reverse the direction in which the KAP pumps air, to take advantage of changes in the direction of natural airflow through the shelter.
- If the KAP is installed on quick-removal brackets, in an emergency a person standing beside the KAP could grasp its frame with both hands, lift it upward a few inches to detach it, and carry it out of the way—all in 3 to 5 seconds. Being able to move the KAP quickly could prevent blast winds from wrecking the pump, which might also be blown into your shelter—possibly injuring occupants. In extensive areas where fallout shelters and their occupants would survive the blast effects of typical large warheads, more than 4 seconds would elapse between the time shelter occupants would see the extremely bright light from the explosion and the arrival of a blast wave strong enough to wreck a KAP or other pumps left exposed in a ventilation opening.

Note in Fig. 19 that the KAP's "fixed" support-board (a $3^1/_2$-in.-wide board to which its hinges are attached) is held in a bracket only 2 inches deep. To prevent too tight a fit in the bracket, be sure to place a $^1/_{32}$-in. shim or spacer (the cardboard back of a writing tablet will do) between two boards of the bracket, as illustrated. Also, make spaces about $^1/_{16}$ inches wide between the lower inner corners of the stop-blocks and the sides of the outer board. To prevent your hands from being cut, you should put tape over the exposed ends of wires near the frame's outer edges of a KAP that you want to be able to remove rapidly.

In a small expedient shelter, a small KAP can be quickly jerked loose if its "fixed" support-board is attached to the roof with only a few small nails.

VI. OPERATION AND MAINTENANCE

A. Pumping

Operate your 3-foot KAP by pulling it with an easy, swinging motion of your arm. To pump the maximum volume of air, you should pull the KAP toward you until its frame swings out to an almost-horizontal position. Then quickly move your hand so that the pull-cord is kept **slack during the entire, free-swinging return stroke.** Figure 24 in Section VIII, LARGE KAPs, illustrates this necessary motion.

Be sure to provide a comfortable hand-hold on the pull-cord (see Fig. 14). Blisters can be serious under unsanitary conditions.

To pull a KAP via an overhead pulley with minimum effort, sit down and pull as if you were tolling a bell—except that you should raise your hand quickly with the return stroke and keep it raised long enough so that the pull-cord remains slack during the entire return stroke. Or, if the pulley is not overhead, operate the KAP by swinging your extended arm back and forth from the shoulder.

B. Placement to Take Advantage of the Natural Direction of Air Flow

A KAP can pump more air into a shelter if it is installed so that it pumps air through the shelter in the direction in which the air naturally flows. Since this direction can be reversed by a wind change outdoors, it is desirable to provide a way to quickly remove your pump and reposition it so that air can be pumped in the opposite direction. This can be done in several ways, including making one set of quick-removal brackets for one air opening and a second set for the other.

C. Maintenance

To operate your KAP efficiently, keep the flaps in good repair and make sure that there is the minimum practical area of open spaces in and around the KAP through which air can flow back around the pump frame, opposite to the pumped direction. So keep at least some extra flap material in your shelter, along with some extra tape and the few tools you may need to make repairs.

VII. NARROW KAPs AND SMALL KAPs

A. Narrow KAPs

To swing efficiently in an entrance or emergency exit of an expedient trench shelter that is 22 in. wide, a KAP is best made 20 in. wide and 36 in. high. One of less height is not as efficient as a 36-in.-high model and has to be pulled uncomfortably fast. So, when ventilation openings can be selected or made at least 38 in. high, make your pump 36 in. high.

In a narrow trench shelter, it is best to have the pull-cord run the full length of the trench, along the trench wall that occupants will face when sitting. Then each occupant can take a turn pulling the pump without having to change seats.

Good metal hinges on a narrow KAP allow it to swing properly if pulled with the pull-cord attached to **one side** of the frame. (Pumps with improvised hinges and large pumps must be pulled from a connection point on their center vertical brace to make them swing properly.) Therefore, if you have small metal hinges and need a KAP no wider than 20 inches, build a rectangular frame **without** a vertical center brace. Make two pull-cord attachment points, one on each side of the frame and each 9 inches below the top of the frame. (For a small KAP, a satisfactory attachment point can readily be made by driving two nails so that their heads cross, and wiring them together.) Then if a change in wind direction outside causes the direction of natural air flow in the trench to become opposite to the direction in which air is being pumped, you can move your KAP to the opening at the other end of the trench. The pull-cord can easily be connected to the other side of the frame, and convenient pumping can be resumed quickly.

So that the horizontal support board can be nailed easily to the roofing poles or boards of an entry trench, it is best to use cabinet hinges. Screw them onto an **edge** of the support board, in the UNusual, OUT-OF-LINE POSITION shown in Fig. 20. This hinge connection allows the pump to swing a full 180 degrees. To facilitate moving the horizontal support board, connect it to the roof with a few small nails, so that it can be pulled loose easily and quickly.

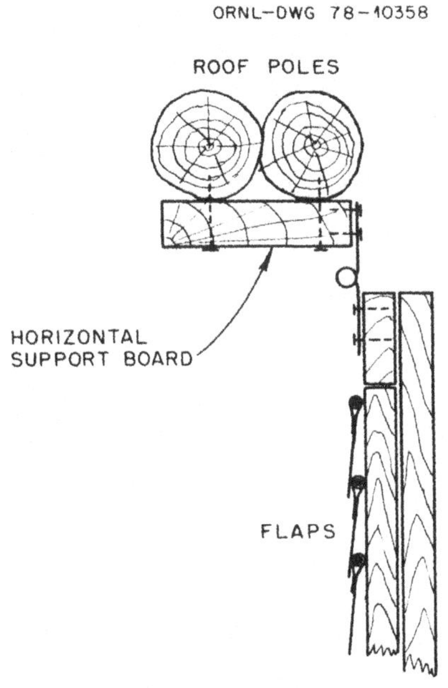

Fig. 20.

B. Small KAPs

If the only available opening in which a KAP can be installed is small, build a KAP to fit it. Use narrower boards to make the frame and make the flaps of thinner material, such as the polyethylene of large plastic trash bags. For pumps 24 inches or less in height, make the finished flaps only $3^1/_2$ inches wide and space their pivot-wires 3 inches apart. The flaps should overlap no more than $^1/_2$ inch. A KAP 24 inches high will pump enough outdoor air for only a few people, except in cold weather.

Small, yet efficient KAPs can be made even if the only materials available are straight sticks about $1^1/_4$ inches in diameter, strips of cloth to tie the frame together and to make the hinges and the pull cord, polyethylene film from large trash bags for the flaps, freezer or duct tape (or needle and thread) to make the flap hems, coat hanger wire or string for the pivot-wire, and string or ordinary thread for the flap-stops. A sharp knife is the only essential tool. Figure 21 shows a way to easily tie sticks securely together and to attach strings or threads for stop-flaps, when small nails and tacks are not available. The flap-stop strings or threads should be secured by wrapping them several times around each stick to which they are attached, so they will be gripped by the out-of-line knife cuts.

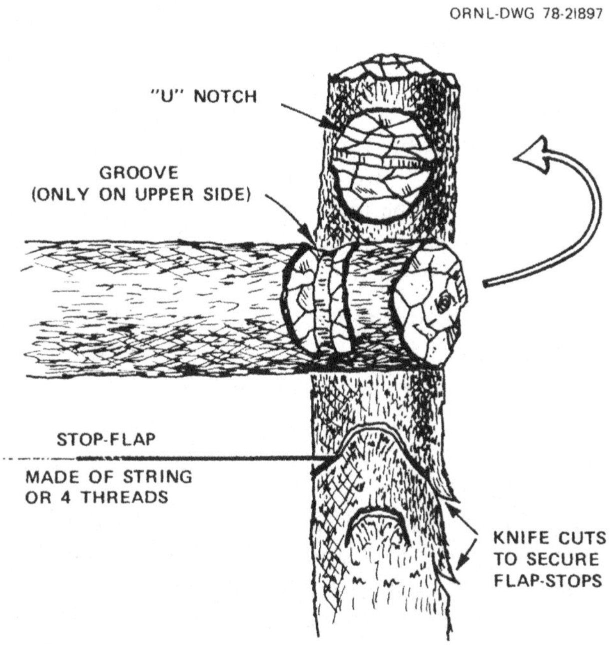

Fig. 21. Sticks ready to be tied together to make a KAP frame.

VIII. LARGE KAPs

A. Construction

A 6-ft-high by 29-in.-wide model can be constructed in the same way as a 3-ft model—except that it should have both horizontal and vertical center braces (1 × 2-in. boards are best). To increase the strength of a 6-ft KAP, all parts of its double-thickness frame and its vertical center brace should be made of two thicknesses of 1 × 2-in. softwood boards, securely held together with clinched nails. Also, to increase the distance that the pump will swing back by itself during its return stroke, it is worthwhile to attach a 6-ft piece of 1 × 2-in. board (not illustrated) to the back of each side of the frame. Do NOT attach weights to the bottom of the frame; this would slow down the pumping rate.

This 6-ft-high pump requires 18 flaps, each the same size as those of the 36-in.-high KAP. The flaps on the lower part of a large KAP must withstand hard use. If $^1/_2$-in.-wide strips of tape are attached along the bottom and side edges of these lower flaps, then even flaps made of ordinary 4-mil polyethylene will remain serviceable for over 1000 hours of pumping. However, the **lower** flaps of large KAPs can advantageously be made of 6-mil polyethylene. The width and spacing of all flaps should be the same as those of the 36-in.-high model.

The pull-cord should be attached to the vertical center brace of a 6-ft KAP about $16^1/_2$ in. below the hinge line. A $^3/_{16}$-in. nylon cord is ideal.

To adequately ventilate and cool very large and crowded shelters in buildings, mines, or caves, KAPs larger than 72 × 29 in. should be used. You can take better advantage of large doorways, elevator shaft openings, etc., by "tailor-making" each large air-supply KAP to the size of its opening—that is, by making it as large as is practical. The frame and brace members should be appropriately strengthened, and one or more "Y" bridles should be provided, as described in the section below. A 7-ft-high × $5^1/_2$-ft-wide KAP, with a $^1/_4$-in.-diameter pull-cord attached 18 in. below its hinge line, and with two "Y" bridles for its two operators, pumped air at the rate of over 11,000 cubic ft per minute through a large basement shelter during tests.

To make a durable connection of the pull-cord to the center vertical brace: (1) Attach a wire loop (Fig. 22) about $16^1/_2$ in. below the hinge line. This loop can be made of coat hanger wire and should go around the center vertical brace. This fixed loop should be kept from slipping on the center brace by bending four 6-penny nails over it in front as illustrated, and two smaller nails in back. (2) Make a free-turning, triple-wire loop connected to the fixed loop. (3) Cover part of the free-turning loop with tape and tie the pull-cord to this loop. Tie the pull-cord tightly over the taped part.

ORNL DWG 72-8204

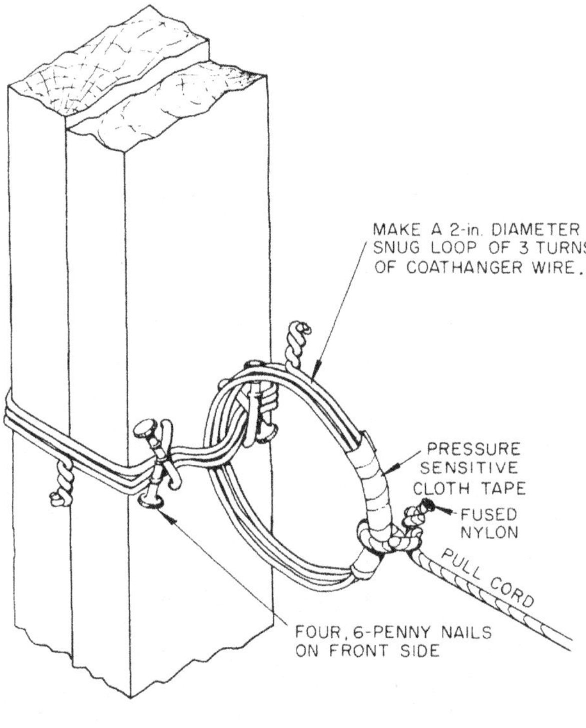

Fig. 22.

B. Operation of Larger KAPs

A larger KAP can be pulled most easily by providing it with a "Y" bridle (see Fig. 23) attached to the end of its pull-cord.

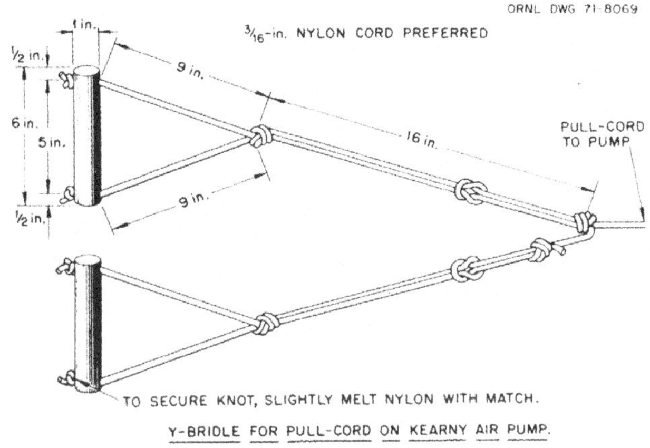

Fig. 23. Y-bridle for pull-cord on KAP.

A man of average size and strength can operate a 6 ft × 29 in. KAP by himself, pumping over 4000 cubic feet per minute through a typical large shelter without working hard; tests have shown that he must deliver only about $^1/_{20}$ of a horsepower. However, most people prefer to work in pairs when pulling a 6-ft KAP equipped with a "Y" bridle, when pumping over 3000 cfm.

To pump the maximum volume of air with minimum effort, study Fig. 24 and follow the instructions given below for operating a large KAP.

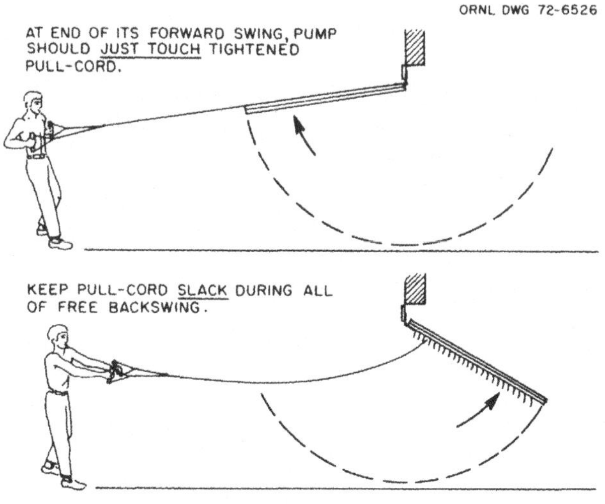

Fig. 24.

1. Gradually start the pump swinging back and forth, moving your arms and body as illustrated and **pulling mostly with your legs and body.**

2. Stand at such a distance from the pump that you can pull the pump toward you until the forward-swinging pump **just touches the tightly stretched pull-cord**—and at such a distance that you can keep the pull-cord **slack** during the whole of the pump's free backswing.

3. To be sure you do not reduce the amount of air pumped, rapidly move your arms forward **as soon as the forward-swinging pump touches the tightened pull-cord.** Hold your arms forward until the pump again starts to swing toward you.

IX. SOLUTIONS TO SPECIAL PROBLEMS

A. Increasing the Usefulness of Shelters by Supplying 40 cfm per Planned Occupant

If a shelter is fully occupied for days during hot weather and is cooled both day and night by pumping through it and distributing at least 40 cubic feet per minute of outdoor air for each occupant—more than is required to maintain tolerable temperatures at night—these advantages result:

- The shelter occupants will be exposed to effective temperatures less than 2° F higher than the current effective temperatures outdoors, and at night will get relief from extreme heat.
- The floors, walls, etc. of a shelter so ventilated will be cooled at night to temperatures well below daytime temperatures. Therefore, during the day a considerable fraction of the occupants' body heat will flow into the floors, walls, and other parts of the shelter and less body heat will have to be carried out by the exhaust air during the hottest hours of the day. Thus daytime temperatures will be reduced.
- Since the shelter occupants will be cooler and will sweat less, especially at night, they will need less water than they would require if the shelter were ventilated at a rate of less than 40 cfm per occupant. (If the outdoor air is very hot and desert-dry, it usually is better to supply less than 40 cfm per occupant during the hottest hours of the day.)
- If the shelter were to be endangered by the entry of outside smoke, carbon monoxide or other poisonous gases, or heavy descending fallout under windy conditions, ventilation of the shelter could be temporarily restricted or stopped for a longer period than would be practical if the shelter itself were warmer at the beginning of such a crisis period.

- The shelter could be occupied beyond its rated capacity without problems caused by overcrowding becoming as serious as would be the case if smaller-capacity air pumps were to be installed and used.

B. Pre-Cooling Shelters

If the shelter itself is cooler than the occupants, more of the body heat of occupants can flow into its cool walls, ceiling, and floor. Therefore, it would be advantageous to pre-cool a shelter that may soon be occupied, especially during hot weather. KAPs (or other air pumps or fans) can be used to pre-cool a shelter by forcing the maximum volume of cooling outdoor air through the shelter and by distributing it within the shelter. A shelter should be pre-cooled at all times when the air temperature outdoors is lower than the air temperature inside the shelter. Then, if the pre-cooled shelter is used, the occupants will be kept cooler at a given rate of ventilation than if the shelter had not been pre-cooled, because the air will not have to carry all of their body heat out of the shelter.

C. Increasing the Effectiveness of a KAP

If you want to increase the volume of air that a KAP with good metal hinges can force through a shelter, install side baffles (see Fig. 25). Side baffles should be rigidly fixed to form two stationary "walls," one on each side of the swinging pump frame. They can be made of plywood, boards, doors, table tops, or even well-braced plastic. A space or clearance of $^1/_2$ to 1 in. should be maintained between the inner side of each baffle and the outer side of the swinging frame.

By installing side baffles you may be able to increase the volume of air your KAP will pump by as much as 20%, if it is in good repair and the openings around it are small.

ORNL-DWG 66-12334R

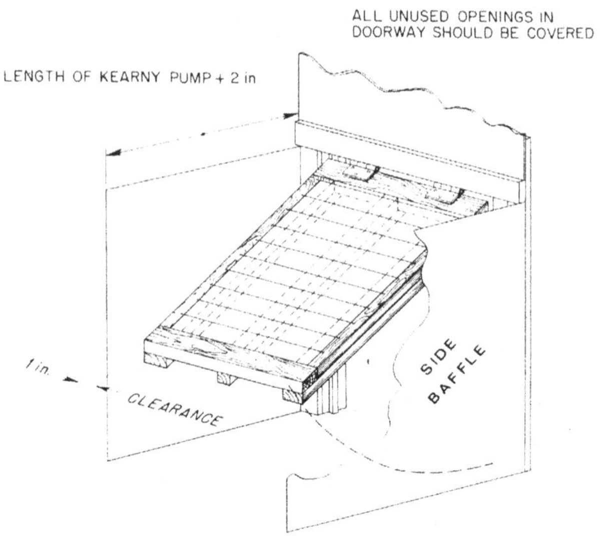

Fig. 25. Side baffles.

D. Operating a KAP as an Exhaust Pump

In some shelters, a KAP can be operated most effectively by using it as an exhaust pump. This can be done by pushing it with a push-pole attached to its center vertical brace. Push-pole operation is sometimes the best way to "suck" outdoor air into a shelter by pumping air out of the shelter in the natural direction of air flow; for example, up an elevator shaft or up a stairwell. This method is especially useful in those basement shelters in which air-intake openings are impractical for installing KAPs. This would be the case if the air-intake openings are small, exposed windows or holes broken in the ceiling of a shelter in a building.

To pump a large KAP most effectively with a push-pole, stand with your back to the KAP and grasp the push-pole with both hands. Using mostly your leg muscles, push the KAP by pulling the free end of its push-pole toward you.

Figure 26 shows an improvised, flexible connection of a push-pole attached to the center brace of a large KAP 28 in. from the top of its frame.

ORNL-DWG 66-12332R

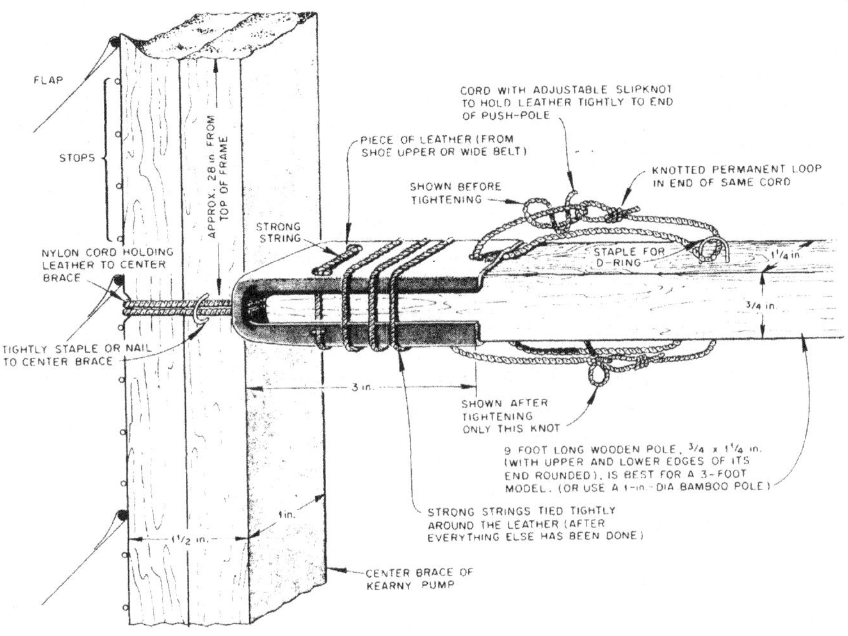

Fig. 26. Push-pole flexible connection.

E. Ventilating a Shelter with Only One Opening

Some basement rooms that may be used as shelters have only one opening, the doorway. A KAP can be used to ventilate such a shelter room if enough well-mixed and distributed air is moving just outside the doorway, or if air from outdoors can be pumped in by another KAP and made to flow in a hallway or room and pass just outside this doorway. Figure 27 indicates how to ventilate such a one-opening room by operating a 3-ft KAP as an air-intake pump in the upper part of the doorway.

Below such a doorway KAP, a "divider" 6 ft to 8 ft long can be installed. The divider permits exhaust air to flow out of the room without much of it being "sucked" back into the room by the KAP swinging above it. Plywood, reinforced heavy cardboard, or even well-braced plastic can be used to make a divider. It should be installed so that, in a possible emergency, it can be jerked out of the way in a few seconds.

When used with a divider, a 36×29 in. KAP can pump almost 1000 cubic feet of air per minute into and out of such a shelter room. Although 1000 cubic feet of well-distributed air is sufficient for several times as many as 25 shelter occupants under most temperate climate conditions, it is enough for only about 25 people in a one-entry room under exceptionally severe heat-wave conditions. Furthermore, to make it habitable for even 25 people under such conditions, the air in this room must be kept from rising more than 2°F above the temperature outdoors. This can be done using a second air-supply KAP to pump enough outdoor air through the building and in some cases also using air-distribution KAPs in spaces outside the one-entry room. The KAP in the doorway of a one-entry room should supply 40 cfm per occupant of this room.

In order to prevent any of the used, warmed, exhaust air from the one-entry room from being "sucked" by the doorway KAP back into the room, a stiffened rectangular duct can be built so as to extend the exhaust-opening (in the lower part of the doorway) several feet outside the room. Such a duct can be built of plastic supported by a frame of small boards. It can be used to discharge the exhaust air far enough away from the KAP and "downstream" in the airflow outside the one-opening room so that no exhausted air can be "sucked" back into the room.

ORNL DWG 72-8203

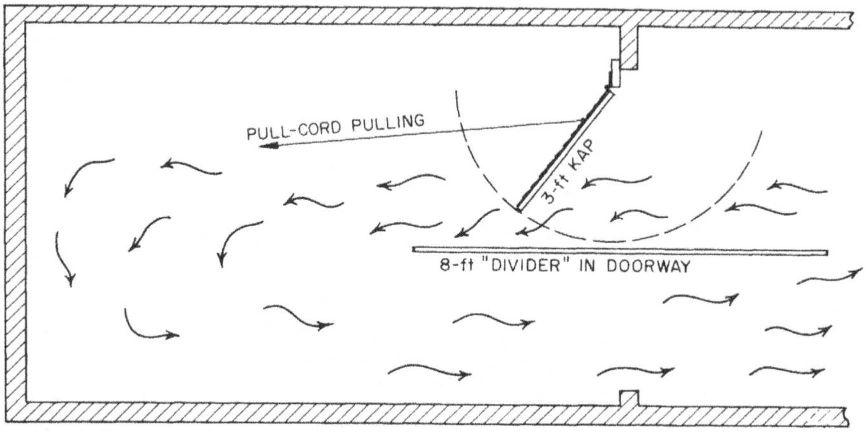

Fig. 27. Use of a "divider" to ventilate a shelter with only one opening.

F. Installing a KAP in a Steel-Framed Doorway

If you need to install a KAP in a steel-framed doorway and it is not feasible to screw or otherwise permanently connect it to the doorway, you can attach the KAP by using a few boards and some cord, as illustrated by Figs. 28 and 29. The two horizontal boards shown extending across the doorway are squeezed tightly against the two sides of the wall in which the doorway is located by tightening two loops of cord, one near each side of the doorway. One loop is illustrated. A cord is first tightened around the two horizontal boards. Then the looped cord is further tightened by binding it in the center with another cord, as illustrated.

Two large "C" clamps serve even better than two looped cords. However, secure support for a swinging KAP still requires the use of a vertical support board on each side of the doorway, as illustrated.

ORNL DWG 72-6364

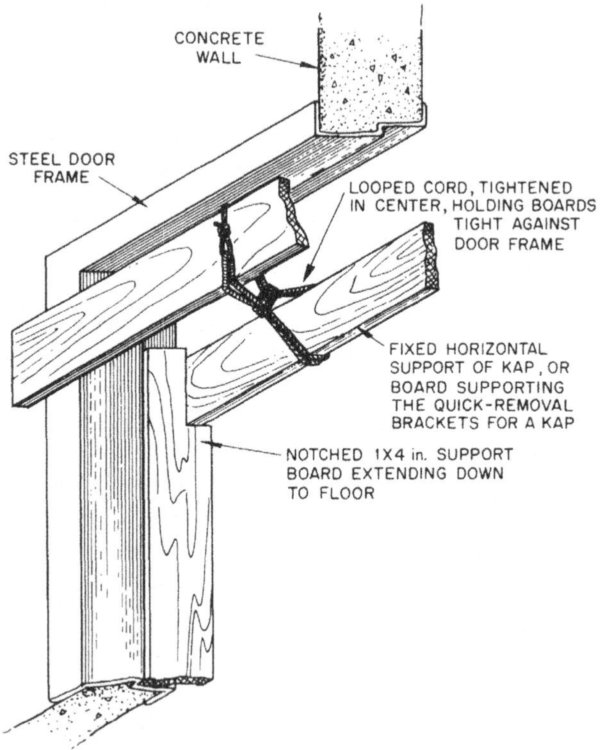

Fig. 28.

Figure 29 shows a quick-removal bracket supported by two horizontal boards tightened across the upper part of a doorway by looped cords, as described above. Also, study Fig. 19 and its accompanying instructions.

ORNL DWG 72-6617

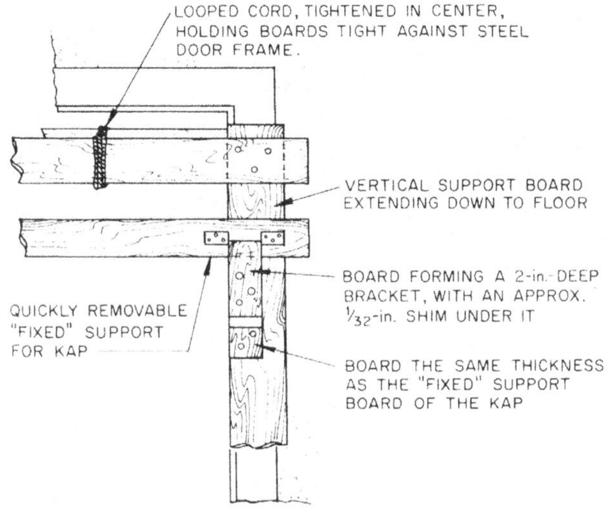

Fig. 29.

G. Building More Durable KAPs

If you are building KAPs in normal times, you may want to use materials that will make your pumps last longer, even though these materials are more difficult to obtain and are more expensive.

Durability tests have shown that the KAP parts that wear out first are the flaps and the pulleys. In 6-ft KAPs, the lower flaps are subject to hard use. Lower flaps made of 6-oz (per sq. yd), clear, nylon-reinforced, plied vinyl have lasted undamaged for over 1000 hours of full-stroke pumping, without having their edges reinforced. Lower flaps made of 6-mil nylon-reinforced polyethylene, without edge reinforcements, have lasted for 1000 hours with only minor damage.

The best pulley tested was a marine pulley such as that used on small sailboats, with a Delrin (DuPont) 2-in.-diameter wheel and 3/16-in. stainless steel shaft. This pulley was undamaged after operating a 6-ft KAP for 324 hours. The pulley appeared to be good for hundreds of hours of further operation.

The best pulley-cords tested were of braided dacron or nylon.

H. Using Air Filters

To supply shelter occupants with filtered air usually would be of **much less** importance to their survival and health than to provide them with adequate volumes of outdoor air to maintain tolerable temperatures. However, filtering the entering air could prove worthwhile, provided:

- Your shelter is not in an area likely to be subjected to blast, or it is a blast shelter with blast doors and blast valves protecting everything inside.
- Work on filters is started *after* you have completed more essential work, including the building of a high-protection-factor shelter, making, installing, and testing the necessary number of KAPs, storing adequate water, making a homemade fallout meter, etc.
- You have enough low-resistance filters (such as fiberglass dust filters used in furnaces and air-conditioners) and other materials for building the necessary large, supported filter in front of your KAP.
- Your KAP can pump an adequate volume of air through the filter and shelter.
- The filter is installed so that it can be easily removed if shelter temperatures rise too high.

To prevent a filter used with a KAP from causing too great a reduction in the volume of air that the KAP can pump through your shelter, you must use **large areas of low-resistance filter material.** An example: In one ventilation test, a large basement shelter was used which had two ordinary doorways at its opposite ends. These served as its air-intake and its air-exhaust openings. A 72×29 in. KAP operating in one doorway pumped almost 5000 cubic feet per minute through the shelter. But when a filter frame holding 26 square feet of 1-in.-thick fiberglass dust filters was placed across the air-intake stairwell, the KAP could pump only about 3400 cfm through this filter and the shelter.

The KFM Instructions This Printout is IMPORTANT

ORIGINALLY PUT IN THIS BOOK SO A NEWSPAPER COULD PRINT IT OUT QUICKLY THE NEXT DAY

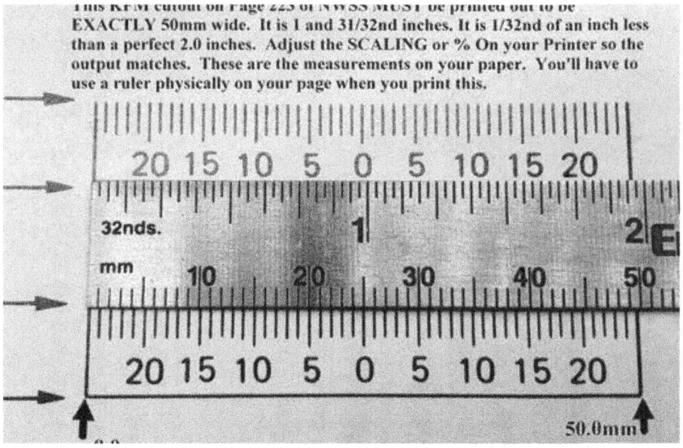

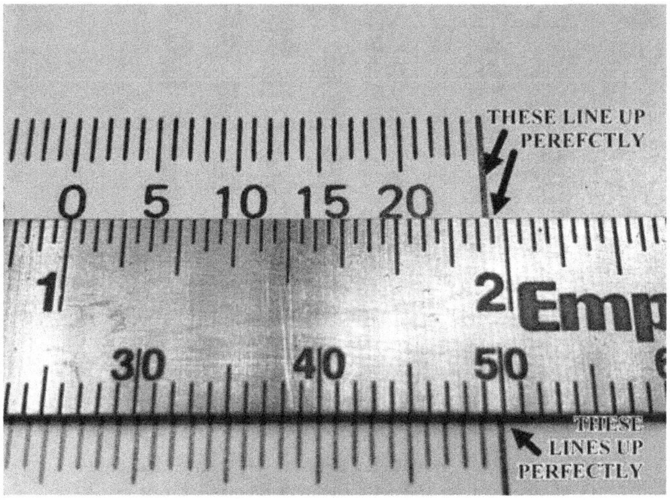

- Newspapers have changed sizes and are -smaller in the format than when this book was updated in 1987.

- Newspapers are no longer a dominant form of daily communication to people from the press and are becoming a thing of the times past.

In case this is printed out and not exactly to scale, here is the exact sale with the exact measurements it should be at, you can change the ratio for printing on your printer until the printed size equals the measured size. This is from the original NWSS book from 1987 and mine is autographed by Cresson.

These measurements are exact. You need to change the % of Size of your print such that 50mm on a ruler you have exactly matches what I put there that must be exactly 50mm in size for accurate radiation readings. Cresson notes that if you photocopied these instructions (used a Xerox or copy machine) that the measurements might not be exact because copiers in that day had a tendency to enlarge the original image by approximately 1% when you put something on the glass and pressed the COPY BUTTON.

I really wanted to delete the blank pages and the layout for the newspapers because it's no longer relevant but I'm leaving everything as it originally was and only adding these addendum pages for enhancement.

I do not know how you are reading these instructions, but the scale on page 223 must be exact for you to get a good radiation reading from your KFM.

You could have this on a PDF, you could be printing it on A4 paper in Europe or 8.5x11 in the USA or the Amazon print might be off by a few % that I do not have control over. A friend could have given you this. Even if you have to take a photo of the scale on page 22 with your camera and then size it to print out exactly, please do so. **MEASURE WITH A RULER WHEN YOUT PRINT IT OUT.**

ADJUST THE PRINT SETTINGS (SCALE, ENLARGEMENT, REDUCTION) SO PAGE 223 WITH THE SCALE ON IT PRINTS EXACTLY TO THE MEASUREMENTS SHOWN HERE.
It must be 50mm from outside edge to outside edge.
It is also 1 31/32 inches. it's 1/32nd shorter than a perfect 2.0 inches in width from the outside of the black line to the outside of the black line.

NOTE: this is NOT page 223 of the PDF, this is the PAGE 223 as listed on the upper right of the paper in the NWSS BOOK. Page 223 from the Original Printing.

223

Look for this in the upper right corner

APPENDIX C

A HOMEMADE FALLOUT METER, THE KFM
HOW TO MAKE AND USE IT

FOLLOWING THESE INSTRUCTIONS MAY SAVE YOUR LIFE

The complete KFM instructions include patterns to be cut out and used to construct the fallout meter. At the end of the instructions are extra patterns on 4 unnumbered pages. The reader is urged to use these extra patterns to make KFM's in normal peacetime and to keep the complete instructions intact for use during a recognized crisis period.

If Xerox copies of the patterns are used, they should be checked against the originals in order to make sure that they are the same size as the originals. Some older copiers make copies with slightly enlarged dimensions. Even slightly enlarged copies of all the KFM patterns can be made satisfactory provided: (1) on the PAPER PATTERN TO WRAP AROUND KFM CAN, the distances between the 4 marks for the HOLES FOR STOP-THREAD are corrected; and (2) the dimensions of the FINISHED-LEAF PATTERN are corrected.

These instructions, including the heading on this page and the illustrative photos, can be photographed without additional screening and rapidly reproduced by a newspaper or printer. If you keep the KFM instructions intact, during a worsening crisis you will be able to use them to help your friends and thousands of your fellow citizens by making them available for reproduction.

Pg 1 — (1) LOGO

I. The Need for Accurate and Dependable Fallout Meters

If a nuclear war ever strikes the United States, survivors of the blast and fire effects would need to have reliable means of knowing when the radiation in the environment around their shelters had dropped enough to let them venture safely outside. Civil defense teams could use broadcasts of surviving radio stations to give listeners a general idea of the fallout radiation in some broadcast areas. However, the fallout radiation can vary widely from point to point and the measurements are likely to be made too far from most shelters to make them accurate enough to use safely. Therefore, each shelter should have some dependable method of measuring the changing radiation dangers in its own area.

During a possible rapidly worsening nuclear crisis, or after a nuclear attack, most unprepared Americans could not buy or otherwise obtain a fallout meter -- an instrument that would greatly improve their chances of surviving a nuclear war. The fact that the dangers from fallout radiation -- best expressed in terms of the radiation dose rate, roentgens per hour (R/hr) -- quite rapidly decrease during the first few days, and then decrease more and more slowly, makes it very important to have a fallout meter capable of accurately measuring the unseen, unfelt and changing fallout dangers. Occupants of a fallout shelter should be able to minimize the radiation doses they receive. In order to effectively minimize the radiation doses, a dependable measuring instrument is needed to determine the doses they receive while they are in the shelter and while they are outside for emergency tasks, such as going out to get badly needed water. Also, such an instrument would permit them to determine when it is safe to leave the shelter for good.

Untrained families, guided only by these written instructions and using only low cost materials and tools found in most homes, have been able to make a KFM by working 3 or 4 hours. By studying the operating sections of these instructions for about 1½ hours, average untrained families have been able to successfully use this fallout meter to measure dose rates and to calculate radiation doses received, permissible times of exposure, etc.

The KFM (Kearny Fallout Meter) was developed at Oak Ridge National Laboratory. It is understandable, easily repairable, and as accurate as most civil defense fallout meters. In the United States in 1986 the least expensive commercially available dose-rate meter that is accurate and dependable and that measures high enough dose rates for wartime use is a British instrument that retails for $375. Comparable American instruments retail for over $1000.

Before a nuclear attack occurs is the best time to build, test and learn how to use a KFM. However, this instrument is so simple that it could be made even after fallout arrives **provided** that all the materials and tools needed (see lists given in Sections V, VI, and VII) and a copy of these instructions have been carried into the shelter.

II. Survival Work Priorities During a Crisis

Before building a KFM, persons expecting a nuclear attack within a few hours or days and already in the place where they intend to await attack should work with the following priorities: (1) build or improve a high-protection-factor shelter (if possible, a shelter covered with 2 or 3 feet of earth and separate from flammable buildings). At the same time, make and install a KAP (a homemade shelter-ventilating pump) -- if instructions and materials are available. If not available, at least make a Directional Fan. Also store at least 15 gallons of water for each shelter occupant -- if containers are available. (2) Assemble all materials for one or two KFM s. (3) Make and store the drying agent (by heating wallboard gypsum, as later described) for both the KFM and its dry-bucket. (4) Complete at least one KFM.

III. How to Use These Instructions to Best Advantage

1. Read ALOUD all of these instructions **through Section VII,** "Tools Needed," before doing anything else.

2. Next assemble all of the needed materials and tools.

3. Then read ALOUD ALL of each section following Section VII before beginning to make the part described in that section.

A FAMILY THAT FAILS TO READ ALOUD ALL OF EACH SECTION DESCRIBING HOW TO MAKE A PART, BEFORE BEGINNING TO MAKE THAT PART, WILL MAKE AVOIDABLE MISTAKES AND WILL WASTE TIME.

4. Have different workers, or pairs of workers, make the parts they are best qualified to make. For example, a less skilled worker should start making the drying agent (as described in Section VIII) before other workers start making other parts. The most skilled worker should make and install the aluminum-foil leaves (Sections X and XI).

5. Give workers the sections of the instructions covering the parts they are to build--so they can follow the step-by-step instructions, checking off with a pencil each step as it is completed.

6. Discuss the problems that arise. The head of the family often can give better answers if he first discusses the different possible interpretations of some instructions with other family members, especially teenagers.

7. After completing one KFM and learning to use it, if time permits make a second KFM--that should be a better instrument.

Pg 1 — (3)

Pg 1 — (2)

IV. What a KFM Is and How It Works

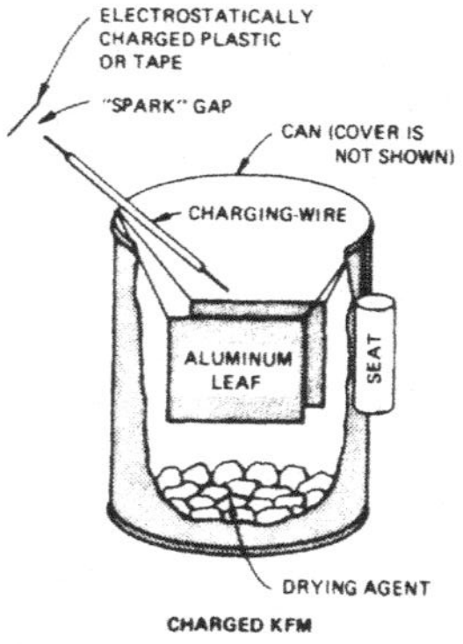

CHARGED KFM

A KFM is a simple electroscope-ionization chamber fallout meter with which fallout radiation can be measured accurately. To use a KFM, an electrostatic charge must first be placed on its **two** separate aluminum-foil leaves. These leaves are insulated by being suspended separately on clean, dry insulating threads.

To take accurate readings, the air inside a KFM must be kept very dry by means of drying agents such as dehydrated gypsum (easily made by heating gypsum wallboard, "sheetrock") or silica gel. (Do not use calcium chloride or other salt.) Pieces of drying agent are placed on the bottom of the ionization chamber (the housing can) of a KFM.

An electrostatic charge is transferred from a homemade electrostatic charging device to the two aluminum-foil leaves of a KFM by means of its charging-wire. The charging-wire extends out through the transparent plastic cover of the KFM.

When the two KFM leaves are charged electrostatically, their like charges (both positive or both negative) cause them to be forced apart. When fallout gamma radiation (that is similar to X rays but more energetic) strikes the air inside the ionization chamber of a KFM, it produces charged ions in this enclosed air. These charged ions cause part or all of the electrostatic charge on the aluminum-foil leaves to be discharged. As a result of losing charge, the two KFM leaves move closer together.

A KFM-maker who wants visual proof that his instrument can be partially or wholly discharged by ionizing radiation should persuade his dentist to place the charged KFM about 20 inches directly below a typical dental X-ray machine. For example, when a typical 90 kvp machine was set at 15 milliamps and for a 1/20th second pulse, its columnated X-ray beam partially discharged the KFM's separated aluminum-foil leaves, promptly reducing the initial reading of 15 mm to 9 mm. Other types of machines will require different settings. Many dental X-ray machines are not accurately calibrated, nor do they produce gamma rays, so such tests should not be used in an attempt to check the accuracy of a KFM.

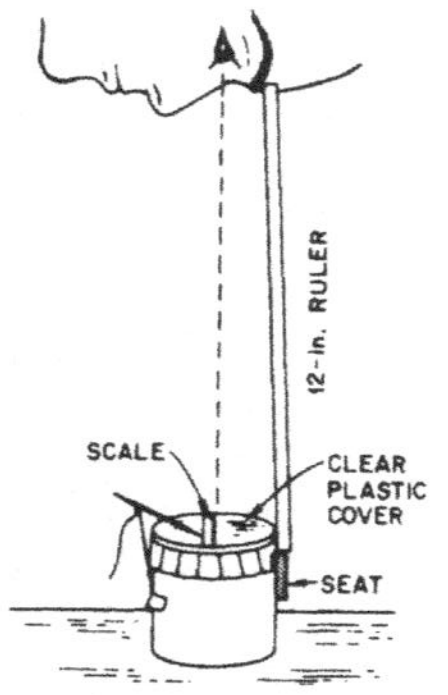

To read the separation of the lower edges of the two KFM leaves with one eye, look straight down on the leaves and the scale on the clear plastic cover. Keep the reading eye 12 inches above the SEAT. The KFM should be resting on a horizontal surface. To be sure the reading eye is always at this exact distance, place the lower end of a 12-inch ruler on the SEAT, while the upper end of the ruler touches the eyebrow above the reading eye. It is best to hold the KFM can with one hand and the ruler with the other. Using a flashlight makes the reading more accurate.

If a KFM is made and maintained with the specified dimensions and of the specified materials, ITS ACCURACY IS AUTOMATICALLY AND PERMANENTLY ESTABLISHED BY UNCHANGING LAWS OF NATURE. Unlike factory made radiation measuring instruments, A KFM NEVER NEEDS TO BE CALIBRATED OR TESTED WITH A RADIATION SOURCE. A KFM is used with a watch and the following table that is based on numerous calibrations made at Oak Ridge National Laboratory.

The millimeter scale is cut out and attached (see photo illustrations on the following page) to the clear plastic cover of the **KFM** so that its zero mark is directly above the two leaves in their discharged position when the **KFM** is resting on a horizontal surface. A reading of the separation of the leaves is taken by noting the number of millimeters that the **lower edge** of one leaf appears to be on, on one side of the zero mark on the scale, and almost at the same time noting the number of millimeters the **lower edge** of the other leaf appears to be on, on the other side of the zero mark. The **sum** of these two apparent positions of the lower edges of the two leaves is called a **KFM** reading. The drawing appearing after the photo illustrations shows the **lower** edges of the leaves of a KFM appearing to be 9 mm on the right of zero and 10 on the left, giving a KFM reading of 19 mm. (Usually the lower edges of the leaves are not at the same distance from the zero mark.)

As will be fully explained later, the radiation dose rate is determined by:

1. **charging and reading the KFM before exposure;**
2. exposing it to radiation for a specified time in the location where measurement of the dose rate is needed -- when outdoors, positioning the KFM about 3 ft. above the ground;
3. reading the **KFM** after its exposure;
4. calculating, by subtraction, the **difference** between the reading taken before exposure and the reading taken after exposure;
5. using this table to find what the dose rate was during the exposure -- as will be **described later.**

TABLE USED TO FIND DOSE RATES (R/HR) FROM KFM READINGS

**DIFFERENCE BETWEEN THE READING BEFORE EXPOSURE AND THE READING AFTER EXPOSURE (8-PLY STANDARD-FOIL LEAVES)*

DIFF.* IN READINGS	TIME INTERVAL OF AN EXPOSURE 15 SEC. R/HR	1 MIN. R/HR	4 MIN. R/HR	16 MIN. R/HR	1 HR. R/HR
2 mm	6.2	1.6	0.4	0.1	0.03
4 mm	12.	3.1	0.8	0.2	0.06
6 mm	19.	4.6	1.2	0.3	0.08
8 mm	25.	6.2	1.6	0.4	0.10
10 mm	31.	7.7	2.0	0.5	0.13
12 mm	37.	9.2	2.3	0.6	0.15
14 mm	43.	11.	2.7	0.7	0.18

Instructions on how to use a KFM are given after those detailing how to make and charge this fallout meter.

Pg 1 — (5)

Pg 1 — (4)

To get a clearer idea of the construction and use of a KFM, look carefully at the following photos and read their captions.

A. An Uncharged KFM. The charging wire has been pulled to one side by its adjustment-thread. This photo was taken looking straight down at the upper edges of the two flat, 8-ply aluminum leaves. At this angle the leaves are barely visible, hanging vertically side by side directly under the zero mark, touching each other and with their ends even. Their suspension-threads insulate the leaves. These threads are almost parallel and touch (but do not cross) each other where they extend over the top of the rim of the can.

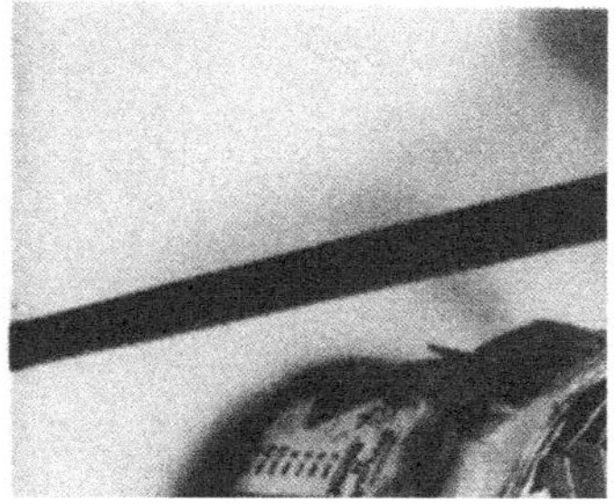

B. Charging a KFM by a Spark-Gap Discharge from a Tape That Has Been Electrostatically Charged by Being Unwound Quickly. Note that the charged tape is moved so that its surface is perpendicular to the charging-wire.

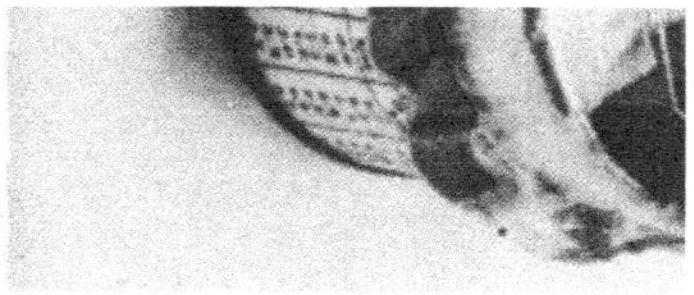

The high-voltage electrostatic charge on the unwound tape (that is an insulator) jumps the spark-gap between the tape and the upper end of the charging-wire, and then flows down the charging-wire to charge the insulated aluminum-foil leaves of the KFM. (Since the upper edges of the two leaves are ¾ inch below the scale and this is a photo taken at an angle, both leaves appear to be under the right side of the scale.)

C. A Charged KFM. Note the separation of the upper edges of its two leaves. The charging-wire has been raised to an almost horizontal position so that its lower end is too far above the aluminum leaves to permit electrical leakage from the leaves back up the charging-wire and into the outside air.

Also note the SEAT, a piece of pencil taped to the right side of the can, opposite the charging wire.

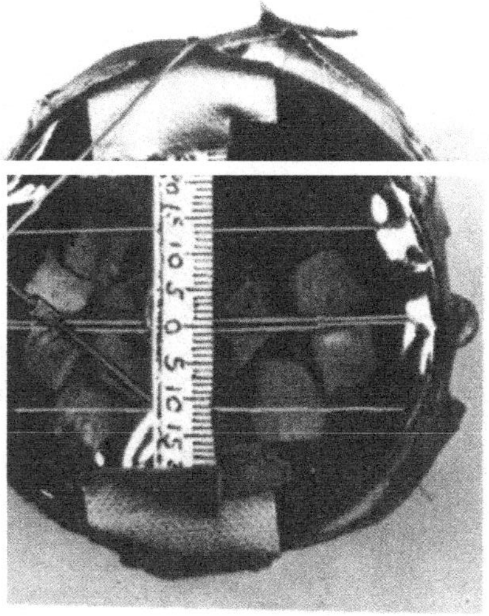

D. Reading a KFM. A 12-inch ruler rests on the SEAT and is held vertical, while the reader's eyebrow touches the upper end of the ruler. The lower edge of the right leaf is under 8 on the scale and the lower edge of the left leaf is under 6 on the scale, giving a KFM reading of 14.

For accurate radiation measurements, a KFM should be placed on an approximately horizontal surface, but the charges on its two leaves and their displacements do not have to be equal.

NOTE: In these photos, the paper scale is taped to the top of the transparent plastic-film cover. It is better to tape the scale to the under side of the cover, where it is less likely to be damaged.

Pg 2 — (7)

Pg 2 — (6)

INSTRUCTIONS, Page 5

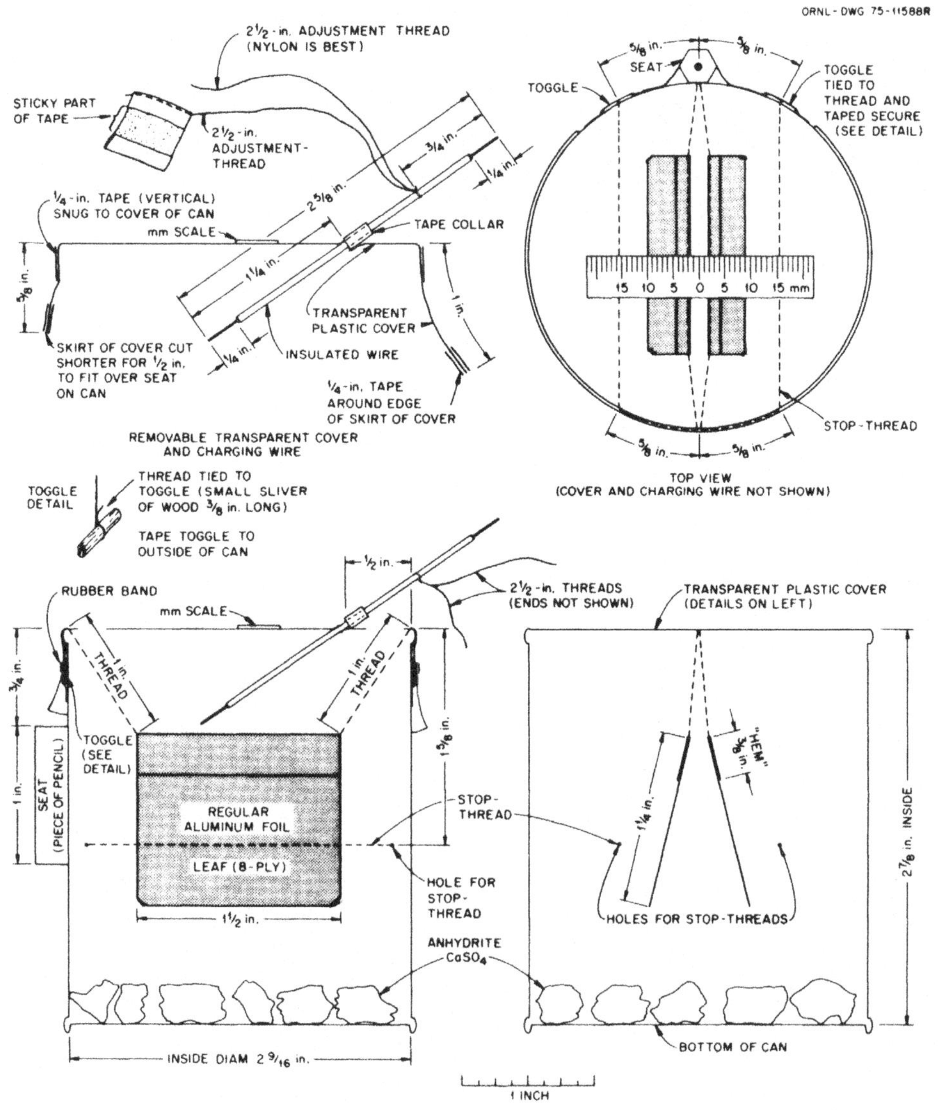

(This is not a Full Scale Drawing).

Pg 2 — (8)

V. Materials Needed

A. For the KFM: (In the following list, when more than one alternative material is given, the **best** material is listed first.)

1. Any type metal can, approximately 2-9/16 inches in diameter inside and 2-7/8 inches high inside, washed clean with soap. (This is the size of a standard 8-ounce can. Since most soup cans, pop cans, and beer cans also are about 2-9/16 inches in diameter inside, the required size of can also can be made by cutting down the height of more widely available cans — as described in Section IX of these instructions.)

2. Standard aluminum foil — 2 square feet. (In 1987, 2 square feet of widely sold U.S. brands of aluminum foil weighed between 8.0 and 8.5 grams. One gram equals 0.035 ounce.) (If only "Heavy Duty" or "Extra Heavy Duty" aluminum foil is available, make 5-ply leaves rather than 8-ply leaves of standard foil; the resultant fallout meter will be almost as accurate.)

3. Doorbell-wire, or other light insulated wire (preferably but not necessarily a single-strand wire inside the insulation — 6 inches.

4. Any type of **clean, fine** thread that has not been anti-static treated will serve to suspend a KFM's leaves. (Almost all kinds of sewing thread and fly-tying thread manufactured in 1987 are anti-static treated, are poor insulators, and are unsatisfactory.) In 1987 the best widely available excellent insulating thread is unwaxed dental floss: floss is not anti-static treated. Most unwaxed dental floss is too thick and stiff for properly suspending KFM leaves, but, since dental floss is not a twisted thread, you can make flexible strand-threads from it. Make each no more than one-quarter as thick as the floss, and about 12 inches long. First separate several strands at the end of the floss outside its dispenser. Then separate strands while pulling one way on the end of the strand-thread that you want and the other way on the unwanted strands. Use only a clean needle to touch and separate the strands in the middle 6 inches of the 12-inch-long piece of unwaxed dental floss.

   A widely sold dental floss, Johnson and Johnson's Extra Fine Unwaxed, drawn out of its dispenser without splitting it, makes quite satisfactory leaf-supporting threads. However, better leaf-supporting threads can be made by first separating any dental floss into thinner, more flexible threads.

   Very thin monofilament fishing line or leader is an excellent insulator. The 2-pound-test strength, such as Du Pont's "Stren" monofilament fishing line, is best. "Trilene" 2-pound "nylon leader," a monofilament manufactured by Berkley and Company, also is excellent. (A 4-pound monofilament line will serve, but is disadvantageously stiff.) Some modern monofilament lines or leaders such as "Trilene" contain an additive that makes them pliant, but also makes them poorer insulators for the first several hours after being taken out of their dispenser and used to suspend the leaves of a KFM. However, in about 6 hours the silica gel or anhydrite drying agent in a KFM removes this additive and the monofilament becomes as good an insulator as even strands of unwaxed dental floss.

   To minimize the chance of using a piece of monofilament or other thread that has been soiled and thus changed into a poor insulator, always first remove and discard the outermost layer of thread on any spool that has not been kept clean in a plastic bag or other packaging after being initially unwrapped.

   During a worsening crisis or after an attack, neither thread that has not been anti-static treated, nor unwaxed dental floss, nor clean 2-pound or 4-pound monofilament line may be available. However, most American homes have an excellent insulator, very thin polyethylene film — especially clean dry cleaners' bags. A narrow insulating strip cut only 1/16 inch wide can be used to suspend each KFM leaf, instead of an insulating thread. (Installed leaves suspended on strips of thin plastic film must be handled with care.)

   To cut 1/16-inch-wide strips from very thin polyethylene film, first cut a piece about 6 x 10 inches. Tape only the two 6-inch-wide ends to a piece of paper (such as a brown grocery bag), so that the film is held flat and smooth on the paper. Make 10 marks, 1/16-inch apart, on each of the two tapes that are holding the film. Place a light so that its reflection on the film enables you to see the edge of the film that you are preparing to cut. Then use a very sharp, **clean** knife or **clean** razor blade, guided by the edge of a firmly held ruler, to cut 9 strips, of which you will select the best two. When cutting, hold the knife **almost horizontal,** with the **plane of its blade perpendicular** to the taped-down film. Throughout this procedure avoid touching the center parts of the strips.

5. A piece of clear plastic film — a 6 x 6 inch square. Clear vinyl (4 mils thick) used for storm-proofing windows is best, but any reasonably stout and clear plastic will serve. The strong clear plastic used to wrap pieces of cheese, if washed with hot water and soap, is good. Do not use weak plastic or cellophane. Plastic film made from cellulose (such as Flex-O-Pane) and roasting bags are too permeable to water vapor.

6. Cloth duct tape ("silver tape"), or masking tape, or freezer tape, or Scotch-type tape —about 10 square inches. (A roll of Scotch Magic Transparent Tape, if available, should be saved for use in charging the KFM).

7. Band-Aid tape, or masking tape, or freezer tape, or Scotch transparent tape, or other thin and very flexible tapes — about 2 square inches.

8. Gypsum wallboard (sheetrock) — about 1/2 square foot, best about 1/2 inch thick, for a good homemade drying agent. (Silica gel with dark blue color indicator is an even better drying agent, but is not available in most communities. Available from chemical supply firms that supply high school chemistry classes. With dark blue silica gel in the bottom of a KFM, white typing correction fluid or white ink is needed to make the lower edges of a KFM's aluminum leaves easier to see.)

9. Glue — not essential, but useful to replace Band-Aid and other thin tapes. "One hour" epoxy is best. Model airplane cement is satisfactory.

10. An ordinary wooden pencil and a small toothpick (or split a small sliver of wood.)

11. Two strong rubber bands, or string.

12. Several small, transparent plastic bags, such as sandwich bags, to cover the KFM when it is exposed where fallout particles may get on it and contaminate it. Or pieces of thin, transparent plastic film, such as that from bread bags. Also small rubber bands, or string.

B. For the Charging Devices:

1. Most hard plastic rubbed on **dry** paper. This is the best method.

   a. Plexiglas and most other hard plastics, such as are used in draftsmen's triangles, common smooth plastic rulers, etc. — at least 6 inches long.

   b. **Dry** paper — Tough paper, such as clean, strong grocery-bag or typing paper. Tissue paper, newspaper, or facial tissue such as Kleenex, or toilet paper are satisfactory for charging, but not as durable.

2. Scotch Magic Transparent Tape (3/4 inch width is best), or Scotch Transparent Tape, or P.V.C. (Polyvinyl chloride) insulating electrical tapes, or a few of the other common brands of Scotch-type tapes. (Some plastic tapes do not develop sufficiently high-voltage electrostatic charges when unrolled quickly.) This method cannot be used for charging a KFM inside a dry-bucket, needed for charging when the air is very humid.

C. For Determining Dose Rates and Recording Doses Received:

1. A watch with a second hand.

2. A flashlight or other light, for reading the KFM in a dark shelter or at night.

3. Pencil and paper — preferably a notebook.

D. For the Dry-Bucket: A KFM must be charged inside a dry-bucket if the air is very humid, as it often is inside a crowded, long-occupied shelter lacking adequate forced ventilation.)

1. A large bucket, pot, or can, preferably with a top diameter of at least 11 inches.

2. Clear plastic (best is 4-mil-thick clear plastic used for storm windows). A square piece 5 inches wider on a side than the diameter of the bucket to be used.

3. Cloth duct tape, one inch wide and 8 feet long (or 4 ft., if 2 inches wide). Or 16 ft. of freezer tape one inch wide.

Pg 3 — (10)

Pg 3 — (9)

4. Two plastic bags 14 to 16 inches in circumference, such as ordinary plastic bread bags. The original length of these bags should be at least 5 inches greater than the height of the bucket.

5. About one square foot of wall board (sheetrock), to make anhydrite drying agent.

6. Two 1-quart Mason jars or other airtight containers, one in which to store anhydrite and another in which to keep dry the KFM charging devices.

7. Strong rubber bands -- enough to make a loop around the bucket. Or string.

VI. **Useful but not Essential Materials**
--Which Could be Obtained Before a Crisis--

1. An airtight container (such as a large peanut butter jar) with a mouth at least 4 inches wide, in which to keep a KFM, along with some drying agent, when it is not being used. Keeping a KFM very dry greatly extends the time during which the drying agent **inside** the KFM remains effective.

2. Commercial anhydrite with a color indicator, such as the drying agent Drierite. This granular form of anhydrite remains light blue as long as it is effective as a drying agent; it turns pink when it becomes ineffective. Or use silica gel with color indicator, that is dark blue when effective and that turns light pink when it becomes ineffective. Heating in a hot oven or in a can over a fire reactivates them as drying agents and restores their blue color. Obtainable from laboratory supply sources. Use enough to cover the bottom of the KFM's can no more than 1/2 inch deep.

3. Four square feet of aluminum foil, to make a moisture-proof cover for the dry-bucket.

VII. Tools Needed

Small nail - sharpened
Stick, or a wooden tool handle
  (best 2-2½ inch diameter and at least 12 inches long)
Hammer
Pliers
Scissors
Needle - quite a large sewing needle, but less than 2½ inches long
Knife with a small blade - sharp
Ruler (12 inches)
Desirable but not essential tools: a file and
  a fine-toothed hacksaw blade.

VIII. **Make the Drying Agent**
-- The Easiest Part to Make, but Time Consuming --

1. For a KFM to measure radiation accurately, the air inside its ionization chamber must be kept **very dry**. An excellent drying agent (anhydrite) can be made by heating the gypsum in ordinary gypsum wallboard (sheetrock). Do NOT use calcium chloride.

2. Take a piece of gypsum wallboard approximately 12 inches by 6 inches, and preferably with its gypsum about 3/8 inches thick. Cut off the paper and glue, easiest done by first wetting the paper. [Since water vapor from normal air penetrates the plastic cover of a KFM and can dampen the anhydrite and make it ineffective in as short a time as two days, fresh batches of anhydrite must be made before the attack and kept ready inside the shelter for replacement. The useful life of the drying agent inside a KFM can be greatly lengthened by keeping the KFM inside an airtight container (such as a peanut butter jar with a 4-inch-diameter mouth) with some drying agent, when the KFM is not being used.]

3. Break the white gypsum filling into small pieces and make the largest no more than 1/2 in. across. (The tops of pieces larger than this may be too close to the aluminum foil leaves.) If the gypsum is dry, using a pair of pliers makes breaking it easier. Make the largest **side** of the largest pieces no bigger than this.

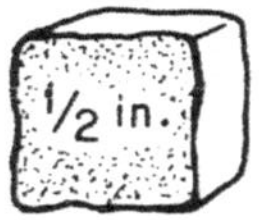

4. Dry gypsum is **not** a drying agent. To drive the water out of the gypsum molecules and produce the drying agent (anhydrite), heat the gypsum in an oven at its **highest** temperature (which should be above 400 degrees F) for one hour. Heat the gypsum after placing the small pieces no more than two pieces deep in a pan. Or heat the pieces over a fire for 20 minutes or more in a pan or can heated to a dull red.

5. If sufficient aluminum foil and time are available, it is best to heat the gypsum and store the anhydrite as follows:

   a. So that the right amount of anhydrite can be taken quickly out of its storage jar, put enough pieces of gypsum in a can with the same diameter as the KFM, measuring out a batch of gypsum that almost covers the bottom of the can with a single layer.

   b. Cut a piece of aluminum foil about 8 in. x 8 in. square, and fold up its edges to form a bowl-like container in which to heat one batch of gypsum pieces.

   c. Measure out 10 or 12 such batches, and put each batch in its aluminum foil "bowl."

   d. Heat all of these filled "bowls" of gypsum in hottest oven for one hour.

Pg 3 — (12)

Pg 3 — (11)

e. As soon as the aluminum foil is cool enough to touch, fold and crumple the edges of each aluminum foil "bowl" together, to make a rough aluminum-covered "ball" of each batch of anhydrite.

f. Promptly seal the batches in airtight jars or other airtight containers, and keep containers closed except when taking out an aluminum-covered "ball."

6. Since anhydrite absorbs water from the air very rapidly, quickly put it in a **dry** airtight container while it is still quite hot. A Mason jar is excellent.

7. To place anhydrite in a KFM, drop in the pieces one by one, being careful not to hit the leaves or the stop-threads. The pieces should almost cover the bottom of the can, with no piece on top of other pieces.
8. To remove anhydrite from a KFM, use a pair of scissors or tweezers as forceps, holding them in a vertical position and not touching the leaves.

IX. **Make the Ionization Chamber of the KFM**
(To Avoid Mistakes and Save Time,
Read All of This Section ALOUD Before Beginning Work.)

1. Remove the paper label (if any) from an ordinary 8-ounce can from which the top has been smoothly cut. Wash the can with soap and water and dry it. (An 8-ounce can has an inside diameter of about 2-9/16 inches and an inside height of about 2-7/8 inches.)

2. Skip to step 3 if an 8-ounce can is available. If an 8-ounce can is not available, reduce the height of any other can having an inside diameter of about 2-9/16 inches (such as most soup cans, most pop cans, or most beer cans). To cut off the top part of a can, first measure and mark the line on which to cut. Then to keep from bending the can while cutting, wrap newspaper tightly around a stick or a round wooden tool handle, so that the wood is covered with 20 to 30 thicknesses of paper and the diameter (ideally) is only slightly less than the diameter of the can.

One person should hold the can over the paper-covered stick while a second person cuts the can little by little along the marked cutting line. If leather gloves are available, wear them. To cut the can off smoothly, use a file, or use a hacksaw drawn backwards along the cutting line. Or cut the can with a sharp, short blade of a pocketknife by: (1) repeatedly stabbing downward vertically through the can into the paper, and (2) repeatedly making a cut about 1/4 inch long by moving the knife into a sloping position, while keeping its point still pressed into the paper covering the stick.

Next, smooth the cut edge, and cover it with small pieces of freezer tape or other flexible tape.

3. Cut out the PAPER PATTERN TO WRAP AROUND KFM CAN. (Cut one pattern out of Pattern Page A.) Glue (or tape) this pattern to the can, starting with one of the two short sides of the pattern. Secure this starting short side directly over the side seam of the can. Wrap the pattern snugly around the can, gluing or taping it securely as it is being wrapped. (If the pattern is too wide to fit flat between the rims of the can, trim a little off its lower edge.)

4. Sharpen a small nail, by filing or rubbing on concrete, for use as a punch to make the four holes needed to install the stop-threads in the ionization chamber (the can). (The stop-threads are insulators that stop the charged aluminum leaves from touching the can and being discharged.)

5. Have one person hold the can over a horizontal stick or a round wooden tool-handle, that ideally has a diameter about as large as the diameter of the can. Then a second person can use the sharpened nail and a hammer to punch four very small holes through the sides of the can at the points shown by the four crosses on the pattern. Make these holes just large enough to run a needle through them, and then move the needle in the holes so as to bend back the obstructing points of metal.

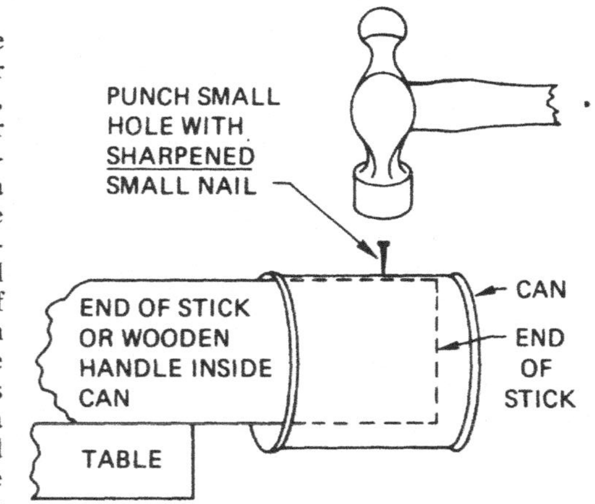

6. The stop-threads can be installed by using a needle to thread a single thread through all four holes. Use a **very clean** thread, preferably nylon, and do not touch the parts of this thread that will be inside the can and will serve as the insulating stop-threads. Soiled threads are poor insulators. (See illustrations.)

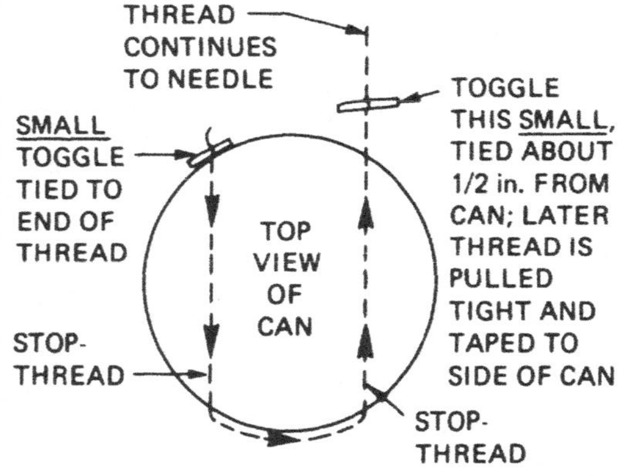

SINGLE THREAD THREADED THROUGH 4 HOLES TO MAKE 2 STOP-THREADS

Pg 4 — (14)

Pg 4 — (13)

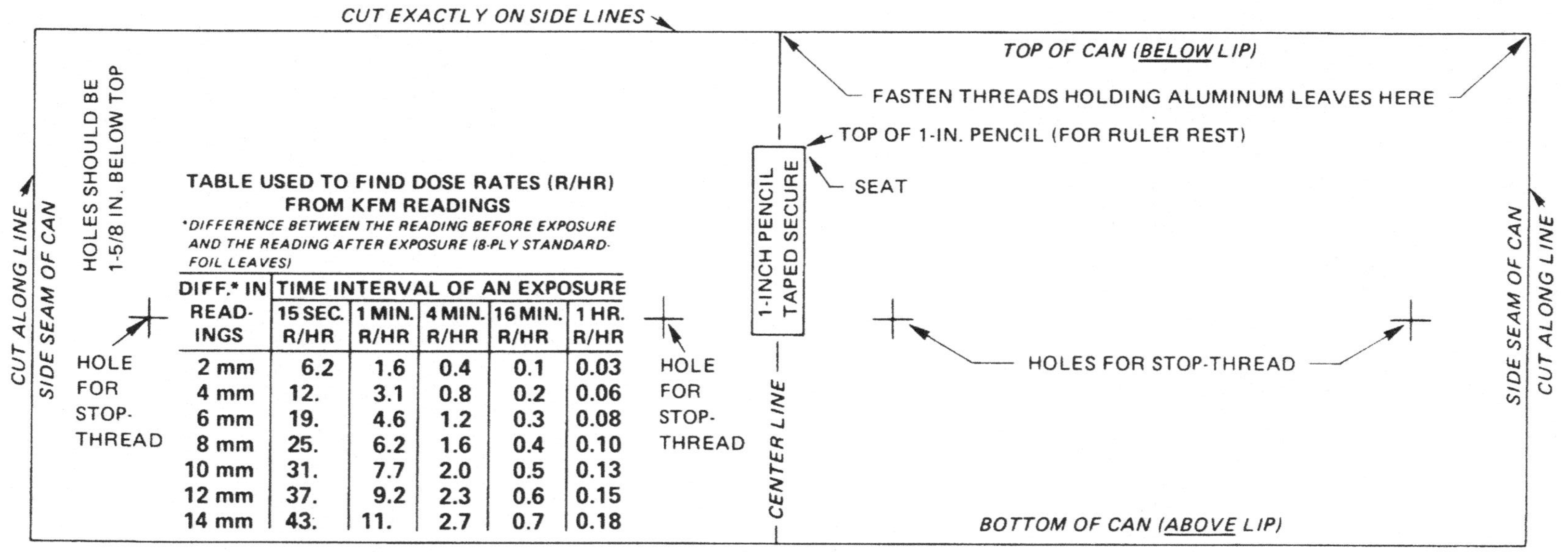

TABLE USED TO FIND DOSE RATES (R/HR) FROM KFM READINGS

*DIFFERENCE BETWEEN THE READING BEFORE EXPOSURE AND THE READING AFTER EXPOSURE (8-PLY STANDARD-FOIL LEAVES)

DIFF.* IN READ-INGS	TIME INTERVAL OF AN EXPOSURE				
	15 SEC. R/HR	1 MIN. R/HR	4 MIN. R/HR	16 MIN. R/HR	1 HR. R/HR
2 mm	6.2	1.6	0.4	0.1	0.03
4 mm	12.	3.1	0.8	0.2	0.06
6 mm	19.	4.6	1.2	0.3	0.08
8 mm	25.	6.2	1.6	0.4	0.10
10 mm	31.	7.7	2.0	0.5	0.13
12 mm	37.	9.2	2.3	0.6	0.15
14 mm	43.	11.	2.7	0.7	0.18

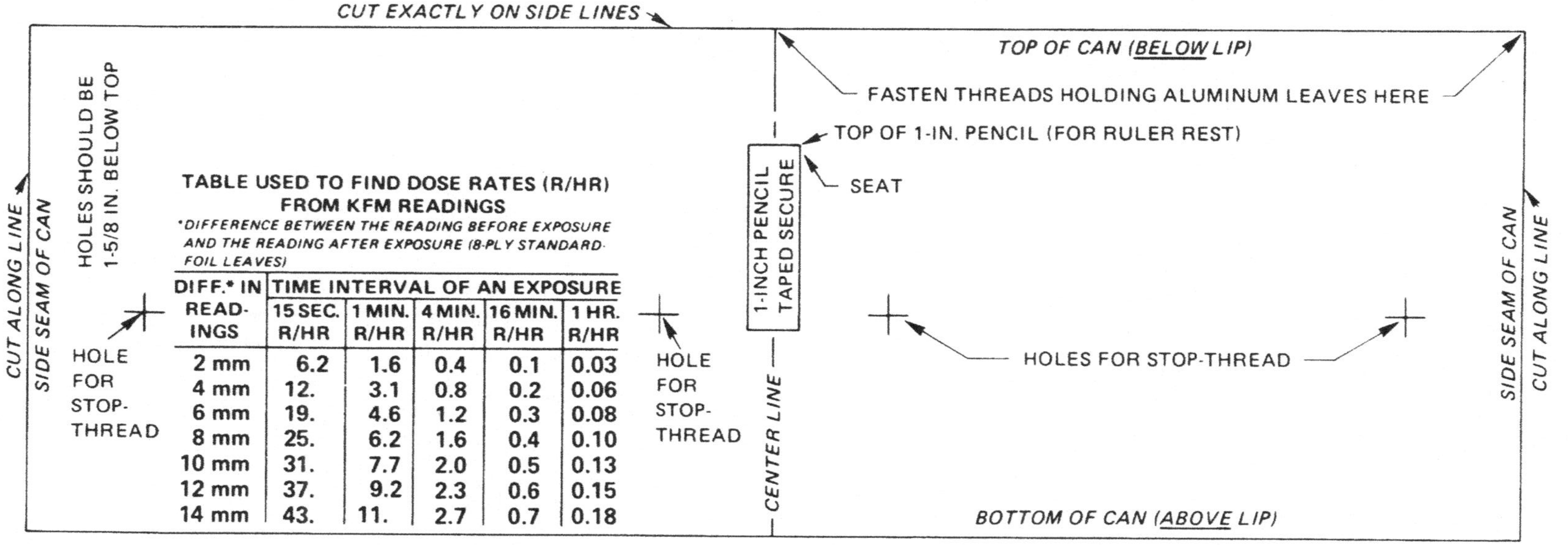

TABLE USED TO FIND DOSE RATES (R/HR) FROM KFM READINGS

*DIFFERENCE BETWEEN THE READING BEFORE EXPOSURE AND THE READING AFTER EXPOSURE (8-PLY STANDARD-FOIL LEAVES)

DIFF.* IN READ-INGS	TIME INTERVAL OF AN EXPOSURE				
	15 SEC. R/HR	1 MIN. R/HR	4 MIN. R/HR	16 MIN. R/HR	1 HR. R/HR
2 mm	6.2	1.6	0.4	0.1	0.03
4 mm	12.	3.1	0.8	0.2	0.06
6 mm	19.	4.6	1.2	0.3	0.08
8 mm	25.	6.2	1.6	0.4	0.10
10 mm	31.	7.7	2.0	0.5	0.13
12 mm	37.	9.2	2.3	0.6	0.15
14 mm	43.	11.	2.7	0.7	0.18

PAPER PATTERN TO WRAP AROUND KFM CAN (GLUE OR TAPE SECURELY TO CAN)

PATTERN PAGE (A)

CUT OUT THESE PATTERNS, EACH OF WHICH IS THE EXACT SIZE FOR A KFM.

CAUTION: XEROX COPIES OF THESE PATTERNS MAY BE TOO LARGE.

Pg 5 — (15)

Before threading the thread through the four holes, tie a **small** toggle (see the preceding sketch) to the long end of the thread. (This toggle can easily be made of a very small sliver of wood cut about 3/8 in. long.) After the thread has been pulled through the four holes, attach a second toggle to the thread, about 1/2 inch from the part of the thread that comes out of the fourth hole. Then the thread can be pulled tightly down the side of the can and the second small toggle can be taped securely in place to the side of the can. (If the thread is taped down without a toggle, it is likely to move under the tape.)

The first toggle and all of the four holes also should be covered with tape, to prevent air from leaking into the can after it has been covered and is being used as an ionization chamber.

X. **Make Two Separate 8-Ply Leaves of Standard [Not Heavy Duty*] Aluminum Foil**

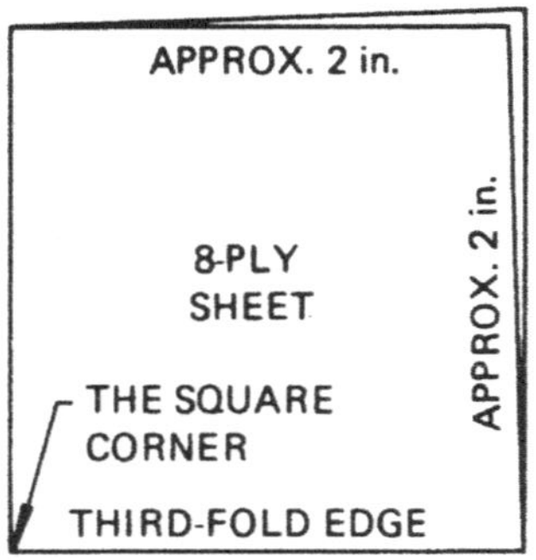

Proceed as follows to make each leaf:

1. Cut out a piece of standard aluminum foil approximately 4 inches by 8 inches.

2. Fold the aluminum foil to make a 2-ply (= 2 thicknesses) sheet approximately 4 inches by 4 inches.

3. Fold this 2-ply sheet to make a 4-ply sheet approximately 2 inches by 4 inches.

4. Fold this 4-ply sheet to make an 8-ply sheet (8 sheets thick) approximately 2 inches by 2 inches, being **sure** that the two halves of the second-fold edge are exactly together. This third folding makes an 8-ply aluminum foil sheet with **one corner exactly square**.

5. **Cut out** the FINISHED-LEAF PATTERN, found on the following Pattern Page B. Note that this pattern is **NOT** a square and that it is **smaller** than the 8-ply sheet. Flatten the 8 thicknesses of aluminum foil with the fingers until they appear to be a single thin, flat sheet.

6. Hold the FINISHED-LEAF PATTERN **on top of** the 8-ply aluminum foil sheet, with the pattern's THIRD-FOLD EDGE on top of the third-fold edge of the 8-ply aluminum sheet. Be sure that one lower **corner** of the FINISHED-LEAF PATTERN is on top of the **exactly square corner** of the 8-ply aluminum sheet.

7. While holding a straight edge along the THREAD LINE of the pattern, press with a sharp pencil so as to make a shallow groove for the THREAD LINE on the 8-ply aluminum sheet. Also using a sharp pencil, trace around the top and side of the pattern, so as to indent (groove) the 8-ply foil.

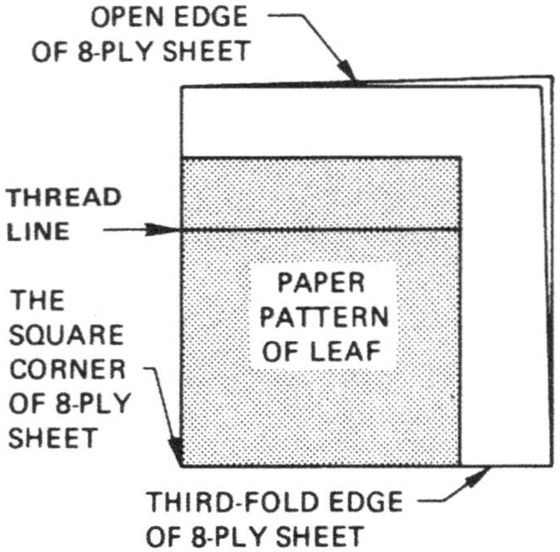

8. Remove the pattern and cut out the 8-ply aluminum foil leaf. Then, in order to prevent possible excessive electrical discharge from overly sharp points on the lower corners of the leaf, cut about 1/16-inch (◢) off each of its two lower corners.

9. While holding a straight edge along the indented THREAD LINE, lift up the OPEN EDGE of the 8-ply sheet (keeping all 8 plies together) until this edge is vertical, as illustrated. Remove the straight edge, and fold the 8-ply aluminum along the THREAD LINE so as to make a **flat-folded** hem.

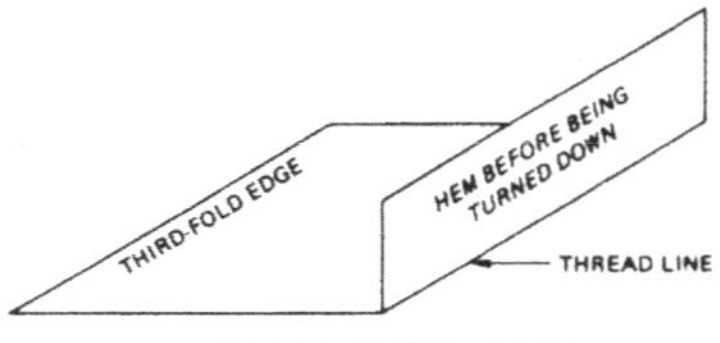

8-PLY LEAF WITH ITS OPEN EDGE FOLDED TO VERTICAL POSITION

10. Open the flat-folded hem of the finished leaf until the 8-ply leaf is almost flat again, as shown by the pattern, from which the FINISHED-LEAF PATTERN has already been cut.

11. Prepare to attach the aluminum-foil leaf to the thread that will suspend it inside the KFM.

---

*If only heavy duty aluminum foil (sometimes called "extra heavy duty") is available, make 5-ply leaves of the same size, and use the table for the 8-ply KFM to determine radiation dose rates. To make a 5-ply leaf, start by cutting out a piece of foil approximately 4 inches by 4 inches. Fold it to make a 4-ply sheet approximately 2 inches by 2 inches, with one corner exactly square. Next from a single thickness of foil cut a square approximately 2 inches by 2 inches. Slip this square into a 4-ply sheet, thus making a 5-ply sheet. Then make the 5-ply leaf, using the FINISHED-LEAF PATTERN, etc. as described for making an 8-ply leaf.

Pg 4 — (17)

Pg 4 — (16)

PATTERN FOR CLEAR-PLASTIC COVER FOR KFM CAN

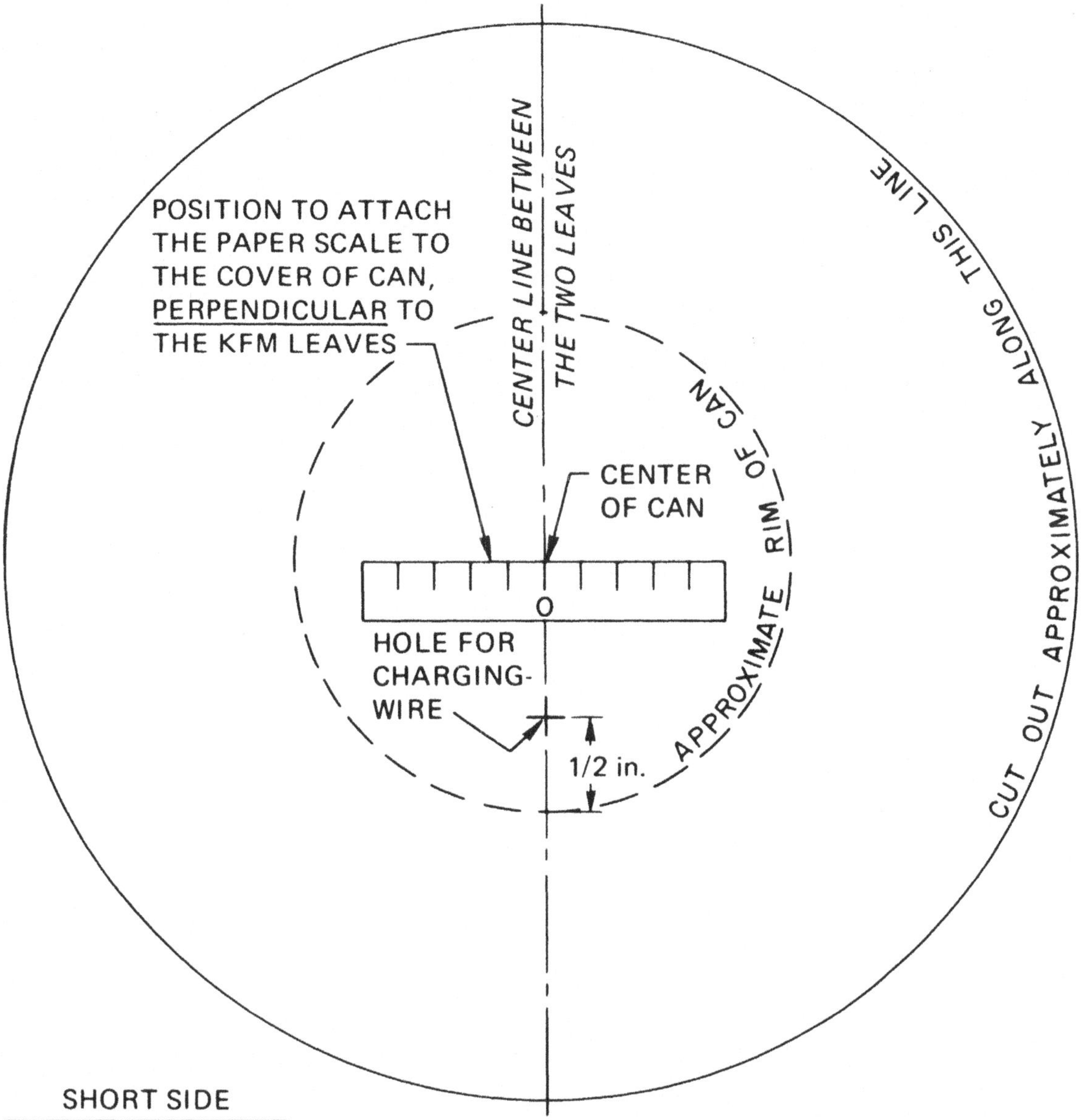

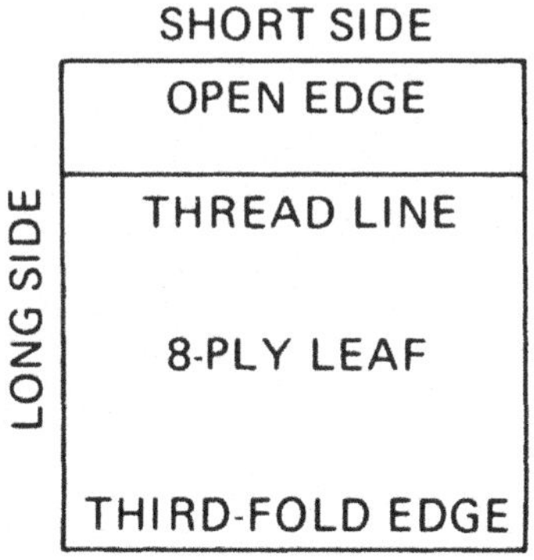

FINISHED-LEAF PATTERN
(CUT OUT EXACTLY ON SIDE LINES)

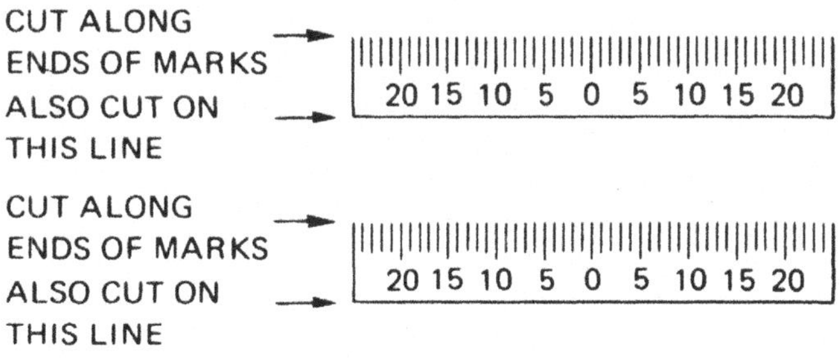

PAPER SCALE (TO BE CUT OUT)

PATTERN PAGE (B)

CAUTION: XEROX COPIES OF THE FINISHED-LEAF AND THE SCALE PATTERNS MAY BE SLIGHTLY TOO LARGE.

Pg 5 — (18)

If no epoxy glue* is available to hold down the hem and prevent the thread from slipping in the hem, cut two pieces of tape (Band-Aid tape is best; next best is masking or freezer tape; next best, Scotch tape). After first peeling off the paper backing of Band-Aid tape, cut each piece of tape 1/8 inch by 1 inch long. Attach these two pieces of tape to the finished 8-ply aluminum leaf with the sticky sides up, except for their ends. As shown by the pattern on the following pattern page, secure 1/8 inch of one end of a tape strip near one corner of the 8-ply aluminum foil leaf by first turning under this 1/8-inch end; that is, with this end's sticky side down. Then turn under the other 1/8-inch-long end, and attach this end below the THREAD LINE. **Slant** each tape strip as illustrated on Pattern (C).

Be sure you have read through step 18 before you do anything else.

12. Cut an 8-1/2 inch piece of fine, unwaxed, **very clean** thread that has not been anti-static treated. See INSTRUCTIONS, Page 6 for excellent insulating threads and substitutes. In 1986 most sewing threads are anti-static treated and are too poor insulators for use in a KFM.

    Cut out Pattern (C), the guide sheet used when attaching a leaf to its suspending thread. Then tape Pattern (C) to the top of a work table. Cover the two "TAPE HERE" rectangles on Pattern (C) with pieces of tape, each piece the size of the rectangle. Then cut two other pieces of tape each the same size and use them to **tape the thread ONTO the guide sheet**, on top of the "TAPE HERE" rectangles.

    Be very careful **not to touch** the two 1-inch parts of the thread next to the outline of the finished leaf, since oil and dirt even on clean fingers will reduce the electrical insulating value of the thread between the leaf and the top rim of the can.

13. With the thread still taped to the paper pattern and while slightly lifting the thread with a knife tip held under the center of the thread, slip the finished leaf **under** the thread and into position exactly on the top of the leaf outlined on the pattern page. Hold the leaf in this position with two fingers.

14. While keeping the thread straight between its two taped-down ends, lower the thread so that it sticks to the two plastic strips. Then press the thread against the plastic strips.

15. With the point of the knife, hold down the center of the thread against the center of the THREAD LINE of the leaf. Then, with two fingers, carefully fold over the hem and press it almost flat. Be sure that the thread comes out of the corners of the hem. Remove the knife, and press the hem down completely flat against the rest of the leaf.

16. Make **small** marks on the thread at the two points shown on the pattern page. Use a ballpoint pen if available.

17. Loosen the second two small pieces of tape from the pattern paper, but leave these tapes stuck to the thread.

18. Cut 5 pieces of Band-Aid tape, each approximately 1/8 inch by 1/4 inch, this small. 

    Use 2 of these pieces of tape to secure the centers of the side edges of the leaf. Place the 5 pieces as illustrated in the SIDE VIEW sketch below. Or use tiny droplets of epoxy, applied with a needle, to secure the side edges and to hold down the hem.

ORNL-DWG 76-6542

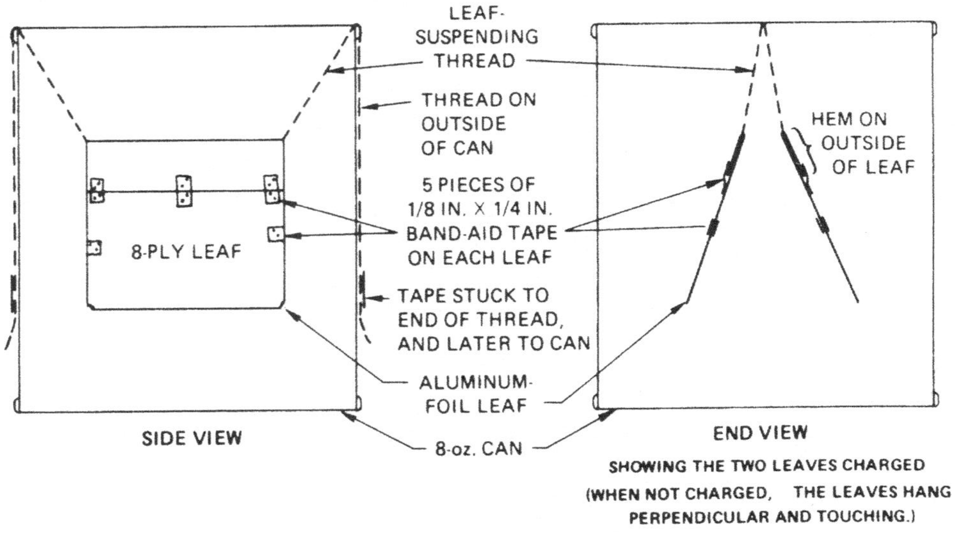

19. To prevent possible partial discharge from overly sharp lower corners of the leaves, use scissors to cut about 1/16 inch (▲) off each lower corner of the two leaves. (Partial discharge from an overly sharp corner may prevent a KRM's leaves from being adequately charged and adequately separated.)

20. To make it easier to take accurate readings:
    a. Make a black stripe 1/8-inch wide on the hem side of the lower edge of each leaf, if the drying agent to be used is white anhydrite made from gypsum, or light blue Drierite. It is best to use a waterproof marker, such as black Marko by Flair.
    b. Make a white stripe, if the drying agent to be used is dark blue silica gel. Liquid Paper correction fluid, or white ink, serves well.

*If using epoxy or other glue, use only a **very** little to hold down the hem, to attach the thread securely to the leaf and to glue together any open edges of the plied foil. Most convenient is "one hour" epoxy, applied with a toothpick. Model airplane cement requires hours to harden when applied between sheets of aluminum foil. To make sure no glue stiffens the free thread beyond the upper corners of the finished leaf, put no glue within 1/4 inch of a point where thread will go out from the folded hem of the leaf.

The instructions in step 11 are for persons lacking "one hour" epoxy or the time required to dry other types of glue. Persons using glue instead of tape to attach the leaf to its thread should make appropriate use of the pattern on the following page and of some of the procedures detailed in steps 12 through 18.

Pg 7 — (20)

Pg 7 — (19)

COVER THE TWO "TAPE HERE" RECTANGLES WITH SAME-SIZED PIECES OF TAPE, IN ORDER TO KEEP FROM TEARING THIS PAPER WHEN REMOVING TWO ADDITIONAL PIECES OF TAPE. THEN, BY PUTTING TWO OTHER PIECES OF TAPE THIS SAME SIZE ON TOP OF THE FIRST TWO PIECES, TAPE THE THREAD ONTO THIS GUIDE SHEET, AND LATER ATTACH A LEAF TO THE TAPED-DOWN THREAD.

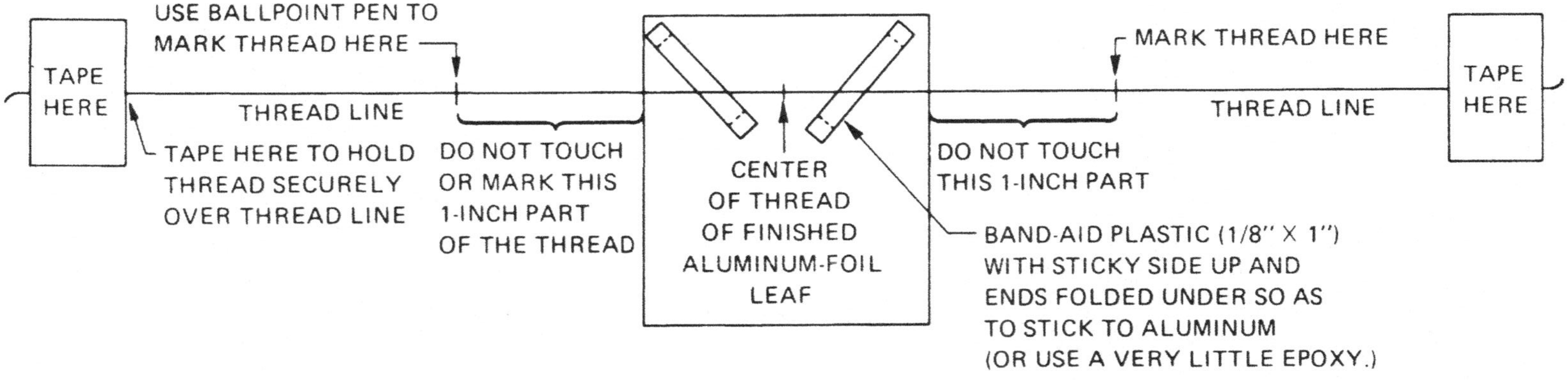

PATTERN (C)
(Cut out this guide along its border lines and tape to the top of a work table.)

WARNING: The parts of the thread that will be inside the can and on which the leaf will be suspended must serve to insulate the high-voltage electrical charges to be placed on the leaf. Therefore, the suspended parts of the thread must be kept very clean.

Pg 9 — (21)

XI. Install the Aluminum-Foil Leaves

1. In preparation for suspending the leaves inside the can, make two shallow notches in the top of the rim of the can. Make one notch above each of the two lines ("FASTEN THREADS HOLDING ALUMINUM LEAVES HERE") on the paper Pattern attached to the outside of the can. Make flat-bottomed notches by first filing a V-shaped notch, and then using a fine-toothed hacksaw blade to make the notch rectangular. (If a file and/or a hacksaw blade are not available, the leaf-suspending threads can be taped to the top of the rim of the can.)

2. Use the two small pieces of tape stuck to the ends of a leaf-suspending thread to attach the thread to the outside of the can. Attach the tapes on opposite sides of the can, so as to suspend the leaf inside the can. See END VIEW sketch. Each of the two **marks** on the attached thread MUST **rest exactly in a notch** (or on the top of the rim of the can, if you are unable to make notches). Be sure that the hem-side of each of the two leaves will face outward. See END VIEW sketch.

3. Position and secure the second leaf, being sure that:

   a. The smooth sides of the two leaves are not wrinkled or bent and face each other, and are flush (= "right together") when not charged. See END VIEW sketch and study the first photo illustration, "An Uncharged KFM".

   b. The upper edges of the two leaves are suspended side by side and at the same distance below the top of the can.

   c. The leaf-suspending threads are in their notches in the top of the rim of the can (or are taped with Band-Aid to the top of the rim of the can) so that putting the cover on will not move the threads.

   d. No parts of the leaf-suspending threads inside the can are taped down to the can or otherwise restricted.

   e. The leaf-suspending parts of the threads inside the can do not cross over, entangle or restrict each other.

   f. The threads come together where they go over the rim of the can, and the leaves are flat and hang together as shown in the first photo illustration, "An Uncharged KFM".

   g. The leaves look like these photographed leaves. If not, make new, better leaves and install them.

4. Cover with tape the parts of the threads that extend down the **outside** of the can, and also cover with more tape the small pieces of tape near the ends of the threads on the outside of the can. Or use epoxy or other waterproof glue to attach the parts of the threads on the <u>outside</u> of the can securely to the can.

5. **To make the SEAT, cut a piece of a wooden pencil, or a stick, about one inch long and tape it securely to the side of the can along the center line marked SEAT on the pattern. Be sure the upper end of this piece of pencil is at the same position as the top of the location for the SEAT outlined on the pattern. The top of the SEAT is 3/4 inch below the top of the can. Be sure not to cover or make illegible any part of the table printed on the paper pattern.**

6. Cut out one of the "Reminders for Operators" and glue and/or tape it to the unused side of the KFM. Then it is best to cover all the sides of the finished KFM with clear plastic tape or varnish. This will keep sticky-tape on the end of an adjustment thread or moisture from damaging the "Reminders" or the table.

XII. Make the Plastic Cover

1. Cut out the paper pattern for the cover from the Pattern Page (B).

2. **From a piece of clear, strong plastic, cut a circle approximately the same size as the paper pattern. (Storm-window vinyl film, 4 mils thick, is best.)**

3. Stretch the center of this circular piece of clear plastic over the open end of the can, and pull it down close to the sides of the can, making small tucks in the "skirt," so that there are no wrinkles in the top cover. Hold the lower part of the "skirt" in place with a strong rubber band or piece of string. (If another can having the same diameter as the KFM can is available, use it to make the cover -- to avoid the possibility of disturbing the leaf-suspending threads.)

4. Make the cover so it fits snugly, but can be taken off and replaced readily.

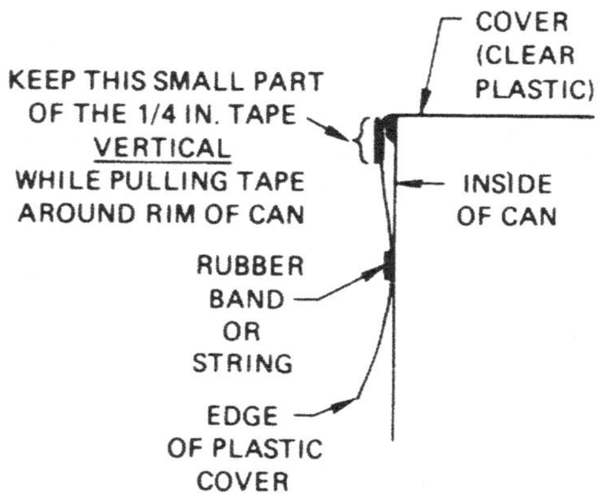

Just below the top of the rim of the can, bind the covering plastic in place with a 1/4-inch-wide piece of strong tape. (Cloth duct tape is best. Use two thicknesses. If only freezer or masking tape is available, use three or four thicknesses.)

Keep vertical the small part of the tape that presses against the rim of the can while pulling the length of the tape horizontally around the can so as to bind the top of the plastic cover snugly to the rim. If this small part of the tape is kept vertical, the lower edge of the tape will not squeeze the plastic below the rim of the can to such a small circumference as to prevent the cover from being removed quite easily.

Pg 7 — (23)

Pg 7 — (22)

REMINDERS FOR OPERATORS

The **drying agent** inside a KFM is O.K. if, when the charged KFM is **not** exposed to radiation, its readings decrease by 1 mm or less in 3 hours.

Reading: With the reading eye 12 inches vertically above the seat, note on the mm scale the separation of the **lower** edges of the leaves. If the right leaf is at 10 mm and the left leaf is at 7 mm, the KFM reads 17 mm. Never take a reading while a leaf is touching a stop-thread. Never use a KFM reading that is less than 5 mm.

Finding a dose rate: If before exposure a KFM reads 17 mm and if after a 1-minute exposure it reads 5 mm, the difference in readings is 12 mm. The attached table shows the dose rate was 9.6 R/hr during the exposure.

Finding a dose: If a person works outside for 3 hours where the dose rate is 2 R/hr, what is his radiation dose? Answer: 3 hr x 2 R/hr = 6 R.

Finding how long it takes to get a certain R dose: If the dose rate is 1.6 R/hr outside and a person is willing to take a 6 R dose, how long can he remain outside? Answer:
6 R ÷ 1.6 R/hr = 3.75 hr =
3 hours and 45 minutes.

Fallout radiation guides for a healthy person not previously exposed to a total radiation dose of more than 100 R during a 2-week period:

6 R per day can be tolerated for up to two months without losing the ability to work.

100 R in a week or less is not likely to seriously sicken.

350 R in a few days results in a 50-50 chance of dying, under post-attack conditions.

600 R in a week or less is almost certain to cause death within a few weeks.

REMINDERS FOR OPERATORS

The **drying agent** inside a KFM is O.K. if, when the charged KFM is **not** exposed to radiation, its readings decrease by 1 mm or less in 3 hours.

Reading: With the reading eye 12 inches vertically above the seat, note on the mm scale the separation of the **lower** edges of the leaves. If the right leaf is at 10 mm and the left leaf is at 7 mm, the KFM reads 17 mm. Never take a reading while a leaf is touching a stop-thread. Never use a KFM reading that is less than 5 mm.

Finding a dose rate: If before exposure a KFM reads 17 mm and if after a 1-minute exposure it reads 5 mm, the difference in readings is 12 mm. The attached table shows the dose rate was 9.6 R/hr during the exposure.

Finding a dose: If a person works outside for 3 hours where the dose rate is 2 R/hr, what is his radiation dose? Answer: 3 hr x 2 R/hr = 6 R.

Finding how long it takes to get a certain R dose: If the dose rate is 1.6 R/hr outside and a person is willing to take a 6 R dose, how long can he remain outside? Answer:
6 R ÷ 1.6 R/hr = 3.75 hr =
3 hours and 45 minutes.

Fallout radiation guides for a healthy person not previously exposed to a total radiation dose of more than 100 R during a 2-week period:

6 R per day can be tolerated for up to two months without losing the ability to work.

100 R in a week or less is not likely to seriously sicken.

350 R in a few days results in a 50-50 chance of dying, under post-attack conditions.

600 R in a week or less is almost certain to cause death within a few weeks.

Pg 9 — (24)

5. **With scissors, cut off the "skirt" of the plastic cover until it extends only about one inch below the top of the rim of the can.**

6. **Make a notch in the "skirt," about one inch wide, where it fits over the pencil SEAT attached to the can. The "skirt" in this notched area should be only about 5/8 of an inch long, measured down from the top of the rim of the can.**

7. **Remove the plastic cover, and then tape the lower edges of the "skirt," inside and out, using short lengths of 1/4-inch-wide tape. Before securing each short piece of tape, slightly open the tucks that are being taped shut on their edges, so that the "skirt" flares slightly outward and the cover can be readily removed.**

8. Make the charging-wire by using the full-size, exact-size pattern on the right.

Doorbell wire with an outside diameter of about 1/16 inch is best, but any lightweight insulated wire, such as part of a lightweight two-wire extension cord split in half, will serve. The illustrated wire is much thicker than bell wire. To stop tape from possibly slipping up or down the wire, use a very little glue.

If a very thin plastic has been used for the cover, a sticky piece of tape may need to be attached to the end of the bare-ended adjustment thread, so both threads can be used to hold the charging wire in a desired position.

The best tape to attach to an end of one of the adjustment-threads is cloth duct tape. A square piece 3/4 inch by 3/4 inch is the sticky base. To keep this tape sticky (free of paper fibers), the paper on the can should be covered with transparent tape or varnish. A piece about 1/8 inch by 3/4 inch serves to stick under one end of the sticky base, to hold the adjustment-thread. A 3/4 inch by 1-1/4 inch rectangular piece of tape is used to make the finger hold -- important for making adjustments inside a dry-bucket.

With a needle or pin, make a hole in the plastic cover 1/2 inch from the rim of the can and directly above the upper end of the CENTER LINE between the two leaves. The CENTER LINE is marked on the pattern wrapped around the can. Carefully push the CHARGING-WIRE through this hole (thus stretching the hole) until all of the CHARGING-WIRE below its Band-Aid-tape stop is inside the can.

9. **From the Pattern Page (B) cut out the SCALE. Then tape the SCALE to the under side of the plastic cover, in the position shown on the pattern for the cover, and also by the drawings. Preferably use transparent tape. Be careful not to cover with tape any of the division lines on the SCALE between 20 on the right and 20 on the left of 0.**

10. **Put the plastic cover on the KFM can.**

EXACT SIZE

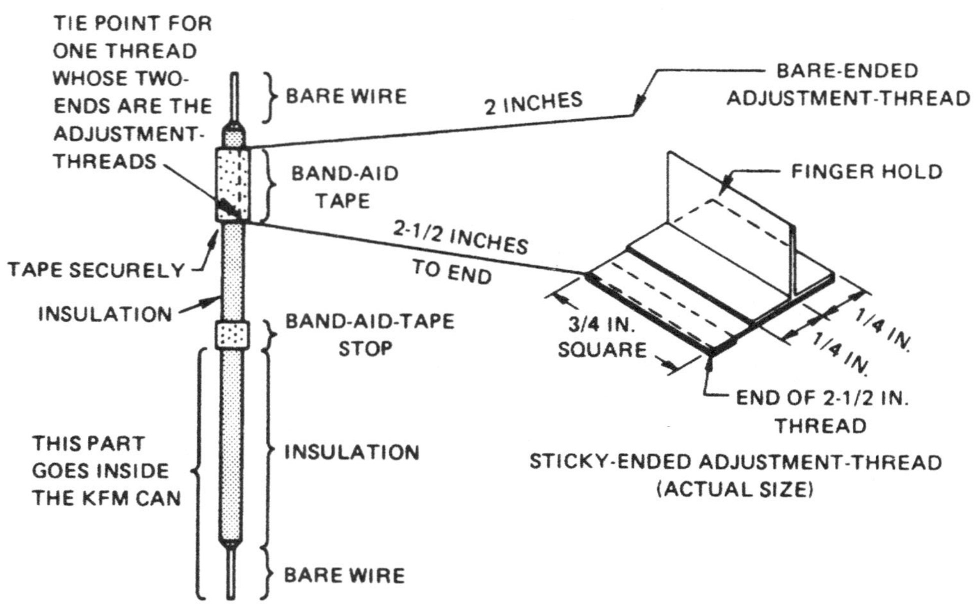

CHARGING-WIRE

(= LIGHT INSULATED WIRE) (BELL-WIRE IS BEST)

STICKY—ENDED ADJUSTMENT—THREAD (OVERSIZED DRAWING)

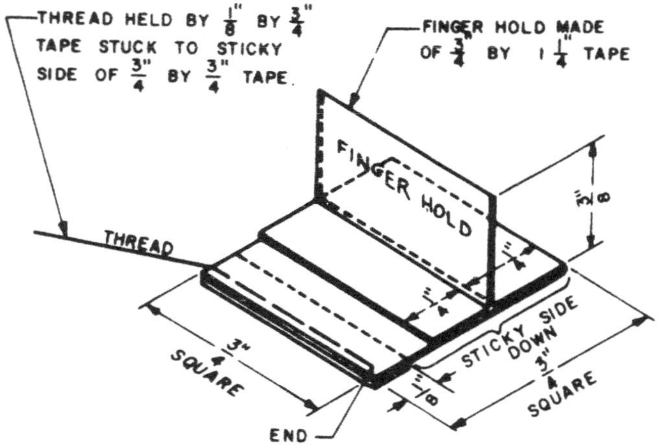

Pg 8 — (26)

Pg 8 — (25)

XIII. Two Ways to Charge a KFM

When preparing to charge a KFM, be sure its anhydrite is fresh. (Under humid conditions, sometimes in only 2 days enough water vapor will go through the plastic cover to make the drying agent ineffective.) Be sure no piece of anhydrite is on top of another piece. Re-read VIII 7 and VIII 8.

1. Charging a KFM with Hard Plastic Rubbed on **Dry** Paper.

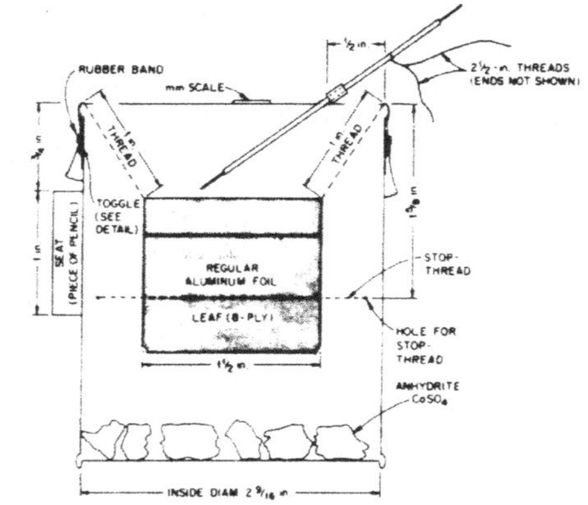

a. Adjust the charging-wire so that its lower end is about 1/16 inch above the upper edges of the aluminum-foil leaves. Use the sticky-tape at the end of one adjustment-thread to hold the charging-wire in this position. Stick this tape approximately in line with the threads suspending the leaves, either on the side of the can or on top of the plastic cover. (If the charging-wire is held loosely by the cover, it may be necessary to put a piece of sticky-tape on the end of each adjustment-thread in order to adjust the charging-wire securely. If a charging-wire is not secure, its lower end may be forced up by the like charge on the leaves before the leaves can be fully charged.)

b. Select a piece of Plexiglas, a draftsman's plastic triangle, a smooth plastic ruler, or other piece of hard, smooth plastic. **(Unfortunately, not all types of hard plastic can be used to generate a sufficient electrostatic charge.)** Be sure the plastic is dry.

For charging a KFM (especially inside a dry-bucket), cut a rectangular piece of hard plastic such as Plexiglas about 1-1/2 by 6 inches. Sharp corners and edges should be smoothed. To avoid contaminating the charging end with sweaty, oily fingers, it is best to mark the other end with a piece of tape, and to hold it only by its taped end.

c. Fold **DRY** paper (a piece of clean paper bag, or other smooth, clean paper) to make an approximate square about 5 inches on a side and 15 to 20 sheets thick. (This many sheets of paper lessens leakage to the fingers of the electrostatic high-voltage charges to be generated on the hard plastic and on the rubbed paper.)

d. Fold the square of paper in the middle, and move the hard plastic rapidly back and forth so that it is rubbed **vigorously** on the paper in the middle of this folded square —while the outside of this folded square of paper is squeezed firmly between thumb and little finger on one side, and the ends of three fingers on the other. To avoid discharging the charge on the plastic to the fingers, keep them away from the edges of the paper. See sketch.

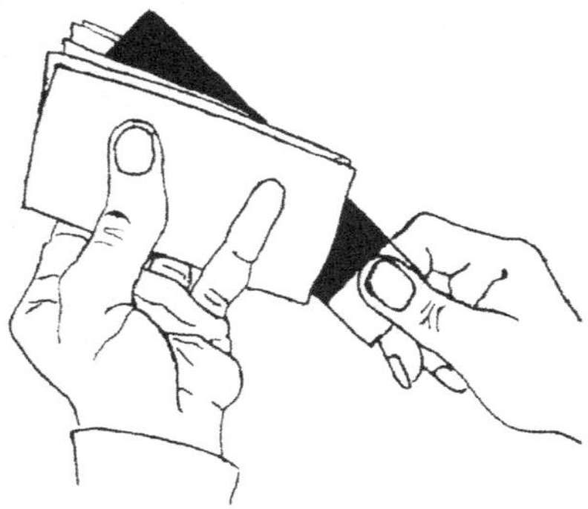

e. Move the electrostatically charged part of the rubbed plastic rather slowly past the upper end of the charging-wire, while looking straight down on the KFM. Keep the hard plastic approximately perpendicular to the charging-wire and about 1/4 to 1/2 inch away from its upper end. The charge jumps the spark gaps and charges the leaves of the KFM. **Charge the leaves sufficiently to give a reading of at least 15 mm.**

f. Pull down on an insulating adjustment-thread to raise the lower end of the charging-wire. (If the charging-wire has been held in its charging position by its sticky-ended adjustment-thread being stuck to the top of the clear plastic cover, to avoid possibly damaging the threads: (1) pull down a little on the bare-ended adjustment-thread; and (2) detach, pull down on, and secure the sticky-ended adjustment-thread to the side of the can, so as to raise and keep the lower end of the charging-wire close to the underside of the clear plastic cover.) **Do not touch the charging-wire,** because its insulation usually is not good enough to prevent the charge from bleeding off into the fingers.

g. To get the most accurate readings possible, lightly bump or shake the charged KFM (to remove any unstable part of the charge) before taking the initial reading.

h. If the initial reading is more than 20 mm, to get the most accurate reading possible carefully partially discharge the leaves (by touching them with the charging-wire while guiding the wire with your fingers on its insulation), to reduce to 20 mm or slightly less the initial reading that you will use. Or completely discharge, and recharge to 20 mm or slightly less.

i. To keep a KFM in excellent condition and to enable its drying agent to last much longer before becoming ineffective, put the whole KFM in an airtight container, such as a large peanut butter jar, with drying agent about an inch deep on its bottom. Or at least keep the charging paper and the hard plastic charging strip dry in a sealable container, such as a Mason jar, with some drying agent.

2. Charging a KFM from a Quickly Unwound Roll of Tape. (Quick unwinding produces a harmless charge of several thousand volts on the tape.)

a. Adjust the charging-wire so that its lower end is about 1/16 inch above the upper edges of the aluminum-foil leaves. Use the sticky-tape at the end of one adjustment-thread to hold the charging-wire in this position. Stick this tape approximately in line with the leaves, either on the side of the can or on the plastic cover. (If the plastic cover is weak, it may be necessary to put a piece of sticky-tape on the end of each adjustment-thread, in order to hold the charging-wire securely. If a charging-wire is not secure, its lower end may be forced up by the like charge on the leaves before the leaves can be fully charged.)

Pg 8 — (28)

Pg 8 — (27)

b. The sketch shows the "GET SET" position, preparatory to unrolling the Scotch Magic Transparent Tape, P.V.C. electrical tape, or other tape. Be sure to first remove the roll from its dispenser. Some of the other kinds of tape will not produce a high enough voltage.

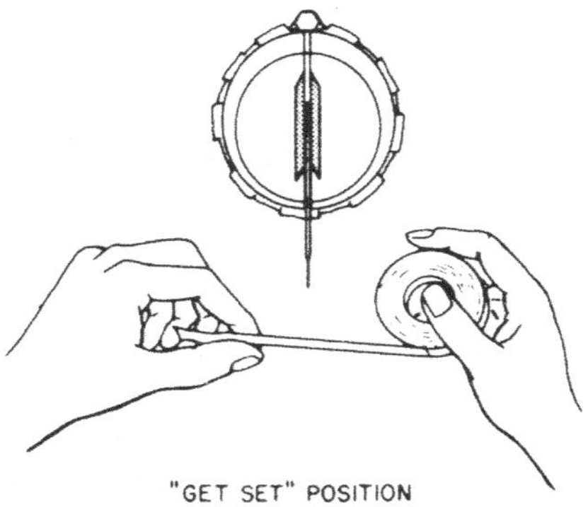

"GET SET" POSITION

c. **QUICKLY** unroll 10 to 12 inches of tape by pulling its end with the left hand, while the right hand allows the roll to unwind while remaining in about the same "GET SET" position only an inch or two away from the KFM.

d. While holding the unwound tape tight, about perpendicular to the charging-wire, and about 1/4 inch away from the end of the charging-wire, **promptly** move both hands and the tape to the right **rather slowly** — taking about 2 seconds to move about 8 inches. The electrostatic charge on the unwound tape "jumps" the spark gaps from the tape to the upper end of the charging-wire and from the lower end of the charging-wire to the aluminum leaves, and charges the aluminum leaves.

Be sure neither leaf is touching a stop-thread.

Try to charge the leaves enough to spread them far enough apart to give a reading of at least 15 mm, but no more than 20 mm after the KFM has been gently bumped or shaken to remove any unstable part of the charge.

e. **Pull down on an insulating adjustment-thread to raise the lower end of the charging-wire. If the charging-wire has been held in charging position by its sticky-ended adjustment-thread being stuck to the top of the clear plastic cover, it is best first to pull down a little on the bare-ended adjustment-thread, and then to move, pull down on, and secure the sticky-ended adjustment-thread to the side of the can so that the lower part of the charging-wire is close to the underside of the clear plastic cover.**

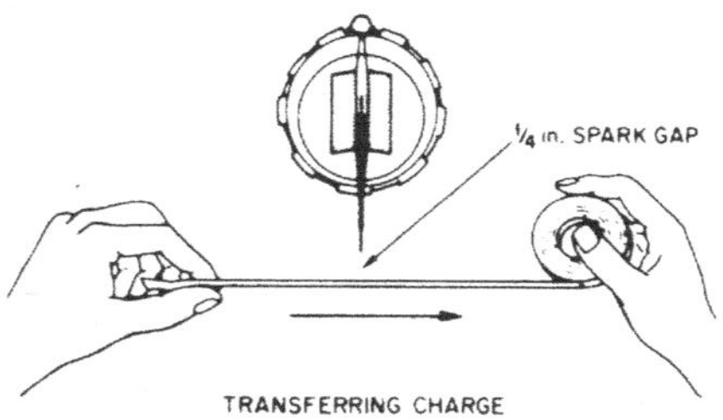

TRANSFERRING CHARGE

Do not touch the charging-wire.

f. Rewind the tape **tight** on its roll, for future use when other tape may not be available.

Testing Your KFM to Learn if it Can Accurately Measure Low Dose Rates

Put fresh drying agent in your KFM and then charge and test the KFM in a location where it is **not** exposed to abnormal radiation. Take an initial reading. If after 3 hours its reading has decreased by 1 mm, or less, this means that its leaf-suspending threads are good insulators and that your KFM can reliably measure dose rates as low as 0.03 roentgens per hour (30 milliroentgens per hour). By post-attack standards, 30 mR/hr is a low dose rate. In a whole month of continuous exposure (an impossibility, because fallout decays), 30 mR/hr would result in a dose of 21.9 roentgens — not enough to incapacitate. **Warning:** In heavy fallout areas, for the first few days after fallout deposition the dose rates inside even most good shelters will be higher than 0.03 R/hr.

Trouble Shooting

If charging does not separate the two leaves sufficiently, take these corrective actions:

1. Be sure the pieces of anhydrite in the bottom of the ionization chamber (the can) are in a single layer, with no piece on top of another and the top of no piece more than 1/2 inch above the bottom of the can.

2. Check to be sure that the threads suspending the leaves are not crossed; then try to charge the KFM again.

3. If the KFM still cannot be charged, replace the used anhydrite with fresh anhydrite.

4. If you cannot charge a KFM when the air is very humid, charge it inside its dry-bucket.

5. If you cannot charge the KFM while in an area of heavy fallout, take it to the place affording the best protection against radiation, and try to charge it there. (A dose rate of several hundred R/hr will neutralize the charges on both the charging device and the instrument so rapidly that a KFM cannot be charged.)

If a KFM or other radiation measuring instrument gives unexpectedly high readings inside a good shelter, wipe all dust off the outside of the instrument and repeat the radiation-measurements. Especially when exposing a fallout meter outdoors where there is fresh fallout, keep the instrument in a lidded pot, plastic bag, or other covering to avoid the possibility of having it contaminated with fallout particles and afterwards getting erroneously high radiation measurements.

Pg 9 — (30)

Pg 9 — (29)

XIV. **Make and Use a Dry-Bucket**

charging a KFM while it is ıde a dry-bucket with a ısparent plastic cover (see stration), this fallout meter be charged and used even the relative humidity is % outside the dry-bucket. ; air inside the dry-bucket is ıt very dry by a drying ınt placed on its bottom. ɔut a cupful of anhydrite ves very well. The pieces of ; dehydrated gypsum need be as uniform in size as is t for use inside a KFM, but not use powdered anhy- :e.

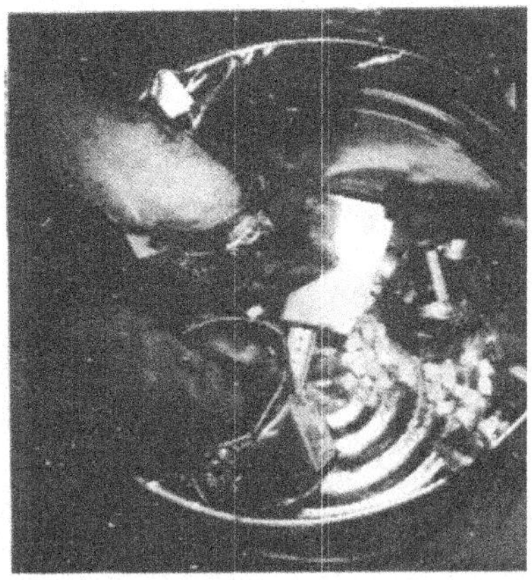

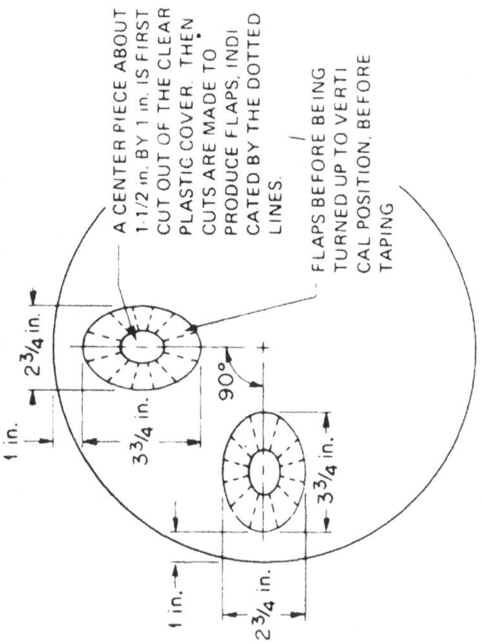

ɟry-bucket can be readily de in about an hour by ceeding as follows:

Remove the handle of a large bucket, pot, or can preferably w diameter of at least 11 inches. A 4-gallon bucket having a top dia about 14 inches and a depth of about 9 inches is ideal. A pl approximately this size is satisfactory. If the handle-supports with stretching a piece of clear plastic film across the top of the remove them, being sure no sharp points remain.

Cut out a circular piece of clear plastic with a diameter about

plastic top that fits snugly but is easily re ɹund the plastic just below the top of the ıct tape, or **one**-inch-wide glass-reinforced Vhen taping, do not permit the lower edge below the rim of the bucket.

XIV. **Make and Use a Dry-Bucket**

By charging a KFM while it is inside a dry-bucket with a transparent plastic cover (see illustration), this fallout meter can be charged and used even if the relative humidity is 100% outside the dry-bucket. The air inside the dry-bucket is kept very dry by a drying agent placed on its bottom. About a cupful of anhydrite serves very well. The pieces of this dehydrated gypsum need not be as uniform in size as is best for use inside a KFM, but do not use powdered anhydrite.

A dry-bucket can be readily made in about an hour by proceeding as follows:

1. Remove the handle of a large bucket, pot, or can preferably with a top diameter of at least 11 inches. A 4-gallon bucket having a top diameter of about 14 inches and a depth of about 9 inches is ideal. A plastic tub approximately this size is satisfactory. If the handle-supports interfere with stretching a piece of clear plastic film across the top of the bucket, remove them, being sure no sharp points remain.

2. Cut out a circular piece of clear plastic with a **diameter** about 5 inches larger than the diameter of the top of the bucket. **Clear vinyl 4 mils thick,** used for storm windows, etc., is best. **Stretch the plastic smooth across** the top of the bucket, and tie it in place, preferably with strong rubber bands looped together to form a circle.

3. Make a plastic top that fits snugly but is easily removable, by taping over and around the plastic just below the top of the bucket. **One**-inch-wide cloth duct tape, or **one**-inch-wide glass-reinforced strapping tape, serves well. When taping, do not permit the lower edge of the tape to be pulled inward below the rim of the bucket.

Pg 10 — (32)

Pg 10 — (31)

4. **Cut two small holes (about 1 inch by 2 inches) in the plastic cover**, as illustrated. Then make the radial cuts (shown by dotted lines) outward from the small holes, out to the solid-line outlines of the 3 inch by 4 inch hand-holes, so as to form small flaps.

5. Fold the small flaps upward, so they are vertical. Then tape them on their outer sides, so they form a vertical "wall" about 3/4 inch high around each hand-hole.

6. Reduce the length of two ordinary plastic bread bags (or similar plastic bags) to a length that is 5 inches greater than the height of the bucket. (Do not use rubber gloves in place of bags; gloves so used result in much more humid outside air being unintentionally pumped into a dry-bucket when it is being used while charging a KFM inside it.)

7. Insert a plastic bag into each hand-hole, and fold the edge of the plastic bag about 1/2 inch over the taped vertical "wall" around each hand-hole.

8. Strengthen the upper parts of the plastic bags by folding 2-inch pieces of tape over the top of the "wall" around each hand-hole.

9. Make about a quart of anhydrite by heating small pieces of wall-board gypsum, and keep this anhydrite dry in a Mason jar or other airtight container with a rubber or plastic sealer.

10. Make a circular aluminum-foil cover to place over the plastic cover when the dry-bucket is not being used for minutes to hours. Make this cover with a diameter about 4 inches greater than the diameter of the top of the bucket, and make it fit more snugly with an encircling loop of rubber bands, or with string. Although not essential, an aluminum-foil cover reduces the amount of water vapor that can reach and pass through the plastic cover, thus extending the life of the drying agent.

11. Charge a KFM inside a dry-bucket by:

    a. Taking off wrist watch and sharp-pointed rings that might tear the plastic bags.

    b. Placing inside the dry-bucket:

        (1) About a cup of anhydrite or silica gel;
        (2) the KFM, with its charging-wire adjusted in its charging position; and
        (3) dry, folded paper and the electrostatic charging device, best a 5-inch-long piece of Plexiglas with smoothed edges, to be rubbed between dry paper folded about 4 inches square and about 20 sheets thick. (Unrolling a roll of tape inside a dry-bucket is an impractical charging method.)

    c. **Replacing the plastic cover, that is best held in place with a** loop of rubber bands.

    d. Charging the KFM with your hands inside the plastic bags, operating the charging device. Have another person illuminate the KFM with a flashlight. When adjusting the charging-wire, move your hands very slowly. See the dry-bucket photos.

12. Expose the KFM to fallout radiation **either** by:

    a. Leaving the KFM inside the dry-bucket while exposing it to fallout radiation for one of the listed time intervals, and reading the KFM before and after the exposure while it remains inside the dry-bucket. (The reading eye should be a measured 12 inches above the SEAT of the KFM, and a flashlight or other light should be used.)

    b. Taking the charged KFM out of the dry-bucket to read it, expose it, and read it after the exposure. (If this is done repeatedly, especially in a humid shelter, the drying agent will not be effective for many KFM chargings, and will have to be replaced.)

XV. How to Use a KFM after a Nuclear Attack

A. Background Information

If during a rapidly worsening crisis threatening nuclear war you are in the place where you plan to take shelter, postpone studying the instructions following this sentence until after you have:

(1) built or improved a high-protection-factor shelter (if possible, a shelter covered with 2 or 3 ft of earth and separate from flammable buildings), and

(2) made a KAP (homemade shelter-ventilating pump) if you have the instructions and materials, and

(3) stored at least 15 gallons of water for each shelter occupant if you can obtain containers.

Having a KFM or any other dependable fallout meter and knowing how to operate it will enable you to minimize radiation injuries and possible fatalities, especially by skillfully using a high-protection-factor fallout shelter to control and limit exposures to radiation. By studying this section you first will learn how to measure radiation **dose rates** (roentgens per hour = R/hr), how to calculate **doses [R]** received in different time intervals, and how to determine **time intervals** (hours and/or minutes) in which specified doses would be received. Then this section lists the sizes of doses (number of R) that the average person can tolerate without being sickened, that he is likely to survive, and that he is likely to be killed by.

Pg 11 — (34)

Pg 11 — (33)

Most fortunately for the future of all living things, the decay of radioactivity causes the sandlike fallout particles to become less and less dangerous with the passage of time. Each fallout particle acts much like a tiny X ray machine would if it were made so that its rays, shooting out from it like invisible light, became weaker and weaker with time.

Contrary to exaggerated accounts of fallout dangers, the radiation **dose rate** from fallout particles when they reach the ground in the areas of the heaviest fallout **will decrease quite rapidly**. For example, consider the decay of fallout from a relatively nearby, large surface burst, at a place where the fallout particles are deposited on the ground one hour after the explosion. At this time one hour after the explosion, assume that the radiation dose rate (the best measure of radiation danger at a particular time) measures 2,000 roentgens per hour (2,000 R/hr) outdoors. Seven hours later the dose rate is reduced to 200 R/hr by normal radioactive decay. Two days after the explosion, the dose rate outdoors is reduced by radioactive decay to 20 R/hr. After two weeks, the dose rate is less than 2 R/hr. When the dose rate is 2 R/hr, people can go out of a good shelter and work outdoors for 3 hours a day, receiving a daily dose of 6 roentgens, without being sickened.

In places where fallout arrives several hours after the explosion, the radioactivity of the fallout will have gone through its time period of most rapid decay while the fallout particles were still airborne. If you are in a location so distant from the explosion that fallout arrives 8 hours after the explosion, two days must pass before the initial dose rate measured at your location will decay to 1/10 its initial intensity.

B. Finding the **Dose Rate**

1. Reread Section IV, "What a KFM Is and How it Works." Also reread Section XIII, "Two Ways to Charge a KFM," and actually do each step immediately after reading it.

2. Charge the KFM so that it reads at least 15 mm. Next raise the lower end of the charging wire. Then gently bump or shake the KFM to remove any unstable part of the charge. Read the apparent separation of the lower edges of the leaves while the KFM rests on an approximately horizontal surface. If the reading is larger than 20 mm, bleed off enough charge to reduce the initial reading to 20 mm or slightly less, for maximum accuracy. Never take a reading while a leaf is touching a stop-thread.

3. To prevent possible contamination of a KFM (or of any other fallout meter) with fallout particles, keep it inside a plastic bag or other covering when there is risk of fallout particles being deposited or blown onto it. An instrument contaminated with fallout particles can give too high readings, especially of the low dose-rate measurements made inside a good shelter.

4. Expose the KFM to fallout radiation for one of the time intervals shown in the vertical columns of the table attached to the KFM. (Study the following table.) If the dose rate is not known even approximately, first expose the fully charged KFM for one minute. For dependable measurements outdoors, expose the charged KFM about **3 feet above the ground.** The longer outdoor exposures usually are best made by attaching the KFM with 2 strong rubber bands to a stick or pole, being careful never to tilt the KFM too much.

5. Read the KFM after the exposure, while the KFM rests on an approximately horizontal surface.

6. Find the time interval that gives a dependable reading — by exposing the fully charged KFM for one or more of the listed time intervals until the **reading after the exposure is;**
(a) Not less than **5 mm.**
(b) At least **2 mm** less than the reading before the exposure.

7. Calculate by simple subtraction the **difference** in the apparent separation of the **lower** edges of the leaves before the exposure and after the exposure. An example: If the reading before the exposure is 18 mm and the reading after the exposure is 6 mm, the **difference** in readings is 18 mm − 6 mm = 12 mm.

8. If an exposure results in a difference in readings of **less** than **2 mm,** recharge the KFM and expose it again for one of the **longer** time intervals listed. (If there appears to be **no** difference in the readings taken before and after an exposure for one minute, this does not prove there is absolutely no fallout danger. Take a longer reading.)

9. If an exposure results in the **reading** after the exposure being **less than 5 mm,** recharge the KFM and expose it again for one of the **shorter** time intervals listed.

10. Use the table attached to the KFM to find the **dose rate** (R/hr) during the time of exposure. The dose rate (R/hr) is found at the intersection of the vertical column of numbers under the time interval used and of the horizontal line of numbers that lists the calculated difference in readings at its left end.

TABLE USED TO FIND DOSE RATES (R/HR FROM KFM READINGS

*DIFFERENCE BETWEEN THE READING BEFORE EXPOSURE AND THE READING AFTER EXPOSURE, 8 PLY STANDARD FOIL LEAVES

DIFF.* IN READINGS	TIME INTERVAL OF AN EXPOSURE 15 SEC. R/HR	1 MIN. R/HR	4 MIN R/HR	16 MIN R/HR	1 HR R/HR
2 mm	6.2	1.6	0.4	0.1	0.03
4 mm	12.	3.1	0.8	0.2	0.06
6 mm	19.	4.6	1.2	0.3	0.08
8 mm	25.	6.2	1.6	0.4	0.10
10 mm	31.	7.7	2.0	0.5	0.13
12 mm	37.	9.2	2.3	0.6	0.15
14 mm	43.	11.	2.7	0.7	0.18

An example: If the time interval of the exposure was **1 MIN.** and the difference in the readings was **12 mm,** the table shows that the **dose rate** during the time interval of the exposure was **9.2 R/HR** (9.2 roentgens per hour).

Another example: If the time interval of the exposure was **15 SEC.** and the difference in readings was **11 mm,** the table shows that the dose rate during the exposure was halfway between **31 R/HR** and **37 R/HR;** that is, the **dose rate** was 34 R/hr.

Pg 11 — (35)

Pg 11 — (36)

11. Note in the table that if an exposure for one of the listed time intervals causes the **difference** in readings to be 2 mm or 3 mm, then an exposure 4 times as long reveals the same dose rate. An example: If a 1-min exposure results in a difference in readings of 2 mm, the table shows the dose rate was 1.6 R/hr; then if the KFM is exposed for 4 minutes at this same dose rate of 1.6 R/hr, the table shows that the resultant difference in readings is 8 mm.

    The longer exposure results in a more accurate determination of the dose rate.

12. If the dose rate is found to be greater than 0.2 R/hr and time is available, recharge the KFM and repeat the dose-rate measurement -- to avoid possible mistakes.

C. Calculating the **Dose Received**

The **dose** of fallout radiation -- that is, the **amount** of fallout radiation received -- determines the harmful effects on men and animals. Being exposed to a high **dose rate** is not always dangerous -- provided the exposure is short enough to result in only a small **dose** being received. For example, if the **dose rate** outside an excellent fallout shelter is 1200 R/hr and a shelter occupant goes outside for 30 seconds, he would be exposed for 1/2 of 1 minute, or 1/2 of 1/60 of an hour, which equals 1/120 hour. Therefore, since the dose he would receive if he stayed outside for 1 hour would be 1200 R, in 30 seconds he would receive 1/120 of 1200, which equals 10 R (1200 R divided by 120 = 10 R). A total daily **dose** of 10 R (10 roentgens) will not cause any symptoms if it is not repeated day after day for a week or more.

In contrast, if the average dose rate of an area were found to be 12 R/hr and if a person remained exposed in that particular area for 24 hours, he would receive a **dose** of 288 R (12 R/hr x 24 hr = 288 R). Even assuming that this person had been exposed previously to very little radiation, there would still be a serious risk that this 288 R **dose** would be fatal under the difficult conditions that would follow a heavy nuclear attack.

Another example: Assume that three days after an attack the occupants of a dry, hot cave giving almost complete protection against fallout are in desperate need of water. The dose rate outside is found to be 20 R/hr. To backpack water from a source 3 miles away is estimated to take 2-1/2 hours. The cave occupants estimate that the water backpackers will receive a dose in 2-1/2 hours of 50 R (2.5 hr x 20 R/hr = 50 R). A dose of 50 R will cause only mild symptoms (nausea in about 10% of persons receiving a 50 R dose) for persons who previously have received only very small doses. Therefore, one of the cave occupants makes a rapid radiation survey for about 1-1/2 miles along the proposed route, stopping to charge and read a KFM about every quarter of a mile. He finds no dose rates much higher than 20 R/hr.

So, the cave occupants decide the risk is small enough to justify some of them leaving shelter for about 2-1/2 hours to get water.

D. Estimating the **Dangers** from Different Radiation Doses

Fortunately, the human body -- if given enough time -- can repair most of the damage caused by radiation. An historic example: A healthy man accidently received a daily **dose** of 9.3 R (or somewhat more) of fallout-type radiation each day for a period of 106 days. His total accumulated **dose** was at least 1000 R. A dose of one thousand roentgens, if received in a few days, is almost three times the dose likely to kill the average man if he receives the whole dose in a few days and after a nuclear attack cannot get medical treatment, adequate rest, etc. However, the only symptom this man noted was serious fatigue.

The occupants of a high-protection-factor shelter (such as a trench shelter covered with 2 or 3 feet of earth and having crawlway entrances) would receive less than 1/200 of the radiation dose they would receive outside. Even in most areas of very heavy fallout, persons who remain continously in such a shelter would receive a total accumulated **dose** of less than 25 R in the first day after the attack, and less than 100 R in the first two weeks. At the end of the first two weeks, such shelter occupants could start working outside for an increasing length of time each day, receiving a **daily dose** of no more than **6 R** for up to two months without being sickened.

Pg 12 — (38)

Pg 12 — (37)

To control radiation exposure in this way, each shelter must have a fallout meter, and a daily record must be kept of the approximate total dose received each day by every shelter occupant, both while inside and outside the shelter. The long-term penalty which would result from a dose of 100 R received within a few weeks is much less than many Americans fear. If 100 average persons received an external dose of 100 R during and shortly after a nuclear attack, the studies of the Japanese A-bomb survivors indicate that no more than one of them is likely to die during the following 30 years as a result of this 100 R radiation dose. These delayed radiation deaths would be due to leukemia and other cancers. In the desperate crisis period following a major nuclear attack, such a relatively small shortening of life expectancy during the following 30 years should not keep people from starting recovery work to save themselves and their fellow citizens from death due to lack of food and other essentials.

A healthy person who previously has received a total accumulated dose of no more than 100 R distributed over a 2-week period should realize that:

100 R, even if all received in a day or less, is unlikely to require medical care -- provided during the next 2 weeks a total additional dose of no more than a few R is received.

350 R received in a few days or less results in a 50-50 chance of being fatal after a large nuclear attack when few survivors could get medical care, sanitary surroundings, a well-balanced diet, or adequate rest.

600 R received in a few days or less is almost certain to cause death within a few days.

E. Finding the **Protection Factor** of a Shelter

To avoid the necessity of repeatedly going outside a shelter to determine the changing dose rates outside, find the shelter's protection factor (PF) by measuring the dose rate inside the shelter as soon as it becomes high enough to be reliably measured. Then promptly measure the dose rate outside. The uncontaminated shelter's

$$PF = \frac{\text{Dose Rate Outside}}{\text{Dose Rate Inside}}$$

An example: If the dose rate inside is found to be 0.2 R/hr and the dose rate outside is 31 R/hr, the shelter's

$$PF = \frac{31\ R/hr}{0.2\ R/hr} = 155$$

Then at future times the **approximate** dose rate outside can be found by measuring the dose rate inside and multiplying it by 155. Approximate Dose Rate Outside = Dose Rate Inside x PF.

F. **Using a KFM to Reduce Radiation Doses Received**

If a charged KFM is discharged and reads zero within a second or two after being taken outside a good shelter, this means that the dose rate outside is hundreds of roentgens per hour. Get back inside! Also remember that a 15-second reading is not as accurate as are readings made in longer specified exposure times.

Inside most shelters, the dose received by an occupant varies considerably, depending on the occupant's location. For example, inside an expedient covered-trench shelter the dose rate is higher near the entrance than in the middle of the trench. In a typical basement shelter the best protection is found in one corner. Especially during the first several hours after the arrival of fallout, when the dose rates and doses received are highest, shelter occupants should use their fallout meters to determine where to place themselves to minimize the doses they receive.

They should use available tools and materials to reduce the doses they receive, especially during the first day, by digging deeper (if practical) and reducing the size of openings by partially blocking them with earth, water containers, etc. -- while maintaining adequate ventilation. To greatly reduce the slight risk of fallout particles entering the body through nose or mouth, shelter occupants should cover nose and mouth with a towel or other cloth while the fallout is being deposited outside their shelter, if at the same time ventilating air is being blown or pumped through their shelter.

The air inside an occupied shelter often becomes very humid. If a good flow of outdoor air is flowing into a shelter -- especially if pumped by briefly operating a KAP or other ventilating pump -- a KFM usually can be charged at the air intake of the shelter room without putting it inside a dry-bucket. However, if the air to which a KFM is exposed has a relative humidity of 90% or higher, the instrument cannot be charged, even by quickly unrolling a roll of tape.

In extensive areas of heavy fallout, the occupants of most home basements, that provide inadequate shielding against heavy fallout radiation, would be in deadly danger. By using a dependable fallout meter, occupants would find that persons lying on the floor in certain locations would receive the smallest doses, and that, if they improvise additional shielding in these locations, the doses received could be greatly reduced. Additional shielding can be provided by making a very small shelter inside the basement where the dose rate is found to be lowest. Furniture, boxes, etc. can be used for walls, doors for the roof, and water containers, books, and other heavy objects for shielding -- especially on the roof. Or, if tools are available, breaking through the basement floor and digging a shelter trench will greatly increase available protection against radiation. If a second expedient ventilating pump, a KAP, (or a small Directional Fan), is made and used as a fan, such an extremely cramped shelter inside a shelter usually can be occupied by several times as many persons as can occupy it without forced ventilation.

END OF INSTRUCTIONS

Pg 12 — (39)

Pg 12 — (40)

INSTRUCTIONS
EXTRA PAGE

ORNL-DWG 76-6535

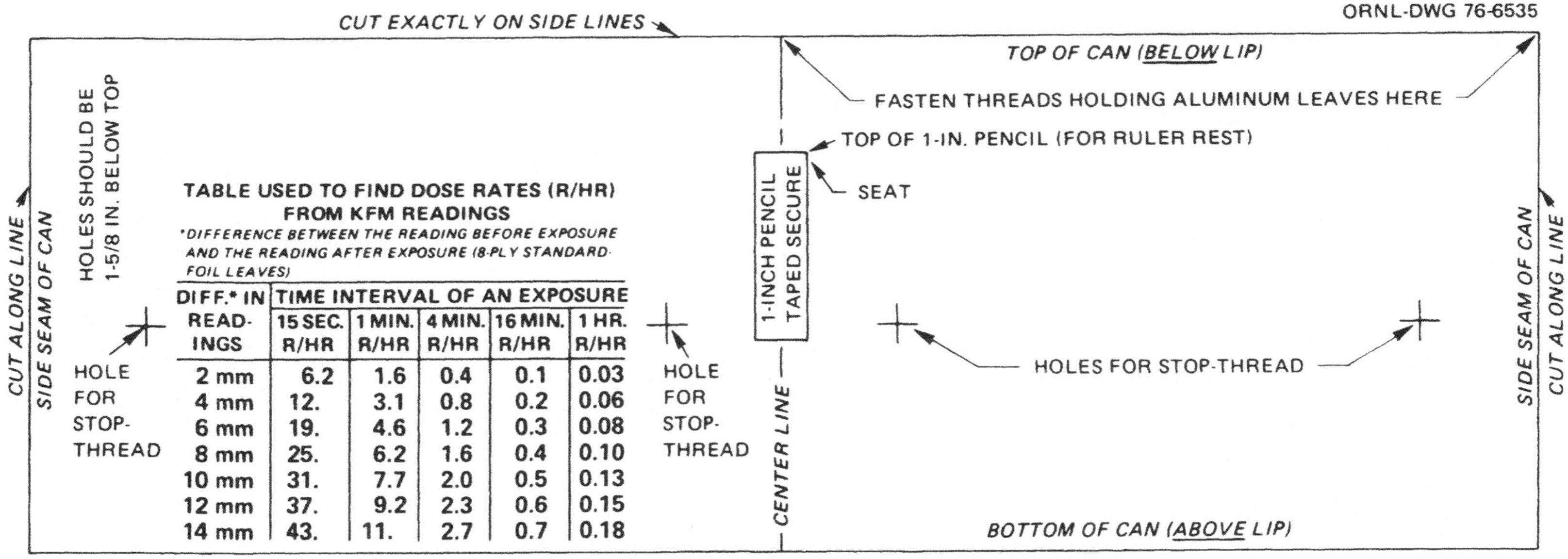

TABLE USED TO FIND DOSE RATES (R/HR) FROM KFM READINGS

**DIFFERENCE BETWEEN THE READING BEFORE EXPOSURE AND THE READING AFTER EXPOSURE (8-PLY STANDARD-FOIL LEAVES)*

DIFF.* IN READINGS	TIME INTERVAL OF AN EXPOSURE: 15 SEC. R/HR	1 MIN. R/HR	4 MIN. R/HR	16 MIN. R/HR	1 HR. R/HR
2 mm	6.2	1.6	0.4	0.1	0.03
4 mm	12.	3.1	0.8	0.2	0.06
6 mm	19.	4.6	1.2	0.3	0.08
8 mm	25.	6.2	1.6	0.4	0.10
10 mm	31.	7.7	2.0	0.5	0.13
12 mm	37.	9.2	2.3	0.6	0.15
14 mm	43.	11.	2.7	0.7	0.18

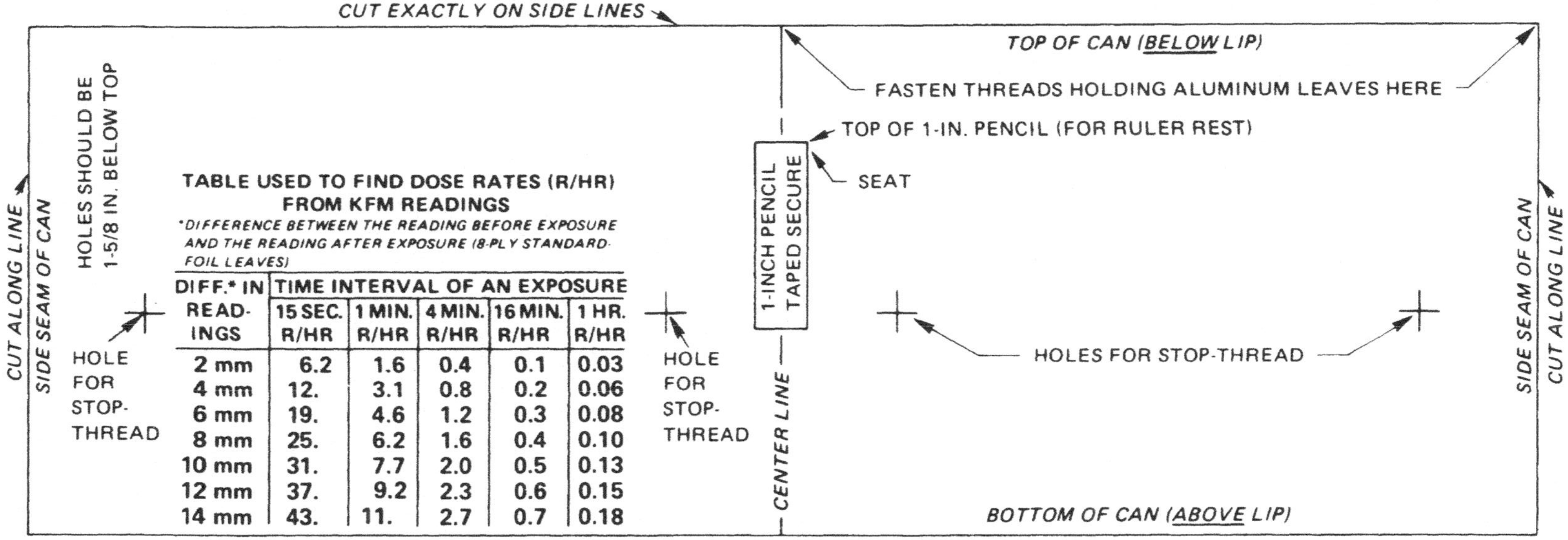

TABLE USED TO FIND DOSE RATES (R/HR) FROM KFM READINGS

**DIFFERENCE BETWEEN THE READING BEFORE EXPOSURE AND THE READING AFTER EXPOSURE (8-PLY STANDARD-FOIL LEAVES)*

DIFF.* IN READINGS	TIME INTERVAL OF AN EXPOSURE: 15 SEC. R/HR	1 MIN. R/HR	4 MIN. R/HR	16 MIN. R/HR	1 HR. R/HR
2 mm	6.2	1.6	0.4	0.1	0.03
4 mm	12.	3.1	0.8	0.2	0.06
6 mm	19.	4.6	1.2	0.3	0.08
8 mm	25.	6.2	1.6	0.4	0.10
10 mm	31.	7.7	2.0	0.5	0.13
12 mm	37.	9.2	2.3	0.6	0.15
14 mm	43.	11.	2.7	0.7	0.18

PAPER PATTERN TO WRAP AROUND KFM CAN (GLUE OR TAPE SECURELY TO CAN)

PATTERN PAGE (A)

CUT OUT THESE PATTERNS, EACH OF WHICH IS THE EXACT SIZE FOR A KFM.
CAUTION: XEROX COPIES OF THESE PATTERNS MAY BE TOO LARGE.

PATTERN FOR CLEAR-PLASTIC COVER FOR KFM CAN

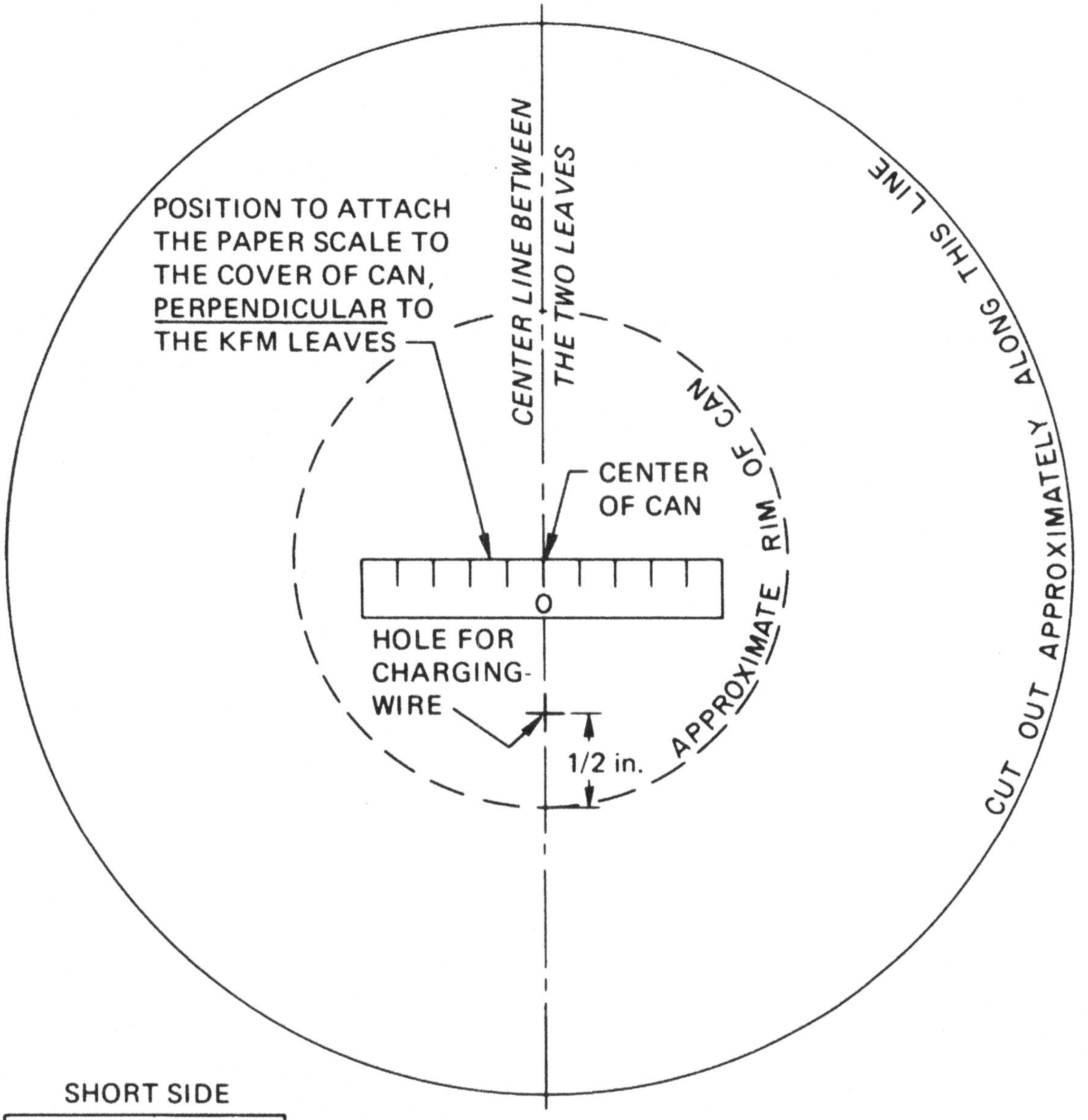

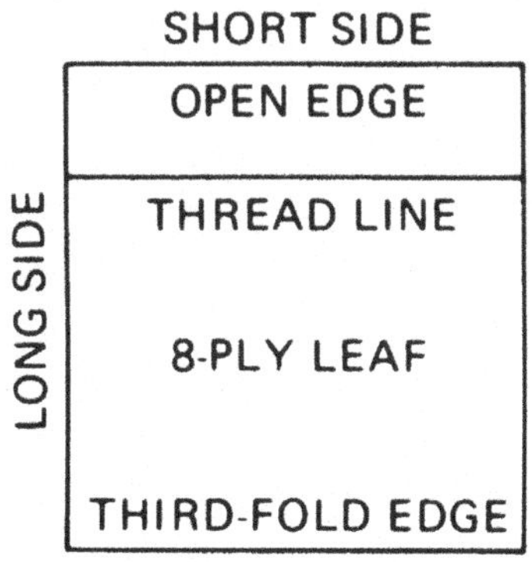

FINISHED-LEAF PATTERN
(CUT OUT EXACTLY ON SIDE LINES)

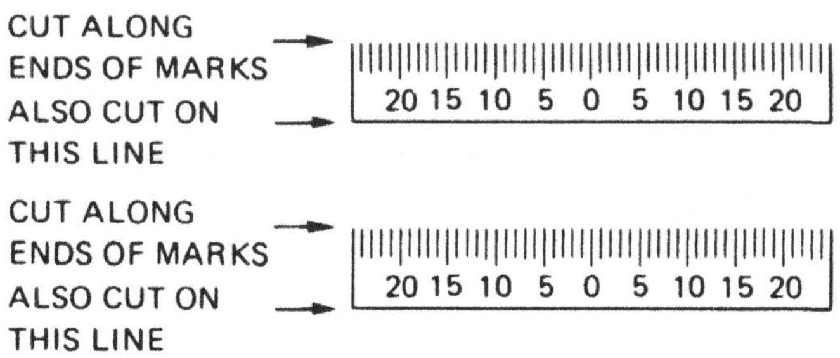

PAPER SCALE (TO BE CUT OUT)

PATTERN PAGE (B)

CAUTION: XEROX COPIES OF THE FINISHED-LEAF AND THE SCALE PATTERNS MAY BE SLIGHTLY TOO LARGE.

COVER THE TWO "TAPE HERE" RECTANGLES WITH SAME-SIZED PIECES OF TAPE, IN ORDER TO KEEP FROM TEARING THIS PAPER WHEN REMOVING TWO ADDITIONAL PIECES OF TAPE. THEN, BY PUTTING TWO OTHER PIECES OF TAPE THIS SAME SIZE ON TOP OF THE FIRST TWO PIECES, TAPE THE THREAD ONTO THIS GUIDE SHEET, AND LATER ATTACH A LEAF TO THE TAPED-DOWN THREAD.

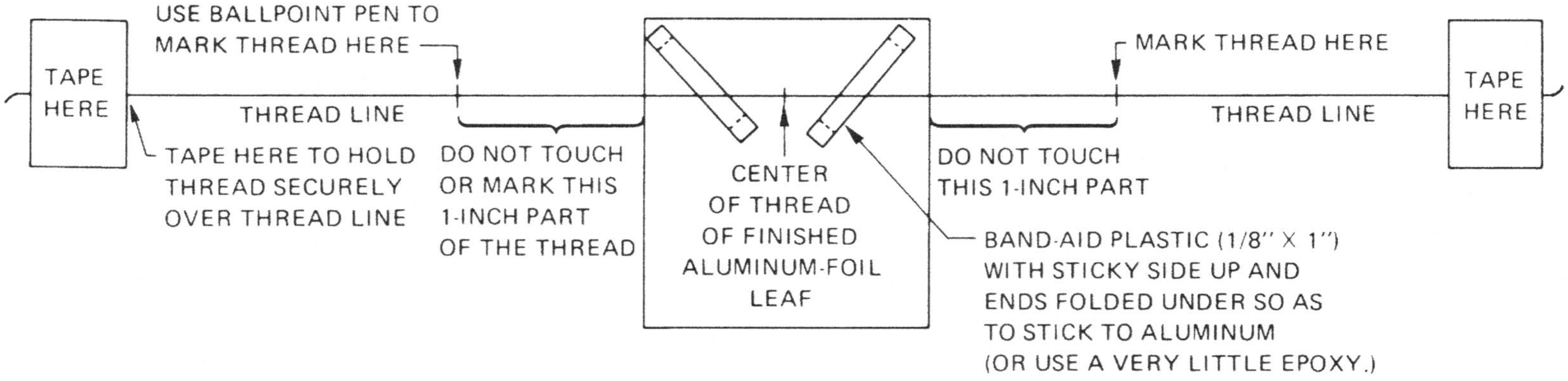

PATTERN (C)
(Cut out this guide along its border lines and tape to the top of a work table.)

WARNING: The parts of the thread that will be inside the can and on which the leaf will be suspended must serve to insulate the high-voltage electrical charges to be placed on the leaf. Therefore, the suspended parts of the thread must be kept very clean.

INSTRUCTIONS
EXTRA PAGE

REMINDERS FOR OPERATORS

The **drying agent** inside a KFM is O.K. if, when the charged KFM is **not** exposed to radiation, its readings decrease by 1 mm or less in 3 hours.

Reading: With the reading eye 12 inches vertically above the seat, note on the mm scale the separation of the **lower** edges of the leaves. If the right leaf is at 10 mm and the left leaf is at 7 mm, the KFM reads 17 mm. Never take a reading while a leaf is touching a stop-thread. Never use a KFM reading that is less than 5 mm.

Finding a dose rate: If before exposure a KFM reads 17 mm and if after a 1-minute exposure it reads 5 mm, the difference in readings is 12 mm. The attached table shows the dose rate was 9.6 R/hr during the exposure.

Finding a dose: If a person works outside for 3 hours where the dose rate is 2 R/hr, what is his radiation dose? Answer: 3 hr x 2 R/hr = 6 R.

Finding how long it takes to get a certain R dose: If the dose rate is 1.6 R/hr outside and a person is willing to take a 6 R dose, how long can he remain outside? Answer:
6 R ÷ 1.6 R/hr = 3.75 hr =
3 hours and 45 minutes.

Fallout radiation guides for a healthy person not previously exposed to a total radiation dose of more than 100 R during a 2-week period:

6 R per day can be tolerated for up to two months without losing the ability to work.

100 R in a week or less is not likely to seriously sicken.

350 R in a few days results in a 50-50 chance of dying, under post-attack conditions.

600 R in a week or less is almost certain to cause death within a few weeks.

REMINDERS FOR OPERATORS

The **drying agent** inside a KFM is O.K. if, when the charged KFM is **not** exposed to radiation, its readings decrease by 1 mm or less in 3 hours.

Reading: With the reading eye 12 inches vertically above the seat, note on the mm scale the separation of the **lower** edges of the leaves. If the right leaf is at 10 mm and the left leaf is at 7 mm, the KFM reads 17 mm. Never take a reading while a leaf is touching a stop-thread. Never use a KFM reading that is less than 5 mm.

Finding a dose rate: If before exposure a KFM reads 17 mm and if after a 1-minute exposure it reads 5 mm, the difference in readings is 12 mm. The attached table shows the dose rate was 9.6 R/hr during the exposure.

Finding a dose: If a person works outside for 3 hours where the dose rate is 2 R/hr, what is his radiation dose? Answer: 3 hr x 2 R/hr = 6 R.

Finding how long it takes to get a certain R dose: If the dose rate is 1.6 R/hr outside and a person is willing to take a 6 R dose, how long can he remain outside? Answer:
6 R ÷ 1.6 R/hr = 3.75 hr =
3 hours and 45 minutes.

Fallout radiation guides for a healthy person not previously exposed to a total radiation dose of more than 100 R during a 2-week period:

6 R per day can be tolerated for up to two months without losing the ability to work.

100 R in a week or less is not likely to seriously sicken.

350 R in a few days results in a 50-50 chance of dying, under post-attack conditions.

600 R in a week or less is almost certain to cause death within a few weeks.

INSTRUCTIONS
(A)

INSTRUCTIONS FOR PERSONS CONCERNED WITH REPRODUCING THE KFM INSTRUCTIONS

The KFM instruction pages are printed so that they can be readily cut out and pasted up (using the "LAYOUT FOR 12-PAGE TABLOID" given on page 242) to expedite rapid reproduction preparatory to mass distribution. No authorization is required to reproduce this survival information.

All of the paste-ups should be photo-reduced to fit your size newspaper, EXCEPT four cut-outs [paste-ups (15), (18), (21) and (24)] and one drawing [paste-up (26)] SHOULD REMAIN AT 100%.

To make the instruction pages fully camera-ready for paste-up and photographing, it is necessary: (1) To cut off each page's title and number (such as "INSTRUCTIONS, Page 2" and "214"); (2) To use a camera-invisible blue pencil to copy the numbers on the back of each page onto the front of that page, writing them in a blank space nearest to the approximate original position of the numbers; (3) To cut out each of the 40 paste-ups.

On the back of each paste-up are the number of the tabloid page to which the paste-up is to be attached and (in parentheses) the number of the paste-up itself. For example, on the back of "INSTRUCTIONS, Page 2" are printed the following: "Pg 1 - (2)" and "Pg 1 - (3)." Thus, this page contains two paste-ups, both of which should be attached to page 1 of the tabloid paste-up. The positions in which they should be attached to page 1 are shown in the layout sketch on page 242.

Timed field tests by two newspapers have shown that less than 40 minutes is required to begin printing a KFM tabloid. Each test began when the newspaper was given only written instructions like this page and the following layout page, along with KFM instructions like those in this book—except that the index numbers were already printed in camera-invisible blue on each half page of the instructions.

The camera-ready copy is for use with a straight lens (100% horizontal and 100% vertical reproduction).

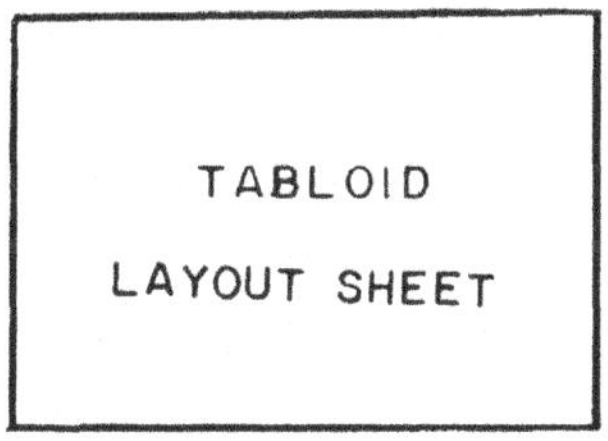

CENTER FOLD OF A 12-PAGE TABLOID, INDICATING TABLOID Page 6 AND Page 7.

All photographs are 85-line screen.

The following layout sketch for a 12-page tabloid indicates where each of the numbered paste-ups [(1), (2), . . . (40)] should be pasted-up and what spaces should be left blank. This positioning of the paste-ups is necessary to permit a KFM-maker to cut out the patterns without destroying any instructions printed on opposite sides of the 12 tabloid pages.

LAYOUT FOR 12-PAGE TABLOID

NUMBERS INSIDE PARENTHESES [(1) THROUGH (40)] ARE PASTE-UPS CUT OUT OF THE INSTRUCTIONS PAGES

Appendix D
Expedient Blast Shelters

INCREASING IMPORTANCE

The majority of urban and suburban Americans would need blast shelters to avoid death or injury if they did not evacuate before an all-out nuclear attack. As nuclear arsenals continue to grow, an increasing majority would need the protection of blast shelters. In an attack on militarily relevant targets, as much as 5% of the total area of the 48 states could be subjected to blast damage severe enough to destroy or damage homes — depending on the number of warheads assigned to each hard target, weapon reliability, etc. If blast shelters affording protection up to the 15-pounds-per-square-inch (15 psi) overpressure range were available to everybody and were occupied at the time of attack, the great majority of the occupants would survive all blast, fire, and radiation effects in the blast areas subjected to less than 15-psi blast effects.

Fifteen-psi blast shelters will survive as close as about 1.5 miles from ground zero of a 1-megaton surface burst, and about 2.3 miles from ground zero or a 1-megaton air burst. Except in high-density urban areas where the air supply openings and exits of shelters are all too likely to be covered with blast-hurled debris, the area in which people inside good earth-covered 15-psi blast shelters would be killed would be only about 1/6th as large as the area in which most people sheltered in typical American homes probably would die from blast and fire effects alone.

Blast tests have indicated that the Small-Pole Shelter (the most blast-resistant of the earth-covered expedient shelters described in Appendix A) should enable its occupants to survive up to the 50-psi overpressure range — if built with the blast-resistant and radiation-protective features described in following sections, and if located outside an urban area. Calculations show that this earth-covered expedient blast shelter also would give adequate protection at the 50-psi blast overpressure range against the intense initial nuclear radiation that is emitted from the fireball of a 1-megaton explosion. However, to make this shelter (see page 258) provide adequate protection against the even more intense initial nuclear radiation that would reach the 50-psi overpressure range from the fireball of a 500-kiloton or smaller explosion, it should have at least 6 feet of earth cover and additional cans of water should be kept ready to be placed in the horizontal parts of the entryways promptly after the shelter is occupied.

The life-saving potential of well designed, well built blast shelters is a demonstrated fact. Millions of Americans living in high-risk areas would be able to build expedient blast shelters within only a few days—provided they were given field-tested instructions, had made some preparations before the crisis arose, had a few days of recognized warning, and during the crisis were motivated by the President. The following information is given in the hope of encouraging more Americans to make preparations for blast protection. Also, it may serve to increase the number who realize the need for *permanent* blast shelters in high-risk blast areas.

Some informed citizens—particularly those who live near large cities or in their outer suburbs—may choose to build earth-covered expedient blast shelters in their backyards, rather than to evacuate. Going into a strange area and trying to build or find good shelter and other essentials of life would entail risks that many people might hesitate to take, particularly if they live outside the probable areas of severe blast damage. For such citizens, the best decision might be to stay at home, build earth-covered expedient blast shelters, supply them with the essentials for long occupancy, and remain with their possessions.

The following descriptions of the characteristics and components of expedient blast shelters should enable many readers to use locally available materials to provide at least 15-psi blast protection. Pre-crisis preparations are essential, as well as the ability to work very hard for two to four days. (Field-tested instructions are not yet available; to date only workers who were supervised have built expedient blast shelters.[5])

PRACTICALITY OF EXPEDIENT BLAST SHELTERS

At Hiroshima and Nagasaki, simple wood-framed shelters with about 3 feet of earth over wooden roofs were undamaged by blast effects in areas where substantial buildings were demolished.[4]

Figure D.1 shows a Hiroshima shelter that people with hand tools could build in a day, if poles or timber were available. This shelter withstood blast and fire at an overpressure range of about 65 psi. Its narrow room and a 3-foot-thick earth cover brought about effective earth arching; this kept its yielding wooden frame from being broken.

Fig. D.1. A small, earth-covered backyard shelter with a crude wooden frame—undamaged, although only 300 yards from ground zero at Hiroshima.

Although the shelter itself was undamaged, its occupants would have been fatally injured because the shelter had no blast door. The combined effect of blast waves, excessive pressure, blast wind, and burns from extremely hot dust blown into the shelter (the popcorning effect) and from the heated air would have killed the occupants. For people to survive in areas of severe blast, their shelters must have strong blast doors.

In nuclear weapons tests in the Nevada desert, box-like shelters built of lumber and covered with sandy earth were structurally undamaged by 10- to 15-psi blast effects. However, none had blast doors, so occupants of these open shelters would have been injured by blast effects and burned as a result of the popcorning effect. Furthermore, blast winds blew away much of the dry, sandy earth mounded over the shelters for shielding; this resulted in inadequate protection against fallout radiation.

Twelve different types of expedient shelters were blast-tested by Oak Ridge National Laboratory during three of Defense Nuclear Agency's blast tests.[5] Two of these tests each involved the detonation of a million pounds or more of conventional explosive; air-blast effects equivalent to those from a 1-kiloton nuclear surface burst were produced by these chemical explosions.

Several of these shelters had expedient blast doors which were closed during the tests. Figure D.2 shows the undamaged interior of the best expedient blast shelter tested prior to 1978, an improved version of the Small-Pole Shelter described in Appendix A. Its two heavy plywood blast doors excluded practically all blast effects; the pressure inside rose only to 1.5 psi—an overpressure not nearly high enough to break eardrums. The only damage was to the expedient shelter-ventilating pump (a KAP) in the stoop-in entryway. Two men worked about 5 minutes to replace the 4 flap-valves that were blown loose.

Fig. D.2. Undamaged interior of a Small-Pole Shelter after blast testing at the 53-psi overpressure range. Large buildings would have been completely demolished.

When blast-tested at 5-psi overpressure, not even the weakest covered-trench shelters with unsupported earth walls (described in Appendix A) were damaged structurally. However, if the covering earth were sandy and dry and if it were exposed to the blast winds of a megaton explosion at the 5-psi overpressure range, so much earth would be blown away that the shelter would give insufficient protection against fallout radiation. Much of the **dry,** shielding earth mounded over some of the above-ground shelters was, in fact, removed by the blast winds of these relatively small test explosions, even at the lower overpressure ranges at which homes would be wrecked. In contrast, in blast tests where the steeply mounded earth was damp, little blast-wind erosion resulted. (The reader should remember that even if shelters without blast doors are undamaged, the occupants are likely to suffer injuries.)

CONSTRUCTION PRINCIPLES

Millions of Americans—if given good instructions, strong motivation, and several days to work—should be able to build blast shelters with materials found in many rural areas and suburban neighborhoods. During a crisis, yard trees could be cut down for poles and sticks, and a garage or part of a house could be torn down for lumber. Many average citizens could build expedient blast shelters if they learn to:

- **Utilize earth arching by making a yielding shelter.** The remarkable protection that earth arching gives to those parts of a shelter designed to use it is illustrated by Fig. D.3.

This picture shows the unbroken roof of a 4-foot-wide Pole-Covered Trench Shelter that was built in rock-like soil and blast tested where the blast pressure outside was 53 psi. Its strong blast doors prevented the blast wave from entering. Without the protection of earth arching that developed in the 5 feet of earth cover over the yielding roof poles, the poles would have been broken like straws. In contrast, the ground shock and earth pressure produced by 1-kiloton blast effects almost completely collapsed the unsupported, rock-like earth walls.

Fig. D.3. Effective earth arching in the earth covering of this 4-ft-wide Pole-Covered Trench Shelter prevented a single pole from being broken by blast forces that exerted a downward force of 53 psi (over $3^1/_2$ tons per square foot) on the overlying earth.

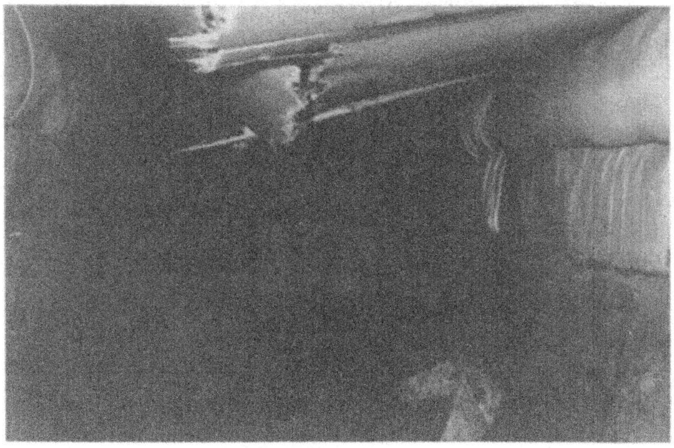

Fig. D.4. Post-blast interior of an Above-ground, Door-Covered Shelter that survived 1-kiloton blast effects at the 5.8-psi overpressure range. The shelter walls were made of bedsheets containing earth, as described in Appendix A.

Figure D.4 also indicates the effectiveness of earth arching. This photo shows the roof of a small, earth-covered fallout shelter, as it appeared after surviving blast effects severe enough to demolish most homes. The roof was made of light, hollow-core, interior doors and looks as though it had been completely broken. In fact, only the lower sheets of $^1/_8$-inch-thick veneer of the hollow-core interior doors were broken. (These breaks were caused by a faulty construction procedure—a front-end loader had dumped several tons of earth onto the uncovered doors.) The upper $^1/_8$-inch-thick sheets of veneer were bowed downward, unbroken, until an earth arch formed in the 2-foot-thick earth covering and prevented the thin sheets from being broken. Earth arching also prevented this roof from being smashed in by blast overpressure that exerted a pressure of 5.8 psi (835 pounds per square foot) on the surface of the earth mounded over this open shelter. (See Appendix A for details of construction.)

- **Make shelters with the minimum practical ceiling height and width.** Most of the narrow covered-trench shelters used by tens of thousands of Londoners during the World War II blitz were built with only $4\frac{1}{2}$-foot ceilings, to maximize blast protection and minimize high water-table problems. These shelters were found to be among the safest for protection against nearby explosions. The Chinese also have a good understanding of this design principle and skillfully utilize the protection provided by earth arching. A Chinese civil defense handbook states: "... the height and width of tunnel shelters should be kept to the minimum required to accommodate the sheltering requirements," and "The thicker the protective layer of earth, the greater the ability to resist blast waves."[21]

- **Shore earth walls to prevent their caving in as a result of ground shock and earth pressure.** Most unshored (that is, unsupported) earth walls are partially collapsed by ground shock at much lower blast overpressures than those at which a flexible roof protected by earth arching is damaged. Figure D.5 is a picture of a seated dummy taken by a high-speed movie camera mounted inside an unshored, Pole-Covered Trench Shelter of the Russian type tested at the 20-psi range. (A second dummy was obscured by blast-torn curtains made of blankets.) The shelter had an open stairway entryway, positioned at right angles to the stand-up-height trench and facing away from the targeted "city" so as to minimize the entry of blast waves and blast wind.

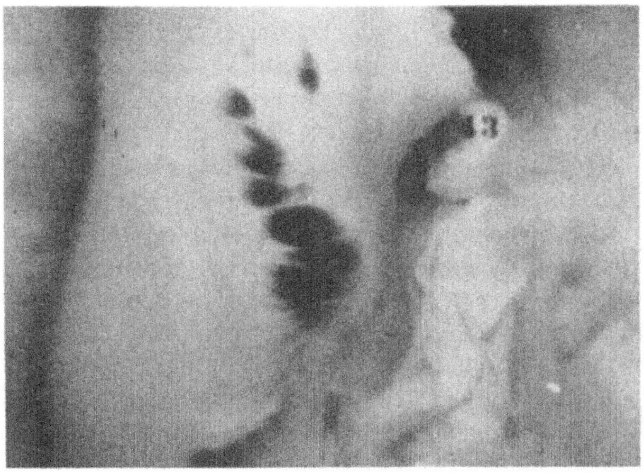

Fig. D.5. A dummy in an unshored Pole-Covered Trench Shelter as it is struck by collapsing rock-like earth walls. The photo also shows the shelter's blanket-curtains as they are torn and blown into the shelter by the 180-mph blast wind. (Immediately after this photo was taken, the dummies were hit by the airborne blast wave and blast wind. Outside, the blast wind peaked at about 490 mph.)

Figure D.6 is a post-blast view of the essentially undamaged earth-covered roof poles and the disastrously collapsed, unshored shelter walls of the Russian shelter tested at 20 psi.[21] Russian civil defense books state that unshored fallout shelters do not survive closer to the blast than the 7-psi overpressure range. This limitation was confirmed by an identical shelter tested at 7 psi; parts of its unshored walls were quite badly collapsed by the ground shock from an explosion producing merely 1-kiloton blast effects.

Fig. D.6. Dummies after ground shock from 1-kiloton blast effects at the 20-psi range had collapsed the rock-like walls of a hardened desert soil called caliche. The dummies' steel "bones" and "joints" prevented them from being knocked down and buried. The fallen caliche all around them kept them from being blown over by the air blast wave and 180-mph blast wind that followed.

Unsupported earth walls should be sloped as much as practical. The length and strength of available roofing material should be considered and, in order to attain effective earth arching, the thickness of the earth cover should be **at least** half as great as the distance between the edges of the trench.

The stability of the earth determines the proper method for shoring the walls of a trench shelter. Methods for shoring both loose, unstable earth and firm, stable earth are described below:

*In loose, unstable earth such as sand, the walls of all underground shelters must be shored. First, an oversized trench must be dug with gently sloping sides. Next, the shoring is built, often as a freestanding, roofless structure. Then earth must be backfilled around the shoring to a level a few inches higher than the uppermost parts of the shoring, as in Fig. D.7. Finally, the roof poles or planks must be placed so that they are supported only by the backfilled earth. Blast tests have indicated that a Pole-Covered Trench Shelter thus proportioned and lightly shored should protect its occupants against disastrous collapse of its walls at overpressure ranges up to 15 psi.

* **In firm, stable earth,** it is best first to dig a trench a few inches wider than 7 feet (the length of the roof poles) and 1 foot deep. Next, dig the part to be shored, down the center of this shallow trench, using the dimensions given for the shoring in Fig. D.7. The trench walls should be sloped and smoothed quite accurately, so that the shoring can be tightened against the earth. If the shoring does not press tightly against the trench walls, large wedges of earth may be jarred loose, hit the shoring, and cause it to collapse.

A different, comparatively simple way to tighten shoring is indicated by Fig. D.8. This sketch shows a 4-pole frame designed to be installed every $2^1/_2$ feet along a trench in stable earth and to be tightened against trench-wall shoring with the same dimensions as those shown in Fig. D.7. Note that the two horizontal brace poles have shallow "V" notches

ORNL–DWG 78-14430R

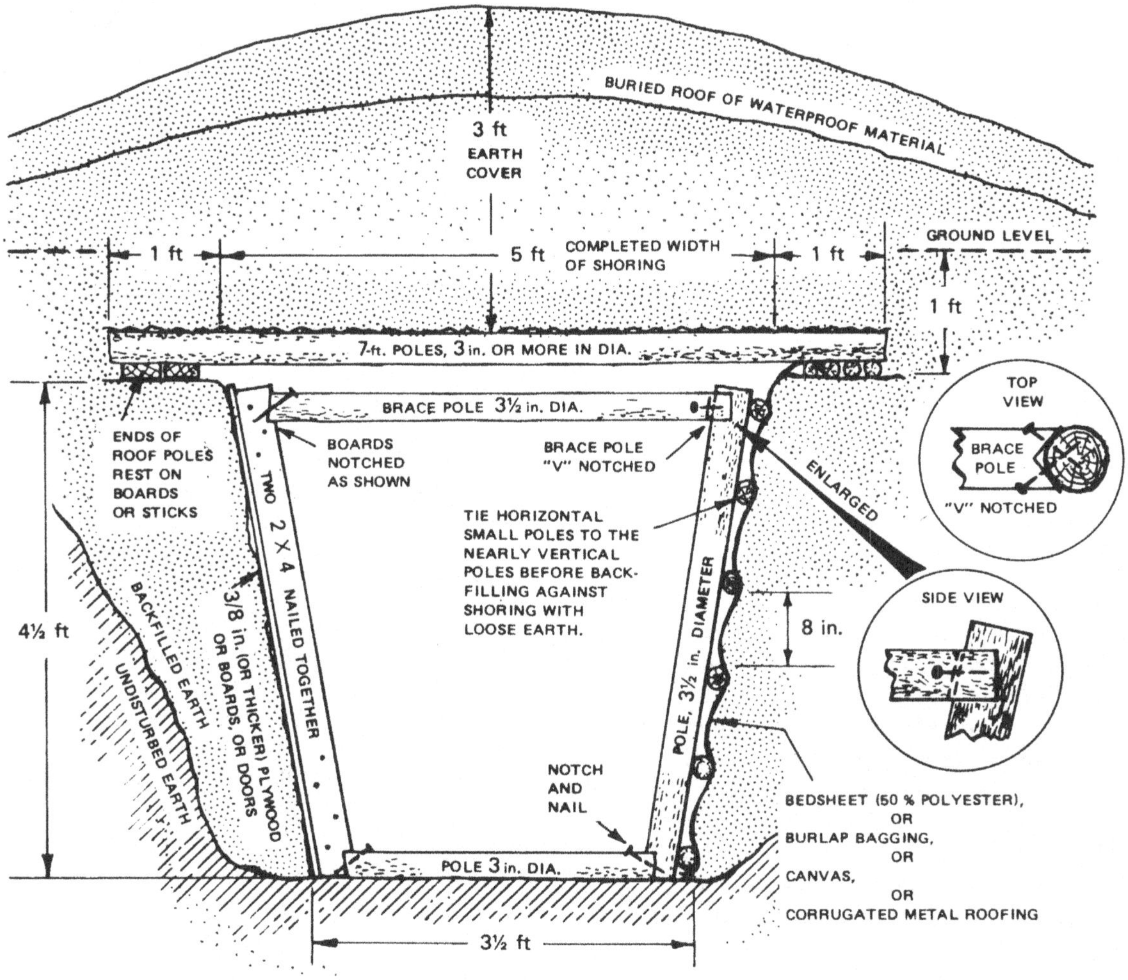

Fig. D.7. An illustration of several ways to shore a trench in unstable earth, using various materials. A 4-piece frame (consisting of 4 poles, or 4 boards, installed as shown above) should be installed every $2^1/_2$ feet along the length of the trench, including the horizontal parts of the entryways. All parts of the shoring should be at least 2 inches below the roof poles, so that the downward forces on the roof will press only on the earth.

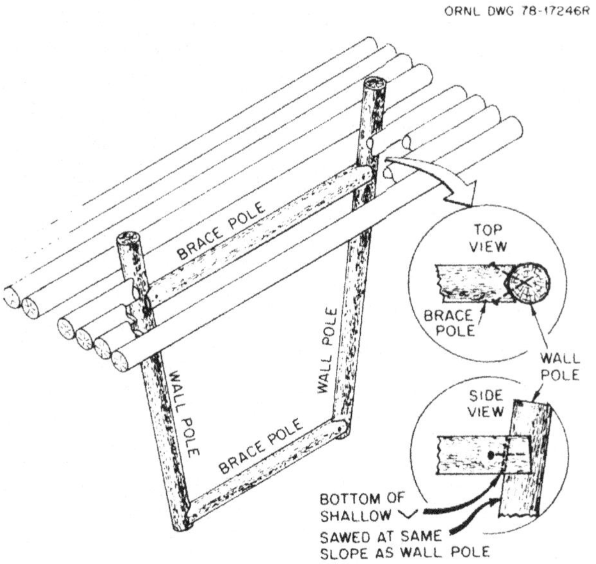

Fig. D.8. A 4-pole frame designed so that it can be tightened against the shoring materials that must press firmly against the walls of a trench dug in stable earth. (In this sketch, the middle sections of three poles have been removed, so that the upper brace pole may be seen more clearly.)

sawed in both ends. If these brace poles are driven downward when positioned as shown, the two wall poles are forced outward against the shoring materials placed between them and the earth walls. An upper brace pole should be cut to the length needed to make it approximately the same height as the roof poles on each side of it (no higher) after the shoring is tightened. Finally, each "V"-notched end should be nailed to its wall pole.

Light, yielding poles can serve simultaneously both to roof and to shore a shelter. A good example is the Chinese "Man" Shelter illustrated in Fig. D.9, requiring comparatively few poles to build.[21] This shelter is too cramped for long occupancy, and its unshored, lower earth walls can be squeezed in by blast pressure. Therefore, it is not recommended if sufficient materials are available for building a well-shored, covered-trench shelter. It is described here primarily to help the reader understand the construction of similarly designed entryways, outlined later in this appendix. The room and the horizontal entryway of the model tested were made of $6^1/_2$-foot poles averaging only 3 inches in diameter. It had two vertical, triangular entries of ORNL design. Each was protected by an expedient triangular blast door made of poles. In Fig. D.9, note the two small horizontal poles at the top of the triangle, one tied inside and the other tied outside the triangle, to hold the wall poles together. Before covering this shelter with earth, a 6-inch-thick covering of small limbs was placed horizontally across the approximately 3-inch-wide spaces between the $6^1/_2$-foot wall poles; the limbs were then covered with bedsheets.

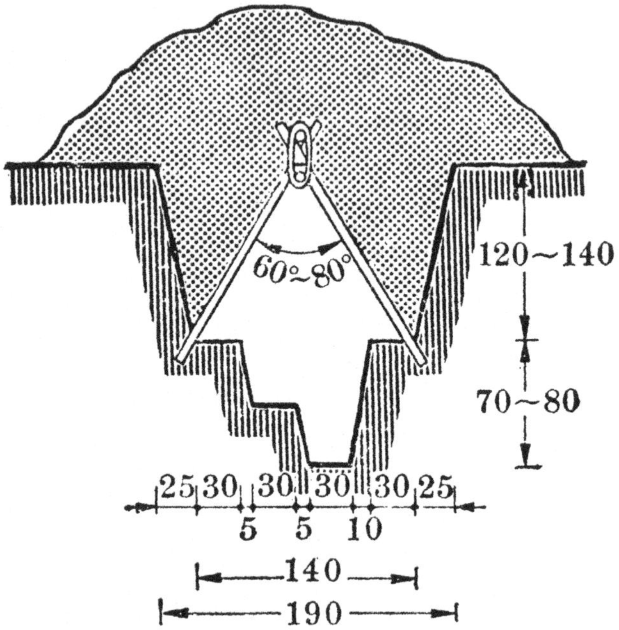

图 3-107 人字形骨架避弹所

Fig. D.9. Chinese "Man" Shelter tested at 20 psi, and undamaged because the thin poles yielded and were protected by earth arching. This drawing was taken from a Chinese civil defense manual. The dimensions are in centimeters.

When blast-tested in loose, unstable soil, the unsupported earth walls of the trench below the wall poles were squeezed in. The 12-inch width of the foot trench was reduced to as little as 4 inches by the short-duration forces produced by 0.2-kiloton blast effects at 50 psi. The much longer duration forces of a megaton explosion would be far more damaging to the shelter at lower overpressure ranges, due to destabilizing and squeezing-in unshored earth at depths many feet below ground level.

Calculations based on blast-test findings indicate that the unsupported earth walls of a shelter are likely to fail if the aboveground maximum overpressure is greater than 5 to 7 psi and this overpressure is caused by an explosion that is a megaton or more.

(Most homes would be severely damaged by the 3-psi blast effects from a 1-megaton or larger weapon. This damage would result one mile closer to ground zero of a 1-megaton surface burst than the distance at which the unshored earth walls of some shelters would be collapsed. For a 20-megaton surface burst, the corresponding reduction in distance would be about 2.7 miles.)

• **Build sufficiently long and strong entryways.** Blast shelters need longer horizontal entryways, taller vertical entryways, and thicker earth cover than do most fallout shelters; these are needed primarily for increased protection against high levels of initial nuclear radiation. The entryways of the Small-Pole Shelter described in Appendix A.3 (with the improvements for increased blast protection outlined in the following section of this appendix) afford protection against both blast and radiation up to the 50-psi overpressure range. However, these entryways require straight poles 14 feet long; these may be difficult to find or transport.

In contrast, both the horizontal and the vertical parts of the triangular entry pictured in Figs. D.10, D.11, and D.12 require only small-diameter, short poles. Triangular entries of this type were undamaged by 1-kiloton blast effects at the 20-psi overpressure range[5] and by 0.2-kiloton blast effects at 50 psi. This type of entry and its blast door (also triangular and made of short poles) can be used with a wide variety of expedient blast shelters and should withstand megaton blast effects at 25 psi. Therefore, their construction is described in considerable detail.

* **The horizontal part of a triangular entry:** If the Chinese "Man" Shelter shown in Fig. D.9 is made without excavating the unshored lower trench that forms its earth seats, it will serve as a horizontal, shored crawlway-entry affording blast protection up to at least the 25-psi overpressure range. Two horizontal entries, one at each end of the shelter, should be provided. Each entry should be 10 feet long. This length is needed to reduce the amount of initial nuclear radiation reaching the blast shelter room while assuring adequate through-ventilation. The outer part of such a horizontal entry is pictured in the background of Fig. D.10.

* **The vertical part of a triangular entry:** The *lower section* of the vertical part is made in a similar manner to the horizontal shelter shown in Fig. D.9. Figure D.10 shows $4\frac{1}{2}$-foot horizontal poles (1) forming a "V", with one end of each pole laid on top of the adjacent lower pole. The other ends of these poles (1) are pressed against the two pairs of vertical posts (2). (After this photo was taken, the tops of these two pairs of vertical posts were sawed off as

Fig. D.10. Uncompleted lower section of a vertical triangular entry.

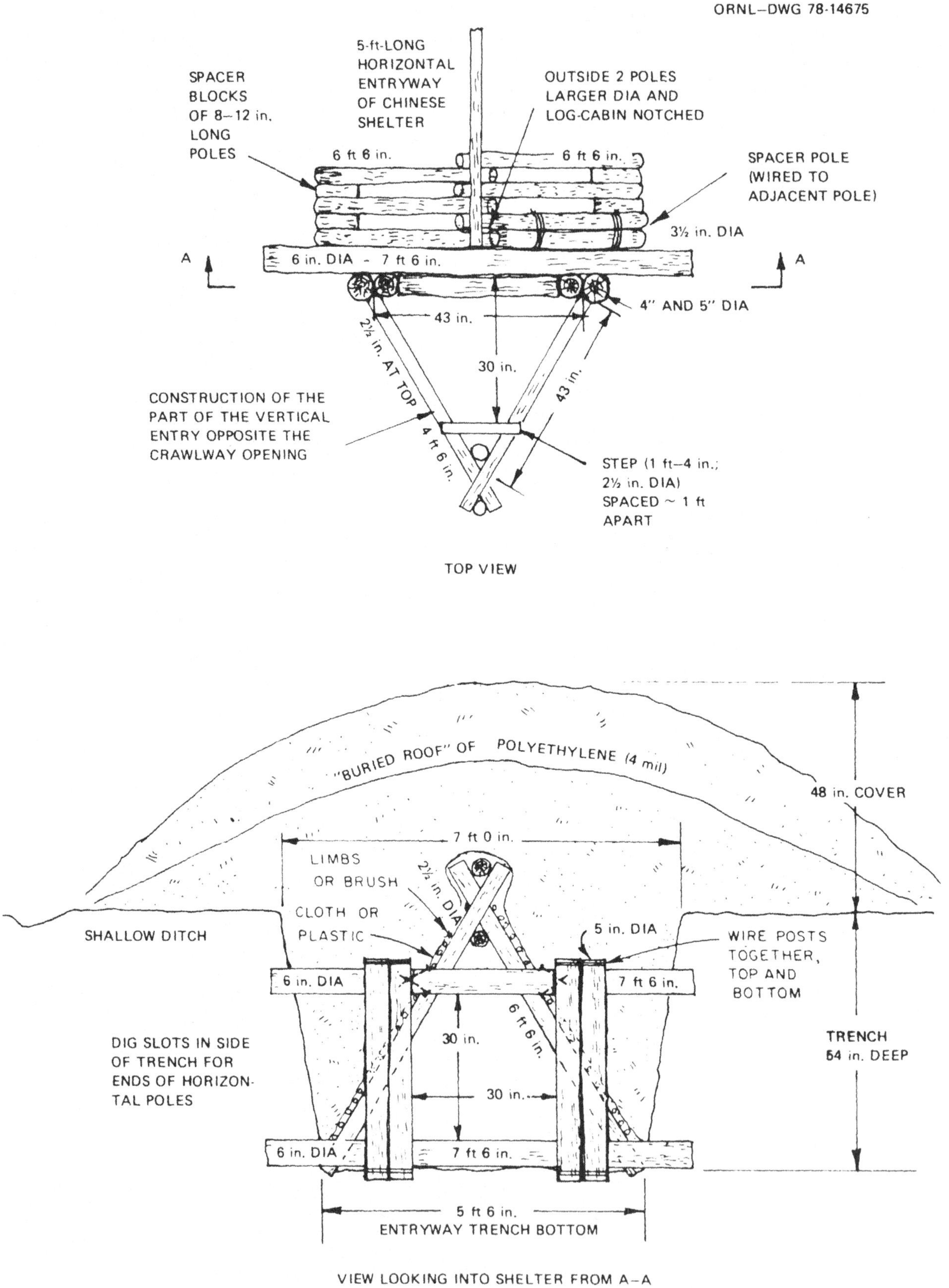

Fig. D.11. Lower part of a vertical triangular entry, showing its connection to the horizontal part of the shelter entry.

Fig. D.12. Completed frame of Chinese "Man" Shelter showing its two ORNL-designed entryways (one at each end) and triangular blast doors made of poles. Before covering the triangular vertical entries with earth, tree branches were placed vertically over the sides; the branches then were covered with bedsheets. Horizontal branches, also covered with bedsheets, were laid over the rest of the shelter frame. After being covered with earth, this shelter was subjected to 1-kiloton blast effects. Multiple earth arching over and around this yielding structure prevented both the small poles and the bedsheets from being damaged at 20 psi.

shown in Fig. D.11.) The $4^1/_2$-foot horizontal poles (1) were kept level by the short spacer-poles (3) that were wired or nailed in place.

Each pair of vertical posts (2) was securely wired together at top and bottom. The two pairs were held apart at top and bottom by two horizontal brace-poles toenailed in place to frame the rectangular 30-×30-inch crawlway "doorway" between the vertical entry and the horizontal entry. Only the upper pole (4) of these two 30-inch-long horizontal brace-poles is shown.

The two pairs of vertical posts (2) were positioned so that they pressed against two $7^1/_2$-foot horizontal poles (5); only the uppermost is shown. These in turn pressed against the outermost two poles (6) of the horizontal entry and against the earth in two slot-trenches dug in the sidewalls of the excavation. These two $7^1/_2$-foot poles (5) should be at least 6 inches in diameter.

Additional details of the lower section of this vertical triangular entry are given in Fig. D.11. If horizontal poles considerably larger in diameter than those illustrated are used, fewer poles are required and strength is increased. However, the space inside the entry is decreased unless the larger-diameter horizontal poles that form the "V" are made longer than $4^1/_2$ feet.

As shown on the left in Fig. D.10, a small, vertical pole (7) was placed in the small "V" between the outer ends of the horizontal poles that form the lower section of the vertical entry. After this photo was taken, a second small, vertical pole was positioned in the adjacent large "V", inside the entry. These two poles (7) were then tightly wired together so as to make a strong, somewhat yielding, outer-corner connection of the horizontal poles (1)—in the same way that the tops of the side-wall poles of the Chinese "Man" Shelter are bound together.

The **upper section** of the vertical part of this entry (the section above the tops of the two pairs of vertical posts shown in Fig. D.10 and Fig. D.11) is made by overlapping the ends of its nearly horizontal poles (Fig. D.12). These poles [marked with a (1) in Fig. D.10] were each 4 feet 6 inches long and varied uniformly in diameter from about $2^1/_2$ inches just above the two pairs of wired-together posts, to 4-inch diameters just below the triangular door frame of poles. The triangular-shaped blast door was hinged to and closed against this door frame. The hinges were strips cut from worn auto tires, to be described shortly.

The upper section is formed by laying poles in a triangular pattern, ends crossing at the angles, with large ends and small ends placed so that the poles are as nearly horizontal as is practical. Each of its three corners is held together by strong wires that tightly bind an outside and an inside small vertical pole, in the same manner as the top of the Chinese "Man" Shelter (shown in Fig. D.9) is secured. (Instead of No. 9 soft steel wire, rope or twisted strips of strong fabric could be used.)

Before starting to install the upper section of a vertical triangular entry, the three outermost of the six small vertical poles that will hold the three corners together should be connected temporarily with three small horizontal poles. Connect them at the height of the door frame planned for the triangular blast door, and space them so as to be the same size as this door frame.

Next, all the horizontal poles should be laid out on the ground in the order of their increasing diameters. The triangular entry then should be started with the smallest poles at the base, with increasingly large-diameter poles used toward the top—so that the three pairs of small vertical poles will press securely against all the horizontal side poles of the entry.

To prevent the negative overpressure ("suction") phase of the blast from yanking out and carrying away the blast door and the upper part of the vertical entry to which it is hinged, the uppermost 4 or 5 horizontal poles of each of the three sides of the vertical entry should be wired or tied securely together. Rope or strips of strong cloth can be used if strong wire is not available.

Before placing earth around this lightly constructed blast-protective entry, the vertical walls must be covered to a thickness of about 6 inches with a yielding, crushable covering of limbs, brush, or innerspring mattresses. Limbs or brush should be placed in three layers, with the innermost layer at right angles to the underlying poles. The yielding thickness then is covered with strong cloth, such as 50% dacron bedsheets, or two thicknesses of 4-mil polyethylene film. This outermost covering keeps loose earth or sand from filling spaces inside the yielding layer or running into the entry. Thus protected, this vertical entry should be undamaged by 25-psi blast effects of megaton weapons.

A vertical blast-protective entry can also be made like a strong box, using 2-inch-thick boards. Such entries afford blast protection up to 50 psi if made as small as shown here and protected with yielding materials such as a 6-inch-thick layer of brush covered with strong cloth.

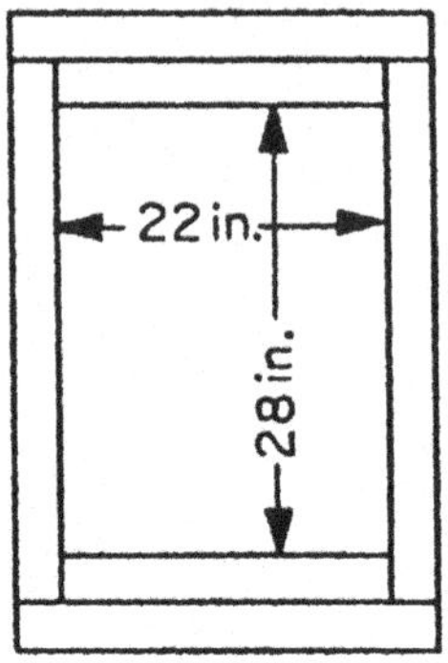

- **Install blast doors** to keep out airborne blast waves, blast wind, overpressure, blast-borne debris, burning-hot dust and air, and fallout.

A fast-rising overpressure of as little as 5 psi will break some people's eardrums. At overpressures of 15 to 20 psi, 50% of the people who are exposed will have their eardrums broken. However, persons near a shelter wall may have their eardrums broken by somewhat less than half of these unreflected overpressures. (Any wall may reflect blast waves and greatly increase overpressures near it.) Broken eardrums are not serious in normal times, but after a nuclear attack this injury is likely to be far more dangerous to persons in crowded shelters without effective medical treatment. Lung damage, that can result from overpressures as low as 10 to 12 psi, would also be more serious under post-attack conditions.

A blast door must withstand blast waves and overpressure. Not only must the door itself be sufficiently strong to withstand forces at least as great as those which the shelter will survive, but in addition the door frame and the entranceway walls must be equally as strong. The expedient blast door pictured in Fig. D.13 was made of rough boards, each a full 2 inches thick. It had a continuous row of hinges made of 18-inch-long strips cut from the treads of worn car tires.

The strips were nailed to the vertical poles on one side of the vertical entry. These and other details of construction are shown in Fig. D.14. Although the two center boards were badly cracked by the shock wave and overpressure at the 17-psi range, the door

Fig. D.13. Blast door surrounded by 4 blast-protector logs that were notched and nailed together. The wet, mounded soil had been compacted by the blast but not blown away.

pictured in Fig. D.13 afforded good protection against all blast effects from a surface explosion of a million pounds of TNT. In Fig. D.14, note the *essential,* strong tie-down attachment of the wires at the bottom of the vertical entry, to prevent the blast door from being yanked open by the negative pressure ("suction") that follows the overpressure.

Blast doors must be protected against reflected pressures from blast waves that could strike an edge of an unprotected door and tear it off its hinges. Note the blast-protector logs installed around the door pictured in Fig. D.14. When the door was closed, the tops of these four logs were about 2 inches higher than the door, thus protecting its edges on all sides.

The closed door must be prevented from rebounding like a spring and opening a fraction of a second after being bowed down by overpressure, or from being opened and perhaps torn off its hinges by the partial vacuum ("suction") that follows the overpressure phase. Figure D.14 gives the details of such a hold-down system for a blast door. Note that near the bottom of the vertical entry the 6 strong wires must encircle a horizontal pole that is flattened on one side and nailed to the vertical wall poles with at least a dozen 6-inch (60-penny) nails. Blast tests up to the 53-psi overpressure range have proved that this hold-down system works.[5]

Figure D.15 shows a blast door made of 5 thicknesses of $^3/_4$-inch exterior plywood, well glued and nailed together with $4^1/_2$-in. nails at 4-in. spacings. This door was protected by 4 blast-protector logs, each 8 feet long and about 8 inches in diameter. The logs were notched, nailed together, and surrounded with earth. For protection against ignition by the thermal pulse from an explosion, exposed wood and rubber should be coated with thick whitewash (slaked lime) or mud, or covered with aluminum foil.

An equally strong blast door and the door base upon which it closes can be made of poles. If poles are fresh-cut, they are easy to work with ax and saw. Figure D.16 shows the best blast-tested design. This door also had a continuous row of hinges made from worn auto tire treads. The pole to which the hinges were attached was 7 inches in diameter after peeling and had been flattened on its top and outer sides. The two other poles of the equal-sided triangle were 8 inches in diameter and had been flattened with an ax on the bottom, top, and inner sides. The three poles were each 55 inches long. They were notched and spiked together with 60-penny nails so that the door would close snugly on its similarly constructed base made of three stout poles. Other poles, at least 7 inches in diameter before being hewn so that they would fit together snugly, were nailed side-by-side on top of the three outer poles.

Many Americans have axes and would be able to cut poles, but not many know how to use an ax to hew flat, square sides on a pole or log. This easily acquired skill is illustrated by Fig. D.17. The worker should first fasten the pole down by nailing two small poles to it and to other logs on the ground. Figure D.17 shows a pole thus secured. When hewing a flat side, the worker stands with his legs spread far apart, and repeatedly moves his feet so that he can look almost straight down at where his ax head strikes. First, vertical cuts with a *sharp* ax are made about 3 or 4 inches apart and at angles of about 45° to the surface of the pole, for the length of the pole. These multiple cuts should be made almost as deep as is needed to produce a flat side of the desired width. Then the worker, again beginning at the starting end, should cut off long strips, producing a flat side.

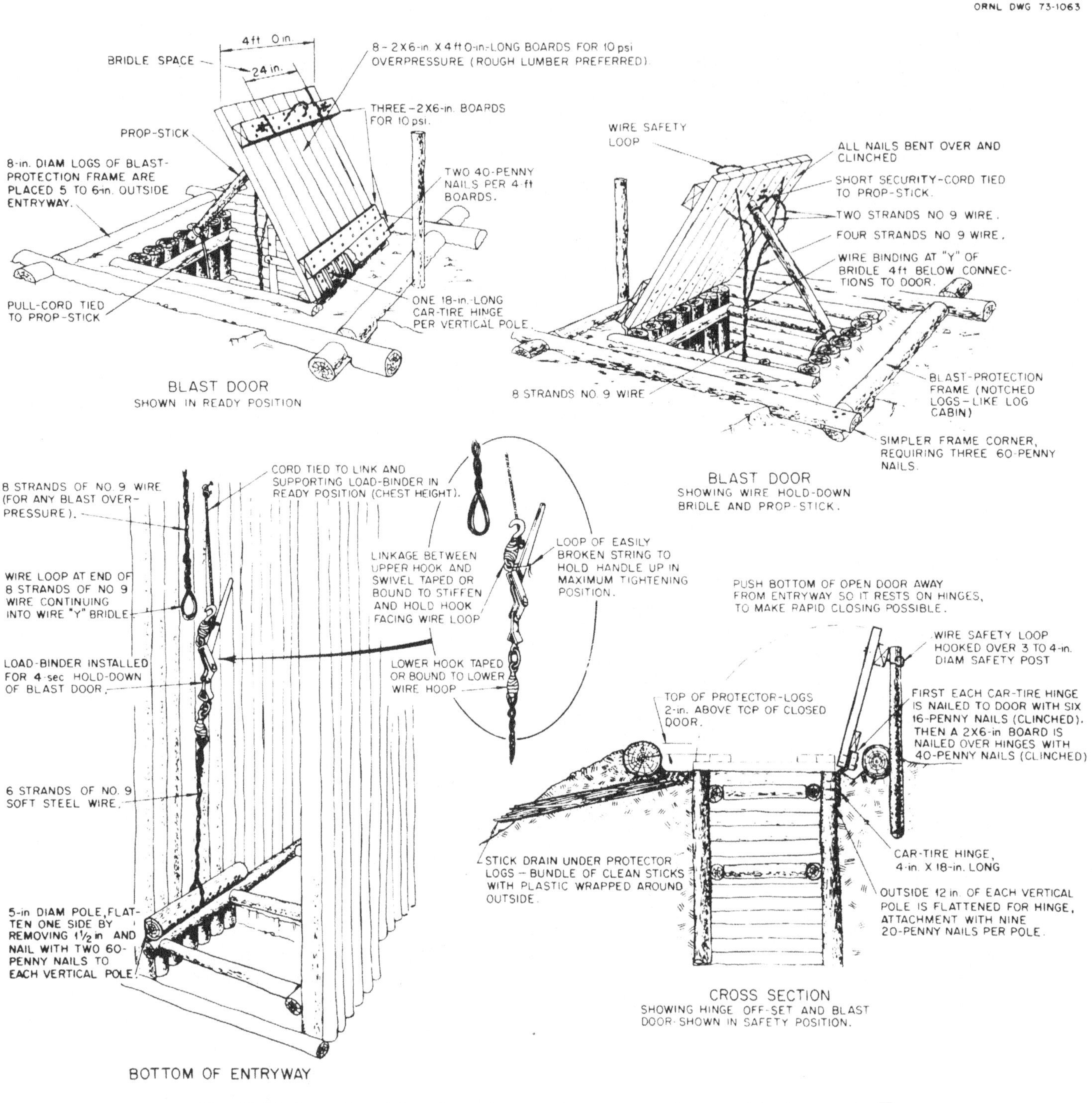

Fig. D.14. Expedient blast door that can be closed and secured in 4 seconds. Four seconds would be too little time if the shelter is at the 15-psi overpressure range from a 550-kiloton or smaller warhead — typical of the 1987 Soviet ICBM arsenal. (See the last paragraph on page 255.) However, this door closure is still the best blast-tested expedient means to secure a closed blast door.

Fig. D.15. Tire-strip hinges nailed to an expedient, 4-inch-thick blast door made of plywood, designed to withstand 50-psi blast effects of very large weapons and undamaged by blast at the 53-psi range.

Fig. D.16. Blast-tested triangular blast door made of hand-hewn pine poles, notched and nailed together. This door closed on a triangular pole base that is concealed in this photo by two of the three blast-protector logs that also withstood 53-psi blast effects.

Fig. D.17. Hewing flat sides on a pole with a sharp ax.

To hew a second flat side at right angles to the first side, rotate the pole 90°, secure it again, and repeat—as pictured in Fig. D.17.

- **Provide blast closures for an adequate ventilation system.** The following two expedient closure systems permit adequate volumes of ventilating air to be pumped through a shelter:

1. **Install two blast doors,** one on each end of the shelter, designed to be left open until the extremely bright light from a large blast is seen. Figure D.14 shows a door held open by a prop-stick that can be yanked away by the attached pull-cord. While propped open, one blast door serves as an extremely low-resistance air-intake opening, and the other serves as an air-exhaust opening. A large KAP can pump air at the rate of several thousand cubic feet per minute through such open doors.

When an attack is expected, each pull-cord should be held by a shelter occupant who stays ready at all times to yank out the prop-stick as soon as he sees the light of an explosion. After the door has fallen closed, the loop at the end of its wire bridle is close to the upper hook of the load-binder and at the same height (Fig. D.14). The person who closes the door should quickly hook the upper hook of the load-binder into the wire loop and pull down on the handle of the load-binder. The door will then be tightly shut. (Sources during an emergency would be the millions of load-binders owned by truckers and farmers.)

At distances from a large explosion where blast wave and overpressure effects are not destructive enough to smash most good expedient blast shelters, there is enough time between the instant the light of the explosion is seen and the arrival of its blast wave for an alert person to shut and securely fasten a well-designed blast door. The smaller the explosion and the greater the overpressure range, the shorter the warning time. Thus at the 15-psi overpressure range from a 1-megaton surface burst (1.5 miles), the blast wave arrives about 2.8 seconds after the light; whereas at the 10-psi overpressure range from a 1-megaton surface burst (1.9 miles), the blast wave arrives about 4.5 seconds after the light. For a 20-megaton surface burst, the warning time at the 15-psi range is about 8 seconds, and at the 30-psi overpressure range, about 4 seconds. Experiments have shown that even people who react quite slowly can close and secure this door within 4 seconds after seeing a spotlight shine on the door without warning.

2. **Build a vertical air shaft next to the outermost side of each vertical entry, with an Overlapping-Flaps Blast Valve** (see Fig. D.18) connecting each entry to its air shaft, as shown in Fig. D.19. These air shafts and blast valves permit forced ventilation to be maintained when the two blast doors are closed. Figure D.18 illustrates the construction of a fast-closing expedient blast valve, a design that was undamaged by the 65-psi shock wave and other effects produced by the explosion of a million pounds of TNT. When blast-tested in a shock-tube at 100-psi, the flaps were undamaged; they closed in 6/1000 of a second (0.006 sec.). This is as fast as the best factory-made blast valves close.

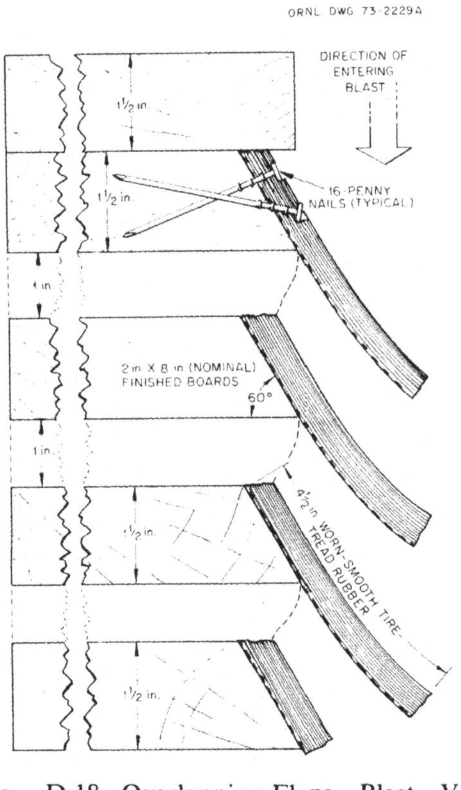

Fig. D.18. Overlapping-Flaps Blast Valve, made of boards, plywood, and strips cut from the treads of worn car tires.

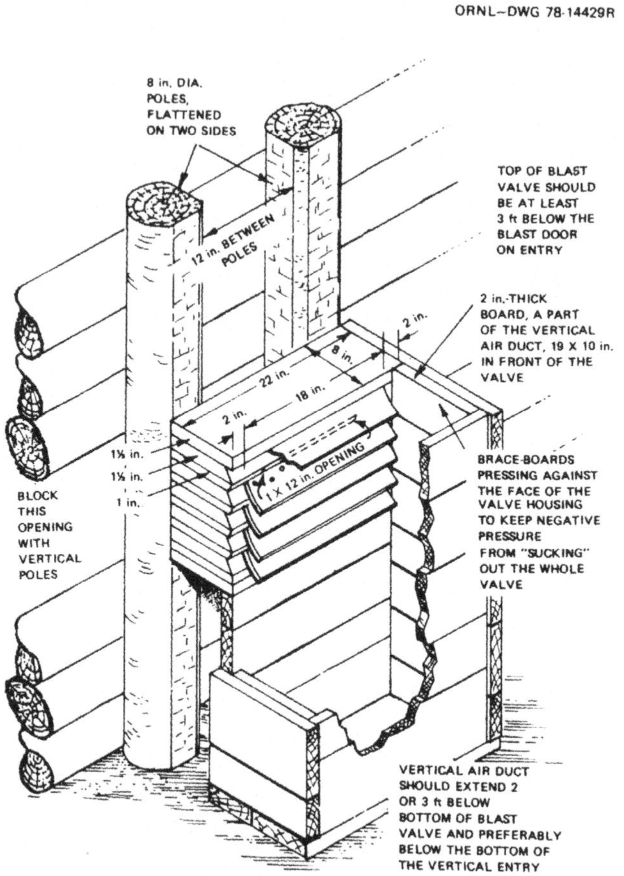

Fig. D.19. Installation of a 50-psi Overlapping-Flaps Blast Valve in such a way that it will not be blown into a shelter by the blast overpressure, nor pulled out by the following negative pressure ("suction") phase.

To withstand 50 psi, the load-bearing "2-inch" boards (actually $1^1/_2$ inches thick) of the valve should be at least 6 inches wide, if the 1-in.-high air openings are each made 12 in. wide, measured between two vertical poles of a shelter entry. See Fig. D.19, that gives the dimensions of a valve that has been blast tested.[5] Note that there are 5 inches of solid wood at each end of each 1-in.-high air opening. If there are 5 such air openings to a valve, a properly installed KAP (Appendix B) can pump air at about 125 cubic feet per minute (125 cfm) through a shelter equipped with such valves. This ventilation rate is ample for at least 40 people in cold weather. Except in hot and humid weather, a constant air supply of about 10 cfm per shelter occupant is enough to maintain tolerable conditions during continuous shelter occupancy for many days.

If a factory-made blower capable of pumping more than 100 cfm is available, use it. Such a hand-operated blower can pump against much higher air flow resistances than a KAP can. It can pump its full-rated volume of outdoor air through a shelter equipped with two Overlapping-Flaps Blast Valves, one at each end of the shelter and each with only 2 air openings—providing a total of 24 square inches of openings per valve. Equally or more effective is a homemakeable Plywood Double-Action Piston Pump, made and operated as described in Appendix E.

Remember that a pressure of 7200 pounds pushes against each square foot of the exposed face of a blast valve when it is subjected to a 50-psi blast overpressure. Also keep in mind that the "suction" that follows can exert an outwardly directed force of up to 700 pounds per square foot on the valve face and can yank it out of position unless it is securely installed. Figure D.19 shows how to securely install a blast valve. (Merely nailing a blast valve in its opening will not enable it to withstand severe blast forces.)

Note in Figure D.19 that an opening is shown between the back edge of the uppermost board of the Overlapping-Flaps Blast Valve and the adjacent horizontal pole of the vertical entry. Both this opening and the similar opening next to the lowermost board of the Blast Valve should be closed off with a stout board, to prevent blast from going through these openings and on into a vertical entry and the shelter room.

The top of an air shaft should be a few inches higher than the earth piled around it, as are the tops of the vertical entries of the Small-Pole Shelter illustrated in Figure A.3.1 on page 174. To minimize the amount of rain that may fall into an air shaft, a shed-like, open-sided miniature roof should be placed over it, a few inches above its top. The roof can be lightly constructed, since it will be blown away by a severe blast.

- **Minimize aboveground construction and the mounding of shielding earth.** At high overpressure ranges, the shock wave and the blast-wind drag can wreck an aboveground shelter entry. For example, the 5-ft-high earth mound over a shelter built with its pole roof at ground level was moved enough by 1-kiloton air-blast effects at the 53-psi overpressure range to break one of the poles of a blast-door frame. The forces of a 1-megaton explosion at the same overpressure range would have operated 10 times as long, and probably would have smashed the vertical entryways of this shelter. Whenever practical, a blast shelter should be built far enough belowground so that the top of its shielding earth cover is at ground level. Avoiding aboveground construction and earth mounds also greatly reduces the chances of damage from blast-hurled, heavy debris, such as tree trunks and pieces of buildings.

Dry earth, steeply mounded over a shelter which is subjected to blast winds from a big explosion, will be mostly blown away. However, blast-wind "scouring" of **wet** earth is negligible. The blast winds from a 1-kiloton explosion at the 31-psi overpressure range scoured away 17 inches of **dry,** sandy soil mounded at a slope of 32°.

If it is impractical to build a blast shelter with its roof belowground, good protection can be attained by mounding even dry earth at slopes not steeper than 10°.

- **Provide adequate shielding against initial nuclear radiation.** Good expedient blast shelters require a greater thickness of earth cover than is needed on good fallout shelters, for these reasons:

  * Blast shelters should also protect against initial nuclear radiation emitted by the fireball. This radiation is reduced by half when it penetrates about 5 inches of packed earth (as compared to a halving-thickness of only about 3½ inches of earth against radiation from fallout).
  * The initial radiation, in some areas where good blast shelters will survive, can be much greater than the fallout radiation is likely to be.
  * Initial nuclear radiation that comes through entryways is more difficult to attenuate (reduce) than fallout radiation. Therefore, longer entryways or additional right-angle turns must be provided.

For these reasons, good blast shelters should be covered with at least 4 ft of well-packed, average-weight earth, or 5 ft of unpacked or light earth. (A 3-ft thickness gives excellent protection against radiation from fallout.)

A 50-PSI SMALL-POLE SHELTER

This expedient blast shelter is described in detail to enable the reader to build this model. The details will help him better understand the design principles of other expedient blast shelters that are capable of preventing injuries from blast effects severe enough to destroy all ordinary buildings and kill the occupants. Blast tests and calculations have indicated that the Small-Pole Shelter described and illustrated in Appendix A.3 will afford protection against all weapon effects at overpressure ranges up to 50 psi that are produced by an explosion of 1 megaton, or *larger,* provided the shelter is:

- Made with horizontal entryways each with ceilings no higher than 7 ft, 2 in., no wider than 3 ft, and each at least 10 ft long—to lessen the radiation coming through the entries (see Fig. D.20). Lower and narrower entryways would give better protection but would increase the time required for entry.

- Constructed with a floor of poles that are 4 in. or more in diameter, laid side-by-side, with the wall poles resting on the floor poles. The ground shock and earth pressures at a depth of 10 ft or more resulting from an overpressure on the surface of more than about 35 psi, if caused by a large explosion, may destabilize and squeeze earth upward into the shelter through an unprotected earth floor. The Small-Pole Shelter described in Appendix A.3 has an earth floor.

- Installed in an excavation about 13 feet deep, with the shelter's vertical entrances appropriately increased in height so that the blast doors are only about one foot above the original ground level.

To prevent possibly life-endangering cave-in of the 13-foot-deep trench that was dug for the blast testing of this model shelter, the trench walls were sloped about 45 degrees. The shelter was built as a braced, free-standing structure, and then covered. During a crisis it would be impractical to safely excavate a deep trench with steeply sloping walls and then safely build a shelter in it. A 13-foot-deep trench is usually too deep to dig by hand—especially since to dig it with safely sloping walls requires the removal of a large amount of earth.

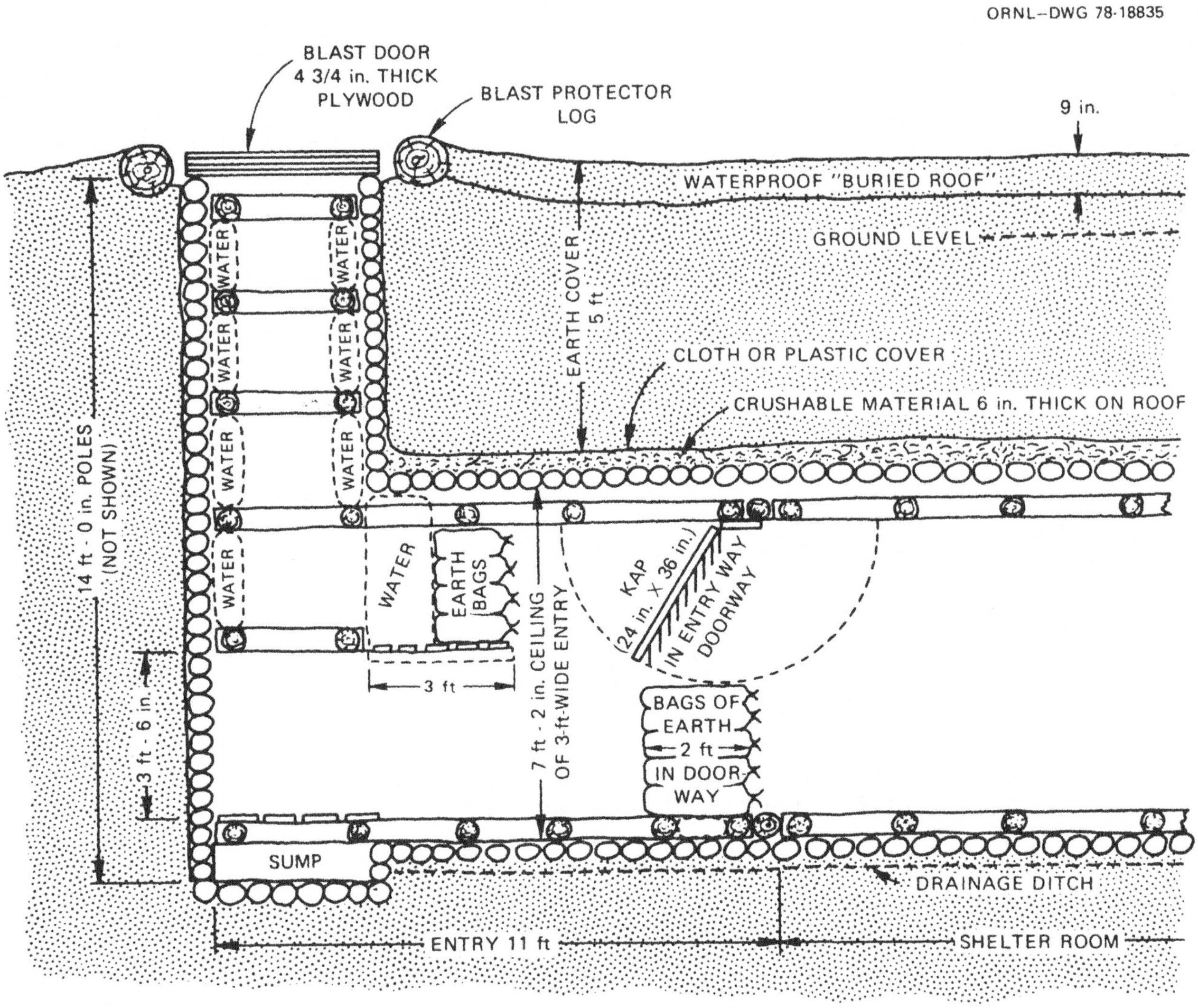

Fig. D.20. Entryway of Small-Pole Blast Shelter shielded against initial nuclear radiation. This sketch is a simplified vertical section through the centerline of one end of the shelter.

- Made with 4 rectangular horizontal braces in each vertical entry, in addition to the ends of the two long, ladder-like braces. The detailed drawings in Appendix A show such braces. The lowest rectangular brace should be positioned $3^1/_2$ feet above the flooring at the bottom of the vertical entry (see Fig. D.20).

- Equipped with blast doors each made of 5 sheets of $^3/_4$-inch exterior plywood (see Fig. D.15) bonded with resin glue and nailed together with $4^1/_2$ in. nails. The nails should be driven on 4-in. spacings and their protruding ends should be clinched (bent over). The blast doors must be secured against being yanked open by negative pressure ("suction") by securing them with a strong wire bridle (see Fig. D.14), and with the lower, fixed wire strongly connected near the bottom of the entry to all of the vertical poles on one side, as shown in Fig. D.14.

- Provided with an adequate ventilation pump and with ventilation openings protected against blast by expedient blast-valves (Fig. D.18) installed in the vertical entries as shown in Fig. D.19, to protect the air-intake and the air-exhaust openings. (Ventilation openings should be as far as practical from buildings and combustible materials. Manually closed ventilation openings are NOT effective at the 50-psi overpressure range of most weapons, because there is insufficient time to close them between the arrival of the warning light from the explosion and the arrival of the blast wave.)

- Made with the roof poles covered by a yielding layer of brush or limbs about 6 inches thick, or of innerspring mattresses. This yielding layer in turn should be covered with bedsheets or other strong cloth, to increase the effectiveness of protective earth arching. Brush or limbs should be laid in 3 layers with sticks of the middle layer perpendicular to those of the other two layers.

- Covered with 5 feet of earth, sloped no steeper than 10°.

- Provided with additional shielding materials in the entryways, as shown in Fig. D.20. Such shielding would be needed to prevent occupants from receiving possibly incapacitating or fatal doses of initial nuclear radiation through the entryways at the 50-psi overpressure range, if the shelter is subjected to the effects of a weapon that is one megaton, *or larger,* in explosive yield.

Damp earth serves better for neutron shielding material than dry earth and can be substituted for water as shielding material if sufficient water containers are not available. (At the 50-psi overpressure range from explosions *smaller* than one megaton, the entry and shielding shown in Fig. D.20 may not provide adequate protection against initial nuclear radiation.)

When the shelter is readied for rapid occupancy, the shelter-ventilating KAP is secured against the ceiling, and the bags of earth in the doorway (under the KAP) are removed. Persons entering the shelter would stoop to go under the platform adjacent to the vertical entry. This platform is attached to vertical wall-poles of the horizontal entry and supports shielding water and earth. When all except the person who will shut and secure the blast door are inside the shelter room, occupants should quickly begin to place bags of earth in the doorway. When the attack has begun, the whole doorway can be closed with bags of earth or other dense objects until ventilation is necessary.

The entries of other types of blast shelters can be shielded in similar ways.

- Protected against fire by being built sufficiently distant from buildings and flammable vegetation and by having its exposed wood covered. For maximum expedient protection against ignition by the thermal radiation from a large explosion, all exposed wood should be free of bark, coated with wet mud or damp slaked lime (whitewash), and covered with aluminum sheet metal or foil to reflect heat. (Most of the thermal radiation from an explosion that was 1 megaton or larger would reach the 50-psi overpressure range after the blast wave had arrived and had torn the expedient protective coverings from the wood. However, as has been observed in megaton nuclear weapon tests, the dust cloud first produced by the popcorning effect and later by the blast winds would screen solid wood near the ground so effectively against thermal radiation that it would not be ignited, provided it had been initially protected as described above.)

PRECAUTIONS FOR OCCUPANTS OF BLAST SHELTERS

Although a well constructed blast shelter may be undamaged at quite high overpressure ranges, its occupants may be injured or killed as a result of rapid ground motions that move the whole shelter several inches in a few thousandths of a second. Rapid ground motions are not likely to cause serious injuries unless the shelter is in an area subjected to 30-psi or greater blast effects. To prevent possible injury, when the occupants of high-protection blast shelters are expecting attack they should avoid:

- Having their heads close to the ceiling. The "air slap" of the air-blast wave may push down the earth and an undamaged shelter much more rapidly than a person can fall. If one's head were to be only a few inches from the ceiling, a fractured skull could result.

- Leaning against a wall, because it may move very rapidly, horizontally as well as vertically.

- Sitting or standing on the floor, because ground shock may cause the whole shelter (including the floor) to rise very fast and injure persons sitting or standing on the floor. The safest thing to do is to sit or lie in a securely suspended, strong hammock or chair, or on thick foam rubber such as that of a mattress, or on a pile of small branches.

In dry areas or in a dry expedient shelter, ground shock may produce choking dust. Therefore, shelter occupants should be prepared to cover their faces with towels or other cloth, or put on a mask. If an attack is expected, they should keep such protective items within easy reach.

Appendix E

How to Make and Use a Homemade Plywood Double-Action Piston Pump and Filter

THE NEED

Ventilating pumps—mostly centrifugal blowers capable of operating against quite high resistance to airflow—are used to force outdoor air through most high-protection-factor fallout shelters and through almost all permanent blast shelters. Low-pressure ventilating devices, including ordinary bladed fans and homemade air pumps such as KAPs and Directional Fans, cannot force enough air through a permanent shelter's usual air-supply system consisting of pipes, or of pipes with a blast valve, a filter, and the valves needed to maintain a positive pressure within the shelter.

Manually cranked centrifugal blowers, or blowers that can either be powered by an electric motor or be hand-cranked, are the preferred means of ventilating permanent shelters from Switzerland to China. The main disadvantages of efficient centrifugal blowers are:

1. They are quite expensive. For example, in 1985 a good American hand-cranked blower, that pumps only about 50 cubic feet per minute (50 cfm) through a shelter's pipes, blast valve and filter, retails for around $250. An excellent foreign blower that enables one man to pump somewhat larger volumes sells for about twice as much.
2. Not enough centrifugal blowers could be manufactured quickly enough to equip all shelters likely to be built during a recognized crisis threatening nuclear attack, and lasting for weeks to several months.

Therefore, there is need for an efficient, manually operated, low-cost ventilating pump that:

1. Can pump adequate volumes of outdoor air through shelter-ventilating systems that have quite high resistances—up to several inches water gauge pressure differential.
2. Will be serviceable after at least several weeks of continuous use.
3. Can be built at low cost in home workshops by many Americans, using only materials available in most towns.
4. Could be made by the millions in thousands of shops all over the U.S., for mass production during a recognized prolonged crisis, using only plywood and other widely available materials.

To produce such a shelter ventilating pump, during the past 20 years I have worked intermittently designing and building several types of homemade air pumps. However, until I was traveling in China as an official guest in October 1982 and saw a wooden double-action piston pump being used, I did not conceive or come across a design that I was able to develop into a shelter-ventilating pump that meets all of the requirements outlined above. Now I have made and tested a simple homemade Plywood Double-Action Piston Pump, described below, that satisfies these requirements. Three other persons have used successively improved versions of these instructions to make this model, and several others have contributed improvements.

HOW A PLYWOOD DOUBLE-ACTION PISTON PUMP WORKS

Fig. 1 pictures the box-like test model described in these instructions.

Fig. 1. Plywood Double-Action Piston Pump, with manometer attached for tests.

Fig. 2 illustrates a vertical section through a slightly improved model, and shows the 12x12-in. plywood piston being pushed from right to left, causing air from the outdoors to be "sucked" down the open air-supply duct in the top of the pump, then down to the right through the open valve in the airtight frame (that is above and near the right end of the PARTITION), and on down into the lower-pressure area behind the leftward-moving piston.

Because the air to the right of the leftward-moving piston is at a lower pressure than the air in the shelter room, the exhaust valves in the front end (the handle end) of the pump are held closed.

During this half of the pumping cycle, the higher-pressure air in the part of the pump's square "cylinder" to the left of the leftward-moving piston opens the air-exhaust valves in the back end of the pump, and fresh air is forced out into the shelter room. The higher-pressure air to the left of the valve in the airtight frame (that is above the left end of the PARTITION) keeps this valve closed, while the lower-pressure air to the right of this valve helps keep it closed.

When the piston is pulled to the right, all of the valves shown closed are quickly opened, and all shown open are quickly closed. Then fresh air is forced into the shelter room through the opened exhaust valves in the front end of the pump.

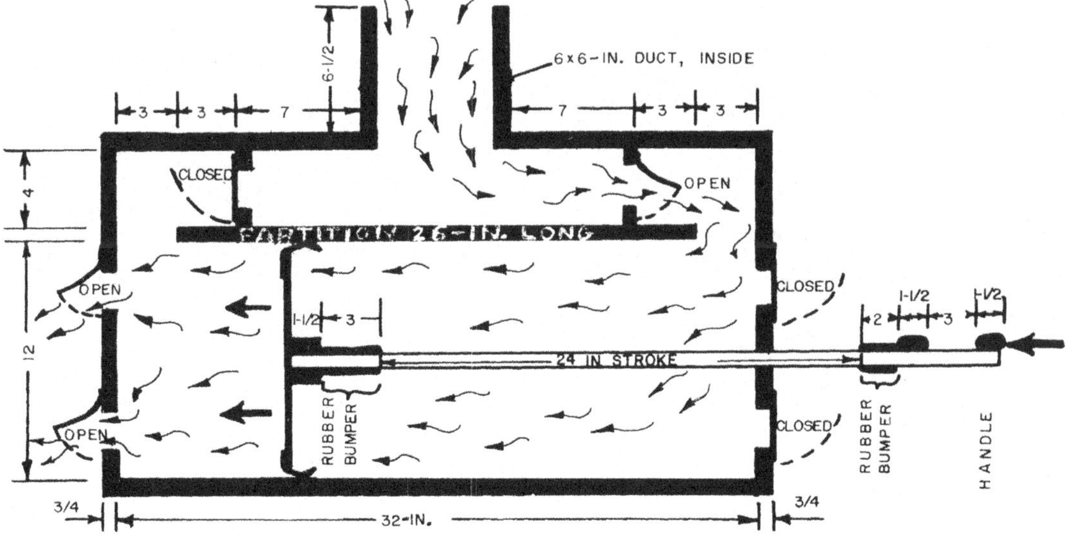

Fig. 2. Vertical Section of the Double-Action Piston Pump showing its square piston being pushed to the left.

PERFORMANCE TESTS

The volumetric and durability tests summarized below are proof that this homemade Plywood Double-Action Piston Pump is better than most hand-cranked centrifugal blowers for supplying a shelter with outdoor air through typical air-intake and exhaust pipes—especially when the ventilation system contains a filter and/or blast valves. The filters that give the best protection, Chemical Biological Radiological (CBR) Filters, have quite high resistance to airflow, as do commercial blast valves that close quickly enough to protect filters.

1. **Volumetric tests.** Because the rapidly pulsating airflows into and out of a piston pump are very hard to measure accurately with an air velocity meter, I made an inflatable cylindrical bag of 2-mil (0.002 inch) polyethylene film; the fully inflated volume of this bag was 256 cubic feet. The bag was suspended on a horizontal strong cord running through its length. A short tube 62 inches in circumference connected the back end of the pump (that is opposite the operator's end) to the suspended bag. Bag and pump were in a below ground shelter that normally has essentially motionless air. See Fig. 1.

Since this type of pump exhausts equal volumes of air from each of its two ends, the total cubic feet per minute (cfm) that it pumps equals twice the cfm that it exhausts into the shelter from one of its ends. See Fig. 1, that shows the pump attached with "C" clamps to a small steel table and being used to pump air into the 256 cubic foot suspended bag.

I measured the pressure differences against which the pump was operated. In a shelter these differences typically are caused by the resistance to airflow in pipes, valves, and a filter. I measured pressure differences in inches water gauge (1 in. w.g. = 0.036 psi) with the small-tube manometer attached to the side of the pump. To produce various pressure differences for several tests, I nailed a piece of plywood over the top of the air-intake duct, so as to produce different sized openings; in most tests I placed different layers of filter materials in a filter box that was fitted airtight over the 6 x 6-in. air-supply duct on the top of the pump. See Fig. 3. (This low-resistance filter removes practically all fallout particles of wartime concern, and also most infective aerosols that may be used in biological warfare. See "Making and Using a Homemade Filter Box and Filter", by Cresson H. Kearny, October 1985.

Fig. 3. Pump with Homemade Filter (20 x 20 x 8-inches inside dimensions) connected airtight on top of the pump's 6 x 6-inch air-intake duct.

The best centrifugal blowers that I have seen or heard about are those manufactured by a Finnish company, Temet Oy. (I cranked a Temet Oy blower in an Israeli shelter used for testing ventilation equipment; the Finnish centrifugal blower was better than Swiss, German and captured Russian blowers also undergoing tests.) Therefore, in Table 1 a few of the volumetric tests of my best model Plywood Double-Action Piston Pump (powered by one and two men) are compared with performance data furnished by Temet Oy for its centrifugal blower when cranked by two men. I have converted Temet Oy's metric units into the common American units.

In Table 1 the pressure difference of 4.3 inches water gauge is the resistance to airflow that Temet Oy realistically gives as typical of a well designed shelter ventilation system of pipes, valves and blower plus a Chemical Biological Radiological (CBR) filter. Temet Oy gives 2.0 inches water gauge as typical of the same ventilation system with only a low resistance dust filter. The much larger volume pumped by the Double-Action Piston Pump when a CBR filter is used (as compared to the cfm pumped by this very good centrifugal blower) is typical of the reduced effectiveness of even the best centrifugal blowers at high pressure differences.

TYPE OF PUMP	PRES. DIFF. (in. w.g.)	CUBIC FEET PER MINUTE	HORSE-POWER
Double-Action Piston Pump			
one man	4.9	134	?
two men	4.3	182	?
Temet Oy Centrifugal Blower			
two men	4.3	90	0.15
Double-Action Piston Pump			
one man	2.3	172	?
two men	2.3	208	?
Temet Oy Centrifugal Blower			
two men	2.0	300	0.18

Table 1. Comparison of Plywood Double-Action Piston Pump with Temet Oy Centrifugal Blower.

In areas devastated by a nuclear explosion, the typical very dusty conditions are likely to result in filters soon becoming dirty and higher in resistance to airflow. Then the greater effectiveness of a piston pump for ventilating a shelter with a high-resistance air-supply system will be even more important than when its filter is clean.

The horsepower requirements of my pump have not yet been measured. However, based on the calculated air pressure on the 12 x 12-in. piston of 22.3 lbs. when the pressure difference was 4.3 in. w.g. (0.155 psi), when two pumpers were making 52 strokes (cycles) per minute while pumping 182 cfm, the horsepower delivered was about 0.14 HP without allowing for friction and the losses of power due to reversals in the directions of piston movements. I estimate that the actual horsepower delivered by the two pumpers (I, a 69 year old with a stiff back in 1983, and a 15-year-old boy) was somewhat less than 0.2 HP. A man in good condition can work for hours delivering 0.1 HP.

When comparing machines powered by human muscles, what muscles are used and how they are used are often as important as are the horsepower requirements. Leg muscles are more efficient and are much stronger than arm muscles. Arm muscles are used much more in cranking a blower than in pushing and pulling the piston of a properly designed reciprocating piston pump back and forth horizontally. See Fig. 3. If this double-action piston pump is placed at a height above the floor so that its handle is approximately at the height of a standing operator's elbows, then the operator can do most of the work with his legs. See Fig. 3. He efficiently moves his body back and forth for over a foot, while moving his hands and forearms horizontally for slightly less than a foot relative to his body. To deliver the same horsepower by cranking a blower uses less efficient muscles inefficiently, and is much more tiring.

As shown in Table 2, the volumetric efficiency of my best model is good for a shelter-ventilating pump. The volumetric efficiency of a piston pump (a positive displacement pump) is found by dividing the cfm actually pumped by the theoretical maximum cfm at the same pumping rate and the same pressure difference, assuming all piston strokes are full length, that all valves open and close instantaneously, and that there is no leakage. Table 2 shows that the greater the pressure difference, the lower the efficiency—as one would expect, because of increased leakage.

PRES. DIFF. (in. w.g.)	STROKES PER MINUTE	cfm	EFFICIENCY
4.0	36	122	84.0%
2.6	45	160	89.0%
0.7	51	188	92.0%
0.4	54	202	94.0%
0.2	55	208	94.5%

Table 2. Volumetric Efficiencies of Double-Action Piston Pump Operated by One Man.

2. **Durability tests.** Finding a homemakeable method to seal the moving piston so as to assure at least one month of continuous efficient pumping was the most difficult problem. Various rubber seals attached to the edges of the piston were unsatisfactory, and aluminum sheetmetal strips (shaped and attached like the galvanized steel sheetmetal strips used in this model) wore out in less than a week, even when oiled every 24 hours.

To save money during weeks of continuous durability testing, the pump was operated by an electric motor that powered a pulley drive that turned a 2-foot-diameter pulley having an attached 40-in.-long steel pitman with a hinged connection to a horizontally-sliding bar connected to the handle of the pump's wooden piston rod. See Fig. 4.

Fig. 4. Mechanized Drive Used in Weeks-Long Durability Tests.

After pumping for 380 hours (15.83 days) at 44 strokes per minute against a pressure difference of 2.3 in. w.g., the worst worn spot on any of the **30-gauge** steel sheetmetal sealing strips on the piston was reduced in thickness from its original 0.0155 in. to 0.0145 in. This worst-spot wear of 0.001 in. is only about a 6% reduction in thickness. The flap valves functioned as well as when new, and appeared unworn.

I conclude that this pump would be serviceable after several months of continuous use—provided it is lubricated after every 24 hours of actual use, as in this durability test. In this test I lubricated the piston, its "cylinder's" four walls, and its rod with Lubriplate No. 105, "the original white grease". This non-sticky "grease-type lubricant" is used extensively, especially to lubricate internal combustion engines before first starting up. Another builder of this model pump found Siloo White Lube, an all-purpose lithium grease, the best of the lubricants that he tested. Judging from my prior durability tests, a very light oil applied daily serves reasonably well. Ordinary bearing grease is unsatisfactory.

MATERIALS

The following materials (that cost about $65. retail in 1985) are needed to make and operate the best model of this pump:

Plywood, 3/4-in. exterior: one 4 x 8-ft. sheet (finished on one side, unwarped).
Plywood, 3/8-in. exterior: 1/4th of a 4 x 8-ft. sheet (finished on one side, unwarped). (Second choice: 1/4-in. exterior plywood).
Oak board, 3/4 x 1-3/4 in., **straight**, well seasoned, 4 ft. long, to make the piston rod. (If oak or other very strong wood is not available, use a **straight** fir or pine board.)
Fir or pine board, about 3/4 x 1-3/4 in., 8 ft. long, to make the piston-rod handle, etc.
28-gauge or lighter galvanized-steel flashing (sold by lumber yards for roofers), no thicker than 0.016 in.; or galvanized steel or flashing no thinner than 0.012 in. Or 30 gauge galvanized steel sheetmetal available in some sheetmetal shops. (Sheetmetal thicker than 0.016 is not springy enough for making this pump's near-equivalent of piston rings.) Best to go to a sheetmetal shop and have 3 strips cut, each 3 in. wide and about 30 in. long.
Screws, round-headed, zinc-plated wood screws:
22 each of No. 12 (2-in. long, 12/32 in. dia.), with flat washers
10 each of No. 10 (1-1/2 in. long, with flat washers)
15 each of No. 6 (3/4 in. long, with flat washers)
Nails, 4-penny (1-1/2 in.), best cement-coated: 1/4 lb.
Nails, 3-penny (1-1/4 in.), galvanized: 1/4 lb.
Staples (if an oak board for the piston rod is not available), No. 17, 3/4-in., galvanized): 1/4 lb.
Tacks, No. 6 upholstery, (1/2-in. long): a small container.
Tacks, No. 3 upholstery (3/8-in. long): a small container.
Felt, weather stripping, 5/8-in. wide: 10 ft.
Tape, silver duct tape, 2-in. wide: a small roll.
Tape, masking tape, 3/4-in. wide: a small roll.
Adhesive, waterproof: "Liquid Nails", or other all purpose construction adhesive: one approx. 11-oz. tube (for use in caulking gun).
Epoxy, 5-minute: 2 tubes.
Rubber cement: a small tube.
Sealer (such as polyurethane clear finish, to reduce absorption of oil or other lubricant of the "cylinder"): 1/2 pint.
Plastic film, transparent storm-window type (such as 4-mil Flex-O-Glass, by Warp Bros.): 3 sq. ft.
Grease-type lubricant, an all-purpose motor-breakin lithium grease such as "Siloo White Lube" or "Lubriplate No. 5 Space Age Lubricant": two approx. 10 oz. tubes.
Inner tube rubber, heavy truck or auto (cut from an old tube): 1 sq. ft.

FUNCTIONAL RELATIONS OF PARTS

Look at Figs. 2, 5, and 6. In Figs. 5 and 6, the lower, fixed part of the front end is pictured below the piston rod. The piston rod slides back and forth on the center of the fixed part of the front end (as indicated more clearly in Fig. 7), and in the notch in the removable part of the front end.

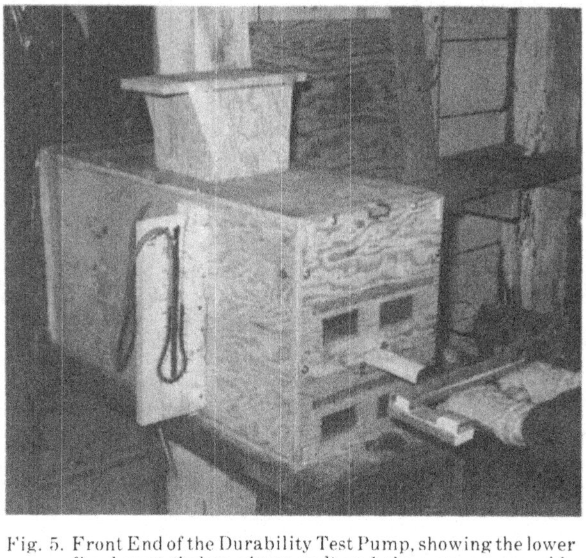

Fig. 5. Front End of the Durability Test Pump, showing the lower fixed part (below piston rod) and the upper removable part, that is held by 6 screws with flat washers. Felt weather-stripping makes the removable part airtight.

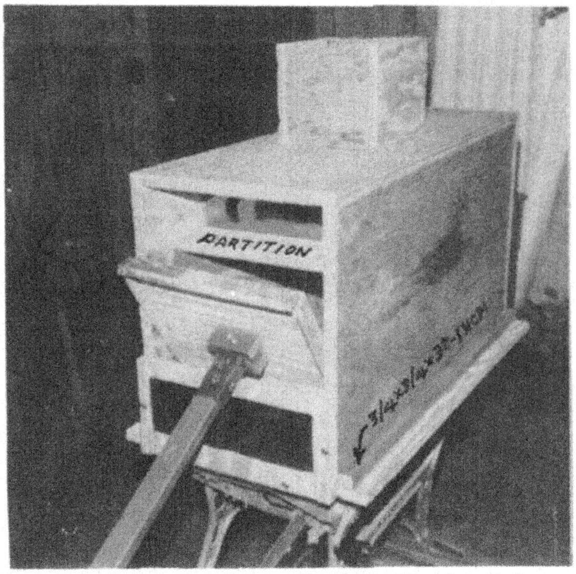

Fig. 6. Pump Built by Dale Huber, of Lake City, Florida in his home workshop, while guided only by the second draft of these repeatedly improved instructions. The removable part of the front end has been taken off, to insert the piston into the 12 x 12-in. "cylinder" under the PARTITION. The plastic flaps of this pump's flap valves are black: transparent plastic film is preferred.

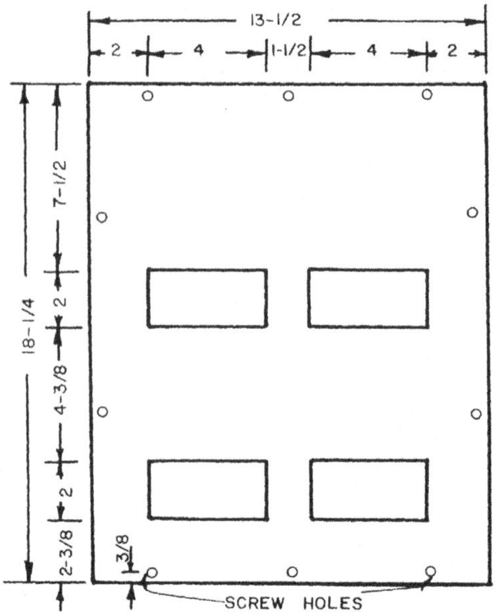

Fig. 8. Back End. Only the plywood is shown.

Note that a single plastic-film flap covers each pair of 2 x 4-in. valve holes, and that, as shown in Fig. 2 (that gives a side view of all six flaps), all flaps open **away** from the vertical center-plane of the pump.

In Fig. 5 the removable (upper) part of the front end is shown in place, secured by six round-head screws with flat washers. In Fig. 7 note the pair of 2 x 4-in. flap-valve holes above the piston rod.

In Fig. 6, the removable part of the front end has been removed, exposing the 26-in.-long, horizontal PARTITION that serves as the top of the 12 x 12-in. "cylinder", in which the piston can make a 24-in.-maximum-length stroke. Also see Figs. 2 and 7. Fig. 6 also shows the piston while it is being removed and one of the two rubber bumpers (made of inner tube rubber) on its piston rod.

The back end of the "box" is made of one piece of plywood, as shown in Fig. 8. The two plastic flaps of its exhaust valves each cover two 2 x 4-in. valve holes, that are positioned the same as the four valve holes in the front end.

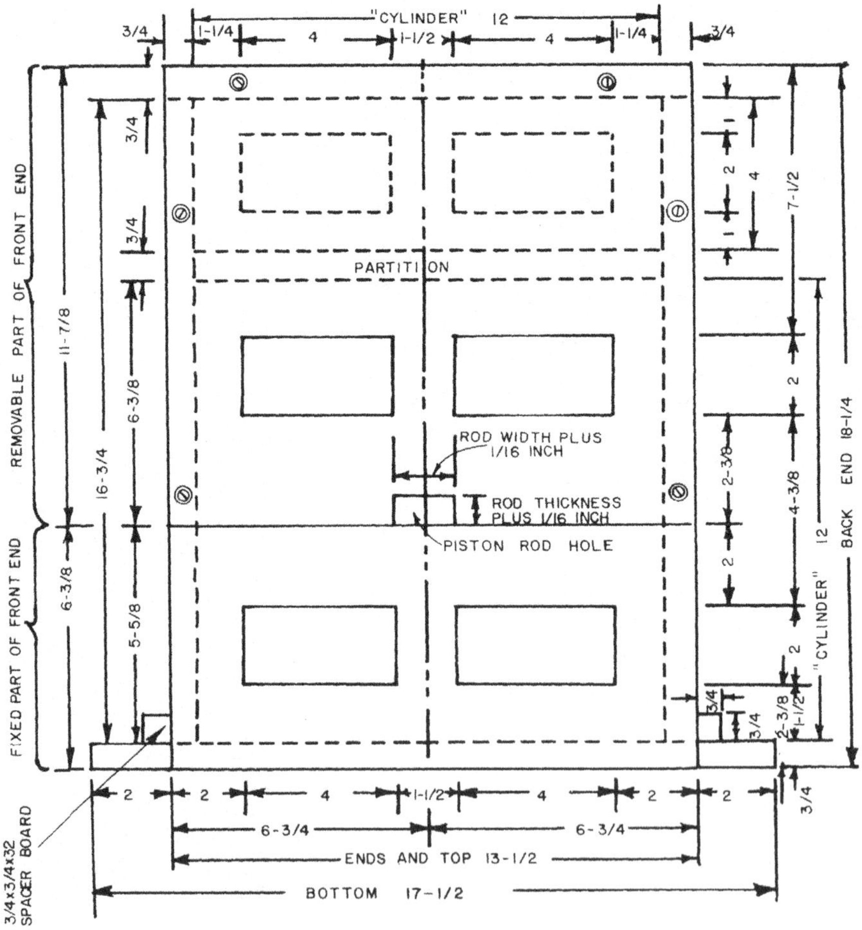

Fig. 7. Front End (Operator's End) of Plywood Double-Action Piston Pump. The two 4 x 12-in. valve frames are shown by dashed lines, as is the 12 x 26-in. PARTITION.

CUTTING OUT THE PLYWOOD PARTS

1. The four parts of the "cylinder" (its bottom, two sides, and the PARTITION: see Fig. 7) should be made with the wood grain of the plywood running in the same direction as the lengths of these parts. This reduces piston friction.

2. Outline on a sheet of **exterior** 3/4-in. plywood all of the plywood parts—except for the 12 x 12-in. piston and the two 12 x 12-in. construction forms, which are made of 3/8-in. **exterior** plywood. (If 3/8-in. plywood is not available, use 1/4-in.) Do not assume that the corners of a sheet of plywood are truly square. Also check the width of the sawcut of the saw to be used, and allow for this width when drawing adjacent outlines of parts on the plywood. Be sure to make all corners **square**.

3. If you do not have a table saw that saws accurately, or a heavy-duty saber saw, you will do well to pay a professional carpenter or cabinet maker to saw out the plywood parts—and also the piston rod if you are making it out of an oak board. A professional can accurately saw out all of the plywood parts and the 10 valve holes in about 2 hours, provided you have accurately outlined all saw lines.

4. Make the following plywood rectangles with tolerances of + or - 1/32 in.:

PARTITION, 12 x 26-in.
Two sides, each 16-3/4 x 32-in. (If your "3/4-in. plywood" actually is less than 11/16-in. thick, make the height of each of your sides 16-3/4-in. less the difference between 3/4-in. and the actual thickness of your plywood. See Fig. 7.)
Bottom, 17-1/2 x 32-in.
Top, 13-1/2 x 32-in.
Two valve frames, each 4 x 12-in.
Piston, 12 x 12-in. (of 3/8-in. plywood).
Two construction forms, each 12 x 12-in. (of 3/8-in. plywood).

5. Make the following plywood rectangles with tolerances of + or - 1/16 in.:

Back end, 13-1/2 x 17-1/4-in. (See Fig. 8.)
Removable (upper) part of front end, 13-1/2 x 10-7/8 in. (See Figs. 7 and 9.)
Fixed (lower) part of front end, 13-1/2 x 6-3/8-in. (See Figs. 7 and 10.)
The four parts of the air-intake duct: two each 6-1/2 x 6-in.; two each 6-1/2 x 7-1/2-in.
Two spacers (to be nailed to the bottom) each 3/4 x 3/4 x 32-in.

6. Saw out the 10 valve holes; a tolerance of + or - 1/8 in. is good enough. (See Figs. 7, 8, 9, and 10.)

7. Saw a square 6 x 6-in. hole in the center of the top, as shown in Fig. 2 — if you are going to install the homemade filter (described in separate instructions) directly on top of your pump. (To connect your pump to a round air-intake pipe, cut an appropriate round hole in the top.)

8. Sandpaper the finished sides of the PARTITION, the two sides, and the bottom, to reduce friction on the reciprocating piston. Use fine sandpaper.

9. Make and attach the 6 valve flaps, to complete the flap valves, that are the lowest resistance, quickest acting type tested.

a. Make a 3-3/4 x 5-3/4-in. cardboard TEMPLATE, using carbon paper to transfer lines of Fig. 11 to cardboard. (See Fig. 11 on page 7, and note that this TEMPLATE outlines the **right** half of the 3-3/4 x 11-1/2-in. plastic-film flap.) Also transfer the dashed tack-line and mark the ends of the 4 horizontal stop-string lines. Drill 8 small holes through the cardboard at the ends of the 4 stop-string lines, so that you can use a pencil to mark these points on plywood.

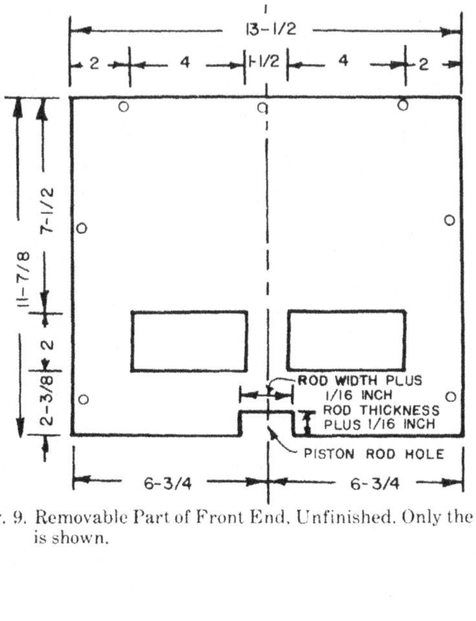

Fig. 9. Removable Part of Front End, Unfinished. Only the plywood is shown.

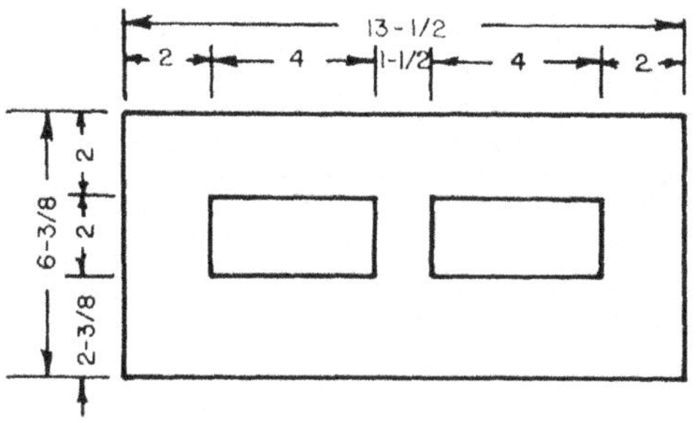

Fig. 10. Fixed Part of Front End, Unfinished. Only the plywood is shown.

b. Use your TEMPLATE to mark around the 2 x 4-in. valve holes in plywood parts: (1) the positions of the ends of each hole's 8 stop-strings, (2) the **right** side-edge and the bottom-edge of each flap after it is attached, and (3) the tack-lines.

c. Drill a 1/16-in. diameter hole through the plywood at each point marked for an end of a stop-string.

d. With nylon kite string (or other nylon string about 1/16-in. in diameter, such as 50-lb-test nylon fishing line) and a big enough needle, string the "four" stop-strings across each 2 x 4-in. hole. (Use a string long enough to make "four" uncut stop-strings.) Start on the unfinished, back side of the plywood, on the opposite side from the future valve flap. To secure the starting end, wrap the string around a half-driven tack, and then drive it in. Keep pulling the string **tight** as you thread it through the holes and as you wrap its finishing end around a half-driven tack. Finally epoxy the string in all of the holes, on the back side of the plywood. (An equally strong nylon string can be made by twisting together 4 pieces of waxed nylon dental floss.)

(Stop-strings also can be positioned by using No. 3 upholstery tacks in place of the 1/16-in. diameter holes. Drive a tack partly in, wind the string around it while pulling the string tight, and drive the tack completely in, to hold the string securely. Finally, coat the tack heads and the adjacent plywood with a smooth covering of adhesive, to provide a smooth seat for the valve flap.)

e. Cut out 6 plastic flaps of transparent 4-mil plastic film (each 3-3/4 x 11-1/2 in.). The easiest way to accurately cut a flap of thin plastic film is to make a cardboard template 3-3/4 x 11-1/2-in., place it on the film, and cut around it with a very sharp knife.

f. In preparation for attaching a flap over each pair of 2 x 4-in. valve holes, cover the plywood **above** each pair of holes with masking tape, up to the straight "tack line" that you already have drawn 1/2 in. **above** each hole. Use your cardboard TEMPLATE. The masking tape will prevent the adhesive (that will be used to attach each valve flap) from being applied too near the 2 x 4-in. holes, where adhesive would keep a flap from opening fully.

g. Position each of the 6 flaps properly in its closed position, with its lower edge on the line that you already have used the TEMPLATE to draw 3/4 in. below each flap's pair of 2 x 4-in. holes. Position its **right** side-edge on the line already drawn 1 in. from the right side of the right hole of each pair of 2 x 4-in. holes. Then put masking tape over the lower edge of each flap and the adjacent plywood, to hold the flap temporarily in its closed position.

h. Gently fold down the upper part of each flap, so that the plywood above its pair of 2 x 4-in. holes is uncovered (except where you have placed the protective tape), and place small pieces of masking tape so as to hold each flap temporarily in this folded-down position.

i. Quickly apply a thin coat of all-purpose construction adhesive (such as Liquid Nails) to a 1/2-in.-wide plywood area above the protective masking tape that covers the plywood up to the "tack line" 1/2 in. above each pair of 2 x 4-in. valve holes. Then promptly detach the small pieces of masking tape holding the flap in its folded-down position, and turn the flap (the lower part of which is still being held in its proper closed position by masking tape) into the whole flap's closed position. Press the upper part firmly against the approximately 1/2-in.-wide coating of adhesive, to secure the valve in its proper closed position. Allow several hours for the adhesive to harden before removing the tape and using the valve.

j. Drive small tacks (No. 3; 3/8 in.) on the "tack line" (see TEMPLATE), to make sure the flap stays securely attached after long use. (Very small tacks are easily driven if held with tweezers or needle-nosed pliers.)

PUTTING THE PUMP "BOX" TOGETHER

1. The following procedure is the best tested construction method for persons who lack experience in putting parts together so that all corners are exactly square, or who do not have the big clamps and other glueing equipment used by cabinet makers. This procedure is best carried out by two persons working together.

2. On the finished side of the top, draw two parallel lines exactly 12 in. apart and parallel to the top's 32-in.-long edges. Each of these lines will be 3/4-in. from an edge. Also draw a line 6 in. from and parallel to each end of the top, to mark the positions of the two valve frames. See Fig. 2.

3. Build the pump's "box" **upside down**; start by placing its top on the floor, as indicated by Fig. 12.

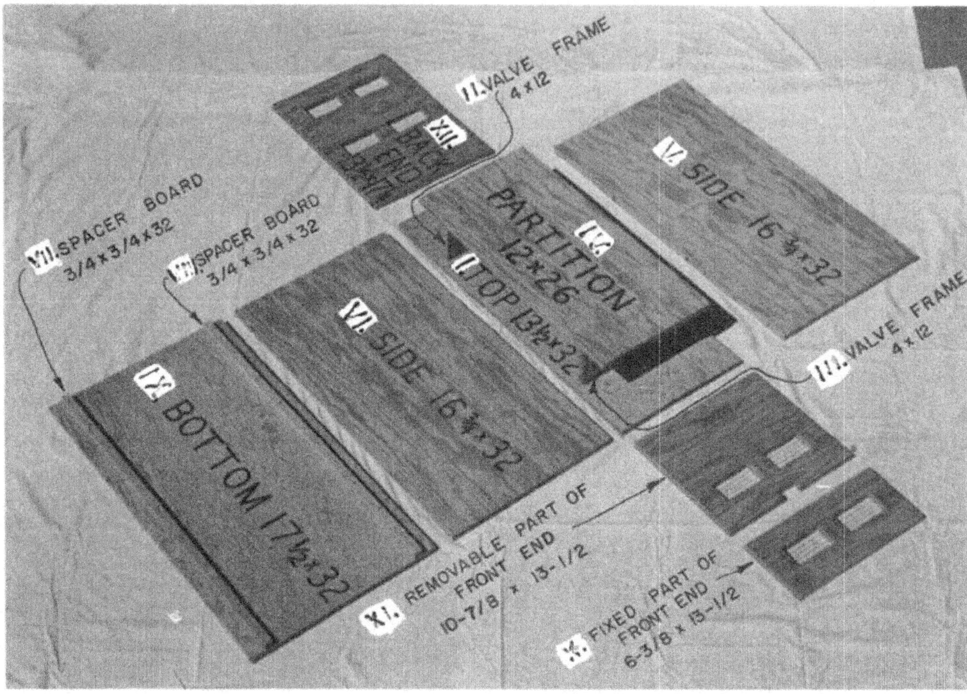

Fig. 12. Parts of the Pump "Box", with Dimensions in Inches. The Roman numbers give the best tested order for attaching these parts to each other.

4. Attach the two valve frames II and III to the top I with construction adhesive, positioning each of them 6 in. from an end of the top I. Make sure that each frame's flap valve is **upside down** and **facing away from the center** of the pump. Remove any adhesive that is on the top beyond the ends of the valve frames.

(When using construction adhesive to make this pump, it is best to apply a rather thin coat to only one of the two plywood surfaces to be joined. Then promptly rub one plywood part slightly back and forth against the other, while pressing them together—thus making sure that both surfaces are coated and in close contact. Wait until the adhesive sets and bonds adequately before attaching more parts.)

5. Draw two parallel lines on the unfinished side of the PARTITION, each 3 inches from one of its ends. Adhere the two 12-in.-long unattached edges of the valve frames to the PARTITION on these two lines, as illustrated by Figs. 2, 7 and 12. Allow time for the adhesive to set.

6. Before permanently attaching side V, position it vertically with a long edge resting on the top, and with a side-edge of the PARTITION and ends of the two valve frames I and II in contact with the finished side of side V. See Fig. 7. On the unfinished (outer) side of side V draw lines showing the positions of the PARTITION and of the two valve frames in contact with the finished side of side V.

7. Preparatory to attaching side V to the PARTITION and to the two valve frames, drill 4 slightly oversize screw holes (for your 2-in. roundhead screws) through side V. Drill these holes so that a screw will go into an end of each valve frame about 1 in. from its adhered edge, and the other 2 screws will go into the side-edge of the PARTITION, at points above the valve frames. Next, with side V temporarily in its final position, drill with a smaller diameter drill through the 4 holes in side V, into the PARTITION and into the two valve frames. Then with the 4 screws temporarily connect side V, the PARTITION, and the two valve frames, and, while checking with a carpenter's square the squareness of the angle between the PARTITION and side V, adjust the two pairs of screws to attain squareness. Remove side V.

8. Apply adhesive to the 3/4-in.-wide area along the long edge of the top, and if necessary a thicker coating of adhesive than normal to unattached edges of the PARTITION and of the two valve frames. Then promptly position side V, and by again screwing in and adjusting the 4 screws, make the angle between the PARTITION and side V **square.** Allow the adhesive to set.

9. Use short pieces of duct tape to temporarily attach the two 12 x 12-in. construction forms to the PARTITION and to side V. (Before using these forms, drive 4 small nails into each form, near its corners, to serve as handles for removing them from the completed "cylinder".) Attach a construction form near each end of the PARTITION.

10. Adhere the finished side of side VI to the top, to the unattached side-edge of the PARTITION, and to end-edges of the valve frames, while keeping side VI pressed against the two **square** construction forms. To keep side VI pressed against the construction forms until the adhesive sets, use small nails to temporarily nail two small boards horizontally across the ends of the sides, at each end of the "box".

11. On the finished side of the bottom IX, draw two parallel lines 13-1/2-in. apart, making each line 6-3/4-in. from the center line of the bottom, as shown in Fig. 7. Nail the two 3/4 x 3/4 x 32-in. spacer boards VII and VIII to the bottom, 13-1/2-in. apart.

12. To attach the bottom, first place it (with its finished side **down**) on the exposed long-edges of the sides. If you find that the bottom rests on the construction forms and is not in contact with the long-edges of the sides, in effect increase the heights of the sides by coating with adhesive both the edges of the sides and the 3/4-in.-wide area of the bottom to which the sides will be adhered. Then adhere the bottom onto the edges of the sides. Before the adhesive hardens, remove any that has been squeezed into the corner of the "cylinder".

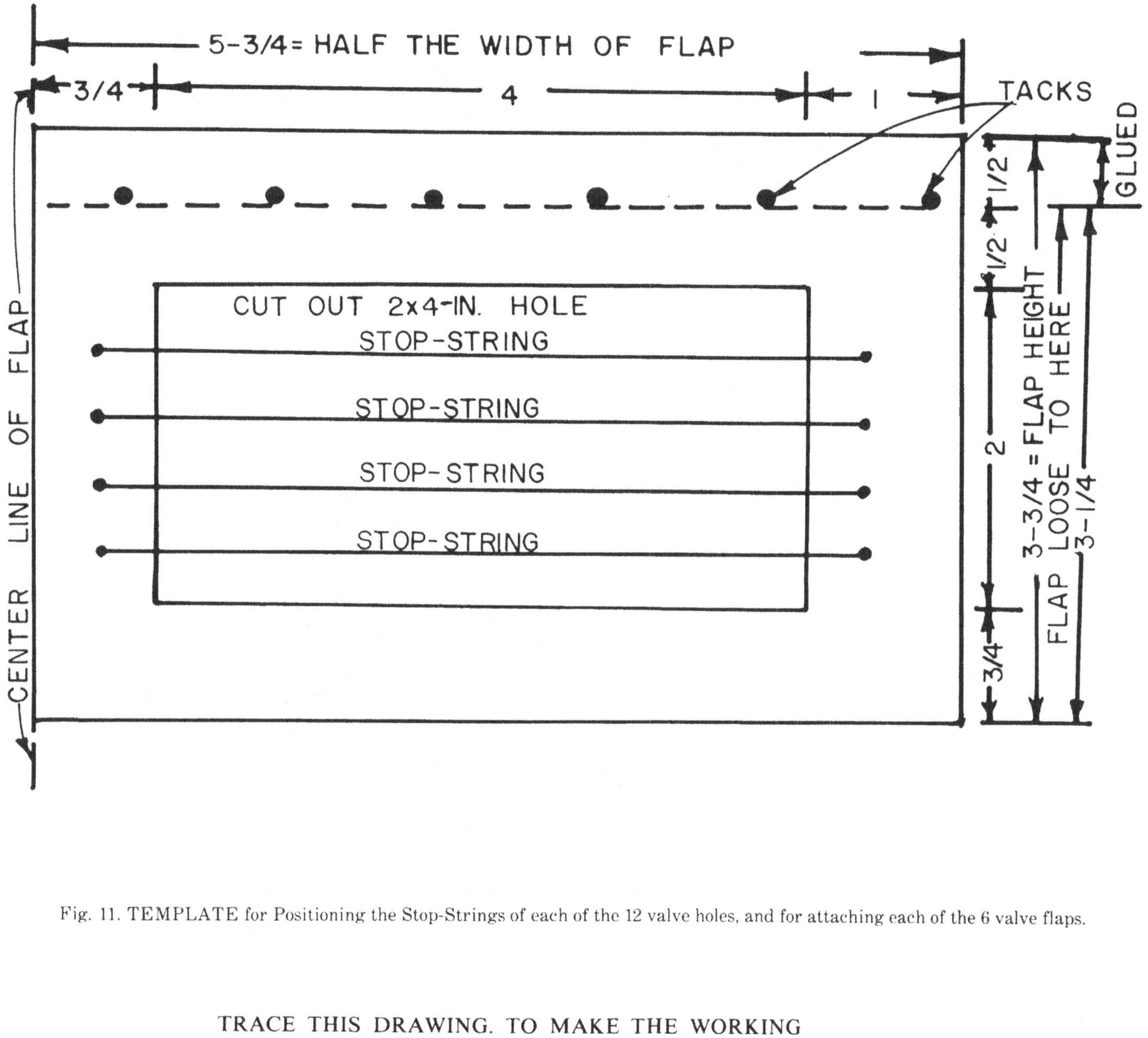

Fig. 11. TEMPLATE for Positioning the Stop-Strings of each of the 12 valve holes, and for attaching each of the 6 valve flaps.

TRACE THIS DRAWING. TO MAKE THE WORKING TEMPLATE, TRANSFER THE TRACING TO A PIECE OF CARDBOARD. CUT OUT THE 2 X 4-INCH HOLE IN THE CARDBOARD, AND MAKE SMALL HOLES SHOWING THE POSITIONS OF THE STOP-STRINGS AND TACKS.

13. Permanently attach the fixed part of the front end X (see Fig. 7, 10 and 12) with adhesive and small nails to the sides and to the bottom. Be sure that its flap valve is **upside down** and is **facing away from the center** of the pump, and that a long edge of this part is level with the outer side of the bottom. Remove the construction forms.

14. Paint the interior of the "cylinder" with sealer—after removing all adhesive that may be in its corners.

15. After the sealer dries, sandpaper the interior of the "cylinder" with fine sandpaper, and paint it again with the final coat of sealer.

16. To attach the removable part of the front end XI, stand the "box" on its completely open end and drill slightly oversize screw holes (for your 2-in. screws) clear through the removable part of the front end, as indicated by Fig. 9. With the flap valve **facing outward**, temporarily attach this part with a few small nails to the end of the top and to ends of the two sides. Then with a smaller-diameter bit, drill the screw holes deep enough into the top and the sides so that the 7 screws will hold securely.

17. So that it will be unnecessary to tightly screw on the removable part of the front end in order to make its repeated temporary attachments airtight, tack felt weatherstripping (best 1/8-in. thick and 5/8-in. wide), or strips made of two thicknesses of flannel, to the contact edges of the top and the sides. No. 3 (3/8-in.) carpet tacks serve well. Then with a razor blade carefully cut the felt covering the screw holes in the edges, and remove these small pieces of covering felt.

18. Attach with screws the removable part of the front end.

19. To prevent damage to the front-end valve flaps when you stand the pump on its front end, epoxy a small piece of 3/8-in. plywood to the front end, near each of its four corners, as pictured in Figs. 3 and 5. Before standing the pump on its front end, use small pieces of masking tape to temporarily secure its valve flaps in their closed positions.

20. Attach the back end XII, using only screws. See Fig. 8. (For repairs, the back end may have to be removed.) To make the attachment of the back end airtight, coat its attachment "crack" only with rubber cement.

MAKING THE PISTON, THE PISTON ROD, AND ITS HANDLE

1. Have a sheetmetal shop cut three 3-ft.-long, 3-in.-wide strips of galvanized steel sheetmetal that is **no more than 0.016-in. thick** and no less than 0.012-in. thick. (Most galvanized steel valley flashing used by roofers and sold by many lumber yards is less than 0.016-in. thick; 30-gauge galvanized sheet metal sold by some sheetmetal shops is about 0.015-in. thick.) Steel sheetmetal thicker than about 0.016 in. is not springy enough and is unsatisfactory.

2. With a tolerance of + or - 1/32-in., cut from these strips two strips each 11-13/16-in. long, and two strips each 11-3/4-in. long. (These four strips first must be bent and then tacked to the four sides of the plywood piston; these piston-sealing strips serve rather like piston rings, by making close, sliding, low-friction contact with the sides of the plywood "cylinder". Steel strips resist wear and if properly lubricated make the pump serviceable for months of continuous use.)

3. Preparing the four sheetmetal sealing strips:

a. Since the strips to be tacked to the top and the bottom of the piston must be bent differently from the strips to be tacked to its two sides, mark "T or B" on each of the two strips that are 11-13/16 in. long, and mark "S" on each of the two strips that are 11-3/4 in. long.

b. On each of the two strips marked "T or B", draw an ink line along which to make the approximately 30 degree bend, and another line for the approximately 90 degree bend. (See the left half of Fig. 13 for the distances from the edges of these two "T or B" strips to their bends.) Also draw two ink lines along which to drive tacks, spaced as shown in the left half of Fig. 13.

Likewise draw four lines on each of the two strips marked "S", as specified in the right half of Fig. 13, noting that some of these lines are spaced differently than corresponding lines on the strips marked "T or B".

c. Using a small sharpened nail for a punch and placing one strip of sheetmetal at a time on a smooth board, punch 2 rows of tack holes in each strip. The tack holes should be about 1-1/2 in. apart.

d. From a nominal 1 x 2-in. **straight** board, make two boards each about 3/4 x 7/8 x 12-1/4 in., for use in bending the sealing strips.

e. Securely sandwich a "T or B" strip of sheetmetal between the two 12-1/4-in.-long boards placed exactly on top of each other, by tightening two "C" clamps on the ends of the two boards, so that the bending line 3/8-in. from one side of the strip is just visible along the straight edge of a board. Then hold the two clamped boards in a vise so that the 3/8-in.-wide part of the sheetmetal strip is uppermost and vertical.

f. Bend the exposed part of the strip about 30 degrees off the vertical, **away** from the side of the strip where the holes have been indented by the punch. To bend evenly, hammer gently and repeatedly on a 3/4 x 3/4 x 18-in. board held against the exposed 3/8-in.-wide part of the strip.

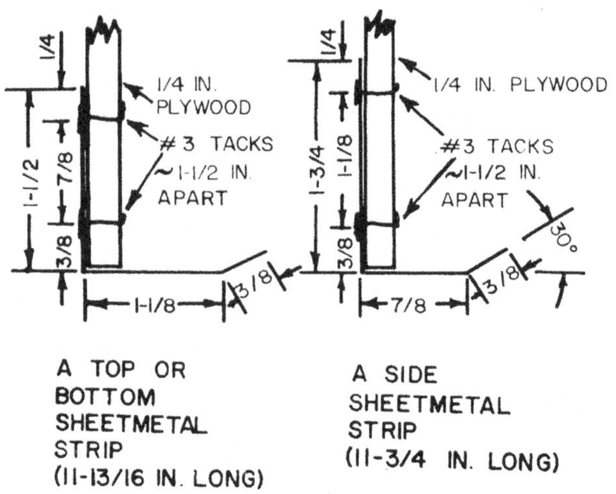

Fig. 13. Piston Sealing Strips, each made of a springy sheetmetal strip 3 in. wide.

g. With the sheetmetal strip held sandwiched between the two 12-1/4-in.-long boards by the two "C" clamps and the vise, so that the bending line for the almost 90-degree bend is barely visible, bend the exposed part of the strip 90 degrees, in the same direction that the 3/8-in.-wide part was bent. See Figs. 13 and 14.

Fig. 14. Plywood Piston with Sheetmetal Sealing Strips Attached.

h. Bend the other "T or B" strip, and similarly bend each of the two "S" strips.

4. Attach the four sheetmetal sealing strips to the plywood piston with No. 6 tacks (1/2-in. long). Place on a solid metal surface the part of the plywood piston opposite the spot to which part of a strip is being tacked, so that when a tack is hammered in its point is **clinched** (bent over) on the far side of the 3/8-in.-thick plywood piston, by being hammered against the solid metal surface.

a. First tack a "T or B" sheetmetal strip to the top of the piston, and a "T or B" strip to its bottom.

b. Then tack the two "S" strips to its sides. The strips should fit together so as to make square corners. If adjacent ends of two strips do not fit neatly together, cut bit by bit a very little off the end(s) of a strip(s) so that the two adjacent ends fit together neatly at their corner.

c. To prevent air leakage between the ends of the sealing strips, put rubber cement in the four corner "cracks" between strips. (This was not done on the test pump's piston.)

5. For the piston rod, saw from a **straight, well-seasoned** oak board a 3/4 x 1-3/4 x 36-1/2-in. board. Sandpaper it smooth. (A piston rod made of well-seasoned oak is less likely to break if abused, but necessitates using screws, in place of nails and staples, for attachments. Piston rods made of nominal 1 x 2-in. fir boards were undamaged in the tests.)

6. To complete the piston rod:

a. For the handle, use 4 pieces of a nominal 1 x 2-in. board cut to the lengths shown in Fig. 15. Also see Fig. 16. Round all edges and corners, to minimize the chances of the operators' blistering their hands.

b. Paint the piston rod and its handle with sealer. When dry, sandpaper. Then apply a final coat of sealer.

c. Use adhesive, screws, and nails (or adhesive and nails if your piston rod is of soft wood) in making the handle illustrated by Fig. 15.

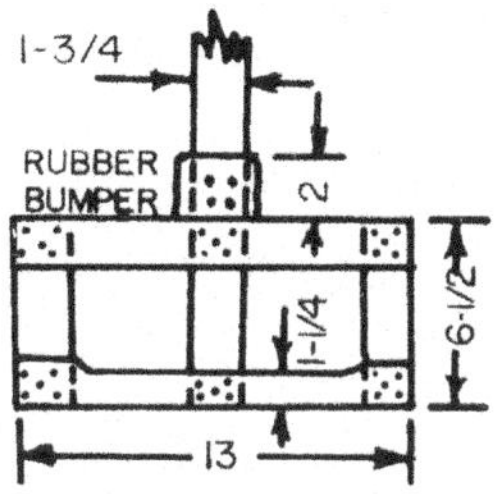

Fig. 15. Piston Rod Handle Made of 3/4 x 1-3/4-in. Boards.

Fig. 16. The Pump Handle of the Durability-Test Pump, showing how one man best holds it when two men are pumping.

d. To reduce friction on the piston rod and resultant enlargement of the piston-rod hole with long use, coat with epoxy all four sides of the piston-rod hole. See Figs. 7 and 16. Be sure that the piston rod slides snugly yet freely in its hole when the removable part of the front end is screwed in place.

e. From a piece of thick truck-tire inner-tube rubber, cut a 2-in.-wide strip 12-in. long. To make the 2-in.-wide rubber bumper (see Figs. 15 and 16), connect one end of this rubber strip to the center of a 3/4-in.-wide side of the piston rod. Do not place any screw or staple in the strip closer than 1 in. from the strip's forward edge, that may repeatedly bump into the front end. Wrap and attach the strip quite tightly around the piston rod next to the handle. (If you have only a piece of passenger-car inner-tube rubber, then to make a 2-in.-wide bumper use a 4-in.-wide strip of this thinner rubber folded double lengthwise.)

7. Attaching the piston rod to the piston:

a. On the back of the 12 x 12-in. plywood piston, mark lines to enable you to attach the piston rod as pictured in Fig. 14. Note that the **lower side** of the piston rod is exactly 5-1/2 in. above the lower edge of the plywood of the piston, and that the center line of the piston rod intersects the vertical center line of the plywood of the piston.

b. To the end of the piston rod (see Fig. 14) adhere and screw (or adhere and nail if your piston rod is not oak) two pieces of nominal 1 x 2-in. boards each 3 in. long. Each of these two small boards and the end of the piston rod are in contact with and securely connected to the plywood piston, and form a perfect "T" at the end of the piston rod.

c. Connect the piston rod to the piston, best with epoxy (or adhesive) and small screws. Make sure that: (1) the four piston sealing strips overlap the piston's plywood in the direction of the piston rod, (2) the 1-3/4-in.-wide sides of the piston rod are parallel to the top and bottom of the piston, and (3) the piston rod is perpendicular to the piston. See Figs. 2 and 14.

d. Make and attach to the piston rod a 3-in.-long rubber bumper, positioned close to the piston as shown in Fig. 2.

OPERATING THE PUMP

1. Check to see that the four sheetmetal strips on the four sides of the piston all make even contact with the walls of the "cylinder" when the piston is moved back and forth. If the piston does not slide back and forth quite easily even when not lubricated, carefully bend a strip or strips so that they press less against the "cylinder" walls. If while someone is shining a flashlight through a valve opening in the other end of the pump you observe that parts of a sheetmetal strip do not make close contact with a "cylinder" wall, gently bend outward that part of the strip.

2. Lubricate all four walls of the "cylinder", the sheetmetal strips that slide against the walls, and the piston rod. Use a very thin motor-breakin white lithium grease (not an ordinary bearing grease, that is too sticky). Or use a thin oil. The pump should be lubricated after no more than each 24 hours of use, and before being used again after days of disuse.

3. Install the pump at a height above the floor so that most of the persons who are going to pump can push and pull with their hands moving at about the same height that their elbows are when they are standing. See Fig. 3 for an example of a pump-supporting table raised to an efficient height for operators who are the height of the pumper pictured.

4. To save work and to minimize wear on the pump, usually operate it with a length of stroke a little shorter than the distance between its two rubber bumpers. To save energy especially when pumping air through a high resistance ventilation system, move the piston back and forth by using mostly your leg and body muscles.

PROLONGED STORAGE

Wipe off all grease and other lubricants if you do not plan to use this pump for months. All lubricants—especially those on wood—tend to become gummy with time.

Keep your supply of pump lubricants taped to your pump.

REQUEST

Suggestions for improving this pump and/or these instructions will be appreciated, and may contribute to improvements likely to save lives.

Cresson H. Kearny

FILTER BOX AND FILTER

PURPOSES

The primary shelter ventilation requirement is to supply enough outdoor air to maintain endurable heat-humidity conditions.

To keep the concentration of respiratory carbon dioxide low enough for survival, very little fresh outdoor air is required. Even for an infant or an infirm person remaining in a crowded shelter for days, 3 cubic feet per minute (3 cfm) is adequate. For a healthy adult or child 1.5 cfm is enough. Too much carbon dioxide, not too little oxygen, is the initial cause of unendurable conditions in inadequately ventilated shelters in which the air does not get unendurably hot.

In contrast, up to 25 cfm of outdoor air per occupant may be needed to maintain endurable heat-humidity conditions inside a crowded shelter occupied for days during a heat wave in a hot, humid part of the U.S. Hence the need for a large-volume ventilating pump, best with a low-resistance filter.

If outdoor air flows into a shelter through a hood, gooseneck pipe, or other air-supply opening that causes all but tiny fallout particles to fall out before the air reaches shelter occupants, breathing this unfiltered air will not result in short-term radiation casualties. However, a very small fraction of the occupants of a shelter supplied with unfiltered air in an area of heavy fallout may contract cancer years later as a result of breathing shelter air containing tiny fallout particles, that a properly designed filter could have removed.

Air that has been in contact with fallout particles before being filtered is not radioactive.

The homemade filter illustrated below, if used with an efficient "suction" pump such as the Plywood Double-Action Piston Pump described separately, will remove practically all fallout particles likely to cause casualties even decades later. This filter also will remove most infective aerosols, the air-borne tiny particles used in biological warfare — an unlikely type of attack on the United States. It will not remove poisonous gasses, an even less likely danger to Americans if all-out war befalls us.

CONSTRUCTION

Filter Box

If 20 x 20-inch furnace filters are available, use plywood or boards to build the filter box shown in the illustration. To make permanent connections airtight, first use waterproof construction adhesive or glue, and then tape. (If only smaller filters are available, reduce the horizontal dimensions of the box accordingly, except for the top and bottom openings.) Check to be sure that your filters will fit snugly in the box of the size you plan to build.

The square frame on the bottom of the filter box should fit snugly over the square air-intake duct on the top of your Plywood Double-Action Piston Pump. Tape the cracks to make the connection airtight and to permit easy removal of the filter box.

Make the illustrated 4 supports of the hardware cloth no thicker than 3/4 inch, thus providing enough space below the filter for low-resistance airflow. (Hardware cloth is a stiff, square-mesh, molten-dipped galvanized wire.)

Make the square top of the filter box so that it covers the upper edges of the box's sides and can be easily removed. Then cut in its center a round hole slightly smaller than 4 inches in diameter. File the hole's edges so that a 4-inch-diameter can (such as a coffee can with its top and bottom cut out) fits **snugly** in this hole. To connect the can securely and airtight, first use waterproof construction adhesive or epoxy, and then tape. (If construction adhesive or epoxy is not available, cut a 2-1/2-inch-diameter hole in the center of the bottom of the 4-inch-diameter can. Then make radial cuts spaced about one-half inch apart, out to the full diameter of the can. Bend these tabs outward 180 degrees, preparatory to tacking them with small tacks to the bottom of the filter box top. Tape airtight.)

So that the top of the filter box can be easily removed, tape it onto its box. A roll of duct tape should be kept with the filter box and pump at all times.

To connect the filter box to the shelter's air-intake pipe, the best widely available air duct is the inexpensive, 4-inch-diameter flexible duct used with clothes dryers.

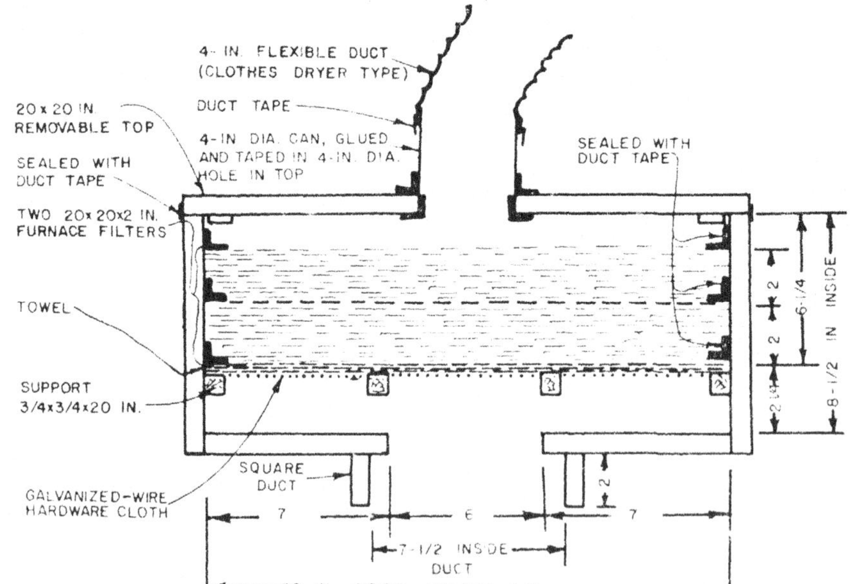

Homemade Filter To Fit On Plywood Double-Action Piston Pump, and To Be Connected to a 4-Inch-Diameter Air-Intake Pipe.

Filter Materials

Furnace or air-conditioner dust filters, those made of oiled fiberglass fibers, will remove practically all but the very smallest fallout particles. Filters that are sold in box-like housings can easily be installed so that all the pumped air will pass through them, by taping them to the inner sides of the filter box. The illustration shows two plain mats of furnace filter material, each taped around its edges. (If commercial dust filters are not available, bath towel cloth will serve. However, in very dusty areas a cloth filter may become overloaded, thus seriously reducing the rate of airflow much sooner than if an oiled fiber filter is used as a prefilter.)

To filter out most of the tiny particles that may pass through one or more furnace filters, place two thicknesses of bath towel on top of the filter-support made of hardware cloth, and tape them around their edges to the box. See illustration.

Tests by U.S. Army specialists have shown that filtering air through two thicknesses of bath towel removes about 85 percent of even microscopic aerosols as small as 1 to 5 microns in diameter. (See "Emergency Respiratory Protection Against Radiological and Biological Aerosols", by H. G. Guyton et al., A.M.A. Archives of Industrial Health, Vol. 20, July through Dec. 1959.) This is the size of most infective aerosols used in biological warfare. In most of an area subjected to a biological attack, if 85 percent of this size-range of infective aerosols and practically all larger particles are removed, then most persons breathing this filtered air will not receive enough infective agents to infect and sicken them.

Persons who are especially desirous of protecting their shelter's occupants against biological warfare aerosols, but who can not afford or obtain expensive High Efficiency Particulate Air filters (HEPA filters), should consider using disposable pleated air filters that meet official ASHRAE standards. One 2-in. pleated air filter, measuring 19-1/2 x 19-1/2 in., will remove over 90 percent of particles in the 1.0-5.0 micron range, yet when clean its resistance to an airflow of 200 cfm is only about 0.2 in. water gauge (about 0.007 psi). Its cost is about twice that of a good ordinary furnace filter of the same size. However, it has approximately three times the life of a standard panel type filter before becoming overloaded. Disposable pleated air filters are available in larger cities.

USE

The illustrated homemade filter has such low resistance to airflow that, when up to about 200 cfm is being pumped through it by a Plywood Double-Action Piston Pump, the air volume is decreased by only about 10 percent, as compared to the volume pumped with no filter in the ventilation system. With a homemade Plywood Double-Action Piston Pump, up to approximately 200 cfm can be pumped through this filter even when the total difference in air pressure (caused by the ventilation pipes, a dirty filter, etc. that restrict airflow) is high, about 5 inches water gauge (0.18 psi).

Even if the United States suffers an all-out Soviet attack, only a small part of its area will be subjected to blast effects severe enough to injure the occupants of fallout shelters. (Fallout shelters are not designed to withstand blast, but especially typical earth-covered ones afford consequential blast protection.) In contrast, an installed filter, unless protected by an efficient blast valve, will be wrecked by a quite low-pressure blast wave that comes down its open air-intake pipe —even if the small part of the blast wave that would enter the shelter room through its open ventilation pipes is not nearly powerful enough to injure the shelter occupants. Thus unprotected installed filters will be wrecked in an area several times as large as the area in which occupants of fallout shelters will be injured by blast.

To be sure of having a filter in good condition, you can:

1. Make and keep in your shelter an extra complete filter, ready to replace your installed filter if it is damaged, or if it becomes overloaded with dust and its resistance to airflow becomes too high. Furthermore, if your filter is installed in your shelter room and becomes so radioactive with retained fallout particles that it is delivering a consequential radiation dose to shelter occupants, it is advantageous to be able to remove it, pitch it out, and install a replacement filter. (To be able to supply your shelter with unfiltered air in peacetime or after the end of consequential fallout danger, you should make and keep ready a duct with appropriate fittings to connect your pump directly to its air-intake pipe.)

2. If you have only one filter, do not install it before you need to filter the air supply. Connect your pump directly to the air-intake pipe, using an appropriate duct and fittings. Then before the attack and before the arrival of fallout (revealed by your fallout-monitoring instrument), keep your shelter well ventilated with unfiltered air. Whether or not your filter is installed, stop ventilating your shelter for a few hours while heavy fallout is being deposited outside — unless heat-humidity conditions become unbearable. If before shelter ventilation is stopped the shelter air does not contain an abnormally high concentration of carbon dioxide, then no outdoor air need be supplied for about 5 hours to prevent building up too high a concentration of respiratory carbon dioxide — provided there is about 70 cubic feet of shelter-room volume for each occupant.

AN ENCOURAGING REMINDER

Persons making preparations to improve their chances of surviving an all-out attack should realize that if the United States is hit with warheads the sizes of those in the 1987 Soviet intercontinental arsenal, the fallout particles of critical concern will be much larger than the extremely small particles (1 to 5 microns in diameter) which are not completely removed by this filter. Fallout particles this small produced by large nuclear explosions do not fall to the ground for many days to months after the nuclear explosions, by which time they have become much less radioactive. Essentially all of the larger particles can be removed merely by filtering the air through a few thicknesses of bath towel cloth.

Appendix F

Means for Providing Improved Natural Ventilation and Daylight to a Shelter with an Emergency Exit

THE NEED

Survivors in areas of heavy fallout can greatly reduce the radiation doses that they will receive, and thus decrease their risks of contracting cancer, if they sleep and spend many of their non-outdoor-working hours inside good shelters during the first several months after an attack. (See *Minimizing Excess Radiogenic Cancer Deaths After a Nuclear Attack,* by Kathy S. Gant and Conrad V. Chester, Health Physics, September 1981.)

A permanent family shelter can serve quite well for months as a post-attack temporary home if it is designed to provide adequate natural ventilation most of the time, to have adequate and easy forced ventilation by a KAP when forced ventilation is needed, and to have daylight illumination. A shelter dependent on ventilation laboriously pumped through pipes and on artificial lights even during daytime is much less practical for use as a post-attack home.

The following instructions should enable a family having an earth-covered shelter with an emergency exit to make it much more livable for months-long occupancy. The means described below for providing improved ventilation and daylight illumination also will supply guidance to survivors who will build shelters post-attack to minimize continuing radiation exposures, especially to children and pregnant women.

BUILDING AND USING A MULTI-PURPOSE EMERGENCY EXIT HOUSING

Build a multi-use emergency exit housing of the design pictured in Fig. F.1 and detailed in Fig. F.2. Size your exit housing to fit snugly over the top of your **completed** vertical exit shaft. This exit housing is made of 3/4-inch exterior plywood, four 2 x 2 x 36-inch boards, and four 16 x 16-inch window panes of 1/8-inch Plexiglas. Plated screws and waterproof adhesives are used to assure sturdiness and durability.

Fig. F.1. Multi-Use Emergency Exit Housing Installed Over the Square Emergency Exit Described by Figs. 17.1, 17.2, and 17.3.

The adjustable top of this exit housing measures 4 x 4 x 1 feet, and can be tilted to make different sized ventilation openings in any of four directions. The top also can be raised straight up to make various sized openings all the way around, or it can be completely closed — as explained by Fig. F.2 and the following descriptions of its uses.

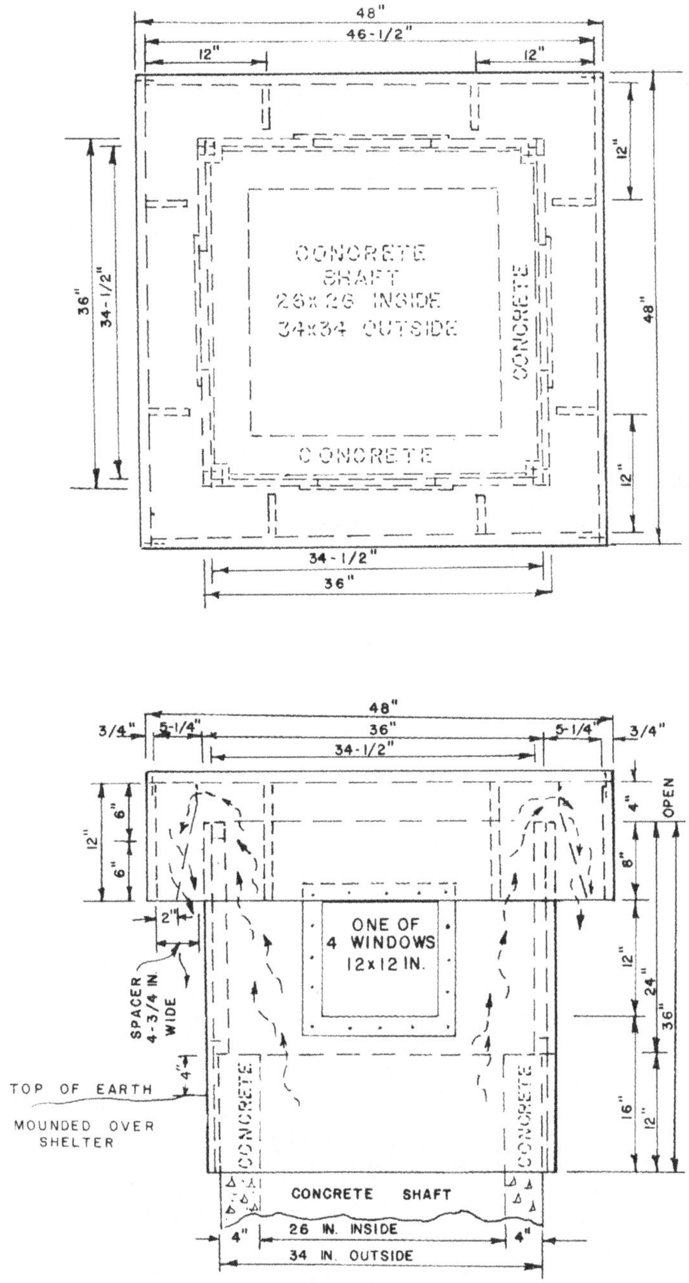

Fig. F.2. Plan and Side View of Multi-Purpose Emergency Exit Housing, on a Square Emergency Exit with 34 x 34-Inch Cross-Sectional Outside Dimensions.

Fig. F.3. The Top and Four Walls of the Multi-Purpose Emergency Exit Housing, Nested Together to Save Storage Space.

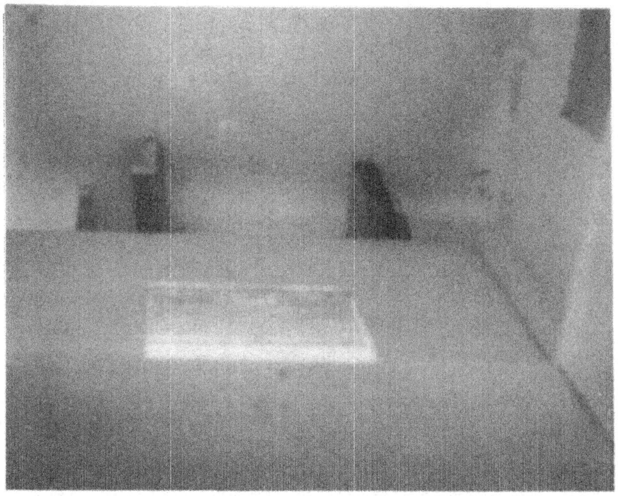

Fig. F.4. View from Below the Exit, Looking Up the Multi-Purpose Emergency Exit Housing. The top is shown supported in a tilted position by two 6-inch-wide boards placed between a wall and the top.

In Figs. F.2 and F.3, note the eight bevelled plywood guides, two on the inside of each side of the top. These guides are needed so that the top can be tilted in the position desired, merely by using a stick to raise it from below. To hold the top in a tilted or raised position, spacer boards are placed between the raised top and the upper edges of a wall or walls, as illustrated by Fig. F.4.

The illustrated housing over a vertical exit provides:

* A means to regulate shelter ventilation, and to increase natural ventilation when the wind is blowing. If, for example, the shelter's opened exit is to the north of its opened entry and a north wind is blowing, shelter airflow will blow in through the exit and out through the entry. This natural ventilating airflow, often inadequate, is increased if the adjustable top of the exit housing is not simply raised 6 inches on all four sides, but is tilted as shown in Fig. F.1, with its south side closed and its north side tilted up 6 inches to provide a 6 x 26-inch ventilation opening between the upper edge of the entry housing's north wall and its top. Then a north wind striking the north wall produces

increased air pressure over and above this wall, forcing more air into the exit and on through the shelter. In contrast, if a south wind is blowing, natural airflow will go in through the shelter's entry and out through its exit. And if the adjustable top still is tilted open to the north as illustrated, then reduced air pressure over and above the downwind north wall will "suck" an increased airflow out of the exit and through the shelter.

The measured increases in airflows through a small shelter resulting from the top of this exit housing being tilted were only 40-50 cfm when an 8-10 mph breeze was blowing. These rather small increases in airflow, however, often would make it unnecessary to supply forced ventilation to a family shelter by intermittently operating a KAP.

* Exclusion of rain, snow, and larger dust and fallout particles. The four 12 x 48-inch vertical sides of the adjustable top overhang the exit housing's walls by 6 to 12 inches. Thus the top serves as a large ventilation hood over the exit, preventing rain, snow, and larger dust and fallout particles from entering while ventilation is continuing. (To prevent entry of flies and mosquitoes, an insect screen panel, made to fit over the bottom of the emergency exit, should be kept stored in the shelter until needed. A screen door for the inner entry doorway also should be stored. Remember that installing screens greatly reduces natural ventilation airflows.)

* A reliable source of daylight. The four 12 x 12-inch windows of this exit housing let enough daylight into the exit shaft, that is painted white, to permit a person on the shelter floor below to read, even for several minutes after sunset. See Fig. F.4.

* A way to observe what is going on all around the shelter, without having to go outside, and with lessened exposure to fallout radiation.

* Quick installation post-attack, after fallout decays sufficiently. In an installation test, dirt was dug away to expose the upper 12 inches of the emergency exit shaft. Then in just 8 minutes the author and a boy carried the 5 parts of this exit housing 80 feet, positioned its four walls around the already exposed upper 12 inches of the reinforced concrete emergency exit, nailed its walls together, and placed its adjustable top in the tilted position pictured in Fig. F.1.

BUILDING AND USING AN ENTRYWAY COVER THAT PROVIDES A LARGE, PROTECTED VENTILATION OPENING

Build a shelter entryway cover that keeps out rain, snow, and the bigger dust and fallout particles while providing a large, protected ventilation opening both for natural ventilation and for easy forced ventilation by a KAP when needed. For an example of one type of entryway cover, see Fig. F.5. This photo shows a 4-piece cover, that two men in a little less than 5 minutes carried out of this shelter and installed over the 4 x 6-foot opening above the shelter's opened stairway doors.

Fig. F.5. A Quickly Installable, 4-Piece Entryway Cover That Provides Easy Access and a Large, Protected Ventilation Opening.

This cover is made of 4 pieces of 1/4-inch chipboard, each 5 feet wide, and short lengths of nailed-on 1 x 2-inch boards. These 4 pieces can be tied quickly with their attached nylon cords to inner parts of the two 2 x 6-foot steel entryway doors, which are pictured in their opened, upright positions.

The lowermost of the 4 chipboard pieces has a groove near each end. The grooves are each made of 2 nailed-on lengths of 1 x 2 lumber spaced apart to fit the lower ends of the doors and hold them in their upright positions 4 feet apart. The upper edge of this lowermost piece is 8 inches below the lower raised corners of the doors, so that an 8 x 48-inch ventilation opening is assured when the lower of the two large covering pieces (pictured being held open) rests on the doors. (This step-over piece of chipboard illustrates a way to reduce the quantity of larger fallout particles that will be blown into many types of shelters, because most sandlike particles and coarse dust are blown along close to the ground. They are not blown upward and over a vertical obstruction by most winds. If an entryway has an inner, ordinary doorway, even more fallout particles can be kept out of the shelter room if an 18 x 18-inch ventilation hole is cut in the door near its top. Then air entering the shelter room will have to rise at least 4 feet above the entryway floor, and most of the larger fallout particles will be deposited on the entryway floor.)

The chipboard piece attached to the upper ends of the doors also has two 1 x 2 boards nailed near each end, forming grooves into which the upper ends of the doors fit. The doors are thus held in their upright positions and rain, etc. is kept from falling or being blown through the upper end into the entryway.

The uppermost of the two large covering pieces of chipboard (or exterior plywood) rests on the opened doors and is kept from slipping down by a 1 x 2-inch board nailed 4 inches from its upper end. This small board "hooks" over the upper edge of the piece of chipboard (or plywood) attached to the upper ends of the steel doors. (See the drawing on the side of this column.) This large piece of chipboard is securely tied to the doors.

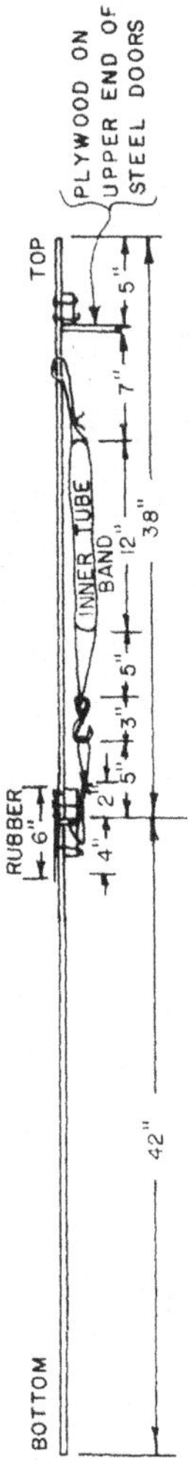

To keep the two large pieces from moving sideways, one 1 x 2-inch board is nailed near each of their side edges, spaced so as to lie against the outside of each opened, upright steel door. To strengthen the hingeline edge of the upper large covering piece, a 1 x 2-inch board is nailed along its lower edge.

The lower of the two large covering pieces also has a reinforcing 1 x 2 nailed near its hinged edge.

The most practical hinge that the author has devised is illustrated by the drawing. This flexible hinge is much less likely to be broken than are conventional hinges, and makes it easier to build the two large covering pieces to fit over the opened doors. Note that the upper edge of the lower large piece goes under the rainproofing, 6-inch-wide rubber flap, which is nailed only along the lower edge of the upper large covering piece. Then the two large pieces are held and hinged together by first stretching each of 2 strong, 2-inch-wide rubber bands (or rustproof springs) attached by cords to the upper large covering piece, and then hooking its attached bent-wire hook onto a nylon cord loop connected to the lower large covering piece. Each strong rubber band (cut from a truck innertube) and its attached hook and nylon cords is 5 inches from an opened door. Thus hinged, the lower large piece can be easily raised to permit a person to step out of or into the stairway entry. When this hinged lower large piece is closed and tied down, a 2.7 square foot protected ventilation opening with a 10-inch overhang results.

OTHER ENTRYWAY COVERS TO PROVIDE LARGE PROTECTED OPENINGS FOR NATURAL AND KAP VENTILATION

The owner of a permanent shelter with an emergency exit may be able to improvise coverings over its entry and exit after fallout decays sufficiently to permit work outdoors — provided that he understands natural ventilation and low-pressure forced ventilation requirements, and has the boards, nails, pieces of chipboard or plywood or canvas, tools, etc. needed. But if you own a permanent shelter your pre-crisis preparations surely should include making and storing ready-to-install entryway and exit coverings of whatever designs you decide will best meet your anticipated needs for high-protection-factor sleeping and living quarters during weeks or months following a nuclear attack.

Selected References

1. *Radiobiological Factors in Manned Space Flight,* Space Radiation Study Panel of the Life Sciences Committee, Space Science Board, National Academy of Sciences, National Research Council, 1967.

2. Personal communication with Dr. C. C. Lushbaugh, Chairman, Medical and Health Science Division, Oak Ridge Associated Universities, in June 1977.

3. *The Effects of Nuclear Weapons,* 1962, Samuel Glasstone, Editor, published by U.S. Atomic Energy Commission, April 1962.

4. "Adequate Shelters and Quick Reactions to Warning: A Key to Civil Defense," Francis X. Lynch, *Science,* Vol. 142, pp. 665–667, 1963.

5. *Blast Tests of Expedient Shelters in the DICE THROW Event,* Cresson H. Kearny and Conrad V. Chester, Oak Ridge National Laboratory Report No. 5347, February 1978.

6. *The Effects of Nuclear Weapons,* 1977, Third Edition, Samuel Glasstone and Philip J. Dolan, Editors, U.S. Department of Defense and U.S. Department of Energy, 1977. This most authoritative publication has numerous sections written for non-technical educated readers. In 1986, a cloth-bound copy can be purchased for $17.00 from the Superintendent of Documents, U.S. Government Printing Office, Washington, D.C. 20402. When ordering, ask for *The Effects of Nuclear Weapons, 1977,* Stock No. 008-046-00093-0. (Since the price may be increased in future years, a buyer should first write requesting the current price.)

7. *The 900 Days,* Harrison E. Salisbury, Harper Row, New York, N.Y., 1969.

8. *Expedient Shelter Construction and Occupancy Experiments,* Cresson H. Kearny, Oak Ridge National Laboratory Report No. 5039, March 1976.

9. *Biological Tolerance to Air Blast and Related Biomedical Criteria,* Clayton S. White et al., Lovelace Foundation for Medical Education and Research, Albuquerque, N.M., April 1965.

10. *Instrument Requirements for Radiological Defense of the U.S. Population in Community Shelters,* Carsten M. Haaland and Kathy S. Gant, Oak Ridge National Laboratory Report No. 5371, August 1978.

11. *Field Testing and Evaluation of Expedient Shelters in Deeply Frozen Ground,* Ren Read, College of Environmental Design, University of Colorado, Denver, Colo., July 1978.

12. "Construction of Hasty Winter Shelters," Cresson H. Kearny, *Annual Progress Report,* Oak Ridge National Laboratory Report No. 4784, March 71–March 72, December 1972.

13. *Shelter Occupancy Studies at the University of Georgia, Final Report,* J. A. Hammes and Thomas R. Ahearn, OCD Contract No. OCD-PS-66-25, 1966.

14. "Environmental Physiology of Shelter Habitation," A. R. Dasler and D. Minard, paper presented at the ASHRAE Semiannual Meeting in Chicago, January 1965.

15. *Studies of the Bureau of Yards and Docks Protective Shelter,* NRL Report 5882, U.S. Naval Research Laboratory, Washington, D.C., December 1962.

16. *Winter Ventilation Tests,* Guy B. Panero, Inc., Subcontract No. B-64212-US for Office of Civil Defense, February 1965.

17. "Interim Standards for Ventilating Systems and Related Equipment for Fallout Shelters," Office of Civil Defense, Washington, D.C., 1962.

18. *Response to DCPA Questions on Fallout,* DCPA Research Report No. 20, prepared by Subcommittee on Fallout, Advisory Committee on Civil Defense, National Academy of Sciences, November 1973.

19. *Personnel Shelters and Protective Construction,* NAVDOCKS P-81, Department of Navy, Bureau of Yards and Docks, September 1961.

20. *The Destruction of Dresden,* David Irving, Wm. Kimber and Co., London, May 1963.

21. *Chinese Civil Defense,* excerpts from *Basic Military Knowledge, Shanghai 1975,* ORNL/tr-4171, edited by Conrad V. Chester and Cresson H. Kearny, Oak Ridge National Laboratory translation, August 1977.

22. *The Effects of Mass Fires on Personnel in Shelters,* A. Broido and A. W. McMasters, Technical Paper 50, Pacific Southwest Forest and Range Experiment Station, Berkeley, Calif., August 1960.

23. *Civil Defense,* N. I. Alabin, et al., Moscow 1970, ORNL/tr-2793, Oak Ridge National Laboratory translation, December 1973.

24. *Manual of Individual Water Supply Systems,* Environmental Protection Agency, Water Supply Division, Washington, D.C., 1973.

25. "Solubility of Radioactive Bomb Debris," D. C. Linsten, et al., *Journal of American Water Work Association,* 53, pp. 256–62, 1961.

26. *Maintaining Nutritional Adequacy During A Prolonged Food Crisis,* Kay B. Franz and Cresson H. Kearny, Oak Ridge National Laboratory Report No. ORNL-5352, July 1979.

27. *Livestock, Fallout and a Plan for Survival,* W. F. Byrne and M.C. Bell, UT-AEC Agricultural Research Laboratory, Oak Ridge, Tenn., R-CD-3, April 1973.

28. "Availability and Shipment of Grain for Survival of the Relocated Population of the U.S. After a Nuclear Attack," Carsten M. Haaland, *American Journal of Agricultural Economics,* May 1977.

29. Personal Communication with Kathy S. Gant and Conrad V. Chester, January 1979.

30. *Food Stockpiling for Emergency Shelters,* Food and Materials Division, Commodity Stabilization Service, U.S. Department of Agriculture, April 1961.

31. *The KFM, a Homemade Yet Accurate and Dependable Fallout Meter,* Cresson H. Kearny, Paul R. Barnes, Conrad V. Chester, and Margaret W. Cortner, Oak Ridge National Laboratory Report No. ORNL-5040 (corrected), January 1978.

32. *Where There Is No Doctor,* David Werner, Hesperian Foundation, Palo Alto, Calif., 1977.

33. Personal communications from Colonel C. Blanchard Henry, M.D., Binghamton, N.Y., to Cresson H. Kearny in 1963.

34. *Emergency Medical Treatment,* TM-11-8, Federal Civil Defense Administration, U.S. Government Printing Office, April 1953.

35. "The Radiation Studies Begin," *Science,* Vol. 204, p. 281, 1979.

36. *Protection of the Thyroid Gland in the Event of Releases of Radioiodine,* National Council on Radiation Protection and Measurements, NCRP Report No. 55, Washington, D.C. 20014, August 1, 1977.

37. *Accidental Radioactive Contamination of Human and Animal Feeds and Potassium Iodide as a Thyroid-Blocking Agent in a Radiation Emergency,* Food and Drug Administration, Federal Register, December 15, 1978, pp. 58790-58800.

38. *Civil Defense,* N. I. Akimov et al., Moscow, 1969, ORNL/tr-2306, Oak Ridge National Laboratory translation, April 1971.

39. "Frantic Team Efforts Brought Vital Chemical to Stricken Plant," Robert Reinhold, *New York Times,* April 4, 1979, p. A16.

40. *Trans-Pacific Fallout and Protective Countermeasures,* Cresson H. Kearny, Oak Ridge National Laboratory Report No. 4900, November 1973.

41. Letter dated May 23, 1979 from William H. Wilcox, Administrator, Federal Disaster Assistance Administration, Washington, D.C. to Robert A. Levetown, Washington Representative of the American Civil Defense Association.

42. *Historical Instances of Extreme Overcrowding,* Bureau of Social Science Research, Inc., Report No. 354-5, March 1963.

43. *After-Action Report, Operation Laboratory Shelter,* Headquarters U.S. Army XXIV Airborne Corps, Ft. Bragg, N.C., 1970.

Selected Index

Definitions and explanations of terms are given on the listed pages. Because some terms are mentioned on up to 55 different pages, all pages on which some terms are listed are not included.

For broad categories of information, see the Contents page.

2001 Addendum on Radiation Hormesis

This is the first addendum to *Nuclear War Survival Skills* that gives an adequately detailed, correct description of Radiation Hormesis: the capability of the human body to repair much of the damage done to its cells that are hit by ionizing radiation. Low level radiation stimulates biological defense mechanisms, and if given before exposure to high level radiation reduces induction of mutations caused by high level radiation.

When I wrote this book, first published in 1979, I knew enough about hormesis to believe it to be a valid explanation of a very important survival process. But I did not even mention hormesis, being sure that if I did so the chances of any U.S. Government organization advocating and using my book would be reduced to almost zero. At that time the idea of any radiation being healthful was unthinkable even to the big majority of well-educated people.

I still believe I made the right decision for the years before the 1990s. That was prior to the collapse of the Soviet Union, which greatly reduced the risk of a massive nuclear attack on the United States. However, in our increasingly unstable world the chances of much smaller attacks on the United States have increased, including attacks by terrorists having only a few small nuclear weapons.

The facts proving the validity of hormesis are now overwhelmingly convincing. Physicist T.D. Luckey's pioneering book, *Radiation Hormesis*, has become a recognized classic. And the studies of Bernard L. Cohen, Ph.D. and of other scientists have unexpectedly revealed that Americans living in homes having relatively high radiation levels from radon and its daughter products have better health, live longer and have less cancer than comparable persons exposed to lower radiation levels in their homes. See Professor B.L. Cohen's irrefutable paper, "Test of the Linear-No Threshold Theory of Radon Carcinogenesis for Inhaled Radon Decay Products," Health Physics, 68 (2): 157-174; 1995.

Bernard L. Cohen's article is the most convincing exposition of radiation hormesis. Attempts to disprove this comprehensive article have all failed. It supplies proof that, contrary to widely accepted theory, persons who receive in their homes relatively high doses of ionizing radiation from the radon and its daughter products that they inhale, do not experience proportionally increased detrimental effects. In fact, "There is a strong tendency for lung cancer rates to decrease with increasing radon exposure." Below a threshold, none of the doses given adversely affected the reported-on persons.

Professor Cohen concluded: "All of this evidence surely leaves linear-no threshold open to serious question in its applications to low level radiation. These applications have had tremendous societal consequences – adding over 100 billion dollars to the cost of U.S. nuclear power plants and largely denying the nation the great potential benefits of that technology, leading to expenditure of a projected 150 billion dollars for clean-up of government facilities, etc. – all this in spite of the fact that linear-no threshold theory has never been verified with experimental data in the low dose, low dose rate region of all the important applications."

Only a very small fraction of the millions of Americans who fear being injured or killed by radiation from nuclear weapons, or by radiation from radon and its daughter products in their homes, have even heard of hormesis.

Those Americans who learn the facts about radiation hormesis will be less likely to panic if subjected to light radioactive fallout, such as may result from terrorists exploding a few small nuclear weapons in the United States. And such well informed Americans will not become fearful if they learn that for years they have been receiving larger than average radiation doses from radon and its daughter products in their homes.

Keep in Touch and Keep UP to Date.

PO BOX

In 1979 and 1987 you just published a book and that was it. Maybe you had a PO Box where people could write you but this is the year 2022 so we will tell you how to keep in touch with us. The field of nuclear expertise is a small one and we will all come together in times of difficulty to feed you the best actionable knowledge (not information) that you can benefit from. In the civil defense field. We all either know each other or are separated by only one person. At the writing of this update, a nuclear device has not been detonated on the earth in anger since 1945. If the situation becomes direr before I do a 2023 update for this book, follow us at the methods below to get the latest information.

WEBSITE

www.NuclearWarSurvivalSkills.com Any updates or notices on changes will be put up on this website.

TWITTER

https://twitter.com/BookNwss or @BookNWSS on twitter.

TELEGRAM

https://t.me/nwssbook Is a Telegram Channel. It can have unlimited members and it allows us to communicate one way, from us to you without limitation and it might be something people younger than me are comfortable with. If we form an NWSS Telegram GROUP where we can all chat and people can ask questions and experts can answer them we will announce that GROUP via the website, Twitter and the above telegram channel.

CONFERENCE CALL.

After the rush of people that got the NWSS book in March of 2022 a good friend told me, "Hey, dummy. Why did you not have a weekly Q&A conference call or something!!". "Great Idea!!!" I stated. If the world situation escalates I will announce when and how we will have some form of a large group meeting, video, audio, text, etc....(at least once a week). You can ask questions and myself and experts more nuclear qualified than myself can answer them directly. We will record these calls and then make them available to everyone. If you are asking a question, a million other people are probably thinking the same thing. If you want to sign up to be on the list for a 'conference call' there is a signup link at www.NuclearWarSurvivalSkills.com Please use your best email that you get daily and this is where I say that I have about a million other things to do in life than to SPAM you. All Subject lines of emails from us will start with "NWSS: blah blah blah. etc..." They will all start with NWSS in the start of the Subject Line.

EMAIL

Email: nwssbook (at) protonmail (dot) com For Personal, Professional, Corporate, or Enterprise Assistance. We know 'everyone' in the field and can get you the help you need. MEDIA: PUT your Media ORG and TIME and DATE Needed in the Subject Line Please. I can't guarantee how often I'll be checking because of the flood of emails I'll get. If you want to help me help people. I'll do it. If you are a large corporate entity with resources that you want to volunteer to help us with what you see we are doing, contact me.

STEVEN HARRIS WEBSITE:

www.Harris1234.com has my other food, water, power, electricity, prepareness subjects on it and I will make this my site that will lead to anything else I have up there to help you.

CRESSON KEARNY COMBAT PROVEN TOOLS

This is a little promo here for Cresson's best practices. I inherited his original items used in the making of the book Jungle Snafus and Remedies. Some of these date back to WWII and Vietnam and the first Gulf War. He gave me specific instructions on how and what to do regarding companies putting these items back into production for the benefit of the NATO War Fighter and the public.

You really need to get a copy of Jungle Snafus and Remedies from the used market or buy a brand new copy from www.RobinsonBooks.com (click on OTHER). The details on everything below are in that book. Please get the book before contacting me.

THE JUNGLE HAMMOCK

Gary Clark did his version of the jungle hammock without knowing about Cresson. I found Gary and called him and Cresson was still alive then. The 3 of us talked and Cresson approved of what Gary had done and I sent Cresson's details and best practices to Gary. Gary has since retired and Dutchware Gear now sells the hammocks at junglehammock.com but I do not know if they are currently keeping up with what Cresson called Jungle Platoon Best Practices. If you want your hammock to be up to Cresson Kearny Warfighter's best practices contact me.

THE PANAMA SOLE.

The panama sole boot pattern or tread has been copied and copied to the point its not like the original that Cresson made and tested when he help found the Jungle Training Center in Panama before/during WW2. I have sent scans of this to 2 boot manufactures but I have no idea of they did anything with it. Does not look like it. Any boot manufactures that want 3D scans or plaster molds of the original pattern, I have Cressons original boots from when he made them in WW2.

THE JUNGLE BOAT.

This is a breath inflatable boat combat-proven and tested to hold 3 warfighters with full pack loads (WW2 / Vietnam Era Loads). It has been under fire, in combat, and the concept is still valid today. It took 87-year-old Cresson about 8 minutes to breathe inflate it, it rolls up, weight is about 7 pounds and it will cross rivers, lakes, and Cresson even took it 25 miles out into the Pacific Ocean off the coast of Panama and had a US Army or Navy boat meet him and pick him up. I have 2 different variants of the boat. Cresson wanted these back in production for use by the WarFighter. NOTE: All of these items do NOT have to go through 'Military Approval". Special Forces today have these things called Military Credit Cards and they buy what they need.

Made in United States
North Haven, CT
20 February 2023

32918481R00187